Numerical Methods for Differential Equations

Fundamental Concepts for Scientific and Engineering Applications

Michael A. Celia
Massachusetts Institute of Technology
and
Princeton University

William G. Gray
University of Notre Dame

PRENTICE HALL
Englewood Cliffs, New Jersey 07632

Library of Congress Cataloging-in-Publication Data

CELIA, MICHAEL ANTHONY.
    Numerical methods for differential equations : fundamental
concepts for scientific and engineering applications / Michael A.
Celia and William G. Gray.
        p.   cm.
    Includes bibliographical references and index.
    ISBN 0-13-626961-3
    1. Differential equations,--Numerical solutions. 2. Differential
equations, Partial--Numerical solutions. I. Gray, William G.
(William Guerin).   II. Title.
QA372.C39 1992
515'.35-dc20
                                                        91-10537
                                                        CIP

Acquisitions editor: Doug Humphrey
Editorial/production supervision
    and interior design: Kathleen Schiaparelli
Copy editor: Zeiders & Associates
Prepress buyer: Linda Behrens
Manufacturing buyer: Dave Dickey
Supplements editor: Alice Dworkin
Editorial assistant: Jaime Zampino

> *To all the students we have taught*
> *and*
> *To Lin and Genny*

©1992 by Prentice-Hall, Inc.
A Simon & Schuster Company
Englewood Cliffs, New Jersey 07632

Printed in the United States of America

10 9 8 7 6 5 4 3 2 1

ISBN 0-13-626961-3

Prentice-Hall International (UK) Limited, *London*
Prentice-Hall of Australia Pty. Limited, *Sydney*
Prentice-Hall Canada Inc., *Toronto*
Prentice-Hall Hispanoamericana, S. A., *Mexico City*
Prentice-Hall of India Private Limited, *New Delhi*
Prentice-Hall of Japan, Inc., *Tokyo*
Simon & Schuster Asia Pte. Ltd., *Singapore*
Editora Prentice-Hall do Brasil, Ltda., *Rio de Janeiro*

Contents

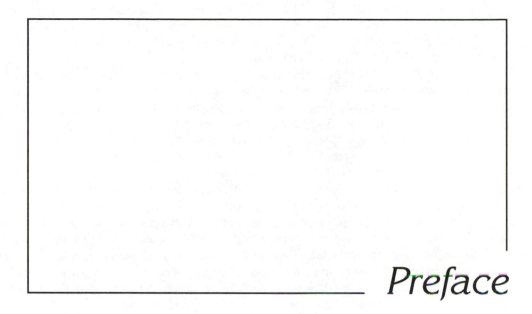

Preface

This book has grown out of several different courses on numerical methods that we have taught at the Massachusetts Institute of Technology, the University of Notre Dame, and Princeton University. These courses focused on numerical methods used to solve ordinary and partial differential equations in science and engineering. In the process of teaching these courses, which were at the advanced undergraduate to beginning graduate level, we developed methods of presentation that were distinct from presentations in standard textbooks on the subject. Through encouragement by, among others, students in these courses, we decided to organize our presentations into a book. The result is this textbook.

In this book, basic numerical methods applicable to many scientific and engineering disciplines are presented in ways that are different from traditional presentations. In this way we hope that the reader will develop both a deeper understanding of fundamental concepts and a broader perspective on the subject. We intend that students who study this book will understand and appreciate the fact that numerical solutions are not simply exercises in computer programming, but that they require understanding and synthesis of many different concepts. Most of all, we hope that students will realize that there is usually no unique "right" answer when designing numerical approximations, and that informed judgments, based on sound principles and careful thought, are required. This book is not a "cookbook" of formulas, but rather a treatise meant to help and encourage students to think. Its purpose is to provide a sound background with which students will be prepared both to solve a wide variety of practical problems and to study more advanced and specialized topics.

The level of presentation is appropriate for advanced undergraduate and first-year graduate students in science and engineering. We assume that students have a standard calculus background, through differential equations. A course in linear algebra would be helpful but is not necessary, as a substantial review of linear algebra is included in the book as Appendix A. Most developments in the book follow from concepts of calculus and linear algebra. In those few instances when more advanced concepts are used, references to outside material are provided.

In planning a course based on this book, the most logical sequence to follow is to begin, if necessary, with Appendix A, which is a review of general concepts of linear algebra. Inclusion of at least some of the material from this appendix will ensure a common background for all students. The chapters may then be gone through sequentially, beginning with Chapter 1. In Chapter 1, partial differential equations are introduced and linked to certain types of physical phenomena. In particular, definition and utilization of special curves or surfaces associated with partial differential equations, which are referred to as characteristic curves or surfaces, provide an analytical tool for understanding the behavior of solutions to those equations. Characteristics are also shown to be important in understanding implementation of initial and boundary conditions. Definition of characteristics is carried out such that a natural hierarchy of characteristics is introduced. This hierarchy takes the specific form of distinct sets of curves called primary characteristics and secondary characteristics. Such a hierarchy is necessary to fully understand solution behaviors, which is in turn necessary to design proper numerical approximation methods.

The first numerical approximation method presented for solution of differential equations is the finite difference method, which is introduced in Chapter 2. After definition of various notation and terminology, including the important concepts of truncation error and consistency, a general formulation is presented for derivation of finite difference approximations to any order derivative in one independent variable. This formulation provides criteria for the minimum number of discrete points needed in a finite difference approximation and is not restricted in any way to constant node spacing. Application of finite difference methods to the solution of boundary value and initial value problems is demonstrated, with emphasis on derivation of several standard families of time-marching algorithms for initial value problems. The chapter concludes with developments of finite difference approximations in multiple dimensions and a discussion of the concepts of strong and weak consistency.

In Chapter 3, basic concepts related to finite element approximations are introduced. The finite element method is presented in the broader context of the method of weighted residuals, which also includes approximation methods such as the collocation and subdomain methods. Examples are used to demonstrate the importance of function continuity and its relationship to the choice of weight or test function in the method of weighted residuals formulation. Finite element computations are then examined in detail to demonstrate certain computational and algorithmic advantages inherent in finite elements. After a brief discussion of mathematical requirements for finite element methods, the method of weighted residuals is extended to two and three dimensions. Finally, other derivations of the finite element method are presented and shown to yield discrete approximations that are identical to those that result from the method of weighted residuals formulation. Because these other formulations are restricted in their application, the weighted residual approach is preferred.

At this point in the presentation, most of the fundamental concepts related to how finite difference or finite element approximations are formulated have been explained and illustrated. There has, however, been little critical analysis of any of the approximations. Such analysis is begun in Chapter 4, where basic questions about how to design an approximation are considered. This includes the underlying choice of a numerical technique, and the subsequent choice of both spatial and temporal discretizations. For spatial discretization, truncation error analysis is employed to develop general heuristic guidelines for node placement. In addition, a variety of irregular gridding patterns are considered, including introduction of coordinate mappings to effectively treat distorted finite element shapes. Problems inherent in high-order coordinate maps are pointed out, and maintenance of linearity in the maps is stressed. Truncation error analysis is also used to develop more appropriate underlying numerical approximations for certain kinds of differential equations. However, truncation error analysis is not sufficient when dealing with time-marching problems. In such cases, stability becomes another important consideration. Various tools for analysis of stability are developed in Chapter 4, with special emphasis on Fourier analysis. Fourier analysis is also extended beyond simple stability considerations to provide quantitative insights into numerical solution behavior. Finally, certain specialized approximation methods are presented, some of which are only appropriate for certain kinds of problems and others which are quite general. These include very simple moving-grid methods, general Petrov-Galerkin methods, localized adjoint methods, and boundary element methods. Each of these methods follows from the fundamental concepts presented in Chapters 1, 2, and 3.

While Chapter 4 focused on relatively simple analytical manipulations, based mostly on truncation and Fourier analysis, to improve numerical approximations and give guidance in grid design, Chapter 5 develops analysis tools based on the numerical solutions themselves. Methods are presented whereby estimates of the actual solution error can be made, such that specific error tolerances can be respected. In addition, methods for improving solution accuracy are presented based on mesh refinement with a fixed approximation and on higher-accuracy approximations on a fixed mesh. These are done in the context of both finite difference and finite element approximations. Quantitative measures are also developed to guide in grid design, such that numerical errors are evenly distributed over the entire domain. The quantitative measures are also used in a dynamic way to provide criteria for dynamic gridding. Examples are used throughout the chapter to illustrate the computational approaches.

Although the five chapters contain exposition of a number of important concepts, we strongly believe that numerical methods are best learned and understood in the context of problem solving. The problems at the end of each chapter reinforce ideas in the text, provide some additional material themselves, and encourage independent and expansive thinking. We hope that by working through these problems, a student will acquire a satisfying mastery of the fundamentals of numerical methods.

After all of the material of Chapters 1–5 is studied, the reader should be ready to delve into a wide variety of specialized areas. In addition, it should be possible to read at least some of the relevant journal articles on a topic of interest. To complete the presentation, Appendix B provides a compendium of tables meant to summarize and complement some of the results presented in the chapters. These include, for example, specific listings of coefficients for different time-marching algorithms, basis function definitions, and various numerical integration formulas. Finally, a list of references is provided in Appendix C. This list includes sources of material for the chapters as well as other textbooks, journal articles, and a listing of journals that are related to applied numerical simulation.

Finally, but perhaps most important, we wish to acknowledge those who have contributed to the completion of this work. Professor David H. Marks of MIT provided invaluable encouragement during this entire writing project. His contributions to this effort are most gratefully acknowledged. We also gratefully acknowledge the financial support provided by the Bernard M. Gordon (1948) Engineering Curriculum Development Fund of MIT. In addition, the MIT, Princeton, and Notre Dame students who read various versions of this text as part of their course work are gratefully acknowledged. Tammy Youngs of the University of Notre Dame and Hope Abramson of MIT provided valuable typing help, for which we are grateful. Professors Alvaro Aldama of Princeton University and Joannes Westerink of the University of Notre Dame read the entire manuscript and provided excellent comments that have improved the text significantly. We are grateful to them. Ingemar Kinnmark also contributed valuable comments on the first two chapters. We also acknowledge Doug Humphrey of Prentice Hall for his prodding encouragement and patience during the completion of this project.

We especially wish to thank our families, especially Lin Ferrand and Genny Gray, for tolerating the (many) years of effort that have gone into the writing of this book.

Michael A. Celia
William G. Gray

Chapter 1

Characteristics and Boundary Conditions for Partial Differential Equations

1.0 INTRODUCTION

Education in mathematical principles and methods typically starts with discrete systems and progresses toward continuous systems. For example, a child's initial exposure to real numbers deals exclusively with integers (and at first, only positive integers). This then develops toward study of fractions, decimals, and finally irrational numbers. Thus understanding of real numbers begins with a few locations on the real number axis and proceeds to include all points on the axis. In learning about calculation of the slope of a curve in (x, y) space, students initially consider straight lines for which the slope is given by the discrete expression $\Delta y / \Delta x$. Understanding of the concept of slope is completed when one is able to calculate the slope at any point on an arbitrary curve using the continuous expression dy/dx. When studying science or engineering, mathematical models for physical processes are presented in terms of algebraic expressions (e.g., $\mathbf{F} = m\mathbf{a}$) before they are seen in terms of differential equations [e.g., $\mathbf{F} = d(m\mathbf{v})/dt$].

The study of numerical methods for the solution of differential equations is complex, in part, because it runs counter to the usual pattern of moving from the discrete to the continuous. Numerical methods, in brief, replace a differential description of a physical process or system with an approximate discrete analog and then solve this analog to represent the solution of the differential system. The challenge to the numerical modeler

1

is twofold: (1) to develop analogs that approximate the differential system with a known and tolerable degree of accuracy, and (2) to employ solution algorithms that are efficient and usable within the constraints of the cost and availability of computing power.

Effective and creative numerical solution of differential equations requires that the modeler (1) have an understanding of the physical processes occurring, (2) be able to describe those processes through differential equations, (3) be able to formulate a discrete analog to the differential system, and (4) be able to solve that analog on the computer. The main focus of this book is on the latter two of these four indispensable components of modeling, as indicated in Figure 1.1. However, because the physical behavior of a system under study influences the selection of a numerical technique, the techniques in this book are more insightfully understood when considered in the context of particular physical phenomena described by differential equations rather than from a purely mathematical viewpoint.

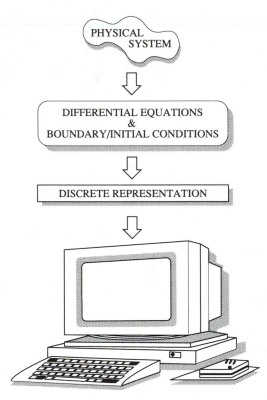

Figure 1.1 Components of a numerical model of a physical process.

1.1 BEHAVIOR OF PHYSICAL SYSTEMS

Differential equations in science and engineering are attempts to describe the actual behavior of physical systems. In determining an appropriate mathematical representation, one must identify the scale, in both time and space, at which the system is to be modeled.

For example, if the behavior of a container of gas subjected to temperature variations is to be modeled, different phenomena could be studied, each at a different scale. In general, as the time or space scale is made larger, the equations describing the system become simpler; but less information is obtained. For the container of gas, phenomena may be described at the molecular, the continuum, or the global scale. At the molecular level, collisions of gas molecules with each other and with the walls of the container must be modeled. At the continuum level, wherein molecular structure and gaps between particles are neglected, temperature and pressure are variables that may be defined at every point in the system. At the global scale, only average properties for the entire system (averaged in time and/or space) can be described. As the scale increases, either spatially or temporally, the ability to describe smaller-scale phenomena is compromised; but the complexity of interactions among equations, of the equation form, or of the boundary conditions usually decreases. The material presented in this book is intended to provide the reader with exposure to and facility with numerical procedures for solution of differential equations that describe phenomena occurring at the continuum scale or larger.

For the equations under study here, at most four independent variables will appear: three spatial dimensions and time. When the problem considered is time invariant, it is called a *steady-state system*. Time-dependent problems are said to be *transient*. The special case of transient but periodic (repeated) behavior is called *dynamic steady state*. The dimensionality of a problem refers to the number of spatial dimensions over which variation is considered. Thus a two-dimensional transient problem would depend on time and two spatial directions. In developing numerical solution procedures or algorithms appropriate for a problem of interest, the domain of the solution must be taken into account such that the portion of time and space which is to be considered is clearly defined. For example, suppose that one is interested in describing the changing pressure field in a groundwater aquifer during a period of constant pumping from a well. The response of the aquifer to the pumping may be considered, rather generally, to depend on the vertical direction, the two lateral directions from the well, and time. Thus the domain of the solution is three spatial dimensions and time. One could develop a general model that allows for variation of pressure in each of these variables. However, this degree of detail is often unnecessary in obtaining a reasonably accurate description of the pressure field. For example, if the flow is primarily horizontal toward the well, the pressure distribution in the vertical tends toward hydrostatic and the vertical dimension can be eliminated. The pressure field can thus be modeled by solving a partial differential equation in time and the two lateral dimensions. If, in addition, the aquifer is homogeneous and isotropic, such that flow to the well may be considered to be radially symmetric, the pressure field may be modeled using an equation that depends only on time and radial distance from the well. If the aquifer is very large in lateral extent but one is only interested in the short-term response of the pressure field, an adequate model may be formulated by describing the changing pressure field in the vicinity of the well but holding it fixed at its initial value at some relatively large distance from the well.

To model any physical system with reasonable accuracy, one must simulate a domain in time and space that includes the region where significant variation of the variables of interest occurs. Supplementary conditions along the edge of the domain must also be prescribed a priori in order to complete the model. Qualitatively, this can be understood in the context of groundwater flow by realizing that the pressure field in the aquifer at any particular time would depend on the field at an earlier time as well as the physical boundaries of the domain (i.e., whether the boundary is a river, impermeable rock, or a slightly permeable formation). Alternatively, modeling of the evolution of a temperature field in a solid body would require that the locations of heat sources and the magnitudes of these sources be known in addition to the initial temperature field and the conditions along the boundary. The mathematical exposition of boundary conditions is provided in Section 1.3.

Before proceeding to definitions pertaining to properties of differential equations, three important behaviors of these equations will be discussed in relation to physical systems and the domain of solution. The purpose of this discussion is to motivate classification of differential equation types from the perspective of properties of the solution rather than from simply the coefficients and terms in the equation. This discussion is less precise than the mathematical section that follows but does provide some insight into important considerations in selecting needed features of numerical solution algorithms.

The first system to be considered is the rectangular plate depicted in Figure 1.2a subjected to an arbitrary temperature distribution around its boundary. Assume, for convenience, that this plate is insulated so that no energy transfer occurs in the direction normal to the plate. A time-invariant temperature profile for this plate will result if the boundary temperature is held fixed for a long period of time. The domain of solution of

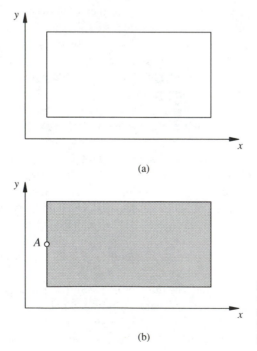

(a)

(b)

Figure 1.2   (a) Rectangular plate with arbitrary temperature distribution specified on its boundary. (b) Change in boundary temperature at point A influences temperature on entire plate.

the differential equation describing this system is the portion of x-y space that the plate covers. Now, if the arbitrary temperature profile imposed at the boundary is changed at just one point on the boundary, the steady-state temperature profile within the plate will change at every point within the domain. For example, if the boundary temperature profile is changed only at point A in Figure 1.2b, the temperature will be altered in the shaded portion of the domain (i.e., every point in the domain except along the edge where the original temperature is specified). A numerical approximation to the differential equation describing the problem must take into account the fact that each point on the boundary affects the solution at every point within the domain.

As a second example, consider the one-dimensional rod in Figure 1.3a. Let the problem of interest be the temporal development of the temperature profile along the

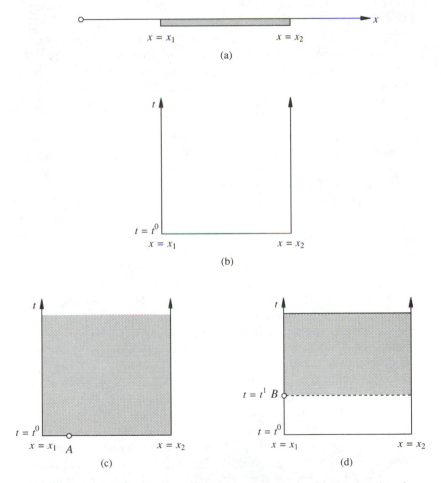

Figure 1.3   (a) One-dimensional rod of length $x_2 - x_1$. (b) Solution domain for the temperature distribution in the rod. (c) Region of solution domain influenced by the temperature specified at point A. (d) Region of solution domain influenced by the temperature specified at point B.

length of the rod and let variations in temperature over the cross section be neglected. The domain of solution is the portion of x-t space depicted in Figure 1.3b which spans the length of the rod and extends infinitely into time beginning from t^0, the time at which a disturbance to an initial temperature profile in the rod is applied. Suppose that at time t^0, a steady-state temperature profile is disturbed by changing the temperatures at the ends of the rods to some new values. If the ends of the rod are held at these new temperatures, the temperature profile will evolve to some final distribution. The differential equation usually selected to model this system is marked by two notable attributes: (1) it predicts that the final, steady-state temperature distribution occurs only after an infinite amount of time; and (2) it predicts that a change in temperature at either end of the rod immediately affects the entire rod. Both of these attributes are mathematical approximations to reality. However, for most systems, the predicted temperature field is negligibly different from that obtained by laboratory experiment.

For this model of heat transfer in a rod, it is interesting to note how changes in the specified temperature along the boundaries of the domain alter the solution. If two initial temperature profiles are considered that differ at just one point, A in Figure 1.3c, the temperature distributions at a later time will be different within the entire domain, the shaded region in the figure (except, of course, when the ultimate steady-state solution is reached).

Next consider two similar temperature evolutions in the rod where initial conditions at t^0 and end conditions at x_1 and x_2 are identical. Now at point B indicated in Figure 1.3d, time $t = t^1$ and $x = x_1$, assume that the temperature of the end of the rod is changed for one of the tests. Thus at all points within the domain of solution for time greater than t^1, the shaded portion of the figure, the temperature fields of the two solutions will be different. However, temperature fields will be the same in the domain for time less than t^1. This is, perhaps, not surprising, because an event occurring at one time can affect only the future, not the past. Of particular note in consideration of this example is the line separating the changed and unchanged portions of the domain in Figure 1.3d. A curve of this sort did not arise in the rectangular plate example nor in the current system when only the initial conditions were modified. The feature of a condition along the edge of the domain affecting portions of the domain differently must be accounted for properly in any numerical approximation to the differential equation. Solution techniques must be designed to deal with domains that are finite as well as those that are infinite in one or more variables.

As a third example, consider a perfectly elastic (nondamping) string that is stretched between $x = x_1$ and $x = x_2$. If the string is given an initial displacement and released from rest (i.e., plucked) at $t = t^0$, the displacement will propagate back and forth along the string as depicted in Figure 1.4a. The domain of solution is the finite section of x occupied by the string and the infinite portion of the time axis that begins at $t = t^0$, as shown in Figure 1.4b. Note that the disturbance will propagate in both the positive and negative x-directions and does not instantaneously affect the entire spatial domain as in the preceding example. If the initial displacement considered is modified at point A, this modification will cause the wave to differ from the original wave along the curves emanating from point A in Figure 1.4c and in the shaded region. Note that there are

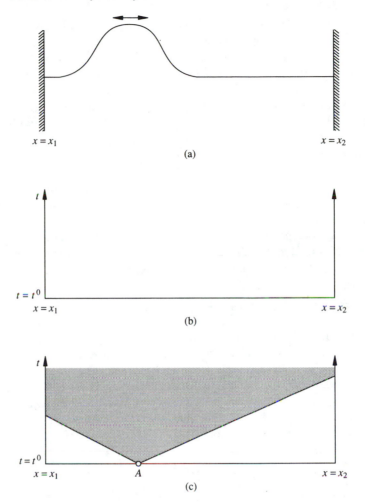

Figure 1.4 (a) Wave propagation in an elastic string plucked at time $t = t^0$. (b) Solution domain for the string displacement. (c) Region of influence of a disturbance applied to the string at point A.

two lines emerging from point A which are important. In the unshaded portion of the domain, the solution is unaffected by changes at point A. This observation contrasts with the previous examples of temperature changes in the rod, where a change of the initial condition influenced the solution at every point in space, and where the change at the x-boundary influenced all points in the spatial domain for time later than the time the disturbance was imposed. In addition, while the impact of a boundary condition perturbation decreases with distance in the domain from the perturbation for the heat conduction examples, perturbations at the boundary persist in the solution for the string displacements and move back and forth along the string with time. A numerical procedure appropriate for simulating the latter phenomenon must be able to preserve the shape of the wave by propagating it at the correct velocity and maintaining its magnitude.

The selection or development of appropriate computational algorithms for the solution of differential equations is aided by a priori knowledge of the behavior of the system under study. If an analytical solution to a differential equation can be obtained, there is no need to obtain a numerical solution (although a comparison between analytical and numerical solutions is a useful step in assessing the performance of a numerical scheme). When an analytical solution is not available, selection of the numerical scheme, discretization of the domain, and application of boundary conditions must all be done judiciously to obtain a good numerical solution. For some problems, this information is well estimated because of the modeler's knowledge of the system under study. In other cases, this information is obtained by successive refinements of the procedures employed based on solutions obtained. Thus numerical models provide insight into the behavior of physical systems as well as quantifying this behavior in systems that are qualitatively well understood.

Before proceeding with the development of numerical methods for the solution of differential equations, it is appropriate to provide a few definitions and conventions which will facilitate the discussion that follows.

1.2 DEFINITIONS AND EQUATION PROPERTIES

Differential equations may be classified as either *ordinary differential equations* (ODEs), in which only one independent variable appears, or as *partial differential equations* (PDEs), in which more than one independent variable appears. Within the scope of the current study, there are four main independent variables: time and the three spatial dimensions. The *order* of a differential equation is the order of the highest derivative that appears. The *degree* of the equation is the greatest power to which the highest-order derivative is raised. Therefore,

$$\frac{d^2u}{dt^2} + u\frac{du}{dt} - \left(\frac{du}{dt}\right)^3 = t^3 \tag{1.2.1}$$

is a second-order, first-degree ODE;

$$\frac{\partial u}{\partial t} + \frac{\partial u}{\partial x} - \frac{\partial^2 u}{\partial x^2} = 0 \tag{1.2.2}$$

is a second-order, first-degree PDE; and

$$\left(\frac{\partial u}{\partial x}\right)^2 + xt^3 u = f(x, t) \tag{1.2.3}$$

is a first-order, second-degree PDE. Differential equations are sometimes rearranged to reduce the explicit appearance of order in the equation. For example, if

$$q = u - \frac{\partial u}{\partial x} \tag{1.2.4a}$$

equation (1.2.2) becomes

$$\frac{\partial u}{\partial t} + \frac{\partial q}{\partial x} = 0 \tag{1.2.4b}$$

Despite the fact that no second derivative appears in equations (1.2.4), this coupled set of first-order equations is second order because combination of these equations into a single form yields a second-order form. Note that a higher-order equation can always be written as a set of first-order equations, but the converse is not true.

A *homogeneous* differential equation does not contain a term involving only the independent variables. Therefore, equation (1.2.1) is nonhomogeneous because of the t^3 term, equation (1.2.2) is homogeneous, and equation (1.2.3) is nonhomogeneous unless the arbitrary function $f(x, t)$ is equal to zero.

Another important concept in classifying differential equations is linearity. An nth-order differential equation is said to be *linear* if the dependent variable and its derivatives appear only to the zero or first degree in an equation and no products of the dependent variable and its derivatives with other derivatives of the variable appear. (This follows from the general definition of linearity given in Appendix A.) Therefore, equation (1.2.2) is linear, whereas equations (1.2.1) and (1.2.3) are not linear because du/dt and $\partial u/\partial x$ are raised to the third and second degree in these equations, respectively. Note that a linear equation may have coefficients of the dependent variable or its derivatives that depend on the independent variables, so that

$$x^3 \frac{\partial^2 u}{\partial x\, \partial t} + e^{-t} \frac{\partial u}{\partial x} + u = 0 \tag{1.2.5}$$

is a linear PDE. The coefficients in this equation—x^3, e^{-t}, and 1—do not depend on u or its derivatives. A differential equation that is not linear is *nonlinear*, and the special case of a nonlinear equation in which the highest-order derivatives occur linearly is said to be *quasilinear*. For example,

$$\left(\frac{\partial u}{\partial x}\right)^2 + \left(\frac{\partial u}{\partial y}\right)^2 = 0 \tag{1.2.6}$$

is a nonlinear equation and

$$\frac{\partial u}{\partial t} + u \frac{\partial u}{\partial x} - \frac{\partial^2 u}{\partial x^2} = 0 \tag{1.2.7}$$

is quasilinear. For convenience, subscripts will be used to indicate derivatives at some places in the text (primarily in this chapter) such that equation (1.2.7) is alternatively expressed as

$$u_t + u u_x - u_{xx} = 0 \tag{1.2.8}$$

Differential equations of importance in science and engineering range from relatively simple linear, homogeneous, first-order ordinary differential equations to highly complex nonlinear, high-order, multidimensional partial differential equations. Although this range of equation types is interesting, for purposes of developing numerical solution algorithms, the behavior of the solution is more important. In Section 1.1, three different types of behavior were discussed, each of which depended on how perturbations influenced the solution domain. In the following section, methods for classifying equations by type are developed and the implications of type in specifying appropriate boundary conditions are explored.

1.3 CHARACTERISTICS AND BOUNDARY CONDITIONS

The solution of a differential equation requires that appropriate boundary conditions, from both a mathematical and a physical viewpoint, be specified. An ODE for which conditions are imposed at only one end of the domain is called an *initial value problem*. However, if conditions are imposed at both ends of the domain, the ODE is called a *boundary value problem*. On the other hand, a PDE may be an initial value problem in one independent variable and a boundary value problem in another. The determination of whether a PDE or system of PDEs forms an initial value problem or a boundary value problem is aided by introducing the concept of characteristics. For the case of a PDE with two independent variables, real characteristics, if they exist, are curves in the plane of the independent variables along which information propagates. When a differential equation has three independent variables, the real characteristics are surfaces; and in higher dimensions, the real characteristics are hypersurfaces.

Perturbations in the boundary conditions influence regions interior to the domain by propagating along characteristics. In some problems, specified boundary conditions may cause the solution to be discontinuous. The locations of these discontinuities can be determined by following them as they propagate into the system along characteristics. Also of importance is the observation that because a characteristic may be a locus of discontinuity, knowledge of the solution only along a characteristic does not necessarily provide knowledge of the solution elsewhere in the domain. For example, given the solution on a characteristic, one could not obtain the solution at a point near the characteristic using the differential equation and a Taylor series expansion because the discontinuity along the characteristic would cause some of the needed derivatives to be indeterminate. This observation implies that boundary conditions should not be specified along characteristics since information cannot propagate from the characteristics into the domain of solution. In fact, as will be shown subsequently, curves or surfaces along which boundary conditions are specified must cut across characteristics. Specification of appropriate boundary conditions for a differential equation is based on an examination of the characteristics and how information on these characteristics influences the solution.

1.3.1 First-Order Partial Differential Equations (Two Independent Variables)

The simplest first-order partial differential equation is

$$\frac{\partial u}{\partial t} + v\frac{\partial u}{\partial x} = 0 \qquad (1.3.1)$$

where v is positive and constant. The restriction to constant v is for convenience, and relaxation of this restriction does not dramatically alter the conclusions that follow. This equation describes, for example, convection in a tube of a dissolved chemical concentration front, moving with uniform velocity v. For purpose of compactness of notation, manipulations will be performed on equation (1.3.1) expressed using the subscript notation as

$$u_t + vu_x = 0 \qquad (1.3.2)$$

The solution to this equation for u is sought in the domain $0 < x < L$ and $0 < t \leq T$. This differential equation only describes how u varies with time and space; it says nothing about the actual value of u. Thus to determine u completely, some auxiliary conditions, also referred to as boundary conditions or initial conditions, must be established. These conditions correspond to specification of the value of u along a curve, or curves, in the x-t plane. As mentioned previously, and as will be discussed further, such a curve must intersect the characteristics and may not be a characteristic. It is therefore important to know the characteristic family for a differential equation prior to specifying a boundary condition.

For this example, the characteristics may be obtained easily. However, for consistency and as an introduction to the procedure needed for more complex systems, the characteristics will be derived formally. Recall that a *characteristic* is a curve along which a singularity may propagate. For the present case, define an arbitrary continuous function in x-t space as $\varphi(x, t)$. When φ is a constant, a relationship between x and t exists and a curve in x-t space is defined. Now assume that $u(x, t)$ of equation (1.3.2) is defined along some curve $\varphi(x, t)$ equal to a constant. Therefore, in general, u_x can be related to u_t through the derivative of u along the curve.

If one is positioned at a point in x-t space and moves an infinitesimal distance dx in x and dt in t, the change in φ will be

$$d\varphi = \varphi_t \, dt + \varphi_x \, dx \tag{1.3.3}$$

Now if the change in position is restricted such that φ has the same value at the beginning and end of the step, then $d\varphi = 0$ and the movement is along the curve of constant $\varphi(x, t)$. This type of motion is particularly important and will be indicated by denoting dt along the curve as Dt, and dx along the curve as Dx. (Note that $D\varphi = 0$ by definition since the capital D indicates movement along a curve of constant φ.) Therefore, equation (1.3.3) becomes

$$D\varphi = 0 = \varphi_t Dt + \varphi_x Dx \tag{1.3.4}$$

or

$$\frac{Dt}{Dx} = -\frac{\varphi_x}{\varphi_t} \tag{1.3.5}$$

Now consider the change in u encountered by moving an infinitesimal distance in space:

$$du = u_t dt + u_x \, dx \tag{1.3.6}$$

If this motion is constrained to be on a curve of constant φ, then

$$Du = u_t Dt + u_x Dx \tag{1.3.7}$$

where Du is not necessarily zero because u may vary along the curve $\varphi(x, t) = $ constant. Equation (1.3.7) may be solved for u_x as

$$u_x = \frac{Du}{Dx} - u_t \frac{Dt}{Dx} \tag{1.3.8}$$

But from equation (1.3.5), $Dt/Dx = -\varphi_x/\varphi_t$, so that equation (1.3.8) becomes

$$u_x = \frac{Du}{Dx} + u_t \frac{\varphi_x}{\varphi_t} \qquad (1.3.9)$$

Note that this equation relates u_x to u_t and a derivative of u along the curve. In addition, the governing equation (1.3.2) relates u_t to u_x at every point in space. Thus substitution of equation (1.3.9) into equation (1.3.2) eliminates u_x and yields

$$\left(1 + v\frac{\varphi_x}{\varphi_t}\right)u_t = -v\frac{Du}{Dx} \qquad (1.3.10)$$

This equation indicates that if u is specified along a curve $\varphi(x,t) = $ constant, u_t may be calculated in terms of a derivative along the curve unless $1 + v(\varphi_x/\varphi_t) = 0$. In matrix form, equation (1.3.10) may be written

$$\left[1 + v\frac{\varphi_x}{\varphi_t}\right][u_t] = \left[-v\frac{Du}{Dx}\right] \qquad (1.3.11)$$

This 1×1 matrix equation has been written to illustrate formally the fact that the ability to solve for u_t requires that the determinant of the coefficient matrix be nonzero. Thus, if the curve on which u is specified is such that

$$1 + v\frac{\varphi_x}{\varphi_t} = 0 \qquad (1.3.12)$$

or

$$\varphi_t + v\varphi_x = 0 \qquad (1.3.13)$$

then u_t cannot be determined from values of u on the curve. This indeterminacy condition serves to define the characteristic curves. The characteristic curves may be solved for using equation (1.3.13) such that

$$\varphi = \varphi\left((x - x_0) - v(t - t^0)\right) \qquad (1.3.14)$$

where x_0 and t^0 are arbitrary constants. Note that because φ will change only when $x - vt$ changes, a different characteristic curve is determined for each value of $x - vt$. Therefore, the family of characteristic curves can be denoted by

$$x - vt = \text{constant} \qquad (1.3.15a)$$

or more simply as

$$(x - x_0) - v(t - t^0) = 0 \qquad (1.3.15b)$$

where selection of different values of the parameters x_0 and t^0 provides different curves in the family of characteristics. By convention, equation (1.3.15b) is referred to as the *characteristic equation* for equation (1.3.2) because it gives rise to a set of characteristic curves for different values of the constants. Although an infinite number of curves exists, each conforms to the single constraint (1.3.15a). Equation (1.3.2) is thus said to have one characteristic.

Selection of various values for x_0 and t^0 and illustration of t versus x leads to the family of characteristic curves in Figure 1.5a. Complete knowledge of u along

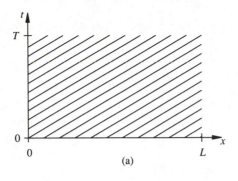

(a)

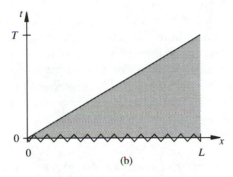

(b)

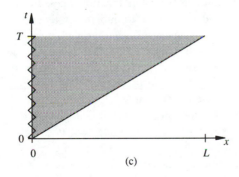

(c)

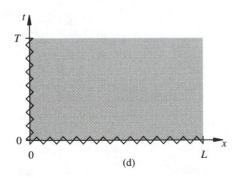

(d)

Figure 1.5   (a) Characteristics of equation (1.3.2) as determined byequation (1.3.15b). (b) Region of influence of conditions specified on x-axis, $0 < x < L$, in solving equation (1.3.2). (c) Region of influence of conditions specified on t-axis, $0 < t < T$, in solving equation (1.3.2). (d) Combined region of influence for conditions specified on x-axis, $0 < x < L$, and t-axis, $0 < t < T$.

one of these curves, together with the differential equation, is insufficient information for calculation of u throughout the domain of interest, $0 < t < T$ and $0 < x < L$ (see Problem 1.2 for further exposition of this point). In contrast, if u were known, for example, along the curve $\varphi = x/L + t/T = 1$, a curve that intersects all the characteristics for this problem, it would be possible to solve for u everywhere in the domain of interest. Although such a specification is mathematically possible, it is unlikely that an experiment would be performed in which u along the curve $x/L + t/T = 1$ is controlled. Therefore, physically realistic as well as mathematically correct boundary conditions will be considered.

Typically, one would expect to be able to specify an initial state for the system, that is, the concentration at all positions along the tube at $t = 0$ as indicated by the wavy line along the x-axis in Figure 1.5b. Specification of only this condition would allow the concentration to be solved for only in the shaded "region of influence" in Figure 1.5b. Concentration above this region and within the problem domain would be affected by more than just the initial condition. Specification of only the inflow concentration (i.e., the concentration along $x = 0$ for time $0 < t \leq T$), as indicated by the wavy line along the t-axis in Figure 1.5c, is sufficient to determine the concentration only in the shaded region of influence indicated in the figure. Thus adequate auxiliary conditions for the problem defined by equation (1.3.1) are initial condition and inlet condition specifications along the portion of the lines $x = 0$ and $t = 0$, as indicated in Figure 1.5d.

As an important physical consideration, one should note that time and space are inherently different. Perturbations at a spatial location may, in general, influence the state of the system in all spatial directions around the point. However, disturbances occurring at a particular time are incapable of affecting the system at an earlier time but can only influence the state at a subsequent time. Thus, in the present problem, where v is positive, the appropriate location for specifying the spatial boundary condition is at $x = 0$ because information along this line propagates into the spatial domain as time increases. If the flow were reversed such that v became negative, characteristics would have a negative slope in the x-t plane; and the appropriate spatial location for specifying a boundary condition would be at $x = L$. With negative v, it is information at $x = L$ that propagates into the spatial domain with increasing time.

The partial differential equation considered in this section is classified as an initial value problem in both time and space because conditions on the boundary of the x-t domain are specified at only one t and one x location. Higher-order PDEs may be either initial value problems, boundary value problems (with conditions specified at both boundaries of the domain), or mixed problems (initial value problems with respect to one or more independent variables, and boundary value problems with respect to other independent variables). The appropriate classification and boundary condition requirements can be obtained from an analysis of characteristics.

1.3.2 Second-Order Partial Differential Equations (Two Independent Variables)

A fairly general second-order differential equation with independent variables x and t may be written as

$$Au_{xx} + 2Bu_{xt} + Cu_{tt} + Du_t + Eu_x = R \qquad (1.3.16)$$

where A, B, C, D, and E may be functions of x, t, u_x, u_t, and u, while R may be a function of x, t, and u. This equation is quasilinear since it is nonlinear and first degree. For consistency of presentation with Section 1.3.1, the single second-order equation will be converted to a system of first-order equations by first defining the variables:

$$f = u_t \qquad (1.3.17)$$

$$g = u_x \qquad (1.3.18)$$

Substitution of these expressions into equation (1.3.16) in order to replace second derivatives of u with first derivatives of f and g yields

$$Ag_x + Bg_t + Bf_x + Cf_t + Du_t + Eu_x = R \qquad (1.3.19)$$

Furthermore, differentiation of equation (1.3.17) with respect to x and of equation (1.3.18) with respect to t demonstrates that

$$f_x = g_t \qquad (1.3.20)$$

These last four equations can be examined to determine whether or not curves exist along which specification of u, f, and g is inadequate to determine the solution of (1.3.16) in a region of interest. If so, these are the characteristic curves.

   The curves to be studied lie in the x-t plane and are indicated in general as $\varphi(x, t) = $ constant. The question that will be explicitly addressed here is: If u, f, and g are specified on a curve $\varphi(x, t)$, can u_t, f_t, and g_t be determined using equations (1.3.17) through (1.3.20)? Of course, if the curve is $\varphi = x$ (i.e., a curve parallel to the t-axis) the partial derivatives with respect to time of u, f, and g are simply their respective derivatives along the curve. In that case, a more interesting question is: Can u_x, f_x, and g_x be determined using equations (1.3.17) through (1.3.20)? Fortunately, if one is careful with the algebraic manipulations, both questions can be answered by doing only one analysis. Arbitrarily, the first question is addressed here, with the second question left to the reader as Problem 1.3.

   In the same manner as the previous analysis, if one is located at a point in x-t space where φ has a particular value and moves an arbitrary infinitesimal distance dx and an arbitrary infinitesimal distance dt, the change in φ will be

$$d\varphi = \varphi_t \, dt + \varphi_x \, dx \qquad (1.3.21)$$

If, however, the movement is constrained such that the value of φ does not change, then equation (1.3.21) becomes

$$D\varphi = 0 = \varphi_t \, Dt + \varphi_x \, Dx \qquad (1.3.22)$$

where the notational change from lowercase d to uppercase D is made to emphasize that movement is on a $\varphi = $ constant curve. Rearrangement of equation (1.3.22) yields

$$\frac{Dt}{Dx} = -\frac{\varphi_x}{\varphi_t} \qquad (1.3.23)$$

The change in u experienced by moving an infinitesimal distance from an initial location x, t is

$$du = u_t \, dt + u_x \, dx \qquad (1.3.24)$$

If this movement is also constrained such that it occurs along a curve of constant φ, then

$$Du = u_t \, Dt + u_x \, Dx \qquad (1.3.25)$$

or

$$\frac{Du}{Dx} = u_t \frac{Dt}{Dx} + u_x \qquad (1.3.26)$$

Substitution of equation (1.3.23) into (1.3.26) and rearrangement yields

$$u_x = \frac{Du}{Dx} + u_t \frac{\varphi_x}{\varphi_t} \qquad (1.3.27a)$$

By analogous arguments using f and g instead of u in equations (1.3.24) through (1.3.27a), the following equations are obtained

$$f_x = \frac{Df}{Dx} + f_t \frac{\varphi_x}{\varphi_t} \qquad (1.3.27b)$$

and

$$g_x = \frac{Dg}{Dx} + g_t \frac{\varphi_x}{\varphi_t} \qquad (1.3.27c)$$

Equations (1.3.27) are now used to eliminate u_x, f_x, and g_x from equation (1.3.19), to obtain

$$A\frac{Dg}{Dx} + Ag_t \frac{\varphi_x}{\varphi_t} + Bg_t + B\frac{Df}{Dx} + Bf_t \frac{\varphi_x}{\varphi_t} + Cf_t + Du_t + E\frac{Du}{Dx} + Eu_t \frac{\varphi_x}{\varphi_t} = R \quad (1.3.28)$$

Because u, f, and g are prescribed along a specified curve φ, the derivatives along the curve may be calculated and the only unknowns in this last equation are u_t, f_t, and g_t. After moving the known quantities to the right side and collecting terms on the left, equation (1.3.28) is rewritten as

$$\left(D + E\frac{\varphi_x}{\varphi_t}\right) u_t + \left(C + B\frac{\varphi_x}{\varphi_t}\right) f_t + \left(B + A\frac{\varphi_x}{\varphi_t}\right) g_t = R - E\frac{Du}{Dx} - B\frac{Df}{Dx} - A\frac{Dg}{Dx}$$

$$(1.3.29)$$

Now recall definition (1.3.17),

$$u_t = f \qquad (1.3.30)$$

Next use equation (1.3.20) to replace f_x with g_t in equation (1.3.27b) and obtain

$$-\frac{\varphi_x}{\varphi_t} f_t + g_t = \frac{Df}{Dx} \qquad (1.3.31)$$

These last three equations may be combined as the matrix equation

$$
\begin{bmatrix}
D + E\dfrac{\varphi_x}{\varphi_t} & C + B\dfrac{\varphi_x}{\varphi_t} & B + A\dfrac{\varphi_x}{\varphi_t} \\
1 & 0 & 0 \\
0 & -\dfrac{\varphi_x}{\varphi_t} & 1
\end{bmatrix}
\begin{bmatrix}
u_t \\ f_t \\ g_t
\end{bmatrix}
=
\begin{bmatrix}
R - E\dfrac{Du}{Dx} - B\dfrac{Df}{Dx} - A\dfrac{Dg}{Dx} \\
f \\
\dfrac{Df}{Dx}
\end{bmatrix}
$$

$$(1.3.32)$$

Because the matrix is square, u_t, f_t, and g_t may be solved for using the known right-side vector and the known coefficients in the matrix unless the determinant of the matrix is zero. A zero determinant indicates that φ is a characteristic curve since the ability to solve for u_t, f_t, and g_t is precluded in this case. Calculation of the determinant and imposition of the constraint that it be equal to zero yields

$$
-\left(C + B\frac{\varphi_x}{\varphi_t}\right) - \left(B + A\frac{\varphi_x}{\varphi_t}\right)\frac{\varphi_x}{\varphi_t} = 0
$$

$$(1.3.33)$$

or, after multiplication by φ_t^2 and rearrangement,

$$
A\varphi_x^2 + 2B\varphi_x\varphi_t + C\varphi_t^2 = 0
$$

$$(1.3.34)$$

It is interesting to note that this expression, which is satisfied if φ is a characteristic, is independent of D and E, the coefficients of the first derivatives. This quadratic equation has two roots and may be solved for φ_x/φ_t (or φ_t/φ_x) by the standard procedure for a quadratic equation. Solution for φ_x/φ_t yields

$$
\frac{\varphi_x}{\varphi_t} = \frac{-B \pm \sqrt{B^2 - AC}}{A}
$$

$$(1.3.35a)$$

while solution for φ_t/φ_x yields

$$
\frac{\varphi_t}{\varphi_x} = \frac{-B \pm \sqrt{B^2 - AC}}{C}
$$

$$(1.3.35b)$$

[Note that equation (1.3.35a) with the $+$ $(-)$ sign is the inverse of (1.3.35b) with the $-$ $(+)$ sign.] From these expressions it can be seen that if $B^2 - AC > 0$, there are two unique real characteristics; if $B^2 - AC = 0$, there is only one unique real characteristic; and if $B^2 - AC < 0$, both characteristics are imaginary. From analytic geometry it is known that, with some restrictions on D, E, and F, an equation of the form

$$
Ax^2 + 2Bxt + Ct^2 = Dx + Et + F
$$

$$(1.3.36)$$

describes a hyperbola if $B^2 - AC > 0$, a parabola if $B^2 - AC = 0$, and an ellipse if $B^2 - AC < 0$. Therefore, by extension of the terminology, the general second-order differential equation given in (1.3.16) may be classified as hyperbolic, parabolic, or elliptic as follows:

If $B^2 - AC > 0$:   the equation is hyperbolic, has two unique real characteristics, and has no complex characteristics.

If $B^2 - AC = 0$:   the equation is parabolic, has one unique real characteristic, and has no complex characteristics.

If $B^2 - AC < 0$:   the equation is elliptic, has no real characteristics, but has two unique complex characteristics. These characteristics are complex conjugates.

Although the general classification scheme discussed above is comprehensive, some particular cases are especially interesting. Often, when solving a second-order differential equation, some of the second derivatives are absent in that one or two of the coefficients A, B, and C become zero in various regions of the solution domain. These cases have been tabulated and information concerning the characteristics has been compiled in Table 1.1. Note that in most cases, only the ratio of derivatives, φ_x/φ_t, has been presented; but for those cases where φ_x or φ_t equals zero, the actual expression for the characteristic is provided. Recall that along a characteristic, φ is constant. Thus the characteristic $t - t^0 = 0$ is in fact a family of straight lines parallel to the x-axis that take on different t values when different values of the arbitrary parameter t^0 are selected.

TABLE 1.1   CHARACTERISTICS FOR EQUATION (1.3.16)

A	B	C	Characteristics
$\neq 0$	$\neq 0$	$\neq 0$	1. $\varphi_x/\varphi_t = (-B + \sqrt{B^2 - AC})/A$ 2. $\varphi_x/\varphi_t = (-B - \sqrt{B^2 - AC})/A$
$\neq 0$	$\neq 0$	0	1. $\varphi_x = 0$ such that $t - t^0 = 0$ 2. $\varphi_x/\varphi_t = -2\,B/A$
$\neq 0$	0	$\neq 0$	1. $\varphi_x/\varphi_t = \sqrt{-C/A}$ 2. $\varphi_x/\varphi_t = -\sqrt{-C/A}$
0	$\neq 0$	$\neq 0$	1. $\varphi_t = 0$ such that $x - x_0 = 0$ 2. $\varphi_x/\varphi_t = -C/2B$
$\neq 0$	0	0	1. $\varphi_x = 0$ such that $t - t^0 = 0$ 2. Double root (see secondary characteristic)
0	$\neq 0$	0	1. $\varphi_t = 0$ such that $x - x_0 = 0$ 2. $\varphi_x = 0$ such that $t - t^0 = 0$
0	0	$\neq 0$	1. $\varphi_t = 0$ such that $x - x_0 = 0$ 2. Double root (see secondary characteristic)
0	0	0	First-order equation (see secondary characteristic)

One additional case presented in Table 1.1 that is appropriate for discussion at this time is the case where A, B, and C are all zero. This is a degenerate case for which the second-order differential equation becomes first order. However, note that when A, B, and C are all zero, equation (1.3.32) becomes

$$
\begin{bmatrix} D + E\dfrac{\varphi_x}{\varphi_t} & 0 & 0 \\[2mm] 1 & 0 & 0 \\[2mm] 0 & -\dfrac{\varphi_x}{\varphi_t} & 1 \end{bmatrix} \begin{bmatrix} u_t \\[2mm] f_t \\[2mm] g_t \end{bmatrix} = \begin{bmatrix} R - E\dfrac{Du}{Dx} \\[2mm] f \\[2mm] \dfrac{Df}{Dx} \end{bmatrix} \tag{1.3.37}
$$

Because the equation has degenerated to a first-order form, the characteristic analysis can also degenerate to the analysis for a first-order problem. For this first-order analysis, further restrict D and E such that they do not depend on u_t or u_x and the equation is quasilinear. Now the question of interest is: If u is specified on a curve $\varphi(x,t)$, can u_t be calculated using information provided by the differential equation? Thus equation (1.3.37) is reduced to the expression

$$
\left[D + E\,\frac{\varphi_x}{\varphi_t} \right][u_t] = \left[R - E\frac{Du}{Dx} \right] \tag{1.3.38}
$$

Here u_t cannot be calculated if the determinant of the matrix is zero, or

$$
D + E\frac{\varphi_x}{\varphi_t} = 0 \tag{1.3.39}
$$

Information concerning these φ curves for various values of D and E is presented in Table 1.2. Note that when A, B, and C are not all zero, these curves are not characteristics for the second-order differential equation. Nevertheless, they still provide some information concerning the behavior of the general second-order problem, as will be demonstrated subsequently. Therefore, these curves are important. To set these curves apart from the characteristics of the problem, they are referred to here as *secondary characteristics*. These secondary characteristics become the primary characteristics if A, B, and C are zero everywhere in the domain such that the differential equation is first-order.

TABLE 1.2   SECONDARY CHARACTERISTICS FOR EQUATION (1.3.16)

D	E	Secondary characteristics
$\neq 0$	$\neq 0$	$\varphi_x/\varphi_t = -D/E$
$\neq 0$	0	$\varphi_t = 0$ such that $x - x_0 = 0$
0	$\neq 0$	$\varphi_x = 0$ such that $t - t^0 = 0$
0	0	None

The mathematical manipulations of these sections have led to information concerning the existence, in real space, of characteristic curves along which discontinuities may propagate. These curves are also extremely useful in determining requirements on boundary conditions for a problem. In the next section, typical model problems from the three classifications of second-order partial differential equations in two independent variables—elliptic, parabolic, and hyperbolic—will be used to illustrate boundary condition requirements.

1.3.3 Example Second-Order Partial Differential Equations (Two Independent Variables)

The first example to be treated in this section is the two-dimensional Laplace equation

$$T_{xx} + T_{yy} = 0 \qquad (1.3.40)$$

This equation, also known as the steady-state heat or diffusion equation, describes, for example, the steady-state temperature profile in a plate where

T is the temperature, and

x, y are Cartesian coordinate directions.

Let the domain of interest be the rectangular region described by $0 < x < L$ and $0 < y < H$. With reference to the standard equation (1.3.16), $A = C = 1$ and $B = D = E = R = 0$. This corresponds to the third row in Table 1.1. Furthermore,

$$B^2 - AC = -1 < 0 \qquad (1.3.41)$$

and equation (1.3.40) is elliptic with no real characteristics. Thus there are no curves emanating from the boundary along which disturbances propagate. A change in conditions at any point on the boundary alters the solution throughout the domain. From physical reasoning, this is not surprising. If the temperature of a plate is changed at any point on the boundary, one would expect to have a different steady-state temperature field.

Boundary conditions for differential equations are restricted to specification of some combination of the dependent variable and derivatives of this variable along the edge of the domain. The derivatives specified must be of lower order than the order of the governing equation. Specification of the value of the dependent variable is referred to as a *first-type* or *Dirichlet boundary condition*. The specification of the derivative of the dependent variable normal to the boundary, the normal derivative, is referred to as a *second-type* or *Neumann boundary condition*. Finally, specification of a linear combination of the dependent variable and its normal gradient along the boundary is a *third-type* or *Robin boundary condition*. Note that where a Robin condition is specified, neither the variable nor its normal gradient is known independently.

For an elliptic problem, one boundary condition must be specified at each point on the boundary. If only the gradient is specified at every point, a unique solution may not be obtainable. On physical grounds, this can be understood by referring to the heat equation (1.3.40) and recognizing that the gradient normal to the boundary is proportional to the heat flux (by Fourier's law). Thus the gradients could be specified so that heat entering the system along one portion of the boundary is precisely balanced by heat leaving along the remainder of the boundary. Although this is an equilibrium situation and the gradients within the domain can be obtained at every point, no information as to the actual temperature of the plate is provided. Alternatively, one could specify fluxes such that, for example, the heat entering the system is greater than that leaving. This would mean that the temperature could not be at a steady-state value and the equation would be inconsistent with the physical problem. To overcome these problems, the temperature must be specified for at least one point on the boundary; and either the temperature, the temperature gradient normal to the boundary, or a Robin condition must be specified at every other point. (In fact, in the present case, a mix of Robin conditions and Neumann conditions along the boundary will provide a unique temperature distribution. However, for some elliptic problems, a unique solution is not obtained without specification of the dependent variable for at least one point on the boundary.) The appropriate boundary conditions for the elliptic problem discussed here are depicted in Figure 1.6. The elliptic problem is a boundary value problem because boundary conditions must be specified at every point on a closed boundary. Problem 1.4 explores the question of nonuniqueness for the case of only Neumann conditions specified along the boundary.

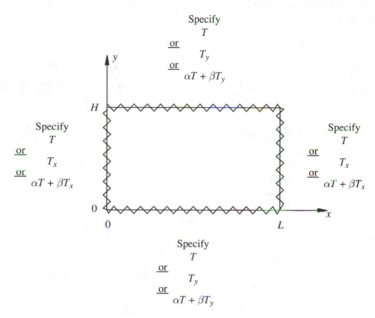

Figure 1.6   Boundary conditions for elliptic equation (1.3.40) solved in region $0 < x < L$ and $0 < y < H$.

As a second example, consider the equation describing the one-dimensional conduction of heat in a rod:

$$T_t - \kappa T_{xx} = 0 \qquad (1.3.42)$$

where

    T is temperature,

    κ is the thermal diffusivity,

    t is time, and

    x is the coordinate along the axis of the rod.

Consider the case where the rod is aligned such that it extends from 0 to L on the x-axis, and the time evolution of the temperature distribution in the rod is to be studied for

$0 < t \le t_{\text{max}}$. Equation (1.3.42) corresponds to equation (1.3.16), with u replaced by T and $A = -\kappa$, $B = 0$, $C = 0$, $D = 1$, $E = 0$, and $R = 0$. Therefore, equation (1.3.42) corresponds to the fifth row in Table 1.1,

$$B^2 - AC = 0 \tag{1.3.43}$$

and the equation is parabolic. Equation (1.3.34) provides the equation for the characteristic

$$-\kappa \varphi_x^2 = 0 \tag{1.3.44}$$

This quadratic equation has two roots, $\varphi_x = 0$, but because they are identical, only one unique characteristic is defined:

$$\varphi = \varphi(t - t^0) \tag{1.3.45}$$

Because φ is constant along a characteristic, the functional form of the dependence of φ on $t - t^0$ is irrelevant and the characteristic curve family is selected as

$$t - t^0 = 0 \tag{1.3.46}$$

A plot of the characteristics is given in Figure 1.7.

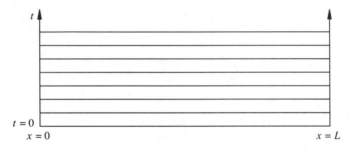

Figure 1.7 Primary characterisics of parabolic equation (1.3.42) in region $0 < x < L$ and $t > 0$ as determined by equation (1.3.46).

Because the characteristics in this figure are parallel to the x-axis, the effects of disturbances at either end of the rod will propagate instantaneously to a point on the interior of the rod. Thus, based on Figure 1.7, one might expect that, for example, if both ends of the rod were set at 100°C, the rod would instantaneously achieve a uniform temperature of 100°C. There is nothing in the analysis of primary characteristics that would indicate otherwise. However, experience indicates that this will not be the case. The rate of approach to a uniform state of 100°C depends upon κ as well as the temperature profile in the rod when the end conditions are imposed. Apparently, the single characteristic family defined by equation (1.3.46) is inadequate for fully describing the behavior of the solution.

There is an additional curve that can be obtained from the secondary characteristic analysis, as discussed in the preceding section and presented in Table 1.2. For conduction in a rod with $D = 1$ and $E = 0$ in the standard equation, the secondary characteristic family has the form

$$x - x_0 = 0 \qquad (1.3.47)$$

These characteristics are presented as dashed lines in Figure 1.8 along with the primary characteristics.

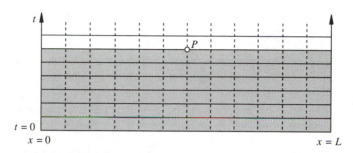

Figure 1.8   Domain of dependence for solution of equation (1.3.42) at point P. Solid lines are primary characteristics from equation (1.3.46), and dashed lines are secondary characteristics from equation (1.3.47).

For point P in Figure 1.8, the domain of dependence is the region $0 < x < L$ below P, the shaded region. Information propagates toward P from both ends of the rod along a horizontal characteristic. Because the characteristic is horizontal, information from both ends of the rod is predicted to propagate instantaneously to any point on the interior of the rod (although the instantaneous effect at points far from the boundary would be small). However, the temperature at a point, such as P, is also influenced by the previous temperature profiles in the rod. Thus the secondary characteristics, which emanate from $t = 0$, are also significant in calculation of the temperature.

Because only one type of characteristic emanates from the x-axis into time, only one initial condition must be specified. This condition must involve derivatives of order less than the highest-order time derivative appearing in the differential equation. Thus the appropriate initial condition is specification of T all along the rod. The primary characteristics are horizontal. Therefore, information may propagate into the rod from both ends, and boundary conditions must be specified at both ends. Because T is specified as an initial condition, the boundary conditions may be either first type, second type, or third type. The sufficient boundary conditions are presented in Figure 1.9. The parabolic problem studied here is a mixed initial (in time) and boundary (in space) value problem.

The third equation to be considered is the wave equation, which describes, for example, propagation of a disturbance in both directions along a plucked string. The governing equation is

$$h_{tt} - c^2 h_{xx} = 0 \qquad (1.3.48)$$

where

h is the magnitude of the disturbance,

c is the velocity or celerity of the disturbance along the string,

t is time, and

x is position along the string.

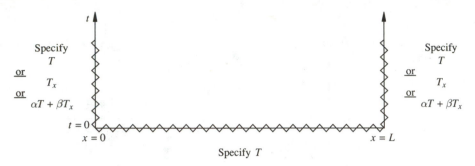

Figure 1.9 Boundary and initial conditions for parabolic equation (1.3.42) solved in region $0 < x < L$ and $t > 0$.

Let the portion of the temporal domain of interest be $0 < t \leq T$ and the portion of the spatial domain be $0 < x < L$. Here the disturbance is assumed small and undamped and the celerity is considered to be constant. With reference to the standard second-order PDE in two independent variables, equation (1.3.16), with h substituted for u, $A = -c^2$, $B = 0$, and $C = 1$. Therefore,

$$B^2 - AC = c^2 > 0 \tag{1.3.49}$$

and equation (1.3.48) is hyperbolic with two real characteristics. From equation (1.3.35a) or the third entry in Table 1.1, the equations for the two characteristics are

$$\frac{\varphi_x}{\varphi_t} = \frac{1}{c} \tag{1.3.50a}$$

$$\frac{\varphi_x}{\varphi_t} = -\frac{1}{c} \tag{1.3.50b}$$

The solutions to these equations are, respectively,

$$\varphi = \varphi\left((x - x_0) + c(t - t^0)\right) \tag{1.3.51a}$$

$$\varphi = \varphi\left((x - x_0) - c(t - t^0)\right) \tag{1.3.51b}$$

The actual form of the functional dependence of φ on its argument in these equations is arbitrary. However, for a constant value of φ, the argument will be a constant. For convenience, for some constant φ, set

$$(x - x_0) + c(t - t^0) = 0 \tag{1.3.52a}$$

$$(x - x_0) - c(t - t^0) = 0 \tag{1.3.52b}$$

Selection of various values for x_0 and t^0 leads to the plot of characteristics in Figure 1.10. Note that this depicts only representative characteristics for particular values of x_0 and t^0.

Now that the characteristics have been determined, the question remains as to what are the required boundary conditions to solve equation (1.3.48) in the domain $0 < t \leq T$ and $0 < x < L$. As a first case, consider point P in Figure 1.11, which

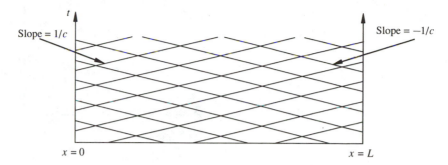

Figure 1.10   Characteristics for hyperbolic equation (1.3.48) in region $0 < x < L$ and $t > 0$ as obtained from equations (1.3.52).

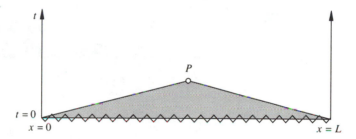

Figure 1.11   Region of influence of the initial conditions for equation (1.3.48) which is unaffected by the boundary conditions at $x = 0$ and $x = L$.

lies at the intersection of the two characteristics that intersect the points $(x, t) = (0, 0)$ and $(x, t) = (L, 0)$, respectively. Point P has coordinates $(x, t) = (L/2, L/2c)$. The solution at point P will depend on the initial condition, the condition along the x-axis at $t = 0$. However, no information specified along the boundary at $x = 0$ or $x = L$ will be transmitted to the position $x = L/2$ until $t > L/2c$. Therefore, to obtain a solution at point P, or anywhere in the shaded portion of Figure 1.11, it is only necessary to have specified initial conditions. Because two families of characteristics emanate from the x-axis, two conditions must be specified at $t = 0$ for all x, these conditions being values of both h and h_t because the order of any derivative in the initial condition for this problem must be less than 2. Specification of both a function and its normal derivative along a boundary is known as a *Cauchy boundary condition*.

If one shifts point P in the x-direction, characteristics that emanate from the boundaries at $x = 0$ and $x = L$ become important, as indicated in Figure 1.12a and b. The location where boundary conditions must be specified, as well as the domain of dependence for the solution at P, are indicated, respectively, by wavy lines and shading. Only one characteristic family originates from the $x = 0$ (and $x = L$) boundary. Information propagates forward in time along these characteristics. Therefore, it is necessary to specify only one boundary condition along $x = 0$ and one along $x = L$. Note that for any point P in the region of interest (e.g., Figure 1.12c) the domain of influence is bounded, at least in part, by the x-axis along which h and h_t are specified. Because h is

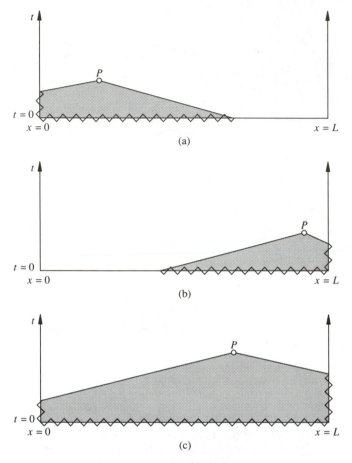

Figure 1.12 Regions of influence of conditions specified on three different portions of the x and t axes (shown by a wavy line) when solving equation (1.3.48).

specified along this part of the boundary, the boundary condition along $x = 0$ or $x = L$ need not include h. Sufficient boundary conditions at these positions are specification of either h, h_x, or a linear combination of the two, such as $\alpha h + \beta h_x$. Figure 1.13 depicts the boundary conditions required to solve hyperbolic equation (1.3.48) in the domain $0 < t \leq T$ and $0 < x < L$.

The differential equation considered is an initial value problem in time because conditions are specified at only the beginning or initial time. However, the equation is a boundary value problem in the spatial domain because conditions must be specified at both ends of the string. Thus the problem of a vibrating string is a mixed initial and boundary value problem.

It is worth noting that the plot of characteristics for the parabolic problem, Figure 1.7, represents a limiting case of the hyperbolic characteristics presented in Figure 1.10. As the magnitude of c, the velocity at which a disturbance propagates into

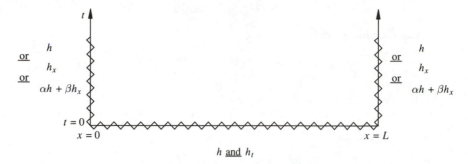

Figure 1.13   Boundary and initial conditions for hyperbolic equation (1.3.48) solved in the region $0 < x < L$ and $t > 0$.

the domain, becomes infinite, Figure 1.10 becomes identical to Figure 1.7. Thus from a study of the primary characteristics, the parabolic problem may be thought of as the limit of the hyperbolic problem where the disturbance propagation velocity becomes infinite. Note, however, that for the parabolic problem, secondary characteristics are needed to provide a full description of information propagation.

A final example of a differential equation in two independent variables is the equation describing propagation of a surface elevation disturbance into a channel where flow is uniform (i.e., flow velocity and depth are initially constant in the channel). The governing equation is

$$h_{tt} + 2vh_{tx} + (v^2 - c^2)h_{xx} = 0 \qquad (1.3.53)$$

where

v is the positive constant uniform flow velocity,

c is the magnitude of the velocity of the disturbance, or celerity,

h is the amplitude of the surface disturbance,

t is time, and

x is space.

Let the temporal domain be $0 < t \leq T$ and the spatial domain be $0 < x < L$. Note that when the flow velocity is zero, this equation becomes identical to equation (1.3.48), the equation for propagation of a disturbance along a string.

With reference to the standard PDE of equation (1.3.16), $A = v^2 - c^2$, $B = v$, $C = 1$, and $D = E = R = 0$. Therefore,

$$B^2 - AC = c^2 > 0 \qquad (1.3.54)$$

and equation (1.3.53) is hyperbolic with two real characteristics. The equations for the characteristics are, from Table 1.1,

$$\varphi_t = (c - v)\varphi_x \qquad (1.3.55a)$$

and

$$\varphi_t = -(c+v)\varphi_x \qquad (1.3.55b)$$

Thus the characteristics are

$$\varphi = \varphi\Big((x-x_0) + (c-v)(t-t^0)\Big) \qquad (1.3.56a)$$

and

$$\varphi = \varphi\Big((x-x_0) - (c+v)(t-t^0)\Big) \qquad (1.3.56b)$$

or

$$(x-x_0) + (c-v)(t-t^0) = 0 \qquad (1.3.57a)$$

$$(x-x_0) - (c+v)(t-t^0) = 0 \qquad (1.3.57b)$$

For these characteristics, three regimes can be identified that require different boundary conditions. The first regime is for the case where $c > v$. The characteristics for this situation are sketched in Figure 1.14a. Note that two families emanate from the x-axis while one family emanates from each end of the domain. Figure 1.14b shows the domain of dependence for point P. Solutions in this domain depend only on the conditions specified at $t = 0$, not upon conditions set at $x = 0$ or $x = L$. Because two families of characteristics intersect the x-axis, two initial conditions are required, both h and h_t. Note that conditions specified at $x = 0$ and $x = L$ propagate along characteristics in the direction of increasing time. For the case of $c > v$, this information propagates into the domain of interest. Therefore, to obtain a solution for the total domain of the problem, one additional condition must be specified at $x = 0$ and one at $x = L$. This condition may be either h, h_x, or a linear combination of the two. The boundary conditions needed to obtain a solution to equation (1.3.53) where $c > v$ in the domain $0 < t \le T$ and $0 < x < L$ are indicated in Figure 1.14c. This problem is an initial value problem in time and a boundary value problem in space.

The second regime of interest in solving equation (1.3.53) is when $c < v$. From equations (1.3.57) it can be seen that both characteristics have a positive slope when plotted in the x-t plane as in Figure 1.15a. In this case, point P, the point of maximum time that is uninfluenced by conditions imposed at the ends of the domain, is located at $x = L$. The domain of dependence for the solution at P is indicated in Figure 1.15b. Note that the solution in this region is dependent only on two specified initial conditions, h and h_t, because information specified at $x = L$ does not propagate into the system but propagates forward in time to x locations greater than L. Physically, the velocity of the flow is greater than the upstream celerity of a condition imposed at $x = L$, and thus any condition imposed there is washed out of the system. Figure 1.15c indicates that the solution to equation (1.3.53) above the domain of dependence of point P for $c < v$ is independent of initial conditions but depends on information propagating along two characteristic families from the $x = 0$ axis. Thus both h and h_x must be specified at $x = 0$ and no conditions are specified at $x = L$. Solution of equation (1.3.53) in the entire domain of interest when $c < v$ requires conditions as indicated in Figure 1.15d. Thus when the velocity of the flow is greater than the celerity of the disturbance, the differential equation is an initial value problem in both time and space.

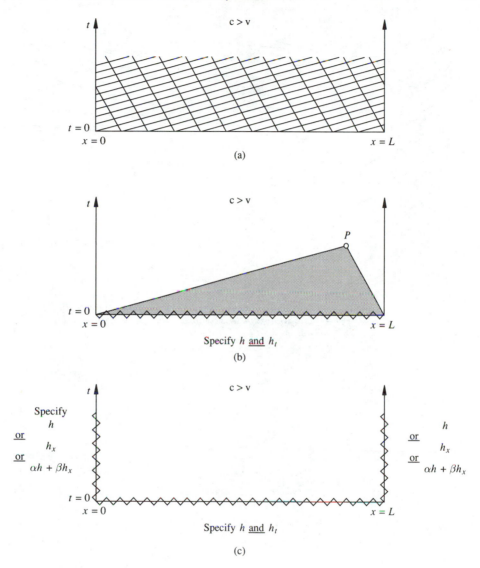

Figure 1.14 For hyperbolic equation (1.3.53) with $c > v$ and characteristics given by equations (1.3.57): (a) Characteristics in region $0 < x < L$ and $t > 0$. (b) Region of influence of the initial conditions which is unaffected by the boundary condition at $x = 0$ and $x = L$. (c) Boundary and initial conditions in region $0 < x < L$ and $t > 0$.

The third possible regime for equation (1.3.53) is the case where $c = v$. Characteristics for this situation are plotted in Figure 1.16a. In this regime, as with the second regime, information specified at the downstream boundary, $x = L$, does not propagate back into the problem domain. Note that two families of characteristics intersect the x-axis while only one family intersects the t-axis. The domain where the solution is

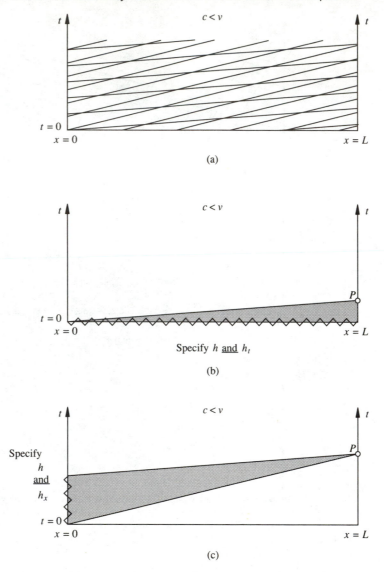

Figure 1.15   For hyperbolic equation (1.3.53) with $c < v$ and characteristics given by equation (1.3.57): (a) Characteristics in region $0 < x < L$ and $t > 0$. (b) Region of influence of the initial conditions where boundary conditions at $x = 0$ have no effect. (c) Region of influence of the boundary conditions at $x = 0$ where the initial conditions have no effect.

dependent only on the initial conditions and is independent of conditions imposed at $x = 0$ and L is indicated in Figure 1.16b. Because two characteristics intersect the x-axis, both h and h_t must be specified at the initial time. The characteristic family that intersects the time axis at $x = 0$ affects the flow in the problem domain above the point

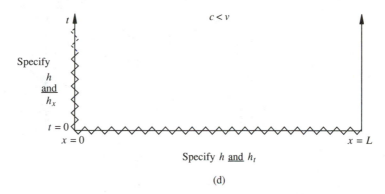

Figure 1.15 (cont'd.)   For hyperbolic equation (1.3.53) with $c < v$ and characteristics given by equation (1.3.57): (d) Boundary and initial conditions in region $0 < x < L$ and $t > 0$.

P region of influence. Thus only one condition must be specified at $x = 0$ and none are specified at $x = L$, as indicated in Figure 1.16c. When $v = c$, equation (1.3.53) is an initial value problem in both time and space.

This last example demonstrates that for a hyperbolic problem, knowledge of the characteristics is essential for imposition of appropriate boundary conditions. Depending on the value of parameters in the problem, the locations where boundary conditions must be imposed and even the number of conditions needed to obtain the solution to a differential equation can be affected.

The examples above are simple in that the coefficients of the equations were selected to be constant. When these coefficients are not constant, the equation type can be different in different regions of the solution domain and the characteristic lines can be curves. Furthermore, explicit solutions for the characteristics may not be readily obtained. However, determination of equation type for the second-order problem in two-independent variables, equation (1.3.16), provides information about required boundary conditions for many problems of physical interest. Elliptic equations are boundary value problems, independent of time, and must be solved in a closed region. A boundary condition is required at each point on the boundary. A parabolic equation is commonly (though not always) a transient problem. The equation is an initial value problem in time and a boundary value problem in space. The region of solution is open-ended in time (i.e., extends to infinity), and an initial condition in time is required, together with boundary conditions at both ends of the spatial domain. A hyperbolic equation requires specification of two initial conditions. Typically, two auxiliary conditions are required in the spatial domain. However, whether the problem is an initial value or boundary value problem in space depends on the celerity, the speed of propagation of a disturbance.

1.3.4 Second-Order Partial Differential Equations (Three Independent Variables)

In Section 1.3.2 second-order partial differential equations were classified as elliptic, parabolic, or hyperbolic, depending on whether the equation had zero, one, or two real

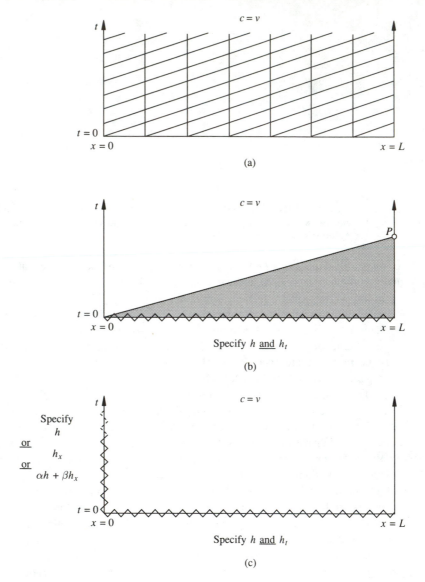

Figure 1.16 For hyperbolic equation (1.3.53) with $c = v$ and characteristics given by equation (1.3.57): (a) Characteristics in region $0 < x < L$ and $t > 0$. (b) Region of influence of the initial conditions where boundary conditions at $x = 0$ have no effect. (c) Boundary and initial conditions in region $0 < x < L$ and $t > 0$.

characteristic curves, respectively. This classification scheme can be extended to the case of three independent variables except that here the characteristic curves are surfaces, and not all equations fall into one of these three categories.

Consider the quasilinear second-order PDE

$$Au_{tt} + Bu_{xx} + Cu_{yy} + 2Du_{xy} + 2Eu_{xt} + 2Fu_{yt} + Gu_t + Hu_x + Ku_y = R \quad (1.3.58)$$

where A, B, C, D, E, F, G, H, and K may be functions of x, y, t, u_x, u_y, u_t, and u, and R may depend on x, y, t, and u. This equation may be converted to a first-order form by defining

$$f = u_t \qquad (1.3.59)$$

$$g = u_x \qquad (1.3.60)$$

$$h = u_y \qquad (1.3.61)$$

Then note that

$$g_y = h_x \qquad (1.3.62)$$

$$f_x = g_t \qquad (1.3.63)$$

$$f_y = h_t \qquad (1.3.64)$$

and replace second derivatives of u in equation (1.3.58) with first derivatives of f, g, and h, to obtain

$$Af_t + Bg_x + Ch_y + D(g_y + h_x) + E(f_x + g_t) + F(f_y + h_t) + Gu_t + Hu_x + Ku_y = R \quad (1.3.65)$$

These last seven equations form the basis of the following effort to define surfaces on which specification of u, f, g, and h is insufficient information for determination of u throughout a domain of interest. These surfaces are the characteristics of the equation.

For problems in three independent variables, surfaces in x, y, and t (or $\mathbf{x}, t$ space) are examined. These surfaces may be defined as

$$\varphi(x, y, t) \equiv \varphi(\mathbf{x}, t) = \text{constant} \qquad (1.3.66)$$

If one moves from point $(\mathbf{x}, t)$ to point $(\mathbf{x} + d\mathbf{x}, t + dt)$ the function φ will undergo a change in value $d\varphi$ where

$$d\varphi = \varphi_x \, dx + \varphi_y \, dy + \varphi_t \, dt \qquad (1.3.67)$$

If the movement is constrained such that φ remains constant, then

$$D\varphi = 0 = \varphi_x \, Dx + \varphi_y \, Dy + \varphi_t \, Dt \qquad (1.3.68)$$

where the notational change from d to D is used to indicate movement in space-time on the surface defined by $\varphi = $ constant. If the motion is further constrained to take place with y constant, then $Dy = 0$ and equation (1.3.68) becomes

$$\left(\frac{Dt}{Dx} \right)_y = -\frac{\varphi_x}{\varphi_t} \qquad (1.3.69)$$

where the y subscripted on Dt/Dx is used to indicate that y is held constant. Similarly, if Dx is zero, motion on φ occurs with only Dy and Dt changing and

$$\left(\frac{Dt}{Dy} \right)_x = -\frac{\varphi_y}{\varphi_t} \qquad (1.3.70)$$

Now consider the change in u due to movement from $(\mathbf{x}, t)$ to $(\mathbf{x} + d\mathbf{x}, t + dt)$. This infinitesimal change is denoted by

$$du = u_t \, dt + u_x \, dx + u_y \, dy \tag{1.3.71}$$

If the motion occurs on a surface φ, this is indicated by

$$Du = u_t \, Dt + u_x \, Dx + u_y \, Dy \tag{1.3.72}$$

where Du is the change in u obtained due to movement on the surface of constant φ. If the movement is constrained such that $Dy = 0$ as well as $D\varphi$, then, after division by Dx, equation (1.3.72) becomes

$$u_x = -u_t \left(\frac{Dt}{Dx} \right)_y + \left(\frac{Du}{Dx} \right)_y \tag{1.3.73}$$

However, equation (1.3.69) provides an alternative expression for $(Dt/Dx)_y$ that can be substituted into equation (1.3.73) to obtain

$$u_x = u_t \frac{\varphi_x}{\varphi_t} + \left(\frac{Du}{Dx} \right)_y \tag{1.3.74a}$$

By an analogous series of steps in which x and y are interchanged in the derivation following equation (1.3.72),

$$u_y = u_t \frac{\varphi_y}{\varphi_t} + \left(\frac{Du}{Dy} \right)_x \tag{1.3.74b}$$

Manipulations identical to those performed on u in this paragraph can be performed on f, g, and h to obtain

$$f_x = f_t \frac{\varphi_x}{\varphi_t} + \left(\frac{Df}{Dx} \right)_y \tag{1.3.75a}$$

$$f_y = f_t \frac{\varphi_y}{\varphi_t} + \left(\frac{Df}{Dy} \right)_x \tag{1.3.75b}$$

$$g_x = g_t \frac{\varphi_x}{\varphi_t} + \left(\frac{Dg}{Dx} \right)_y \tag{1.3.76a}$$

$$g_y = g_t \frac{\varphi_y}{\varphi_t} + \left(\frac{Dg}{Dy} \right)_x \tag{1.3.76b}$$

$$h_x = h_t \frac{\varphi_x}{\varphi_t} + \left(\frac{Dh}{Dx} \right)_y \tag{1.3.77a}$$

$$h_y = h_t \frac{\varphi_y}{\varphi_t} + \left(\frac{Dh}{Dy} \right)_x \tag{1.3.77b}$$

If u, f, g, and h are specified on a surface φ, these last eight equations provide expressions for partial derivatives of these functions with respect to a spatial variable in terms of a partial derivative with respect to time and some known quantities. [For example, if h is known on a specified surface φ, then φ_x, φ_y, φ_t, $(Dh/Dy)_x$, and $(Dh/Dx)_y$ can be calculated so that h_x and h_y in equation (1.3.77) may be expressed in terms of h_t and these known quantities.]

Substitution of equations (1.3.74)–(1.3.77) into (1.3.65) to eliminate derivatives with respect to spatial coordinates followed by regrouping of terms yields

$$\frac{u_t(G\varphi_t + H\varphi_x + K\varphi_y)}{\varphi_t} + \frac{f_t(A\varphi_t + E\varphi_x + F\varphi_y)}{\varphi_t} + \frac{g_t(E\varphi_t + B\varphi_x + D\varphi_y)}{\varphi_t}$$

$$+\frac{h_t(F\varphi_t + D\varphi_x + C\varphi_y)}{\varphi_t} = \mathcal{R} \qquad (1.3.78)$$

where the known quantities are grouped in $\mathcal{R}$, which is given by

$$\mathcal{R} = R - B\left(\frac{Dg}{Dx}\right)_y - C\left(\frac{Dh}{Dy}\right)_x - D\left(\frac{Dg}{Dy}\right)_x - D\left(\frac{Dh}{Dx}\right)_y$$

$$-E\left(\frac{Df}{Dx}\right)_y - F\left(\frac{Df}{Dy}\right)_x - H\left(\frac{Du}{Dx}\right)_y - K\left(\frac{Du}{Dy}\right)_x \qquad (1.3.79)$$

Now recall equation (1.3.59):

$$u_t = f \qquad (1.3.80)$$

Also combine (1.3.63) with (1.3.75a) to obtain

$$g_t = f_t\frac{\varphi_x}{\varphi_t} + \left(\frac{Df}{Dx}\right)_y \qquad (1.3.81)$$

and combine (1.3.64) with (1.3.75b) to obtain

$$h_t = f_t\frac{\varphi_y}{\varphi_t} + \left(\frac{Df}{Dy}\right)_x \qquad (1.3.82)$$

These last three equations can be combined with equation (1.3.78) to obtain the matrix equation

$$\begin{bmatrix} \dfrac{G\varphi_t + H\varphi_x + K\varphi_y}{\varphi_t} & \dfrac{A\varphi_t + E\varphi_x + F\varphi_y}{\varphi_t} & \dfrac{E\varphi_t + B\varphi_x + D\varphi_y}{\varphi_t} & \dfrac{F\varphi_t + D\varphi_x + C\varphi_y}{\varphi_t} \\ 1 & 0 & 0 & 0 \\ 0 & \varphi_x & -\varphi_t & 0 \\ 0 & \varphi_y & 0 & -\varphi_t \end{bmatrix} \begin{bmatrix} u_t \\ f_t \\ g_t \\ h_t \end{bmatrix}$$

$$= \begin{bmatrix} \mathcal{R} \\ f \\ -\varphi_t\left(\dfrac{Df}{Dx}\right)_y \\ -\varphi_t\left(\dfrac{Df}{Dy}\right)_x \end{bmatrix} \qquad (1.3.83)$$

This equation indicates that u_t, f_t, g_t, and h_t may be obtained on a surface φ where u, f, g, and h are specified unless the determinant of the matrix is zero. If the determinant is zero, the surface φ is a characteristic. Thus the equation of the characteristic may be obtained by setting the determinant equal to zero, or

$$A\varphi_t^2 + B\varphi_x^2 + C\varphi_y^2 + 2D\varphi_x\varphi_y + 2E\varphi_x\varphi_t + 2F\varphi_y\varphi_t = 0 \tag{1.3.84}$$

The equation for the secondary characteristic (which is the primary characteristic of the first-order equation obtained when A, B, C, D, E, and F are all zero) is given by

$$G\varphi_t + H\varphi_x + K\varphi_y = 0 \tag{1.3.85}$$

The explicit determination of characteristics for a second-order differential equation in three independent variables is, in general, complex. A table such as Table 1.1 prepared for characteristics of equations in two independent variables is not readily constructed. In the next section, some relatively simple though important specific equations in three variables are analyzed.

1.3.5 Example Second-Order Partial Differential Equations (Three Independent Variables)

For steady-state conduction in a homogeneous isotropic block of material, the governing equation is

$$T_{xx} + T_{yy} + T_{zz} = 0 \tag{1.3.86}$$

If z is used in place of t in the model equation (1.3.58), then $A = B = C = 1$ and the other coefficients are zero. The equation for the characteristics, (1.3.84), becomes

$$\varphi_x^2 + \varphi_y^2 + \varphi_z^2 = 0 \tag{1.3.87}$$

This equation cannot be satisfied if φ_x, φ_y, and φ_z are constrained to be real with at least one of these terms being nonzero. Therefore, no real characteristics exist and equation (1.3.86) is elliptic. Either T, T_n (the normal gradient of T), or a linear combination of these quantities must be specified at every point on the boundary surface. As with the two-independent-variable case, T must be specified for at least one point on the boundary to ensure a unique solution.

A second example that indicates some of the utility of the characteristic analysis is the equation describing transient transport of a dissolved chemical species. Assume that this process is to be modeled as pure advection in the x-direction and pure diffusion in the y-direction. Let the spatial boundaries of the domain be $0 < x < L$ and $0 < y < b$. The equation describing this process is

$$\frac{\partial u}{\partial t} + v\frac{\partial u}{\partial x} - \mathcal{D}\frac{\partial^2 u}{\partial y^2} = 0 \tag{1.3.88}$$

where the velocity, v, and diffusion coefficient, $\mathcal{D}$, are constants. This equation corresponds to equation (1.3.53) with $G = 1$, $H = v$, and $C = -\mathcal{D}$. From equation (1.3.84), the characteristic equation is

$$-\mathcal{D}\varphi_y^2 = 0 \tag{1.3.89}$$

This expression has a double root and describes a characteristic, $\varphi(x - x_0, t - t^0)$, which spans the y-domain of the problem for any fixed coordinate values of x and t. Thus boundary conditions are needed at both y boundaries. Equation (1.3.89) defines only one unique characteristic family, but another may be obtained from the secondary characteristic equation (1.3.85) as

$$\varphi_t + v\varphi_x = 0 \qquad (1.3.90)$$

Therefore, the secondary characteristic has the functional form

$$\varphi = \varphi\left((x - x_0) - v(t - t^0), y - y_0\right) \qquad (1.3.91)$$

This secondary characteristic, at a fixed y location, demonstrates that information propagates into the system from the $t = 0$ axis and from the $x = 0$ position. Thus auxiliary conditions are needed at the initial time ($t = 0$) and at the inlet ($x = 0$). Notice that no information need be prescribed at the outflow boundary in the x-direction. Equation (1.3.88) may be thought of as being hyperbolic with respect to t and x and parabolic with respect to t and y.

It is very important to note that if the x-direction velocity, v, and the y-direction width, b, were allowed to be functions of x, with the constraint that $vb =$ constant still imposed, the application of boundary conditions for equation (1.3.88) is greatly complicated. (This case is discussed in Problems 1.5 and 1.6.) Often the reason that a numerical solution to a problem is sought rather than an analytic solution is that the boundaries of the domain of interest are not parallel to coordinate axes. In these instances, application of appropriate boundary conditions can be a matter of art and requires engineering judgment as well as mathematical rigor.

As a third example, consider the equation of propagation of a disturbance in a two-dimensional domain, such as the movement of sound waves in a drumhead. Dissipation of the wave will be neglected. The governing differential equation is

$$h_{tt} - c^2(h_{xx} + h_{yy}) = 0 \qquad (1.3.92)$$

where c is the wave celerity and h is the displacement of a point on the drumhead from its rest position. Based on the general equation (1.3.58), $A = 1$, $B = -c^2$, $C = -c^2$, and the other coefficients are zero. Then the expression for the characteristics can be obtained from equation (1.3.84) as

$$\varphi_t^2 - c^2(\varphi_x^2 + \varphi_y^2) = 0 \qquad (1.3.93)$$

which has the solutions

$$\varphi = \varphi\left(c(t - t^0) + [(x - x_0)^2 + (y - y_0)^2]^{1/2}\right) \qquad (1.3.94a)$$

and

$$\varphi = \varphi\left(c(t - t^0) - [(x - x_0)^2 + (y - y_0)^2]^{1/2}\right) \qquad (1.3.94b)$$

Therefore, the equations for the characteristic surfaces are the conoidal sections

$$c(t - t^0) + [(x - x_0)^2 + (y - y_0)^2]^{1/2} = 0 \qquad (1.3.95a)$$

and

$$c(t - t^0) - [(x - x_0)^2 + (y - y_0)^2]^{1/2} = 0 \qquad (1.3.95b)$$

Because two real characteristics exist, equation (1.3.92) is hyperbolic. As with the example in one space dimension, because two characteristics emanate from the constant time plane, two initial conditions are required. In addition, one condition is needed at each point on the spatial boundary. For the case of the drumhead, the initial conditions would be the state of displacement and the rate of change of this displacement (h and h_t) while the boundary conditions would be zero displacement ($h = 0$) all along the rim of the drum.

These three examples provide some insight into the use of characteristics to obtain appropriate boundary conditions for multidimensional problems. However, not all equations can be analyzed easily using characteristics. For example, when the coefficients in equation (1.3.58) are strong functions of space, time, or the first derivatives, the analysis to obtain characteristics may become virtually impossible. Also, the geometry of the characteristic surfaces can be complex. In these instances, specification of the correct boundary conditions for a numerical simulation is subject to approximations. Irregular geometry of the solution domain can also contribute to difficulty in specifying appropriate boundary conditions. Finally, the analysis here has been restricted to quasilinear first- and second-order differential equations. For nonlinear equations the analysis for characteristics is more complex. However, virtually all equations of physical interest can be classified.

1.3.6 Second-Order Partial Differential Equations (Four Independent Variables)

The derivations in the preceding section for the characteristics of second-order differential equations may be extended to equations in four or more independent variables. For these cases, the characteristics are hypersurfaces. The derivation follows the same reasoning as was used in the previous cases and is left as an exercise in Problem 1.7.

Without performing the formal derivation of the equation for the characteristics, the result can be inferred by comparison of equations (1.3.84) and (1.3.85) with equation (1.3.58). The primary characteristics depend only on the coefficients of the second derivatives. These coefficients multiply products of first derivatives of the characteristic functions in the corresponding independent variables. The secondary characteristics are obtained in a similar manner using the first derivative terms.

For example, the three-dimensional transient equation describing advection and diffusion of a reacting chemical species is

$$u_t + U u_x + V u_y + W u_z - \mathcal{D}(u_{xx} + u_{yy} + u_{zz}) - ku = 0 \qquad (1.3.96)$$

where u is concentration; U, V, and W are x, y, and z velocity components, respectively, $\mathcal{D}$ is the diffusion coefficient, and k is the reaction rate constant. This equation has characteristics given by

$$\varphi_{xx} + \varphi_{yy} + \varphi_{zz} = 0 \qquad (1.3.97)$$

and secondary characteristics given by

$$\varphi_t + U\varphi_x + V\varphi_y + W\varphi_z = 0 \qquad (1.3.98)$$

From equation (1.3.97), only one real characteristic may be obtained,

$$\varphi = \varphi(t - t^0) \qquad (1.3.99a)$$

or

$$t - t^0 = 0 \qquad (1.3.99b)$$

Thus equation (1.3.96) is parabolic and the secondary characteristic is of interest. If U, V, and W are constant, solution of equation (1.3.98) yields

$$\varphi\left((U^2 + V^2 + W^2)(t - t^0) - U(x - x_0) - V(y - y_0) - W(z - z_0)\right) = 0 \quad (1.3.100a)$$

or

$$(U^2 + V^2 + W^2)(t - t^0) - U(x - x_0) - V(y - y_0) - W(z - z_0) = 0 \quad (1.3.100b)$$

If U, V, or W is not constant, the secondary characteristics will include some curvature. Otherwise, equation (1.3.100b) defines a hyperplane that is analogous to the simpler curves of equation (1.3.15b).

Numerical simulation in time and three spatial dimensions becomes very difficult because large amounts of computer time and storage are typically needed, irregular geometry of a domain of interest is difficult to incorporate into a model, differential equations being simulated are often quasilinear or nonlinear, and knowledge and proper application of boundary conditions is complex. Preliminary analytical analysis for characteristics of such an equation may not yield explicit forms of the characteristics, but it can provide insight into the behavior of the solution and guidance in the selection of an appropriate numerical method.

1.4 CONCLUSION

This chapter is intended to provide some physical as well as mathematical understanding of the behavior of partial differential equations through analysis of their characteristics and boundary conditions. The examples presented are relatively simple in that they involve linear equations with constant coefficients. Therefore, processes such as the formation of shocks or those which cause the classification of a differential equation to be dependent on location in the solution domain are not considered. Additionally, in all the examples presented the characteristics did not exhibit any curvature. Nevertheless, the insights that can be gained from understanding of the mechanisms of information propagation along characteristics are very helpful in developing computational algorithms capable of capturing the physics of a problem.

At times numerical simulation is viewed abstractly as an approximate tool for solution of a differential equation. However, when a simulation is attempted in the context of understanding of the physical processes of interest, the opportunity for a real growth in knowledge is greatly enhanced. Characteristics are valuable tools that contribute to such understanding, assist in the identification of necessary and sufficient boundary conditions, and help in formulation and selection of computational algorithms.

PROBLEMS

1.1. Classify the following differential equations (1) as ordinary or partial; (2) as to order; (3) as to degree; (4) as linear, nonlinear, or quasilinear; and (5) as homogeneous or nonhomogeneous.

(a) $\dfrac{\partial u}{\partial t} + v\dfrac{\partial u}{\partial x} - \dfrac{\partial}{\partial x}\left(D\dfrac{\partial u}{\partial x}\right) + ku^2 = 0$

where v, D, and k are constants

(b) $\dfrac{\partial T}{\partial t} - \dfrac{\partial}{\partial x}\left(\kappa\dfrac{\partial T}{\partial x}\right) = 0$

where $\kappa = \kappa(T)$

(c) $\dfrac{\partial \zeta}{\partial t} + h\dfrac{\partial u}{\partial x} = 0$

$\dfrac{\partial u}{\partial t} + \tau u + g\dfrac{\partial \zeta}{\partial x} = 0$

where h, τ, and g are constants

(d) $\dfrac{d^2 f}{dx^2} + M\left[1 + \left(\dfrac{df}{dx}\right)^2\right]^{1.5} = 0$

where $M = M(x)$

(e) $S\dfrac{\partial h}{\partial t} - \dfrac{\partial}{\partial x}\left(T\dfrac{\partial h}{\partial x}\right) - \dfrac{\partial}{\partial y}\left(T\dfrac{\partial h}{\partial y}\right) = Q$

where

$$Q = Q(x, y, t)$$
$$T = T(x, y, h)$$
$$S = S(x, y)$$

1.2. Given the differential equation

$$\frac{\partial u}{\partial t} + v\frac{\partial u}{\partial x} = 0$$

where $u = u(x, t)$, x has units of feet, and t has units of seconds, determine the following solutions, if possible.

(a) If $u(0, t) = 1$, $u(x, 0) = 0$, and $v = 2$ ft/sec, find $u(1, 1)$, $u(3, 2)$, and $u(7, 2)$.

(b) If $u(0, t) = 1$, $u\left(x, (x - 2)/v\right) = 2$, and $v = 1$ ft/sec, find $u(1, 3)$, $u(1, 2)$, $u(4, 1)$, and $u(4, 4)$.

(c) If $u(0, t) = t/\text{sec}$, $u(x, 0) = x/\text{ft}$, and $v = 3$ ft/sec, find $u(1, 1)$, $u(3, 2)$, $u(4, 4)$, and $u(1, 3)$.

(d) If $u(0, t) = t/\text{sec}$, $u(x, 0) = x/\text{ft}$, and $v = x/\text{sec}$, find $u(1, 1)$, $u(3, 2)$, $u(4, 4)$, and $u(1, 3)$.

(e) If $u(0, t) = 1$ for $3 \geq t > 0$ and $u(x, x/2 - 1) = 2$, and $v = 1$ ft/sec, find the domain where a solution may be obtained and the solution within that domain.

1.3. Equation (1.3.16), the second-order PDE in x and t, can be reexpressed by equations (1.3.17) through (1.3.20). Develop a series of manipulations analogous to those in Section 1.3.2 to obtain the equation for characteristics as follows.

(a) Show that

$$u_t = \frac{Du}{Dt} + u_x \frac{\varphi_t}{\varphi_x}$$

$$f_t = \frac{Df}{Dt} + f_x \frac{\varphi_t}{\varphi_x}$$

$$g_t = \frac{Dg}{Dt} + g_x \frac{\varphi_t}{\varphi_x}$$

(b) Use the relations in part (a) to eliminate u_t, f_t, and g_t from equation (1.3.19).

(c) Use equation (1.3.18), $g = u_x$, and equation (1.3.27c), with g_t replaced by f_x, together with the result of part (b) to obtain a 3×3 matrix equation with u_x, f_x, and g_x as unknowns.

(d) Obtain the equation for the characteristics and compare with equation (1.3.34).

1.4. The equation describing two-dimensional, steady-state diffusion and first-order decay of a chemical species is

$$\mathcal{D}[u_{xx} + u_{yy}] + ku = 0$$

where $\mathcal{D}$ is the constant diffusion coefficient and k is the chemical reaction rate constant. Assume that this equation applies in a two-dimensional region Ω with boundary $\partial\Omega$.

(a) Classify this equation as elliptic, hyperbolic, or parabolic and obtain the equation for the characteristics.

(b) Let the boundary conditions for this problem be of Neumann type such that

$$\frac{\partial u}{\partial n} = f(x, y) \text{ on } \partial\Omega$$

where n is the direction normal to the boundary. If u_1 is a solution to this problem such that it satisfies the differential equation and the boundary conditions, show that this solution is unique unless k or f is zero.

1.5. Consider flow and transport between two plates of length L where the distance between the plates is given by $b = b_0 + \alpha x$, as shown in the figure. Assume that all properties are constant in the direction normal to x and y. If diffusion in the x-direction is considered negligible, the velocity in the x-direction is independent of y, and the flow rate through the aperture is constant, then the equation describing the transport is

$$\frac{\partial u}{\partial t} + v\frac{\partial u}{\partial x} - \mathcal{D}\frac{\partial^2 u}{\partial y^2} = 0$$

where $vb = Q = $ constant.

(a) Show that the characteristics for this problem are given by $\varphi_y^2 = 0$ such that

$$\varphi(x - x_0, t - t^0) = 0$$

(b) Show that the secondary characteristic has the functional form

$$\varphi = \varphi\left\{\frac{1}{Q}\left[b_0(x - x_0) + \frac{1}{2}\alpha x^2\right] - [t - t^0], y - y_0\right\}$$

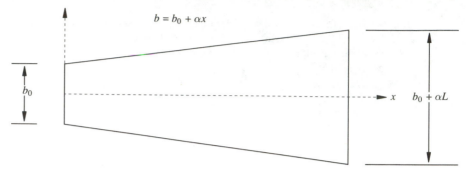

$$b = b_0 + \alpha x$$

(c) Sketch the primary and secondary characteristics for this problem.

(d) The following boundary conditions have been proposed for this problem for the function $u(x, y, t)$:

   (i) $u(0, y, t) = f(y)$ where $f(y)$ is known

   (ii) $\dfrac{\partial u}{\partial n}\left(x, \dfrac{1}{2}(\alpha x + b_0), t\right) = 0$

   (iii) $\dfrac{\partial u}{\partial n}\left(x, -\dfrac{1}{2}(\alpha x + b_0), t\right) = 0$

   (iv) $u(x, y, 0) = 0$

   Note that conditions (ii) and (iii) indicate no diffusion into the walls of the aperture. Discuss whether or not these conditions are sufficient to obtain a unique solution to the problem.

1.6. One proposal for simplifying the analysis and solution of Problem 1.5 is to include a term in the governing equation that allows for a very small amount of diffusion in the x-direction. Thus the problem solution is essentially unchanged, but the equation is modified to the form

$$\frac{\partial u}{\partial t} + v\frac{\partial u}{\partial x} - D\frac{\partial^2 u}{\partial y^2} - \epsilon\frac{\partial^2 u}{\partial x^2} = 0$$

where ϵ is very small.

(a) Obtain the characteristics for this equation and classify the equation by type.

(b) Obtain the secondary characteristics, if any.

(c) Sketch the characteristics for the problem.

(d) Pose suitable boundary conditions for the problem.

(e) Discuss differences between this problem and Problem 1.5.

1.7. (a) Write the quasilinear second-order PDE analogous to equation (1.3.58) with three spatial variables and time.

   (b) Show that if the characteristics are defined by $\varphi(\mathbf{x}, t) = \text{constant}$, then

$$\left(\frac{Dt}{Dx}\right)_{y,z} = -\frac{\varphi_x}{\varphi_t}$$

$$\left(\frac{Dt}{Dy}\right)_{x,z} = -\frac{\varphi_y}{\varphi_t}$$

$$\left(\frac{Dt}{Dz}\right)_{x,y} = -\frac{\varphi_z}{\varphi_t}$$

(c) Show that for a function u,

$$u_x = u_t \frac{\varphi_x}{\varphi_t} + \left(\frac{Du}{Dx}\right)_{y,z}$$

$$u_y = u_t \frac{\varphi_y}{\varphi_t} + \left(\frac{Du}{Dy}\right)_{x,z}$$

(d) Obtain the equations of the characteristics and the secondary characteristics.

Chapter 2

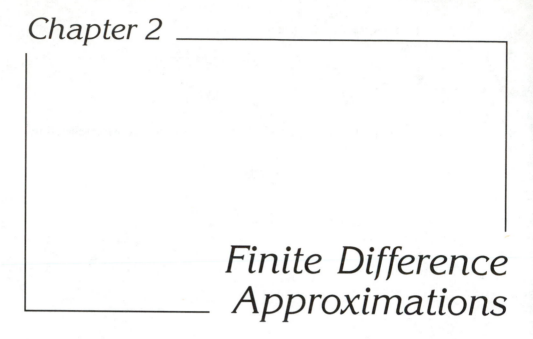

Finite Difference Approximations

2.0 INTRODUCTION

A fundamental tenet of numerical methods is the reduction of a differential equation to an approximation in terms of algebraic equations. This reduction replaces a continuous differential equation, whose solution space is generally infinite dimensional, with a finite set of algebraic equations whose solution space is finite dimensional. One avenue by which this reduction can be achieved is the finite difference method.

In broad outline form, the finite difference method proceeds by first identifying a finite number of discrete points within the domain of interest. These points are called *nodes*, and it is at these locations that approximations to the true solution are computed. Definition of the node locations is called the *discretization step*. Next the derivatives that appear in the governing differential equation are replaced by discrete difference approximations. These approximations are written in terms of nodal evaluations of the unknown function. This step, called the *approximation step*, produces a set of algebraic equations with discrete nodal values as unknowns. If the original differential operator is linear, the resulting algebraic system is also linear; otherwise, the algebraic equations may be nonlinear. The final step follows the approximation step and involves solution of the resulting algebraic system of equations. Upon completion of this step, a discrete approximation to the solution of the original differential equation is obtained.

The procedure described above provides a methodology for computation of an approximate solution. For the procedure to be of any general use, the approximate solution must demonstrably be a "good approximation" to the true solution. This consideration leads to two very important questions: (1) What is meant by the term *good approximation*? and (2) How can the quality of the approximate solution be assessed in comparison to the actual solution? The first question can be addressed in the context of the definition of a norm (Appendix A, Definition A.3.9). Let u be the true solution and U a finite difference approximation to u. While the definition of "good approximation" is always subjective, a general mathematical definition can be proposed as

$$\|u - U\| < \epsilon \qquad (2.0.1)$$

where $\| \cdot \|$ denotes a valid norm and ϵ is subjectively chosen to be sufficiently small. Showing a solution to be a good approximation is not trivial because, even if ϵ is given, the exact solution u is typically unknown. (If u were available, the approximation given by U would not be needed!) To determine the adequacy of an approximation requires analysis of each of the three steps (discretization, approximation, solution) involved in deriving the finite difference solution. This analysis takes place, in various ways, throughout this book.

The present chapter proceeds by first presenting the fundamental ideas that form the foundation of finite difference theory. Next standard finite difference nomenclature is introduced, including definition of a set of difference operators. The difference operators facilitate presentation of finite difference concepts, and also illustrate the underlying philosophy of the finite difference method: the replacement of a differential operator by a (finite) difference operator. The process of analyzing difference approximations is then initiated using Taylor series to define the important concepts of truncation error and consistency. A general procedure for deriving finite difference approximations in one dimension is then presented. The derivation enables all difference formulas to be viewed as particular cases of a universal formulation. Several examples are solved to illustrate practical implementations of the finite difference method. Among these examples is the use of finite difference analysis to derive several general classes of approximations for first-order initial value problems. Many of the traditional solution methods for initial value problems, including Runge-Kutta methods, Gear's methods, Adams-Bashforth methods, and Adams-Moulton methods, are shown to be subsets of these general formulations. Finite difference procedures are then extended to multiple dimensions and partial differential equations. The chapter concludes with example solutions for several partial differential equations that are important in many fields of science and engineering.

2.1 DISCRETE APPROXIMATIONS TO DERIVATIVES IN ONE DIMENSION

The underlying concept of a finite difference approximation can be viewed as a reversal of the limit process that is used to define derivatives. Given the standard definition for the derivative of a continuous function $u(x)$,

$$\frac{du}{dx} \equiv \lim_{h \to 0} \frac{u(x+h) - u(x)}{(x+h) - x} = \lim_{h \to 0} \frac{u(x+h) - u(x)}{h} \qquad (2.1.1)$$

a finite difference approximation to du/dx can be viewed as equation (2.1.1) without the limit process. That is, a finite value of h is used, so that an estimate of du/dx may be obtained algebraically from $u(x)$. Furthermore, in the finite difference method, the locations x and $x + h$ are usually chosen to coincide with predetermined node points. Thus a finite difference approximation to du/dx might be written as

$$\left.\frac{du}{dx}\right|_{x_i} \simeq \frac{u(x_i + h) - u(x_i)}{(x_i + h) - x_i} = \frac{u_{i+1} - u_i}{x_{i+1} - x_i} \qquad (2.1.2a)$$

where $u_i \equiv u(x_i)$, $u_{i+1} \equiv u(x_{i+1})$, x_i is a fixed spatial location, and $x_{i+1} \equiv x_i + h$. The points x_i and x_{i+1} are referred to as *node points*. The right side of equation (2.1.2a) provides an algebraic approximation to du/dx evaluated at the node point x_i. The geometric interpretation of equation (2.1.2a) is illustrated in Figure 2.1.

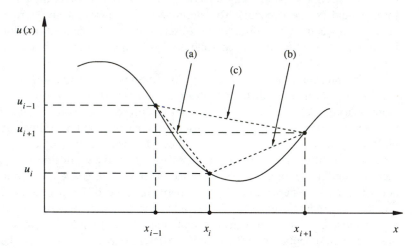

Figure 2.1   Location of nodes x_{i-1}, x_i, x_{i+1} and associated values of u_{i-1}, u_i, u_{i+1}. Slopes of lines (a), (b), and (c) correspond to approximations of $du/dx|_{x_i}$ used in equations (2.1.2a), (2.1.2b), and (2.1.2c), respectively.

A derivative does not have a unique finite difference approximation. Many possible approximate formulas may be found. For example, two additional approximations to $du/dx|_{x_i}$ are

$$\left.\frac{du}{dx}\right|_{x_i} \simeq \frac{u_i - u_{i-1}}{x_i - x_{i-1}} \qquad (2.1.2b)$$

$$\left.\frac{du}{dx}\right|_{x_i} \simeq \frac{u_{i+1} - u_{i-1}}{x_{i+1} - x_{i-1}} \qquad (2.1.2c)$$

where x_{i-1} is a node to the left of x_i (see Figure 2.1) and $u_{i-1} \equiv u(x_{i-1})$. These different approximations are illustrated geometrically in Figure 2.1. Whether any of the approximations in equations (2.1.2) qualifies as a good approximation, and which among the three is best, are topics that require a method of analysis for finite difference approximations.

Approximations similar in concept to those for first derivatives can be written for higher derivatives. For example, an approximation for the second derivative of $u(x)$ may be derived as follows:

$$\frac{d^2 u}{dx^2}\bigg|_{x_i} \simeq \frac{\dfrac{du}{dx}\bigg|_{x_{i+1/2}} - \dfrac{du}{dx}\bigg|_{x_{i-1/2}}}{x_{i+1/2} - x_{i-1/2}}$$

$$\simeq \frac{\dfrac{u_{i+1} - u_i}{x_{i+1} - x_i} - \dfrac{u_i - u_{i-1}}{x_i - x_{i-1}}}{x_{i+1/2} - x_{i-1/2}} \tag{2.1.3a}$$

where $x_{i \pm 1/2}$ represents the x-location of the midpoint between x_i and x_{i+1}. If the node spacing is constant, so that $x_{i+1/2} - x_{i-1/2} = x_{i+1} - x_i = x_i - x_{i-1} \equiv \Delta x$, equation (2.1.3a) simplifies to

$$\frac{d^2 u}{dx^2}\bigg|_{x_i} \simeq \frac{u_{i+1} - 2u_i + u_{i-1}}{(\Delta x)^2} \tag{2.1.3b}$$

Questions concerning the applicability of the approximations (2.1.3) again necessitate development of methods of analysis for finite difference formulas. A variety of mathematical tools and analytical methodologies are presented throughout this chapter, beginning in Section 2.3. Section 2.2 first defines basic notation and nomenclature associated with the finite difference method.

2.2 OPERATOR NOTATION AND THE PHILOSOPHY OF FINITE DIFFERENCES

2.2.1 Finite Difference Operators

Finite difference approximations are based on replacement of a continuous, differential operator with a discrete approximation written in terms of a finite number of nodal values of the unknown. The algebraic expressions that arise in finite difference approximations are often written using difference operators. Difference operators provide a compact notational representation of algebraic relations that commonly occur in finite difference approximations. They can also provide direct correspondence between the differential operator and the difference approximation to that operator.

A standard set of symbols, called *finite difference operators*, has evolved to represent basic algebraic relations that occur in finite difference approximations. The most common difference operators are defined as follows:

Forward difference operator, Δ $\qquad$ $\Delta u_i \equiv u_{i+1} - u_i$

Backward difference operator, ∇ $\qquad$ $\nabla u_i \equiv u_i - u_{i-1}$

Central difference operator, δ $\qquad$ $\delta u_i \equiv u_{i+1/2} - u_{i-1/2}$

Average operator, μ $\qquad$ $\mu u_i \equiv \frac{1}{2}(u_{i+1/2} + u_{i-1/2})$

Shift operator, E $\qquad$ $E u_i \equiv u_{i+1}$

Identity operator, I $\qquad$ $I u_i \equiv u_i$

The operators listed above are linear (see Problem 2.2). Many standard finite difference approximations can be expressed as combinations of these operators, including the simple approximations developed in Section 2.1.

Example 2.1

Problem Write the approximations of equations (2.1.2) using difference operator notation.

Solution Approximation (2.1.2a) can be written in terms of the forward difference operator,

$$\left.\frac{du}{dx}\right|_{x_i} \simeq \frac{u_{i+1} - u_i}{x_{i+1} - x_i} = \frac{\Delta u_i}{\Delta x_i} \qquad \text{(forward difference)} \qquad (2.2.1a)$$

Similarly, the approximation of equation (2.1.2b) can be written in operator notation as

$$\left.\frac{du}{dx}\right|_{x_i} \simeq \frac{u_i - u_{i-1}}{x_i - x_{i-1}} = \frac{\nabla u_i}{\nabla x_i} \qquad \text{(backward difference)} \qquad (2.2.1b)$$

while approximation (2.1.2c) requires combination of two operators,

$$\left.\frac{du}{dx}\right|_{x_i} \simeq \frac{u_{i+1} - u_{i-1}}{x_{i+1} - x_{i-1}} = \frac{\delta(\mu u_i)}{\delta(\mu x_i)} \qquad \text{(centered difference)} \qquad (2.2.1c)$$

Notice that the operator representation of these approximations is not unique. For example, since $\Delta u_i = \nabla u_{i+1}$, the forward difference of equation (2.2.1a) could be written equivalently as $\nabla u_{i+1}/\nabla x_{i+1}$. However, operators are usually chosen to correspond to the location at which the approximation is being written. In the current example, the derivative is being evaluated at point x_i. Therefore, the appropriate difference operator is that which acts on values of u and x at point x_i (i.e., u_i and x_i) and not any other spatial locations (such as x_{i+1}). This criterion provides a standard for writing difference operators, and leads to the nomenclature of forward, backward, and centered (or central) difference approximation, respectively, for the expressions of equations (2.2.1a) through (2.2.1c). Use of operators that are associated with the point at which a derivative is evaluated also facilitates comparison between differential and difference operators.

Example 2.2

Problem Using operator notation, write the three-point approximation for $d^2u/dx^2|_{x_i}$ given in equation (2.1.3).

Solution The difference approximation is written as

$$\left.\frac{d^2u}{dx^2}\right|_{x_i} \simeq \frac{\dfrac{u_{i+1} - u_i}{x_{i+1} - x_i} - \dfrac{u_i - u_{i-1}}{x_i - x_{i-1}}}{x_{i+1/2} - x_{i-1/2}} = \frac{\delta\left(\dfrac{\delta u}{\delta x}\right)_i}{\delta x_i} \tag{2.2.2}$$

Notice that when dealing with higher derivatives, difference operators must be applied repeatedly. The approximation for a second derivative, for example equation (2.2.2), requires two applications of a difference operator such as $\delta/\delta x$. It seems reasonable that for an mth-order derivative, an operator such as $\delta/\delta x$ would be applied m times in a repeated, or nested way; equation (2.2.2) is an example of an approximation for $m = 2$. However, careful analysis based on concepts presented in the next section shows that such a procedure must be used with care. In particular, use of simple nesting is generally acceptable only when node spacing is constant. Problems 2.5 and 2.6 explore this point further.

When node points are chosen so that spacing between any adjacent pair of nodes is constant, then $\Delta x_i = \Delta x_{i+1} = \nabla x_i = \delta x_i = \cdots \equiv \Delta x$. For this circumstance, the subscript on x is usually dropped, and spacing between any two adjacent nodes is usually represented by Δx, although δx and ∇x may also be used. The key is that lack of a subscript implies constant spacing. Problem 2.3 revisits approximations (2.2.1) and (2.2.2) under the assumption of constant nodal spacing. Constant spacing is often used for convenience of presentation. However, results that apply to cases of constant node spacing will usually differ from those for nonconstant spacing (as the example of nested operators demonstrates). Therefore, the complexities due to the general case of nonconstant grid spacing should be taken into account when developing general finite difference expressions.

2.2.2 Philosophy of Differences

Implementation of finite difference approximations to differential equations may be viewed as the replacement of a continuous, differential operator by a discrete, difference operator. In this way, finite differences are philosophically rooted in approximation of the differential operator. For example, the finite difference approximations presented in Example 2.1 can be viewed, respectively, as the replacement of the differential operator d/dx by the difference operators $\Delta/\Delta x_i$, $\nabla/\nabla x_i$, and $\mu\delta/\mu\delta x_i$. This *operator approximation* achieves the overall objective of a numerical solution in that use of a discrete operator reduces the solution space from infinite dimensional (for the original differential operator) to finite dimensional. Thus tractability in terms of algebraic computation is achieved.

2.2.3 Notation

Through most of this chapter, the dependent variable of interest is denoted as u. Independent variables are x for one-dimensional space, $\mathbf{x} = (x, y)$ for two-dimensional Euclidean space, $\mathbf{x} = (x, y, z)$ for three-dimensional Euclidean space, and t for time. A lowercase variable such as $u(\mathbf{x}, t)$ denotes the exact representation of a function, and an uppercase variable such as U denotes the corresponding discrete finite difference approximation. Subscripts are used to denote discrete locations in space, and superscripts denote discrete locations in time. When there is only one independent spatial variable, a single subscript is used. When more than one spatial coordinate is involved, a separate subscript is used for each coordinate direction, with the subscripts separated by commas. For example, a finite difference approximation to $u(x_i, y_j, z_k)$ is denoted by $U_{i,j,k}$. When both space and time are independent variables, discrete spatial locations are indexed using subscripts and discrete temporal locations are indexed using superscripts. Thus a one-dimensional, transient problem would use notation U_i^n, with i corresponding to the spatial location and n corresponding to time level. Similarly, $U_{i,j,k}^n$ is the finite difference approximation to the discrete value $u(x_i, y_j, z_k, t^n)$ of the three-dimensional, transient variable u.

2.3 ANALYSIS OF APPROXIMATIONS IN ONE DIMENSION: TRUNCATION ERROR AND CONSISTENCY

Analysis of finite difference approximations is rooted in Taylor series expansions. In preparation for what follows, Taylor's theorem is stated.

Theorem 2.3.1: Taylor's Theorem in One Dimension. Consider the function $u(x)$ which is continuous on the interval $[\omega_1, \omega_2]$, and which has derivatives through order N also continuous on $[\omega_1, \omega_2]$ (i.e., $u(x) \in \mathbb{C}^N[\omega_1, \omega_2]$; see Appendix A). Given a point $x_* \in [\omega_1, \omega_2]$, then for any point $x \in [\omega_1, \omega_2]$,

$$u(x) = u(x_*) + \left.\frac{du}{dx}\right|_{x_*}(x - x_*) + \left.\frac{d^2u}{dx^2}\right|_{x_*}\frac{(x - x_*)^2}{2!} + \cdots$$

$$+ \left.\frac{d^{N-1}u}{dx^{N-1}}\right|_{x_*}\frac{(x - x_*)^{N-1}}{(N-1)!} + R^N \tag{2.3.1}$$

where

$$R^N \equiv \left.\frac{d^N u}{dx^N}\right|_{\xi}\frac{(x - x_*)^N}{N!}, \qquad \xi \in [x, x_*]$$

Proof of this theorem may be found in standard mathematics textbooks, as listed in Appendix C. Taylor's theorem is fundamental to most analyses of numerical approximations. Note that for infinitely differentiable functions, $u(x) \in \mathbb{C}^\infty[\omega_1, \omega_2]$, the series (2.3.1) may be written as an infinite series,

$$u(x) = \sum_{n=0}^{\infty} \left.\frac{d^n u}{dx^n}\right|_{x_*}\frac{(x - x_*)^n}{n!} \tag{2.3.2}$$

only when $u(x)$ is analytic in the interval $[\omega_1, \omega_2]$ (see references in Appendix C). In what follows, equation (2.3.1) will generally be employed when using Taylor series.

Given Taylor's theorem, the previous finite difference approximations can be analyzed as follows. Assume that $u(x)$ is sufficiently smooth over some finite region of the real axis, denoted by $[\omega_1, \omega_2]$. Then consider the following Taylor series expansions, written with respect to the distinct points x_{i-1}, x_i, x_{i+1}, each of which lies within $[\omega_1, \omega_2]$:

$$u(x_{i+1}) \equiv u_{i+1} = u(x_i) + \left.\frac{du}{dx}\right|_{x_i} \frac{x_{i+1} - x_i}{1!} + \left.\frac{d^2u}{dx^2}\right|_{x_i} \frac{(x_{i+1} - x_i)^2}{2!} + \cdots \quad (2.3.3a)$$

$$u(x_{i-1}) \equiv u_{i-1} = u_i + \left.\frac{du}{dx}\right|_{x_i} \frac{x_{i-1} - x_i}{1!} + \left.\frac{d^2u}{dx^2}\right|_{x_i} \frac{(x_{i-1} - x_i)^2}{2!} + \cdots \quad (2.3.3b)$$

In equations (2.3.3), the notation "$\cdots$" implies additional terms up to and including the remainder term R^N, where N is assumed to be larger than the highest-order derivative written explicitly in the expansion [for the case of equations (2.3.3), the highest-order derivative is 2, so it is implied that $N > 2$]. Subtraction of u_i from both sides of equation (2.3.3a) produces

$$u_{i+1} - u_i = \left.\frac{du}{dx}\right|_{x_i} (x_{i+1} - x_i) + \left.\frac{d^2u}{dx^2}\right|_{x_i} \frac{(x_{i+1} - x_i)^2}{2} + \cdots$$

or

$$\left.\frac{du}{dx}\right|_i = \frac{u_{i+1} - u_i}{x_{i+1} - x_i} - \frac{x_{i+1} - x_i}{2} \left.\frac{d^2u}{dx^2}\right|_{x_i} - \cdots$$

$$= \frac{\Delta u_i}{\Delta x_i} - \frac{\Delta x_i}{2} \left.\frac{d^2u}{dx^2}\right|_{x_i} - \cdots \quad (2.3.4)$$

Comparison of equations (2.2.1a) and (2.3.4) indicates that the finite difference approximation (2.2.1a) neglects the terms

$$\left.\frac{du}{dx}\right|_{x_i} - \frac{\Delta u_i}{\Delta x_i} = -\frac{\Delta x_i}{2} \left.\frac{d^2u}{dx^2}\right|_{x_i} - \frac{(\Delta x_i)^2}{3!} \left.\frac{d^3u}{dx^3}\right|_{x_i} - \cdots$$

$$\equiv \text{T.E.}_{(a)} \quad (2.3.5a)$$

The finite difference approximation thus truncates the series (2.3.4), leading to the *truncation error*, T.E., defined as the difference between the true derivative and the finite difference approximation to it. Equation (2.3.5a) thus defines the truncation error, T.E.$_{(a)}$, associated with the approximation (2.2.1a). The truncation error is due to higher-order terms in the Taylor series being neglected in finite difference approximations.

Truncation errors for the approximations (2.2.1b) and (2.2.1c) can be derived in a similar way. Under constant node spacing, the truncation errors are

$$\left.\frac{du}{dx}\right|_{x_i} - \frac{\nabla u_i}{\nabla x_i} \equiv \text{T.E.}_{(b)} = \frac{(\Delta x)}{2!} \left.\frac{d^2u}{dx^2}\right|_{x_i} - \frac{(\Delta x)^2}{3!} \left.\frac{d^3u}{dx^3}\right|_{x_i} + \cdots \quad (2.3.5b)$$

$$\left.\frac{du}{dx}\right|_{x_i} - \frac{\delta(\mu u_i)}{\delta(\mu x_i)} \equiv \text{T.E.}_{(c)} = -\frac{(\Delta x)^2}{6}\left.\frac{d^3 u}{dx^3}\right|_{x_i} - \frac{(\Delta x)^4}{5!}\left.\frac{d^5 u}{dx^5}\right|_{x_i} - \cdots (2.3.5c)$$

where T.E.$_{(b)}$ is the truncation error associated with approximation (2.2.1b) and T.E.$_{(c)}$ is that associated with approximation (2.2.1c). As Problems 2.3 and 2.4 point out, the truncation error associated with a finite difference approximation can change depending on whether the node spacing is constant or not. For example, the truncation error for the central difference of equation (2.2.1c) is generally of the form

$$\left.\frac{du}{dx}\right|_{x_i} - \frac{\delta(\mu u_i)}{\delta(\mu x_i)} = \text{T.E.}_{(c')}$$

$$= -\frac{(\Delta x_i)^2 - (\nabla x_i)^2}{4(\delta x_i)}\left.\frac{d^2 u}{dx^2}\right|_{x_i} - \frac{(\Delta x_i)^3 + (\nabla x_i)^3}{2(3!)(\delta x_i)}\left.\frac{d^3 u}{dx^3}\right|_{x_i} - \cdots (2.3.5d)$$

Equation (2.3.5d) reduces to equation (2.3.5c) when $\Delta x_i = \nabla x_i = \delta x_i = \Delta x$. Notice that in this reduction, the leading term in the series disappears, since under constant nodal spacing $\Delta x_i = \nabla x_i$.

A fundamental requirement that must be met by any finite difference approximation is that when the limit process of equation (2.1.1) is reimposed on it, the actual derivative must be recovered. Therefore, as the node spacing Δx becomes arbitrarily small, the finite difference expression must become arbitrarily close to the derivative that it is meant to approximate. Therefore, the truncation error must vanish as $\Delta x \rightarrow 0$. When this is the case, the finite difference approximation is said to be *consistent*. Consistency is defined by the requirement that

$$\lim_{\Delta x \rightarrow 0} \text{T.E.} = 0 \qquad \text{(consistency)} \qquad (2.3.6)$$

The approximations of equations (2.2.1) are thus seen to be consistent finite difference expressions because equations (2.3.5) satisfy the constraint of equation (2.3.6).

The rate at which the truncation error approaches zero as Δx is decreased can be an important consideration. For example, if Δx is decreased by a factor of 2, the rth-order term in the truncation error is decreased by a factor $(2)^r$. As Δx becomes sufficiently small, the term with the lowest-order exponent will assume a dominant role in the truncation error, and in the limit as $\Delta x \rightarrow 0$, the lowest-order term dominates all others. The order of the lowest-order term is referred to as the *order of the approximation*; if the lowest order is p, then the order is written symbolically as $\mathcal{O}((\Delta x)^p)$ [read "of order" $(\Delta x)^p$]. Thus equations (2.2.1a) and (2.2.1b) are first-order approximations, while equation (2.2.1c) is second-order for constant spacing ($\Delta x_i = \nabla x_i$) and first-order otherwise. The higher the order of the approximation, the faster the truncation error decreases as Δx goes toward zero. Thus higher-order approximations might be expected to be more accurate. This is generally the case for problems with solutions that are smooth. However, higher-order approximations generally make use of information at more nodes than do low-order approximations. Therefore, the computational effort needed to approximate a derivative, as well as the potential for arithmetic roundoff error, increases with order. Acceptable accuracy in computing a finite difference approximation involves finding a reasonable trade-off between small values of Δx used with low-order approximations and larger values of Δx used with higher-order expressions. For any approximation that is $\mathcal{O}((\Delta x)^p)$, consistency demands that $p > 0$.

2.4 A GENERALIZED FORMULATION OF DIFFERENCE APPROXIMATIONS IN ONE DIMENSION

A general procedure exists for deriving finite difference approximations for derivatives of arbitrary order. The procedure is presented here for functions of a single independent variable. Partial derivatives of multivariate functions are treated in Section 2.7.

Consider the mth-order derivative $d^m u/dx^m$, and a collection of q node points which are to be used in a finite difference approximation to this derivative. Let these nodes be numbered consecutively from 1 to q, with node spacing $\Delta x_j \equiv x_{j+1} - x_j (1 \leq j \leq q-1)$ not necessarily constant. For convenience, denote the largest value of Δx_j as Δx_{max}. Let the derivative be evaluated at an arbitrary point x_*, where x_* may or may not coincide with one of the node points (see Figure 2.2). A finite difference approximation expresses the derivative at the point x_* as a linear combination of the function values at each of the q node points. Thus the general form of the difference approximation to $d^m u/dx^m |_{x_*}$ is written as

$$\frac{d^m u}{dx^m}\bigg|_{x_*} \simeq \gamma_1 u_1 + \gamma_2 u_2 + \cdots + \gamma_q u_q = \sum_{i=1}^{q} \gamma_i u_i \qquad (2.4.1)$$

Imposition of the consistency requirement implies that the linear combination on the right side of equation (2.4.1) must be of the form

$$\sum_{i=1}^{q} \gamma_i u_i = \frac{d^m u}{dx^m}\bigg|_{x_*} + \mathcal{O}((\Delta x_{max})^p), \qquad p > 0 \qquad (2.4.2)$$

where Δx_{max}, the largest spacing, is used as a general measure of the node spacing. Now consider Taylor series expansions for each of the $u_i (i = 1, 2, ..., q)$ about the point of interest x_*. These expansions take the form

$$u_i = u_* + (x_i - x_*)\frac{du}{dx}\bigg|_{x_*} + \frac{1}{2}(x_i - x_*)^2 \frac{d^2 u}{dx^2}\bigg|_{x_*} + \cdots \qquad (2.4.3)$$

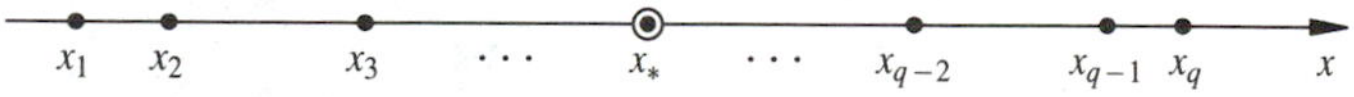

Figure 2.2   General one-dimensional grid of q node points $x_1, x_2, ..., x_q$. Location x_* is arbitrary.

Substitution of these expansions into the linear combination of equation (2.4.1) leads to

$$
\sum_{i=1}^{q} \gamma_i u_i = \sum_{i=1}^{q} \gamma_i \left[u_* + (x_i - x_*) \left. \frac{du}{dx} \right|_{x_*} + \frac{1}{2}(x_i - x_*)^2 \left. \frac{d^2 u}{dx^2} \right|_{x_*} + \cdots \right]
$$

$$
= \left[\sum_{i=1}^{q} \gamma_i \right] u_* + \left[\sum_{i=1}^{q} \gamma_i (x_i - x_*) \right] \left. \frac{du}{dx} \right|_{x_*} + \left[\sum_{i=1}^{q} \gamma_i \frac{(x_i - x_*)^2}{2} \right] \left. \frac{d^2 u}{dx^2} \right|_{x_*} + \cdots
$$

$$
= B_0(\gamma_1, \gamma_2, ..., \gamma_q) u_* + B_1(\gamma_1, ..., \gamma_q) \left. \frac{du}{dx} \right|_{x_*} + \cdots
$$

$$
+ B_m(\gamma_1, ..., \gamma_q) \left. \frac{d^m u}{dx^m} \right|_{x_*} + B_{m+1}(\gamma_1, ..., \gamma_q) \left. \frac{d^{m+1} u}{dx^{m+1}} \right|_{x_*} + \cdots \tag{2.4.4}
$$

In equation (2.4.4), the B_i are (linear) functions of the γ_j and are defined, by inspection of equation of (2.4.4), as

$$
B_0 = \gamma_1 + \gamma_2 + \cdots + \gamma_q \tag{2.4.5a}
$$

$$
B_1 = \gamma_1(x_1 - x_*) + \gamma_2(x_2 - x_*) + \cdots + \gamma_q(x_q - x_*) \tag{2.4.5b}
$$

$$
\vdots
$$

$$
B_m = \gamma_1 \frac{(x_1 - x_*)^m}{m!} + \cdots + \gamma_q \frac{(x_q - x_*)^m}{m!} \tag{2.4.5c}
$$

$$
B_{m+1} = \gamma_1 \frac{(x_1 - x_*)^{m+1}}{(m+1)!} + \cdots + \gamma_q \frac{(x_q - x_*)^{m+1}}{(m+1)!} \tag{2.4.5d}
$$

Examination of equations (2.4.5) shows that each B_j is proportional to $\Sigma_i[\gamma_i(\alpha_i \Delta x_{max})^j / j!]$, where α_i is an appropriate length proportion such that $\alpha_i = (x_i - x_*)/\Delta x_{max}$. If equation (2.4.2) is to be satisfied, then the coefficient of the mth-order derivative must be 1, so that, by equation (2.4.4), $B_m(\gamma_1, \gamma_2, ..., \gamma_q) = 1$. Furthermore, consistency demands that any terms other than B_m must be at least $\mathcal{O}((\Delta x_{max})^1)$. Because each γ_i in the expression for B_m is multiplied by a term proportional to $(\Delta x_{max})^m$, each γ_i must be proportional to $(\Delta x_{max})^{-m}$ if B_m is to equal 1; all other B_j will then be proportional to $(\Delta x_{max})^{j-m}$. Consistency then dictates that each B_j, $j < m$, must be identically zero. Thus the following conditions are necessary for the existence of a consistent difference approximation for $d^m u/dx^m |_{x_*}$:

$$
B_0 = B_1 = B_2 = \cdots = B_{m-1} = 0 \tag{2.4.6a}
$$

$$
B_m = 1 \tag{2.4.6b}
$$

Conditions (2.4.6) combine with equations (2.4.5) to produce the following set of linear algebraic equations for the coefficients γ_i:

$$
\begin{bmatrix}
1 & 1 & \cdots & 1 \\
x_1 - x_* & x_2 - x_* & \cdots & x_q - x_* \\
(x_1 - x_*)^2 & (x_2 - x_*)^2 & \cdots & (x_q - x_*)^2 \\
\vdots & \vdots & & \vdots \\
(x_1 - x_*)^m & (x_2 - x_*)^m & \cdots & (x_q - x_*)^m
\end{bmatrix}
\begin{bmatrix}
\gamma_1 \\ \gamma_2 \\ \vdots \\ \\ \gamma_q
\end{bmatrix}
=
\begin{bmatrix}
0 \\ 0 \\ \vdots \\ 0 \\ m!
\end{bmatrix}
\tag{2.4.7a}
$$

or

$$
\mathbf{A} \cdot \mathbf{g} = \mathbf{b} \tag{2.4.7b}
$$

The matrix $\mathbf{A}$ is $((m + 1) \times q)$, $\mathbf{g}$ is $(q \times 1)$, and $\mathbf{b}$ is $((m + 1) \times 1)$.

When the matrix $\mathbf{A}$ is square ($q = m + 1$), a unique solution for $\mathbf{g}$ can be guaranteed, because the determinant of $\mathbf{A}$ is a so-called *Vandermonde determinant*, which is always nonzero (Davis, 1975, pp. 24–25). A unique solution for $\mathbf{g}$ thus exists by Corollary A.2.1.1. Furthermore, the nonzero determinant implies that the rows (and columns) of $\mathbf{A}$ are linearly independent. This linear independence leads to the conclusion that a solution to equation (2.4.7) exists (by Theorem A.2.1) whenever $q \geq m + 1$, and no solution exists when $q < m + 1$. Thus at least $m + 1$ points must be used to derive a consistent finite difference approximation for an mth-order derivative. This is a fundamentally important fact about finite difference approximations.

Solutions to equation (2.4.7) will have $q - (m+1)$ free parameters, with uniqueness of solution only occurring when $q = m + 1$. Different values of the free parameters lead to different approximations of the derivative. Higher-order approximations can be obtained by judicious choice of the free parameters. This judicious choice corresponds to imposition of the conditions $B_j = 0$, $j = m + 1, m + 2, ..., q - 1$. In general, approximations up to $\mathcal{O}((\Delta x_{max})^{q-m})$ can be achieved. When $q = m + 1$, the minimum number of points is used, and the resulting approximation will in general be first order, although second-order approximations may be obtained when Δx_i is constant and m is even (see Problem 2.7).

Example 2.3

Problem   Derive a finite difference approximation for $du/dx|_{x_i}$ using the three node points x_{i-1}, x_i, x_{i+1}. Assume constant node spacing, so that $\Delta x_i = \nabla x_i = \delta x_i = \Delta x_{max} = \Delta x$.

Solution   Let the finite difference approximation be expressed as

$$
\frac{du}{dx}\bigg|_{x_i} \simeq \gamma_{i-1} u_{i-1} + \gamma_i u_i + \gamma_{i+1} u_{i+1}
$$

In terms of the preceding development, the number of points, q, equals 3, and the order of the derivative is $m = 1$. Direct imposition of the conditions (2.4.6) leads to

$$
\begin{bmatrix}
1 & 1 & 1 \\
-\Delta x & 0 & \Delta x
\end{bmatrix}
\begin{bmatrix}
\gamma_{i-1} \\ \gamma_i \\ \gamma_{i+1}
\end{bmatrix}
=
\begin{bmatrix}
0 \\ 1
\end{bmatrix}
$$

Solution of this equation produces $\gamma_{i-1} = \gamma_{i+1} - 1/\Delta x$, $\gamma_i = 1/\Delta x - 2\gamma_{i+1}$, with γ_{i+1} being arbitrary. If the parameter β is defined as $\beta = (\Delta x)\gamma_{i+1}$, then the general finite difference approximation can be written as

$$\frac{du}{dx}\bigg|_{x_i} \simeq \frac{(\beta - 1)u_{i-1} + (1 - 2\beta)u_i + \beta u_{i+1}}{\Delta x} \tag{2.4.8}$$

where β may be selected arbitrarily. This equation encompasses the cases of equation (2.2.1a) when $\beta = 1$, equation (2.2.1b) when $\beta = 0$, and equation (2.2.1c) when $\beta = 0.5$. Alternatively, imposition of the additional constraint $B_3 = 0$ requires $\beta = 0.5$ such that $\gamma_{i+1} = 1/2\Delta x$. This is the second-order, centered approximation of equation (2.2.1c). Problem 2.3 explores the case of nonconstant nodal spacing, for which $\beta = 0.5$ no longer produces second-order accuracy.

Example 2.4

Problem   Derive an approximation for $d^2u/dx^2\big|_{x_{i+1}}$ using the points x_{i-1}, x_i, x_{i+1}, with constant node spacing again assumed.

Solution   While the point at which the derivative is evaluated is not centered, the procedure developed previously still applies, with $q = 3$ and $m = 2$. After observation that three points are sufficient to ensure a consistent approximation to the second derivative, equation (2.4.7) is applied directly as

$$\begin{bmatrix} 1 & 1 & 1 \\ -2\Delta x & -\Delta x & 0 \\ 4(\Delta x)^2 & (\Delta x)^2 & 0 \end{bmatrix} \begin{bmatrix} \gamma_{i-1} \\ \gamma_i \\ \gamma_{i+1} \end{bmatrix} = \begin{bmatrix} 0 \\ 0 \\ 2 \end{bmatrix}$$

Solution of this system produces $\gamma_{i-1} = 1/(\Delta x)^2$, $\gamma_i = -2/(\Delta x)^2$, $\gamma_{i+1} = 1/(\Delta x)^2$. Thus

$$\frac{d^2u}{dx^2}\bigg|_{x_{i+1}} \simeq \frac{u_{i-1} - 2u_i + u_{i+1}}{(\Delta x)^2} \tag{2.4.9}$$

This approximation is identical to that for $d^2u/dx^2\big|_{x_i}$ given in equation (2.1.3b). However, equation (2.4.9) is a first-order approximation at point x_{i+1} [B_4 of equation (2.4.4) is not zero], while equation (2.1.3b) is second order at point x_i. The latter case is special; in general, three-point approximations to second-order derivatives can be expected to be only first-order accurate.

Example 2.5

Problem   Derive a finite difference expression for $u\big|_{x_i}$ using the three nodes x_{i-1}, x_i, x_{i+1}, with Δx_i not necessarily equal to ∇x_i.

Solution   Let the finite difference approximation be expressed as

$$u\big|_{x_i} \simeq \gamma_{i-1}u_{i-1} + \gamma_i u_i + \gamma_{i+1}u_{i+1}$$

Direct imposition of conditions (2.4.6) with $m = 0$ and $q = 3$ leads to

$$[1 \quad 1 \quad 1] \begin{bmatrix} \gamma_{i-1} \\ \gamma_i \\ \gamma_{i+1} \end{bmatrix} = [1] \tag{2.4.10}$$

Solution of this equation produces $\gamma_i = 1 - \gamma_{i-1} - \gamma_{i+1}$, with γ_{i-1} and γ_{i+1} arbitrary. Thus a general three-point approximation to $u\big|_{x_i}$ is of the form

$$u|_{x_i} \simeq \gamma_{i-1}(u_{i-1} - u_i) + u_i + \gamma_{i+1}(u_{i+1} - u_i) \qquad (2.4.11)$$

Equation (2.4.11) represents a first-order approximation, with $B_0 = 1$ and B_1 not necessarily zero. Imposition of the condition $B_1 = 0$ provides the constraint

$$-(\nabla x_i)\gamma_{i-1} + (\Delta x_i)\gamma_{i+1} = 0 \qquad (2.4.12)$$

or

$$\gamma_{i+1} = \frac{\nabla x_i}{\Delta x_i}\gamma_{i-1}$$

Thus a general second-order approximation is given by

$$u|_{x_i} \simeq \gamma_{i-1}(u_{i-1} - u_i) + u_i + \frac{\nabla x_i}{\Delta x_i}\gamma_{i-1}(u_{i+1} - u_i) \qquad (2.4.13)$$

Because one arbitrary parameter, γ_{i-1}, remains in this expression, a higher (third)-order approximation may be obtained by requiring that $B_2 = 0$,

$$\frac{(\nabla x_i)^2}{2}\gamma_{i-1} + \frac{(\Delta x_i)^2}{2}\gamma_{i+1} = 0 \qquad (2.4.14)$$

Solution of equation (2.4.14), given constraint (2.4.12), is $\gamma_{i-1} = \gamma_{i+1} = 0$. Thus

$$u|_{x_i} \simeq u_i \qquad (2.4.15)$$

constitutes a third-order approximation. However, this representation also satisfies $B_3 = B_4 = \cdots = B_n = \cdots = 0$. Equation (2.4.15) is therefore an exact representation.

Example 2.5 illustrates that a point evaluation of the function u may or may not be chosen as u evaluated at that point. Alternative representations that employ combinations of values at neighboring points can also be used. These latter expressions have a nonzero truncation error, which may in fact be advantageous for certain problems. In addition, if the point at which u is evaluated is not a node, then representation of the function must use values at neighboring nodes.

The procedure presented in this section provides consistent finite difference approximations for any order derivative (say m) on an arbitrary array of q node points, provided only that $q \geq m + 1$. Simpler procedures for deriving finite difference expressions are not as general. For example, the nested operator approach discussed in Section 2.2 is applicable to constant node spacing only (see Problems 2.5 and 2.6). The procedure based on Taylor series presented in this section is recommended for development of all finite difference approximations.

2.5 EXAMPLE CALCULATIONS IN ONE DIMENSION

To demonstrate the application of the finite difference method, several example ordinary differential equations are solved in this section. Notation is adopted wherein uppercase variables are used to denote finite difference approximations to the exact (lowercase) function. For example, the finite difference approximation of a function $u(x_i) \equiv u_i$ is written as U_i. Furthermore, if $f = f(x, u)$, then $f_i = f(u_i, x_i)$ and $F_i = f(U_i, x_i)$.

Example 2.6

Problem   Derive a finite difference approximation to the equation that describes steady-state diffusion of a dissolved substance into a quiescent fluid body in which a first-order reaction occurs:

$$D\frac{d^2u}{dx^2} - Ku = 0, \qquad 0 < x < 1 \text{ cm} \qquad\qquad (2.5.1)$$

$$u(0) = 0$$

$$u(1) = C_1$$

where $u(x)$ (dimensions of mass/volume, or M/L^3) is the concentration of the dissolved substance, D (L^2/T) is the diffusion coefficient, K ($1/T$) is the reaction rate, and C_1 (M/L^3) is a specified concentration at the right boundary. The coefficients D, K, and C_1 are constants that, for this calculation, will be assigned the following values: $D = 0.01 \text{ cm}^2/\text{s}$, $K = 0.1 \text{ s}^{-1}$, and $C_1 = 1.0 \text{ g/cm}^3$. Because the dimensions of all variables and parameters are consistent, they are not explicitly carried along in the subsequent solution and discussion.

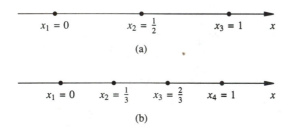

(a)

(b)

Figure 2.3   Finite difference discretizations used in Example 2.6.

Solution   The first step in deriving an approximate solution to equation (2.5.1) is the discretization step. Let the simple discretization of Figure 2.3a be imposed, so that three nodes are chosen, one at each boundary point and a third at $x = 0.5$. Thus three discrete values, (U_1, U_2, U_3), will be computed to approximate the true solution values $(u(0), u(0.5), u(1)) = (u_1, u_2, u_3)$. Because three unknowns are to be determined, three algebraic equations are needed. Whenever a first-type boundary condition is given, and a node is located at that boundary location, the boundary condition is written as the appropriate equation corresponding to that node. Thus two equations come directly from the boundary conditions, namely

$$U_1 = 0 \qquad\qquad (2.5.2a)$$

$$U_3 = C_1 \qquad\qquad (2.5.2b)$$

The finite difference approximation to the exact solution is thus required to exactly satisfy the first-type boundary conditions. For all other nodes (in this case, only node 2), finite difference equations are written. Because the governing equation must hold at all points in the region $0 < x < 1$, it must be the case that the equation holds at $x = x_2 = 0.5$. Thus

$$D\frac{d^2u}{dx^2}\bigg|_{x_2} - Ku\big|_{x_2} = 0$$

Taylor series expansion for the second derivative leads to the equality

$$D\left[\frac{u_1 - 2u_2 + u_3}{(\Delta x)^2} + \text{T.E.}\right] - Ku_2 = 0 \tag{2.5.3a}$$

where the truncation error, T.E., is $\mathcal{O}((\Delta x)^2)$ (see Problem 2.4), $u\big|_{x_2}$ is represented without error as u_2, and the constant spacing is denoted by Δx, with $\Delta x = 0.5$. Equation (2.5.3a) involves exact nodal values $u_j(j = 1, 2, 3)$. To write the appropriate finite difference approximation, the truncation error terms are neglected, resulting in the finite difference equation

$$D\frac{U_1 - 2U_2 + U_3}{(\Delta x)^2} - KU_2 = 0 \tag{2.5.3b}$$

(Note that for this problem $U_1 = u_1$ and $U_3 = u_3$ while $U_2 \simeq u_2$.) Equation (2.5.3b) is the algebraic equation used to solve for the nodal (finite difference) approximations $U_j(j = 1, 2, 3)$. Combination of equations (2.5.2) and (2.5.3b) leads to

$$\begin{bmatrix} 1 & 0 & 0 \\ \dfrac{D}{(\Delta x)^2} & -K - \dfrac{2D}{(\Delta x)^2} & \dfrac{D}{(\Delta x)^2} \\ 0 & 0 & 1 \end{bmatrix} \begin{bmatrix} U_1 \\ U_2 \\ U_3 \end{bmatrix} = \begin{bmatrix} 0 \\ 0 \\ C_1 \end{bmatrix} \tag{2.5.4}$$

The solution of this set of equations is $U_1 = 0$, $U_2 = C_1 D/[2D + K(\Delta x)^2]$, $U_3 = C_1$. For the prescribed parameter values of $D = 0.01$, $K = 0.1$, $C_1 = 1$, and $\Delta x = 0.5$, the solution is $U_2 = 0.222$. This compares to the exact solution $u(0.5) = 0.171$.

If the discretization of Figure 2.3b is chosen, with four nodes and $\Delta x = 1/3$, then the boundary conditions produce

$$U_1 = 0 \tag{2.5.5a}$$

$$U_4 = 1 \tag{2.5.5b}$$

and two interior finite difference equations must be written, one corresponding to each interior node. The finite difference approximations analogous to equation (2.5.3b) are

$$D\frac{U_1 - 2U_2 + U_3}{(\Delta x)^2} - KU_2 = 0 \tag{2.5.6a}$$

$$D\frac{U_2 - 2U_3 + U_4}{(\Delta x)^2} - KU_3 = 0 \tag{2.5.6b}$$

Given $\Delta x = 1/3$, and the previous values of D, K, and C_1, the approximation step produces the following set of linear algebraic equations:

$$\begin{bmatrix} 1 & 0 & 0 & 0 \\ 0.09 & -0.28 & 0.09 & 0 \\ 0 & 0.09 & -0.28 & 0.09 \\ 0 & 0 & 0 & 1 \end{bmatrix} \begin{bmatrix} U_1 \\ U_2 \\ U_3 \\ U_4 \end{bmatrix} = \begin{bmatrix} 0 \\ 0 \\ 0 \\ 1 \end{bmatrix} \tag{2.5.7}$$

The solution step then produces the approximate solution $\mathbf{U} = (0, 0.094, 0.291, 1)$; this compares to the analytical solution $(0, 0.083, 0.320, 1)$.

The matrices generated in the solutions of Example 2.6 are not symmetric. However, simple manipulation of the boundary information allows the matrices to be made symmetric for this problem. Because the finite difference solution at the boundary nodes is known, the boundary equations can be eliminated from the matrices. This is achieved by eliminating the first and last rows and columns of the matrices of equations (2.5.4) and (2.5.7). Elimination of columns involves transferring the known (boundary) information to the right-side vector. The reduced form of matrix equation (2.5.4) is

$$\left[\frac{-K-2D}{(\Delta x)^2}\right][U_2] = \left[\frac{-C_1 D}{(\Delta x)^2}\right] \tag{2.5.8}$$

while the reduced version of equation (2.5.7) is

$$\begin{bmatrix} -0.28 & 0.09 \\ 0.09 & -0.28 \end{bmatrix} \begin{bmatrix} U_2 \\ U_3 \end{bmatrix} = \begin{bmatrix} 0 \\ -0.09 \end{bmatrix} \tag{2.5.9a}$$

Solution of equation (2.5.8) for U_2 and (2.5.9a) for U_2 and U_3 produces solutions identical to those calculated above. The reduced matrices are preferable because they are usually symmetric whenever the original differential operator is self-adjoint (see Appendix A for a definition of self-adjoint), and they are smaller in size. Because only the diagonal and the numbers above the diagonal completely determine a symmetric matrix, symmetric matrices require less computer storage and are therefore more computationally efficient. A second procedure that produces a symmetric matrix from equation (2.5.4) or (2.5.7) involves transfer of the first-type boundary information to the right-side vector for every column associated with a Dirichlet node except for the entry on the main diagonal. For example, equation (2.5.7) can be written in an equivalent symmetric form as

$$\begin{bmatrix} 1 & 0 & 0 & 0 \\ 0 & -0.28 & 0.09 & 0 \\ 0 & 0.09 & -0.28 & 0 \\ 0 & 0 & 0 & 1 \end{bmatrix} \begin{bmatrix} U_1 \\ U_2 \\ U_3 \\ U_4 \end{bmatrix} = \begin{bmatrix} 0 \\ 0 \\ -0.09 \\ 1 \end{bmatrix} \tag{2.5.9b}$$

Reduction of matrices using boundary information is explored further in Problems 2.8 and 2.9.

Example 2.7

Problem   Solve the steady-state reaction-diffusion equation subject to a flux-type boundary condition at the right end of the domain,

$$D\frac{d^2 u}{dx^2} - Ku = 0, \qquad 0 < x < 1 \tag{2.5.10}$$

$$u(0) = 0$$

$$D\frac{du}{dx}\bigg|_{x=1} = C_2$$

Solution   The finite difference solution procedure is the same as that for Example 2.6, except at the right boundary node. Let the discretization of Figure 2.3a be applied. At node 1, the first-type boundary condition is written as $U_1 = 0$. Next, the finite difference approximation (2.5.3b) is written at node 2:

$$D\frac{U_1 - 2U_2 + U_3}{(\Delta x)^2} - KU_2 = 0 \qquad (2.5.3b)$$

When second (or third)-type boundary conditions are imposed at a node, the usual approach in finite difference methods is to write both the finite difference approximation to the governing differential equation and a finite difference approximation to the boundary condition at the node. To allow both of these equations to be written, a commonly employed strategy is to artificially extend the domain by placing an *imaginary node* a distance $\Delta x_N = \nabla x_N$ beyond the right boundary node x_N. For the discretization of Figure 2.3a, where $N = 3$ and $x_N = x_3 = 1$, the imaginary node is placed at $x_4 = 1.5$. If the value of the finite difference solution at node 4 is denoted by U_4, then the two equations written at the boundary node 3 are

$$D\frac{U_2 - 2U_3 + U_4}{(\Delta x)^2} - KU_3 = 0 \qquad (2.5.11)$$

$$D\frac{U_4 - U_2}{2\Delta x} = C_2 \qquad (2.5.12)$$

Equation (2.5.12) can be rearranged to express the "imaginary" value U_4 in terms of values within the domain, in this case U_2,

$$U_4 = U_2 + \frac{2\Delta x}{D}C_2 \qquad (2.5.13)$$

Substitution of equation (2.5.13) into equation (2.5.11) results in an algebraic equation in which U_4 does not appear,

$$D\frac{2U_2 - 2U_3}{(\Delta x)^2} - KU_3 = -\frac{2}{\Delta x}C_2 \qquad (2.5.14)$$

Equation (2.5.14) is used as the finite difference equation at node 3. Equations (2.5.2a), (2.5.3b), and (2.5.14) are then written in matrix form as

$$\begin{bmatrix} 1 & 0 & 0 \\ \dfrac{D}{(\Delta x)^2} & -K - \dfrac{2D}{(\Delta x)^2} & \dfrac{D}{(\Delta x)^2} \\ 0 & \dfrac{2D}{(\Delta x)^2} & -K - \dfrac{2D}{(\Delta x)^2} \end{bmatrix} \begin{bmatrix} U_1 \\ U_2 \\ U_3 \end{bmatrix} = \begin{bmatrix} 0 \\ 0 \\ -\dfrac{2C_2}{\Delta x} \end{bmatrix} \qquad (2.5.15a)$$

or, after reducing out the first row and column (first-type boundary condition) and dividing the last row by 2,

$$\begin{bmatrix} -K - \dfrac{2D}{(\Delta x)^2} & \dfrac{D}{(\Delta x)^2} \\ \dfrac{D}{(\Delta x)^2} & -\dfrac{K}{2} - \dfrac{D}{(\Delta x)^2} \end{bmatrix} \begin{bmatrix} U_2 \\ U_3 \end{bmatrix} = \begin{bmatrix} 0 \\ -\dfrac{C_2}{\Delta x} \end{bmatrix} \qquad (2.5.15b)$$

The matrix of equation (2.5.15b) is symmetric, whereas that of equation (2.5.15a) is not. Problem 2.10 explores implementation of second- and third-type boundary conditions in more detail.

Example 2.8

Problem   Derive a finite difference approximation to the (nonlinear) initial value problem

$$\frac{du}{dt} = f(u, t), \qquad t > t^0 \tag{2.5.16}$$

$$u(t^0) = \alpha$$

where f is a given function of both u and t. Equations of this type arise in many fields of science and engineering. For example, a continuous-stirred tank reactor (CSTR) that involves a high-order chemical reaction is described by equation (2.5.16), with u being the concentration of the dissolved substance and $f(u, t)$ being the functional representation of the chemical reaction.

Solution   A large number of difference approximations have been developed to solve this equation. For now, as a first try, consider the following approximation. Let the domain be discretized using nodes located at time levels t^0, t^1, t^2, ..., t^n, ..., where superscripts are used to denote discrete temporal locations and the time domain is open-ended. Let the value of the exact solution at time t^n be denoted by $u^n \equiv u(t^n)$, while the discrete finite difference approximation to this value is denoted by U^n. A finite difference approximation to the derivative appearing in the governing equation (2.5.16) can be written as

$$\left.\frac{du}{dt}\right|_{t=t^n} \simeq \frac{U^{n+1} - U^n}{t^{n+1} - t^n} = \frac{\Delta U^n}{\Delta t^n} \tag{2.5.17}$$

Because the governing equation (2.5.16) must hold for all t, it must hold at $t = t^n$. Imposition of this requirement, given equation (2.5.17), leads directly to the following difference approximation:

$$0 = \left[\frac{du}{dt} - f(u, t)\right]\bigg|_{t^n} \simeq \frac{U^{n+1} - U^n}{t^{n+1} - t^n} - f(U^n, t^n)$$

$$= \frac{U^{n+1} - U^n}{\Delta t^n} - F^n \tag{2.5.18}$$

where $F^n \equiv f(U^n, t^n)$. The computational algorithm associated with equation (2.5.18) proceeds stepwise, beginning with $n = 0$. When $n = 0$, U^1 is calculated from equation (2.5.18), with U^0 known from the initial condition, $U^0 = \alpha$. The approximation at the next time step is then calculated by setting $n = 1$ in equation (2.5.8), to obtain the solution U^2. The procedure continues into the open-ended time domain. The approximation given by equation (2.5.18) is called a *forward Euler approximation*.

Example 2.9

Problem   Use the forward Euler method to solve the equation

$$\frac{du}{dt} = -u, \qquad t > 0 \tag{2.5.19}$$

$$u(0) = 1$$

Assume constant node spacing, so that $\Delta t^n = \nabla t^n = \Delta t^{n+1} = \cdots = \Delta t$.

Solution   The computational algorithm begins with $n = 0$ in equation (2.5.18), using the resulting expression to calculate U^1. From equation (2.5.18),

$$\frac{U^1 - U^0}{\Delta t} = -U^0$$

or

$$U^1 = (1 - \Delta t)U^0 \tag{2.5.20a}$$

where U^0 is known from the initial condition $u(0) = 1$. With U^1 calculated, equation (2.5.18) with $n = 1$ can be used to compute U^2:

$$U^2 = (1 - \Delta t)U^1 \tag{2.5.20b}$$

Solution at later times are computed in an analogous way. Once the first n solutions, U^1, U^2, ..., U^n, are known, the next value is calculated by

$$U^{n+1} = (1 - \Delta t)U^n \tag{2.5.20c}$$

In this way, the finite difference proceeds forward in time.

This last problem provides a simple example of two important concepts. The first involves the fact that the time dimension is open ended. Thus the finite difference algorithm relies only on information at times $t \leq t^{n+1}$ when solving for U^{n+1}. The procedure thus "marches" through time, providing solutions sequentially, and the forward Euler method is an example of a *time-marching algorithm*. From a physical point of view, this can be understood since an event occurring at a particular time does not influence things that occurred previously. Thus a solution depends only upon history, not on the future. This is in contrast to the boundary value problem of Example 2.6, wherein boundary information given at both ends of the domain created the need for simultaneous (matrix) solution for all nodal values. The discussion of characteristics in Chapter 1 provides insight to this distinction. Information specified at spatial boundaries may (mathematically) instantaneously affect the entire spatial domain. Thus the solution to a problem at one location depends on the solution at all neighboring spatial locations.

A second point related to solution of Example 2.9 is that while equation (2.5.18) is consistent, only certain values of Δt may be used in the finite difference approximation (2.5.20c). The solution of equation (2.5.19) is $u(t) = e^{-t}$, indicating that as t becomes large, u approaches zero. Examination of equations (2.5.20) reveals that successive substitution allows U^{n+1} to be expressed as $U^{n+1} = (1 - \Delta t)U^n = (1 - \Delta t)^2 U^{n-1} = \cdots = (1 - \Delta t)^{n+1} U^0 = (1 - \Delta t)^{n+1}$. Whenever Δt is larger than 2, the finite difference approximation not only fails to approach zero as t becomes large, it becomes unbounded. This simple example provides a preview of the concept of stability (which is treated in detail in Section 4.2) in that when $\Delta t > 2$, the numerical approximation is unstable. When $1 < \Delta t \leq 2$, the solution decreases in magnitude as t increases (it is therefore stable), but it does so by oscillating between positive and negative values. Only when $0 < \Delta t < 1$ does the finite difference solution decrease monotonically, which is the behavior of the exact solution.

2.6 SOLUTION OF INITIAL VALUE PROBLEMS BY FINITE DIFFERENCES

The general initial value problem

$$\frac{du}{dt} = f(u, t), \qquad t > t^0 \tag{2.6.1}$$

$$u(t^0) = u^0$$

has application to a wide variety of physical systems. This is especially true when the unknown $u(t)$ is a vector, so that equation (2.6.1) represents a system of differential equations. This section expands on the previous example problems (Examples 2.8 and 2.9) and presents four general families of solution methodologies for equation (2.6.1). As before, superscripts are used to denote discrete time levels. The finite difference theory developed earlier in this chapter is applied directly to obtain approximations of interest.

2.6.1 Euler Methods

The forward Euler method was introduced in Example 2.8. It is an approximation to equation (2.6.1) that takes the form, for constant time steps Δt,

$$\frac{U^{n+1} - U^n}{\Delta t} = f(U^n, t^n)$$

or

$$U^{n+1} = U^n + (\Delta t)F^n \qquad \text{(forward Euler)} \tag{2.6.2}$$

This equation arises from a Taylor expansion about the time level t^n using information at the discrete time levels t^n and t^{n+1}. By analogous development, the *backward Euler method* can be obtained through Taylor expansion about the point t^{n+1}. This produces

$$\frac{U^{n+1} - U^n}{\Delta t} = f(U^{n+1}, t^{n+1})$$

or

$$U^{n+1} = U^n + (\Delta t)F^{n+1} \qquad \text{(backward Euler)} \tag{2.6.3}$$

While similar in appearance to equation (2.6.2), equation (2.6.3) is much more difficult to solve when f is nonlinear in u. This is because the unknown solution U^{n+1} would appear implicitly, through F^{n+1}, on the right side of equation (2.6.3), thus precluding simple algebraic solution. The forward method always leads to a simple calculation whether or not f is linear. Forward methods are often referred to as explicit, due to the direct nature of the computations, while backward methods are referred to as implicit.

Finally, a general difference approximation can be formulated about the time level $t^{n+\theta}$, where θ is arbitrary although usually bounded by $0 \leq \theta \leq 1$, using information from levels t^n and t^{n+1}. For this case the approximation for du/dt remains unchanged, while $f^{n+\theta}$ is approximated with a two-point $\mathcal{O}((\Delta t)^2)$ approximation, $f^{n+\theta} \simeq \theta f^{n+1} + (1 - \theta)f^n$. The finite difference approximation to equation (2.6.1) thus takes the form

$$U^{n+1} = U^n + (\Delta t)[\theta F^{n+1} + (1 - \theta)F^n] \qquad \text{(weighted Euler)} \qquad (2.6.4)$$

This approximation is referred to as a *weighted Euler method*, since it is equivalent to a weighted average of a forward and backward Euler method. With θ selected as 0, the forward Euler method results, while $\theta = 1$ is the backward Euler method.

From a computational point of view, the simplicity of the forward Euler method seems to make it the Euler method of choice. However, it is only a first-order approximation, and Example 2.9 alluded to potential stability problems. To obtain a second-order approximation while maintaining the computational benefits of forward methods, a *corrected Euler method* can be implemented:

$$U^* = U^n + (\Delta t)F^n \tag{2.6.5a}$$

$$U^{n+1} = U^n + \frac{\Delta t}{2}[f(U^n, t^n) + f(U^*, t^{n+1})] \qquad \text{(corrected Euler)} \qquad (2.6.5b)$$

There are several important features about this approximation. First, the method is a two-stage procedure in that two distinct calculations are performed in moving forward one step to obtain the desired solution U^{n+1}. The first stage, equation (2.6.5a), is a standard forward Euler method which provides an estimate, or prediction, of the value at time t^{n+1}. The second stage, equation (2.6.5b), is similar to a weighted Euler method with $\theta = 0.5$. The modification introduced is the use of U^* to estimate U^{n+1}. Equation (2.6.5b) is used to calculate an updated, or corrected, value of U^{n+1}. This corrected value is accepted as the approximate solution at t^{n+1}, and the calculation proceeds to the next time level. Although this method is not stable for all values of Δt, its ability to provide stable solutions is improved over the standard forward Euler approximation. For example, in solving $du/dt = -u$, the corrected Euler method is unstable for $\Delta t > 2$ but produces a monotonically decreasing solution for $0 < \Delta t < 2$. The corrected Euler method is an example of a two-stage, predictor-corrector method.

In standard terminology of initial value problems, forward, backward, and weighted Euler methods are one-step, one-stage calculations, because they use one previous time step (n) and one calculation (or stage) to obtain the solution at the new time level, U^{n+1}. The corrected Euler method is a one-step, two-stage method. One-stage Euler methods are first-order approximations to equation (2.6.1), except for the weighted Euler method using $\theta = 0.5$, which is second order. The corrected Euler method of equations (2.6.5) is also second order (see Problem 2.11). In addition to these standard Euler methods, more general multistage implicit Euler methods can be developed. For example, when f depends on u and t, the solution U^{n+1} can be calculated iteratively until equation (2.6.3) is satisfied. This can be accomplished using a variety of nonlinear solution methods, including, for example, Picard or Newton-Raphson procedures.

Example 2.10

   Problem   Solve the nonlinear initial value problem

$$\frac{du}{dt} = -(u)^2, \qquad t > 1 \tag{2.6.6}$$

$$u(1) = 1$$

using the forward Euler method. Examine the effect of the time step by solving the problem three different times using constant time steps $\Delta t = 0.5$, 1.0, and 2.0.

Solution　The forward Euler algorithm is given by

$$U^{n+1} = U^n - (\Delta t)(U^n)^2$$

A table of calculated values follows.

t^n	$\Delta t = 0.5$		$\Delta t = 1.0$		$\Delta t = 2.0$	
	n	U^n	n	U^n	n	U^n
1.0	0	1.0	0	1.0	0	1.0
1.5	1	0.5	—	—	—	—
2.0	2	0.375	1	0.0	—	—
2.5	3	0.305	—	—	—	—
3.0	4	0.258	2	0.0	1	−1.0
3.5	5	0.225	—	—	—	—
4.0	6	0.200	3	0.0	—	—
4.5	7	0.180	—	—	—	—
5.0	8	0.164	4	0.0	2	−3.0
5.5	9	0.150	—	—	—	—
6.0	10	0.139	5	0.0	—	—
6.5	11	0.129	—	—	—	—
7.0	12	0.121	6	0.0	3	−21.
7.5	13	0.114	—	—	—	—
8.0	14	0.107	7	0.0	—	—
8.5	15	0.101	—	—	—	—
9.0	16	0.096	8	0.0	4	−903.
9.5	17	0.092	—	—	—	—
10.0	18	0.087	9	0.0	—	—
10.5	19	0.084	—	—	—	—
11.0	20	0.081	10	0.0	5	-1.6×10^6

The stability limit for the forward Euler method for equation (2.6.6) is $\Delta t \leq 1$. In fact, for the general problem $du/dt = -(u)^p$, p a positive integer, and $u(1) = \alpha$, it can be shown (Problem 2.12) that the stability bound for the forward Euler method is

$$\Delta t \leq \frac{1}{\alpha^{p-1}}, \qquad p \text{ even}$$

$$\Delta t \leq \frac{2}{\alpha^{p-1}}, \qquad p \text{ odd}$$

Thus for nonlinear problems, stability depends not only on the value of Δt but also on the degree of nonlinearity and the initial value of the solution. Because of this dependence, general stability bounds for nonlinear equations are often difficult, if not impossible, to obtain.

To derive higher-order approximations to equation (2.6.1), either additional stages or additional steps need to be used in the finite difference approximation. The most popular family of one-step, multistage methods are Runge-Kutta methods. These are discussed in the next section. This is followed by presentation of a general family of multistep methods in Section 2.6.3. Specific examples of this general formulation include several standard algorithms, including Adams-Bashforth, Adams-Moulton, and Gear methods. Finally, multivalue methods are developed in Section 2.6.4.

2.6.2 One-Step, Multistage Methods: Runge-Kutta Methods

Runge-Kutta (R-K) methods form a family of one-step, multistage approximations to equation (2.6.1). The first, and simplest, member of the family is a general two-stage procedure that uses the same computational philosophy as the corrected Euler method. That is, a forward and a backward calculation are used in tandem so that the computational advantage of forward methods is maintained throughout. A very general form of a one-step, two-stage calculation is

$$U^* = U^n + \alpha_1 (\Delta t) F^n \tag{2.6.7a}$$

$$U^{n+1} = U^n + (\Delta t)[\alpha_2 F^n + \alpha_3 F^*] \tag{2.6.7b}$$

where

$$F^n \equiv f(U^n, t^n) \tag{2.6.7c}$$

$$F^* \equiv f(U^*, t^n + \alpha_1 (\Delta t)) \tag{2.6.7d}$$

In equation (2.6.7), U^* can be interpreted as an approximation to $U^{n+\alpha_1}$, while F^* is interpreted as an approximation to $F^{n+\alpha_1}$. Different choices of α_1, α_2, and α_3 lead to different members of the two-stage R-K family. However, these choices are not arbitrary. At a minimum, the approximation (2.6.7) must be consistent with the governing equation (2.6.1). This leads to restrictions on the parameters α_1, α_2, and α_3. Imposition of second-order accuracy leads to additional restrictions.

To derive the appropriate constraints, the following Taylor series are used:

$$\frac{du}{dt}\bigg|_{t^n} = \frac{u^{n+1} - u^n}{\Delta t} - \frac{\Delta t}{2} \frac{d^2 u}{dt^2}\bigg|_{t^n} - \frac{(\Delta t)^2}{6} \frac{d^3 u}{dt^3}\bigg|_{t^n} - \cdots = f^n \tag{2.6.8a}$$

$$f^* = f(u^{n+\alpha_1}, t^n + \alpha_1 (\Delta t)) = f(u^n, t^n) + \alpha_1 (\Delta t) \frac{df}{dt}\bigg|_{u^n, t^n} + \mathcal{O}((\Delta t)^2) \tag{2.6.8b}$$

The expansion provided in equation (2.6.8b) makes use of the fact that although f is written explicitly as a funciton of u and t, it may be considered to be a function only of t because u is a function of t. However, it is worth noting (for use in derivations of higher order Runge-Kutta methods) that the total and partial derivatives of $f(u, t)$ may be related by

$$\frac{df}{dt} = \frac{\partial f}{\partial t} + \frac{\partial f}{\partial u} \frac{du}{dt} = \frac{\partial f}{\partial t} + \frac{\partial f}{\partial u} f \tag{2.6.8c}$$

Finally, by repeated differentiation of the governing equation (2.6.1), the following relationships hold:

$$\frac{d^m u}{dt^m} = \frac{d^{m-1} f}{dt^{m-1}} \tag{2.6.8d}$$

With equations (2.6.8a), (2.6.8b), and (2.6.8d), the two-stage Runge-Kutta algorithm of equations (2.6.7) can be analyzed. By equation (2.6.8a),

$$\frac{u^{n+1} - u^n}{\Delta t} = \left.\frac{du}{dt}\right|_{t^n} + \frac{\Delta t}{2!} \left.\frac{d^2 u}{dt^2}\right|_{t^n} + \mathcal{O}((\Delta t)^2) \tag{2.6.9a}$$

Similarly, by equation (2.6.8b),

$$\alpha_2 f^n + \alpha_3 f^* = (\alpha_2 + \alpha_3) f^n + (\alpha_3 \alpha_1 \Delta t) \left.\frac{df}{dt}\right|_{u^n, t^n} + \mathcal{O}((\Delta t)^2) \tag{2.6.9b}$$

Combination of equations (2.6.9a) and (2.6.9b), with equation (2.6.8d) used to replace (total) time derivatives of f by time derivatives of u, produces

$$\frac{u^{n+1} - u^n}{\Delta t} - [\alpha_2 f^n + \alpha_3 f^*]$$

$$= \left[\left.\frac{du}{dt}\right|_{t^n} - (\alpha_2 + \alpha_3) f^n\right] - \left(\alpha_3 \alpha_1 - \frac{1}{2}\right)(\Delta t) \left.\frac{d^2 u}{dt^2}\right|_{t^n} + \mathcal{O}((\Delta t)^2) \tag{2.6.10}$$

$$= \left.\frac{du}{dt}\right|_{t^n} - f^n + (1 - \alpha_2 - \alpha_3) f^n + (\Delta t) \left(\frac{1}{2} - \alpha_1 \alpha_3\right) \left.\frac{d^2 u}{dt^2}\right|_{t^n} + \mathcal{O}((\Delta t)^2)$$

The finite difference approximation of equation (2.6.7b) must be consistent with $du/dt|_{t^n} - f^n = 0$. Therefore, all terms on the right side of equation (2.6.10) should vanish as $\Delta t \to 0$. This occurs whenever $1 - \alpha_2 - \alpha_3 = 0$. Therefore, the constraint $\alpha_2 + \alpha_3 = 1$ is a consistency requirement for two-stage Runge-Kutta methods. Satisfaction of this condition leads to a first-order approximation. Second-order accuracy is achieved by setting $1/2 - \alpha_1 \alpha_3 = 0$, since the $\mathcal{O}(\Delta t)$ error term of equation (2.6.10) vanishes when this condition is met. Thus the requirements for equation (2.6.7) to be a second-order, two-stage Runge-Kutta method are

$$\alpha_2 = 1 - \frac{1}{2\alpha_1} \tag{2.6.11a}$$

$$\alpha_3 = \frac{1}{2\alpha_1} \tag{2.6.11b}$$

where α_1 is an arbitrary positive number. Notice that the corrected Euler method is a member of this Runge-Kutta family, in that equations (2.6.5) are of the form of equations (2.6.7) and satisfy equations (2.6.11) with $\alpha_1 = 1$.

Higher-order Runge-Kutta algorithms are obtained from the use of more than two stages in the calculation from one time level to the next. Derivation of higher-order formulas follows the same logic that was presented for second-order, two-stage methods, although the algebra becomes quite tedious. Four-stage, fourth-order methods have been derived, the most popular of which is given by the following algorithm:

$$U^* = U^n + \left(\frac{\Delta t}{2}\right) F^n \tag{2.6.12a}$$

$$U^{**} = U^n + \left(\frac{\Delta t}{2}\right) F^* \tag{2.6.12b}$$

$$U^{***} = U^n + (\Delta t)F^{**} \tag{2.6.12c}$$

$$U^{n+1} = U^n + \left(\frac{\Delta t}{6}\right) [F^n + 2F^* + 2F^{**} + F^{***}] \tag{2.6.12d}$$

where

$$F^* \equiv f\left(U^*, t^n + \frac{\Delta t}{2}\right) \tag{2.6.12e}$$

$$F^{**} \equiv f\left(U^{**}, t^n + \frac{\Delta t}{2}\right) \tag{2.6.12f}$$

$$F^{***} \equiv f(U^{***}, t^n + \Delta t) \tag{2.6.12g}$$

In these equations, U^* and U^{**} are a predictor and a corrector, respectively, for $U^{n+1/2}$, while U^{***} and U^{n+1} form a predictor and a corrector for U^{n+1}. The terms F^* and F^{**} are estimates of $F^{n+1/2}$ based on, respectively, the predicted and corrected values of $U^{n+1/2}$ (i.e., U^* and U^{**}), while F^{***} approximates F^{n+1} based on the predicted value U^{***}. Very tedious Taylor series analysis demonstrates that this algorithm is fourth order.

Example 2.11

Problem   Solve the equation

$$\frac{du}{dt} = -u^2, \qquad t > 1 \tag{2.6.6}$$

$$u(1) = 1$$

using the corrected Euler method (a two-stage, second-order Runge-Kutta scheme) and compare the three sets of results obtained using $\Delta t = 0.5$, 1.0, and 2.0.

Solution   The corrected Euler algorithm is given by

$$U^* = U^n - (\Delta t)(U^n)^2$$

$$U^{n+1} = U^n - \left(\frac{\Delta t}{2}\right) [(U^n)^2 + (U^*)^2]$$

A table of calculated values follows.

t^n	$\Delta t = 0.5$		$\Delta t = 1.0$		$\Delta t = 2.0$	
	n	U^n	n	U^n	n	U^n
1.0	0	1.0	0	1.0	0	1.0
1.5	1	0.687	—	—	—	—
2.0	2	0.518	1	0.5	—	—
2.5	3	0.414	—	—	—	—
3.0	4	0.344	2	0.344	1	$-11.$
3.5	5	0.294	—	—	—	—
4.0	6	0.257	3	0.259	—	—
4.5	7	0.228	—	—	—	—
5.0	8	0.205	4	0.207	2	-6.4×10^5
5.5	9	0.186	—	—	—	—
6.0	10	0.170	5	0.172	—	—
6.5	11	0.157	—	—	—	—
7.0	12	0.145	6	0.147	3	-6.8×10^{20}
7.5	13	0.136	—	—	—	—
8.0	14	0.127	7	0.129	—	—
8.5	15	0.119	—	—	—	—
9.0	16	0.113	8	0.114	4	$< -1 \times 10^{30}$
9.5	17	0.107	—	—	—	—
10.0	18	0.101	9	0.102	—	—
10.5	19	0.096	—	—	—	—
11.0	20	0.091	10	0.093	5	$< -1 \times 10^{30}$

These results indicate that the stability bound for the corrected Euler approximation to equation (2.6.6) lies between $\Delta t = 1.0$ and $\Delta t = 2.0$. Furthermore, the solutions that converge can be seen to be significantly more accurate than those calculated in Example 2.10 using the forward Euler method, given the exact solution $u(t) = 1/t$. This improved accuracy is consistent with the fact that the corrected Euler approximation is a higher-order method. Notice, however, that two-stage calculations require twice the computational effort as one-stage procedures; this is the price paid for increased accuracy.

2.6.3 Multistep Methods

Multistep methods using constant step size obtain U^{n+1}, the approximate solution to $du/dt = f(u, t)$ at time t^{n+1}, using values of U and F from more than one previous time level. A general $(q + 2)$-step method uses the time levels $n + 1, n, n - 1, ..., n - q$. For a one-stage calculation, the unknown U^{n+1} must occur linearly in the finite difference approximation. Therefore, because $f(u, t)$ is generally nonlinear, F^{n+1} should not appear in a one-stage formulation.

The most general, constant-Δt, $(q + 2)$-step approximation is of the form

$$\left.\frac{du}{dt}\right|_{t^n} - f^n = \frac{1}{\Delta t}\left[\beta_1 U^{n+1} + \beta_0 U^n + \beta_{-1} U^{n-1} + \beta_{-2} U^{n-2} + \cdots + \beta_{-q} U^{n-q}\right]$$

$$+\alpha_1 F^{n+1} + \alpha_0 F^n + \alpha_{-1} F^{n-1} + \alpha_{-2} F^{n-2} + \cdots + \alpha_{-q} F^{n-q} = 0 \qquad (2.6.13)$$

The multiplier $1/\Delta t$ is used strictly for convenience to allow the coefficients β_i to be obtained as dimensionless numbers independent of Δt. If a one-stage algorithm is desired, then α_1 in equation (2.6.13) is set to zero. Such multistep algorithms are usually referred to as *open* (or *forward* or *explicit*) *methods*. Through use of the general development of Section 2.4, the $q+2$ coefficients β_i $(i = 1, 0, -1, ..., -q)$ can be chosen to produce an approximation to $du/dt|_{t^n}$ that is, at best, $\mathcal{O}((\Delta t)^{q+1})$. Similarly, the coefficients $\alpha_i (i = 1, 0, -1, ..., -q)$ can be chosen to approximate f^n to $\mathcal{O}((\Delta t)^{q+2})$. Therefore, the equation can be approximated directly to $\mathcal{O}((\Delta t)^{q+1})$.

However, the order of approximation can be improved substantially by a more judicious choice of the parameters β_i and α_i. The key is to notice that because the governing equation is $du/dt = f$, successive differentiation with respect to time yields

$$\frac{d^2u}{dt^2} = \frac{df}{dt}, \frac{d^3u}{dt^3} = \frac{d^2f}{dt^2}, ..., \frac{d^mu}{dt^m} = \frac{d^{m-1}f}{dt^{m-1}}$$

These relationships can be used to significant advantage in the Taylor series analysis of approximation (2.6.13). To illustrate this idea, propose a linear combination of the nodal values used in equation (2.6.13):

$$\frac{du}{dt}\bigg|_{t^n} - f^n = \frac{1}{\Delta t}\left[\beta_1 u^{n+1} + \beta_0 u^n + \beta_{-1} u^{n-1} + \beta_{-2} u^{n-2} + \cdots + \beta_{-q} u^{n-q}\right]$$

$$+\alpha_1 f^{n+1} + \alpha_0 f^n + \alpha_{-1} f^{n-1} + \alpha_{-2} f^{n-2} + \cdots + \alpha_{-q} f^{n-q} = 0 \qquad (2.6.14)$$

Next expand each u^{n-k} and $f^{n-k} (k = -1, 0, 1, ..., q)$ in Taylor series about the time level n:

$$u^{n-k} = u^n - (k\Delta t) \frac{du}{dt}\bigg|_{t^n} + \frac{(k\Delta t)^2}{2!} \frac{d^2u}{dt^2}\bigg|_{t^n} - \frac{(k\Delta t)^3}{3!} \frac{d^3u}{dt^3}\bigg|_{t^n} + \cdots \quad (2.6.15a)$$

$$f^{n-k} = f^n - (k\Delta t) \frac{df}{dt}\bigg|_{t^n} + \frac{(k\Delta t)^2}{2!} \frac{d^2f}{dt^2}\bigg|_{t^n} - \frac{(k\Delta t)^3}{3!} \frac{d^3u}{dt^3}\bigg|_{t^n} + \cdots \quad (2.6.15b)$$

Substitution of equations (2.6.15) into equation (2.6.14) produces the following equation:

$$\frac{du}{dt}\bigg|_{t^n} - f^n = \frac{1}{\Delta t}\left[\sum_{k=-1}^{q} \beta_{-k}\right] u^n$$

$$- \left[\sum_{k=-1}^{q} k\beta_{-k}\right] \frac{du}{dt}\bigg|_{t^n}$$

$$+ \frac{\Delta t}{2!}\left[\sum_{k=-1}^{q} k^2\beta_{-k}\right] \frac{d^2u}{dt^2}\bigg|_{t^n}$$

$$- \cdots$$

$$+ \left[\sum_{k=-1}^{q} \alpha_{-k}\right] f^n$$

$$-\Delta t \left[\sum_{k=-1}^{q} k\alpha_{-k} \right] \frac{df}{dt} \bigg|_{t^n}$$

$$+\frac{\Delta t^2}{2!} \left[\sum_{k=-1}^{q} k^2\alpha_{-k} \right] \frac{d^2 f}{dt^2} \bigg|_{t^n}$$

$$-\cdots$$

$$= 0 \tag{2.6.16}$$

The trivial way to satisfy equation (2.6.10) is to set all α_i and β_i to zero. However, this would not lead to any useful difference expressions. Alternatively, a nontrivial approximation to equation (2.6.10) can be obtained by requiring some of the coefficients to be nonzero while constraining the summations in a consistent manner. Following the procedures of Section 2.4, derivation of an $\mathcal{O}((\Delta t)^{q+1})$ approximation for $du/dt|_{t^n}$ would proceed by choosing the coefficients β_{-k} $(k = -1, 0, 1, ..., q)$ to satisfy the $q+2$ constraints.

$$\sum_{k=-1}^{q} \beta_{-k} = 0 \tag{2.6.17a}$$

$$\sum_{k=-1}^{q} k\beta_{-k} = -1 \tag{2.6.17b}$$

$$\sum_{k=-1}^{q} k^2\beta_{-k} = 0 \tag{2.6.17c}$$

$$\vdots$$

$$\sum_{k=-1}^{q} k^{q+1}\beta_{-k} = 0 \tag{2.6.17d}$$

Similarly, an $\mathcal{O}((\Delta t)^{q+2})$ approximation can be developed for f^n by setting the bracketed terms that multiply f^n and the derivatives of f as follows:

$$\sum_{k=-1}^{q} \alpha_{-k} = -1 \tag{2.6.18a}$$

$$\sum_{k=-1}^{q} k\alpha_{-k} = 0 \tag{2.6.18b}$$

$$\sum_{k=-1}^{q} k^2\alpha_{-k} = 0 \tag{2.6.18c}$$

$$\vdots$$

$$\sum_{k=-1}^{q} k^{q+1} \alpha_{-k} = 0 \qquad (2.6.18d)$$

If an open approximation is desired such that f^{n+1} does not appear in the approximation, an $\mathcal{O}((\Delta t)^{q+1})$ approximation for f^n is obtained by setting $\alpha_1 = 0$ and not imposing constraint (2.6.18d). However, because $d^m u/dt^m = d^{m-1}f/dt^{m-1}$, the derivatives of f in equation (2.6.16) can be replaced by derivatives of u to obtain

$$\left. \frac{du}{dt} \right|_{t^n} - f^n = \frac{1}{\Delta t} \left[\sum_{k=-1}^{q} \beta_{-k} \right] u^n$$

$$- \left[\sum_{k=-1}^{q} k\beta_{-k} - \sum_{k=-1}^{q} \alpha_{-k} \right] \left. \frac{du}{dt} \right|_{t^n}$$

$$+ \frac{\Delta t}{2!} \left[\sum_{k=-1}^{q} k^2 \beta_{-k} - 2 \sum_{k=-1}^{q} k\alpha_{-k} \right] \left. \frac{d^2 u}{dt^2} \right|_{t^n} \qquad (2.6.19)$$

$$\vdots$$

$$+ (-1)^m \frac{(\Delta t)^{m-1}}{m!} \left[\sum_{k=-1}^{q} k^m \beta_{-k} - m \sum_{k=-1}^{q} k^{m-1} \alpha_{-k} \right] \left. \frac{d^m u}{dt^m} \right|_{t^n} + \cdots$$

The only way that equation (2.6.19) can be satisfied exactly is for all α_i and β_i to be zero. This is the trivial solution and is not useful. A nontrivial consistent approximation is obtained by setting one coefficient, or combination of coefficients, to a nonzero value and also requiring that each grouping of coefficients in equation (2.6.19) that multiplies Δt^r, where $r < 1$, be zero. For convenience, let equation (2.6.18a) provide the nonzero condition. The first two bracketed terms in equation (2.6.19) must be zero for consistency, and thus a nontrivial, consistent approximation to the differential equation is given by

$$\sum_{k=-1}^{q} \beta_{-k} = 0 \qquad (2.6.20a)$$

$$\sum_{k=-1}^{q} k\beta_{-k} - \sum_{k=-1}^{q} \alpha_{-k} = 0 \qquad (2.6.20b)$$

$$\sum_{k=-1}^{q} \alpha_{-k} = -1 \qquad (2.6.20c)$$

Any choice of the $2q + 4$ parameters α_i and β_i $(i = 1, 0, -1, ..., -q)$ that satisfies equations (2.6.20) will produce a consistent approximation to equation (2.6.1) that is at least first-order accurate. Higher-order accuracy can be achieved by forcing successively higher-order truncation error terms to zero in equation (2.6.19). The highest possible order, $\mathcal{O}((\Delta t)^{2q+2})$, is achieved when the following $2q + 1$ additional constraints are satisfied:

$$\sum_{k=-1}^{q} k^2 \beta_{-k} - 2 \sum_{k=-1}^{q} k \alpha_{-k} = 0 \qquad (2.6.21a)$$

$$\sum_{k=-1}^{q} k^3 \beta_{-k} - 3 \sum_{k=-1}^{q} k^2 \alpha_{-k} = 0 \qquad (2.6.21b)$$

$$\vdots$$

$$\sum_{k=-1}^{q} k^{2q+2} \beta_{-k} - (2q+2) \sum_{k=-1}^{q} k^{2q+1} \alpha_{-k} = 0 \qquad (2.6.21c)$$

The highest-order open approximation, $\mathcal{O}((\Delta t)^{2q+1})$, is obtained by setting $\alpha_1 = 0$ and satisfying the set of constraints given by equations (2.6.20) as well as those implied by equations (2.6.21), except for the last one. Note that although methods of varying accuracy may be obtained using the formulation described, some of the methods will have stringent stability constraints or will be unconditionally unstable. Thus optimal accuracy does not necessarily imply the best solution. To examine stability properties, the general analysis described in Chapter 4 can be used.

Many traditional approximations are subsets of this general formulation. For illustration, the Adams and Gear families of formulas will be presented here.

Adams open, also called Adams-Bashforth, formulas use $q+1$ values of f (f^n, f^{n-1}, ..., f^{n-q}) but only two values of u (u^{n+1} and u^n). In the context of the approximation (2.6.13), α_1 and the coefficients β_{-i} must be constrained such that $\alpha_1 = 0$, $\beta_{-i} = 0$ ($i = 1, 2, ..., q$). These $q + 1$ constraints replace the last $q + 1$ of the $2q + 1$ higher-order constraints given in equation (2.6.21). With only β_1 and β_0 nonzero among the β_{-i}'s, consistency equations (2.6.20) imply that $\beta_1 = 1$ and $\beta_0 = -1$.

Coupled with the consistency requirement (2.6.20c), substitution of the values for β_i into the first q constraints of equations (2.6.21) leads to the following $q+1$ constraints on the coefficients α_i (with $\alpha_1 = 0$):

$$\sum_{k=-1}^{q} \alpha_{-k} = -1 \qquad (2.6.22a)$$

$$\sum_{k=-1}^{q} k^m \alpha_{-k} = \frac{(-1)^{m+1}}{m + 1}, \qquad 0 < m \le q, \quad m \text{ integer} \qquad (2.6.22b)$$

Solution of the $q + 1$ equations (2.6.22) for the $q + 1$ unspecified values of α_{-i} ($i = 0, 1, ..., q$) produces the desired $(q + 1)$-order Adams open or Adams-Bashforth formula.

A similar development can be followed to derive approximations in which f^{n+1} is included (i.e., $\alpha_1 \ne 0$). The $(q + 2)$-order Adams closed, or Adams-Moulton, formulas are obtained by setting $\beta_{-i} = 0$ ($i = 1, 2, ..., q$). Consistency, as required by equations (2.6.20), again provides that $\beta_1 = 1$ and $\beta_0 = -1$. Thus the $q + 2$ constraints needed to determine α_{-i} ($i = -1, 0, 1, ..., q$) are the same as given in equations (2.6.22), together with the additional equation obtained by letting $m = q+1$ in equation (2.6.22b).

Examples of third-order ($q = 2$) Adams-Bashforth and third-order ($q = 1$) Adams-Moulton formulas are given by (see Problem 2.14)

$$U^{n+1} = U^n + \frac{\Delta t}{12} \left[23F^n - 16F^{n-1} + 5F^{n-2} \right] \qquad \text{(open)} \qquad (2.6.23a)$$

$$U^{n+1} = U^n + \frac{\Delta t}{12} \left[5F^{n+1} + 8F^n - F^{n-1} \right] \qquad \text{(closed)} \qquad (2.6.23b)$$

Open and closed methods are frequently coupled to produce a two-stage, multistep, predictor-corrector algorithm. One of the most popular of these is the following fourth-order algorithm, which uses open and closed Adams formulas with $q = 3$ and $q = 2$, respectively:

$$U^* = U^n + \frac{\Delta t}{24} \left[55F^n - 59F^{n-1} + 37F^{n-2} - 9F^{n-3} \right] \qquad (2.6.24a)$$

$$U^{n+1} = U^n + \frac{\Delta t}{24} \left[9F^* + 19F^n - 5F^{n-1} + F^{n-2} \right] \qquad (2.6.24b)$$

where $F^* \equiv f(U^*, t^{n+1})$. More than two stages may be employed by using the value of U^{n+1} computed by equation (2.6.24b) as an improved prediction to reevaluate F^* and obtaining a better solution for U^{n+1}. Whether this additional calculation is worth the computational effort depends on the equation being solved. In addition, when applying multistep methods and when using iterative procedures, instabilities due to excessive step size, as well as failure of the iterative procedure to converge, must be considered. Coefficients for Adams-Bashforth approximations of order p ($p = q + 1$) and for Adams-Moulton approximations of order p ($p = q + 2$) are provided in Appendix B.

Many other traditional approximations are subsets of the general formula (2.6.13). For example, the class of approximations known as Gear's methods have the form of equation (2.6.13) with $\alpha_{-i} = 0$ ($i = 1, 2, ..., q$). Open Gear's formulas use the additional constraint that $\alpha_1 = 0$ such that α_0 is the only nonzero α coefficient. Closed Gear's formulas use the extra constraint that $\alpha_0 = 0$ with α_1 being the only nonzero α coefficient. To obtain general relationships for the coefficients in ($q + 2$)-step Gear formulas, the constraints imposed to determine the $2q + 4$ coefficients are $q + 1$ values of α_{-i} set to zero, the three consistency relations [equations (2.6.20)], and the first q constraints given by equation (2.6.21); these lead to an approximation that is of order $q + 1$. For the ($q + 1$)-order Gear's open method, the consistency relations reduce to

$$\sum_{k=-1}^{q} \beta_{-k} = 0 \qquad (2.6.25a)$$

$$\sum_{k=-1}^{q} k\beta_{-k} = -1 \qquad (2.6.25b)$$

$$\alpha_0 = -1 \qquad (2.6.25c)$$

The constraints provided by equations (2.6.21) are

$$\sum_{k=-1}^{q} k^m \beta_{-k} = 0, \qquad 2 \le m \le q+1, \quad m \text{ integer} \tag{2.6.25d}$$

For the $(q + 1)$-order Gear's closed method (with $\alpha_{-i} = 0$ for $i = 0, 1, ..., q$) the consistency relations are

$$\sum_{k=-1}^{q} \beta_{-k} = 0 \tag{2.6.26a}$$

$$\sum_{k=-1}^{q} k\beta_{-k} = -1 \tag{2.6.26b}$$

$$\alpha_1 = -1 \tag{2.6.26c}$$

while the high-order conditions from equations (2.6.21) are

$$\sum_{k=-1}^{q} k^m \beta_{-k} = (-1)^m m, \qquad 2 \le m \le q+1, \quad m \text{ integer} \tag{2.6.26d}$$

Examples of third-order Gear approximations include the following open formula ($q = 2$, $\alpha_1 = 0$, which yields $\alpha_0 = -1$, $\beta_1 = 1/3$, $\beta_0 = 1/2$, $\beta_{-1} = -1$, and $\beta_{-2} = -1/6$):

$$U^{n+1} = -\frac{1}{2}\left[3U^n - 6U^{n-1} + U^{n-2}\right] + 3(\Delta t)F^n \tag{2.6.27a}$$

and the following closed formula ($q = 2$, $\alpha_0 = 0$, yielding $\alpha_1 = -1$, $\beta_1 = 11/6$, $\beta_0 = -3$, $\beta_{-1} = 3/2$, and $\beta_{-2} = -1/3$):

$$U^{n+1} = \frac{1}{11}\left[18U^n - 9U^{n-1} + 2U^{n-2}\right] + \frac{6}{11}(\Delta t)F^{n+1} \tag{2.6.27b}$$

These two third-order methods may be combined in a two-stage predictor-corrector algorithm. Note that for both open and closed Gear approximations, the order of accuracy is equal to $q+1$ (i.e., $p = q+1$). Coefficients for these formulas are provided in Appendix B.

Example 2.12

   Problem   Solve the equation

$$\frac{du}{dt} = -u^2, \qquad t > 1 \tag{2.6.6}$$

$$u(1) = 1$$

using the second-order ($q = 1$) Adams forward, or open, method with three different constant time steps, $\Delta t = 0.5$, 1.0, and 2.0.

Solution   The appropriate algorithm is (Problem 2.15)

$$U^{n+1} = U^n - (\Delta t)\left[\frac{3}{2}(U^n)^2 - \frac{1}{2}(U^{n-1})^2\right]$$

As with all Adams open formulas using more than one step ($q > 1$), a different start-up algorithm must be used (since the solution at time step $n - q$, $q > n$, is undefined). For this example the second-order, corrected Euler method is used for the first time step, because it maintains the second-order accuracy of the Adams method. The Adams formula given above is used for all subsequent time steps. A table of calculated values follows.

t^n	$\Delta t = 0.5$		$\Delta t = 1.0$		$\Delta t = 2.0$	
	n	U^n	n	U^n	n	U^n
1.0	0	1.0	0	1.0	0	1.0
1.5	1	0.687	—	—	—	—
2.0	2	0.583	1	0.5	—	—
2.5	3	0.446	—	—	—	—
3.0	4	0.382	2	0.625	1	−1.
3.5	5	0.322	—	—	—	—
4.0	6	0.281	3	0.164	—	—
4.5	7	0.248	—	—	—	—
5.0	8	0.221	4	0.319	2	−3.0
5.5	9	0.200	—	—	—	—
6.0	10	0.182	5	0.180	—	—
6.5	11	0.167	—	—	—	—
7.0	12	0.155	6	0.182	3	−29.
7.5	13	0.144	—	—	—	—
8.0	14	0.134	7	0.149	—	—
8.5	15	0.126	—	—	—	—
9.0	16	0.118	8	0.132	4	−2540.
9.5	17	0.112	—	—	—	—
10.0	18	0.106	9	0.117	—	—
10.5	19	0.101	—	—	—	—
11.0	20	0.096	10	0.105	5	-1.9×10^7

A stability bound for this algorithm apparently resides between $\Delta t = 1.0$ and $\Delta t = 2.0$.

It has been stated several times that backward or closed approximations suffer computational difficulties when f is nonlinear in u. However, when f is linear in u [i.e., $f(u, t) = \gamma(t)u(t) + \delta(t)$, with γ, δ arbitrary functions of time] backward methods become much more attractive because nonlinear algebra is no longer required to solve for U^{n+1}. In addition, backward methods tend to have much better stability properties than forward approximations. General stability analysis of time-marching algorithms is postponed until Chapter 4. The stability results of the last four example problems are, for now, simply observed in the solution behavior.

2.6.4 Multivalue Methods

Although multistep methods, such as Adams-Bashforth, Adams-Moulton, and Gear's methods described in the preceding section, are widely used for solution of initial value problems, they suffer from two significant shortcomings. First, they require information at more than one previous time level to proceed to the solution at a new level. Therefore, start-up of the method is complicated by the fact that for the first step, information is known at only one level. For example, use of the fourth-order Adams-Moulton predictor-corrector formulas, equations (2.6.24), requires information at four levels to obtain a solution at the next level. Therefore, two steps must be taken using some start-up procedure, such as the single-step Runge-Kutta method, to provide the needed information for an implementation of this equation method. This need for a special start-up algorithm is, at best, inconvenient. A second shortcoming arises from the fact that multistep methods are based on the use of equal time step sizes. To allow for unequal step sizes, one must derive special formulas that are significantly more complex than those presented earlier in this section. The general procedure follows the presentation of Section 2.4; the resulting algorithms are complex, awkward, and unwieldly. However, the utilization of variable time step sizes in a numerical algorithm is an important feature of effective error control.

A variation on multistep methods, which use the values of the dependent variable at multiple locations, is multivalue methods, which use the values of the dependent variable and its derivatives at one location. Two of the most easily developed multivalue formula families are variants on the Adams and Gear methods. These will be derived here. The derivation proceeds as if a $(q + 2)$-step method with constant spacing is to be employed to solve for the dependent variables. Then, after needed coefficients have been obtained, Taylor expansions are used to convert to a single-step algorithm which solves for the dependent variable and its first $p + 1$ derivatives.

The pth-order Adams-Moulton formula for solution of

$$\frac{du}{dt} - f(u, t) = 0 \tag{2.6.28}$$

makes use of estimates of f at $q + 2$ levels $(n + 1, n, ..., n - q)$ and estimates of u at the n and $n + 1$ levels when $p = q + 2$. The desired equation for u^{n+1} can be expressed as

$$u^{n+1} - u^n - (\Delta t) \sum_{\ell=-1}^{q} \alpha_{-\ell,0} f^{n-\ell} \simeq 0 \tag{2.6.29}$$

where the $q + 2$ coefficients $\alpha_{1,0}$, $\alpha_{0,0}$, $\alpha_{-1,0}$, ..., $\alpha_{-q,0}$ are to be determined. As was shown in the preceding section, these coefficients can only be determined if equation (2.6.29) is allowed to be satisfied with some truncation error neglected. For the multivalue method, equations providing solutions for the first through $q + 1$ derivatives of u^{n+1} will also be needed. For the first derivative, an Adams-Moulton formula can be written in terms of the derivative. This approximation involves two values of du/dt (at n and $n + 1$) and $q + 2$ values of f (at $n + 1$, n, ..., $n - q$). The difference equation is

$$(\Delta t) \left. \frac{du}{dt} \right|_{t^{n+1}} - (\Delta t) \left. \frac{du}{dt} \right|_{t^n} - (\Delta t) \sum_{\ell=-1}^{q} \alpha_{-\ell,1} f^{n-\ell} \simeq 0 \qquad (2.6.30)$$

Here the use of Δt as a multiplier of du/dt is simply for dimensional convenience, and the second subscript on the α coefficients denotes the order of derivative being investigated. Including these last two equations a total of $q+2$ equations must be written for derivatives up to order $q + 1$. These equations can be written compactly as

$$\frac{(\Delta t)^k}{k!} \left. \frac{d^k u}{dt^k} \right|_{t^{n+1}} - \frac{(\Delta t)^k}{k!} \left. \frac{d^k u}{dt^k} \right|_{t^n} - (\Delta t) \sum_{\ell=-1}^{q} \alpha_{-\ell,k} f^{n-\ell} \simeq 0, \qquad k = 0, 1, ..., q+1$$

$$(2.6.31)$$

The use of $(\Delta t)^k / k!$ is again a convenience, as this multiplier could be accounted for in the unknown coefficients $\alpha_{-\ell,k}$. Now $d^k u/dt^k|_{t^{n+1}}$ and $f^{n-\ell}$ are each expanded in Taylor series around time level n using

$$\left. \frac{d^k u}{dt^k} \right|_{t^{n+1}} = \left. \frac{d^k u}{dt^k} \right|_{t^n} + (\Delta t) \left. \frac{d^{k+1} u}{dt^{k+1}} \right|_{t^n} + \frac{(\Delta t)^2}{2!} \left. \frac{d^{k+2} u}{dt^{k+2}} \right|_{t^n} + \cdots \qquad (2.6.32)$$

and

$$f^{n-\ell} = f^n - (\ell \, \Delta t) \left. \frac{df}{dt} \right|_{t^n} + \frac{(\ell \, \Delta t)^2}{2!} \left. \frac{d^2 f}{dt^2} \right|_{t^n} - \cdots \qquad (2.6.33)$$

Substitution of equations (2.6.32) and (2.6.33) into (2.6.31) results in

$$\sum_{m=k+1}^{\infty} \frac{(\Delta t)^m}{k!(m-k)!} \left. \frac{d^m u}{dt^m} \right|_{t^n} - \left[\sum_{\ell=-1}^{q} \alpha_{-\ell,k} \right] (\Delta t) f^n + \left[\sum_{\ell=-1}^{q} \ell \alpha_{-\ell,k} \right] (\Delta t)^2 \left. \frac{df}{dt} \right|_{t^n}$$

$$- \left[\sum_{\ell=-1}^{q} \ell^2 \alpha_{-\ell,k} \right] \frac{(\Delta t)^3}{2!} \left. \frac{d^2 f}{dt^2} \right|_{t^n} + \cdots \simeq 0, \qquad k = 0, 1, ..., q+1 \qquad (2.6.34)$$

However, because $d^{n+1} u/dt^{n+1} = d^n f/dt^n$, f and its derivatives in equation (2.6.34) may be replaced by derivatives of u to obtain

$$\sum_{m=k+1}^{\infty} \frac{(\Delta t)^m}{k!(m-k)!} \left. \frac{d^m u}{dt^m} \right|_{t^n} - \left[\sum_{\ell=-1}^{q} \alpha_{-\ell,k} \right] (\Delta t) \left. \frac{du}{dt} \right|_{t^n} + \left[\sum_{\ell=-1}^{q} \ell \alpha_{-\ell,k} \right] (\Delta t)^2 \left. \frac{d^2 u}{dt^2} \right|_{t^n}$$

$$- \left[\sum_{\ell=-1}^{q} \ell^2 \alpha_{-\ell,k} \right] \frac{(\Delta t)^3}{2!} \left. \frac{d^3 u}{dt^3} \right|_{t^n} + \cdots \simeq 0, \qquad k = 0, 1, ..., q+1 \qquad (2.6.35)$$

To obtain the highest possible order of accuracy, the multipliers of the first $q + 2$ derivatives of u should be zero. Thus the approximation will be of order $q + 2$. The constraints that provide this accuracy are obtained from equation (2.6.35) as

$$\frac{m!}{k!(m + 1 - k)!} - (-1)^m \sum_{\ell=-1}^{q} \ell^m \alpha_{-\ell,k} = 0, \quad 0 \leq k \leq m, \ 0 < m \leq q + 1 \quad (2.6.36a)$$

$$\sum_{\ell=-1}^{q} \ell^m \alpha_{-\ell,k} = 0, \qquad m < k \leq q + 1, \quad 0 < m \leq q + 1 \quad (2.6.36b)$$

$$\delta_{0,k} - \sum_{\ell=-1}^{q} \alpha_{-\ell,k} = 0, \qquad 0 \leq k \leq q + 1, \quad m = 0 \quad (2.6.36c)$$

where $\delta_{0,k}$ is the Kronecker delta, equal to 1 when $k = 0$ and 0 when $k \neq 0$. Solution of equation (2.6.36) for the $(q + 2) \times (q + 2)$ coefficients $\alpha_{-\ell,k}$ determines the set of equations (2.6.31).

The form of equation (2.6.31) is multivalue (using estimates of u and its first $q + 1$ derivatives) and multistep (requiring estimates of f at $q + 2$ levels). The multilevel usage of f at levels $n - \ell$ for $1 \leq \ell \leq q$ can be removed from equation (2.6.31) by replacing $f^{n-\ell}$ with a $(q + 1)$-term Taylor series expansion around f^n:

$$f^{n-\ell} \simeq \sum_{m=0}^{q} \frac{(-\ell \Delta t)^m}{m!} \left. \frac{d^m f}{dt^m} \right|_{t^n}, \qquad 1 \leq \ell \leq q \quad (2.6.37)$$

Substitution of this equation back into (2.6.31) yields

$$\left. \frac{(\Delta t)^k}{k!} \frac{d^k u}{dt^k} \right|_{t^{n+1}} - \left. \frac{(\Delta t)^k}{k!} \frac{d^k u}{dt^k} \right|_{t^n} - (\Delta t)\alpha_{1,k} f^{n+1} - (\Delta t)\alpha_{0,k} f^n$$

$$-\Delta t \sum_{m=0}^{q} \sum_{\ell=1}^{q} \alpha_{-\ell,k} \frac{(-\ell \Delta t)^m}{m!} \left. \frac{d^m f}{dt^m} \right|_{t^n} \simeq 0, \qquad k = 0, 1, ..., q + 1 \quad (2.6.38)$$

or

$$\left. \frac{(\Delta t)^k}{k!} \frac{d^k U^{n+1}}{dt^k} \right. = \left. \frac{(\Delta t)^k}{k!} \frac{d^k U^n}{dt^k} \right. + (\Delta t)\alpha_{1,k} F^{n+1} + (\Delta t) \left[\sum_{\ell=0}^{q} \alpha_{-\ell,k} \right] F^n$$

$$+\Delta t \sum_{m=1}^{q} \sum_{\ell=1}^{q} \alpha_{-\ell,k} \frac{(-\ell \Delta t)^m}{m!} \frac{d^m F^n}{dt^m}, \qquad k = 0, 1, ..., q + 1 \quad (2.6.39)$$

where

$$\left. \frac{d^k U^{n+1}}{dt^k} \simeq \frac{d^k u}{dt^k} \right|_{t^{n+1}}, \quad F^{n+1} = f(U^{n+1}, t^{n+1}), \quad \text{and} \quad \frac{d^m F^n}{dt^m} = \frac{d^{m+1} U^n}{dt^{m+1}}$$

for $m = 0, 1, ..., q$. Note that equation (2.6.39) is the end product of the conversion of the $(q + 2)$-step method to a single-step method using $q + 1$ values of the function and its first

$q+1$ derivatives. The quantity $\Delta t = t^{n+1} - t^n$ may be easily varied from time step to time step as the solution for U^{n+1} and the approximate derivatives, $d^k U^{n+1}/dt^k$, depend only on corresponding values at one time level. The development of a particular formula is demonstrated in the following example, and additional multivalue approximations appear in Appendix B.

Example 2.13

Problem   Derive the three-value Adams-Moulton method for solution of

$$\frac{du}{dt} = f(u, t)$$

Solution   For this problem, $q = 1$, so constraint equations (2.6.36) may be satisfied for $k = 0, 1$, and 2 with $m = 0, 1$, and 2. These equations are

$$k = 0, m = 0: \qquad 1 - (\alpha_{1,0} + \alpha_{0,0} + \alpha_{-1,0}) = 0 \qquad (2.6.40a)$$

$$k = 0, m = 1: \qquad \tfrac{1}{2} + (-\alpha_{1,0} + \alpha_{-1,0}) = 0 \qquad (2.6.40b)$$

$$k = 0, m = 2: \qquad \tfrac{1}{3} - (\alpha_{1,0} + \alpha_{-1,0}) = 0 \qquad (2.6.40c)$$

$$k = 1, m = 0: \qquad \alpha_{1,1} + \alpha_{0,1} + \alpha_{-1,1} = 0 \qquad (2.6.41a)$$

$$k = 1, m = 1: \qquad 1 + (-\alpha_{1,1} + \alpha_{-1,1}) = 0 \qquad (2.6.41b)$$

$$k = 1, m = 2: \qquad 1 - (\alpha_{1,1} + \alpha_{-1,1}) = 0 \qquad (2.6.41c)$$

$$k = 2, m = 0: \qquad \alpha_{1,2} + \alpha_{0,2} + \alpha_{-1,2} = 0 \qquad (2.6.42a)$$

$$k = 2, m = 1: \qquad -\alpha_{1,2} + \alpha_{-1,2} = 0 \qquad (2.6.42b)$$

$$k = 2, m = 2: \qquad 1 - (\alpha_{1,2} + \alpha_{-1,2}) = 0 \qquad (2.6.42c)$$

Solution of equations (2.6.40) yields

$$\alpha_{1,0} = \frac{5}{12}$$

$$\alpha_{0,0} = \frac{8}{12} \qquad (2.6.43)$$

$$\alpha_{-1,0} = \frac{-1}{12}$$

Solution of equations (2.6.41) yields

$$\alpha_{1,1} = 1$$

$$\alpha_{0,1} = -1 \qquad (2.6.44)$$

$$\alpha_{-1,1} = 0$$

Finally, solution of equations (2.6.42) gives

$$\alpha_{1,2} = \frac{1}{2}$$

$$\alpha_{0,2} = -1 \qquad (2.6.45)$$

$$\alpha_{-1,2} = \frac{1}{2}$$

Thus equations (2.6.39) for $k = 0, 1, 2$ are, respectively,

$$U^{n+1} = U^n + \frac{\Delta t}{12}\left[5F^{n+1} + 7F^n + (\Delta t)\frac{dF^n}{dt}\right] \qquad (2.6.46a)$$

$$(\Delta t)\frac{dU^{n+1}}{dt} = (\Delta t)\frac{dU^n}{dt} + (\Delta t)\left[F^{n+1} - F^n\right] \qquad (2.6.46b)$$

$$\frac{(\Delta t)^2}{2}\frac{d^2U^{n+1}}{dt^2} = \frac{(\Delta t)^2}{2}\frac{d^2U^n}{dt^2} + \frac{\Delta t}{2}\left[F^{n+1} - F^n - (\Delta t)\frac{dF^n}{dt}\right] \qquad (2.6.46c)$$

The form of equation (2.6.46b) indicates that if du/dt is initially equal to f, this equality will be preserved approximately at each step in the form

$$\frac{dU^{n+1}}{dt} = f(U^{n+1}, t^{n+1}) \qquad (2.6.47)$$

Notice that equation (2.6.46a) is an implicit equation that is satisfied for a particular value of U^{n+1}. Once this equation has been solved, the approximate derivatives of u may be obtained explicitly from the remaining equations.

The Adams multivalue equations (and, in fact, all multivalue formulas) lend themselves to a convenient predictor-corrector form for computation. If Taylor series analogs are used to predict the solution using

$$\frac{(\Delta t)^k}{k!}\frac{d^k \tilde{U}^{n+1}}{dt^k} = \sum_{\ell=k}^{q+1} \frac{(\Delta t)^\ell}{k!(\ell - k)!}\frac{d^\ell U^n}{dt^\ell}, \qquad k = 0, 1, ..., q+1 \qquad (2.6.48)$$

then equations (2.6.39) may be written in the form (see Problem 2.16)

$$\frac{(\Delta t)^k}{k!}\frac{d^k U^{n+1}}{dt^k} = \frac{(\Delta t)^k}{k!}\frac{d^k \tilde{U}^{n+1}}{dt^k} + \alpha_{1,k}(\Delta t)\left[F^{n+1} - \frac{d\tilde{U}^{n+1}}{dt}\right], \qquad k = 0, 1, ..., q+1 \qquad (2.6.49)$$

Written in this form, only the $q+2$ parameters $\alpha_{1,k}$, $k = 0, 1, ..., q+1$ appear explicitly and need to be utilized to define a multivalue scheme. Furthermore, $\alpha_{1,1}$ will always equal 1, to ensure that condition (2.6.47) is satisfied. However, because the predictor equation (2.6.48) is one order less accurate than the corrector equation (2.6.49), some iteration on the corrector formula is generally appropriate.

An alternative predictor may be developed by considering the last term in equation (2.6.49) to be an $\mathcal{O}((\Delta t)^{q+2})$ term. If this term is assumed to differ between consecutive time steps by a term that is $\mathcal{O}(\Delta t)$, then a predictor of the same order as equation (2.6.49) is

$$\frac{(\Delta t)^k}{k!}\frac{d^k \hat{U}^{n+1}}{dt^k} = \frac{(\Delta t)^k}{k!}\frac{d^k \tilde{U}^{n+1}}{dt^k} + \alpha_{1,k}(\Delta t)\left[F^n - \frac{d\tilde{U}^n}{dt}\right], \qquad k = 0, 1, ..., q+1$$

(2.6.50)

Note that if the time step changes such that $\Delta t^n \neq \Delta t^{n-1}$, then equation (2.6.50) must be written

$$\frac{(\Delta t^n)^k}{k!}\frac{d^k \hat{U}^{n+1}}{dt^k} = \frac{(\Delta t^n)^k}{k!}\frac{d^k \tilde{U}^{n+1}}{dt^k} + \alpha_{1,k}\frac{\Delta t^n}{\Delta t^{n-1}}\left[F^n - \frac{d\tilde{U}^n}{dt}\right], \qquad k = 0, 1, ..., q+1$$

(2.6.51)

Although the predictor formula is one order higher accuracy than equation (2.6.48) and the same order as equation (2.6.49), it is best used only to obtain a prediction of U^{n+1}. Subsequent iteration using equation (2.6.49) will generally provide a more accurate solution. Nevertheless, the fact that predicted and corrected solutions are of the same order of accuracy provides a useful tool for estimation of error and control of accuracy, as discussed in Section 5.1.2.

Explicit multivalue Adams-Bashforth methods of order $q + 1$ can be obtained by setting $\alpha_{1,0} = 0$ in lieu of satisfying equation (2.6.36a) for $k = 0$ and $m = q + 1$. Thus for $k > 0$, the coefficients $\alpha_{1,k}$ in equation (2.6.49) will be unchanged although the explicit method is one order less accurate than the implicit method.

Example 2.14

Problem   Solve the equation

$$\frac{du}{dt} = -u^2, \qquad t > 1$$

(2.6.6)

$$u(1) = 1$$

using the three-value Adams method. Use both implicit (Adams-Moulton) and explicit (Adams-Bashforth) formulations with step sizes of 0.5 and 2.0.

Solution   The implicit formulation uses equation (2.6.49) with $\alpha_{1,0} = 5/12$, $\alpha_{1,1} = 1$, and $\alpha_{1,2} = 1/2$, while the explicit formulation uses $\alpha_{1,0} = 0$, $\alpha_{1,1} = 1$, and $\alpha_{1,2} = 1/2$. For equation (2.6.6), with $u(1) = 1$, $du/dt|_1 = -1$. Differentiation of equation (2.6.6) yields

$$\frac{d^2 u}{dt^2} = -2u\frac{du}{dt} = 2u^3$$

Therefore, $d^2u/dt^2|_1 = 2$. A table of solutions based on the three-value Adams method and iteration on the corrector follows. Although first and second derivatives are also computed at each step, these are not included in the table.

t^n	n	$\Delta t = 0.5$ Open U^n	$\Delta t = 0.5$ Closed U^n	n	$\Delta t = 2.0$ Open U^n	$\Delta t = 2.0$ Closed U^n
1.0	0	1.0	1.0	0	1.0	1.0
1.5	1	0.750	0.659	—	—	—
2.0	2	0.578	0.503	—	—	—
2.5	3	0.468	0.403	—	—	—
3.0	4	0.387	0.336	1	3.0	0.380
3.5	5	0.329	0.288	—	—	—
4.0	6	0.285	0.252	—	—	—
4.5	7	0.251	0.224	—	—	—
5.0	8	0.225	0.201	2	−23.0	0.286
5.5	9	0.203	0.183	—	—	—
6.0	10	0.184	0.168	—	—	—
6.5	11	0.169	0.155	—	—	—
7.0	12	0.156	0.143	3	−1601.	0.175
7.5	13	0.145	0.134	—	—	—
8.0	14	0.135	0.125	—	—	—
8.5	15	0.126	0.118	—	—	—
9.0	16	0.119	0.112	4	-7.7×10^6	0.133
9.5	17	0.113	0.105	—	—	—
10.0	18	0.107	0.100	—	—	—
10.5	19	0.101	0.0955	—	—	—
11.0	20	0.0965	0.0912	5	-1.8×10^{14}	0.105

Note that the explicit scheme is unstable with the larger time step, while the implicit scheme is stable using this step size. This is consistent with the fact that implicit algorithms are generally more stable than explicit ones. Further, it should be noted that the explicit three-value scheme is only second-order accurate, while the implicit three-value scheme is third-order accurate. Thus when the same step size is used, the better agreement of the implicit scheme than of the explicit scheme with the analytical solution, $u = 1/t$, is not unexpected.

A second multivalue approximation, based on Gear's method and of order of accuracy $q + 1$, can be derived from the general equation set

$$\frac{(\Delta t)^k}{k!} \frac{d^k u}{dt^k}\bigg|_{t^{n+1}} - \sum_{\ell=0}^{q} \beta_{-\ell,k} u^{n-\ell} - (\Delta t)\alpha_{1,k} f^{n+1} \simeq 0, \qquad k = 0, 1, ..., q+1 \quad (2.6.52)$$

A Taylor series expansion is made for all terms in equation (2.6.52) around time level n. The procedure is similar to that used for the Adam's method, and the resulting equation is

$$\sum_{m=k}^{\infty} \frac{(\Delta t)^m}{k!(m-k)!} \frac{d^m u^n}{dt^m} - \left[\sum_{\ell=0}^{q} \beta_{-\ell,k}\right] u^n + \left[\sum_{\ell=0}^{q} \ell\beta_{-\ell,k}\right] (\Delta t)\frac{du^n}{dt}$$

$$- \left[\sum_{\ell=0}^{q} \ell^2 \beta_{-\ell,k}\right] \frac{(\Delta t)^2}{2} \frac{d^2 u^n}{dt^2} + \cdots$$

$$-(\Delta t)\alpha_{1,k} \sum_{m=0}^{\infty} \frac{(\Delta t)^m}{m!} \frac{d^m f^n}{dt^m} \simeq 0, \qquad k = 0, 1, ..., q+1 \qquad (2.6.53)$$

Additionally, use is made of the relation

$$\frac{d^m f^n}{dt^m} = \frac{d^{m+1} u^n}{dt^{m+1}}$$

to express all terms in equation (2.6.53) as derivatives of u. The highest order of accuracy $(q + 1)$ for equation (2.6.53) is achieved when the multipliers of the zero through $q + 1$ derivatives of u are zero. Thus the constraint equations are

$$\frac{m!}{k!(m-k)!} - (-1)^m \sum_{\ell=1}^{q} \ell^m \beta_{-\ell,k} - m\alpha_{1,k} = 0, \qquad 0 \le k \le m, \quad 0 < m \le q+1$$

$$(2.6.54a)$$

$$(-1)^m \sum_{\ell=1}^{q} \ell^m \beta_{-\ell,k} + m\alpha_{1,k} = 0 \qquad m < k \le q+1, \quad 0 < m \le q+1 \qquad (2.6.54b)$$

$$\delta_{0,k} - \sum_{\ell=0}^{q} \beta_{-\ell,k} = 0 \qquad 0 \le k \le q+1, \quad m = 0 \qquad (2.6.54c)$$

Equations (2.6.54) may be solved for $(q + 1) \times (q + 2)$ coefficients $\beta_{-\ell,k}$ and $q + 2$ coefficients $\alpha_{1,k}$. Use of these coefficients in equation (2.6.52) yields a multivalue and multistep set of equations. These equations are converted to a $q + 2$ multivalue form by a $(q + 1)$-term Taylor series expansion for $u^{n-\ell}$ around u^n such that

$$u^{n-\ell} \simeq \sum_{m=0}^{q} \frac{(-\ell)^m (\Delta t)^m}{m!} \frac{d^m u}{dt^m}\bigg|_{t^n}, \qquad 1 \le \ell \le q \qquad (2.6.55)$$

Substitution of equation (2.6.55) into equation (2.6.52) yields the Gear multivalue, single-step form of order $q + 1$:

$$\frac{(\Delta t)^k}{k!} \frac{d^k u}{dt^k}\bigg|_{t^{n+1}} - \beta_{0,k} u^n - \sum_{m=0}^{q} \sum_{\ell=1}^{q} \beta_{-\ell,k} \frac{(-\ell)^m (\Delta t)^m}{m!} \frac{d^m u}{dt^m}\bigg|_{t^n} - (\Delta t)\alpha_{1,k} f^{n+1} \simeq 0,$$

$$k = 0, 1, ..., q+1 \qquad (2.6.56)$$

Constraints (2.6.54) can be used to rearrange this equation to the equation pair (2.6.48) and (2.6.49) (see Problem 2.17).

Example 2.15

Problem   Derive the three-value Gear multivalue method for solution of $du/dt = f(u, t)$.

Solution   For this problem, $q = 1$, so constraint equations (2.6.54) must be satisfied for k and m taking on values of 0, 1, and 2. These equations are

$$k = 0, m = 0: \qquad 1 - (\beta_{0,0} + \beta_{-1,0}) = 0 \qquad (2.6.57a)$$

$$k = 0, m = 1: \qquad 1 + \beta_{-1,0} - \alpha_{1,0} = 0 \qquad (2.6.57b)$$

$$k = 0, m = 2: \qquad 1 - \beta_{-1,0} - 2\alpha_{1,0} = 0 \qquad (2.6.57c)$$

$$k = 1, m = 0: \qquad \beta_{0,1} + \beta_{-1,1} = 0 \qquad (2.6.58a)$$

$$k = 1, m = 1: \qquad 1 + \beta_{-1,1} - \alpha_{1,1} = 0 \qquad (2.6.58b)$$

$$k = 1, m = 2: \qquad 2 - \beta_{-1,1} - 2\alpha_{1,1} = 0 \qquad (2.6.58c)$$

$$k = 2, m = 0: \qquad \beta_{0,2} + \beta_{-1,2} = 0 \qquad (2.6.59a)$$

$$k = 2, m = 1: \qquad -\beta_{-1,2} + \alpha_{1,2} = 0 \qquad (2.6.59b)$$

$$k = 2, m = 2: \qquad 1 - \beta_{-1,2} - 2\alpha_{1,2} = 0 \qquad (2.6.59c)$$

Solution of equations (2.6.57), (2.6.58), and (2.6.59) yields, respectively

$$\alpha_{1,0} = \frac{2}{3} \qquad \beta_{-1,0} = -\frac{1}{3} \qquad \beta_{0,0} = \frac{4}{3} \qquad (2.6.60)$$

$$\alpha_{1,1} = 1 \qquad \beta_{-1,1} = 0 \qquad \beta_{0,1} = 0 \qquad (2.6.61)$$

$$\alpha_{1,2} = \frac{1}{3} \qquad \beta_{-1,2} = \frac{1}{3} \qquad \beta_{0,2} = -\frac{1}{3} \qquad (2.6.62)$$

With $q = 1$ in equations (2.6.48) and (2.6.49), use of the parameters $\alpha_{1,k}$ in equation (2.6.49) defines the Gear three-value method.

Example 2.16

Problem   Solve the equation

$$\frac{du}{dt} = -u^2, \qquad t > 1 \qquad (2.6.6)$$

$$u(1) = 1$$

using the three-value Gear's method. Use both implicit ($\alpha_{1,0} = 2/3$) and explicit ($\alpha_{1,0} = 0$) formulations with step sizes of 0.5 and 2.0.

Solution   For the three-value Gear's method, from Example 2.15, $\alpha_{1,1} = 1$ and $\alpha_{1,2} = 1/3$ in equation (2.6.49). With $du/dt|_1 = -1$ and $d^2u/dt^2|_1 = -2$, solutions were successfully computed with $\Delta t = 0.5$. With $\Delta t = 2$, the open Gear's method was unstable, while the closed method, perhaps surprisingly, did not converge to any solution. The calculated solutions for U^n are given in the following table.

Gear's Three-value

t^n	n	$\Delta t = 0.5$ Open U^n	Closed U^n	n	$\Delta t = 2.0$ Open U^n	Closed U^n
1.0	0	1.0	1.0	0	1.0	N
1.5	1	0.750	0.621	—	—	O
2.0	2	0.625	0.433	—	—	
2.5	3	0.510	0.333	—	—	C
3.0	4	0.429	0.274	1	3.0	O
3.5	5	0.366	0.236	—	—	N
4.0	6	0.317	0.209	—	—	V
4.5	7	0.278	0.188	—	—	E
5.0	8	0.247	0.171	2	$-19.$	R
5.5	9	0.222	0.158	—	—	G
6.0	10	0.201	0.146	—	—	E
6.5	11	0.184	0.136	—	—	D
7.0	12	0.169	0.127	3	$-977.$	
7.5	13	0.156	0.119	—	—	S
8.0	14	0.145	0.113	—	—	O
8.5	15	0.136	0.107	—	—	L
9.0	16	0.127	0.101	4	-2.5×10^6	U
9.5	17	0.120	0.096	—	—	T
10.0	18	0.113	0.092	—	—	I
10.5	19	0.107	0.088	—	—	O
11.0	20	0.102	0.084	5	1.7×10^{13}	N

The Gear closed three-value method is second-order accurate, the same order as three-value Adams open. Indeed, the solutions with $\Delta t = 0.5$ using Gear closed (here) and Adams open (in Example 2.14) are comparable in accuracy. The Gear open three-value method is only first-order accurate, and the solution in the table is inferior to that of the closed method.

The inability of the Gear's closed method to provide an approximate solution with $\Delta t = 2$ can be understood by a hand calculation. With $q = 1$ and $k = 0$, equation (2.6.49) is

$$U^{n+1} = \left[U^n + (\Delta t)\frac{dU^n}{dt} + \frac{1}{2}(\Delta t)^2 \frac{d^2U^n}{dt^2} \right] + \alpha_{1,0}(\Delta t)\left[F^{n+1} - \frac{dU^n}{dt} - (\Delta t)\frac{d^2U^n}{dt^2} \right]$$

$$(2.6.63)$$

In the first computational step, $n = 0$, $U^0 = 1$, $dU^0/dt = -1$, and $d^2U^0/dt^2 = 2$. Also $F^1 = -(U^1)^2$, so that equation (2.6.63) becomes

$$U^1 = [1 - (\Delta t) + (\Delta t)^2] + \alpha_{1,0}\Delta t[-(U^1)^2 + 1 - (\Delta t)^2] \qquad (2.6.64)$$

This is a quadratic equation in U^1 whose roots are real, with $\Delta t = 2$, for $-0.038675 < \alpha_{1,0} < 0.538675$. However, for Gear's three-value method, $\alpha_{1,0} = 2/3$, so that the solution for U^1 in this example is complex and therefore unattainable using real arithmetic.

Multivalue methods combine the high-order accuracy of multistep methods with the ability to alter the time step easily as the solution progresses, in order to control error. The accuracy of the method is dependent on the cancellation of errors among approximations to U^{n+1} and its derivatives. Therefore, the first step of a multivalue method for computation of U^1 can be lower order than expected because U^0 and the derivatives are exact and provide no error to be used in cancellation. This is the reason for the difficulty with the three-value Gear's closed method using $\Delta t = 2.0$ in Example 2.16. A very simple demonstration of this phenomenon is given in Problem 2.21. This difficulty can be reduced by using special values of $\alpha_{1,0}$ or small values of Δt in the first few time steps if necessary or desired. Thus although the multivalue methods do not require special start-up algorithms as multistep methods do, start-up does require attention.

2.6.5 Systems of Equations

The methods presented in Sections 2.6.1–2.6.4 extend directly to systems of first-order initial value problems of the form

$$\frac{du_1}{dt} = f_1(u_1, u_2, ..., u_m, t)$$

$$\frac{du_2}{dt} = f_2(u_1, u_2, ..., u_m, t) \qquad (2.6.65)$$

$$\vdots$$

$$\frac{du_m}{dt} = f_m(u_1, u_2, ..., u_m, t)$$

or, using matrix notation,

$$\frac{d\mathbf{u}}{dt} = \mathbf{f}(\mathbf{u}, t), \qquad t > t_0 \qquad (2.6.66)$$

$$\mathbf{u}(t_0) = \mathbf{u}_0$$

For example, the forward Euler method takes the form

$$\mathbf{U}^{n+1} = \mathbf{U}^n + (\Delta t)\mathbf{f}(\mathbf{U}^n, t^n) \qquad (2.6.67a)$$

while the corrected Euler method is written as

$$\mathbf{U}^* = \mathbf{U}^n + (\Delta t)\mathbf{f}(\mathbf{U}^n, t^n)$$

$$\mathbf{U}^{n+1} = \mathbf{U}^n + \frac{\Delta t}{2}[\mathbf{f}(\mathbf{U}^n, t^n) + \mathbf{f}(\mathbf{U}^*, t^{n+1})] \qquad (2.6.67b)$$

$$= \mathbf{U}^n + \frac{\Delta t}{2}[\mathbf{F}^n + \mathbf{F}^*]$$

Also, when $\mathbf{f}$ is linear in $\mathbf{u}$, each f_i can be expressed as

$$f_i(\mathbf{u}, t) = \gamma_{i,1}(t)u_1 + \gamma_{i,2}(t)u_2 + \cdots + \gamma_{i,m}(t)u_m + \beta_i(t)$$

and the system (2.6.65) is equivalent to

$$\frac{d\mathbf{u}}{dt} = \mathbf{A} \cdot \mathbf{u} + \mathbf{b} \tag{2.6.68}$$

where

$$\mathbf{A} = \begin{bmatrix} \gamma_{11} & \gamma_{12} & \cdots & \gamma_{1m} \\ \gamma_{21} & \gamma_{22} & \cdots & \gamma_{2m} \\ \vdots & \vdots & & \vdots \\ \gamma_{m1} & \gamma_{m2} & \cdots & \gamma_{mm} \end{bmatrix}, \qquad \mathbf{b} = \begin{bmatrix} \beta_1 \\ \beta_2 \\ \vdots \\ \beta_m \end{bmatrix}$$

For this case, forward (or open or explicit) methods allow each U_i^{n+1} to be calculated separately from the other U_k^{n+1}, $k \neq i$. This is because in each of the m equations, only one unknown appears at the new time level. Conversely, for backward (or closed or implicit) methods, $\mathbf{U}$ on the right side of equation (2.6.65) is evaluated at the new $(n + 1)$ time level, so that the matrix $\mathbf{A}$ introduces coupling of all unknowns $U_i^{n+1}(i = 1, 2, ..., m)$. Thus a system of linear algebraic equations must be solved to obtain $\mathbf{U}^{n+1}$. This again is a computational price that is associated with backward methods.

2.6.6 Higher-Order Initial Value Problems

Higher-order initial value problems can always be written as an equivalent system of first-order initial value problems. Consider the mth-order ordinary differential equation for the unknown $w(t)$,

$$\frac{d^m w}{dt^m} + c_{m-1}\frac{d^{m-1} w}{dt^{m-1}} + c_{m-2}\frac{d^{m-2} w}{dt^{m-2}} + \cdots + c_1\frac{dw}{dt} + c_0 w = f(t), \qquad t \geq t^0 \tag{2.6.69a}$$

subject to the initial conditions

$$w(t^0) = d_0 \tag{2.6.69b}$$

$$\frac{dw}{dt}(t^0) = d_1 \tag{2.6.69c}$$

$$\vdots$$

$$\frac{d^{m-1} w}{dt^{m-1}}(t^0) = d_{m-1} \tag{2.6.69d}$$

Coefficients c_k $(k = 0, 1, ..., m-1)$ are arbitrary functions of t (linear case) and possibly $w, dw/dt, ..., d^{m-1}w/dt^{m-1}$ (quasilinear case). If the following definitions are used,

$$u_1 = w \tag{2.6.70a}$$

$$u_2 = \frac{du_1}{dt} = \frac{dw}{dt} \tag{2.6.70b}$$

$$u_3 = \frac{du_2}{dt} = \frac{d^2 w}{dt^2} \tag{2.6.70c}$$

$$\vdots$$

$$u_m = \frac{du_{m-1}}{dt} = \frac{d^{m-1}w}{dt^{m-1}} \tag{2.6.70d}$$

then equation (2.6.69) may be rewritten as the following set of m first-order equations:

$$\frac{du_m}{dt} + c_{m-1}\frac{du_{m-1}}{dt} + c_{m-2}\frac{du_{m-2}}{dt} + \cdots + c_1\frac{du_1}{dt} + c_0 u_1 = f(t) \tag{2.6.71a}$$

$$\frac{du_1}{dt} - u_2 = 0 \tag{2.6.71b}$$

$$\frac{du_2}{dt} - u_3 = 0 \tag{2.6.71c}$$

$$\vdots$$

$$\frac{du_{m-1}}{dt} - u_m = 0 \tag{2.6.71d}$$

subject to the initial conditions

$$u_1(t^0) = d_0 \tag{2.6.72a}$$

$$u_2(t^0) = d_1 \tag{2.6.72b}$$

$$\vdots$$

$$u_m(t^0) = d_{m-1} \tag{2.6.72c}$$

Equations (2.6.71) and (2.6.72) can be written in matrix form as

$$\frac{d}{dt}\begin{bmatrix} u_1 \\ u_2 \\ \vdots \\ u_m \end{bmatrix} + \begin{bmatrix} 0 & -1 & 0 & 0 & \cdots & 0 \\ 0 & 0 & -1 & 0 & \cdots & 0 \\ \vdots & & & & & \vdots \\ 0 & 0 & \cdots & 0 & & -1 \\ c_0 & c_1 & \cdots & c_{m-1} & & 0 \end{bmatrix}\begin{bmatrix} u_1 \\ u_2 \\ \vdots \\ u_m \end{bmatrix} = \begin{bmatrix} 0 \\ 0 \\ \vdots \\ 0 \\ f(t) \end{bmatrix} \tag{2.6.73a}$$

$$\begin{bmatrix} u_1(t^0) \\ u_2(t^0) \\ \vdots \\ u_m(t^0) \end{bmatrix} = \begin{bmatrix} d_0 \\ d_1 \\ \vdots \\ d_{m-1} \end{bmatrix} \tag{2.6.73b}$$

or

$$\frac{d\mathbf{u}}{dt} + \mathbf{C} \cdot \mathbf{u}(t) = \mathbf{f}(t) \tag{2.6.74a}$$

$$\mathbf{u}(t^0) = \mathbf{d} \tag{2.6.74b}$$

Solution procedures of Section 2.6.4 can be applied to equations (2.6.74).

Any mth-order initial value problem can be reduced to the system (2.6.73), although the converse is not true (see Problem 2.22). If any of the coefficients c_k in equation (2.6.69) are nonlinear, then the set of first-order equations will also be nonlinear; if equation (2.6.69) is linear, then equation (2.6.74) is also linear.

Reduction to a system of first-order equations provides approximate values $(u_1, u_2, ..., u_m)$ at each discrete time level. These values correspond to w and its first $m - 1$ derivatives. As Problem 2.23 points out, solution of equations of order larger than one [e.g., the original mth-order equation (2.6.69)] requires fewer discrete values to be calculated at each time step, but involves approximation of higher derivatives and therefore requires coupling of more time steps in the finite difference approximation. This trade-off is explored further in Problem 2.23.

2.7 MULTIPLE DIMENSIONS AND PARTIAL DIFFERENTIAL EQUATIONS

The development of finite difference approximations in multiple dimensions can be approached using an extension of the methodology of Section 2.4. In that section a general formulation of difference approximations was presented which was based on extensive use of one-dimensional Taylor series. A similar approach for approximations to partial derivatives in multiple dimensions is presented in this section. Approximations are first derived for rectangular finite difference grids. The approach is then extended to discretizations that use node points located arbitrarily in space. The latter analysis demonstrates that existence of a consistent finite difference approximation cannot, in general, be guaranteed when the node spacing lacks regularity. It also prompts a broader definition of consistency.

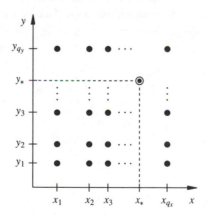

Figure 2.4 Typical rectangular array of node points. The location (x_*, y_*) is arbitrary.

2.7.1 Rectangular Grids

Consider the rectilinear grid of Figure 2.4, wherein a rectangular array of q_x nodes along x and q_y nodes along y is to be used to approximate the general mixed partial derivative $\partial^n u / \partial x^m \partial y^{n-m}|_{x_*, y_*}$, with (x_*, y_*) within the domain of interest but not necessarily corresponding to a node point. This derivative can be rewritten as $\left[\partial^m/\partial x^m(\partial^{n-m}u/\partial y^{n-m}|_{y_*})\right]_{x_*}$. Because the term

$$\left.\frac{\partial^{n-m}u}{\partial y^{n-m}}\right|_{y_*} = \frac{\partial^{n-m}u}{\partial y^{n-m}}(x, y_*)$$

is only a function of x, partial differentiation of this term with respect to x can be treated exactly as the ordinary differentiation of Section 2.4. The following finite difference expansion is therefore proposed:

$$\left[\frac{\partial^m}{\partial x^m}\left(\left.\frac{\partial^{n-m}u}{\partial y^{n-m}}\right|_{y_*}\right)\right]_{x_*} \simeq \sum_{i=1}^{q_x}\alpha_i\left.\frac{\partial^{n-m}u}{\partial y^{n-m}}\right|_{x_i,y_*} \tag{2.7.1}$$

where the partial derivative $(\partial^{n-m}u/\partial y^{n-m})|_{y_*}$ is treated in the same way as the function $u(x)$ in equation (2.4.1), and the coefficients α_i are analogous to γ_i of equation (2.4.1). From the constraints of equations (2.4.5) and (2.4.6), consistency dictates that

$$\sum_{i=1}^{q_x}\frac{(x_i - x_*)^k}{k!}\alpha_i = 0, \qquad k = 0, 1, 2, \ldots, m-1 \tag{2.7.2a}$$

$$\sum_{i=1}^{q_x}\frac{(x_i - x_*)^m}{m!}\alpha_i = 1 \tag{2.7.2b}$$

From these constraints the coefficients α_i can be determined.

The y derivative is treated in an analogous way. That is, for each i, $u|_{x_i} = u(x_i, y)$ is treated as a function of only y. Therefore, the following (one-dimensional) expansion is written:

$$\left.\frac{\partial^{n-m}u}{\partial y^{n-m}}\right|_{x_i,y_*} = \sum_{j=1}^{q_y}\beta_j u_{i,j} \tag{2.7.3}$$

In equation (2.7.3), $u_{i,j}$ is the value of u at location (x_i, y_j), $u_{i,j} \equiv u(x_i, y_j)$. Equations (2.4.5) and (2.4.6) imply the following consistency requirements for the coefficients β_j:

$$\sum_{j=1}^{q_y}\frac{(y_j - y_*)^k}{k!}\beta_j = 0, \qquad k = 0, 1, 2, \ldots, n-m-1 \tag{2.7.4a}$$

$$\sum_{j=1}^{q_y}\frac{(y_j - y_*)^{n-m}}{(n-m)!}\beta_j = 1 \tag{2.7.4b}$$

Based on the presentation in Section 2.4, the minimum node requirements $q_x \geq m+1$ and $q_y \geq n-m+1$ apply. The resulting finite difference approximation takes the form

$$\frac{\partial^n u}{\partial x^m \partial y^{n-m}}\bigg|_{x_*,y_*} \simeq \sum_{i=1}^{q_x} \alpha_i \left[\sum_{j=1}^{q_y} \beta_j u_{i,j} \right]$$

$$= \sum_{i=1}^{q_x} \sum_{j=1}^{q_y} \alpha_i \beta_j u_{i,j}$$

$$= \sum_{i=1}^{q_x} \sum_{j=1}^{q_y} \gamma_{i,j} u_{i,j} \tag{2.7.5}$$

where $\gamma_{i,j} \equiv \alpha_i \beta_j$.

Example 2.17

Problem   Derive a consistent finite difference approximation for $\partial^2 u/\partial x \partial y|_{x_i,y_j}$ using the node points (x_i, y_j), (x_{i+1}, y_j), (x_i, y_{j+1}), (x_{i+1}, y_{j+1}).

Solution   For this case, $n = 2$, $m = n - m = 1$, and the difference approximation is written in the general form

$$\frac{\partial^2 u}{\partial x \partial y}\bigg|_{x_i,y_j} \simeq \gamma_{i,j} u_{i,j} + \gamma_{i+1,j} u_{i+1,j} + \gamma_{i,j+1} u_{i,j+1}$$

$$+ \gamma_{i+1,j+1} u_{i+1,j+1} \tag{2.7.6}$$

where $\gamma_{r,s} = \alpha_r \beta_s$. Requirements (2.7.2) translate to the following equations:

$$\alpha_i + \alpha_{i+1} = 0 \tag{2.7.7a}$$

$$0 + (\Delta x)\alpha_{i+1} = 1 \tag{2.7.7b}$$

whose solution is $\alpha_{i+1} = -\alpha_i = 1/\Delta x$. Similarly, equations (2.7.4) are written as

$$\beta_j + \beta_{j+1} = 0 \tag{2.7.7c}$$

$$0 + (\Delta y)\beta_{j+1} = 1 \tag{2.7.7d}$$

and thus $\beta_{j+1} = -\beta_j = 1/\Delta y$. Therefore, by equation (2.7.5), the consistent finite difference approximation is

$$\frac{\partial^2 u}{\partial x \partial y}\bigg|_{x_i,y_j} \simeq \frac{u_{i,j} - u_{i+1,j} - u_{i,j+1} + u_{i+1,j+1}}{(\Delta x)(\Delta y)}. \tag{2.7.8}$$

Truncation error analysis indicates that this approximation is $\mathcal{O}(\Delta x, \Delta y)$.

2.7.2 Irregular Grids

When the grid of node points used to approximate a derivative is not chosen in a geometrically regular way, the approach of Section 2.7.1 can no longer be used. That is, combinations of one-dimensional Taylor series cannot be applied, and two-dimensional Taylor series must be employed. Furthermore, when the node point locations lack geometrical regularity, it may not be possible to derive a consistent finite difference approximation for a given partial derivative.

This section presents a general method for deriving finite difference approximations in two dimensions, using two-dimensional Taylor series. Analysis of Taylor series expansions leads to several different definitions of consistency, which are referred to as strict consistency, weak consistency, and conditional consistency. Strict consistency can, in general, be achieved only on *regular grids*, which are defined as grids in which nodal points are arranged in a fixed geometric pattern, or lattice. The rectangular grids used in Section 2.7.1 are thus classified as regular (classification of different gridding patterns is discussed in more detail in Section 4.1).

To initiate the general two-dimensional development, Taylor's theorem is written for two independent variables.

Theorem 2.7.1: Taylor Series in Two Dimensions.   Consider a function $u(x, y)$ that is continuous within a region Ω and which has continuous mixed derivatives through order N on Ω (i.e., $u(x, y) \in \mathbb{C}^{N+1}[\Omega]$; see Appendix A). Given a point $\mathbf{x}_* \equiv (x_*, y_*) \in \Omega$, the value of u at any point $\mathbf{x} \equiv (x, y) \in \Omega$ can be written as

$$u(\mathbf{x}) = u(\mathbf{x}_*) + (x - x_*) \left. \frac{\partial u}{\partial x} \right|_{\mathbf{x}_*} + (y - y_*) \left. \frac{\partial u}{\partial y} \right|_{\mathbf{x}_*} + \frac{(x - x_*)^2}{2!} \left. \frac{\partial^2 u}{\partial x^2} \right|_{\mathbf{x}_*}$$

$$+ (x - x_*)(y - y_*) \left. \frac{\partial^2 u}{\partial x \partial y} \right|_{\mathbf{x}_*} + \frac{(y - y_*)^2}{2!} \left. \frac{\partial^2 u}{\partial y^2} \right|_{\mathbf{x}_*} + \cdots$$

$$+ \frac{(x - x_*)^{N-m}}{(N - m)!} \frac{(y - y_*)^m}{m!} \left. \frac{\partial^N u}{\partial x^{N-m} \partial y^m} \right|_{\mathbf{x}_*} + R^{N+1}$$

$$= \sum_{i=0}^{N} \sum_{j=0}^{N-i} \frac{(x - x_*)^i (y - y_*)^j}{i! j!} \left. \frac{\partial^{i+j} u}{\partial x^i \partial y^j} \right|_{\mathbf{x}_*} + R^{N+1} \qquad (2.7.9)$$

where R^{N+1} is a multidimensional remainder term analogous to the remainder of equation (2.3.1).

Consider a collection of Q distinct (node) points, $\{\mathbf{x}_1, \mathbf{x}_2, \ldots, \mathbf{x}_Q\}$, which are arbitrarily located in a two-dimensional domain Ω. Next consider a finite difference approximation to the general mixed partial derivative $\partial^n u / \partial x^m \partial y^{n-m} \big|_{\mathbf{x}_*}$, written as a linear combination of the function values at the Q node points. That is,

$$\left. \frac{\partial^n u}{\partial x^m \partial y^{n-m}} \right|_{\mathbf{x}_*} = \sum_{i=1}^{Q} \Gamma_i u |_{\mathbf{x}_i} \qquad (2.7.10)$$

By analogy to the one-dimensional treatment of Section 2.4, solution for the coefficients Γ_i takes place by expanding each $u |_{\mathbf{x}_i}$ in a (two-dimensional) Taylor series about $\mathbf{x}_* \equiv (x_*, y_*)$. Application of equation (2.7.9) leads directly to

$$u(\mathbf{x}_i) = u(\mathbf{x}_*) + (x_i - x_*) \left.\frac{\partial u}{\partial x}\right|_{\mathbf{x}_*} + (y_i - y_*) \left.\frac{\partial u}{\partial y}\right|_{\mathbf{x}_*} + \frac{(x_i - x_*)^2}{2!} \left.\frac{\partial^2 u}{\partial x^2}\right|_{\mathbf{x}_*} + \cdots \quad (2.7.11)$$

Substitution of equation (2.7.11) into (2.7.10) and subsequent grouping of terms generates the following expression:

$$\left.\frac{\partial^n u}{\partial x^m \partial y^{n-m}}\right|_{\mathbf{x}_*} = B_{0,0} u\big|_{\mathbf{x}_*} + B_{1,0} \left.\frac{\partial u}{\partial x}\right|_{\mathbf{x}_*} + B_{0,1} \left.\frac{\partial u}{\partial y}\right|_{\mathbf{x}_*} + B_{2,0} \left.\frac{\partial^2 u}{\partial x^2}\right|_{\mathbf{x}_*} + \cdots \quad (2.7.12a)$$

where

$$B_{0,0} = \sum_{i=1}^{Q} \Gamma_i \qquad\qquad (2.7.12b)$$

$$B_{1,0} = \sum_{i=1}^{Q} (x_i - x_*)\Gamma_i \qquad\qquad (2.7.12c)$$

$$B_{0,1} = \sum_{i=1}^{Q} (y_i - y_*)\Gamma_i \qquad\qquad (2.7.12d)$$

$$B_{2,0} = \sum_{i=1}^{Q} \frac{(x_i - x_*)^2}{2!}\Gamma_i \qquad\qquad (2.7.12e)$$

$$\vdots$$

$$B_{r,s} = \sum_{i=1}^{Q} \frac{1}{r!s!}(x_i - x_*)^r (y_i - y_*)^s \Gamma_i \qquad\qquad (2.7.12f)$$

Equations (2.7.12) are the two-dimensional analogs of the one-dimensional equations (2.4.4) and (2.4.5) of Section 2.4.

By arguments that parallel those of Section 2.4, the coefficient in equation (2.7.12a) that corresponds to the derivative being approximated, $\partial^n u / \partial x^m \partial y^{n-m}\big|_{\mathbf{x}_*}$, must be unity, so that $B_{m,n-m} = 1$. This implies that each Γ_i, $i = 1, 2, \ldots, Q$, is proportional to $(\Delta x)^{-m}(\Delta y)^{-(n-m)}$, where Δx, Δy are some general measures of grid spacing along each coordinate direction. The strictest criterion for consistency is the requirement that the truncation error vanish as each increment (Δx and Δy in the two-dimensional case) goes to zero, independent of the other increments. This means that the truncation error must remain bounded as only one of the increments goes to zero. This requirement is referred to as *strict consistency*.

A finite difference approximation of the form (2.7.10) exhibits strict consistency if and only if all terms in the truncation error are proportional to grid spacings raised to positive exponents, $(\Delta x)^r (\Delta y)^s$, $r > 0$, $s > 0$. By the definitions of equations (2.7.12), given that each Γ_i is proportional to $(\Delta x)^{-m}(\Delta y)^{-(n-m)}$, strict consistency requires that

$$B_{m,n-m} = 1 \tag{2.7.13a}$$

$$B_{r,s} = 0, \qquad s < n-m, \quad r = 0, 1, 2, \ldots \tag{2.7.13b}$$

$$B_{r,s} = 0, \qquad r < m, \quad s = n-m, n-m+1, n-m+2, \ldots \tag{2.7.13c}$$

Equations (2.7.13b) and (2.7.13c) constitute an infinite number of linear algebraic equations in terms of the finite number of unknowns $\Gamma_1, \Gamma_2, \ldots, \Gamma_Q$. Such a system generally possesses no solution. When there is no geometric regularity of node locations, a finite number of nodes (Q) is insufficient to satisfy equations (2.7.13). Thus a strictly consistent finite difference approximation having the form of equation (2.7.10) is, in general, not possible when an irregular grid of node points is used. Only on regular grids can strict consistency be assured.

A weaker restriction on consistency can be imposed to allow finite difference approximations to be generated on irregular grids. This weaker condition requires the truncation error to go to zero as all increments are reduced, at the same rate, toward zero. This means that truncation error terms that have the form of, for example,

$$\frac{(\Delta y)^r}{(\Delta x)^m}, \qquad r > m$$

will go to zero in the limit of $\Delta x \to 0$, $\Delta y \to 0$, with $\Delta x / \Delta y$ constant. These types of terms do not go to zero under strict consistency, because strict consistency requires these terms to go to zero as only $\Delta x \to 0$, with Δy finite (and vice versa). For weak consistency, the set of infinite constraints listed in equations (2.7.13) are replaced by the finite set of weak consistency constraints,

$$B_{m,n-m} = 1 \tag{2.7.14a}$$

$$B_{r,s} = 0, \qquad r+s \le n, \qquad [(r,s) \ne (m, n-m)] \tag{2.7.14b}$$

For mixed derivatives of (total) order n, constraints (2.7.14) comprise

$$M \equiv 1 + 2 + \cdots + (n+1) = \frac{(n+1)(n+2)}{2}$$

equations. Thus, as long as the matrix of coefficients formed by these equations is nonsingular, a weakly consistent approximation can be guaranteed by using M node points. In the one-dimensional case, the coefficient matrix that resulted was always nonsingular, because it possessed a Vandermonde determinant (Section 2.4). However, it appears that this result cannot be generalized to multiple dimensions.

General results can be stated for rectangular grids. For example, when approximating the derivative $\partial^n u / \partial x^m \partial y^{n-m} \big|_{\mathbf{x}_*}$, a rectangular grid of at least $m+1$ points in x and $n-m+1$ points in y will always allow a strictly consistent finite difference approximation to be formulated. This fact is demonstrated in Examples 2.18 and 2.19, which follow, as well as in Problem 2.24. Because it is significantly easier to work with regular grids, and because the analysis presented above indicates that regular grids are the only type for which strict consistency can be guaranteed, the vast majority of finite difference applications use regular grids of node points.

Example 2.18

Problem   Rederive the four-point approximation to $\partial^2 u/\partial x \partial y|_{(x_i,y_j)}$ that was given in Example 2.13 by using two-dimensional Taylor series. Prove that the approximation is strictly consistent.

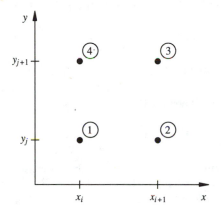

Figure 2.5   Node locations and node numbers for Example 2.18.

Solution   Let the four nodes be numbered 1 through 4 as illustrated in Figure 2.5. The finite difference approximation that is sought is thus of the form

$$\left.\frac{\partial^2 u}{\partial x \partial y}\right|_{\mathbf{x}_1} \simeq \sum_{i=1}^{4} \Gamma_i u|_{\mathbf{x}_i} = \sum_{i=1}^{4} \Gamma_i u_i \tag{2.7.15}$$

Substitution of the appropriate Taylor series from equation (2.7.11) and subsequent regrouping leads to the following expressions for the coefficients $B_{r,s}$ in equations (2.7.12):

$$B_{0,0} = \Gamma_1 + \Gamma_2 + \Gamma_3 + \Gamma_4 \tag{2.7.16a}$$

$$B_{1,0} = \Delta x(\Gamma_2 + \Gamma_3) \tag{2.7.16b}$$

$$B_{0,1} = \Delta y(\Gamma_3 + \Gamma_4) \tag{2.7.16c}$$

$$B_{1,1} = (\Delta x)(\Delta y)(\Gamma_3) \tag{2.7.16d}$$

$$B_{2,0} = \frac{(\Delta x)^2}{2!}(\Gamma_2 + \Gamma_3) \tag{2.7.16e}$$

$$B_{0,2} = \frac{(\Delta y)^2}{2!}(\Gamma_3 + \Gamma_4) \tag{2.7.16f}$$

$$B_{3,0} = \frac{(\Delta x)^3}{3!}(\Gamma_2 + \Gamma_3) \tag{2.7.16g}$$

$$B_{0,3} = \frac{(\Delta y)^3}{3!}(\Gamma_3 + \Gamma_4) \tag{2.7.16h}$$

$$B_{2,1} = \frac{(\Delta x)^2 (\Delta y)}{2!} (\Gamma_3) \tag{2.7.16i}$$

$$B_{1,2} = \frac{(\Delta x)(\Delta y)^2}{2!} (\Gamma_3) \tag{2.7.16j}$$

$$\vdots$$

Imposition of constraint (2.7.13a) requires that $B_{1,1} = 1$, so that

$$\Gamma_3 = \frac{1}{(\Delta x)(\Delta y)} \tag{2.7.17a}$$

Constraints (2.7.13b) imply that $B_{0,0}$, $B_{1,0}$, $B_{2,0}$, $B_{3,0}$, ... must all equal zero. For this example, each constraint $B_{r,0} = 0$, $r \geq 1$, implies the same algebraic relationship: $\Gamma_2 + \Gamma_3 = 0$. Thus, given the solution for Γ_3, it must be that

$$\Gamma_2 = -\Gamma_3 = \frac{-1}{(\Delta x)(\Delta y)} \tag{2.7.17b}$$

Equation (2.7.17b) guarantees that the infinite number of constraints of equation (2.7.13b) are satisfied. Similarly, constraints (2.7.13c) require that $B_{0,0} = B_{0,1} = B_{0,2} = \cdots = 0$. Each constraint $B_{0,s} = 0$, $s \geq 1$ implies that $\Gamma_3 + \Gamma_4 = 0$. Thus

$$\Gamma_4 = -\Gamma_3 = \frac{-1}{(\Delta x)(\Delta y)} \tag{2.7.17c}$$

satisfies the infinite number of constraints (2.7.13c). Finally, the constraint that $B_{0,0} = 0$ requires that

$$\Gamma_1 = \Gamma_3 = \frac{1}{(\Delta x)(\Delta y)} \tag{2.7.17d}$$

Thus the approximation is given by

$$\frac{\partial^2 u}{\partial x \partial y}\bigg|_{x_1} \simeq \frac{u_1 - u_2 + u_3 - u_4}{(\Delta x)(\Delta y)} \tag{2.7.18}$$

This approximation is strictly consistent because each of the constraints of equations (2.7.13) is satisfied. This means that neither Δx nor Δy appears in the denominator of any term in the truncation error. This is easily seen to be the case because all $B_{r,s}$ with either $r = 0$ or $s = 0$ are zero. The repeat pattern for the coefficients that appear in constraints (2.7.13) (e.g., $\Gamma_2 + \Gamma_3 = 0$ for all $B_{r,0} = 0$, $r \geq 1$) is characteristic of regular grids. It is this property that allows strictly consistent approximations to be derived.

Example 2.19

Problem   Derive the most general finite difference approximation for $\partial^2 u / \partial x^2 \big|_{(x_i, y_j)}$ using the nine points shown in Figure 2.6. Notice that the grid spacing shown in Figure 2.6 is not constant, although the grid is rectangular.

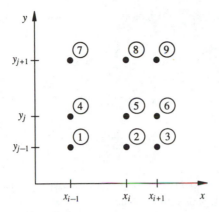

Figure 2.6 Node locations and node numbers for Example 2.19.

Solution   Let the nodes be identified by the numbers 1 through 9, as indicated in Figure 2.6. The finite difference approximation is then of the form

$$\left.\frac{\partial^2 u}{\partial x^2}\right|_{\mathbf{x}_5} \simeq \sum_{i=1}^{9} \Gamma_i u_i \qquad (2.7.19)$$

The procedure to be followed here parallels that of the last example. Each of the u_i, $i = 1, 2, \ldots, 9$, in equation (2.7.19) is expanded in a Taylor series, and the approximation is written in the form of equation (2.7.12). Since $n = 2$, $m = 2$, and $n - m = 0$ for the derivative in equation (2.7.19), the conditions for strict consistency, as stated by equations (2.7.13), are

$$B_{2,0} = 1$$

$$B_{0,0} = 0$$

$$B_{0,1} = B_{0,2} = B_{0,3} = \cdots = 0$$

$$B_{1,0} = B_{1,1} = B_{1,2} = \cdots = 0$$

Examination of the expressions for each coefficient $B_{r,s}$ reveals that the constraint from all $B_{0,s} = 0$, $s = 1, 2, \ldots$, is of the form

$$\frac{(\nabla y_5)^s}{s!}(\Gamma_1 + \Gamma_2 + \Gamma_3) + \frac{(\Delta y_5)^s}{s!}(\Gamma_7 + \Gamma_8 + \Gamma_9) = 0 \qquad (2.7.20a)$$

This can be satisfied for all s if

$$\Gamma_1 + \Gamma_2 + \Gamma_3 = 0 \qquad (2.7.20b)$$

$$\Gamma_7 + \Gamma_8 + \Gamma_9 = 0 \qquad (2.7.20c)$$

Combination of constraints (2.7.20b) and (2.7.20c) with the constraint that $B_{0,0} = 0$ leads to the intermediate consistency conditions,

$$\Gamma_1 + \Gamma_2 + \Gamma_3 = 0 \qquad (2.7.21a)$$

$$\Gamma_4 + \Gamma_5 + \Gamma_6 = 0 \qquad (2.7.21b)$$

$$\Gamma_7 + \Gamma_8 + \Gamma_9 = 0 \qquad (2.7.21c)$$

Similarly, the constraints $B_{1,s} = 0$, $s = 0, 1, 2, \ldots$, lead to the following three equations:

$$\Gamma_1 - \frac{\Delta x_5}{\nabla x_5}\Gamma_3 = 0 \qquad\qquad (2.7.22a)$$

$$\Gamma_4 - \frac{\Delta x_5}{\nabla x_5}\Gamma_6 = 0 \qquad\qquad (2.7.22b)$$

$$\Gamma_7 - \frac{\Delta x_5}{\nabla x_5}\Gamma_9 = 0 \qquad\qquad (2.7.22c)$$

Constraints (2.7.21) and (2.7.22) satisfy all requirements for strict consistency except the constraint that $B_{2,0} = 1$, which implies that

$$\frac{(\nabla x_5)^2}{2!}(\Gamma_1 + \Gamma_4 + \Gamma_7) + \frac{(\Delta x_5)^2}{2!}(\Gamma_3 + \Gamma_6 + \Gamma_9) = 1$$

The final set of constraints is therefore given by

$$\Gamma_3 = \frac{\nabla x_5}{\Delta x_5}\Gamma_1 \qquad\qquad \Gamma_6 = \frac{\nabla x_5}{\Delta x_5}\Gamma_4 \qquad\qquad \Gamma_9 = \frac{\nabla x_5}{\Delta x_5}\Gamma_7$$

$$\Gamma_2 = -\left(1 + \frac{\nabla x_5}{\Delta x_5}\right)\Gamma_1 \qquad \Gamma_5 = -\left(1 + \frac{\nabla x_5}{\Delta x_5}\right)\Gamma_4 \qquad\qquad (2.7.23)$$

$$\Gamma_8 = -\left(1 + \frac{\nabla x_5}{\Delta x_5}\right)\Gamma_7 \qquad \Gamma_1 + \Gamma_4 + \Gamma_7 = \frac{2/\nabla x_5}{\nabla x_5 + \Delta x_5}$$

Substitution of these relations into equation (2.7.19) (after writing all coefficients in terms of Γ_1 and Γ_7) produces the following general finite difference approximation:

$$\left.\frac{\partial^2 u}{\partial x^2}\right|_{x_5} \simeq \Gamma_1\left[u_1 - \left(1 + \frac{\nabla x_5}{\Delta x_5}\right)u_2 + \frac{\nabla x_5}{\Delta x_5}u_3\right]$$

$$+ \left(\frac{2/\nabla x_5}{\Delta x_5 + \nabla x_5} - \Gamma_1 - \Gamma_7\right)\left[u_4 - \left(1 + \frac{\nabla x_5}{\Delta x_5}\right)u_5 + \frac{\nabla x_5}{\Delta x_5}u_6\right]$$

$$+ \Gamma_7\left[u_7 - \left(1 + \frac{\nabla x_5}{\Delta x_5}\right)u_8 + \frac{\nabla x_5}{\Delta x_5}u_9\right] \qquad\qquad (2.7.24)$$

This approximation is first order in x, first order in y, and is strictly consistent for any values of the parameters Γ_1 and Γ_7. Second-order accuracy in y can be achieved by requiring all $\mathcal{O}(\Delta y)$ terms to be zero. This translates into the requirement that $B_{r,1} = 0$ for all $r \geq 0$, which leads to the constraint that $\Gamma_7 = (\nabla y_5/\Delta y_5)\Gamma_1$. Therefore, a one-parameter, $\mathcal{O}(\Delta x, (\Delta y)^2)$ approximation is written as

$$\frac{\partial^2 u}{\partial x^2}\bigg|_{x_5} \simeq \Gamma_1 \left[u_1 - \left(1 + \frac{\nabla x_5}{\Delta x_5} \right) u_2 + \frac{\nabla x_5}{\Delta x_5} u_3 \right]$$

$$+ \left[\frac{2/\nabla x_5}{\Delta x_5 + \nabla x_5} - \left(1 + \frac{\nabla y_5}{\Delta y_5} \right) \Gamma_1 \right] \left[u_4 - \left(1 + \frac{\nabla x_5}{\Delta x_5} \right) u_5 + \frac{\nabla x_5}{\Delta x_5} u_6 \right]$$

$$+ \frac{\nabla y_5}{\Delta y_5} \Gamma_1 \left[u_7 - \left(1 + \frac{\nabla x_5}{\Delta x_5} \right) u_8 + \frac{\nabla x_5}{\Delta x_5} u_9 \right] \qquad (2.7.25)$$

where Γ_1 is an arbitrary parameter. The only additional accuracy that can be achieved is $\mathcal{O}((\Delta y)^3)$, which forces $\Gamma_1 = 0$. In this case, there is no error in y (infinite-order accuracy), and the approximation lies along the $y = y_5$ line. Problem 2.25 explores this approximation further.

As shown in Problem 2.26, the coefficients Γ_k can always be written as products of effectively one-dimensional coefficients when the node points align along the coordinate axes in a regular array. Therefore, the development based on two-dimensional Taylor series expansions is consistent with the development of two-dimensional approximations using one-dimensional analyses along each direction, as presented earlier in this section. Because the earlier development is generally easier to implement, it is usually used to develop and analyze finite difference approximations on regular grids.

Whenever geometric regularity is absent in the finite difference grid, strict consistency cannot generally be achieved. Weak consistency then becomes the next best option. It is in these cases of irregular node spacing that the fully two-dimensional analysis is necessary. The following example illustrates the underlying concepts.

Example 2.20

Problem Derive a finite difference approximation to $\partial^2 u/\partial x \partial y|_{(x_i, y_j)}$ using the four points shown in Figure 2.7.

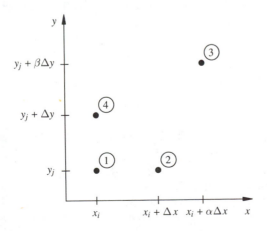

Figure 2.7 Node locations and node numbers for Example 2.20.

Solution   Let the four nodes be numbered 1 through 4, as indicated in Figure 2.7. A finite difference approximation of the following form is sought:

$$\frac{\partial^2 u}{\partial x \partial y}\bigg|_{\mathbf{x}_1} = \Gamma_1 u_1 + \Gamma_2 u_2 + \Gamma_3 u_3 + \Gamma_4 u_4 \tag{2.7.26}$$

Following the procedures outlined in the previous examples, the coefficients of interest are

$$B_{0,0} = \Gamma_1 + \Gamma_2 + \Gamma_3 + \Gamma_4 \tag{2.7.27a}$$

$$B_{1,0} = \Delta x (\Gamma_2 + \alpha \Gamma_3) \tag{2.7.27b}$$

$$B_{0,1} = \Delta y (\beta \Gamma_3 + \Gamma_4) \tag{2.7.27c}$$

$$B_{1,1} = (\alpha \Delta x)(\beta \Delta y)(\Gamma_3) \tag{2.7.27d}$$

$$B_{2,0} = \frac{(\Delta x)^2}{2!}(\Gamma_2 + \alpha^2 \Gamma_3) \tag{2.7.27e}$$

$$B_{0,2} = \frac{(\Delta y)^2}{2!}(\beta^2 \Gamma_3 + \Gamma_4) \tag{2.7.27f}$$

$$B_{3,0} = \frac{(\Delta x)^3}{3!}(\Gamma_2 + \alpha^3 \Gamma_3) \tag{2.7.27g}$$

$$B_{2,1} = \frac{(\alpha \Delta x)^2 (\beta \Delta y)}{2!}(\Gamma_3) \tag{2.7.27h}$$

$$B_{1,2} = \frac{(\alpha \Delta x)(\beta \Delta y)^2}{2!}(\Gamma_3) \tag{2.7.27i}$$

$$B_{0,3} = \frac{(\Delta y)^3}{3!}(\beta^3 \Gamma_3 + \Gamma_4) \tag{2.7.27j}$$

$$\vdots$$

Conditions of strict consistency, as given by equations (2.7.13), dictate that

$$B_{1,1} = 1 \tag{2.7.28a}$$

$$B_{0,0} = 0 \tag{2.7.28b}$$

$$B_{r,0} = 0, \qquad r = 1, 2, 3, \dots \tag{2.7.28c}$$

$$B_{0,s} = 0, \qquad s = 1, 2, 3, \dots \tag{2.7.28d}$$

The first condition, $B_{1,1} = 1$, implies that $\Gamma_3 = 1/(\alpha \Delta x)(\beta \Delta y)$. The condition $B_{1,0} = 0$ implies that $\Gamma_2 = -\alpha \Gamma_3$, while $B_{2,0} = 0$ requires that $\Gamma_2 = -\alpha^2 \Gamma_3$ (for any $r > 0$, $B_{r,0} = 0$ implies that $\Gamma_2 = -\alpha^r \Gamma_3$). Similarly, $B_{0,s} = 0$ requires that $\Gamma_4 = -\beta^s \Gamma_3$. Conditions (2.7.28c) can be met only if $\alpha = 1$, while conditions (2.7.28d) can be met only when $\beta = 1$. This means that strict consistency can only be achieved when a rectangular grid is used, since $\alpha = \beta = 1$ implies a rectangular grid.

Given that strict consistency is not possible, the next step is to attempt to derive an approximation that possesses weak consistency. This will be achieved if the conditions of equation (2.7.14) can be satisfied. Since $n = 2$, $m = 1$, and $n - m = 1$, the appropriate conditions for weak consistency are

$$B_{1,1} = 1 \tag{2.7.29a}$$

$$B_{0,0} = B_{1,0} = B_{0,1} = B_{2,0} = B_{0,2} = 0 \tag{2.7.29b}$$

Equations (2.7.29) represent six constraints on the four unknown coefficients $\Gamma_1, \Gamma_2, \Gamma_3, \Gamma_4$. If more than four of the six equations are linearly independent, there will be no solution for the four Γ_i. The number of independent equations reduces to four only when $\alpha = \beta = 1$ (rectangular grid; see Problem 2.27). Therefore, four points are generally insufficient to achieve weak consistency; a minimum of six nodes is required.

Weak consistency is a special case of the more general classification of conditional consistency. Conditional consistency means that a finite difference approximation is consistent only when the grid spacings are made to approach zero under particular constraints. Weak consistency is a specific example of conditional consistency in that the spacing in each of the independent variables must go to zero at the same rate. Other conditions may exist in certain approximations (such as requiring a ratio like $\Delta x / \Delta y$ to go to zero as Δx and Δy go to zero, implying that Δx must decrease faster than Δy), although such conditions are usually undesirable.

2.8 TWO-DIMENSIONAL EXAMPLE CALCULATIONS

This section presents two example finite difference solutions to partial differential equations. The first is a solution for steady-state potential problems subjected to an external source or sink term (Poisson equation). The second is a solution for the two-dimensional transient heat equation, which is a model equation for many physical phenomena.

Example 2.21

Problem   Obtain a finite difference solution to the partial differential equation that describes steady-state temperature distribution in a homogeneous rectangular plate, subject to a spatially variable source of heat,

$$\nabla^2 u = f(x, y), \qquad (x, y) \in \Omega \tag{2.8.1}$$

The domain and boundary conditions selected for study are shown in Figure 2.8a. Because equation (2.8.1) is a second-order elliptic partial differential equation, one boundary condition is provided at each point along the boundary $\partial \Omega$ of the closed region Ω.

Solution   The solution procedure begins with the discretization step. Figure 2.8b shows a discretization into 25 nodes, which will be used for this example solution. Next, a finite difference approximation to equation (2.8.1) is written in terms of nodal values. Let nodal values be denoted by $u_{i,j} \equiv u(x_i, y_j)$. The finite difference approximation (2.7.25), with

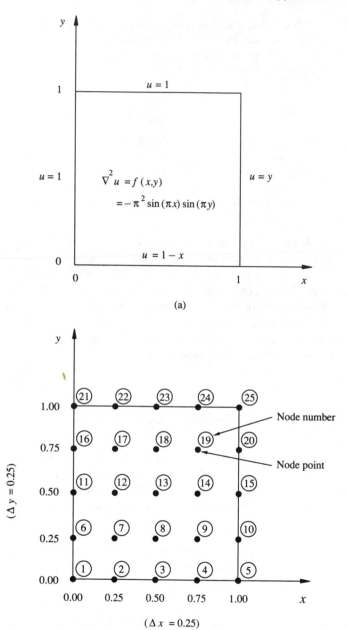

(a)

(b)

Figure 2.8   (a) Domain and boundary conditions for the problem of Example 2.21; (b) finite difference discretization for Example 2.21.

$\Gamma_1 = 0$, is chosen to approximate $\partial^2 u/\partial x^2$, while an analogous approximation is written for $\partial^2 u/\partial y^2$:

$$\left.\frac{\partial^2 u}{\partial x^2}\right|_{x_i,y_j} \simeq \frac{2/\nabla x_i}{\Delta x_i + \nabla x_i} u_{i-1,j} - \frac{2/\Delta x_i + 2/\nabla x_i}{\Delta x_i + \nabla x_i} u_{i,j}$$

$$+ \frac{2/\Delta x_i}{\Delta x_i + \nabla x_i} u_{i+1,j} + \mathcal{O}(\Delta x) \tag{2.8.2a}$$

$$\left.\frac{\partial^2 u}{\partial y^2}\right|_{x_i,y_j} \simeq \frac{2/\nabla y_j}{\Delta y_j + \nabla y_j} u_{i,j-1} - \frac{2/\Delta y_j + 2/\nabla y_j}{\Delta y_j + \nabla y_j} u_{i,j}$$

$$+ \frac{2/\Delta y_j}{\Delta y_j + \nabla y_j} u_{i,j+1} + \mathcal{O}(\Delta y) \tag{2.8.2b}$$

Because the discretization of Figure 2.8b exhibits constant nodal spacing, $\Delta x_i = \nabla x_i$ and $\Delta y_j = \nabla y_j$. Therefore, approximations (2.8.2a) and (2.8.2b) can be written in the following simplified form:

$$\left.\frac{\partial^2 u}{\partial x^2}\right|_{x_i,y_j} = \frac{u_{i-1,j} - 2u_{i,j} + u_{i+1,j}}{(\Delta x)^2} + \mathcal{O}((\Delta x)^2) \tag{2.8.2c}$$

$$\left.\frac{\partial^2 u}{\partial y^2}\right|_{x_i,y_j} = \frac{u_{i,j-1} - 2u_{i,j} + u_{i,j+1}}{(\Delta y)^2} + \mathcal{O}((\Delta y)^2) \tag{2.8.2d}$$

where $\Delta x_i = \nabla x_i \equiv \Delta x$ and $\Delta y_j = \nabla y_j \equiv \Delta y$, for all i and j. Notice that the approximation is second order rather than first order when the node spacing is constant. The right-side forcing function $f(x, y)$ can be approximated without error by the expression

$$f|_{x_i,y_j} = f(x_i, y_j) \equiv f_{i,j} \tag{2.8.3}$$

Application of these approximations at each interior node leads to nine independent linear algebraic equations, each of which has the form

$$\frac{1}{(\Delta x)^2} U_{i-1,j} + \frac{1}{(\Delta x)^2} U_{i+1,j} + \frac{1}{(\Delta y)^2} U_{i,j-1} + \frac{1}{(\Delta y)^2} U_{i,j+1}$$

$$-2\left(\frac{1}{(\Delta x)^2} + \frac{1}{(\Delta y)^2}\right) U_{i,j} = f_{i,j} \tag{2.8.4}$$

These equations are written for the nodes numbered 7, 8, 9, 12, 13, 14, 17, 18, 19 in Figure 2.8b. When the boundary information specified at the 16 first-type boundary nodes is brought to the right side, there results a 9×9 symmetric coefficient matrix. This matrix has a five-diagonal (or pentadiagonal) structure, characteristic of the five-point finite difference approximation of equations (2.8.2). Problem 2.27 examines this matrix in more detail, and Problem 2.29 considers implementation of second-type boundary conditions. The following table presents the finite difference solution for the special case where the forcing function $f(x, y) = -\pi^2 \sin(\pi x) \sin(\pi y)$, using the boundary conditions of Figure 2.8a and the discretization of Figure 2.8b. The analytic solution to this equation is $u(x, y) = 1 - x +$

$xy + (1/2) \sin(\pi x) \sin(\pi y)$. Nodal values of both the finite difference approximation and the analytic solution are given in the table.

TABLE OF RESULTS

Node	x	y	F.D. solution	Exact solution
1	0.	0.	1.0	1.0
2	0.25	0.	0.75	0.75
3	0.5	0.	0.50	0.50
4	0.75	0	0.25	0.25
5	1.0	0.	0.0	0.0
6	0.	0.25	1.0	1.0
7	0.25	0.25	1.076	1.063
8	0.5	0.25	0.997	0.979
9	0.75	0.25	0.701	0.688
10	1.0	0.25	0.25	0.25
11	0.	0.5	1.0	1.0
12	0.25	0.5	1.247	1.229
13	0.5	0.5	1.277	1.250
14	0.75	0.5	0.997	0.979
15	1.0	0.5	0.50	0.50
16	0.	0.75	1.0	1.0
17	0.25	0.75	1.201	1.188
18	0.5	0.75	1.247	1.229
19	0.75	0.75	1.076	1.063
20	1.0	0.75	0.75	0.75
21	0.	1.0	1.0	1.0
22	0.25	1.0	1.0	1.0
23	0.5	1.0	1.0	1.0
24	0.75	1.0	1.0	1.0
25	1.0	1.0	1.0	1.0

Figure 2.9 presents finite difference approximations for $u(0.5, 0.5)$ using three different grids: $\Delta x = \Delta y = 0.5$, $\Delta x = \Delta y = 0.25$, and $\Delta x = \Delta y = 0.125$. Figure 2.9 shows that the logarithm of the error at the center node ($x = 0.5$, $y = 0.5$) is linearly related to the logarithm of Δx, with constant of proportionality (slope of the line on the plot) equal to 2. This value of the slope reflects the leading truncation error term, since the leading-order term is proportional to $(\Delta x)^2$. That is, error $e \approx C(\Delta x)^2$, with C approximately constant. Therefore, $\log e \approx \log C + 2 \ \log \Delta x$, so that the slope of the plot $\log e$ versus $\log \Delta x$ represents the order of the approximation. This idea is explored in detail in Chapter 5.

Example 2.22

Problem Derive a finite difference approximation for the parabolic partial differential equation that describes transient temperature distribution in a homogeneous rectangular plate,

$$\frac{\partial u}{\partial t} - \kappa \nabla^2 u = f(x, y, t), \qquad (x, y) \in \Omega, \quad t > 0 \tag{2.8.5}$$

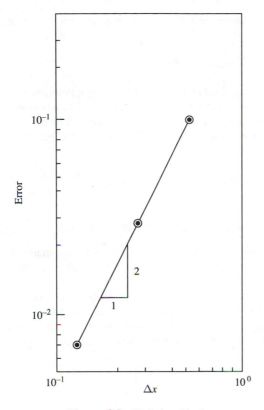

Δx	$\lvert u(0.5,\ 0.5) - U(0.5,\ 0.5)\rvert$
0.125	0.00648
0.25	0.0265
0.5	0.117

Figure 2.9 Relationship between error at center node ($x = 0.5$, $y = 0.5$) and grid spacing Δx for three different grids. Solutions are for the problem of Example 2.21, with $\Delta x = \Delta y$.

In this equation, u represents temperature, κ is thermal diffusivity, f represents external sources or sinks of heat, and Ω is a closed spatial region. One boundary condition is required at every point along $\partial\Omega$, the boundary of Ω, and one initial condition specifying $u(x, y, 0)$ for all $(x, y) \in \Omega$ must be provided for this parabolic problem. A specific set of boundary and initial conditions are given in Problem 2.28.

Solution This problem is similar to that of Example 2.21 except that transient behavior has been introduced. Consider application of a finite difference discretization in the spatial dimensions only. Although a variety of approximations could be developed, equations (2.8.2) are employed with the understanding that $u_{i,j}$, and the finite difference approximations $U_{i,j}$, are now functions of time. The finite difference approximation that results is thus of the form

$$\frac{dU_{i,j}}{dt} - \kappa \left[\frac{U_{i-1,j} - 2U_{i,j} + U_{i+1,j}}{(\Delta x)^2} + \frac{U_{i,j-1} - 2U_{i,j} + U_{i,j+1}}{(\Delta y)^2} \right] = f_{i,j}(t) \qquad (2.8.6)$$

where constant nodal spacing is assumed in both the x and y directions, the time derivative $\partial u / \partial t \big|_{x_i, y_j}$ is represented without spatial error as $dU_{i,j}/dt$, and $f(x_i, y_j, t)$ is also represented without spatial error. Upon combination of all finite difference equations (all i, j

for which first-type boundary conditions are not given), there results a system of first-order differential equations,

$$\frac{d\mathbf{U}}{dt} + \mathbf{A} \cdot \mathbf{U} = \mathbf{F}(t) \tag{2.8.7}$$

The matrix $\mathbf{A}$ is identical to that generated in Example 2.21, with appropriate modification for κ. This set of coupled, linear initial value problems can be solved by any of the methods discussed in Section 2.6. Because the system is linear, either forward (open) or backward (closed) methods can be used. For example, a one-step, variably weighted Euler formula can be written as

$$\frac{\mathbf{U}^{n+1} - \mathbf{U}^n}{\Delta t} + \mathbf{A} \cdot [\theta \mathbf{U}^{n+1} + (1 - \theta)\mathbf{U}^n] = \mathbf{F}^{n+\theta} \tag{2.8.8a}$$

or,

$$[\mathbf{I} + \theta(\Delta t)\mathbf{A}] \cdot \mathbf{U}^{n+1} = (\Delta t)\mathbf{F}^{n+\theta} + [\mathbf{I} - (1 - \theta)(\Delta t)\mathbf{A}] \cdot \mathbf{U}^n \tag{2.8.8b}$$

This matrix equation must be solved at each successive time step, beginning with $n = 0$ and proceeding forward into the open-ended time domain. Problem 2.28 examines particular solutions to this equation.

Reduction of a space-time partial differential equation to a system of ordinary differential equations in time, by means of a discrete spatial approximation such as finite differences, is referred to as a *semidiscretization procedure*. Equation (2.8.7) therefore represents a semidiscrete system. Solution of this set of first-order ordinary differential equations leads to the desired solution.

2.9 CONCLUSION

This chapter presented the underlying theory of finite difference approximations. General procedures for deriving finite difference approximations to ordinary and partial derivatives were presented. These procedures apply to virtually all partial differential equations of interest in science and engineering. Practical considerations such as choice of spatial discretization and time step size are addressed in Chapter 4. Chapters 4 and 5 also address general concepts of error reduction and tie the developments of the present chapter to practical methods of error control in simulation of engineering problems.

PROBLEMS

2.1. Provide a geometric interpretation for the approximation of equation (2.1.3b), similar to those of Figure 2.1 for the approximations of equations (2.1.2).

2.2. Prove that the finite difference operators listed in Section 2.2.1 are linear.

2.3. Derive expressions for the truncation error associated with equations (2.2.1a), (2.2.1b), and (2.2.1c) when the node spacing is not constant ($\Delta x_i \neq \nabla x_i$). State the order of the approximations. How do these compare to the case of constant spacing ($\Delta x_i = \nabla x_i$)?

2.4. Show that the approximation (2.2.2) is consistent, and state the order of approximation. Does the order change when $\Delta x_i = \nabla x_i$?

2.5. Write the algebraic form of the nested approximation for $d^2 u/dx^2|_{x_i}$,

$$\left.\frac{d^2 u}{dx^2}\right|_{x_i} \simeq \frac{\Delta(\Delta u/\Delta x)_i}{\Delta x_i}$$

Analyze the approximation for consistency. Is the approximation consistent when $\Delta x_{i+1} \neq \nabla x_{i+1}$? When $\Delta x_{i+1} = \nabla x_{i+1}$? What is the order of approximation?

2.6. Write the algebraic form of the nested approximation

$$\left.\frac{d^4 u}{dx^4}\right|_{x_i} \simeq \frac{\delta \left\{ \frac{\delta}{\delta x} \left[\frac{\delta}{\delta x} \left(\frac{\delta u}{\delta x} \right) \right] \right\}_i}{\delta x_i}$$

Show that the approximation is in general not consistent unless the node spacings are constant. For the case of arbitrary (nonconstant) node spacing, write a consistent approximation to $d^4 u/dx^4|_{x_i}$ using the five nodes $x_{i-2}, x_{i-1}, x_i, x_{i+1}, x_{i+2}$ and the general procedure of Section 2.4.

2.7. Prove that the nested central difference on $m+1$ nodes centered about x_i for the derivative $d^m u/dx^m|_{x_i}$ produces a second-order approximation whenever m is even and constant node spacing is used. Notice that for this case, $m+1$ points are used to produce an $\mathcal{O}(\Delta x^2)$ approximation.

2.8. Show that the reduced matrix form for the approximations used in Example 2.7 will be symmetric no matter how many nodes are used (consider the case of N nodes, where N is arbitrary, $2 < N < \infty$).

2.9. Write a finite difference approximation for the steady-state advection-diffusion-reaction equation,

$$\mathcal{L}u \equiv D\frac{d^2 u}{dx^2} - V\frac{du}{dx} - ku = f(x), \qquad 0 < x < \ell$$

$$u(0) = 1$$

$$u(\ell) = 0$$

Is the resulting matrix symmetric? Is the operator $\mathcal{L}$ self-adjoint? Can a difference approximation be written that leads to a symmetric matrix structure for this equation?

2.10. Consider the problem and resulting finite difference approximation of Example 2.7.

    (a) Instead of the central difference of equation (2.5.12), use the one-sided difference

$$D\frac{U_3 - U_2}{\Delta x} = C_2$$

as an approximation for the boundary condition $Ddu/dx|_{x_3} = C_2$. Write the resulting matrix, and explain how the finite difference equation written for the interior node (node 2) affects the solution. What happens in the general case of N nodes (N arbitrary)? Discuss the merits of the central difference equation (2.5.12) as compared to the one-sided difference equation proposed above.

(b) Explain how a third-type boundary condition, for example

$$D\frac{du}{dx} - Vu = C_3 \text{ at } x = \ell$$

would be implemented into the finite difference approximation. Write the resulting matrix for the discretization of Figure 2.3a.

2.11. Prove that the corrected Euler method of equation (2.6.5) is a second-order approximation.

2.12. Prove that the stability limit for the forward Euler approximation to

$$\frac{du}{dt} = -(u)^p, \qquad t > 1$$

$$u(1) = \alpha > 0$$

with p a positive integer, is given by

$$\Delta t \le \frac{1}{(\alpha)^{p-1}}, \qquad p \text{ even}$$

$$\Delta t \le \frac{2}{(\alpha)^{p-1}}, \qquad p \text{ odd}$$

(*Hint*: Examine the first time step and require that $|U^1| \le |U^0|$. Then continue to the next time steps.)

2.13. Consider the two-stage Runge-Kutta scheme of equation (2.6.7). Let the evaluation of F^* in equation (2.6.7d) be replaced by

$$F^* \equiv f(U^*, t^n + \beta(\Delta t))$$

What conditions must be placed on β for the resulting Runge-Kutta scheme to be consistent? to be second-order $\mathcal{O}((\Delta t)^2)$?

2.14. Derive the constraints, analogous to those of equations (2.6.22), for an $\mathcal{O}((\Delta t)^{q+2})$, closed Adams formula for the general ordinary differential equation (2.6.1).

2.15. Derive the third-order Adams formulas given in equations (2.6.23a) and (2.6.23b) as well as the second-order formula used in Example 2.12.

2.16. Show that for Adams-Moulton multivalue methods with $\alpha_{-\ell,k}$ constrained by equation (2.6.36), equation (2.6.39) can be rearranged to the form of equation (2.6.49).

2.17. Show that for Gear's multivalue methods with $\alpha_{1,k}$ and $\beta_{-\ell,k}$ constrained by equations (2.6.54), equations (2.6.56) can be rearranged to the form of equation (2.6.49).

2.18. Show that the coefficients $\alpha_{1,k}$ for the four-value ($p = 2$) Adam's-Moulton method obtained from equation (2.6.36) are $\alpha_{1,0} = 3/8$, $\alpha_{1,1} = 1$, $\alpha_{1,2} = 3/4$, and $\alpha_{1,3} = 1/6$.

2.19. Show that the coefficients $\alpha_{1,k}$ for the four-value ($p = 2$) Gear's closed method obtained from equations (2.6.54) are $\alpha_{1,0} = 6/11$, $\alpha_{1,1} = 1$, $\alpha_{1,2} = 6/11$, and $\alpha_{1,3} = 1/11$.

2.20. Write a computer code to solve equation (2.6.6),

$$\frac{du}{dt} = -u^2, \qquad t > 1$$

$$u(1) = 1$$

using four-value multivalue methods. Compare the accuracy of the numerical solutions obtained using Gear's and Adam's open and closed methods with the analytical solution,

$u = 1/t$. Estimate the values of Δt for which the methods become unstable for this problem.

2.21. Solve the differential equation

$$\frac{du}{dt} = 3t^2, \qquad u(0) = 0$$

using the Adams-Moulton three-value method. This method is third-order accurate and thus is expected to provide an exact solution for $u(t)$. Determine the error in the numerical solution after each of the first five time steps. Repeat these calculations; but for the first time step only, use $\alpha_{1,0} = 1/3$. Compare the error here with that of the previous set of calculations. Hypothesize reasons for any differences observed.

2.22. Prove that a general system of first-order ordinary differential equations, $d\mathbf{u}/dt + \mathbf{A} \cdot \mathbf{u} = \mathbf{f}$, cannot be written equivalently as one mth-order equation.

2.23. Consider a second-order initial value problem

$$\frac{d^2 w}{dt^2} + \mu_1(t)\frac{dw}{dt} + \mu_0(t)w = f(t), \qquad t \geq 0$$

$$w(0) = 0$$

$$\frac{dw}{dt}(0) = 1$$

(a) Write a consistent finite difference approximation to this equation for $w(t)$, stating the minimum number of node points required for consistency.

(b) Consider the fourth-order equation

$$\frac{d^4 w}{dt^4} + \mu_3\frac{d^3 w}{dt^3} + \mu_2\frac{d^2 w}{dt^2} + \mu_1\frac{dw}{dt} + \mu_0 w = f(t)$$

How many nodes are required for a consistent finite difference approximation to this equation? Next, consider the following scheme for order reduction. Define two variables, $u_1(t)$ and $u_2(t)$, as

$$u_1 = w$$

$$u_2 = \frac{d^2 w}{dt^2} = \frac{d^2 u_1}{dt^2}$$

so that

$$\frac{d^2 u_2}{dt^2} + \mu_3\frac{du_2}{dt} + \mu_2 u_2 + \mu_1\frac{du_1}{dt} + \mu_0 u_1 = f(t)$$

$$\frac{d^2 u_1}{dt^2} - u_2 = 0$$

How many nodes are now required to derive a consistent approximation to this set of equations? How many unknowns must be approximated at each node?

(c) Considering the trade-off between number of nodal unknowns (number of variables) and the maximum order of derivatives in the resulting set of equations, discuss the advantages and disadvantages of reducing the order of an mth-order initial value problem.

(d) If the second-order equation in part (a) is a boundary value problem instead of an initial value problem,

$$\frac{d^2 w}{dx^2} + \mu_1 \frac{dw}{dx} + \mu_0 w = f(x), \qquad 0 \le x \le \ell$$

$$w(0) = 0$$
$$w(\ell) = 1$$

can the same order reduction be applied? If so, write the system of equations and the appropriate boundary conditions. If not, explain why.

2.24. Consider the general derivative $\partial^n u / \partial x^m \partial y^{n-m}|_{x^*}$. Let the derivative be approximated on a rectangular grid of $m + 1$ points in x and $n - m + 1$ points in y. Show that each equation in the set of constraints $F_{0,s} = 0$, $s = 1, 2, \ldots$, leads to the same algebraic relation for the coefficients Γ_i. Show the same fact for $F_{1,s} = 0$, $F_{2,s} = 0, \ldots, F_{m-1,s} = 0$, $s = 1, 2, \ldots$. Impose all remaining strict consistency constraints to prove that a strictly consistent approximation can always be derived.

2.25. (a) Rederive the approximation of equation (2.7.25) using the one-dimensional analysis of Section 2.7.1.
 (b) Write the approximation (2.7.25) for the case of constant grid spacing.
 (c) Show that the only way to achieve a higher-order approximation is to set $\Gamma_1 = 0$.

2.26. Show that the coefficients Γ_i that arise in two-dimensional finite difference approximations can be written as the product of one-dimensional coefficients whenever the finite difference grid is rectangular. Show that the one-dimensional formulation of Section 2.7.1 guarantees a strictly consistent finite difference approximation.

2.27. Write the full (9×9) matrix equation for the approximation to the Poisson equation presented in Example 2.21. Identify the five nonzero diagonals. Next, observe that the structure of the matrix is also "block tridiagonal" in that it has the form

$$\begin{bmatrix} \mathbf{T} & \mathbf{D}_2 & \mathbf{O} & \cdots & \mathbf{O} \\ \mathbf{D}_1 & \mathbf{T} & \mathbf{D}_2 & \mathbf{O} & \mathbf{O} \\ & \ddots & \ddots & \ddots & \\ & \mathbf{D}_1 & \mathbf{T} & \mathbf{D}_2 & \\ \mathbf{O} & & \ddots & \ddots & \ddots \end{bmatrix}$$

where $\mathbf{T}$ is a submatrix which is itself tridiagonal and $\mathbf{D}$ are diagonal matrices. For a general discretization of N_x nodes in x and N_y nodes in y, define the matrices $\mathbf{T}$, $\mathbf{D}_1$, and $\mathbf{D}_2$ for the five-point approximation to the Poisson equation. Define the total bandwidth in terms of N_x and N_y. Notice that nodes should be numbered consecutively along the direction of minimum nodes to minimize the bandwidth of the resulting matrix.

2.28. Write a computer code using the variably weighted Euler method to solve equation (2.8.8) for an arbitrary rectangular grid of N_x nodes in x and N_y in y. Solve the following problem:

$$\frac{\partial u}{\partial t} - \nabla^2 u = -\pi^2 \sin(\pi x) \sin(\pi y), \qquad 0 < x < 1$$

$$0 < y < 1$$

$$t > 0$$

$$u(0, y, t) = 1$$

$$u(1, y, t) = y$$

$$u(x, 0, t) = 1 - x$$

$$u(x, 1, t) = 1$$

$$u(x, y, 0) = 0$$

Set the time weighting parameter $\theta = 0.5$, and show that the solution at large time approaches the steady-state solution given in the table on page 106 (use the 5×5 grid of Example 2.21 for this case).

2.29. Consider the parabolic equation of Problem 2.28 with the boundary condition at $x = 0$ replaced by $\partial u(0, y, t)/\partial x = g_1(y)$. Formulate the appropriate finite difference approximations for nodes that lie along this boundary. Modify the computer code developed in Problem 2.28 to accommodate second-type boundary conditions along any of the spatial boundaries.

Chapter 3

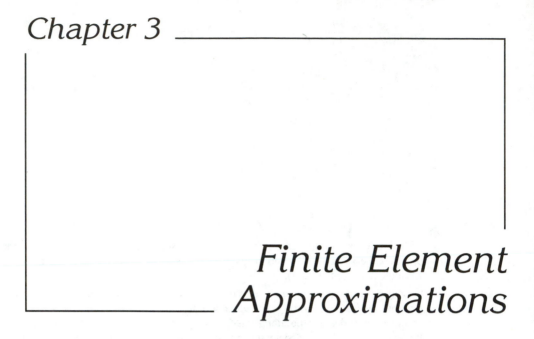

Finite Element Approximations

3.0 INTRODUCTION

This chapter extends the ideas of Chapter 2 by presenting a second alternative for derivation of numerical approximations to differential equations. This method is referred to as the *finite element method*. It is based on an approach that is fundamentally different from the finite difference method. However, the overall objective, and ultimately the results, are the same in that a continuous differential operator is replaced by a finite set of algebraic equations.

In this chapter finite element methods are presented in the broad context of a family of approximation methods referred to as the *method of weighted residuals*. This allows related methods, such as collocation, to be presented in a unified framework. Other formulations of the finite element equations are also discussed, but the weighted residual approach is favored for reasons that are presented in the chapter. The formulations presented are restricted to one dimension and relatively simple geometries in two and three dimensions. More complex geometric shapes and the associated mathematical complexities are presented in Chapter 4. This chapter focuses on the underlying principles on which finite element approximations are built.

114

3.1 METHOD OF WEIGHTED RESIDUALS

The *method of weighted residuals* (MWR) encompasses a general family of approximation methods used for solution of ordinary and partial differential equations. As opposed to the finite difference method, wherein the differential operator is approximated by a (finite) difference operator (see Section 2.2), the method of weighted residuals approximates the actual solution of the differential equation while maintaining the original differential operator. This is accomplished by explicitly defining a functional form for the solution which is approximate in that it satisfies the differential operator only in an approximate way.

The approximate solution is sought from a finite-dimensional function space, denoted here by S_N. This space can be characterized by a set of basis functions $\{\phi_1, \phi_2, \ldots, \phi_N\}$, with N being the dimension of the space (see Appendix A, Definitions A.3.5 and A.3.6). A fundamental property of basis functions is that any member of the space S_N can be expressed as a unique linear combination of the basis functions. Therefore, if an approximation to some function $u(\mathbf{x})$, call it $U(\mathbf{x})$, is sought from S_N, it can always be expressed in the form

$$U(\mathbf{x}) = \sum_{j=1}^{N} \gamma_j \phi_j(\mathbf{x}) \tag{3.1.1}$$

where the $\gamma_j (j = 1, 2, \ldots, N)$ are scalars and the vector $\mathbf{x}$ contains the independent variables. In MWR, the approximating space S_N is chosen a priori, and the problem is then to determine the coefficients $\{\gamma_j\}$ so that $U(\mathbf{x})$ is a good approximation to $u(\mathbf{x})$. MWR algorithms provide a systematic methodology that ultimately produces algebraic equations with the γ_j as unknowns. As such, MWR algorithms achieve the fundamental tenet of numerical methods in that a differential equation is replaced by a related system of algebraic equations, finite in number. For linear differential operators, these algebraic equations are usually linear; solution of these algebraic equations defines $U(\mathbf{x})$ by providing values for $\{\gamma_j\}$ in equation (3.1.1).

An overview of the method of weighted residuals can be presented as follows. Consider a differential equation that is written using general operator notation as

$$\mathcal{L}u(\mathbf{x}) = f(\mathbf{x}), \qquad \mathbf{x} \in \Omega \tag{3.1.2}$$

where $\mathcal{L}$ is a differential operator [e.g., $\mathcal{L} = D(d^2/dx^2) - V(d/dx)$; $\mathcal{L} = \partial^2/\partial x^2 + \partial^2/\partial y^2 + \partial^2/\partial z^2$], $u(\mathbf{x})$ is the unknown solution of interest, $f(\mathbf{x})$ is a known forcing function, Ω denotes the domain over which the differential equation applies, $\partial\Omega$ is the boundary of Ω, and the proper number and type of boundary conditions are specified along $\partial\Omega$. MWR proceeds by first choosing a finite-dimensional function space, S_N, from which an approximate solution to equation (3.1.2) is sought. This space is called the *trial space*. As discussed above, for S_N N-dimensional, with basis functions $\{\phi_1(\mathbf{x}), \phi_2(\mathbf{x}), \ldots, \phi_N(\mathbf{x})\}$, the approximate solution can always be expressed as

$$U(\mathbf{x}) = \sum_{j=1}^{N} \gamma_j \phi_j(\mathbf{x}) \tag{3.1.3}$$

The function $U(\mathbf{x})$ is called the *trial function*. Determination of the N scalars γ_j, $j = 1, 2, \ldots, N$, is the objective of MWR.

The method of weighted residuals seeks to minimize the amount by which $U(x)$ fails to satisfy the original governing equation. A measure of this failure can be defined by

$$R(\mathbf{x}) \equiv \mathcal{L}U(\mathbf{x}) - f(\mathbf{x}) \qquad (3.1.4)$$

where $R(\mathbf{x})$ is called the *residual*. Let the original problem defined by the differential equation $\mathcal{L}u = f$ and its associated boundary conditions be well-posed. Then there exists a unique solution $u(\mathbf{x})$ which generally resides in an infinite-dimensional space. Since U is from a finite-dimensional space, it is generally the case that $U(\mathbf{x}) \neq u(\mathbf{x})$ and therefore $R(\mathbf{x}) \neq 0$. The method of weighted residuals seeks to minimize $R(\mathbf{x})$ by forcing it to zero in a weighted average sense over the entire domain. Mathematically, this is expressed as

$$\int_{\Omega} R(\mathbf{x}) w_i(\mathbf{x}) \, d\mathbf{x} = 0 \qquad (3.1.5)$$

where $w_i(\mathbf{x})$ is a member of a set of weight, or test, functions, $\{w_i(\mathbf{x})\}_{i=1}^{M}$. The number of weight functions, M, is related to N (the number of undetermined coefficients γ_j) and the number and type of boundary conditions specified, as illustrated later in this section. Different choices of weight functions lead to different MWR approximations. Once a weight function $w_i(\mathbf{x})$ is specified, integrations in equation (3.1.5) can be performed, in conjunction with equations (3.1.3) and (3.1.4), to produce an algebraic equation in terms of the coefficients γ_j.

To apply MWR, two choices must be made. The first is a choice of trial space S_N, with concomitant definition of basis functions $\{\phi_1, \ldots, \phi_N\}$. The second is choice of the weight or test functions $\{w_i(\mathbf{x})\}$. Each of these choices is important. Furthermore, the two choices are not independent.

3.1.1 Choice of Basis Functions in One Dimension

In practice, the trial space is almost always chosen as a finite-dimensional polynomial space. This is due mainly to convenience, because polynomials are simple to define and have well-known properties. Choice of an N-dimensional polynomial space for S_N implies that the basis functions are polynomials. For an nth-degree polynomial space, $N = n + 1$ and one choice of a basis set is $\{1, x, x^2, \ldots, x^{N-1}\}$. However, for any linear vector space, there is no unique choice of basis set. As such, there is flexibility in the choice of basis functions. It is usually convenient for the coefficients $\{\gamma_j\}$ of equation (3.1.3) to have a direct relationship to the unknown solution $U(\mathbf{x})$. This reasoning leads to the very popular choice of Lagrange polynomials as basis functions for polynomial spaces, because the coefficients γ_j correspond exactly to nodal values of $U(\mathbf{x})$. For example, consider a space S_N of $(N-1)$th-degree polynomials defined over $\Omega = [\omega_1, \omega_2]$, $\Omega \in \mathbb{R}^1$. Lagrange polynomials are then defined with respect to a set of N discrete points within Ω (see Problem A.7 in Appendix A). These points, called *node points*, are denoted by $\{x_1, x_2, \ldots, x_N\}$. An $(N-1)$th-degree polynomial is associated with each x_j, $j = 1, 2, \ldots, N$, such that the polynomial achieves a value of one at $x = x_j$ and is zero at all other nodes x_i, $i \neq j$. That is,

$$\ell_j(x) = \prod_{\substack{i=1 \\ i \neq j}}^{N} \frac{x - x_i}{x_j - x_i} \tag{3.1.6}$$

where $\ell_j(x)$ is the Lagrange polynomial associated with node j. The polynomial $\ell_j(x)$ exhibits the property that

$$\ell_j(x_i) = \begin{cases} 0, & i \neq j \\ 1, & i = j \end{cases} \tag{3.1.7}$$

The dimension of S_N is N, and the N Lagrange polynomials associated with the N nodes form a basis for S_N (see Problem A.6).

Given the choice of Lagrange polynomials as basis functions, equation (3.1.3) implies that the trial function evaluated at any node is simply equal to the coefficient γ_i associated with that node, that is,

$$U(x_i) = \sum_{j=1}^{N} \gamma_j \ell_j(x_i) = \gamma_i \ell_i(x_i) = \gamma_i \equiv U_i \tag{3.1.8}$$

So each coefficient γ_j has the meaning of the approximate solution U evaluated at the node location x_j. These nodal values are denoted by U_j, and their equality to γ_j allows equation (3.1.3) to be rewritten as

$$U(x) = \sum_{j=1}^{N} U_j \phi_j(x) \tag{3.1.9}$$

whenever the ϕ_j, $j = 1, 2, \ldots, N$, are Lagrange polynomials. Notice that the choice of Lagrange polynomials is one of convenience and not one of necessity, since basis sets are not unique.

The Lagrange polynomials defined above are nonzero over the entire domain Ω, except for a finite number of node points. In addition, they are infinitely differentiable, belonging to $\mathbb{C}^\infty[\Omega]$ (see Appendix A for a definition of continuity and associated notation). It is often advantageous to choose *piecewise* Lagrange polynomials as basis functions instead of the *global* Lagrange polynomials defined above. Reasons for preferring this choice will be illustrated shortly.

Piecewise polynomials are functions that have different polynomial definitions over different subregions of the domain and which maintain a specified degree of global continuity. For example, if a one-dimensional domain contains m subregions separated by $m + 1$ nodes, a polynomial of degree 1 might be defined within each subregion, under the constraint that $\mathbb{C}^0[\Omega]$ continuity be maintained over the entire domain. Such a function is depicted in Figure 3.1. This function is a piecewise linear, $\mathbb{C}^0[\Omega]$ polynomial.

When the linear polynomial over any subregion $[x_j, x_{j+1}]$ is formed by linearly interpolating between nodal values U_j and U_{j+1}, the resulting polynomial basis functions

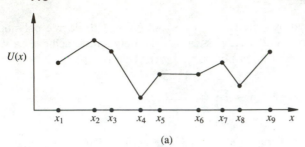

(a)

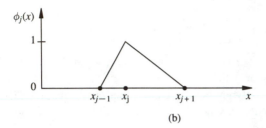

(b)

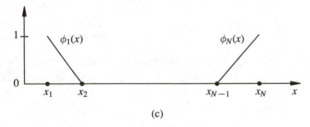

(c)

Figure 3.1 (a) Example of piecewise linear polynomial; (b) typical piecewise linear Lagrange polynomial; (c) basis functions associated with nodes at boundaries of domain.

can be chosen as piecewise linear Lagrange polynomials. As is demonstrated in detail in Problem 3.1, the function $U(x)$ for the piecewise linear polynomial space is still written as

$$U(x) = \sum_{j=1}^{N} U_j \phi_j(x)$$

with the piecewise linear Lagrange bases defined by

$$\phi_j(x) = \begin{cases} \dfrac{x - x_{j-1}}{x_j - x_{j-1}}, & x_{j-1} \le x \le x_j \\[2mm] \dfrac{x_{j+1} - x}{x_{j+1} - x_j}, & x_j \le x \le x_{j+1} \\[2mm] 0, & \text{all other } x \end{cases} \qquad (3.1.10)$$

A typical function $\phi_j(x)$ is shown in Figure 3.1. Notice that each ϕ_j is defined for all x, with the function being equal to zero in the region outside $[x_{j-1}, x_{j+1}]$. When x_j resides at the boundary of the domain Ω, only that portion of ϕ_j that is defined within Ω is used in the definition (see Figure 3.1). Notice that each $\phi_j(x)$ maintains the fundamental property of Lagrange polynomials in that

$$
\phi_j(x_i) = \begin{cases} 1, & i = j \\ 0, & i \neq j \end{cases}
$$

Higher-degree polynomials can also be pieced together to form higher-degree piece-wise polynomial trial spaces, still maintaining overall $\mathbb{C}^0[\Omega]$ continuity. For example, piecewise quadratic Lagrange polynomial expansions are of the form (Problem 3.2)

$$
U(x) = \sum_{j=1}^{N} U_j \phi_j(x) \tag{3.1.11}
$$

where $\{\phi_j(x)\}$ are piecewise quadratic Lagrange polynomials. For this case, as illustrated in Figure 3.2, three nodes are required to define each separate quadratic polynomial. In any group of three nodes used to define a quadratic, the left and right nodes (the *end nodes*) are shared by two adjacent groups, while the *center node* is associated with only one group of nodes. Figure 3.2 also shows graphs of the associated piecewise quadratic Lagrange polynomials. The function definitions now have two general forms, one for the end nodes (which are identified by odd numbers) and one for the center or interior (even-numbered) nodes. These two quadratic polynomials have the general functional form

$$
\phi_j(x) = \begin{cases} \dfrac{(x - x_{j-1})(x - x_{j-2})}{(x_j - x_{j-1})(x_j - x_{j-2})}, & x_{j-2} \leq x \leq x_j \\[2ex] \dfrac{(x_{j+1} - x)(x_{j+2} - x)}{(x_{j+1} - x_j)(x_{j+2} - x_j)}, & x_j \leq x \leq x_{j+2} \\[2ex] 0, & \text{all other } j \end{cases} \tag{3.1.12a}
$$

for end nodes (j odd), and

$$
\phi_j(x) = \begin{cases} \dfrac{(x - x_{j-1})(x_{j+1} - x)}{(x_j - x_{j-1})(x_{j+1} - x_j)}, & x_{j-1} \leq x \leq x_{j+1} \\[2ex] 0, & \text{all other } x \end{cases} \tag{3.1.12b}
$$

for interior nodes (j even). Because each piece of the polynomial is itself a Lagrange polynomial, the function $U(x)$ of equation (3.1.11), with definitions (3.1.12), maintains the property that $\phi_j(x_i) = 0$, $i \neq j$, and $\phi_j(x_j) = 1$. The trial function of equation (3.1.11) consists of quadratic Lagrange polynomials over clusters of three nodes, with the overall function being $\mathbb{C}^0[\Omega]$. The procedure can extend to piecewise polynomials of degree m, with $m + 1$ nodes defining each polynomial and $\mathbb{C}^0[\Omega]$ continuity being maintained (see Problem 3.2).

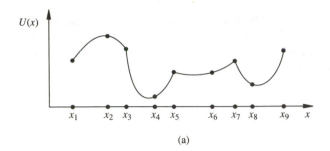

(a)

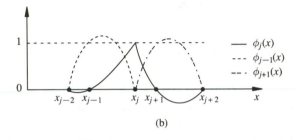

(b)

Figure 3.2 (a) Example of piecewise quadratic polynomial; (b) typical piecewise quadratic Lagrange polynomials (j odd integer).

Higher orders of global continuity can be achieved by choosing different trial spaces and associated basis functions. The most common choice of basis functions to achieve $\mathbb{C}^1[\Omega]$ continuity is the set of *piecewise Hermite polynomials*. Their popularity is due to the fact that the coefficients appearing in the linear combination of these functions, analogous to the $\{\gamma_j\}$ of equation (3.1.3), again contain very convenient information about nodal values of the solution. In particular, the form of $\mathbb{C}^1[\Omega]$ piecewise Hermite polynomials is

$$U(x) = \sum_{j=1}^{N} U_j \phi_{0j}(x) + \frac{dU_j}{dx}\phi_{1j}(x) \tag{3.1.13}$$

In this equation, U_j is the approximate value of u at node j, while dU_j/dx is the approximate value of du/dx at node j. The functions $\phi_{0j}(x)$ and $\phi_{1j}(x)$ are piecewise Hermite polynomials. These are usually chosen to be cubic polynomials (this is the minimum degree required to achieve $\mathbb{C}^1[\Omega]$); these cubic polynomials have the following functional form:

$$\phi_{0j}(x) = \begin{cases} \dfrac{(x-x_{j-1})^2}{(x_j - x_{j-1})^3}[2(x_j - x) + (x_j - x_{j-1})], & x_{j-1} \le x \le x_j \\[3mm] \dfrac{(x-x_{j+1})^2}{(x_{j+1}-x_j)^3}[2(x-x_j) + (x_{j+1}-x_j)], & x_j \le x \le x_{j+1} \\[3mm] 0, & x < x_{j-1}, \quad x > x_{j+1} \end{cases} \tag{3.1.14a}$$

$$\phi_{1j}(x) = \begin{cases} \dfrac{(x - x_{j-1})^2(x - x_j)}{(x_j - x_{j-1})^2}, & x_{j-1} \le x \le x_j \\[3mm] \dfrac{(x - x_{j+1})^2(x - x_j)}{(x_{j+1} - x_j)^2}, & x_j \le x \le x_{j+1} \\[3mm] 0, & x < x_{j-1}, \quad x > x_{j+1} \end{cases} \tag{3.1.14b}$$

These functions exhibit the properties that at any node x_i,

$$\phi_{0j}(x_i) = \begin{cases} 1, & i = j \\ 0, & i \ne j \end{cases} \tag{3.1.15a}$$

$$\phi_{1j}(x_i) = 0 \qquad \forall i \tag{3.1.15b}$$

$$\frac{d\phi_{0j}}{dx}(x_i) = 0 \qquad \forall i \tag{3.1.15c}$$

$$\frac{d\phi_{1j}}{dx}(x_i) = \begin{cases} 1, & i = j \\ 0, & i \ne j \end{cases} \tag{3.1.15d}$$

These properties are required for the coefficients of equation (3.1.13) to have the proper meaning. Figure 3.3 illustrates typical functions $\phi_{0j}(x)$ and $\phi_{1j}(x)$. Higher-degree piecewise Hermite polynomials, still of $\mathbb{C}^1[\Omega]$, are explored in Problem 3.3. Notice that $\mathbb{C}^1[\Omega]$ Hermite expansions involve two nodal coefficients $[U_j, dU_j/dx]$, as opposed to only one for the Lagrange case (U_j).

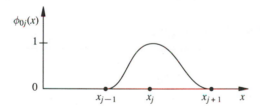

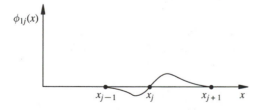

Figure 3.3 Typical piecewise cubic Hermite polynomial basis functions.

When piecewise polynomials are used, different polynomials (of continuity $\mathbb{C}^\infty$) are "pieced together," with their points of intersection possessing lower continuity. Each subregion of infinite differentiality, which occurs between points of least continuity, is called an *element* or *finite element*. The points of least continuity usually correspond to node points. For piecewise linear Lagrange polynomial bases, the space between consecutive nodes defines each element, and N nodes produce $N - 1$ elements. For piecewise quadratic Lagrange polynomials, three nodes are associated with each element, and N nodes define $(N - 1)/2$ elements, where N is restricted to an odd integer. For general piecewise mth-order Lagrange polynomials, each element is composed of $m + 1$ nodes, and the total number of nodes, N, must satisfy $N = Km + 1$, K being a positive integer that is equal to the number of elements. Piecewise cubic Hermite spaces have $N - 1$ elements per N nodes, which is the same number of elements, per N nodes, as piecewise linear Lagrange polynomials. However, Hermite and Lagrange interpolators differ fundamentally in the number of coefficients associated with each node as well as in their global continuity.

Other polynomial forms, as well as nonpolynomial functions, can be used as basis functions. Problem 3.4 touches on one such possibility. What follows is essentially restricted to the polynomial spaces discussed above. This is because these spaces are by far the most commonly employed in practice. In addition, understanding of the fundamental ideas of the method of weighted residuals and finite element methods should readily allow for development and implementation of methodologies that use alternative trial spaces.

3.1.2 Choice of Weight Functions in One Dimension

Specific choice of weight functions in equation (3.1.5) defines the different members of the method of weighted residuals family of approximations. The three most important members are defined and discussed herein, with several others mentioned but referenced to other literature.

Subdomain method. Recall that the idea of MWR is to minimize the residual $R(x)$ by forcing it to zero in a weighted average sense over the domain Ω. The subdomain method attempts to minimize $R(x)$ over Ω by forcing the arithmetic average of $R(x)$, taken over discrete intervals (or *subdomains*) of Ω, to be zero. As such, the weight functions are chosen as

$$w_i(x) = \begin{cases} 1, & x \in \Omega_i \\ 0, & x \notin \Omega_i \end{cases} \tag{3.1.16}$$

where $\{\Omega_i\}_{i=1}^E$ are nonintersecting subregions within Ω whose union covers all of Ω.

For piecewise Lagrange polynomial trial functions defined on nodes $\{x_i\}_{i=1}^N$, the usual choice of Ω_i is

$$\left(x_i - \frac{x_i - x_{i-1}}{2} \right) < x < \left(x_i + \frac{x_{i+1} - x_i}{2} \right)$$

As such, equation (3.1.16) becomes

$$w_i(x) = \begin{cases} 1, & x_i - \dfrac{\nabla x_i}{2} < x < x_i + \dfrac{\Delta x_i}{2} \\ 0, & \text{all other } x \end{cases} \tag{3.1.17}$$

where $\Delta x_i \equiv x_{i+1} - x_i$ and $\nabla x_i \equiv x_i - x_{i-1}$. When x_i is a boundary node, the subdomain Ω_i is taken as only that region which resides within Ω.

The following example calculations illustrate the method. Within the presentation of these examples, important concepts of continuity and differentiation of functions of limited continuity are introduced.

Example 3.1

Problem   Solve the equation

$$\frac{du}{dx} + u = 1, \qquad 0 < x < 1 \tag{3.1.18}$$

$$u(0) = 2$$

using the subdomain method.

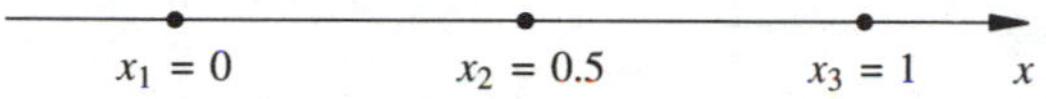

Figure 3.4   Discretization used for Example 3.1.

$x_1 = 0 \qquad x_2 = 0.5 \qquad x_3 = 1 \qquad x$

Solution   Let piecewise linear Lagrange polynomials be defined on the grid of Figure 3.4. From the boundary conditions, it is known that at node 1, $u = 2$. Imposition of the condition $U(0) = 2$ leads directly to $U_1 = 2$. When first-type boundary information is given, the subdomain equation associated with that boundary node is not written, because the boundary condition is used instead. Approximating equations are written for the subdomains that are associated with all other nodes, in this case for nodes 2 and 3. These equations derive from equations (3.1.17), (3.1.10), and (3.1.5) as

$$\int_\Omega R(x)w_2(x)\, dx = \int_0^1 \left(\frac{dU}{dx} + U - f\right) w_2(x)\, dx$$

$$= \int_{0.25}^{0.75} \left(\frac{dU}{dx} + U - f\right) dx$$

$$= \int_{0.25}^{0.75} \left[\frac{d}{dx}\left(\sum_{j=1}^3 U_j \phi_j\right) + \left(\sum_{j=1}^3 U_j \phi_j\right) - f\right] dx$$

$$= \sum_{j=1}^3 U_j \int_{0.25}^{0.75} \left(\frac{d\phi_j}{dx} + \phi_j\right) dx - \int_{0.25}^{0.75} (1)\, dx$$

$$= U_1 \left(-\frac{7}{16}\right) + U_2 \left(\frac{3}{8}\right) + U_3 \left(\frac{9}{16}\right) - \frac{1}{2} = 0 \tag{3.1.19a}$$

$$\int_\Omega R(x)w_3(x)\, dx = \sum_{j=1}^3 U_j \int_{0.75}^{1.0} \left(\frac{d\phi_j}{dx} + \phi_j\right) dx - \int_{0.75}^{1.0} (1)\, dx$$

$$= U_1(0) + U_2 \left(-\frac{7}{16}\right) + U_3 \left(\frac{11}{16}\right) - \frac{1}{4} = 0 \tag{3.1.19b}$$

Thus the following set of algebraic equations results for the unknown nodal coefficients U_1, U_2, U_3:

$$\begin{bmatrix} 1 & 0 & 0 \\ -\dfrac{7}{16} & \dfrac{3}{8} & \dfrac{9}{16} \\ 0 & -\dfrac{7}{16} & \dfrac{11}{16} \end{bmatrix} \begin{bmatrix} U_1 \\ U_2 \\ U_3 \end{bmatrix} = \begin{bmatrix} 2 \\ \dfrac{1}{2} \\ \dfrac{1}{4} \end{bmatrix} \qquad (3.1.20)$$

Solution of equation (3.1.20) is $(U_1, U_2, U_3) = (2.0, 1.597, 1.380)$. The analytic solution for this example is $u(x) = 1 + e^{-x}$, which has nodal values given by $(2, 1.607, 1.368)$.

Evaluation of the integrals of equation (3.1.19) requires careful accounting of the different functional forms of the basis functions in different elements. Problem 3.5 provides details for this example, and Section 3.3 provides a more general discussion of computational procedures.

Example 3.2

Problem   Obtain a solution to

$$\frac{d^2u}{dx^2} + u = 0, \qquad 0 < x < 1$$

$$u(0) = 1 \qquad\qquad (3.1.21)$$

$$u(1) = 0$$

using the subdomain method.

Solution   Let the trial space coincide with that of the previous example, namely a piecewise linear polynomial space defined on the discretization of Figure 3.4. Application of the subdomain method is then analogous to Example 3.1 except that evaluation of the integrals is somewhat different.

As stated above, when first-type boundary conditions are present, they are written as direct constraints on the trial function. Thus two equations are written for this case, $U_1 = 1$ and $U_3 = 0$. Subdomain equations are written for all remaining nodes, in this case only node 2. The subdomain equation corresponding to node 2 is

$$\int_0^1 R(x)w_2(x)\,dx = 0$$

or

$$\sum_{j=1}^{3} U_j \int_{0.25}^{0.75} \left(\frac{d^2\phi_j}{dx^2} + \phi_j \right) dx = 0 \qquad (3.1.22)$$

Equation (3.1.22) involves second derivatives of each of the three basis functions. Figure 3.5 shows graphs of $\phi_2(x)$, $d\phi_2/dx$, and $d^2\phi_2/dx^2$. Notice that the first derivative has

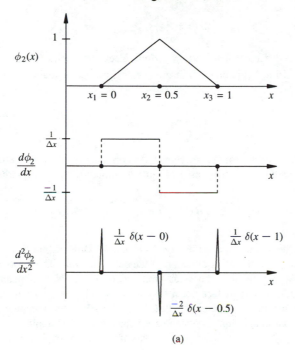

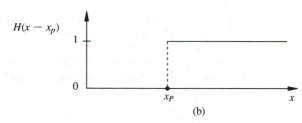

Figure 3.5 (a) Basis function $\phi_2(x)$ and associated derivatives; (b) Heaviside step function $H(x - x_p)$.

finite jump discontinuities that occur at node points. These discontinuities can be described mathematically using the *Heaviside step function*, $H(x - x_j)$, which is defined by

$$H(x - x_j) \equiv \begin{cases} 1, & x > x_j \\ 0, & x < x_j \end{cases} \tag{3.1.23}$$

The derivative $d\phi_2/dx$ can thus be written as

$$\frac{d\phi_2}{dx} = \frac{1}{\Delta x} H(x - 0) + \left(-\frac{2}{\Delta x}\right) H(x - 0.5) + \frac{1}{\Delta x} H(x - 1.0) \tag{3.1.24}$$

The coefficient of each Heaviside step function is equal to the magnitude of the jump at each point of discontinuity.

Because the second derivative appears in equation (3.1.22), an additional differentiation must be performed. This means that the Heaviside step function must be differentiated, necessitating the following additional definition:

$$\delta(x - x_j) \equiv \frac{d}{dx} H(x - x_j) \tag{3.1.25}$$

where $\delta(x - x_j)$ is called the *Dirac delta function*. The Dirac delta function is zero at all $x \neq x_j$ and is undefined (unbounded) at $x = x_j$. However, it maintains the integral property that

$$\int_{\omega_1}^{\omega_2} \delta(x - x_j) \, dx = 1 \qquad \omega_1 < x_j < \omega_2 \tag{3.1.26}$$

since the Heaviside step function must be recovered upon integration of the delta function. Furthermore, for any well-defined function $F(x)$ that is smooth in the neighborhood of x_j,

$$\int_{\omega_1}^{\omega_2} F(x)\delta(x - x_j) \, dx = F(x_j), \qquad \omega_1 < x_j < \omega_2 \tag{3.1.27}$$

That is, an integral of the product of any function $F(x)$ and the Dirac delta function is simply equal to the value of $F(x)$ at the point of action of the delta function. This property follows from equation (3.1.26) and the smoothness assumption for $F(x)$. Notice, parenthetically, that the Dirac delta function is in fact not a "function" at all, since its definition is not consistent with the elementary definition of a function. As such, it has meaning only when used in the context of an integration, in which case equation (3.1.27) applies.

Given definition (3.1.25), the second derivative of ϕ_2 can be expressed as

$$\frac{d^2\phi_2}{dx^2} = \frac{1}{\Delta x}\delta(x - 0) + \left(-\frac{2}{\Delta x}\right)\delta(x - 0.5) + \left(\frac{1}{\Delta x}\right)\delta(x - 1.0) \tag{3.1.28}$$

Similar equations can be written for the second derivatives of the other basis functions, as required by equation (3.1.22). Substitution of expressions for $d^2\phi_j/dx^2$ into equation (3.1.22), and subsequent recognition of equation (3.1.27), allows equation (3.1.22) to be expressed as

$$U_1 \int_{0.25}^{0.75} \left[\frac{1}{\Delta x}\delta(x - 0.5) + \phi_1(x)\right] dx + U_2 \int_{0.25}^{0.75} \left[\left(-\frac{2}{\Delta x}\right)\delta(x - 0.5) + \phi_2(x)\right] dx$$

$$+ U_3 \int_{0.25}^{0.75} \left[\frac{1}{\Delta x}\delta(x - 0.5) + \phi_3(x)\right] dx = 0 \tag{3.1.29a}$$

or, because $\Delta x = 0.5$,

$$U_1 \left[2 + \frac{1}{16}\right] + U_2 \left[(-4) + \frac{3}{8}\right] + U_3 \left[2 + \frac{1}{16}\right] = 0 \tag{3.1.29b}$$

Combination of equation (3.1.29b) with the first-type boundary equations $U_1 = 1$, $U_3 = 0$ leads to

$$\begin{bmatrix} 1 & 0 & 0 \\ \dfrac{33}{16} & -\dfrac{29}{8} & \dfrac{33}{16} \\ 0 & 0 & 1 \end{bmatrix} \begin{bmatrix} U_1 \\ U_2 \\ U_3 \end{bmatrix} = \begin{bmatrix} 1 \\ 0 \\ 0 \end{bmatrix} \tag{3.1.30}$$

In practice, equation (3.1.30) would be symmetrized by reduction of the first and last equations, as discussed for the finite difference approximations in Section 2.5. The solution of equation (3.1.30) is $(U_1, U_2, U_3) = (1, 33/58, 0) = (1.0, 0.569, 0.0)$. The analytic solution for this example is $u(x) = \cos(x) - \cot(1) \sin(x)$, which has nodal values $(1.0, 0.570, 0.0)$.

Collocation method.   The collocation method attempts to minimize the residual $R(x)$ by forcing it to pass through zero at a finite number of discrete points within the domain Ω. Given the property of the Dirac delta function in equation (3.1.27), point evaluations of $R(x)$ can be achieved in the context of the method of weighted residuals by choosing $w_i(x)$ to be a Dirac delta function. Thus, for the collocation method,

$$w_i(x) \equiv \delta(x - x_i^c), \qquad x_i^c \in \Omega \tag{3.1.31}$$

where x_i^c is referred to as a *collocation point*. Choice of collocation points is an important consideration in the collocation method. This is discussed in Example 3.4 below.

Given the definition of $w_i(x)$ in equation (3.1.31) and that of the Dirac delta function in equation (3.1.27), the MWR equation (3.1.5) can be written as

$$\int_\Omega R(x) w_i(x)\, dx = \int_\Omega R(x) \delta(x - x_i^c)\, dx = R(x_i^c) = 0 \tag{3.1.32}$$

According to equation (3.1.32), at each collocation point the trial function is **required** to satisfy the differential operator equation exactly. The number of collocation points chosen is directly related to the number of undetermined coefficients in the trial function. Each collocation point gives rise to an algebraic equation in terms of the undetermined coefficients. The following examples illustrate the method.

Example 3.3

Problem   Solve the equation

$$\frac{du}{dx} + u = 1, \qquad 0 < x < 1 \tag{3.1.18}$$

$$u(0) = 2$$

using the collocation method.

Solution   Let the discretization of Figure 3.4 be chosen, with piecewise linear Lagrange polynomials chosen as a basis for the trial space. Thus the trial function is expressed as

$$U(x) = \sum_{j=1}^{3} U_j \phi_j(x) \tag{3.1.33}$$

First-type boundary information implies that $U_1 = 2$. This means that U_2 and U_3 remain to be determined. As such, two collocation equations are required. It turns out (see the discussion in Example 3.4) that for this problem optimal accuracy results from choosing collocation points located at the midpoint of each element; that is, $x_1^c = (x_1 + x_2)/2 = 0.25$, $x_2^c = (x_2 + x_3)/2 = 0.75$. The corresponding collocation equations are

$$\left. \left(\frac{dU}{dx} + U \right) \right|_{x=0.25} = 1 \tag{3.1.34a}$$

$$\left(\frac{dU}{dx} + U\right)\Bigg|_{x=0.75} = 1 \tag{3.1.34b}$$

Substitution of equation (3.1.33) into equations (3.1.34), and recognition of definition (3.1.10), leads to

$$\left(\frac{dU}{dx} + U\right)\Bigg|_{x=0.25} = \left[\sum_{j=1}^{3} U_j \frac{d\phi_j}{dx}\Bigg|_{x=0.25}\right] + \left[\sum_{j=1}^{3} U_j \phi_j\Big|_{x=0.25}\right]$$

$$= \left[U_1\left(-\frac{1}{\Delta x}\right) + U_2\frac{1}{\Delta x} + U_3(0)\right] + \left[U_1\left(\frac{1}{2}\right) + U_2\left(\frac{1}{2}\right) + U_3(0)\right]$$

$$\left(\frac{dU}{dx} + U\right)\Bigg|_{x=0.75} = \left[\sum_{j=1}^{3} U_j \frac{d\phi_j}{dx}\Bigg|_{x=0.75}\right] + \left[\sum_{j=1}^{3} U_j \phi_j\big|_{0.75}\right]$$

$$= \left[U_1(0) + U_2\left(-\frac{1}{\Delta x}\right) + U_3\frac{1}{\Delta x}\right] + \left[U_1(0) + U_2\left(\frac{1}{2}\right) + U_3\left(\frac{1}{2}\right)\right]$$

Thus the collocation equations are (given $\Delta x = 0.5$)

$$\left(-\frac{3}{2}\right)U_1 + \left(\frac{5}{2}\right)U_2 \qquad\quad = 1$$

$$\left(-\frac{3}{2}\right)U_2 + \left(\frac{5}{2}\right)U_3 = 1$$

Coupled with the boundary condition $U_1 = 2$, the resulting set of linear algebraic equations is

$$\begin{bmatrix} 1 & 0 & 0 \\ -\dfrac{3}{2} & \dfrac{5}{2} & 0 \\ 0 & -\dfrac{3}{2} & \dfrac{5}{2} \end{bmatrix} \begin{bmatrix} U_1 \\ U_2 \\ U_3 \end{bmatrix} = \begin{bmatrix} 2 \\ 1 \\ 1 \end{bmatrix} \tag{3.1.35}$$

Solution of this matrix equation produces the collocation approximation of $(U_1, U_2, U_3) = (2, 8/5, 68/50) = (2, 1.60, 1.36)$. The analytic solution for this example is $u(x) = \cos(x) - \cot(1)\sin(x)$, which has nodal values $(2, 1.61, 1.37)$.

Example 3.4

Problem Solve the equation

$$\frac{d^2u}{dx^2} + u = 0, \qquad 0 < x < 1 \tag{3.1.21}$$

$$u(0) = 1$$

$$u(1) = 0$$

using the collocation method.

Solution   As discussed later in Section 3.5, a necessary property of any MWR approximation is that the integrals involved be well defined. This particular requirement leads to continuity constraints on the trial space. For the previous three examples, $\mathbb{C}^0[\omega_1, \omega_2]$ spaces have sufficed. For this fourth example, $\mathbb{C}^0[\omega_1, \omega_2]$ is not sufficient. This is because when a Dirac delta function is present in an integrand, a requirement is that any function in the integrand that multiplies the delta function must be bounded at every point within the range of the integral. Therefore, since the residual $R(x)$ multiplies the Dirac delta function in the collocation MWR equations [equation (3.1.32)], $R(x)$ must be bounded at all points within $[0, 1]$. Because $R(x)$ involves a second derivative of the trial function, the trial space must be at least $\mathbb{C}^1[\Omega]$ for $R(x)$ to remain bounded.

A natural choice for $U(x)$ for collocation approximations to second-order differential equations is a piecewise cubic Hermite polynomial expansion,

$$U(x) = \sum_{j=1}^{N} U_j \phi_{0j}(x) + \frac{dU_j}{dx} \phi_{1j}(x) \tag{3.1.36}$$

Let $N = 2$, so that nodes are located only at $x = 0$ and $x = 1$. For second-order differential equations, with a piecewise cubic Hermite trial space, two collocation points should be chosen per element. Coupled with two boundary conditions, this always leads to the proper number of algebraic equations for the $2N$ unknown nodal coefficients. Furthermore, a special choice of collocation points within each element leads to enhanced accuracy of the solution. In particular, enhanced accuracy [in this case, $\mathcal{O}((\Delta x)^4)$] occurs when collocation points are chosen as the roots of the shifted quadratic Legendre polynomial, defined over each element (these are the Gauss-Legendre integration points used in numerical integration; see Section 4.1).[1] For this example there is one element, and the two collocation points are $x_1^c = 0.5 - (\sqrt{3}/6) = 0.211$; $x_2^c = 0.5 + (\sqrt{3}/6) = 0.789$.

Application of equation (3.1.32), in light of equations (3.1.36) and (3.1.21), produces the following approximating equations:

$$R(x_1^c) = 0 = \sum_{j=1}^{2} U_j \left. \frac{d^2\phi_{0j}}{dx^2} \right|_{x=x_1^c} + \left. \frac{dU_j}{dx} \frac{d^2\phi_{1j}}{dx^2} \right|_{x=x_1^c}$$

$$+ \sum_{j=1}^{2} U_j \left. \phi_{0j} \right|_{x=x_1^c} + \left. \frac{dU_j}{dx} \phi_{1j} \right|_{x=x_1^c} = 0 \tag{3.1.37a}$$

$$R(x_2^c) = 0 = \sum_{j=1}^{2} U_j \left. \frac{d^2\phi_{0j}}{dx^2} \right|_{x=x_2^c} + \left. \frac{dU_j}{dx} \frac{d^2\phi_{1j}}{dx^2} \right|_{x=x_2^c}$$

$$+ \sum_{j=1}^{2} U_j \left. \phi_{0j} \right|_{x=x_2^c} + \left. \frac{dU_j}{dx} \phi_{1j} \right|_{x=x_2^c} = 0 \tag{3.1.37b}$$

---

[1]It can generally be stated that the natural choice of trial space for an mth-order equation is a piecewise polynomial of degree $(2m-1)$, possessing $C^{m-1}[\Omega]$ continuity. Optimal accuracy occurs when m collocation points are chosen within each element, located at the roots of the mth-degree Legendre polynomial defined over each element.

Given the definitions (3.1.14), the functions ϕ_{0j}, ϕ_{1j} can be differentiated and evaluated at the collocation points. This leads to

$$
R(x_1^c) = \sum_{j=1}^{2} U_j \left(\frac{d^2\phi_{0j}}{dx^2} + \phi_{0j} \right) \Bigg|_{x=x_1^c}
$$

$$
+ \frac{dU_j}{dx} \left(\frac{d^2\phi_{1j}}{dx^2} + \phi_{1j} \right) \Bigg|_{x=x_1^c}
$$

$$
= U_1[-2.58] + \frac{dU_1}{dx}[-2.60] + U_2[3.58] + \frac{dU_2}{dx}[-0.767]
$$

$$
= 0
$$

Similarly, the second collocation equation is

$$
R(x_2^c) = U_1[3.58] + \frac{dU_1}{dx}[0.767] + U_2[-2.58] + \frac{dU_2}{dx}[2.60]
$$

$$
= 0
$$

Coupled with the boundary equations $U_1 = 1$, $U_2 = 0$, there results

$$
\begin{bmatrix}
1 & 0 & 0 & 0 \\
-2.58 & -2.60 & 3.58 & -0.767 \\
3.58 & 0.767 & -2.58 & 2.60 \\
0 & 0 & 1 & 0
\end{bmatrix}
\begin{bmatrix}
U_1 \\
\dfrac{dU_1}{dx} \\
U_2 \\
\dfrac{dU_2}{dx}
\end{bmatrix}
=
\begin{bmatrix}
1 \\
0 \\
0 \\
0
\end{bmatrix}
\tag{3.1.38}
$$

Solution of this linear algebraic system is $(U_1, dU_1/dx, U_2, dU_2/dx) = (1, -0.642, 0.0, -1.19)$. The analytic solution to equation (3.1.21) is $u(x) = \cos(x) - \cot(1)\sin(x)$, and $du(x)/dx = -\cot(1)\cos(x)$, which have nodal values given by $(1, -0.642, 0.0, -1.19)$.

Galerkin method.   While the previous two methods had some intuitive foundation on which the choice of weight functions was based, the Galerkin method lacks a simple intuitive foundation. However, as will be shown later in this chapter, the Galerkin method actually has a very solid mathematical and, ultimately, physical foundation for its definition.

The Galerkin method chooses weight functions $w_i(x)$ to be equal to the basis functions of the trial space, $\phi_i(x)$. Therefore, the Galerkin method of weighted residuals statement is

$$
\int_\Omega R(x)\phi_i(x)\,dx = 0
\tag{3.1.39}
$$

The method is again illustrated through several example calculations.

Example 3.5

   Problem   Solve the equation

$$\frac{du}{dx} + u = 1, \qquad 0 < x < 1 \tag{3.1.18}$$

$$u(0) = 2$$

using the Galerkin method.

Solution   Let the trial space be that of piecewise linear Lagrange polynomials defined on the discretization of Figure 3.4. As before, first-type boundary information is imposed directly on $U(x)$, so that $U_1 = 2$. Galerkin approximating equations are written for all other nodes i, in this case $i = 2, 3$. For $i = 2$, $w_i(x) = \phi_i(x) = \phi_2(x)$, and the MWR equation is

$$\int_0^1 \left(\frac{dU}{dx} + U - 1\right) \phi_2(x)\, dx = 0$$

or

$$\sum_{j=1}^3 U_j \int_0^1 \left(\frac{d\phi_j}{dx} + \phi_j\right) \phi_2\, dx = \int_0^1 (1)\phi_2(x)\, dx \tag{3.1.40a}$$

Use of definition (3.1.10) for $\phi_j(x)$ allows the integrals to be evaluated (detailed computational procedures for integral evaluations are discussed in Section 3.3), so that equation (3.1.40) is equivalent to

$$U_1 \left[-\frac{1}{2} + \frac{\Delta x}{6}\right] + U_2 \left[0 + \frac{2\Delta x}{3}\right] + U_3 \left[\frac{1}{2} + \frac{\Delta x}{6}\right] = \frac{1}{2}$$

or because $\Delta x = 0.5$,

$$U_1 \left(-\frac{5}{12}\right) + U_2 \left(\frac{1}{3}\right) + U_3 \left(\frac{7}{12}\right) = \frac{1}{2} \tag{3.1.40b}$$

Similarly, the equation for $w_i(x) = \phi_3(x)$ is

$$U_1(0) + U_2 \left(-\frac{5}{12}\right) + U_3 \left(\frac{2}{3}\right) = \frac{1}{4} \tag{3.1.40c}$$

The resulting set of algebraic equations is

$$\begin{bmatrix} 1 & 0 & 0 \\ -\dfrac{5}{12} & \dfrac{1}{3} & \dfrac{7}{12} \\ 0 & -\dfrac{5}{12} & \dfrac{2}{3} \end{bmatrix} \begin{bmatrix} U_1 \\ U_2 \\ U_3 \end{bmatrix} = \begin{bmatrix} 2 \\ \dfrac{1}{2} \\ \dfrac{1}{4} \end{bmatrix} \tag{3.1.41}$$

whose solution is $(U_1, U_2, U_3) = (2, 1.60, 1.37)$. Again, the analytic solution is $u(x) = 1 + e^{-x}$, which has nodal values $(2, 1.61, 1.37)$.

Example 3.6

Problem   Solve the equation

$$\frac{d^2u}{dx^2} + u = 0, \qquad 0 < x < 1 \tag{3.1.21}$$

$$u(0) = 1$$

$$u(1) = 0$$

using the Galerkin method of weighted residuals.

Solution   Let the trial space again be chosen as a piecewise linear polynomial space defined on the discretization of Figure 3.4. For the Galerkin method, as with the other MWR methods, first-type boundary condition equations are imposed directly on the trial function $U(x)$. Therefore, given

$$U(x) = \sum_{j=1}^{3} U_j \phi_j(x) \tag{3.1.42}$$

two of the algebraic approximating equations come directly from the boundary conditions,

$$U_1 = 1$$

$$U_3 = 0$$

Galerkin approximating equations are written for all remaining nodes, in this case only node 2. This equation takes the form

$$\int_0^1 \left(\frac{d^2U}{dx^2} + U \right) \phi_2(x) dx = 0 \tag{3.1.43a}$$

or

$$\sum_{j=1}^{3} U_j \left(\frac{d^2\phi_j}{dx^2} + \phi_j \right) \phi_2 dx = 0 \tag{3.1.43b}$$

As discussed previously, the second derivatives of $\phi_j(x)$, and thus of $U(x)$, contain Dirac delta functions. Because they appear in the context of integration, and because the multiplying function $\phi_2(x)$ is sufficiently smooth, the integrals can be evaluated using definition (3.1.27). However, it is generally more convenient computationally to eliminate the delta functions through integration by parts. The appropriate formula is (see the references in Appendix C for a thorough discussion of integration by parts)

$$\int_0^1 \frac{d^2U}{dx^2} \phi_i(x) \, dx = \left(\frac{dU}{dx} \phi_i \right)\Big|_0^1 - \int_0^1 \frac{dU}{dx} \frac{d\phi_i}{dx} \, dx \tag{3.1.44}$$

The integration by parts formula (3.1.44) replaces an integral involving Dirac delta functions with one that contains only finite jump discontinuities (Heaviside step functions). The latter integrations are calculated more easily. In general, for any $U \in C^{m_1}[\Omega]$ and $\phi_i \in C^{m_2}[\Omega]$, equation (3.1.44) applies whenever $m_1 + m_2 \geq -1$. Also, notice that equation (3.1.44) is written for integration over the entire domain $\Omega = [0, 1]$. Whenever the integrand contains Dirac delta functions, such as the one on the left side of equation (3.1.44), the integration-by-parts formula should only be applied to integration over the entire domain. The integral should not be broken into a sum of elemental integrals prior to application of integration by parts, because information may be lost. Such loss of information occurs when Dirac delta functions are present at node points. Thus the integration-by-parts formula (3.1.44) should be used only when the integration applies over all of Ω. In addition, it should be remembered that integration by parts is not a requirement but is chosen based on computational convenience.

Application of equation (3.1.44) to equation (3.1.43a) leads to

$$\int_0^1 \left(\frac{d^2U}{dx^2} + U \right) \phi_2 \, dx = \int_0^1 \left(-\frac{dU}{dx}\frac{d\phi_2}{dx} + U\phi_2 \right) dx + \left(\frac{dU}{dx}\phi_2 \right)\Big|_0^1 = 0$$

$$(3.1.45)$$

The boundary term $[(dU/dx)\phi_2]\big|_0^1$ is zero because ϕ_2 is zero at every node except node 2 ($x_1 = 0$ and $x_3 = 1$ are node points). Definition (3.1.10) can be used with the trial function definition (3.1.42) to evaluate equation (3.1.45),

$$\int_0^1 \left(-\frac{dU}{dx}\frac{d\phi_2}{dx} + U\phi_2 \right) dx = \sum_{j=1}^3 U_j \int_0^1 \left(-\frac{d\phi_j}{dx}\frac{d\phi_2}{dx} + \phi_j\phi_2 \right) dx$$

$$= U_1 \left[\frac{1}{\Delta x} + \frac{\Delta x}{6} \right] + U_2 \left[-\frac{2}{\Delta x} + \frac{2\Delta x}{3} \right] + U_3 \left[\frac{1}{\Delta x} + \frac{\Delta x}{6} \right]$$

$$= 0 \tag{3.1.46}$$

Given $\Delta x = 0.5$ and the boundary information $U_1 = 1$, $U_3 = 0$, the relevant matrix equation is

$$\begin{bmatrix} 1 & 0 & 0 \\ \dfrac{25}{12} & -\dfrac{11}{3} & \dfrac{25}{12} \\ 0 & 0 & 1 \end{bmatrix} \begin{bmatrix} U_1 \\ U_2 \\ U_3 \end{bmatrix} = \begin{bmatrix} 1 \\ 0 \\ 0 \end{bmatrix} \tag{3.1.47}$$

This matrix should again be symmetrized by elimination of the first and last rows, and zeroing the first and third entries in row two by bringing the known information in the second row to the right side. Solution of this equation is $(U_1, U_2, U_3) = (1, 25/44, 0) = (1, 0.568, 0)$. Again, the analytic solution is given by $u(x) = \cos(x) - \cot(1)\sin(x)$, which has nodal values $(1, 0.570, 0)$.

3.2 NOMENCLATURE

Whenever piecewise trial functions are used in the method of weighted residuals, the domain Ω is inherently broken into subregions or elements. A finite number of such elements exists. These elements are nonintersecting and their union covers all of Ω. As such, each MWR scheme that is formulated using piecewise trial spaces can be called a "finite element method." However, the terminology *finite element method* has traditionally been restricted to the Galerkin method of weighted residuals using piecewise polynomial trial spaces. In deference to tradition, "finite element method" will be used herein to denote the Galerkin method on piecewise trial spaces.

The various functions that appear in MWR are summarized as follows. The functional approximation to the true solution is called the *trial function*. The trial function approximation to the true solution, $u(\mathbf{x}, t)$, is denoted by $U(\mathbf{x}, t)$. The finite-dimensional function space from which the trial function is chosen is called the *trial space*. The trial function is written as a linear combination of *basis functions*. The latter functions form a basis for the trial space. Finally, the functions that multiply the residual in the weighted residual formulation are called *weight functions* or *test functions*. In general, the test and trial spaces are different. Only for Galerkin's method are they identical. MWR methods in which the trial and test spaces are different are often referred to by the general title *Petrov-Galerkin methods*.

3.3 COMPUTATIONAL PROCEDURES IN ONE DIMENSION

3.3.1 Elementwise Integrations

Finite element methods usually involve piecewise polynomial trial spaces. This choice of trial space has significant implications regarding evaluation of integrals. In particular, because piecewise basis functions have different functional definitions in different elements, the evaluation of an integral over the domain Ω must be performed element by element.

As an example, consider the integral in one-dimensional space $\int_{\Omega} \phi_j(x)\phi_i(x)\,dx$, with ϕ_j and ϕ_i piecewise linear Lagrange polynomials. Because $\phi_j(x)$ and $\phi_i(x)$ have different definitions in different elements [see equation (3.1.10)], the integral must be evaluated element by element,

$$\int_{\Omega} \phi_j(x)\phi_i(x)\,dx = \sum_{e=1}^{E} \int_{\Omega^e} \phi_j(x)\phi_i(x)\,dx \qquad (3.3.1)$$

where Ω^e refers to that region of Ω occupied by element e, and E is the total number of elements.[2] As a specific example, let $j = i - 1$. Then the integral evaluation is performed as follows:

$$\int_{\Omega} \phi_{i-1}(x)\phi_i(x)\,dx = \sum_{e=1}^{E} \int_{\Omega^e} \phi_{i-1}(x)\phi_i(x)\,dx$$

$$= \sum_{e=1}^{E} \int_{x_e}^{x_{e+1}} \phi_{i-1}(x)\phi_i(x)\,dx$$

[2]Note that the conversion of an integral over a total domain to a sum of integrals over subdomains, or elements, is valid only when the integrand is bounded at the interelement boundaries.

$$= \int_{x_1}^{x_2} (0)(0)\; dx + \cdots + \int_{x_{i-3}}^{x_{i-2}} (0)(0)\; dx$$

$$+ \int_{x_{i-2}}^{x_{i-1}} \left(\frac{x - x_{i-2}}{x_{i-1} - x_{i-2}} \right) (0)\; dx$$

$$+ \int_{x_{i-1}}^{x_i} \left(\frac{x_i - x}{x_i - x_{i-1}} \right) \left(\frac{x - x_{i-1}}{x_i - x_{i-1}} \right) dx$$

$$+ \int_{x_i}^{x_{i+1}} (0) \left(\frac{x_{i+1} - x}{x_{i+1} - x_i} \right) dx + \int_{x_{i+1}}^{x_{i+2}} (0)(0)\; dx$$

$$+ \cdots + \int_{x_{N-1}}^{x_N} (0)(0)\; dx$$

$$= \int_{x_{i-1}}^{x_i} \left(\frac{x_i - x}{x_i - x_{i-1}} \right) \left(\frac{x - x_{i-1}}{x_i - x_{i-1}} \right) dx$$

$$= \frac{x_i - x_{i-1}}{6} \tag{3.3.2}$$

Notice that most element integrations in the summation are zero. The only nonzero entries occur for elements in which both ϕ_{i-1} and ϕ_i are nonzero. In this case, this occurs only in element $\Omega^{i-1} = [x_{i-1}, x_i]$. For the more general integral (3.3.1), with ϕ_j and ϕ_i piecewise linear Lagrange polynomials, overlapping nonzero segments of ϕ_j, ϕ_i occur only when $|i - j| \leq 1$. This is equivalent to saying that nodes i and j must be part of a common element. In fact, a fundamental property of a piecewise Lagrange polynomial of any degree, associated with a given node, is that the function is nonzero only within elements that include the given node. As such, integral (3.3.1) will only be nonzero when nodes i and j reside in a common element. Otherwise the integral is zero.

This observation can be used to significant advantage in finite element formulations on piecewise Lagrange polynomial trial spaces. The idea is to recognize the element integrals that are nonzero and to perform the requisite integrations on those elements only. All others are ignored, since they are zero.

Recall that one finite element equation is generated for each basis function ϕ_i, unless node i is a first-type boundary node. Within each equation, a summation is performed over all nodes [sum over j in, for example, equation (3.1.40a)]. This gives rise to integrals whose integrands are products of basis functions, or their derivatives. The product $\phi_j \phi_i$ used above is one such example. As Examples 3.5 and 3.6 demonstrate, these integrals define appropriate matrix entries in row i, column j of the resulting matrix equation. Knowledge that the only combinations of i, j that lead to nonzero integrals are those for which both i and j reside in the same element leads to the following elementwise computational algorithm, written for a discretization of N nodes and $E = N - 1$ elements.

1. Begin with an $N \times N$ coefficient matrix[3] that has all zero entries. This matrix will be filled in with appropriate values during the computational procedure. The matrix multiplies the unknown vector of nodal values $(U_1, U_2, \ldots, U_N)^T$ and is referred to as the *global coefficient matrix*.

2. For each element, provide a list of nodes that make up that element. (For piecewise linear interpolation in one dimension, element e is made up of nodes e and $e + 1$.)

3. Derive the appropriate form of the integrals using MWR, with integration by parts applied to eliminate Dirac delta functions at inter-element boundaries.

4. Compute all element integrals that are nonzero in element 1. For the piecewise linear case, these will only involve basis functions ϕ_1 and ϕ_2, so that combinations $i = 1, j = 1; i = 1, j = 2; i = 2, j = 1; i = 2, j = 2$ should be calculated. All others are ignored since they are known to be zero in element 1. Values calculated for different combinations of (i, j) are added to the corresponding (i, j) location in the $N \times N$ coefficient matrix.

5. Repeat step 4 for all remaining elements, $e = 2$ through $e = E$. For each element e, combinations of basis functions e and $e + 1$ will be calculated and added to their appropriate locations in the global coefficient matrix.

6. Calculate the right-side integral $\int_\Omega f\phi_i \, dx$ for each finite element equation.

7. Impose boundary conditions by modifying the matrix and right side as necessary. For a first-type boundary condition at node k, row k and column k can be eliminated from the global matrix, with the boundary information (column k) being brought to the right-side vector for the other equations (rows of the matrix). This is analogous to imposition of first-type boundary conditions for finite difference approximations, as discussed in Section 2.5. Procedures for second- and third-type boundary conditions are discussed in Section 3.3.4.

8. Solve the resulting matrix equation for the vector of nodal unknowns **U**.

3.3.2 Master Elements in One Dimension

For any element e, the basis functions within the element have a functional form that is analogous to those in any other element, generally differing by scale factors. For example, piecewise linear bases in one dimension scale by the length of the element. Therefore, "typical" integrals can be computed on a so-called *master element*. For nth-degree piecewise Lagrange polynomials, the master element, denoted by Ω^M, has $n+1$ nodes, denoted by $x_1^M, x_2^M, \ldots, x_{n+1}^M$, and associated master basis functions $\phi_1^M(x), \ldots, \phi_{n+1}^M(x)$. For piecewise linear polynomials, $n = 1$, so that the master element has two nodes, x_1^M, x_2^M, and associated master basis function, $\phi_1^M(x)$, $\phi_2^M(x)$, as illustrated in Figure 3.6. The following master integrals can be calculated for the linear case:

---

[3]Most matrices will be both banded and sparse, so that actual storage schemes should take advantage of these features. The $N \times N$ matrix is used here to demonstrate the integration procedure but only some subset of the full matrix is stored in the computer in practice (i.e., stored in banded form or using some sparse matrix storage scheme).

$$\int_{\Omega^M} \phi_1^M \phi_2^M \, dx = \int_{\Omega^M} \phi_2^M \phi_1^M \, dx$$

$$= \int_{x_1}^{x_2} \left(\frac{x - x_1^M}{x_2^M - x_1^M} \right) \left(\frac{x_2^M - x}{x_2^M - x_1^M} \right) dx = \frac{x_2^M - x_1^M}{6} \qquad (3.3.3a)$$

$$\int_{\Omega^M} (\phi_1^M)^2 \, dx = \int_{\Omega^M} (\phi_2^M)^2 \, dx = \frac{x_2^M - x_1^M}{3} \qquad (3.3.3b)$$

$$\int_{\Omega^M} \frac{d\phi_1^M}{dx} \phi_2^M \, dx = -\int_{\Omega^M} \phi_1^M \frac{d\phi_2^M}{dx} \, dx = -\frac{1}{2} \qquad (3.3.3c)$$

$$\int_{\Omega^M} \frac{d\phi_1^M}{dx} \frac{d\phi_2^M}{dx} \, dx = \int_{\Omega^M} \frac{d\phi_2^M}{dx} \frac{d\phi_1^M}{dx} \, dx \qquad (3.3.3d)$$

$$= -\int_{\Omega^M} \left(\frac{d\phi_1^M}{dx} \right)^2 dx = -\int_{\Omega^M} \left(\frac{d\phi_2^M}{dx} \right)^2 dx = -\frac{1}{x_2^M - x_1^M}$$

These can be summarized by the following general integral for piecewise linear bases in one dimension:

$$\int_{\Omega^M} \left(\frac{d\phi_1^M}{dx} \right)^\gamma \left(\frac{d\phi_2^M}{dx} \right)^\epsilon (\phi_1^M)^\alpha (\phi_2^M)^\beta \, dx = \frac{(-1)^\gamma \alpha! \beta!}{(1 + \alpha + \beta)!} (x_2^M - x_1^M)^{1-\gamma-\epsilon} \qquad (3.3.3e)$$

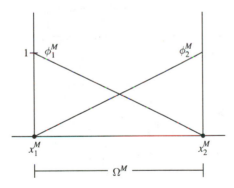

Figure 3.6 Master element Ω^M with associated piecewise linear master basis functions ϕ_1^M and ϕ_2^M.

Given these integrals, the computational procedure involves identification of the nodes that make up the element, and definition of the one-to-one correspondence between the node numbers associated with that element (known from step 2 of the computational procedure of Section 3.3.1) and the master element nodes $x_1^M, x_2^M, \ldots, x_{n+1}^M$. Any integral that arises in the MWR formulation is computed by simple substitution of the appropriate spatial locations into the results of the master integrals, such as equations (3.3.3) for the piecewise linear case. The value is then added to the global matrix in the row and column corresponding to the actual node numbers. The numbering in the master element (1 through $n + 1$) is referred to as *local node numbering*, while the actual node numbers are referred to as *global node numbers*.

3.3.3 Example Calculation

Example 3.7

Problem   Solve the equation

$$\mathcal{L}u \equiv \frac{d^2u}{dx^2} + u = 0, \qquad 0 < x < 1$$

$$u(0) = 1$$

$$u(1) = 0$$

using piecewise linear Lagrange basis functions on a uniform discretization of five nodes.

Solution   Since there are five nodes, there are five undetermined coefficients to be found, U_1, U_2, U_3, U_4, U_5. According to the computational procedure of Section 3.3.1, the first step is to initialize a 5×5 matrix as

$$\begin{bmatrix} 0 & 0 & 0 & 0 & 0 \\ 0 & 0 & 0 & 0 & 0 \\ 0 & 0 & 0 & 0 & 0 \\ 0 & 0 & 0 & 0 & 0 \\ 0 & 0 & 0 & 0 & 0 \end{bmatrix}$$

Note that depending on the matrix solution algorithm employed, matrix storage may be reduced to include only the nonzero entries, only the nonzero band, or some other subset of the full 5×5 matrix. Furthermore, symmetry of the matrix may be exploited to further reduce storage for this example.

Next the *element incidence list* is generated to identify the nodes that occur in each element. In this case, the list is as follows.

Element	Nodes
1	1, 2
2	2, 3
3	3, 4
4	4, 5

Next the integrals of interest are derived using the method of weighted residuals. After application of integration by parts (see Example 3.6), the equations are of the form

$$\sum_{j=1}^{5} U_j \int_0^1 \left(-\frac{d\phi_j}{dx}\frac{d\phi_i}{dx} + \phi_j\phi_i \right) dx = 0, \qquad i = 2, 3, 4 \qquad (3.3.4)$$

where the equation is written for all nodes except those at which first-type boundary conditions are specified. Notice that for all equations indicated by equation (3.3.4), boundary terms that arise in integration by parts vanish as they did in Example 3.6.

Evaluation of the integrals now commences, beginning with element 1. For the first element, the only (i, j) values of interest are[4] $i = 2$ and $j = 1, 2$, since nodes 1 and 2 are present in element 1. The appropriate integrals are

$i = 2$, $j = 1$ (local numbers 2, 1)

$$-\int_{\Omega^1} \frac{d\phi_j}{dx} \frac{d\phi_i}{dx}\, dx = \frac{1}{\Delta x} = 4.0, \qquad \int_{\Omega^1} \phi_j \phi_i\, dx = \frac{\Delta x}{6} = \frac{1}{24}$$

$i = 2$, $j = 2$ (local numbers 2, 2)

$$-\int_{\Omega^1} \frac{d\phi_j}{dx} \frac{d\phi_i}{dx}\, dx = -\frac{1}{\Delta x} = -4.0, \qquad \int_{\Omega^1} \phi_j \phi_i\, dx = \frac{\Delta x}{3} = \frac{1}{12}$$

Into row 2, column 1 of the global matrix is added $(1/\Delta x + \Delta x/6) = 4.0417$, and into row 2, column 2 is added $(-1/\Delta x + \Delta x/3) = -3.9167$. This completes element 1. The global matrix at this point is

$$\begin{bmatrix} 1 & 0 & 0 & 0 & 0 \\ 4.042 & -3.917 & 0 & 0 & 0 \\ 0 & 0 & 0 & 0 & 0 \\ 0 & 0 & 0 & 0 & 0 \\ 0 & 0 & 0 & 0 & 0 \end{bmatrix}$$

For element 2, the indices of interest are $i = 2, 3$, $j = 2, 3$. The various combinations of these are

$i = 2$, $j = 2$ (local numbers 1, 1)

$$-\int_{\Omega^2} \frac{d\phi_j}{dx} \frac{d\phi_i}{dx}\, dx = \frac{-1}{\Delta x} = -4.0, \qquad \int_{\Omega^2} \phi_j \phi_i\, dx = \frac{\Delta x}{3} = \frac{1}{12}$$

$i = 2$, $j = 3$ (local numbers 1, 2)

$$-\int_{\Omega^2} \frac{d\phi_j}{dx} \frac{d\phi_i}{dx}\, dx = \frac{1}{\Delta x} = 4.0, \qquad \int_{\Omega^2} \phi_j \phi_i\, dx = \frac{\Delta x}{6} = \frac{1}{24}$$

$i = 3$, $j = 2$ (local numbers 2, 1)

$$-\int_{\Omega^2} \frac{d\phi_j}{dx} \frac{d\phi_i}{dx}\, dx = \frac{1}{\Delta x} = 4.0, \qquad \int_{\Omega^2} \phi_j \phi_i\, dx = \frac{\Delta x}{6} = \frac{1}{24}$$

$i = 3$, $j = 3$ (local numbers 2, 2)

$$-\int_{\Omega^2} \frac{d\phi_j}{dx} \frac{d\phi_i}{dx}\, dx = \frac{-1}{\Delta x} = -4.0, \qquad \int_{\Omega^2} \phi_j \phi_i\, dx = \frac{\Delta x}{3} = \frac{1}{12}$$

Therefore, to row 2, column 2 is added $(-1/\Delta x + \Delta x/3) = -3.917$, to row 2, column 3 is added $(1/\Delta x + \Delta x/6) = 4.042$, to row 3, column 2 is added $(1/\Delta x + \Delta x/6) = 4.402$,

---

[4]Evaluations for $i = 1$ are unnecessary since this corresponds to a first-type boundary node, and as such, no finite element equation is written.

and to row 3, column 3 is added $(-1/\Delta x + \Delta x/3) = -3.917$. The global matrix now has the following entries:

$$\begin{bmatrix} 1 & 0 & 0 & 0 & 0 \\ 4.042 & -7.834 & 4.042 & 0 & 0 \\ 0 & 4.042 & -3.917 & 0 & 0 \\ 0 & 0 & 0 & 0 & 0 \\ 0 & 0 & 0 & 0 & 0 \end{bmatrix}$$

Integrals associated with element 3 are evaluated next. These produce entries that are added to positions (3,3), (3,4), (4,3), (4,4). Next, element 4 is interrogated and leads to entries in positions (4,4) and (4,5) ($i = 5$ is not used due to the first-type boundary condition at $x_5 = 1$). Finally, boundary conditions are imposed as $U_1 = 1$ and $U_5 = 0$. The resulting matrix equation is

$$\begin{bmatrix} 1 & 0 & 0 & 0 & 0 \\ 4.042 & -7.834 & 4.042 & 0 & 0 \\ 0 & 4.042 & -7.834 & 4.042 & 0 \\ 0 & 0 & 4.042 & -7.834 & 4.042 \\ 0 & 0 & 0 & 0 & 1 \end{bmatrix} \begin{bmatrix} U_1 \\ U_2 \\ U_3 \\ U_4 \\ U_5 \end{bmatrix} = \begin{bmatrix} 1 \\ 0 \\ 0 \\ 0 \\ 0 \end{bmatrix} \qquad (3.3.5a)$$

The tridiagonal (bandwidth $= 3$) structure of the matrix can be seen in equation (3.3.5a), and storage of the zeros outside the bandwidth is unnecessary. Because U_1 and U_5 are known, all information in columns 1 and 5 can be brought to the right side, so that the reduced matrix is

$$\begin{bmatrix} -7.834 & 4.042 & 0 \\ 4.042 & -7.834 & 4.042 \\ 0 & 4.042 & -7.834 \end{bmatrix} \begin{bmatrix} U_2 \\ U_3 \\ U_4 \end{bmatrix} = \begin{bmatrix} -4.042 \\ 0 \\ 0 \end{bmatrix} \qquad (3.3.5b)$$

This matrix is now symmetric, whereas the previous one was not. As in the finite difference case (Section 2.5), symmetric matrices may also be obtained by keeping the boundary equations in (3.3.5a) and zeroing columns 1 and 5, that is,

$$\begin{bmatrix} 1 & 0 & 0 & 0 & 0 \\ 0 & -7.834 & 4.042 & 0 & 0 \\ 0 & 4.042 & -7.834 & 4.042 & 0 \\ 0 & 0 & 4.042 & -7.834 & 0 \\ 0 & 0 & 0 & 0 & 1 \end{bmatrix} \begin{bmatrix} U_1 \\ U_2 \\ U_3 \\ U_4 \\ U_5 \end{bmatrix} = \begin{bmatrix} 1 \\ -4.042 \\ 0 \\ 0 \\ 0 \end{bmatrix} \qquad (3.3.5c)$$

If the right-side forcing function $f(x)$ were not zero, the additional evaluation of $\int_\Omega f\phi_i \, dx$ would need to be carried out for each $i = 2, 3, 4$. Solution of matrix equation (3.3.5b) yields the finite element approximation of $(U_1, U_2, U_3, U_4, U_5) = (1, 0.810, 0.569, 0.294, 0)$. The analytic solution for this example is $u(x) = \cos(x) - \cot(1)\sin(x)$, which has nodal values $(1, 0.810, 0.570, 0.294, 0)$.

The idea of elementwise integration, with calculations carried out on a master element, are fundamental to the finite element method. They carry over to more complex elements in both one and higher dimensions. Problems 3.6 and 3.7 explore these concepts further. The multidimensional case is treated in Sections 3.5 and 3.6.

3.3.4 Implementation of Boundary Conditions in One Dimension

As stated previously, first-type boundary conditions are implemented directly into finite element algorithms by forcing the trial function to exactly satisfy the boundary condition. This provides algebraic equations that are additional to finite element equations. For second-order differential equations, second- and third-type boundary conditions are treated differently from first-type boundary conditions.

For an ordinary differential equation, second-type boundary conditions take the form

$$\left. \frac{du}{dx} \right|_{x=\ell} = C \tag{3.3.6}$$

where ℓ refers to a boundary point and C is a constant. When a second-type boundary condition is specified for a second-order differential equation, the computational procedure is to write the finite element equation associated with the boundary node and then to impose the boundary information within this equation. For a governing equation of the form

$$\mathcal{L}u \equiv \frac{d^2u}{dx^2} + a\frac{du}{dx} + bu = f(x), \qquad 0 < x < \ell \tag{3.3.7}$$

the general finite element equation is, after integrating the second-order derivative by parts,

$$\int_0^\ell \left(-\frac{dU}{dx}\frac{d\phi_i}{dx} + a\frac{dU}{dx}\phi_i + bU\phi_i \right) dx = \int_0^\ell f\phi_i \, dx - \left. \left(\phi_i \frac{dU}{dx} \right) \right|_0^\ell \tag{3.3.8}$$

Let the boundary location correspond to x_N, so that $x_N = \ell$. To accommodate the second-type boundary condition, equation (3.3.8) is written with $i = N$. Definition of $\phi_N(x)$ indicates that $\phi_N(0) = 0$ but $\phi_N(\ell) = 1$. Therefore, as opposed to the finite element equation of previous examples, the boundary term arising from integration by parts no longer vanishes (due to the nonzero value of ϕ_N at $x = \ell$). Instead, equation (3.3.8) becomes

$$\sum_{j=1}^N U_j \int_0^\ell \left[-\frac{d\phi_j}{dx}\frac{d\phi_N}{dx} + \left(a\frac{d\phi_j}{dx} + b\phi_j \right)\phi_N \right] dx = \int_0^\ell f\phi_N dx - \left. \frac{dU}{dx} \right|_{x=\ell} \tag{3.3.9}$$

The left side of equation (3.3.9) is evaluated using standard elementwise integration, and the forcing function f is also integrated. The remaining term is the derivative dU/dx, evaluated at the boundary $x_N = \ell$. However, the second-type boundary condition provides information about du/dx at $x = \ell$, namely that $du/dx|_{x=\ell} = C$. Therefore, $dU/dx|_{x=\ell}$ is replaced by the value given by the boundary condition, in this case the constant C. In this way, the boundary information is incorporated into the algebraic equation written at that boundary node.

When a third-type boundary condition is given,

$$\frac{du}{dx} + \alpha u = C \tag{3.3.10}$$

two different treatments are possible. The first is again to write equation (3.3.9) and to impose the boundary condition

$$\left.\frac{dU}{dx}\right|_{x=\ell} = C - \alpha U|_{x=\ell} = C - \alpha U_N \tag{3.3.11}$$

The constant C then remains on the right side while the term αU_N is brought to the left side, and α is incorporated into the global coefficient matrix [in position (N, N)]. The algebraic equations are then solved. A second option is to integrate both the second and first derivatives by parts to produce

$$\sum_{j=1}^{N} U_j \int_0^\ell \left[-\left(\frac{d\phi_j}{dx} + a\phi_j\right) \frac{d\phi_N}{dx} + b\phi_j\phi_N \right] dx$$

$$= \int_0^\ell f\phi_N dx - \left[\phi_N \left(\frac{dU}{dx} + aU\right) \right]\Bigg|_{x=\ell} \tag{3.3.12}$$

Given boundary condition (3.3.11), the boundary term on the right side of equation (3.3.12) can be replaced using

$$\left[\phi_N \left(\frac{dU}{dx} + aU\right) \right]\Bigg|_{x=\ell} = C + (a - \alpha)U_N \tag{3.3.13}$$

When $\alpha = a$, this term is simply equal to C. Otherwise, the contribution to U_N must be added to the matrix. Evaluation of the resulting integrals shows that the algebraic equations that result are the same whether or not the first-order term is integrated by parts. Therefore, the choice of which procedure to use becomes one of convenience. In many physical systems, the coefficients a and α are equal, so that implementation of third-type boundary conditions is easier when both the second- and first-order terms are integrated by parts. This often happens, for example, in the physical systems of transport of a passive scalar in a flowing fluid. Finally, boundary condition implementation for Hermite collocation approximations, such as that of Example 3.4, are explored in Problem 3.9.

3.4 MATHEMATICAL REQUIREMENTS

A rich mathematical theory exists for most members of the method of weighted residuals family, especially the Galerkin finite element method. Several of the most fundamental ideas are discussed below. These include basic requirements for trial spaces (and associated basis functions) and the notion of consistency for finite elements. A detailed discussion of mathematical analysis is beyond the scope of this book. For an introduction to detailed analysis, the texts of Prenter (1975), Strang and Fix (1973), and the

Texas Finite Element Series (Carey and Oden; see the reference list in Appendix C) are recommended.

3.4.1 Requirements for Trial Space

Choice of trial space (and its associated basis functions) is a pivotal decision in finite element methods. Overall, a wide variety of functions exists from which to choose. The choice is restricted only by the following three constraints:

1. The set of basis functions must be members of a complete set.
2. The approximating MWR equations must form a set of well-defined algebraic equations. In particular, all integrals must be well defined.
3. The trial function should satisfy all essential boundary conditions.

The first constraint ensures that the trial function is capable of representing, in an interpolation sense, any function in the actual solution space to an arbitrary degree of accuracy by choosing sufficiently many basis functions. That is,

$$\lim_{N \to \infty} \left\| \sum_{j=1}^{N} U_j \phi_j(\mathbf{x}) - u(\mathbf{x}) \right\| = 0 \tag{3.4.1}$$

Equation (3.4.1), in which $\|\cdot\|$ denotes a valid norm, should hold for all possible solutions $u(\mathbf{x})$ of the governing differential equation. Equation (3.4.1) represents a completeness criterion. Notice that for piecewise linear Lagrange polynomial bases in one dimension, increasing N implies use of additional node points, with concomitant decrease in node spacing Δx.

The second constraint requires that each integral appearing in the MWR statement must be well defined in the sense of being integrable. This leads directly to continuity constraints on the trial function. Such constraints arose in the discussion of Examples 3.4 and 3.6. In general, for second-order governing differential equations, the trial function $U(\mathbf{x})$ must be $\mathbb{C}^0[\Omega]$ for the Galerkin and subdomain methods and $\mathbb{C}^1[\Omega]$ for the collocation method.

The third constraint requires the trial function to satisfy all essential boundary conditions. For second-order partial differential equations, essential boundary conditions correspond to first-type boundary conditions. For general equations of order $2m$, essential boundary conditions are those that involve derivatives through mth order.

3.4.2 Consistency

Recall from Chapter 2 that consistency is a necessary requirement for any finite difference approximation. This means that the truncation error associated with the finite difference approximation must go to zero as the node spacing approaches zero. For a differential equation of the form

$$\mathcal{L}u = f \tag{3.4.2}$$

consider a finite difference approximation, written symbolically as

$$\hat{\mathcal{L}}U = f \tag{3.4.3}$$

Notation is consistent with the discussion of Section 2.3, in that finite difference methods approximate the differential operator $\mathcal{L}$ by a difference operator $\hat{\mathcal{L}}$. Consistency for finite difference approximations is then stated by

$$(\mathcal{L}u)\big|_{\mathbf{x}_i} - (\hat{\mathcal{L}}u)\big|_{\mathbf{x}_i} = \mathcal{O}(h^p), \qquad p > 0 \tag{3.4.4}$$

where h is a measure of the distance between nodes. This can be seen to correspond directly to the definition of consistency presented in Section 2.3 as equation (2.3.6).

Next recall that whereas finite difference methods approximate $\mathcal{L}$ by $\hat{\mathcal{L}}$, weighted residual methods approximate the solution u by the trial function U while maintaining the original differential operator. Note that error in solution U is due to failure of the basis functions to exactly match the actual interpolation behavior of u between nodes. Therefore, if an interpolation is defined that is exact at the nodes but makes use of the finite element basis functions such that

$$\hat{u} = \sum_{j=1}^{N} u_j \phi_j \tag{3.4.5}$$

then a measure of consistency that considers the weighted average inherent in MWR can be defined as

$$(\mathcal{L}u)\big|_{\mathbf{x}_i} - \frac{\int_\Omega (\mathcal{L}\hat{u})w_i \, d\mathbf{x}}{\int_\Omega w_i \, d\mathbf{x}} = \mathcal{O}(h^p), \qquad p > 0 \tag{3.4.6}$$

where h is again a measure of node spacing.

A weighted residuals approximation is consistent with the original differential equation when equation (3.4.6), with $p > 0$, is satisfied.

Example 3.8

Problem Show that the finite element approximation of Example 3.6 is consistent.

Solution The governing differential equation is

$$\frac{d^2u}{dx^2} + u = 0$$

The associated finite element approximation, using piecewise linear bases, is of the form

$$\int_\Omega \left(\frac{d^2\hat{u}}{dx^2} + \hat{u} \right) \phi_i(x) \, dx = \frac{u_{i+1} - 2u_i + u_{i-1}}{\Delta x} + \frac{\Delta x}{6}(u_{i+1} + 4u_i + u_{i-1})$$

The consistency requirement is then tested as follows:

$$\frac{\int_\Omega (\mathcal{L}\hat{u})w_i \, dx}{\int_\Omega w_i \, dx} = \frac{\dfrac{u_{i+1} - 2u_i + u_{i-1}}{\Delta x} + \dfrac{\Delta x}{6}[u_{i+1} + 4u_i + u_{i-1}]}{\Delta x}$$

$$= \frac{u_{i+1} - 2u_i + u_{i-1}}{(\Delta x)^2} + \left[\left(\frac{1}{6} \right) (u_{i+1} + 4u_i + u_{i-1}) \right]$$

$$= \left[\left. \frac{d^2 u}{dx^2} \right|_{x_i} + \mathcal{O}((\Delta x)^2) \right] + \left[u_i + \mathcal{O}((\Delta x)^2) \right]$$

$$= \left. \left[\frac{d^2 u}{dx^2} + u \right] \right|_{x_i} + \mathcal{O}((\Delta x)^2)$$

$$= \left. \mathcal{L}u \right|_{x_i} + \mathcal{O}((\Delta x)^2) \tag{3.4.7}$$

Therefore,

$$\left. \mathcal{L}u \right|_{x_i} - \frac{\int_\Omega (\mathcal{L}\hat{u}) w_i \, dx}{\int_\Omega w_i \, dx} = \mathcal{O}((\Delta x)^2)$$

and the approximation is consistent.

3.5 METHOD OF WEIGHTED RESIDUALS IN TWO DIMENSIONS

The philosophy of weighted residual methods presented in Section 3.1 is invariant with respect to problem dimensionality. The only changes occur in the definitions of elements, basis functions, and weight functions. This section presents a variety of piecewise polynomial basis functions defined on both rectangular and triangular elements. These include multidimensional versions of both Lagrange and Hermite polynomials. Appropriate weight functions are defined for the different MWR approximations.

3.5.1 Rectangular Elements

When rectangular elements are used to discretize a two-dimensional domain Ω, node points are usually located at the four corners of the element. While additional nodes may reside along the sides of the element, or interior to the element, the four corner nodes serve to define the geometry of the element.

On rectangular discretizations, two-dimensional piecewise Lagrange polynomials can be formed by taking products of associated one-dimensional piecewise Lagrange polynomials. For example, consider the discretization of Figure 3.7, where each element contains four corner nodes. On this discretization, piecewise bilinear Lagrange polynomials can be formed by multiplying two one-dimensional piecewise linear polynomials, one defined along x, the other along y. Let $\ell_i(x)$ be the one-dimensional piecewise linear Lagrange polynomial associated with x-location x_i, and $\ell_j(y)$ the corresponding function associated with y-location y_j. Then the piecewise bilinear basis function associated with node k, located at (x_i, y_j), is defined by

$$\phi_k(x, y) = \ell_i(x)\ell_j(y) \tag{3.5.1a}$$

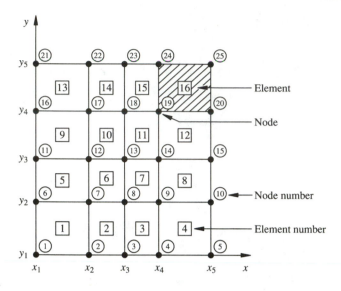

Element

Node

Node number

Element number

Figure 3.7 Typical rectangular discretization showing nodes and elements.

or,

$$\phi_k(x,y) = \begin{cases} \left(\dfrac{x - x_{i-1}}{x_i - x_{i-1}}\right)\left(\dfrac{y - y_{j-1}}{y_j - y_{j-1}}\right), & \begin{array}{l} x_{i-1} \le x \le x_i \\ y_{j-1} \le y \le y_j \end{array} \\[2ex] \left(\dfrac{x_{i+1} - x}{x_{i+1} - x_i}\right)\left(\dfrac{y - y_{j-1}}{y_j - y_{j-1}}\right), & \begin{array}{l} x_i \le x \le x_{i+1} \\ y_{j-1} \le y \le y_j \end{array} \\[2ex] \left(\dfrac{x - x_{i-1}}{x_i - x_{i-1}}\right)\left(\dfrac{y_{j+1} - y}{y_{j+1} - y_j}\right), & \begin{array}{l} x_{i-1} \le x \le x_i \\ y_j \le y \le y_{j+1} \end{array} \\[2ex] \left(\dfrac{x_{i+1} - x}{x_{i+1} - x_i}\right)\left(\dfrac{y_{j+1} - y}{y_{j+1} - y_j}\right), & \begin{array}{l} x_i \le x \le x_{i+1} \\ y_j \le y \le y_{j+1} \end{array} \end{cases}$$ (3.5.1b)

where $\phi_k(x,y)$ is zero at any (x,y) location not included in equation (3.5.1). These functions are two-dimensional polynomials that include the terms 1, x, y, and xy. Figure 3.8 illustrates a typical bilinear function. Notice that the function has curvature within element interiors and is not a planar surface (this results from the xy term in the functional definition). The function maintains a linear shape along element boundaries. In addition, the property of Lagrange polynomials, that ϕ_k is 1 at node k and 0 at all other nodes, is maintained in two dimensions.

Higher-degree piecewise Lagrange polynomial bases can be constructed in an analogous way. For example, piecewise biquadratic polynomials can be defined as direct products of one-dimensional piecewise quadratic Lagrange polynomials. For this case, each two-dimensional element requires three nodes along x and three nodes along y, resulting in the nine nodes indicated in Figure 3.9. Basis functions associated with the four corner nodes span four elements, since each corner node resides in four different

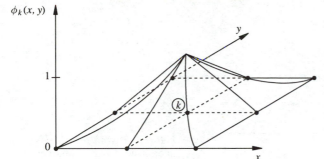

Figure 3.8   Typical piecewise bilinear basis function associated with node k.

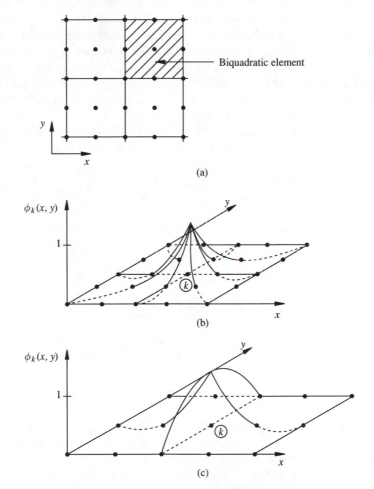

Figure 3.9   (a) Biquadratic finite element discretization; (b) typical corner-node biquadratic basis functions; (c) typical midside-node biquadratic basis function.

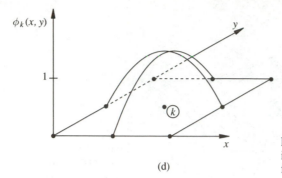

Figure 3.9 (cont'd.)   (d) Typical interior-node biquadratic basis function.

(d)

two-dimensional elements. Nodes along the element sides are shared by two elements, so that their associated basis functions are nonzero only over those two elements, while the basis function associated with the node interior to an element is nonzero only within that element. Each basis function is a two-dimensional polynomial that has the terms 1, x, y, xy, x^2, y^2, xy^2, x^2y, x^2y^2. Typical basis functions for corner, side, and interior nodes are illustrated in Figure 3.9. Construction of two-dimensional piecewise Lagrange polynomial bases can be continued for higher-degree polynomials. Product-type functions are often referred to as *Lagrangian functions*.

The master element concept of Section 3.3 applies to the multidimensional case as well as the one-dimensional case. In two dimensions, the master element is a rectangular element that has node locations in x at $x_1^M, x_2^M, \ldots, x_p^M$ and in y at $y_1^M, y_2^M, \ldots, y_p^M$, for product bases of degree $p - 1$ in both x and y. For the piecewise bilinear case, four nodes located at $\mathbf{x}_1^M = (x_1^M, y_1^M)$, $\mathbf{x}_2^M = (x_2^M, y_1^M)$, $\mathbf{x}_3^M = (x_2^M, y_2^M)$, $\mathbf{x}_4^M = (x_1^M, y_2^M)$ define the master element, as shown in Figure 3.10. Master basis functions associated with master nodes 1, 2, 3, and 4 are then defined as

$$\phi_1^M(x,y) = \left(\frac{x_2^M - x}{x_2^M - x_1^M} \right) \left(\frac{y_2^M - y}{y_2^M - y_1^M} \right) \tag{3.5.2a}$$

$$\phi_2^M(x,y) = \left(\frac{x - x_1^M}{x_2^M - x_1^M} \right) \left(\frac{y_2^M - y}{y_2^M - y_1^M} \right) \tag{3.5.2b}$$

$$\phi_3^M(x,y) = \left(\frac{x - x_1^M}{x_2^M - x_1^M} \right) \left(\frac{y - y_1^M}{y_2^M - y_1^M} \right) \tag{3.5.2c}$$

$$\phi_4^M(x,y) = \left(\frac{x_2^M - x}{x_2^M - x_1^M} \right) \left(\frac{y - y_1^M}{y_2^M - y_1^M} \right) \tag{3.5.2d}$$

Notice that these functions can be derived by starting with a general bilinear polynomial $\gamma_1 + \gamma_2 x + \gamma_3 y + \gamma_4 xy$, and imposing the nodal constraints that ϕ_i^M is 1 at node i and 0 at the other three nodes (see Problem 3.12).

Similar definitions apply to master elements associated with any degree polynomials. For the quadratic case, the master element contains nine nodes, located as shown in Figure 3.10. Typical master basis functions (see Table B.9 of Appendix B and Problem 3.13 for a complete list of the nine master basis functions) are

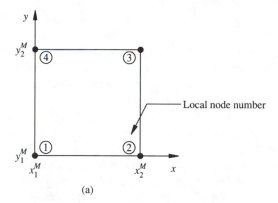

(a)

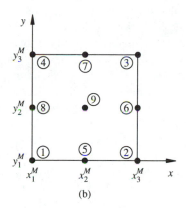

(b)

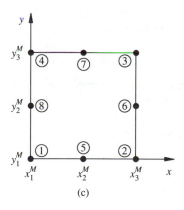

(c)

Figure 3.10 Master elements for (a) piecewise bilinear, (b) piecewise biquadratic, and (c) piecewise serendipity quadratic basis functions.

$$\phi_1^M(x, y) = \frac{(x - x_2^M)(x - x_3^M)}{(x_1^M - x_2^M)(x_1^M - x_3^M)} \frac{(y - y_2^M)(y - y_3^M)}{(y_1^M - y_2^M)(y_1^M - y_3^M)} \qquad (3.5.3a)$$

$$\phi_9^M(x, y) = \frac{(x - x_1^M)(x - x_3^M)}{(x_2^M - x_1^M)(x_2^M - x_3^M)} \frac{(y - y_1^M)(y - y_3^M)}{(y_2^M - y_1^M)(y_2^M - y_3^M)} \qquad (3.5.3b)$$

As in the one-dimensional case, master elements will again play a key role when finite element integrals are evaluated and the subsequent global matrix is formed.

Product-type basis functions are not the only polynomial bases that can be defined on rectangular elements. A family of polynomial basis functions that maintains many properties of Lagrange polynomials but involves fewer nodes per element than product-type functions can be defined. This family uses elements that have no (for linear, quadratic, and cubic functions) or very few (for quartic and higher-degree functions) interior nodes, while retaining the same nodes as product-type functions along element boundaries. For the piecewise bilinear case, there is no change as compared to the product-type functions, since no interior nodes are involved in either case. For piecewise quadratics, the one interior node that appears in the product formulation is eliminated. Thus eight nodes remain, one at each of the four corners of the element, and one along each element side. To derive the functional form of these polynomial basis functions, constraints that each function equal 1 at the node with which it is associated and 0 at the other seven nodes are imposed. The function should also reduce to a standard one-dimensional Lagrange polynomial along each element side. These functions are referred to as *serendipity basis functions*, and the associated elements as *serendipity elements*.

For the quadratic case, each serendipity element has eight nodes, as illustrated in Figure 3.10c. To derive the appropriate basis functions, the following procedure can be used. Consider first a basis function associated with a corner node, for example node 1 of Figure 3.10c. This basis function must be zero at all nodes except node 1, where it has a value of unity. Thus ϕ_1^M must be zero at nodes 2, 3, and 6. Since each of these nodes resides at the same x location ($x = x_3^M$), the functional form along this side must be a quadratic function of y only. But the only quadratic that is zero at three points (in this case, ϕ_1^M is zero at y_1^M, y_2^M, y_3^M) is the zero polynomial. Thus ϕ_1^M is zero along the line $x = x_3^M$. Similarly, ϕ_1^M must be zero along $y = y_3^M$. Thus both x_3^M and y_3^M are roots of the function $\phi_1^M(x, y)$, and the functional form is

$$\phi_1^M(x, y) = (x - x_3^M)(y - y_3^M)(\gamma_1 + \gamma_2 x + \gamma_3 y) \qquad (3.5.4)$$

Because the center node (node 9 of Figure 3.10b) is absent, one constraint on ϕ_1^M is removed. To accommodate one fewer constraint, the biquadratic term $x^2 y^2$ is not included in the serendipity function. This leads to the expansion of equation (3.5.4). The three coefficients γ_1, γ_2, γ_3 are determined from the three constraints

$$\phi_1^M(x_1, y_1) = 1 \qquad (3.5.5a)$$

$$\phi_1^M(x_2, y_1) = 0 \qquad (3.5.5b)$$

$$\phi_1^M(x_1, y_2) = 0 \qquad (3.5.5c)$$

Imposition of these constraints and subsequent solution for the three coefficients leads to the following function definition:

$$\phi_1^M(x, y) = \frac{(x - x_3^M)(y - y_3^M)}{(x_1^M - x_3^M)(y_1^M - y_3^M)} \left(1 - \frac{x - x_1^M}{x_2^M - x_1^M} - \frac{y - y_1^M}{y_2^M - y_1^M} \right) \qquad (3.5.6)$$

This functional form may also be derived from a general polynomial involving eight unknown coefficients multiplying the eight terms 1, x, y, xy, x^2, y^2, x^2y, xy^2. Imposition of the eight constraints $\phi_1^M(\mathbf{x}_1) = 1$ and $\phi_1^M(\mathbf{x}_j) = 0$ ($j = 2, 3, \ldots, 8$) leads to an 8×8 linear algebraic system of equations. Solution of this matrix equation yields equation (3.5.6), although the calculation is much more tedious.

Side-node basis functions are easier to derive than those for corner nodes, since the three sides on which the side node does not reside all correspond to roots of the polynomial. For example, the basis function associated with node 5 of Figure 3.10c must be zero at $x = x_1^M$, $x = x_3^M$, and $y = y_3^M$. Thus the functional form is

$$\phi_5^M(x, y) = \gamma_1(x - x_1^M)(x - x_3^M)(y - y_3^M) \tag{3.5.7}$$

All nodal constraints are satisfied except the constraint that $\phi_5^M(x_2^M, y_1^M) = 1$. Imposition of this constraint allows γ_1 to be determined, leading to the final functional form

$$\phi_5^M(x, y) = \frac{(x - x_1^M)(x - x_3^M)(y - y_3^M)}{(x_2^M - x_1^M)(x_2^M - x_3^M)(y_1^M - y_3^M)} \tag{3.5.8}$$

This form could again be derived from an 8×8 matrix system, as discussed for the function ϕ_1^M, although such a procedure is again much more computationally tedious. Derivation of the other quadratic serendipity basis functions is addressed in Problem 3.13. Table B.9 lists all master basis functions for bilinear, biquadratic, and serendipity quadratic elements. Problem 3.13 also considers cubic elements.

Each of the basis functions discussed above maintains the fundamental property that $\phi_i(\mathbf{x}_i) = 1$, $\phi_i(\mathbf{x}_j) = 0$ ($i \neq j$). As such, the trial function associated with these basis functions is of the form

$$U(x, y) = \sum_{k=1}^{N} U_k \phi_k(x, y) \tag{3.5.9}$$

The global basis functions $\phi_k(x, y)$ are composed of the appropriate element definitions, taking the forms illustrated in Figures 3.8 and 3.9.

The two-dimensional functions considered to this point all possess $\mathbb{C}^0[\Omega]$ continuity, since the functions are continuous but normal derivatives across element boundaries exhibit discontinuities. Higher continuity functions can be defined on two-dimensional rectangular discretizations. The most common $\mathbb{C}^1[\Omega]$ functions are formed as products of one-dimensional Hermite polynomials. For example, piecewise cubic Hermite polynomials can be multiplied to form piecewise bicubic polynomials that possess $\mathbb{C}^1[\Omega]$ continuity. In two dimensions, there are four different types of basis functions associated with each node. These correspond to various combinations of $\phi_{0i}(x)$, $\phi_{1i}(x)$, $\phi_{0j}(y)$, $\phi_{1j}(y)$. The appropriate trial function takes the form

$$U(x, y) = \sum_{k=1}^{N} U_k \phi_{00k}(x, y) + \frac{\partial U_k}{\partial x} \phi_{10k}(x, y) + \frac{\partial U_k}{\partial y} \phi_{01k}(x, y)$$

$$+ \frac{\partial^2 U_k}{\partial x \partial y} \phi_{11k}(x, y) \tag{3.5.10}$$

where the coefficients U_k, $\partial U_k/\partial x$, $\partial U_k/\partial y$, and $\partial^2 U_k/\partial x \partial y$ denote nodal approximations to the function u and its appropriate derivatives. If node number k corresponds to the location (x_i, y_j) in a rectangular discretization, then the two-dimensional basis functions are defined as

$$\phi_{00k}(x,y) = \phi_{0i}(x)\phi_{0j}(y) \tag{3.5.11a}$$

$$\phi_{10k}(x,y) = \phi_{1i}(x)\phi_{0j}(y) \tag{3.5.11b}$$

$$\phi_{01k}(x,y) = \phi_{0i}(x)\phi_{1j}(y) \tag{3.5.11c}$$

$$\phi_{11k}(x,y) = \phi_{1i}(x)\phi_{1j}(y) \tag{3.5.11d}$$

These equations can be written more succinctly as

$$\phi_{\ell m k}(x,y) = \phi_{\ell i}(x)\phi_{mj}(y), \qquad \ell = 0,1, \quad m = 0,1 \tag{3.5.11e}$$

Figure 3.11 illustrates typical two-dimensional, piecewise cubic Hermite basis functions.

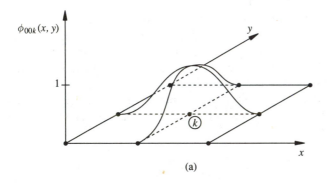

(a)

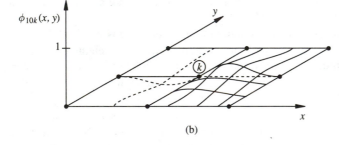

(b)

Figure 3.11 Piecewise bicubic Hermite basis functions associated with (a) function at node k, (b) x-derivative, $\partial u/\partial x$, at node k.

Equation (3.6.10) demonstrates that as the dimensionality of the problem increases, the number of nodal coefficients to achieve $\mathbb{C}^1[\Omega]$ increases. In one dimension, two coefficients per node are required; in two dimensions, four is the minimum number of nodal coefficients needed to obtain $\mathbb{C}^1[\Omega]$ continuity. This means that the cross-derivative coefficient must be present to achieve $\mathbb{C}^1[\Omega]$ continuity. In general, for n-dimensional regions, the number of nodal coefficients that appear in the $\mathbb{C}^1[\Omega]$ Hermite expansion is 2^n. These coefficients involve the function and various derivatives, including mixed derivatives. A modified two-dimensional Hermite expansion that does not use the mixed derivatives (and thus is not fully $\mathbb{C}^1[\Omega]$ continuous) is investigated in Problem 3.24.

3.5.2 Two-Dimensional Example

Consider the two-dimensional Poisson equation,

$$\nabla^2 u = f(x, y), \qquad (x, y) \in \Omega, \quad \Omega \text{ rectangular} \qquad (3.5.12)$$

$$u(x, y) = u_B(x, y), \qquad (x, y) \in \partial\Omega_1$$

$$\frac{\partial u}{\partial x}(x, y) = g(x, y), \qquad (x, y) \in \partial\Omega_2$$

where the boundary of the rectangular domain Ω is denoted by $\partial\Omega = \partial\Omega_1 + \partial\Omega_2$ (see Figure 3.12). First-type boundary conditions are given along the portion of the boundary denoted by $\partial\Omega_1$, and second-type boundary conditions pertain along $\partial\Omega_2$. A Galerkin finite element approximation will be developed for equation (3.5.12), using a piecewise bilinear trial space on the discretization shown in Figure 3.12.

The trial function for this example has the standard form of

$$U(x, y) = \sum_{j=1}^{16} U_j \phi_j(x, y) \qquad (3.5.13)$$

The general Galerkin method of weighted residuals statement is next written as

$$\int_\Omega (\nabla^2 U) \phi_i(x, y) \, dx \, dy = \int_\Omega f(x, y) \phi_i(x, y) \, dx \, dy \qquad (3.5.14)$$

The left side of equation (3.5.14) can be rewritten by application of Green's theorem (multidimensional integration by parts), which produces

$$\int_\Omega (\nabla^2 U) \phi_i(x, y) \, dx \, dy = \int_{\partial\Omega} (\nabla U \cdot \mathbf{n}) \phi_i \, ds - \int_\Omega \nabla U \cdot \nabla \phi_i \, dx \, dy$$

$$= \int_{\partial\Omega} \frac{\partial U}{\partial n} \phi_i \, ds - \int_\Omega \nabla U \cdot \nabla \phi_i \, dx \, dy \qquad (3.5.15)$$

where $\mathbf{n}$ denotes the unit normal to the boundary $\partial\Omega$, directed outward. The first term on the right side of equation (3.5.15) is a line integral over the boundary of the domain, while the second term is a standard area integral that now involves products of first derivatives. Equation (3.5.15) therefore eliminates the second-order derivatives and exhibits the same benefits as integration by parts in one dimension. Use of equations (3.5.13) and (3.5.15) allows equation (3.5.14) to be rewritten as

$$\int_{\partial\Omega} \frac{\partial U}{\partial n} \phi_i \, ds - \sum_{j=1}^N U_j \int_\Omega \nabla \phi_j \cdot \nabla \phi_i \, dx \, dy = \int_\Omega f \phi_i \, dx \, dy \qquad (3.5.16)$$

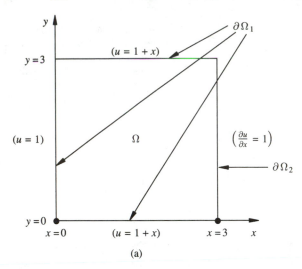

(a)

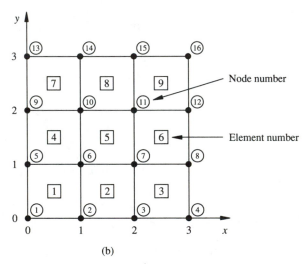

(b)

Figure 3.12 (a) Domain and boundary conditions for example problem of Section 3.5.2; (b) finite element piecewise bilinear discretization for the example problem.

By analogy to the one-dimensional case, the boundary integral is used to accommodate second (and third) -type boundary conditions. The interior integrations produce matrix entries in row i, column j, and the forcing function integrals contribute to the right-side vector.

Construction of the global coefficient matrix proceeds in exactly the same way as in the one-dimensional case (see Example 3.7 of Section 3.3). Master integrals are computed for the expression

$$\int_{\Omega^M} \nabla \phi_\ell^M \cdot \nabla \phi_m^M \, dx \, dy \qquad (\ell = 1, 2, 3, 4; \quad m = 1, 2, 3, 4)$$

By use of the definitions of equations (3.5.2), the master integrals can be tabulated as follows:

ℓ	m	$\int_{\Omega M} \nabla \phi_\ell^M \cdot \nabla \phi_m^M \ dx \ dy$
1	1	$\dfrac{\Delta y}{3\Delta x} + \dfrac{\Delta x}{3\Delta y} = \dfrac{2}{3}$
1	2	$\dfrac{-\Delta y}{3\Delta x} + \dfrac{\Delta x}{6\Delta y} = \dfrac{-1}{6}$
1	3	$\dfrac{-\Delta y}{6\Delta x} + \dfrac{-\Delta x}{6\Delta y} = \dfrac{-1}{3}$
1	4	$\dfrac{\Delta y}{6\Delta x} + \dfrac{-\Delta x}{3\Delta y} = \dfrac{-1}{6}$
2	2	$\dfrac{\Delta y}{3\Delta x} + \dfrac{\Delta x}{3\Delta y} = \dfrac{2}{3}$
2	3	$\dfrac{\Delta y}{6\Delta x} + \dfrac{-\Delta x}{3\Delta y} = \dfrac{-1}{6}$
2	4	$\dfrac{-\Delta y}{6\Delta x} + \dfrac{-\Delta x}{6\Delta y} = \dfrac{-1}{3}$
3	3	$\dfrac{\Delta y}{3\Delta x} + \dfrac{\Delta x}{3\Delta y} = \dfrac{2}{3}$
3	4	$\dfrac{-\Delta y}{3\Delta x} + \dfrac{\Delta x}{6\Delta y} = \dfrac{-1}{6}$
4	4	$\dfrac{\Delta y}{3\Delta x} + \dfrac{\Delta x}{3\Delta y} = \dfrac{2}{3}$

where the discretization lengths $\Delta x = \Delta y = 1$ have been used. The integrals possess symmetry, so that $\ell = 3$, $m = 1$ produces the same result as $\ell = 1$, $m = 3$. Thus this tabulation accommodates all possible combinations of ℓ and m. To apply element integrations, the element incidence list must also be provided. Based on the numbering of Figure 3.12b, the following incidence list applies:

Element	Global incidences
1	1, 2, 6, 5
2	2, 3, 7, 6
.	.
.	.
.	.
9	11, 12, 16, 15

In this list, the counterclockwise numbering used in the master element is adhered to, since the proper one-to-one correspondence must be maintained between the global node numbers in an element and the local node numbers of the master element. Given these two tables of information, the global coefficient matrix is constructed by element-by-element integration. Beginning with a null matrix, all elements are interrogated and the nonzero integrals in each element are evaluated, with the value of the integrals added to the proper location in the global matrix. These integrals are calculated from the master integrals, which have been tabulated a priori. Upon interrogation of all elements, the global coefficient matrix is complete (excepting possible influence of boundary conditions).

As an example of an equation (row) that appears in the global coefficient matrix, consider the equation corresponding to $i = 10$. Node 10 appears in the incidence list of four elements (4, 5, 7, 8), so that entries in row 10 of the matrix arise from integrations in elements 4, 5, 7, and 8. The algebraic equation that results from the matrix assembly procedure is

$$\left(\frac{1}{3}\right) U_5 + \left(\frac{1}{3}\right) U_6 + \left(\frac{1}{3}\right) U_7 + \left(\frac{1}{3}\right) U_9 + \left(\frac{-8}{3}\right) U_{10} + \left(\frac{1}{3}\right) U_{11} + \left(\frac{1}{3}\right) U_{13}$$

$$+ \left(\frac{1}{3}\right) U_{14} + \left(\frac{1}{3}\right) U_{15} = \int_\Omega f \phi_{10} \, dx \, dy - \int_{\partial\Omega} \frac{\partial U}{\partial n} \phi_{10} \, ds \qquad (3.5.17)$$

The left side of equation (3.5.17) represents a nine-point approximation to $\nabla^2 u$ at node 10. It can be shown by Taylor series analysis that this nine-point approximation is second-order accurate in both x and y (see Problem 3.14). Note that the last term in equation (3.5.17) is zero.

For this example, finite element equations are written at nodes 6, 7, 8, 10, 11, and 12. At all other nodes the solution is known by first-type boundary conditions. For all interior nodes ($i = 6, 7, 10, 11$), the boundary integral term in equation (3.5.16) is zero, because ϕ_i is zero along the entire boundary $\partial\Omega$. Therefore, the finite element equations for these nodes involve only the global assembly discussed above and the evaluation of the forcing function integral. However, for nodes 8 and 12, the boundary integral cannot be neglected because ϕ_8 and ϕ_{12} are nonzero along a portion of the boundary $\partial\Omega$. For these two equations, the integral

$$\int_{\partial\Omega} \frac{\partial U}{dn} \phi_i \, ds$$

must be evaluated.

As an example, consider $i = 8$. The basis function $\phi_8(x, y)$ is illustrated in Figure 3.13. The function is nonzero along the segment of $\partial\Omega$ at $x = 3$, $y_1 < y < y_3$. Furthermore, along this segment, the boundary condition is given as $\partial u/\partial x = \partial u/\partial n = 1$. Using the corresponding condition of the trial function that $\partial U/\partial x = \partial U/\partial n = 1$ along this segment, the boundary integral is calculated as

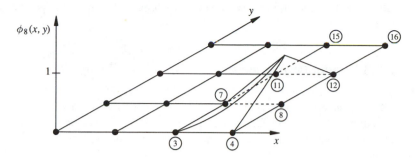

Figure 3.13   Piecewise bilinear basis function associated with boundary node 8.

$$\int_{\partial\Omega} \frac{\partial U}{\partial n}\phi_8 \, ds = \int_{y_1}^{y_3} (1)\phi_8 \, dy$$

$$= \int_{y_1}^{y_2} (1)\frac{y - y_1}{y_2 - y_1} \, dy + \int_{y_2}^{y_3} (1)\frac{y_3 - y}{y_3 - y_2} \, dy$$

$$= (1)\frac{y_2 - y_1}{2} + (1)\frac{y_3 - y_2}{2} \tag{3.5.18}$$

$$= (1)\left(\frac{1}{2}\right) + (1)\left(\frac{1}{2}\right)$$

$$= 1$$

Therefore, the finite element equation associated with node 8 is

$$-\sum_{j=1}^{16} U_j \int_\Omega \nabla\phi_j \cdot \nabla\phi_8 \, dx \, dy = \int_\Omega f(x,y)\phi_8(x,y) \, dx \, dy - 1 \tag{3.5.19a}$$

Upon elementwise assembly of the global coefficient matrix, there results

$$\left(\frac{1}{3}\right)U_3 + \left(\frac{1}{6}\right)U_4 + \left(\frac{1}{3}\right)U_7 + \left(\frac{-4}{3}\right)U_8 + \left(\frac{1}{3}\right)U_{11} + \left(\frac{1}{6}\right)U_{12}$$

$$= \int_{\Omega^3+\Omega^6} f \, \phi_8 \, dx \, dy - 1 \tag{3.5.19b}$$

Analogous arguments pertain to the finite element equation associated with node 12. The boundary flux integral is

$$\int_{\partial\Omega} \frac{\partial U}{\partial n}\phi_{12} \, ds = 1 \tag{3.5.20}$$

and the finite element equation is similar in form to equation (3.5.19b) (see Problem 3.15).

Given a specific functional form for the forcing function $f(x,y)$, the right-side vector can be evaluated and the system of linear algebraic equations generated by the finite element method can be solved. Problem 3.16 addresses specific solutions for this example.

3.5.3 Triangular Elements

One of the major advantages of the finite element method is the ease with which non-rectangular geometries can be accommodated. This is achieved by use of elements that are themselves nonrectangular. The simplest of the nonrectangular elements is the linear triangular element.

Consider a general triangular finite element such as that depicted in Figure 3.14. The element is characterized by three nodes, located at the three vertices of the triangle. Basis functions associated with these three nodes can be developed to maintain the important properties of piecewise Lagrange polynomials, including (1) basis functions exhibit global $\mathbb{C}^0[\Omega]$ continuity; (2) basis functions are unique, $\mathbb{C}^\infty$ polynomials within each element; (3) each function is one at the node with which it is associated and zero at all other nodes; and (4) the function associated with node k is nonzero only in elements of which node k is a part. Basis functions exhibiting all of these properties will be developed, beginning at the element level and then defining the global bases by construction.

Within an element, linear triangular basis functions take the form

$$\phi_i(x, y) = \gamma_1^i + \gamma_2^i x + \gamma_3^i y \tag{3.5.21}$$

Using local node numbering as illustrated in Figure 3.14, in which nodes are numbered 1 through 3 in counterclockwise order, the constraints associated with property (3) above are written as

$$\phi_i(x_i, y_i) = 1 \tag{3.5.22a}$$

$$\phi_i(x_j, y_j) = 0, \qquad j \neq i \tag{3.5.22b}$$

As an example, consider $i = 1$. Then equations (3.5.21) and (3.5.22) combine to produce

$$\phi_1(x_1, y_1) = \gamma_1^1 + \gamma_2^1 x_1 + \gamma_3^1 y_1 = 1 \tag{3.5.23a}$$

$$\phi_1(x_2, y_2) = \gamma_1^1 + \gamma_2^1 x_2 + \gamma_3^1 y_2 = 0 \tag{3.5.23b}$$

$$\phi_1(x_3, y_3) = \gamma_1^1 + \gamma_2^1 x_3 + \gamma_3^1 y_3 = 0 \tag{3.5.23c}$$

Solution of these three linear algebraic equations for the coefficients $\gamma_1^1, \gamma_2^1, \gamma_3^1$ produces

$$\gamma_1^1 = \frac{x_2 y_3 - x_3 y_2}{2A} \tag{3.5.24a}$$

$$\gamma_2^1 = \frac{y_2 - y_3}{2A} \tag{3.5.24b}$$

$$\gamma_3^1 = \frac{x_3 - x_2}{2A} \tag{3.5.24c}$$

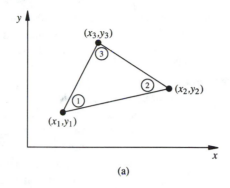

(a)

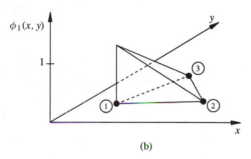

(b)

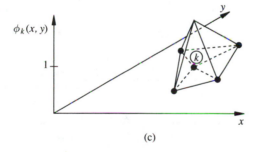

(c)

Figure 3.14 (a) Triangular element with local node numbering; (b) planar basis function $\phi_1(x, y)$, local numbering; (c) piecewise planar basis function $\phi_k(x, y)$.

$$A = \frac{1}{2} \begin{vmatrix} 1 & 1 & 1 \\ x_1 & x_2 & x_3 \\ y_1 & y_2 & y_3 \end{vmatrix} \tag{3.5.24d}$$

where A is the area of the triangle.

The other two basis functions that are nonzero in the element of Figure 3.14, namely ϕ_2 and ϕ_3, are of the same form. This general form can be written as

$$\phi_i(x, y) = \frac{1}{2A} \left[(x_{i+1}y_{i+2} - x_{i+2}y_{i+1}) + (y_{i+1} - y_{i+2})x + (x_{i+2} - x_{i+1})y \right] \tag{3.5.25}$$

where the special indicial operations are such that $2 + 2 = 3 + 1 = 1 + 3 = 1$ and $3 + 2 = 2 + 3 = 2$. Counterclockwise local node numbering, as used in Figure 3.14, is assumed.

The basis function associated with any node i has a value of 1 at node i and goes to 0 as a planar surface over each of the elements that contain node i. It remains at zero in all other elements. An example of this piecewise planar function is shown in Figure 3.14.

These linear triangular elements possess a significant computational advantage in that irregular geometries are easily accommodated while the elementwise integrals remain very simple. This is generally not the case with other types of nonrectangular elements, as discussed in Chapter 4. Any integrals involving gradients, such as those in the example of Section 3.5.2, become especially simple for planar triangular elements because the gradient of the planar surfaces is a constant within each element. Thus the general integral of equation (3.5.15), with local numbering ℓ and m ($\ell = 1, 2, 3$; $m = 1, 2, 3$) used to correspond to global numbers j and i, results in the following simple expression:

$$
\int_{\Omega^e} \nabla \phi_\ell \cdot \nabla \phi_m \, dx \, dy = \int_{\Omega^e} \left(\frac{\partial \phi_\ell}{\partial x} \frac{\partial \phi_m}{\partial x} + \frac{\partial \phi_\ell}{\partial y} \frac{\partial \phi_m}{\partial y} \right) dx \, dy
$$

$$
= \int_{\Omega^e} \left[\left(\frac{y_{\ell+1} - y_{\ell+2}}{2A} \right) \left(\frac{y_{m+1} - y_{m+2}}{2A} \right) \right.
$$

$$
\left. + \left(\frac{x_{\ell+2} - x_{\ell+1}}{2A} \right) \left(\frac{x_{m+2} - x_{m+1}}{2A} \right) \right] dx \, dy
$$

$$
= \left[\left(\frac{y_{\ell+1} - y_{\ell+2}}{2A} \right) \left(\frac{y_{m+1} - y_{m+2}}{2A} \right) \right.
$$

$$
\left. + \left(\frac{x_{\ell+2} - x_{\ell+1}}{2A} \right) \left(\frac{x_{m+2} - x_{m+1}}{2A} \right) \right] \int_{\Omega^e} dx \, dy
$$

$$
\tag{3.5.26}
$$

Because the terms in brackets are all constants, and the remaining integral is equal to the area of the triangle, the original integral can be written as

$$
\int_{\Omega^e} \nabla \phi_\ell \cdot \nabla \phi_m \, dx \, dy = \frac{1}{4A} \left[(y_{\ell+1} - y_{\ell+2})(y_{m+1} - y_{m+2}) \right.
$$

$$
\left. + (x_{\ell+2} - x_{\ell+1})(x_{m+2} - x_{m+1}) \right] \tag{3.5.27}
$$

When the basis function appears in the integral without differentiation, the following integration formula again allows for simple, direct calculation:

$$
\int_{\Omega^e} (\phi_1)^{p_1} (\phi_2)^{p_2} (\phi_3)^{p_3} \, dx \, dy = (2A) \frac{(p_1!)(p_2!)(p_3!)}{(p_1 + p_2 + p_3 + 2)!} \tag{3.5.28}
$$

In equation (3.5.28), ϕ_i are standard planar basis functions, p_i are positive integer exponents, and A is the area of the triangular finite element Ω^e.

3.5.4 Example Calculation

Consider a finite element solution of the two-dimensional Poisson equation,

$$\nabla^2 u = f(x, y), \qquad (x, y) \in \Omega \tag{3.5.29}$$

$$u(x, y) = u_B(x, y), \qquad (x, y) \in \partial\Omega_1$$

$$\frac{\partial u}{\partial n}(x, y) = g(x, y), \qquad (x, y) \in \partial\Omega_2$$

with the regions Ω, $\partial\Omega_1$, and $\partial\Omega_2$ defined in Figure 3.15. Because the region Ω is nonrectangular, let the Galerkin method be applied with a piecewise planar trial space defined on the triangular discretization of Figure 3.15b.

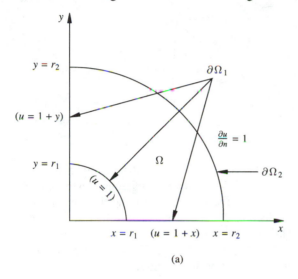

(a)

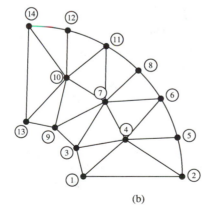

(b)

Figure 3.15   (a) Domain and boundary conditions for example problem of Section 3.5.4; (b) finite element discretization.

In this case, each element has three associated nodes. Therefore, the element incidence list includes only three nodes per element. These nodes can be listed in any

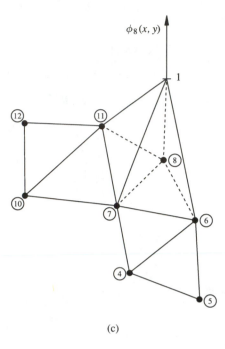

Figure 3.15 (cont'd.) (c) Piecewise planar basis function $\phi_8(x, y)$.

(c)

order, as long as counterclockwise ordering is used so that the global numbers correspond to the local numbering of Figure 3.14. Element integrals can be calculated directly from the expression (3.5.27). Given the incidence list and the element integrations, the computational procedure of Section 3.3.1 can again be followed to derive all relevant finite element equations. This results in the complete assembly of the global coefficient matrix. As in the rectangular case of Section 3.5.2, second-type boundary nodes require the additional evaluation of the boundary flux integral,

$$\int_{\partial\Omega} \frac{\partial U}{\partial n} \phi_i \, ds$$

which is zero for all interior nodes, because those ϕ_i are zero along all of $\partial\Omega$. As an example, consider $i = 8$. Figure 3.15c illustrates the function $\phi_8(x, y)$. The nonzero portion of ϕ_8 along $\partial\Omega$ spans the line segments between nodes 6 and 8 and between nodes 8 and 11. Along these segments, ϕ_8 is piecewise linear. Therefore, the boundary integral is evaluated as

$$\int_{\partial\Omega} \frac{\partial U}{\partial n} \phi_8 \, ds = \int_{\text{node 6}}^{\text{node 8}} (1)\phi_8 \, ds + \int_{\text{node 8}}^{\text{node 11}} (1)\phi_8 \, ds$$

$$= \int_0^{\ell_{6-8}} (1)\frac{s}{\ell_{6-8}} \, ds + \int_0^{\ell_{8-11}} (1)\frac{\ell_{8-11} - s}{\ell_{8-11}} \, ds$$

$$= (1)\frac{\ell_{6-8}}{2} + (1)\frac{\ell_{8-11}}{2}$$

$$= (1)\frac{\ell_{6-8} + \ell_{8-11}}{2} \tag{3.5.30}$$

In equation (3.5.30), ℓ_{6-8} refers to the length of the line segment that connects nodes 6 and 8, while ℓ_{8-11} is the length of the segment between nodes 8 and 11. The functional forms for ϕ_8 reflect the piecewise linear nature of the basis function along these boundary segments.

Similar expressions pertain to nodes 5, 6, 11, and 12. Finite element equations are written for nodes 4, 5, 6, 7, 8, 10, 11, and 12, while first-type boundary condition information is imposed at nodes 1, 2, 3, 9, 13, 14, and 15. Problem 3.16 addresses specific solutions for this example.

3.6 METHOD OF WEIGHTED RESIDUALS IN THREE DIMENSIONS

Extension of the method of weighted residuals from two dimensions to three dimensions is analogous to the extension from one dimension to two dimensions. Various element types can be defined that combine one-dimensional piecewise polynomial functions or piecewise planar (triangular) elements in two dimensions. Combination of one-dimensional piecewise polynomials along each of the three Cartesian coordinate directions leads to piecewise trilinear, triquadratic, and so on, elements in three dimensions. This produces rectangular parallelepiped elements ("bricks"). Triangular elements in two dimensions can be combined with one-dimensional piecewise polynomials in the third dimension to form prismatic elements. Finally, tetrahedral elements can be constructed. Each of these different elements is briefly discussed.

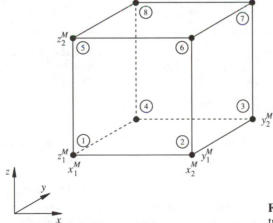

Figure 3.16   Master element for trilinear basis functions.

3.6.1 Parallelepiped Elements

A typical trilinear element is illustrated in Figure 3.16. For the master coordinates of the element of Figure 3.16, the basis function $\phi_1^M(x, y, z)$ has the form

$$\phi_1^M(x, y, z) = \left(\frac{x_2^M - x}{x_2^M - x_1^M} \right) \left(\frac{y_2^M - y}{y_2^M - y_1^M} \right) \left(\frac{z_2^M - z}{z_2^M - z_1^M} \right) \qquad (3.6.1)$$

This function is a simple combination of three one-dimensional piecewise linear polynomials. The other seven master basis functions are constructed in an analogous way. Piecewise triquadratic, tricubic, and so on, bases are formed in the same way. Piecewise trilinear elements have 8 ($= 2^3$) nodes, triquadratic elements have 27 ($= 3^3$) nodes, and tricubic elements have 64 ($= 4^3$) nodes.

Combinations of polynomials of different degrees along different coordinate directions can also be used to define basis functions in two and three dimensions. For example, Figure 3.17 illustrates a 12-node element that uses piecewise linear functions in x and y and piecewise quadratic functions in z. Basis function $\phi_1^M(x, y, z)$ takes the form

$$\phi_1^M(x, y, z) = \left(\frac{x_2^M - x}{x_2^M - x_1^M} \right) \left(\frac{y_2^M - y}{y_2^M - y_1^M} \right) \left(\frac{z_2^M - z}{z_2^M - z_1^M} \right) \left(\frac{z_3^M - z}{z_3^M - z_1^M} \right) \qquad (3.6.2)$$

Other product bases follow directly by construction.

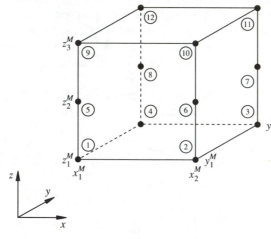

Figure 3.17 Product-type element using piecewise linear functions in x and y, and piecewise quadratic in z.

3.6.2 Prismatic Elements

Prismatic elements are constructed from a triangular base in two dimensions, with a straight-line extension in the third dimension. Figure 3.18 illustrates this type of element, assuming a piecewise linear function along the third dimension. Basis functions are formed by multiplying the piecewise planar (triangular) two-dimensional functional form by the one-dimensional piecewise polynomial along the third dimension. For example, if the triangle resides in the $x - y$ plane, and if the z-direction uses piecewise linear expansion, then $\phi_1(x, y, z)$ of Figure 3.18 is given by

$$\phi_1(x, y, z) = \left(\frac{z_2 - z}{z_2 - z_1} \right) \left(\frac{1}{2A^\Delta} \right) [(x_2 y_3 - x_3 y_2) + (y_2 - y_3)x + (x_3 - x_2)y] \quad (3.6.3)$$

where A^Δ is the area of the triangle. Other bases follow an analogous formulation.

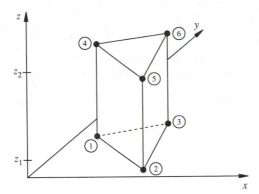

Figure 3.18 Typical prismatic element; piecewise planar in x and y, piecewise linear in z.

3.6.3 Tetrahedral Elements

Tetrahedral elements are composed of four nodes, any three of which defines a triangular face of the element. None of the four triangular faces needs to reside in a coordinate plane. Therefore, like triangular elements in two dimensions, tetrahedral elements allow arbitrary geometries to be represented in three dimensions. For the tetrahedral element of Figure 3.19, the relevant basis functions are hyperplanes defined by

$$\phi_i(x, y, z) = \gamma_1^i + \gamma_2^i x + \gamma_3^i y + \gamma_4^i z \tag{3.6.4}$$

subject to the usual constraints of

$$\phi_i(x_i, y_i, z_i) = 1$$
$$\phi_i(x_j, y_j, z_j) = 0, \qquad i \neq j$$

For an element composed of nodes numbered 1 through 4, the basis function associated with node 1 is of the form (3.6.4) with coefficients γ_k^1, $k = 1, 2, 3, 4$, defined by the following system of linear algebraic equations:

$$\begin{bmatrix} 1 & x_1 & y_1 & z_1 \\ 1 & x_2 & y_2 & z_2 \\ 1 & x_3 & y_3 & z_3 \\ 1 & x_4 & y_4 & z_4 \end{bmatrix} \begin{bmatrix} \gamma_1^1 \\ \gamma_2^1 \\ \gamma_3^1 \\ \gamma_4^1 \end{bmatrix} = \begin{bmatrix} 1 \\ 0 \\ 0 \\ 0 \end{bmatrix} \tag{3.6.5}$$

The solution of these equations is

$$\gamma_1^1 = \frac{1}{D}\{x_2(y_3 z_4 - y_4 z_3) - y_2(x_3 z_4 - x_4 z_3) + z_2(x_3 y_4 - x_4 y_3)\} \tag{3.6.6a}$$

$$\gamma_2^1 = \frac{-1}{D}\{(y_3 z_4 - y_4 z_3) - (y_2 z_4 - y_4 z_2) + (y_2 z_3 - y_3 z_2)\} \tag{3.6.6b}$$

$$\gamma_3^1 = \frac{1}{D}\{(x_3 z_4 - x_4 z_3) - (x_2 z_4 - x_4 z_2) + (x_2 z_3 - x_3 z_2)\} \tag{3.6.6c}$$

$$\gamma_4^1 = \frac{-1}{D}\{(x_3 y_4 - x_4 y_3) - (x_2 y_4 - x_4 y_2) + (x_2 y_3 - x_3 y_2)\} \qquad (3.6.6d)$$

where D is the determinant of the coefficient matrix of equation (3.6.5). The other three basis functions follow in an analogous way (see Problem 3.23).

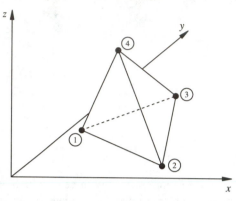

Figure 3.19   Typical tetrahedral element.

Combination of the element functions into global functions associated with each node results in piecewise hyperplane Lagrange polynomials. These bases maintain the standard Lagrange polynomial properties that $\phi_i(\mathbf{x}_i) = 1$ and $\phi_i(\mathbf{x}_j) = 0\,(i \neq j)$. In addition, ϕ_i is only nonzero over those elements to which node i belongs.

3.7 MATHEMATICAL PROPERTIES OF THE GALERKIN FINITE ELEMENT METHOD

Choice of weight functions in the Galerkin method of weighted residuals is the least intuitive of any of the MWR algorithms. However, as was stated in Section 3.1.2, strong mathematical arguments can be developed to accompany and justify this choice. This section presents some of these arguments, with several principal results given as theorems.

3.7.1 Best Approximation Property

The Galerkin finite element algorithm possesses a special minimization property for a certain class of differential equations. This section reviews the background needed to explain this property and then states the result as a fundamental theorem. The material utilizes general concepts of linear algebra, as developed in Appendix A.

To begin, recall the definitions of inner product and norm from Appendix A. Specifically, an inner product (Definition A.3.7) of two elements of a linear vector space, call them u and v, is a scalar quantity, denoted by $\langle u, v \rangle$, that satisfies the following three conditions:

1. $\langle u, u \rangle > 0$ for all $u \neq 0$

     $\langle 0, 0 \rangle = 0$

$$\qquad (3.7.1a)$$

2. $\langle u, v \rangle = \langle v, u \rangle$ (3.7.1b)

3. $\langle u, (\alpha v + \beta w) \rangle = \alpha \langle u, v \rangle + \beta \langle u, w \rangle,$ α, β scalar constants   (3.7.1c)

Conditions (3.7.1) must hold for all u, v, w in the vector space and for all scalars α and β. A measure of distance is introduced to the linear vector space by means of a norm (Definition A.3.9). The norm of u is a scalar function that is denoted by $\|u\|$. In any linear vector space for which an inner product is defined, a norm can always be defined from that inner product as

$$\|u\| \equiv \sqrt{\langle u, u \rangle} \tag{3.7.2}$$

For function spaces, the standard inner product is given by

$$\langle f(x), g(x) \rangle = \int_\Omega f(x) g(x)\, dx \tag{3.7.3}$$

The associated norm is the so-called L_2 *norm*, defined by

$$\|f(x)\| = \left[\int_\Omega f^2\, dx \right]^{1/2} \tag{3.7.4}$$

Two other concepts from linear algebra must also be reviewed. These relate to a general linear operator, call it $\mathcal{L}$, given in the general operator equation $\mathcal{L}u = f$. The linear operator is called *positive definite* (Definition A.3.12) whenever

$$\langle \mathcal{L}u, u \rangle > 0 \qquad \text{for all } u \neq 0 \tag{3.7.5}$$

where u resides in the domain of $\mathcal{L}$. In addition, $\mathcal{L}$ is called *self-adjoint* [Definition (A.3.13)] if the following inner product relationship holds:

$$\langle \mathcal{L}u, v \rangle = \langle u, \mathcal{L}v \rangle \tag{3.7.6}$$

Given this terminology and definitions, two fundamentally important theorems can be presented.

    Theorem 3.7.1. Every positive definite, self-adjoint linear operator $\mathcal{L}$, defined on an inner product space with inner product given by $\langle \cdot, \cdot \rangle$, gives rise to a second inner product, called the *energy inner product*, denoted by $\langle \cdot, \cdot \rangle_{\mathcal{L}}$ and defined by

$$\langle u, v \rangle_{\mathcal{L}} \equiv \langle \mathcal{L}u, v \rangle \tag{3.7.7}$$

Equation (3.7.7) holds for all elements u, v of the inner product space.

    A proof of this theorem is left as an exercise (Problem 3.17). The proof involves demonstration that the inner product $\langle \cdot, \cdot \rangle_{\mathcal{L}}$ satisfies the three criteria of equation (3.7.1).

    Energy inner products are the underlying inner product for the Galerkin finite element method. Replacement of u by U and v by ϕ_i in equation (3.7.7) makes the correspondence clear. The energy norm takes its name because the energy inner product corresponds to a measure of energy in many physical systems. Furthermore, the Galerkin finite element equations represent a minimization of this energy measure (e.g., potential energy of a system) for a certain class of physical problems.

An associated statement is that for a certain class of problems, the Galerkin finite element method minimizes the error committed in the numerical approximation when this error is measured in the energy norm. That is, given a trial space S_N from which an approximate solution, call it U, is sought, the Galerkin procedure leads to that special solution in S_N that minimizes the difference between the exact solution $u(x)$ and the approximate solution $U(x)$ when the difference is measured in the energy norm. The following theorem states this formally.

Theorem 3.7.2.   Consider the linear differential operator equation $\mathcal{L}u(\mathbf{x}) = f(\mathbf{x})$, $\mathbf{x} \in \Omega$, with $\mathcal{L}$ positive definite and self-adjoint. Let the inner product be defined by

$$\langle f(\mathbf{x}), g(\mathbf{x}) \rangle \equiv \int_\Omega f(\mathbf{x})g(\mathbf{x}) \, d\mathbf{x}$$

Let an approximate solution be sought from the finite-dimensional space S_N, which has associated basis functions $\{\phi_j\}_{j=1}^N$. Then for an approximation to $u(\mathbf{x})$ of the form

$$U(\mathbf{x}) = \sum_{j=1}^N U_j \phi_j(\mathbf{x}) \tag{3.7.8}$$

the Galerkin finite element algorithm for computing the coefficients $\{U_j\}_{j=1}^N$ minimizes the error $(u - U)$ under the energy norm

$$\|u - U\|_\mathcal{L} = \left[\langle (u - U), (u - U) \rangle_\mathcal{L} \right]^{1/2} \tag{3.7.9}$$

Proof. To begin, it is noted that $\|u - U\|_\mathcal{L}^2$ has a minimum at the same point as $\|u - U\|_\mathcal{L}$. Therefore, for convenience, let the squared measure be used in the search for the minimum point. By definition (3.7.7),

$$\|u - U\|_\mathcal{L}^2 = \langle \mathcal{L}(u - U), (u - U) \rangle$$
$$= \langle \mathcal{L}u, u \rangle - \langle \mathcal{L}U, u \rangle - \langle \mathcal{L}u, U \rangle + \langle \mathcal{L}U, U \rangle$$
$$= \langle \mathcal{L}u, u \rangle - 2\langle \mathcal{L}u, U \rangle + \langle \mathcal{L}U, U \rangle \tag{3.7.10}$$

In the second line of equation (3.7.10), the fundamental properties of inner products [equations (3.7.1b) and (3.7.1c)] are used, while in the third line, the self-adjoint nature of the operator $\mathcal{L}$ is used to equate and combine the two terms $\langle \mathcal{L}U, u \rangle$ and $\langle \mathcal{L}u, U \rangle$. Next, the functional form of U given in equation (3.7.8) is substituted into equation (3.7.10), so that

$$\|u - U\|_\mathcal{L}^2 = \langle \mathcal{L}u, u \rangle - 2 \left\langle \mathcal{L}u, \left(\sum_{j=1}^N U_j \phi_j \right) \right\rangle$$
$$+ \left\langle \mathcal{L}\left(\sum_{j=1}^N U_j \phi_j \right), \left(\sum_{k=1}^N U_k \phi_k \right) \right\rangle$$

$$= \langle \mathcal{L}u, u \rangle - 2 \sum_{j=1}^{N} U_j \langle \mathcal{L}u, \phi_j \rangle$$

$$+ \sum_{j=1}^{N} \sum_{k=1}^{N} U_j U_k \langle \mathcal{L}\phi_j, \phi_k \rangle \qquad (3.7.11)$$

The error measure $\|u - U\|_{\mathcal{L}}^2$ can be minimized with respect to the free coefficients U_j by choosing that set of values for which

$$\frac{\partial}{\partial U_i} \|u - U\|_{\mathcal{L}}^2 = 0 \qquad \text{for all free coefficients } U_i \qquad (3.7.12)$$

Differentiation of equation (3.7.11), as indicated by equation (3.7.12), leads to

$$\frac{\partial}{\partial U_i} \|u - U\|_{\mathcal{L}}^2 = -2 \langle \mathcal{L}u, \phi_i \rangle + 2 \sum_{j=1}^{N} U_j \langle \mathcal{L}\phi_j, \phi_i \rangle$$

$$= 0 \qquad (3.7.13)$$

Thus $\|u - U\|_{\mathcal{L}}^2$ is minimized when $\{U_j\}$ is chosen such that

$$\sum_{j=1}^{N} U_j \langle \mathcal{L}\phi_j, \phi_i \rangle = \langle f, \phi_i \rangle \qquad (3.7.14a)$$

or

$$\left\langle \mathcal{L} \left(\sum_{j=1}^{N} U_j \phi_j \right), \phi_i \right\rangle = \langle f, \phi_i \rangle \qquad (3.7.14b)$$

or finally,

$$\int_{\Omega} (\mathcal{L}U - f) \phi_i \, d\mathbf{x} = 0 \qquad (3.7.14c)$$

Equation (3.7.14c) is the Galerkin method of weighted residuals statement. Therefore, whenever $\mathcal{L}$ is both positive definite and self-adjoint, the Galerkin method produces a solution from the chosen trial space that minimizes the error $(u - U)$, measured in the energy norm. As such, the Galerkin solution can be viewed as a "best approximation."

3.7.2 Energy Methods and the Ritz Approximation

An alternative approach to the Galerkin method of weighted residuals formulation derives from theoretical results that exist for special classes of linear operators. The most widely used approach involves operators that are both positive definite and self-adjoint. For these systems, the analytical solution possesses certain minimization properties, such as minimum potential energy. Given this minimum property of the solution $u(\mathbf{x})$, a numerical approximation can be derived by forcing the approximate solution to obey an analogous minimum property. For a given trial space, the numerical solution is chosen as that element of the trial space that minimizes the relevant measure, for example potential energy. For a general expression of elements of the trial space of the form $U(x) = \sum_{j=1}^{N} U_j \phi_j(x)$, this minimization leads to algebraic equations for the coefficients $\{U_j\}_{j=1}^{N}$. Algorithms that use the property of minimization of potential energy to derive solutions are often called *energy methods*. The general principle on which energy methods are based is the minimum functional theorem (Mikhlin, 1964, p. 75). The theorem is restated as follows:

Theorem 3.7.3: Minimum Functional Theorem.   Consider the linear operator equation $\mathcal{L}u = f$, with $\mathcal{L}$ positive definite and self-adjoint, and domain $\mathcal{D}$, with $u \in \mathcal{D}$. Then of all values that are assumed by the quadratic functional $F(u)$, defined by

$$F(u) \equiv \langle \mathcal{L}u, u \rangle - 2\langle u, f \rangle$$

$$= \int_{\Omega} (\mathcal{L}u - 2f)u(\mathbf{x})\, d\mathbf{x} \tag{3.7.15}$$

by all possible choices of $u(\mathbf{x}) \in \mathcal{D}$, the least is the value given to this functional by the solution of the original differential equation $\mathcal{L}u = f$. That is, the solution of the differential equation $\mathcal{L}u = f$ coincides with the function $u(\mathbf{x})$ that minimizes $F(u)$.

To derive a numerical solution based on the minimization of equation (3.7.15), consider a choice of a finite-dimensional trial space, call it S_N, with definition of the associated trial function $U(\mathbf{x})$ in terms of a set of basis functions $\{\phi_j(\mathbf{x})\}_{j=1}^{N}$, that is,

$$U(\mathbf{x}) = \sum_{j=1}^{N} U_j \phi_j(\mathbf{x}) \tag{3.7.16}$$

Next form the functional $F(U)$, and minimize $F(U)$ with respect to all possible choices of trial functions $U \in S_N$. Because different functions $U(\mathbf{x}) \in S_N$ are defined by different choices of the coefficients $\{U_j\}_{j=1}^{N}$, this is equivalent to minimization with respect to all free coefficients $\{U_j\}$. Mathematically, this is stated as

$$\frac{\partial}{\partial U_i}(\langle \mathcal{L}U, U \rangle - 2\langle U, f \rangle) = 0 \tag{3.7.17}$$

Substitution of the trial function definition (3.7.16) into equation (3.7.17), and subsequent differentiation, produces

$$\frac{\partial}{\partial U_i}\left[\sum_{j=1}^{N}\sum_{k=1}^{N} U_j U_k \langle \mathcal{L}\phi_j, \phi_k \rangle - 2\sum_{j=1}^{N} U_j \langle \phi_j, f \rangle\right]$$

$$= 2\sum_{j=1}^{N} U_j \langle \mathcal{L}\phi_j, \phi_i \rangle - 2\langle f, \phi_i \rangle$$

$$= 0 \tag{3.7.18}$$

Thus the computational algorithm based on the minimum functional theorem leads directly to the Galerkin MWR algorithm, since equation (3.7.18) is identical to

$$\int_\Omega (\mathcal{L}U - f)\phi_i \, d\mathbf{x} = 0 \qquad (3.7.19)$$

which is the Galerkin statement.

The numerical approach derived from the minimum functional theorem is usually called the Ritz method, or the Rayleigh-Ritz method. Derivation of a Ritz approximation is dependent on the existence of a functional such as $F(u)$ of equation (3.7.15) that possesses minimum properties. This usually restricts Ritz methods to positive definite, self-adjoint operators.

3.7.3 Variational Methods, Weak Solutions, Orthogonality Properties

In general, when a solution to the differential equation $\mathcal{L}u = f$ corresponds to an extremum (usually minimum) of a related functional $F(u)$, use of the functional minimization to determine the solution is referred to as a *variational method*. The functional extremum equation is referred to as a *variational principle*. Problems 3.18, 3.19, and 3.20 provide examples of standard variational principles from the field of mechanics.

When variational principles exist, they not only lead directly to a Ritz approximation, but they can also provide additional physical insights into the physical system under investigation. Examples include Hamilton's principle of particle motion, and the more general statements of energy minimization. For many problems in solid mechanics (see Problems 3.18, 3.19, and 3.20), variational principles exist and concomitant Ritz approximations can be formulated. However, for many other physical systems, no variational principle exists; the associated Ritz approximation can therefore not be formulated. In contrast, the Galerkin method of weighted residuals can be applied to any differential equation, independent of the existence of a variational principle. Finlayson (1972) provides the following observations on Galerkin methods as compared to variational formulations,

> There is always a Galerkin method which is equivalent to the variational method .... The variational method cannot always be applied because there may be no variational principle for the problem, but the Galerkin method is always applicable because it does not depend on the existence of a variational principle. (p. 229)

> Many problems are not characterized by variational principles, others do not entail minimum or maximum principles, and the ones that are amenable to variational treatment are often classical problems or ones which have already been solved. (p. 211)

Because of the more general nature of the Galerkin method of weighted residuals, and because any variational method that does exist leads to a computational procedure that is identical to the Galerkin formulation, the Galerkin approach to derive finite element methods is preferred herein. The method of weighted residuals approach has the additional advantage of encompassing a family of numerical approximations, including collocation and subdomain methods. These methods do not arise naturally from variational formulations.

In addition to its equivalence to variational formulations, the Galerkin method can be seen as a search for a weak solution to the original differential equation. For an equation of the form $\mathcal{L}u = f$, a weak solution is one that satisfies the less stringent equation given by

$$\int_\Omega (\mathcal{L}u)w(\mathbf{x})\,d\mathbf{x} = \int_\Omega f(\mathbf{x})w(\mathbf{x})\,d\mathbf{x} \qquad (3.7.20)$$

where $w(\mathbf{x})$ is referred to as a *weight* or *test function*. The general idea of weak solutions is that equation (3.7.20) allows for a solution u with lower (or weaker) smoothness constraints (see Problem 3.21). The test function $w(\mathbf{x})$ should be chosen to be sufficiently smooth to allow meaningful integration by parts. In addition, $w(\mathbf{x})$ is required to satisfy the homogeneous version of the essential boundary conditions associated with the original governing equation. Let the set W encompass all test functions that possess required smoothness and satisfy the proper boundary conditions. In general, if equation (3.7.20) is satisfied for all $w(\mathbf{x}) \in W$, then the weak solution can be shown (see, e.g., Hughes, 1987) to be equivalent to the solution to the original differential equation (the so-called *strong solution*). Development of the Galerkin method from the point of view of a weak form of the governing differential equation proceeds by choosing a trial space S_N from which an approximation is sought and then choosing W to correspond to S_N. A finite number of test functions is then chosen, with each function corresponding to a basis function for S_N. As such, equation (3.7.20) is satisfied for all $w(\mathbf{x}) \in S_N$ (see Problem 3.22).

Finally, the Galerkin MWR equation

$$\int_\Omega (\mathcal{L}U - f)\phi_i\,d\mathbf{x} = 0 \qquad (3.7.21)$$

can be viewed as forcing the residual $(\mathcal{L}U - f)$ to be orthogonal (see Definition A.3.8) to each of the basis functions $\phi_i(\mathbf{x})$. If $\{\phi_i(\mathbf{x})\}$ are chosen to be members of a complete set, as they should be in light of the requirements of Section 3.4.1, then in the limit as $N \to \infty$, the residual becomes orthogonal to every member of a complete set. The only function that possesses this orthogonality property is the zero function. Thus the Galerkin method can be viewed as requiring the residual to be zero in an approximate sense by forcing $R(\mathbf{x})$ to be orthogonal to every function in the trial space. As the dimension of the trial space increases, the residual should be reduced and, in the limit of $N \to \infty$, $R(\mathbf{x}) \to 0$.

3.8 CONCLUSION

The general concepts of method of weighted residual approximations were presented, with an emphasis on subdomain, collocation, and especially Galerkin finite element methods. Specific formulations and computational procedures for the finite element methods were given. The mathematical properties of the method as well as alternative derivations were presented. Depending on the type of physical problem, one or another formulation may be most advantageous. For example, if the governing differential operator is both self-adjoint and positive definite, then a minimization principle exists and some physical insights may be gained by use of the minimum functional theorem. However, the resulting algebraic equations will be identical to those derived from the Galerkin formulation. Because the Galerkin formulation does not rely on a minimization principle, it is more general and is therefore the recommended approach.

The real advantage of finite element formulations compared to finite differences is their ability to effectively accommodate irregular geometries. This was seen in Section 3.5, where the finite element method was developed using triangular elements, as well as Section 3.6. Even more general geometries may be used in element definitions; the formulation and potential difficulties of more general finite elements are presented in Chapter 4.

PROBLEMS

3.1. Consider a piecewise linear polynomial defined over m subregions (with $N = m+1$ nodes). Prove that the functional form of this piecewise polynomial is given by equation (3.1.9) with the $\phi_j(x)$ defined by equation (3.1.10).

3.2. **(a)** Consider a piecewise quadratic polynomial defined on m subregions (with $N = 2m + 1$ nodes). Prove that the functional form of this piecewise polynomial is given by equation (3.1.11) with the $\phi_j(x)$ defined by equations (3.1.12).

(b) Next consider a piecewise nth-degree polynomial, defined on m subregions (with $N = nm + 1$ nodes). Define the piecewise Lagrange polynomials for this general case, and show that the piecewise nth degree Lagrange polynomials maintain the property that $\phi_j(x_j) = 1$, $\phi_j(x_i) = 0$, $i \neq j$. Prove that the expression for $U(x)$ given by equation (3.1.9) continues to apply. Sketch typical basis functions and show that the piecewise linear [equation (3.1.10), Figure 3.1] and piecewise quadratic [equation (3.1.12), Figure 3.2] cases are specific cases of this general formulation.

3.3. Consider piecewise quintic polynomials of continuity $\mathbb{C}^1[\Omega]$. Let three nodes be associated with each subregion, and derive the functional form for the Hermite quintic polynomials $\phi_{0j}(x)$, $\phi_{1j}(x)$ that arise in the following representation of the piecewise quintic polynomial,

$$U(x) = \sum_{j=1}^{N} U_j \phi_{0j}(x) + \frac{dU_j}{dx} \phi_{1j}(x)$$

Sketch the resulting functions. Compare these to the Hermite cubic functions of equations (3.1.14) and Figure 3.3.

3.4. Write the Galerkin finite element approximation for equation (3.1.21) using as a trial function a finite Fourier series, so that the basis functions over region $[0, \ell]$ are $\{\cos(k\pi x/\ell),$ $\sin(k\pi x/\ell)\}_{k=0}^{N}$. Discuss the possible merits of this approximation as compared to a Galerkin approximation that uses piecewise polynomial bases.

3.5. Consider the integrations of Example 3.1.

   (a) Sketch the three basis functions $\phi_1(x)$, $\phi_2(x)$, and $\phi_3(x)$, given the discretization of Figure 3.4.

   (b) Sketch the weight functions $w_2(x)$, $w_3(x)$.

   (c) Evaluate the integrals

$$\int_{\Omega_2} \left(\frac{d\phi_j}{dx} + \phi_j \right) dx, \qquad j = 1, 2, 3$$

Be sure to account properly for the fact that within $\Omega_2 \equiv [0.25, 0.75]$, the functions $\phi_j(x)$ have two different functional definitions. That is, $\phi_1(x) = (x_2 - x)/(x_2 - x_1) = (0.5 - x)/(0.5)$ for $0.25 \leq x \leq 0.5$ and $\phi_1(x) = 0$ for $x \geq 0.5$. Similar expressions pertain to $\phi_2(x)$ and $\phi_3(x)$. Through evaluation of the integral above, show that equation (3.1.19a) is correct.

   (d) Repeat part (c) for integration over Ω_3, and show that equation (3.1.19b) is correct.

3.6. **(a)** Derive the master integrals analogous to those of equations (3.3.4) for the case of piecewise quadratic Lagrange basis functions.

   (b) Solve the equation of Example 3.7 using a uniform discretization of five nodes with piecewise quadratic basis functions. Follow the computational procedure of Section 3.3.1, using the master element integration of part (a).

3.7. **(a)** Consider a discretization of four nodes, $\{x_1, x_2, x_3, x_4\}$, such that nodes x_1, x_2, and x_3 define a quadratic element, and x_3 and x_4 define a linear element. Define the associated piecewise Lagrange polynomial basis functions for each of the four nodes. Prove that both $\mathbb{C}^0[\Omega]$ continuity and the piecewise polynomial nature of the trial function are maintained. Show that the properties $\phi_j(x_j) = 1$ and $\phi_j(x_i) = 0$, $i \neq j$, are preserved.

   (b) Extend the analysis of part (a) to the case of two adjacent elements of degree n_1 and n_2, so that the left element has $n_1 + 1$ nodes and the right one has $n_2 + 1$ nodes, with one node common to both elements. Define and sketch the $(n_1 + n_2 + 2)$ basis functions.

3.8. **(a)** Design a computer code that builds a coefficient matrix based on the elementwise integration and master element concepts for a Galerkin method of weighted residuals approximation. Allow the algorithm to accommodate piecewise linear basis functions, piecewise quadratic basis functions, or a combination of the two. The latter option means that some elements may be linear, involving two nodes, while others may be quadratic, involving three nodes. Notice that elementwise integration allows the latter (mixed) case to be accommodated easily.

   (b) Write the computer code and solve equation (3.1.21) using a discretization of your choice.

3.9. Consider equation (3.1.21) with the modified boundary conditions

$$\left. \frac{du}{dx} \right|_{x=0} = 1, \qquad u(\ell) = 0$$

   (a) Write the appropriate Galerkin finite element approximating equations using piecewise linear bases on a discretization of N nodes.

   (b) Next consider a collocation approximation that uses piecewise cubic Hermite polynomials as a basis, defined on a discretization of N nodes. Because of the lack of integration in the collocation method and the concomitant higher continuity of basis function, all boundary condition types are imposed directly on the trial function. Since both U_j and

(dU_j/dx) are nodal coefficients, the boundary conditions are imposed as

$$\left.\frac{dU}{dx}\right|_{x=0} = \frac{dU_1}{dx} = 1$$

$$U(\ell) = U_N = 0$$

Show that the correct number of equations (2N) are generated by application of the collocation method, given these two boundary equations. Based on this treatment of second-type boundary conditions, explain how third-type boundary conditions are imposed in Hermite-collocation approximations. Write the system of collocation equations for the boundary conditions

$$\left.\frac{du}{dx}\right|_{x=0} = 1, \qquad \left.\left(\frac{du}{dx}+2u\right)\right|_{x=\ell} = 1$$

(c) Propose a computational procedure for a Galerkin finite element method that uses piecewise cubic Hermite bases. Be sure to properly impose boundary conditions, and be sure that the number of resulting algebraic equations is 2N.

3.10. Show that when $\phi_i \in \mathbb{C}^{-1}[0,\ell]$, equation (3.1.44) pertains as long as $U \in \mathbb{C}^1[0,\ell]$. Discuss the case of $U \in \mathbb{C}^0[0,\ell]$, $\phi_i \in \mathbb{C}^{-1}[0,\ell]$.

3.11. (a) Solve equation (3.1.21) using a Galerkin approximation with a piecewise linear trial space on the discretization of Figure 3.4, without using integration by parts. That is, equation (3.1.21) is to be used, and equation (3.1.44) is to be eschewed.

(b) Repeat part (a) using a piecewise quadratic trial space defined on a uniform discretization of five nodes.

3.12. Derive the master basis functions $\phi_i^M(x,y)$, $i = 1, 2, 3, 4$, for the piecewise bilinear case by imposing the nodal constraints of $\phi_i^M(\mathbf{x}_i) = 1$, $\phi_i^M(\mathbf{x}_j) = 0$, $i \neq j$, on the general functional form $\phi_i^M(x,y) = \gamma_1^i + (\gamma_2^i)x + (\gamma_3^i)y + (\gamma_4^i)xy$. Show that the function is identical to the product of one-dimensional bilinear functions.

3.13. (a) Derive the nine master basis functions for the master biquadratic element.

(b) Repeat part (a) for the case of product-type bicubic basis functions (in this case there are 16 functions per element).

(c) Derive the eight master basis functions for the master biquadratic serendipity element.

(d) Propose a set of serendipity basis functions for the cubic case. How many nodes appear on the interior of the element?

3.14. Consider a rectangular discretization with node k located at location (x_i, y_j). Assume that $x_i - x_{i-1} \neq x_{i+1} - x_i$, $y_j - y_{j-1} \neq y_{j+1} - y_j$, and that a piecewise bilinear expansion for $U(x,y)$ is defined on this rectangular grid. Evaluate the integral

$$\int_\Omega (\nabla^2 U)\phi_k(x,y)\,dx\,dy$$

in terms of nodal values of the trial function. Observe how the approximation changes when constant spacing is used (constant Δx, constant Δy, and finally, $\Delta x = \Delta y$). Derive order-of-approximation estimates using Taylor series analysis.

3.15. Develop the finite element equation associated with node 12 for the example problem of Section 3.5.2.

3.16. Write a computer code to solve the two-dimensional Poisson equation [equation (3.5.12)] using the Galerkin finite element method with piecewise bilinear elements on a rectangular discretization. Allow the code to incorporate an arbitrary number of first- and second-type boundary nodes. Write an analogous code that uses triangular elements. Use the latter code to solve equation (3.5.29) given the boundary conditions of Figure 3.15 and $f(x, y) = 0$.

3.17. Prove that the energy inner product defined by equation (3.7.7) is in fact a valid inner product. This provides a proof of Theorem 3.7.1 of Section 3.7.1.

3.18. A suspended cable, under a transverse loading P and normal loading $w(x)$, is illustrated in the accompanying figure. For small displacements $u(x)$, the governing equation is given by

$$P\frac{d^2u}{dx^2} = -w(x)$$

$$u(0) = 0$$

$$u(\ell) = 0$$

The solution to this equation also minimizes the potential energy, measured by the functional

$$F(u) \equiv \int_0^\ell \left[\frac{P}{2}\left(\frac{du}{dx}\right)^2 - wu \right] dx$$

Show that the Ritz approximation based on minimization of $F(U)$ yields the same set of approximating equations as the Galerkin method applied to the original differential equation.

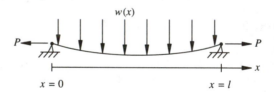

3.19. Small deflection of a beam on an elastic foundation is governed by

$$EI\frac{d^4u}{dx^4} = w(x) - Ku$$

where E is the modulus of elasticity, I is the second moment if inertia of the beam's cross section, $w(x)$ is the applied loading, K is the modulus of the foundation, and $u(x)$ is the beam deflection. A typical configuration is illustrated on the next page. The potential energy associated with this system is given by

$$F(u) \equiv \int_0^\ell \left[\frac{EI}{2}\left(\frac{d^2u}{dx^2}\right)^2 + \frac{K}{2}u^2 - wu \right] dx$$

This potential energy is the sum of the elastic strain energy of the beam, the elastic strain energy of the foundation, and the potential energy of the loading. Develop a Ritz approximation to this equation and compare it to the Galerkin formulation. What is the minimum continuity required for the trial space?

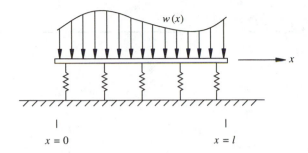

3.20. The Laplace equation is given by

$$\nabla^2 u = 0, \qquad \mathbf{x} \in \Omega$$

The solution to this equation coincides with the extremum point of the functional

$$F(u) \equiv \int_\Omega \left[\left(\frac{\partial u}{\partial x} \right)^2 + \left(\frac{\partial u}{\partial y} \right)^2 \right] dx\, dy$$

Formulate both the Ritz approximation and the Galerkin approximation. (Note that when u is temperature, so that the physical system is that of steady-state temperature distribution in a plate, there is no known physical principle that corresponds to the functional F. This is in contrast to the functionals of Problems 3.18 and 3.19, which were measures of energy in the physical system under consideration.)

3.21. Consider the linear differential operator equation

$$\frac{d^2 u}{dx^2} = f(x), \qquad 0 < x < \ell$$

$$u(0) = u(\ell) = 0$$

Assume that $f(x) \in \mathbb{C}^0[0, \ell]$. Show that a weak formulation of this equation can reduce the continuity requirement on $u(x)$ from $u(x) \in \mathbb{C}^2[0, \ell]$ to $u(x) \in \mathbb{C}^0[0, \ell]$.

3.22. Show that if equation (3.7.20) is satisfied for every $w(\mathbf{x}) = \phi_i(\mathbf{x})$, $i = 1, 2, \ldots, N$, with $\{\phi_j(\mathbf{x})\}_{j=1}^N$ a basis for S_N, then equation (3.7.20) holds for any $w(\mathbf{x}) \in S_N$.

3.23. Derive the four basis functions that correspond to the four nodes of a tetrahedral element. Observe the pattern of index change for each basis function and attempt to write a generally indexed functional form for ϕ_i analogous to the two-dimensional equation (3.5.25).

3.24. Derive a "serendipity" Hermite basis function family such that the trial function is of the form

$$U(x, y) = \sum_{j=1}^N U_j \phi_{00j}^s(x, y) + \frac{\partial U_j}{\partial x} \phi_{10j}^s(x, y) + \frac{\partial U_j}{\partial y} \phi_{01j}^s(x, y)$$

The basis functions must be such that the trial function satisfies the following constraints:

$$U(\mathbf{x}_j) = U_j, \qquad \frac{\partial U}{\partial x}(\mathbf{x}_j) = \frac{\partial U_j}{\partial x}, \qquad \frac{\partial U}{\partial y}(\mathbf{x}_j) = \frac{\partial U_j}{\partial y}$$

and maintains $\mathbb{C}^0[\Omega]$ continuity.

Chapter 4

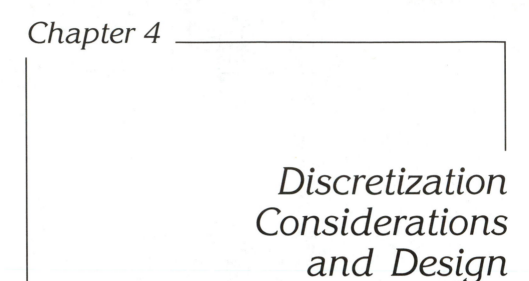

Discretization Considerations and Design of Approximations

4.0 INTRODUCTION

The first three chapters have provided background in fundamental concepts of partial differential equations and in finite difference and finite element methods. These concepts are essential to proper development and understanding of reliable numerical approximations for partial differential equations in science and engineering. Chapter 1 provided general descriptions of the physical processes that correspond to various equations, and provided mathematical analyses to relate the physical processes to the differential equations and the needed boundary conditions. Chapters 2 and 3 described the underlying ideas and fundamental mathematical developments for the two most standard approximation methods: the finite difference method and the method of weighted residuals with emphasis on finite element methods. In each of these chapters, simple model problems were solved to illustrate the basic procedures. In addition, expressions for truncation error were derived, and it was argued that a necessary requirement for an approximation to be acceptable is that the truncation error must go to zero as the grid spacing goes to zero. This is the concept of consistency.

However, for practical simulations, the grid spacing is almost never decreased arbitrarily toward zero. In fact, a very coarse grid may be chosen to perform a given simulation. It is therefore reasonable to ask how the concept of truncation error provides any information on the accuracy of the actual solution, since the grid spacing is finite and may in fact be quite large. Such a question was ignored in the previous chapters. The questions of how to design a grid, how to use truncation error analysis as an aid in such design, and how to devise methods to reduce discretization errors are discussed in this chapter and in the next chapter. This is done for both spatial discretizations and temporal discretizations.

In this chapter, truncation error analysis is used to explain general guidelines for grid design in both space and time. Some simple guidelines are presented for both selection of node placement and for the general design of numerical approximations. It is also shown that truncation error and consistency are not the only important considerations for time-marching algorithms; stability of the marching algorithm is also critical. Together, consistency and stability are shown to lead to convergence of the approximate solution to the correct (analytical) solution.

The chapter begins by considering the design of spatial discretizations. Simple design criteria are presented for one-dimensional problems based on combinations of truncation error analysis and knowledge of the underlying physical processes described by the governing differential equation. A particular example problem is analyzed to demonstrate the arguments. While this example is relatively simple, it illustrates more general guidelines for grid design in more complex systems. Truncation error analysis is also used to derive enhanced numerical approximations on both fixed and variable grids. In addition, a variety of multidimensional gridding procedures are presented for both regular and irregular geometries.

While many of the concepts developed for spatial grids also apply to the temporal domain, the additional concept of stability applies to time. Methods for analyzing stability of numerical approximations are presented, with emphasis on Fourier analysis. The Fourier analysis method is shown to be a powerful tool in that significant insight into solution behavior and accuracy can be gained, in addition to basic information about stability.

The material described above essentially treats the space and time domains as independent. The next section of the chapter demonstrates the importance of treating both space and time simultaneously when designing approximations. Because the design of "optimal" space-time grids and approximations is a difficult and very active area of ongoing research, the presentation of such design is kept to a brief introduction, with in-depth developments being beyond the scope of this book. Finally, the chapter concludes with a presentation of several methodologies that are alternatives to the standard finite difference and finite element methods. These provide evidence of the diversity of approximations available and demonstrate that knowledge of the basic principles presented earlier in this book allow many such alternative methods to be derived and understood.

4.1 SPATIAL DISCRETIZATION

Design of a reasonable spatial discretization requires an understanding of the underlying mathematics of the governing equation, the physical processes being described by that equation, and the numerical methods used to obtain the approximate solution. With such an understanding, general expectations concerning the behavior of the solution can be formulated. These expectations then influence the discretization chosen through combination with knowledge of the truncation errors. This section illustrates these general principles and ideas by analytically developing grid design criteria for some simple example problems. These examples yield results that can be used as design guides for a wide variety of practical problems. A variety of discretization types are developed and presented, ranging from simple rectangular grids to finite elements of irregular shapes, including elements with curved sides.

The presentation begins by looking at one-dimensional and rectangular two-dimensional grids applied to problems defined on simple (one-dimensional or rectangular two-dimensional) domains. Approximations based on node points arranged in regular but nonrectangular patterns are then discussed, followed by presentation of approximations on general, irregular grids. Both finite difference and finite element methods are used for the regular grids, while only finite element methods are presented for irregular grids.

4.1.1 Discretization Criteria for Approximations on Simple Domains

A simple domain is defined as one in which the boundaries align with the coordinate axes. All one-dimensional domains are defined as simple. In multidimensional Cartesian coordinates, a simple domain is one whose boundaries align with the x and y axes in two dimensions and the x, y, and z axes in three dimensions; in radial coordinates, boundaries must align with the r, θ, and z directions, and so on. The analyses presented in this subsection are restricted to problems defined on simple domains. In addition, only numerical approximations defined on simple grid patterns, that is, lattices of nodes that align with the coordinate axes, will be considered. In Cartesian coordinates, this implies a rectangular discretization; in radial coordinates, this implies a discretization that aligns with the r, θ, and z axes. In one dimension, all discretizations are classified as simple.

As a model problem, consider the one-dimensional diffusion equation in a nonhomogeneous medium, with diffusion coefficient $K(x)$ equal to $\alpha + \beta x$, that is,

$$\frac{d}{dx}\left[K(x)\frac{du}{dx}\right] = \frac{d}{dx}\left[(\alpha + \beta x)\frac{du}{dx}\right] = 0, \qquad 0 < x < \ell \tag{4.1.1}$$

$$u(0) = 0$$

$$u(\ell) = 1$$

The analytical solution to this equation is

$$u(x) = \frac{\ln\left(\dfrac{\alpha + \beta x}{\alpha}\right)}{\ln\left(\dfrac{\alpha + \beta \ell}{\alpha}\right)} = \frac{\ln(1 + \beta x/\alpha)}{\ln(1 + \beta \ell/\alpha)} \tag{4.1.2}$$

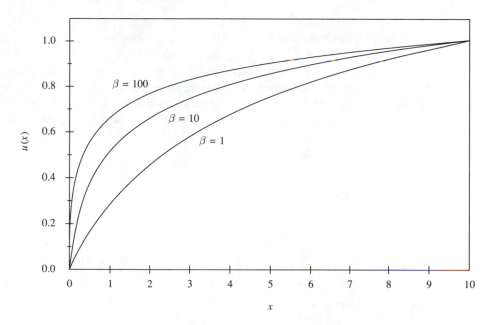

Figure 4.1   Solutions of equation (4.1.2) using $\alpha = 1$, $\ell = 10$.

Several solutions are plotted in Figure 4.1; these correspond to parameter values of $\ell = 10$, $\alpha = 1$, and $\beta = 1, 10, 100$. The solution is characterized by a region of rapid change that develops toward $x = 0$, becoming more pronounced as β increases.

A standard finite difference approximation to equation (4.1.1) is

$$\frac{d}{dx}\left[K(x)\frac{du}{dx}\right] \simeq \frac{K_{i+1/2}\dfrac{U_{i+1}-U_i}{\Delta x_i} - K_{i-1/2}\dfrac{U_i - U_{i-1}}{\nabla x_i}}{\delta x_i} = 0 \qquad (4.1.3a)$$

where $\Delta x_i \equiv x_{i+1} - x_i$, $\nabla x_i \equiv x_i - x_{i-1}$, $\delta x_i \equiv (\Delta x_i + \nabla x_i)/2$, $K_{i\pm 1/2} \equiv K(x_{i\pm 1/2})$, and $x_{i\pm 1/2} \equiv (x_i + x_{i\pm 1})/2$. These forward, backward, and central difference operators (Δ, ∇, and δ, respectively) are consistent with the definitions of difference operators presented in Chapter 2. A finite element approximation to equation (4.1.1), using a piecewise linear trial space, yields equation (4.1.3a) with $K_{i\pm 1/2}$ defined as the arithmetic average of K between x_i and $x_{i\pm 1}$:

$$\frac{\left[\dfrac{1}{\Delta x_i}\displaystyle\int_{x_i}^{x_{i+1}} K(x)\,dx\right]\dfrac{U_{i+1}-U_i}{\Delta x_i} - \left[\dfrac{1}{\nabla x_i}\displaystyle\int_{x_{i-1}}^{x_i} K(x)\,dx\right]\dfrac{U_i - U_{i-1}}{\nabla x_i}}{\delta x_i} = 0$$

$$(4.1.3b)$$

Because $K(x)$ is linear in equation (4.1.1), the integrals in equation (4.1.3b) are equal to $K_{i\pm 1/2}$ defined above. When $K(x)$ is not linear, use of a one-point (at $x = x_{i\pm 1/2}$)

integration rule still makes equation (4.1.3b) equivalent to (4.1.3a). Other rules give slightly modified approximations: for example, expansion of nodal values of K using piecewise linear interpolators results in the modified definition $K_{i\pm1/2} = (K_i + K_{i\pm1})/2$ (see Table B.10 for a list of other numerical integration schemes). Again, when $K(x)$ is linear in x, this modified definition becomes equal to the definition of $K_{i\pm1/2}$ in equation (4.1.3a). The difference formula (4.1.3a) will be used in the following analysis.

The truncation error associated with the approximation (4.1.3a) is (see Problem 4.2)

$$\text{T.E.} = \frac{1}{\delta x_i} \left\{ \left[\frac{(\Delta x_i)^2 - (\nabla x_i)^2}{8} \frac{d^2}{dx^2} \left(K \frac{du}{dx} \right) \right|_{x_i} \right. $$
$$+ \frac{(\Delta x_i)^3 + (\nabla x_i)^3}{48} \frac{d^3}{dx^3} \left(K \frac{du}{dx} \right) \Bigg|_{x_i} + \cdots \Bigg]$$
$$+ \left[\frac{(\Delta x_i)^2}{24} \left(K \frac{d^3u}{dx^3} \right) \right|_{x_{i+1/2}} - \frac{(\nabla x_i)^2}{24} \left(K \frac{d^3u}{dx^3} \right) \Bigg|_{x_{i-1/2}} + \cdots \Bigg] \right\} \quad (4.1.4)$$

Equation (4.1.4) indicates that the finite difference approximation (4.1.3) is generally first order. Only when $\Delta x_i = \nabla x_i$ does the truncation error become second order, reducing to the expansion

$$\text{T.E.} = \frac{(\Delta x)^2}{24} \frac{d^3}{dx^3} \left(K \frac{du}{dx} \right)\Bigg|_{x_i} + \frac{(\Delta x)^2}{24} \frac{d}{dx} \left(K \frac{d^3u}{dx^3} \right)\Bigg|_{x_i} + \text{H.O.T.} \quad (4.1.5)$$

where H.O.T. denotes higher-order terms.

Because equal spacing of nodes produces an approximation that is $\mathcal{O}((\Delta x)^2)$, constant spacing might seem to be the preferred strategy for generating the finite difference approximation. Use of this strategy results in the solution shown in Figure 4.2a for the case of $\alpha = 1$, $\beta = 10$, $\ell = 10$, and $\Delta x = 0.625$ (a 17-node discretization). Figure 4.2b illustrates the effect of changing the number of nodes in the discretization, always maintaining constant spacing. The figure shows a measure of solution error as a function of node spacing Δx. The error measure used is a discrete L_2 error norm, defined by

$$E_{L_2} \equiv \left[\Sigma_{i=1}^N (u_i - U_i)^2 \delta x_i \right]^{1/2} \equiv \|u_i - U_i\|_{(i,N)} \quad (4.1.6)$$

with $u_i \equiv u(x_i)$ denoting the exact solution at node i and U_i the corresponding finite difference approximation. The overall error behavior follows the truncation error estimate in that the slope of the curve approaches the theoretical value of 2 as the grid spacing Δx is decreased. The lower slope at greater values of Δx indicates that other truncation terms beyond the leading term are affecting the error in this range of Δx values. The idea of estimating the order of error by plotting error versus Δx is discussed further in Section 2.8 (see, e.g., Figure 2.9), in Problem 4.4, and in Chapter 5.

While this result is interesting, and the approximation is behaving as expected, much more can be gleaned from this simple example solution. For example, in Figure 4.3 nodal values of the error $|u_i - U_i|$ are plotted as a function of x location, x_i, for the

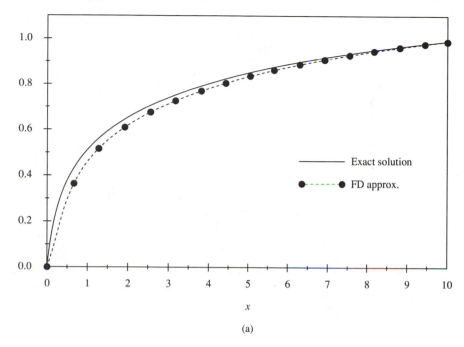

Figure 4.2   (a) Exact solution and finite difference approximation (constant node spacing $\Delta x = 0.625$) for equation (4.1.2) using $\alpha = 1$, $\ell = 10$, $\beta = 10$.

particular solution using $\ell = 10$, $\beta = 10$, and $\Delta x = 0.625$ (17 nodes). This figure shows that the largest errors occur at the left end of the domain, with progressively smaller errors as x increases. Upon reflection, this is not surprising because the logarithmic nature of the solution (Figure 4.1) causes more rapid changes in space as x decreases. Intuitively, for a given discretization with constant Δx, larger errors might be expected to occur in regions of rapid change in solution as compared to regions in which the solution is slowly varying because the discretization is unable to resolve regions of rapid change as effectively as regions of slow change.

This intuitive reasoning is reinforced by analytical evaluation of the truncation error. The leading term in the truncation error equation (4.1.5) is

$$\text{T.E.}_{\text{leading}} = \frac{(\Delta x)^2}{24} \frac{d}{dx}\left(K\frac{d^3 u}{dx^3}\right)\bigg|_{x_i} = \frac{(\Delta x)^2}{12} \frac{-4C\beta^4}{(\alpha + \beta x_i)^3} \tag{4.1.7}$$

where $C = 1/\ln(1 + \beta\ell/\alpha)$ and the expression $d^3/dx^3(K\,du/dx)$ in equation (4.1.5) is zero [because the governing equation is $d/dx(K\,du/dx) = 0$]. Equation (4.1.7) demonstrates that the leading truncation error term changes significantly from $x = 0$ to $x = \ell$. This corresponds to the fact that in regions where the solution changes rapidly, higher-order derivatives are correspondingly large. Therefore, to control truncation error, smaller Δx is required in these regions than in regions of slow change in the solution. In the latter regions, the higher-order derivatives will be small and larger values Δx are

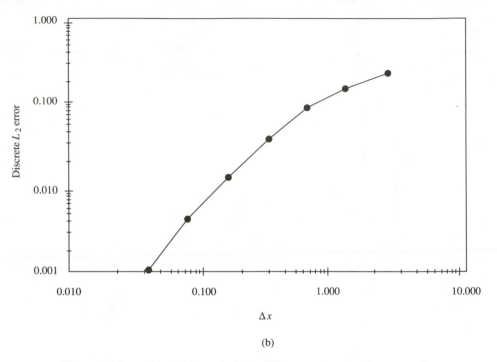

(b)

Figure 4.2 (cont'd.)   (b) Error in finite difference approximation versus (constant) node spacing Δx, using $\alpha = 1$, $\ell = 10$, $\beta = 10$.

admitted. This truncation error analysis confirms the intuitive arguments and leads to the following general rule for grid design: Finer resolution is required in regions of rapid changes of solution than in regions of slow changes. This basic observation is simple but in fact forms the conceptual basis for a variety of important concepts in grid design, such as adaptive grid refinement and general grid generation.

Examination of Figure 4.3 leads to the conjecture that use of variable grid spacing might achieve a more accurate solution than that using constant spacing, for the same number of nodes. For example, consider a grid of 17 nodes, with a geometric progression of node locations such that $\nabla x_i / \Delta x_i = \rho_i$ for all interior nodes x_i, with ρ_i constant. An arbitrary choice of $\rho_i = 0.7$ results in the solution shown in Figure 4.4. The E_{L_2} error associated with this solution is 1.66×10^{-3}, as compared to the E_{L_2} error of the constant spacing case, which is 8.66×10^{-2}. A significant improvement, of nearly two orders of magnitude, is achieved with the same number of nodes but with a more appropriate choice of grid. This is an example of a lower-order approximation producing a more accurate solution than a higher-order method when the same number of nodes is used. For solutions that exhibit regions of rapid change, lower-order methods often perform better that higher-order methods.

A natural next question is whether a different choice of grid, based on a different value of ρ or perhaps on a completely different strategy, might produce an even better

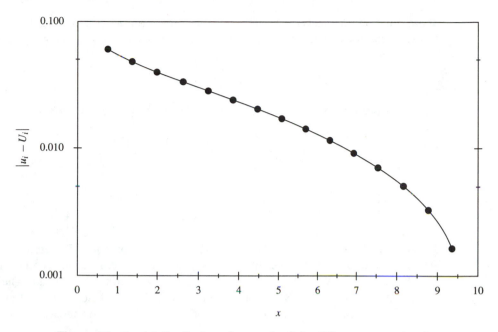

Figure 4.3   Spatial distribution of errors for finite difference approximation using $\Delta x = 0.625$, $\alpha = 1$, $\ell = 10$, $\beta = 10$.

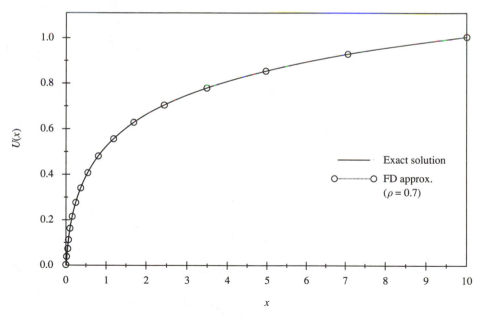

Figure 4.4   Finite difference approximation using 17 unequally spaced nodes with $\rho = \nabla x_i / \Delta x_i = 0.7$, $\alpha = 1$, $\ell = 10$, $\beta = 10$.

approximation. To answer this question, truncation error analysis may again be applied. Consider the truncation error of equation (4.1.4). Because the governing equation is

$$\frac{d}{dx}\left(K\frac{du}{dx} \right) = 0$$

all higher derivatives of $(K\,du/dx)$ are zero. Thus the truncation error is given by

$$\text{T.E.} = \frac{1}{\delta x_i}\left\{ \left[\frac{(\Delta x_i)^2}{24}\left(K\frac{d^3u}{dx^3} \right)\bigg|_{x_{i+1/2}} - \frac{(\nabla x_i)^2}{24}\left(K\frac{d^3u}{dx^3} \right)\bigg|_{x_{i-1/2}} \right] \right.$$
$$\left. + \left[\frac{2(\Delta x_i)^4}{2^5(5!)}\left(K\frac{d^5u}{dx^5} \right)\bigg|_{x_{i+1/2}} - \frac{2(\nabla x_i)^4}{2^5(5!)}\left(K\frac{d^5u}{dx^5} \right)\bigg|_{x_{i-1/2}} \right] + \cdots \right\} \qquad (4.1.8)$$

Because $d/dx[K(du/dx)] = 0$, $K(du/dx) = q = $ constant. Therefore, $du/dx = q/K(x)$, and higher derivatives of u can be calculated in terms of the coefficient $K(x)$. Let the ratio $\rho_i \equiv \nabla x_i/\Delta x_i$ be a free parameter that is to be determined. The leading error term in equation (4.1.8) can be set to zero by judicious choice of ρ_i. Differentiation of $q/K(x)$ twice and substitution into the leading error term [to replace $K(d^3u/dx^3)$] produces

$$\text{T.E.}_{\text{leading}} = \frac{1}{\delta x_i}\left\{ \frac{(\Delta x_i)^2}{24}q\left[\frac{2}{K^2}\left(\frac{dK}{dx} \right)^2 - \frac{1}{K}\frac{d^2K}{dx^2} \right]\bigg|_{x_{i+1/2}} \right.$$
$$\left. - \frac{(\nabla x_i)^2}{24}q\left[\frac{2}{K^2}\left(\frac{dK}{dx} \right)^2 - \frac{1}{K}\frac{d^2K}{dx^2} \right]\bigg|_{x_{i-1/2}} \right\}$$
$$= \frac{q}{24\delta x_i}\left[(\Delta x_i)^2\kappa_{i+1/2} - (\nabla x_i)^2\kappa_{i-1/2} \right] \qquad (4.1.9)$$

where

$$\kappa(x) \equiv K\frac{d^3u}{dx^3} = \frac{2}{K^2}\left(\frac{dK}{dx} \right)^2 - \frac{1}{K}\frac{d^2K}{dx^2}$$

This truncation error term is zero whenever

$$\rho_i \equiv \frac{\nabla x_i}{\Delta x_i} = \left(\frac{\kappa_{i+1/2}}{\kappa_{i-1/2}} \right)^{1/2} \qquad (4.1.10)$$

Notice that this rule is specific to the equation

$$\frac{d}{dx}\left[K(x)\frac{du}{dx} \right] = 0$$

but is not restricted to any particular form of the coefficient $K(x)$.

Now consider application of this rule to the example of equation (4.1.1). In that case, $K(x) = \alpha + \beta x$, so that $\kappa(x) = 2\beta^2/(\alpha + \beta x)^2$. Substitution of this expression for κ into equation (4.1.10) yields

$$\rho_i = \frac{\nabla x_i}{\Delta x_i} = \frac{\alpha + \beta x_{i-1/2}}{\alpha + \beta x_{i+1/2}} = \frac{\alpha + \beta(x_i - \nabla x_i/2)}{\alpha + \beta(x_i + \Delta x_i/2)}$$

Substitution of $\rho_i \Delta x_i$ for ∇x_i and subsequent rearrangement allows this expression to be written as

$$\rho_i = \frac{\nabla x_i}{\Delta x_i} = \frac{\alpha + \beta x_i}{\alpha + \beta x_{i+1}} \tag{4.1.11}$$

For this case of K being a linear function of x, the ratio $\rho_i = \nabla x_i/\Delta x_i$ is constant for all x_i and x_{i+1} (this can be shown by simple geometric arguments; see Problem 4.5). Therefore, nodal spacing in a constant geometric progression is dictated for this special case. In addition, for this simple model problem, choice of ρ_i given by equation (4.1.11) forces all other terms in the truncation error to zero (see Problem 4.6). Therefore, the finite difference approximation of equation (4.1.3), with the grid design rule (4.1.11), produces exact nodal values. This is true for any combinations of α, β, ℓ, and number of nodes. Finally, to design a grid with N nodes over $[0, \ell]$, with $K = \alpha + \beta x$, $x_1 = 0$, and $x_N = \ell$, a rule for generation of the optimal node locations is given by

$$\rho_{\text{opt}} = \left(1 - \frac{\beta\ell}{\alpha + \beta\ell}\right)^{1/(N-1)} \tag{4.1.12a}$$

$$\nabla x_N = \frac{1}{\beta}(\alpha + \beta\ell)(1 - \rho_{\text{opt}}) \tag{4.1.12b}$$

Details of the development of these equations are provided in Problem 4.7. That problem also explores the more general case when $K(x)$ is not linear.

Figure 4.5 illustrates the sensivity of the finite difference approximation to the parameter ρ. One important observation is that for the larger β values, a significant range of ρ values exists over which the approximation errors are at least one order of magnitude smaller that those for the constant node spacing case. Thus even when an exact rule such as (4.1.12) is unavailable, which is the usual case, choice of ρ based on some approximate rule will probably provide a significant improvement in solution. A second important observation is that the improvement of the variable spacing over the constant spacing increases as β increases. This is consistent with the previous analysis and the discussion of the behavior of the solution. A final important observation is that finite difference approximations that give exact nodal solutions can be derived for this problem. In general, any differential equation for which an analytical solution can be written using only a finite number of independent functions (i.e., for which the solution space is finite dimensional) has an associated finite difference approximation that produces exact nodal values.

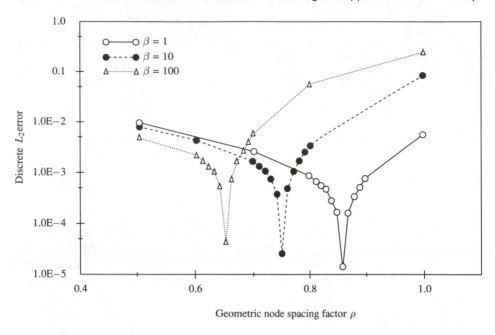

Figure 4.5   Errors in finite difference solutions versus ρ for $\alpha = 1$, $\ell = 10$.

While equation (4.1.1) is relatively simple, it serves to illustrate several fundamental concepts. These include:

1. A priori knowledge of actual solution behavior, even approximate knowledge, is very important in grid design. Thus knowledge of the underlying physical, chemical, and/or biological principles is required, as is understanding of the fundamental mathematical properties of differential equations presented in Chapter 1.

2. Truncation error analysis can be used to significant advantage. This is true in grid design as well as design of the overall numerical approximation.

3. Nonconstant grid spacing is more the rule than the exception for many practical applications. Thus the concepts of Chapter 2, especially Sections 2.4 and 2.7, must be well understood. Further concepts of nonconstant, irregular grid spacing will be discussed later in this section.

These general concepts carry over to problems in higher dimensions and to problems of significantly more complexity. The idealized one-dimensional problem presented above serves to illustrate the underlying concepts in a simple setting.

An example of some practical relevance is steady-state flow of mass or heat to a concentrated source or sink. An example of this type of system is underground flow of water to a pumping well. The governing equation in a homogeneous medium is the two-dimensional Laplace equation, which in radial coordinates is written as

$$\nabla^2 u = \frac{1}{r}\frac{d}{dr}\left(r\frac{du}{dr}\right) = 0, \qquad r_w < r < R \tag{4.1.13a}$$

$$2\pi r_w \left(\frac{du}{dr}\bigg|_{r_w}\right) = Q$$

$$u(R) = 0$$

where r_w is the radius of the well borehole for the groundwater system, or the radius of the extraction device for any other diffusive type of system, and Q is related to an extraction or injection rate. Equation (4.1.13a) may be written equivalently as

$$\frac{d}{dr'}\left[(r_w + r')\frac{du}{dr'}\right] = 0, \qquad 0 < r' < R' \tag{4.1.13b}$$

where $r' \equiv r - r_w$ and $R' \equiv R - r_w$. Equation (4.1.13b) is of the general form

$$\frac{d}{dx}\left[(\alpha + \beta x)\frac{du}{dx}\right] = 0, \qquad 0 < x < \ell \tag{4.1.14}$$

with $\alpha = r_w$, $\beta = 1$, and $r' = x$. Therefore, the analysis and results of the preceding section apply directly, with

$$\rho_{opt} = \frac{\alpha + \beta x_i}{\alpha + \beta x_{i+1}} = \frac{r_w + r'_i}{r_w + r'_{i+1}} \tag{4.1.15a}$$

For a domain of length ℓ with N nodes used in the discretization, the geometric spacing factor ρ_{opt} becomes

$$\rho_{opt} = \left(1 - \frac{\beta\ell}{\alpha + \beta\ell}\right)^{1/(N-1)} = \left(1 - \frac{R'}{r_w + R'}\right)^{1/(N-1)} \tag{4.1.15b}$$

The associated start-up value for the spacing, ∇x_N, is given by

$$\nabla x_N = \frac{\alpha + \beta\ell}{\beta}(1 - \rho_{opt}) = (r_w + R')(1 - \rho_{opt}) = \nabla r'_N \tag{4.1.15c}$$

These are the grid design equations for the equation (4.1.14).

For the one-dimensional system, application of equations (4.1.15) leads to an optimal grid with exact nodal values, $U_i = u_i$. In practice, the shape of the domain Ω dictates that simple radial coordinates used to write the Laplacian operator [equation (4.1.13)] cannot be used. This is because the boundaries of Ω virtually never coincide with a line of constant r value (Ω would need to be an annular region). Therefore, the governing Laplace equation is usually written in Cartesian coordinates, with the associated grid defined in Cartesian coordinates as well. Use of Cartesian coordinates usually precludes achievement of exact nodal values. However, the criteria of equations (4.1.15) still provide general guidance for grid design, leading to improved numerical solutions.

When the governing equation is written in Cartesian coordinates, and $r_w << R$, with R being a characteristic length from the source to the boundary of Ω, the effect of the concentrated source may be described by a Dirac delta function acting at the location of the source ($r = 0$). If the source is assumed to be centered at $x = 0$, $y = 0$, then the governing equation in Cartesian coordinates is

$$\nabla^2 u = \frac{\partial^2 u}{\partial x^2} + \frac{\partial^2 u}{\partial y^2} = Q\delta(\mathbf{x} - \mathbf{0}) \tag{4.1.16}$$

When this equation is solved analytically, the values of u that lie within $0 < r < r_w$ are ignored, as they are nonphysical (in fact, the solution is unbounded at $r = 0$ due to its logarithmic nature). Numerically, when working in Cartesian coordinates, a node is usually placed at the well location, and a numerical approximation is obtained at that point. This approximation is interpreted as the solution at the radial location r_w. In finite difference approximations, the equation written at this point must use a different right side in equation (4.1.16) to calculate the influence of the pumping well. This is because the finite difference approximation requires a point value of the right side function, and point values of the Dirac delta function are not meaningful. The usual approximation of the delta function, call it $f_\delta(x, y)$, is a $\mathbb{C}^{-1}[\Omega]$ function that is as compact as the grid will allow and maintains the correct volume of extraction, $\int_\Omega f_\delta dx\,dy = \int_\Omega Q\,\delta(\mathbf{x} - \mathbf{0})dx\,dy = Q$. The function $f_\delta(x, y)$ is usually defined as

$$f_\delta(x, y) = \begin{cases} \dfrac{Q}{\delta x_w \delta y_w}, & \left(x_w - \dfrac{\nabla x_w}{2}\right) < x < \left(x_w + \dfrac{\Delta x_w}{2}\right) \\ & \left(y_w - \dfrac{\nabla y_w}{2}\right) < y < \left(y_w + \dfrac{\Delta y_w}{2}\right) \\ 0, & \text{all other } (x, y) \in \Omega \end{cases} \tag{4.1.17}$$

where $(x_w, y_w) = (0, 0)$ is the location of both the concentrated source and node number w. Implementation of singularities into finite element approximations does not require any replacement of the delta function. This is due to the fact that finite element equations are based on integrations, and the delta function is well defined in this context (see Problem 4.8).

Consider solution of equation (4.1.16) with $\Omega = [-100, 100] \times [-100, 100]$, Dirichlet boundary conditions on all of $\partial\Omega$, and $Q = 10$. Since Ω lacks radial symmetry, the rules of equations (4.1.15) cannot be applied because the outer boundary distance R is not unique, and more important, a regular (rectangular) discretization in Cartesian space inherently lacks radial symmetry. Inspection of Figure 4.6 indicates that a reasonable strategy might be to use the lengths along the x and y coordinate axes to approximate the rules of equations (4.1.15). In this case, $\alpha = r_w$, $\beta = 1$, and $\ell = 100 - r_w$. For the 11×11 grid shown in Figure 4.6, N is equal to 6. Therefore,

$$\rho_{opt} \simeq \left(1 - \frac{100 - r_w}{100}\right)^{1/5} \tag{4.1.18}$$

If r_w is equal to 0.1, then $\rho_{opt} = 0.251$. Figure 4.7 shows finite difference approximations to $u(x, 0)$ versus x for the cases of constant grid spacing ($\rho = 1$), geometric spacing with $\rho = 0.5$ (this is a common choice for grid design), and geometric spacing with

$\rho = \rho_{opt} = 0.251$. The improvement associated with the near optimal spacing can be seen in the figure.

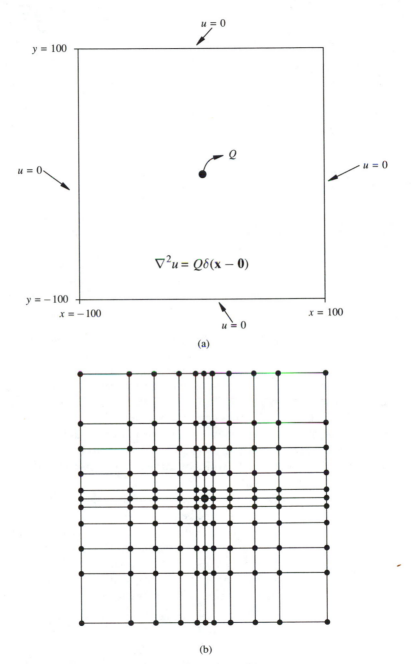

(a)

(b)

Figure 4.6   (a) Problem definition; (b) finite difference grid.

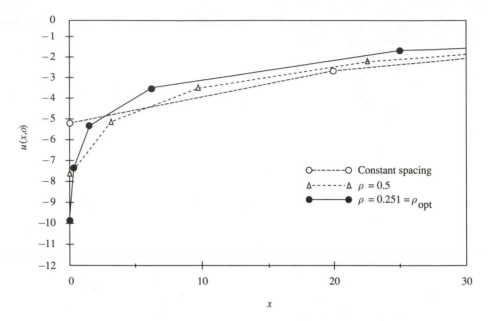

Figure 4.7   Finite difference solutions along x-axis for problem illustrated in Figure 4.6. Maximum drawdown for exact solution is approximately -11.

Notice that the length ℓ used to determine ρ_{opt} in this problem is not unique. For example, the diagonal ($45°$) line could also have been used to determine ρ. This results in a slight change in the numerical result. The point to be made is that the rules which arise from the analysis of the simple one-dimensional system can serve as guidelines for more complex problems. Later analysis will examine the influence of the time dimension and will extend the simple rules derived above to address combined space-time problems. The general principles discussed earlier will remain invariant in all of these analyses, and the importance of understanding the underlying physics and mathematics, as well as the ability to deal effectively with nonconstant node spacing and simple error analysis, will continue to be stressed.

A final point to be made in this section is that control of discretization errors through intelligent grid design is only one, albeit important, way to control errors. Another mechanism is judicious modification of the actual finite difference or finite element approximation. An example of this idea has already been presented in Section 2.6, where combination of truncation errors allowed for higher-order approximations to initial value problems. Similar concepts apply to other systems. For example, consider the one-dimensional, steady-state advection-diffusion equation,

$$V\frac{du}{dx} - D\frac{d^2u}{dx^2} = 0, \qquad 0 < x < \ell \tag{4.1.19}$$

subject to suitable boundary conditions. A general three-point finite difference approximation to this equation may be written as

$$V\left[\beta\frac{U_{i+1}-U_i}{\Delta x_i}+(1-\beta)\frac{U_i-U_{i-1}}{\nabla x_i}\right]$$

$$-D\frac{1}{\delta x_i}\left[\frac{1}{\Delta x_i}U_{i+1}-\left(\frac{1}{\Delta x_i}+\frac{1}{\nabla x_i}\right)U_i+\frac{1}{\nabla x_i}U_{i-1}\right]=0 \qquad (4.1.20)$$

where β is an arbitrary parameter. This approximation for the advection term corresponds to that of equation (2.4.8). As in the previous examples, this set of equations can be made to produce exact nodal values with proper choice of parameters. In this case, both the grid distortion factor $\rho\equiv\nabla x_i/\Delta x_i$ and the parameter β can be chosen to achieve exact results. For example, after truncation error expansions, coupled with the observation that $d^m u/dx^m=(V/D)^{m-1}(du/dx)$ (this follows from the governing equation), one set of (ρ,β) that produces exact values is $\rho=1$, $\beta=(1/\text{Pe})+(1/2)[1-\coth(\text{Pe}/2)]$, where Pe is the grid Peclet number, $\text{Pe}\equiv V(\Delta x)/D$, and coth denotes hyperbolic cotangent.

This criterion for β, given $\rho=1$, was first proposed by Allen and Southwell in 1955 (see Appendix C for the complete reference). It has since been used by many numerical modelers to approximate advection-diffusion processes, using both finite difference and finite element models. The finite element models use Petrov-Galerkin formulations, as discussed later in this chapter. This rule has generally been used as a guide for defining approximations in complicated linear and nonlinear systems in one and more dimensions, for both steady-state and transient problems. While details of the different uses of this simple rule are beyond the scope of the present work, the important point is that this is another example of a general rule, based on a simple model equation, that has widespread application. In addition, careful truncation error analysis (see Problems 4.10 and 4.11) shows that while the only combination of ρ and β that has been reported in the literature is that given above, a general family of (ρ,β) combinations may be defined which give exact solutions at the nodes.

The examples presented above attempt to use all possible information available, including that contained in the differential equation (e.g., to relate higher derivatives to one another in the truncation error terms), to understand numerical behavior and to derive improved approximations. The overall concept of error control and judicious choice of numerical approximations, including both the discretization and the actual approximating equations, will continue to be a focal point in this and the next chapter.

4.1.2 Approximations on Irregular Domains Using Regular Grids

Many practical problems are defined on domains that are irregular in shape. In these cases, the boundary of the domain does not align with the coordinate axes. This lack of alignment precludes analytical solution and makes numerical solutions somewhat more challenging. This section develops approximations to problems defined on irregular domains, using regular grids. A regular grid is defined as one in which nodal points are arranged in a fixed geometric pattern, or lattice. This includes both rectangular and nonrectangular lattices.

When designing grids for irregular domains, there are several key considerations that determine the suitability of a particular scheme. These can be stated by the following three general criteria:

1. The method should provide sufficiently accurate geometric definition of the irregular boundary. Determination of sufficiency should be based on the relative influence that boundary conditions have on the solution of interest.

2. The method should allow relatively easy implementation of boundary conditions. This consideration applies mostly to second- and third-type conditions, where proper imposition of normal flux conditions may become difficult.

3. The method should allow for systematic and efficient development of the discrete approximation equations. This applies to the development of approximating equations interior to the domain.

All of these criteria must be considered when designing a numerical approximation method for irregular domains. In fact, they should be considered when designing any approximation method, although approximations to equations defined on regular, simple domains, using grids defined on simple lattices, generally satisfy these constraints.

As Section 2.7 indicated, development of finite difference equations on general irregular grids is very complicated; therefore, finite differences on irregular grids might be expected to fail the third criterion. This is generally true, and it is rare to find finite difference approximations defined directly on irregular grids. However, finite difference methods have been used, with much success, to solve problems defined on irregular domains. This has been done by using grids of nodal points defined on regular lattices, both rectangular and nonrectangular.

Figure 4.8 shows an example of a numerical grid defined on a rectangular lattice that is used to approximate an irregular domain. In such a case, the boundaries are approximated as discrete steps that are restricted to the directions of the coordinate axes, in this case the x and y axes. In Figure 4.8, the actual domain Ω is bounded by the curved line, while the domain associated with the numerical approximation, call it $\hat{\Omega}$, is the union of the rectangular regions. This kind of approximation introduces the most error in definition of the boundary locations (excepting a simple rectangular domain $\hat{\Omega}$) of any of the methods to be considered. Because of this it is generally acceptable only in the cases where the influence of the boundary conditions is not dominant.

Imposition of boundary conditions along a stepped boundary such as that of Figure 4.8 can be achieved in a variety of ways. As an example, consider a second-order partial differential equation defined on Ω. For Dirichlet conditions, direct assignment of the boundary values to the appropriate boundary nodes is the usual treatment for both finite difference and finite element methods. This is consistent with the presentations in Chapters 2 and 3. For second- and third-type boundary conditions, the finite element method naturally accommodates the flux terms via the boundary integrals that arise from application of integration by parts (Green's theorem). Implementation of flux-type boundary conditions in finite difference approximations on stepped boundaries is somewhat more involved. The concept of imaginary nodes introduced in Chapter 2,

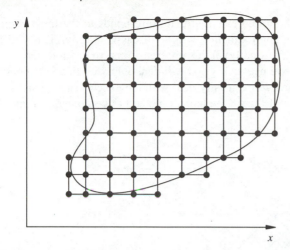

Figure 4.8 Finite difference grid used to approximate an irregular domain.

which essentially involves domain extension, needs to be used. This domain extension is analogous to that required for regular (rectangular) domains. Details of this procedure were presented in Section 2.5 and in Problem 2.10. When the boundary is stepped, the procedure is complicated only by the fact that a node on a convex-out (with respect to $\hat{\Omega}$) corner of the boundary requires an additional node in both the x and y directions, while a node on a concave-out corner requires no additional nodes. In both finite element and finite difference approximations, an underlying difficulty in stepped boundary approximations is that the actual normal direction of the boundary $\partial\Omega$ is poorly approximated by the normal to the numerical boundary $\partial\hat{\Omega}$. Because $\partial\hat{\Omega}$ can only have normals in the x or y directions, strategies need to be developed to impose the boundary fluxes properly. As stated previously, when boundary conditions, in this case flux conditions, are important to the solution of interest, rectangular grids may be inappropriate. This concept of boundary fluxes is explored further in Problem 4.12.

A significant advantage of rectangular discretizations such as that of Figure 4.8 is that the interior approximation equations are simple to derive. For the Laplace operator, for example, the standard five- or nine-point finite difference formulas [equation (2.7.25)], or the standard nine-point (piecewise bilinear) finite element approximation [equation (3.5.17)], can be used for all interior nodes. Thus the equation formulation step, which is usually an important computational consideration, is simple and efficient. Rectangular discretizations also allow certain matrix solution techniques (e.g., those based on approximate factorization such as alternating-direction methods) to be implemented efficiently. This again may be an important consideration.

To approximate more closely the domain boundary $\partial\Omega$, grids of node points may be used that do not form a rectangular lattice. In this way segments of the boundary that are not parallel to either the x or y axis may be better represented. As mentioned earlier, use of finite difference methods on arbitrary grids is very difficult, as the analysis of Section 2.7 indicates. Derivation of appropriate finite difference approximations can easily become overwhelming. However, regular, nonrectangular lattice patterns can be used in a consistent and systematic way to generate both finite difference and finite element approximations. A simple example that corresponds to the most common non-rectangular finite difference approximation will be discussed briefly. This will constitute the most complicated (geometrically) finite difference approximation derived here; all later developments on general irregular grids will deal only with finite elements, because systematic finite element procedures easily deal with the general case. This is one of the most significant advantages of the finite element method as compared to finite difference methods.

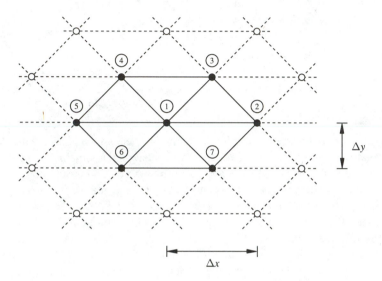

Figure 4.9   Triangular finite difference grid.

Consider the regular triangular lattice of nodal points depicted in Figure 4.9. The grid has associated with it three fundamental directions, as indicated in the figure. Thus the grid can better capture nonrectangular geometries. To derive a finite difference approximation for a second-order partial differential equation, the weak consistency constraints of Section 2.7 indicate that six node points are sufficient to define a weakly consistent approximation, although fewer may be acceptable, depending on the actual geometry. As an example, let the governing equation be the Poisson equation,

$$\nabla^2 u = f(x, y), \qquad (x, y) \in \Omega \qquad (4.1.21)$$

subject to suitable boundary conditions. For the grid of Figure 4.9, let the seven points indicated in the figure be used to approximate the Laplace operator. These nodes are numbered 1 through 7, with the Laplace operator evaluated at node 1. The appropriate finite difference approximation for the x-derivative is

$$\left.\frac{\partial^2 u}{\partial x^2}\right|_{x_1} \simeq \sum_{j=1}^{7} \Gamma_j U_j \qquad (4.1.22)$$

Equations (2.7.14) of Section 2.7 provide the criteria that the coefficients Γ_i must satisfy for the finite difference approximation to be weakly consistent. These constraints are

$$B_{0,0} = B_{0,1} = B_{1,0} = B_{1,1} = 0 \tag{4.1.23a}$$

$$B_{2,0} = 1 \tag{4.1.23b}$$

$$B_{0,2} = 0 \tag{4.1.23c}$$

where

$$B_{r,s} \equiv \sum_{j=1}^{7} \frac{(x_j - x_1)^r}{r!} \frac{(y_j - y_1)^s}{s!} \Gamma_j \tag{4.1.23d}$$

Expansion and solution of this set of six equations in the seven unknowns $\{\Gamma_i\}_{i=1}^{7}$ results in the following values: $\Gamma_1 = -2/(\Delta x)^2$, $\Gamma_2 = (1-\alpha)/(\Delta x)^2$, $\Gamma_3 = \Gamma_7 = \alpha/(\Delta x)^2$, $\Gamma_4 = \Gamma_6 = -\alpha/(\Delta x)^2$, and $\Gamma_5 = (1+\alpha)/(\Delta x)^2$, where α is an arbitrary constant. The approximation for $\partial^2 u/\partial x^2$ thus takes the following form:

$$\frac{\partial^2 u}{\partial x^2} \sim \frac{1}{(\Delta x)^2} \left\{ \begin{array}{ccc} & -\alpha & \alpha \\ 1+\alpha & -2 & 1-\alpha \\ & -\alpha & \alpha \end{array} \right\} \tag{4.1.24}$$

This equation shows the factors Γ_j for each of the seven nodes by writing each of these Γ_j at the respective location of node j. Because of the geometric regularity along the x-direction, the approximation of equation (4.1.24) is in fact strictly consistent (see Problem 4.13).

An analogous procedure for the approximation to $\partial^2 u/\partial y^2$ yields the following coefficient values:

$$\frac{\partial^2 u}{\partial y^2} \sim \frac{1}{(\Delta y)^2} \left\{ \begin{array}{ccc} & \beta & 1-\beta \\ \dfrac{1-4\beta}{4} & -\dfrac{3}{2} & \dfrac{4\beta-3}{4} \\ \beta & 1-\beta \end{array} \right\} \tag{4.1.25}$$

where β is an arbitrary constant. This approximation is weakly consistent and cannot be made strongly consistent using only these seven nodes. Finally, equations (4.1.24) and (4.1.25) can be combined to give the general finite difference approximation for the Laplacian operator

$$\nabla^2 u \sim \left\{ \begin{array}{ccc} & \left(\dfrac{-\alpha}{(\Delta x)^2} + \dfrac{\beta}{(\Delta y)^2}\right) & \left(\dfrac{\alpha}{(\Delta x)^2} + \dfrac{1-\beta}{(\Delta y)^2}\right) \\[2ex] \left(\dfrac{1+\alpha}{(\Delta x)^2} + \dfrac{1-4\beta}{4(\Delta y)^2}\right) & \left(\dfrac{-2}{(\Delta x)^2} + \dfrac{-3}{2(\Delta y)^2}\right) & \left(\dfrac{1-\alpha}{(\Delta x)^2} + \dfrac{4\beta-3}{4(\Delta y)^2}\right) \\[2ex] & \left(\dfrac{-\alpha}{(\Delta x)^2} + \dfrac{\beta}{(\Delta y)^2}\right) & \left(\dfrac{\alpha}{(\Delta x)^2} + \dfrac{1-\beta}{(\Delta y)^2}\right) \end{array} \right\} \tag{4.1.26}$$

A common grid design uses equilateral triangles, so that the angle between the x-axis and either of the diagonal lines is 60° (see Figure 4.9). In this case, $\Delta y = (\Delta x)\sin 60° = (\Delta x)(\sqrt{3})/2$, and $(\Delta y)^2 = 3(\Delta x)^2/4$. Assignment of the arbitrary parameters α and β so that $4\beta - 3\alpha = 2$ results in the following symmetric approximation for the Laplacian operator:

$$\nabla^2 u \sim \frac{1}{(\Delta x)^2} \left\{ \begin{array}{ccc} & \dfrac{2}{3} & \dfrac{2}{3} \\[2ex] \dfrac{2}{3} & -4 & \dfrac{2}{3} \\[2ex] \dfrac{2}{3} & \dfrac{2}{3} & \end{array} \right\} \tag{4.1.27}$$

While this result demonstrates the potential use of finite difference approximations on nonrectangular grids, the utility of these approximations appears to be limited. This is due to the inherent geometric limitations of regular grids, which are required for practical derivation of the finite difference approximations. The use of nonrectangular node patterns improves boundary flux approximation, so that regular but nonrectangular lattices may be a reasonable alternative for finite difference approximations on irregular domains. Another promising and very active area of current research involves transformation of the original irregular domain into a rectangular domain via a coordinate transformation. Finite difference approximations may then be defined on simple lattices of nodes. However, such treatment is sometimes geometrically (mathematically) difficult, and the governing equation is usually made significantly more complicated in the transformation process.

One of the major advantages of the finite element method compared to the finite difference method is the systematic treatment of fully irregular grids. It is at this point in the progression of geometric complexity that finite element methods supersede finite difference methods. The remaining discussion in this section and in the next section focuses on finite element approximations.

The finite element method can be applied to a linear triangular discretization of the grid of Figure 4.9. Use of the discretization of Figure 4.9 results in the following discrete approximation for the Laplace operator:

$$\nabla^2 u \sim$$

$$\left\{ \begin{array}{cccc} & \dfrac{1}{2(\Delta y)^2} & & \dfrac{1}{2(\Delta y)^2} \\[3ex] \dfrac{1}{(\Delta x)^2} - \dfrac{1}{4(\Delta y)^2} & & \dfrac{-2}{(\Delta x)^2} + \dfrac{-3}{2(\Delta y)^2} & & \dfrac{1}{(\Delta x)^2} - \dfrac{1}{4(\Delta y)^2} \\[3ex] & \dfrac{1}{2(\Delta y)^2} & & \dfrac{1}{2(\Delta y)^2} \end{array} \right\}$$

$$\tag{4.1.28}$$

This can be seen to be a subset of the finite difference formula (4.1.26) with parameters $\alpha = 0$, $\beta = 1/2$. With this choice of α and β, the finite difference approximation for $\nabla^2 u$ becomes equivalent to the finite element approximation. However, approximation of the right-side forcing function is different in that the finite difference method commonly uses the point value $f|_1$ while the finite element method uses the integrated value $(1/(\Delta x)(\Delta y)) \int_{\hat{\Omega}} f\phi_1 \, dx \, dy$ (although a one-point approximation to the integral can be made to yield the standard finite difference representation). In addition, the finite element formulation easily accommodates changes in the nodal locations as well as different patterns of connectivity. The finite difference approach does not exhibit such flexibility.

Before leaving this section, it is important to point out that irregular domain shape is not the only reason for desiring more flexibility in grid design. Consider the example of flow to a singularity that was presented in Section 4.1.1. The grid used in that example was rectangular with nonconstant node spacing, and the domain Ω was rectangular (see Figure 4.6). Because of the restriction to rectangular element geometries, the close x-direction spacing around the x-location of the singularity, $x = 0$, persists for all y; similarly, the y-spacing persists for all x. The result is the development of elements with large aspect ratios (ratio of largest side length to smallest side length) away from the origin along the coordinate axes. While in the extreme such increasing aspect ratios can cause computational problems due to excessive round-off errors, the more important observation is that the persistence of fine grid spacing away from the singularity is unnecessary. For problems with multiple singularities or with other localized features that require fine discretization, restriction to rectangular grids (or any other regular lattice pattern) imposes high grid resolution in regions that do not require it. Furthermore, this resolution is asymmetric and leads to adverse aspect ratios. Unless the grid is purposely chosen in a regular pattern to facilitate a special algorithm for solution of the resulting matrix equation (this is sometimes done for certain approximate factorization or "splitting" algorithms for matrix solution), restriction to a regular grid can significantly increase the computational burden with no improvement in solution accuracy and may even cause the accuracy to degenerate. Restriction to rectangular grids also precludes designs with radial symmetry. The error analysis of Section 4.1.1 indicates that such symmetry can be very advantageous for the case of flow to or from a concentrated source. For all of these reasons, the ability to design irregular grids on arbitrary geometries is important in numerical simulation.

4.1.3 Irregular Grids

Arrangements of nodal points that exhibit no geometric regularity are called *irregular grids*. When numerical approximations are sought on irregular grids, finite element methods are usually employed because they effectively accommodate irregular element and domain shapes. The overall finite element formulation on irregular grids is the same as that presented in Chapter 3. However, the complicated geometries inherent in irregular grids usually require additional effort to define basis functions and to evaluate the resulting integrals. This section presents the general approach for finite element approximations on irregular geometries. Different element shapes are considered, and a critical evaluation of different element types is included.

The simplest example of finite elements on irregular grids has already been presented: piecewise planar trial space defined on linear triangular elements. In fact, this will turn out to be an extremely attractive method for many problems of practical interest. There are also a variety of other finite elements that are inherently irregular in shape. These differ from the triangular elements in that basis functions cannot easily be defined in the x, y coordinate system. In addition, evaluation of the element integrals that arise in the finite element formulation may be difficult because simple formulas such as that of equation (3.5.28) for triangular elements are not readily available. However, by proper definition of a new coordinate system and a transformation, or mapping, that relates the original x, y space to this new system, both the basis function definition and the subsequent integration problem can readily be accomplished. The basic idea is to define the new coordinate system so that an element that is irregular in the x, y system is regular in the new coordinate system. The result is a systematic procedure that allows finite element approximations to be generated on a wide variety of irregular discretizations.

To illustrate the general procedure, consider an irregular grid on which four-node quadrilateral elements are defined, such as that depicted in Figure 4.10a. These quadrilateral elements are restricted only by the requirement that interior angles be less than 180° (the mathematical analysis that gives rise to this restriction will be explained below). The finite element formulation proceeds along the lines presented in Chapter 3: nodes are numbered and their locations recorded, an element incidence list is defined, the finite element approximating equations are derived, and elementwise integration is used to evaluate the resulting integrals. Because all finite element integrations are performed at the element level, the concept of a master element applies. The finite element integrals are evaluated in a general way on a typical ("master") element, and all elemental integrals are related to the master integrals. This master element concept applies equally well to the present case of irregular element shapes. Consider the general quadrilateral element depicted in Figure 4.10b, with four nodes with local node numbers 1, 2, 3, and 4. Definition of basis functions on this element is difficult because the sides of the element do not align with the coordinate axes. In fact, a simple bilinear function of x and y is generally not possible for this element, with more complicated functional forms difficult to derive.

To remedy this problem, consider a change of coordinate systems such that the irregular element in the x-y system becomes a simple element, say a square, in the new coordinate system. If such a coordinate system can be found and easily related to the original x-y system, then the formulation of basis functions could be performed in the new system and the functions could simply be mapped back to the x-y space. To this end, let a coordinate transformation, or coordinate mapping, be defined such that the four nodes of the element in x-y space are mapped to corresponding nodes in a new coordinate system. Let this new coordinate system be denoted by the coordinates ξ, η. In this new system, the four nodes are required to occupy the corners of a square, with coordinate values $(-1, -1)$, $(1, -1)$, $(1, 1)$, $(-1, 1)$ (see Figure 4.10c). The x-y space will be referred to as the *global space*, while the transformed space (ξ, η) is called the *local space*.

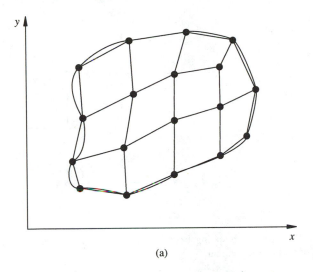

(a)

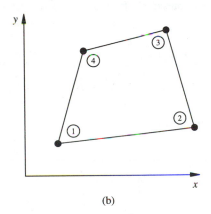

(b)

Figure 4.10 (a) Irregular (nonrectangular) grid of quadrilateral finite elements; (b) typical quadrilateral finite element.

A functional relationship is needed to relate these two coordinate systems. In this way, information derived in one system can readily be transferred to the other. Inspection of Figure 4.10c indicates that there are four constraints that can be imposed on such a coordinate map: the point (X_1, Y_1) should map to $(-1, -1)$, (X_2, Y_2) to $(1, -1)$, (X_3, Y_3) to $(1,1)$, and (X_4, Y_4) to $(-1, 1)$. These constraints may be written in compact form as: (X_i, Y_i) maps to (ξ_i, η_i). The latter notation serves to define the values of ξ_i and η_i $(i = 1, 2, 3, 4)$. A simple mapping to relate the two coordinate systems is a polynomial map. Given the four nodal constraints, the highest order complete polynomial expression that can be used to relate x and y to ξ and η is of the form

$$x(\xi, \eta) = \gamma_1 + \gamma_2 \xi + \gamma_3 \eta + \gamma_4 \xi \eta \qquad (4.1.29a)$$

$$y(\xi, \eta) = \beta_1 + \beta_2 \xi + \beta_3 \eta + \beta_4 \xi \eta \qquad (4.1.29b)$$

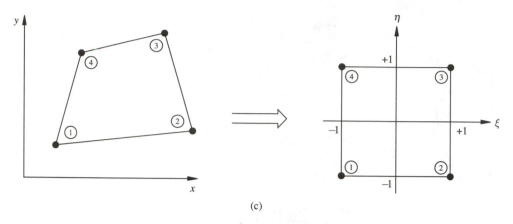

(c)

Figure 4.10 (cont'd.)   (c) Coordinate mapping between global (x, y) and local (ξ, η) coordinates for a typical quadrilateral element.

Solution for the coefficients β_i and γ_i, based on the four nodal constraints on x and y, produces

$$x(\xi, \eta) = \frac{1}{4}\left[(X_1 + X_2 + X_3 + X_4) + (X_1 - X_2 - X_3 + X_4)\xi \right.$$
$$\left. + (X_1 + X_2 - X_3 - X_4)\eta + (X_1 - X_2 + X_3 - X_4)\xi\eta\right]$$
$$= \sum_{i=1}^{4} X_i \left[\frac{1}{4}(1 + \xi\xi_i)(1 + \eta\eta_i)\right] \tag{4.1.30a}$$

$$y(\xi, \eta) = \sum_{i=1}^{4} Y_i \left[\frac{1}{4}(1 + \xi\xi_i)(1 + \eta\eta_i)\right] \tag{4.1.30b}$$

Equations (4.1.30) constitute a bilinear mapping that relates (x, y) to (ξ, η).

The coordinate transformation equations (4.1.30) allow information to be passed from one coordinate system to the other. Because the transformed element is square, functional definitions of basis functions are simple in the transformed space. The bilinear bases in the local coordinates follow directly from the definitions of equation (3.5.1) or (3.5.2), and are defined as

$$\phi_i(\xi, \eta) = \frac{1}{4}(1 + \xi\xi_i)(1 + \eta\eta_i), \qquad i = 1, 2, 3, 4 \tag{4.1.31}$$

where ξ_i and η_i are the ξ and η values, respectively, of node i. Given these definitions, the trial function can be defined within the element in the local space as

$$U(\xi, \eta) = \sum_{i=1}^{4} U_i \phi_i(\xi, \eta) \tag{4.1.32}$$

This functional form (and its appropriate derivatives) may now be used to define the integrands required in finite element formulations.

Notice that the basis functions of equation (4.1.31) are identical to those functions that appear in the coordinate transformation equations. Therefore, the coordinate transformation equations can be rewritten as

$$x(\xi, \eta) = \sum_{i=1}^{4} X_i \phi_i(\xi, \eta) \tag{4.1.33a}$$

$$y(\xi, \eta) = \sum_{i=1}^{4} Y_i \phi_i(\xi, \eta) \tag{4.1.33b}$$

Whenever the basis functions used in the trial function expansion are also used to define the coordinate mapping, the coordinate mapping is referred to as an *isoparametric coordinate transformation*. Thus equations (4.1.33) define a bilinear isoparametric coordinate transformation. When the functions defining the coordinate map are higher order than the trial function, the mapping is referred to as a *superparametric coordinate transformation*; when the functions in the map are lower order than the trial function, the mapping is referred to as a *subparametric coordinate transformation*. Examples of both super- and subparametric transformations are given below.

To demonstrate the application of a coordinate mapping in the context of the finite element method, consider solution of the model Poisson equation,

$$\nabla^2 u = f(x, y), \qquad (x, y) \in \Omega \tag{4.1.34}$$

subject to suitable boundary conditions. As stated above, the finite element formulation is the same as the formulations of Chapter 3, except that here the integral evaluation step is more involved. The Galerkin approach to finite elements can be followed to arrive at the integrals of interest. Substitution of the trial function $U(x, y)$ into equation (4.1.34), multiplication of the equation by a basis function ϕ_i and integration over $\hat{\Omega}$ (Ω is replaced by $\hat{\Omega}$ because the numerical domain does not in general coincide with the analytical domain) leads to

$$\int_{\hat{\Omega}} (\nabla^2 U) \phi_i \, d\mathbf{x} = \int_{\hat{\Omega}} f \phi_i \, d\mathbf{x} \tag{4.1.35}$$

Application of integration by parts (Green's theorem) leads to the following equation:

$$\int_{\partial \hat{\Omega}} (\nabla U \cdot \mathbf{n}) \phi_i \, ds - \int_{\hat{\Omega}} \nabla U \cdot \nabla \phi_i \, d\mathbf{x} = \int_{\hat{\Omega}} f \phi_i \, d\mathbf{x} \tag{4.1.36}$$

The domain integral can now be written as a simple sum of elemental integrals (the original integral required Dirac delta functions to be evaluated, as discussed in Chapter 3). Thus

$$\int_{\hat{\Omega}} \nabla U \cdot \nabla \phi_i \, d\mathbf{x} = \sum_{e=1}^{NE} \int_{\hat{\Omega}_e} \nabla U \cdot \nabla \phi_i \, d\mathbf{x} = \sum_{j=1}^{N} U_j \sum_{e=1}^{NE} \int_{\hat{\Omega}_e} \nabla \phi_j \cdot \nabla \phi_i \, d\mathbf{x} \tag{4.1.37}$$

where j denotes node number, e denotes element number, N is the total number of nodes, NE is the total number of elements, and $\hat{\Omega}_e$ denotes the region of $\hat{\Omega}$ occupied by element e. Given equations (4.1.36) and (4.1.37), the only remaining task is evaluation of the element integrals of equation (4.1.37).

The gradient operators in these integrals are defined with respect to x and y, since that is the coordinate system in which the governing equation is written. However, the elemental definitions of ϕ_i, and therefore U, are in terms of ξ and η. Therefore, some manipulation of the integrands is required. Because the basis functions are defined in the local space [equation (4.1.31)], and because the element shape is much more convenient in that space, the elemental integrals will be evaluated in the local space.

To illustrate the computational procedure, consider the element defined in Figure 4.10. Two relationships from calculus and analytical geometry are required to evaluate the integral of equation (4.1.37) over the element of Figure 4.10. The first is the chain rule of differentiation, which is applied to the gradient operator as follows:

$$\nabla \phi_j = \frac{\partial \phi_j}{\partial x} \iota_1 + \frac{\partial \phi_j}{\partial y} \iota_2$$

$$= \left(\frac{\partial \phi_j}{\partial \xi} \frac{\partial \xi}{\partial x} + \frac{\partial \phi_j}{\partial \eta} \frac{\partial \eta}{\partial x} \right) \iota_1 + \left(\frac{\partial \phi_j}{\partial \xi} \frac{\partial \xi}{\partial y} + \frac{\partial \phi_j}{\partial \eta} \frac{\partial \eta}{\partial y} \right) \iota_2$$

where ι_1 and ι_2 are unit vectors along the x and y directions, respectively. The second relationship involves the area (or volume) calculations in different coordinate systems and is stated by

$$dx\, dy = (\det \mathbf{J}) d\xi\, d\eta \qquad (4.1.38)$$

Equation (4.1.38) states that a differential element of area in global space, $dx\, dy$, is equal to a differential element of area in local space, $d\xi d\eta$, multiplied by the determinant of the Jacobian matrix $\mathbf{J}$ of the coordinate map. The Jacobian matrix is defined by

$$\mathbf{J} \equiv \begin{bmatrix} \dfrac{\partial x}{\partial \xi} & \dfrac{\partial y}{\partial \xi} \\[2ex] \dfrac{\partial x}{\partial \eta} & \dfrac{\partial y}{\partial \eta} \end{bmatrix} \qquad (4.1.39)$$

This matrix is important in any coordinate map because it provides a measure of relative length scales between the two coordinate systems. In addition, it provides a necessary criterion for a coordinate map or transformation to be well defined: The determinant of the Jacobian matrix must be nonzero at all points within the area being mapped, in this case the element being mapped. The determinant of the Jacobian matrix, $\det \mathbf{J}$, is often called simply the *Jacobian*.

Given equations (4.1.37) through (4.1.39), the finite element integral over the element of Figure 4.10 may be expressed as an integral over the transformed element as

$$\int_{\hat{\Omega}_e} (\nabla \phi_j \cdot \nabla \phi_i) dx\, dy$$

$$= \int_{-1}^{+1} \int_{-1}^{+1} \left\{ \left[\left(\frac{\partial \phi_j}{\partial \xi} \frac{\partial \xi}{\partial x} + \frac{\partial \phi_j}{\partial \eta} \frac{\partial \eta}{\partial x} \right) \iota_1 + \left(\frac{\partial \phi_j}{\partial \xi} \frac{\partial \xi}{\partial y} + \frac{\partial \phi_j}{\partial \eta} \frac{\partial \eta}{\partial y} \right) \iota_2 \right] \right.$$

$$\left. \cdot \left[\left(\frac{\partial \phi_i}{\partial \xi} \frac{\partial \xi}{\partial x} + \frac{\partial \phi_i}{\partial \eta} \frac{\partial \eta}{\partial x} \right) \iota_1 + \left(\frac{\partial \phi_i}{\partial \xi} \frac{\partial \xi}{\partial y} + \frac{\partial \phi_i}{\partial \eta} \frac{\partial \eta}{\partial y} \right) \iota_2 \right] \right\} (\det \mathbf{J})\, d\xi\, d\eta$$

$$= \int_{-1}^{+1} \int_{-1}^{+1} \left\{ \left[\left(\frac{\partial \phi_j}{\partial \xi} \frac{\partial \xi}{\partial x} + \frac{\partial \phi_j}{\partial \eta} \frac{\partial \eta}{\partial x} \right) \left(\frac{\partial \phi_i}{\partial \xi} \frac{\partial \xi}{\partial x} + \frac{\partial \phi_i}{\partial \eta} \frac{\partial \eta}{\partial x} \right) \right. \right.$$

$$\left. \left. + \left(\frac{\partial \phi_j}{\partial \xi} \frac{\partial \xi}{\partial y} + \frac{\partial \phi_j}{\partial \eta} \frac{\partial \eta}{\partial y} \right) \left(\frac{\partial \phi_i}{\partial \xi} \frac{\partial \xi}{\partial y} + \frac{\partial \phi_i}{\partial \eta} \frac{\partial \eta}{\partial y} \right) \right] \right\} (\det \mathbf{J})\, d\xi\, d\eta \qquad (4.1.40)$$

The final expression in equation (4.1.40) is significantly more complicated than the original expression on the left side appears to be. However, the integral needs still further expansion to allow it to be evaluated easily. Examination of (4.1.40) indicates that the derivatives of basis functions with respect to ξ and η can be readily evaluated via equation (4.1.31). However, the geometric derivatives $\partial \xi/\partial x$, $\partial \xi/\partial y$, $\partial \eta/\partial x$, and $\partial \eta/\partial y$ must be expressed in terms of the derivatives $\partial x/\partial \xi$, $\partial x/\partial \eta$, $\partial y/\partial \xi$, and $\partial y/\partial \eta$ because the coordinate transformation (4.1.30) is defined by $x(\xi, \eta)$ and $y(\xi, \eta)$, not by $\xi(x, y)$ and $\eta(x, y)$. The appropriate expressions for the coordinate derivatives are

$$\frac{\partial \xi}{\partial x} = \frac{1}{\det \mathbf{J}} \frac{\partial y}{\partial \eta} \qquad (4.1.41a)$$

$$\frac{\partial \xi}{\partial y} = \frac{-1}{\det \mathbf{J}} \frac{\partial y}{\partial \xi} \qquad (4.1.41b)$$

$$\frac{\partial \eta}{\partial x} = \frac{-1}{\det \mathbf{J}} \frac{\partial x}{\partial \eta} \qquad (4.1.41c)$$

$$\frac{\partial \eta}{\partial y} = \frac{1}{\det \mathbf{J}} \frac{\partial x}{\partial \xi} \qquad (4.1.41d)$$

Substitution of these relations into equation (4.1.40) allows the elemental integral $\int_{\hat{\Omega}} \nabla \phi_j \cdot \nabla \phi_i dx\, dy$ to be expressed in terms of known functions of the local coordinates ξ and η. Thus

$$\int_{\hat{\Omega}} \nabla \phi_j \cdot \nabla \phi_i \, dx\, dy = \int_{-1}^{+1} \int_{-1}^{+1} \left\{ \frac{\dfrac{\partial \phi_j}{\partial \xi} \dfrac{\partial y}{\partial \eta} - \dfrac{\partial \phi_j}{\partial \eta} \dfrac{\partial x}{\partial \eta}}{\det \mathbf{J}} \cdot \frac{\dfrac{\partial \phi_i}{\partial \xi} \dfrac{\partial y}{\partial \eta} - \dfrac{\partial \phi_j}{\partial \eta} \dfrac{\partial x}{\partial \eta}}{\det \mathbf{J}} \right.$$

$$\left. + \frac{-\dfrac{\partial \phi_j}{\partial \xi} \dfrac{\partial y}{\partial \xi} + \dfrac{\partial \phi_j}{\partial \eta} \dfrac{\partial x}{\partial \xi}}{\det \mathbf{J}} \cdot \frac{-\dfrac{\partial \phi_i}{\partial \xi} \dfrac{\partial y}{\partial \xi} + \dfrac{\partial \phi_i}{\partial \eta} \dfrac{\partial x}{\partial \xi}}{\det \mathbf{J}} \right\} (\det \mathbf{J})\, d\xi\, d\eta \qquad (4.1.42)$$

where, from equations (4.1.33),

$$\frac{\partial x}{\partial \xi} = \sum_{k=1}^{4} X_k \frac{\partial \phi_k}{\partial \xi} \qquad \frac{\partial x}{\partial \eta} = \sum_{k=1}^{4} X_k \frac{\partial \phi_k}{\partial \eta}$$

$$\frac{\partial y}{\partial \xi} = \sum_{k=1}^{4} Y_k \frac{\partial \phi_k}{\partial \xi} \qquad \frac{\partial y}{\partial \eta} = \sum_{k=1}^{4} Y_k \frac{\partial \phi_k}{\partial \eta}$$

While this integral is quite involved, all terms can be evaluated as functions of ξ and η. Thus the integral has been written in the general form $\int_{-1}^{+1} \int_{-1}^{+1} F(\xi, \eta) \, d\xi \, d\eta$, with F corresponding to the integrand of equation (4.1.42). For irregular elements, this integrand is a ratio of polynomials and is not easily evaluated analytically. For this reason numerical integration is used to approximate the integral of the form (4.1.42) over each element.

A wide variety of numerical integration algorithms can be used to approximate the integral (4.1.42). The most common choice in finite element analysis is Gaussian integration (also called Gauss-Legendre integration). In one dimension, Gauss-Legendre integration uses I discrete values of the integrand to approximate the integral. Judicious choice of the location of these points produces an $\mathcal{O}((\Delta x)^{2I})$ approximation to the integral. The general formula for Gaussian integration in one dimension is

$$\int_{-1}^{+1} F(\xi) d\xi = \sum_{k=1}^{I} W_k F(\xi_k) + R \tag{4.1.43}$$

where W_k is a scalar weight associated with the discrete point ξ_k, and R is an error term, $R \sim \mathcal{O}((\Delta x)^{2I})$. Table B.10 lists weights W_k and locations ξ_k for different values of I. Derivations of the expressions for the weights W_k and the locations ξ_k may be found in references listed in Appendix C.

In two dimensions, integrals of the form $\int_{-1}^{+1} \int_{-1}^{+1} F(\xi, \eta) d\xi d\eta$ are approximated using products of I_ξ points in ξ and I_η points in η, that is,

$$\int_{-1}^{+1} \int_{-1}^{+1} F(\xi, \eta) \, d\xi \, d\eta \simeq \sum_{k=1}^{I_\xi} \sum_{\ell=1}^{I_\eta} W_k W_\ell F(\xi_k, \eta_\ell) \tag{4.1.44}$$

In finite element methods I_ξ and I_η are usually chosen to be equal, although this is not necessary.

To demonstrate the evaluation procedure, consider the element depicted in Figure 4.11. For this element the isoparametric coordinate transformation equations are

$$x(\xi, \eta) = \sum_{i=1}^{4} X_i \phi_i(\xi, \eta) = \frac{1}{8}[7 + 5\xi - \eta + \xi\eta] \tag{4.1.45a}$$

$$y(\xi, \eta) = \sum_{i=1}^{4} Y_i \phi_i(\xi, \eta) = \frac{1}{4}[3 + 2\eta + \xi\eta] \tag{4.1.45b}$$

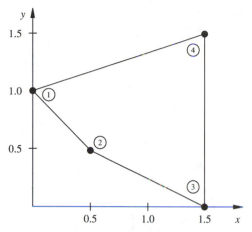

Figure 4.11 Quadrilateral element used to derive equation (4.1.45).

These expressions can be differentiated to give the geometric derivatives required in equation (4.1.42), from which the Jacobian is also calculated, $\det \mathbf{J} = (\partial x/\partial \xi)(\partial y/\partial \eta) - (\partial x/\partial \eta)(\partial y/\partial \xi)$. The basis functions $\phi_i(\xi, \eta)$ of equation (4.1.31) can also be readily differentiated. Therefore, all terms in equation (4.1.42) can be calculated. Choice of the number of Gauss points I_ξ and I_η and algebraic evaluation of the terms then yields the approximation to the desired integral.

For the integral corresponding to the element of Figure 4.11, with $j = 2$, $i = 1$, use of 1 integration point ($\xi = 0$, $\eta = 0$) yields an estimate to the integral of 0.2. Use of 2×2 Gaussian quadrature to estimate the integral gives 0.036, while 3×3 quadrature yields 0.026, which is the same as 4×4 integration. Therefore, in this case, a one-point estimate provides a poor approximation, with 3×3 integration being most appropriate.

In general, integrals become more difficult to evaluate, and therefore require more integration points, as the amount of distortion of the element increases. When the distortion becomes too severe, the integral can no longer be evaluated and the finite element approximation fails. For the linear quadrilateral elements used above, the distortion limit corresponds to interior angles of 180°. Whenever two sides (in global space) meet to form an interior angle of 180° or greater, the coordinate map becomes ill-defined and the Jacobian passes through zero within the element of interest. Of course, elements that approach the limit of 180° become progressively more poorly behaved, and high amounts of distortion should be avoided when designing irregular grids. Problems 4.14–4.16 address aspects of coordinate transformations, including the singular nature of transformations when the Jacobian vanishes and the limit of 180° cited above.

Higher-order finite element basis functions and coordinate transformations may also be defined. Higher-order bases generally give better accuracy, and higher-order transformations allow for elements with curved sides. As an example, consider the eight-node (serendipity) quadratic quadrilateral element of Figure 4.12. Three cases are shown in the figure: (a) an element with straight sides and with side nodes placed midway between corner nodes, (b) the same element but with side nodes offset from the midpoint of the element sides, and (c) an eight-node element with curved sides.

(a)

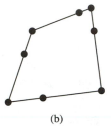

(b)

(c)

Figure 4.12 (a) Serendipity quadratic element with straight sides and side nodes placed midway between corner nodes; (b) serendipity quadratic element with straight sides; (c) serendipity quadratic element with curved sides.

Traditional isoparametric coordinate maps, analogous to those of equation (4.1.33), may be applied to this quadratic case. The transformation for each of these elements is of the same general isoparametric form:

$$x(\xi, \eta) = \sum_{j=1}^{8} X_j \phi_j(\xi, \eta) \qquad (4.1.46a)$$

$$y(\xi, \eta) = \sum_{j=1}^{8} Y_j \phi_j(\xi, \eta) \qquad (4.1.46b)$$

where the transformed quadratic element in local space is a 2×2 square with nodes equally spaced along each side. The eight basis functions in the local space can be obtained from the formulas for quadratic serendipity basis functions on rectangles presented in Table B.9. They are written in compact form here as

$$\phi_j(\xi, \eta) = -\frac{1}{4}(1 + \xi\xi_j)(1 + \eta\eta_j)(1 - \xi\xi_j - \eta\eta_j), \qquad j = 1, 2, 3, 4 \quad (4.1.47a)$$

$$\phi_j(\xi,\eta) = \frac{1}{2}(1-\xi^2)(1+\eta\eta_j), \qquad j = 5,7 \tag{4.1.47b}$$

$$\phi_j(\xi,\eta) = \frac{1}{2}(1-\eta^2)(1+\xi\xi_j), \qquad j = 6,8 \tag{4.1.47c}$$

Formulation of the finite element approximating equations proceeds in the standard way, with equation (4.1.42) used to evaluate the elemental integrals. In this case, there are eight nodes per element, so that, given the symmetry of the integrand, 36 integrals need to be evaluated per element. In addition, each evaluation involves significant computational effort because the coordinate derivatives in the integrand require eight terms to be summed instead of four in the bilinear case, and many more numerical integration points are likely to be required. Nonetheless, the finite element procedure remains systematic.

Other higher-order elements may also be defined. These include higher-order quadrilateral elements in both the serendipity and Lagrangian families. Higher-order triangular elements may also be defined, using both straight and curved sides. An example of a quadratic triangular element is given in Figure 4.13. When straight sides are maintained, such as the element of Figure 4.13, no coordinate transformation is required because definition can proceed easily in the global space. Higher-order basis functions on triangles can also be written very conveniently in terms of the linear functions derived in Section 3.5, assuming that the side nodes are placed at the midpoint of the respective side of the triangle. If $\Psi_j(x,y)$, $j = 1,2,3$, denotes the piecewise planar functions associated with the three-node linear triangular element, then the quadratic functions associated with the six nodes shown in Figure 4.13 can be written as

$$\phi_j(x,y) = \Psi_j(2\Psi_j - 1), \qquad j = 1,2,3 \quad \text{(corner nodes)}$$

$$\phi_j(x,y) = 4\Psi_{j-3}\Psi_{j-5}, \qquad j = 4,5,6 \quad \text{(side nodes with } \Psi_{-1} \equiv \Psi_2, \Psi_0 \equiv \Psi_3)$$

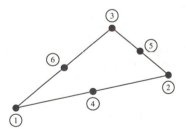

Figure 4.13   Quadratic triangular finite element.

Only when curved sides are present should a coordinate map be used for triangular elements, unless some special effect is desired, such as deliberate distortion of the trial function or singular behavior in the coordinate map. This type of behavior is discussed below.

Other higher-order elements include the Hermite family of interpolation functions. When $\mathbb{C}^1$-continuous Hermite polynomials are used as a basis for the trial space and nonrectangular elements are also used, then more care must be exercised in defining the coordinate map. In particular, because the trial function possesses continuity of both function and derivative, the mapping requires additional smoothness as well. In general, transformations must respect the smoothness of the trial space when moving between global and local coordinates. Several mappings have been proposed in the literature, and some of these are discussed in Problem 4.17.

It appears that finite element discretizations can be defined using almost any order of polynomial for the trial space and for the coordinate transformation. A requirement that must be imposed is that the elements be compatable in that the mapping maintains $\mathbb{C}^0$ continuity of trial functions (except for the Hermite case, which requires $\mathbb{C}^1$ continuity). The $\mathbb{C}^0$ continuity requirement is satisfied by all of the elements considered above. However, when using higher-order elements, other problems may arise, resulting in poor approximations. These have to do with the effect that the coordinate map itself has on the numerical solution. In particular, higher-order elements tend to impart more distortion to the coordinate map than lower-order maps. As discussed previously for the bilinear case, significant distortion away from rectangular can cause numerical difficulties in quadrilateral elements, eventually leading to degeneracy in the form of a zero Jacobian. In the bilinear case, simple geometric consideration (interior angles less than $180°$) were sufficient to provide an acceptable coordinate map. However, for higher-order elements, distortion problems are increased and other more stringent rules apply, at least to the conventional isoparametric transformations that are currently in widespread use. Therefore, while high-order elements with curved sides may appear to be very attractive, they must be used with care.

To illustrate the problem inherent in high-order coordinate maps, consider a simple example of a one-dimensional quadratic element. This element is composed of three nodes, located at X_1, X_2, X_3. Let the nodes be restricted only in that $X_1 < X_2 < X_3$. For this element, the one-dimensional quadratic isoparametric coordinate transformation is defined by

$$x(\xi) = \sum_{j=1}^{3} X_j \phi_j(\xi) \qquad (4.1.48)$$

A typical quadratic element is shown in Figure 4.14, as is the local coordinate system ξ with three nodes corresponding to $\xi_1 = -1$, $\xi_2 = 0$, and $\xi_3 = 1$. The appropriate basis functions in the local space are

$$\phi_1(\xi) = -\frac{1}{2}\xi(1 - \xi) \qquad (4.1.49a)$$

$$\phi_2(\xi) = 1 - \xi^2 \qquad (4.1.49b)$$

$$\phi_3(\xi) = \frac{1}{2}\xi(1 + \xi) \qquad (4.1.49c)$$

Substitution of equations (4.1.49) into (4.1.48) leads to the following general quadratic coordinate map:

$$x(\xi) = \frac{X_1 - 2X_2 + X_3}{2}\xi^2 + \frac{X_3 - X_1}{2}\xi + X_2 \qquad (4.1.50)$$

Figure 4.14 Quadratic finite element in global (x) and local (ξ) coordinates.

Notice that only when the nodes are spaced evenly in the global space is the coordinate map linear. The Jacobian of this transformation is computed as

$$\det \mathbf{J} = \det \left[\frac{dx}{d\xi} \right] = \frac{dx}{d\xi} = (X_3 - 2X_2 + X_1)\xi + \frac{X_3 - X_1}{2} \tag{4.1.51}$$

As a minimum constraint, the Jacobian must be nonzero for all $-1 \le \xi \le 1$. Examination of equation (4.1.51) leads to the conclusion that $dx/d\xi > 0$ for all $-1 \le \xi \le 1$ whenever

$$X_1 + \frac{X_3 - X_1}{4} < X_2 < X_3 - \frac{X_3 - X_1}{4} \tag{4.1.52}$$

This equation requires that the interior node in the quadratic element be within the middle half of the element (between one-fourth and three-fourths of the distance from X_1 to X_3) for the isoparametric coordinate transformation (4.1.48) to be well defined. This defines the limit of acceptable distortion introduced by unequal node spacing within an element. The actual length of the element is unrestricted, as is the ratio of adjacent element lengths.

Avoidance of a singular coordinate transformation does not necessarily eliminate distortion problems. For example, consider finite element solution of the one-dimensional Poisson equation

$$\frac{d^2 u}{dx^2} = -2, \qquad 0 < x < 2 \tag{4.1.53}$$

$$u(0) = 0$$

$$u(2) = 0$$

using one quadratic finite element with $X_1 = 0$, $X_3 = 2$, and X_2 as yet unspecified. Let the finite element calculation be done using the isoparametric coordinate transformation of equation (4.1.50). The finite element equation associated with node 2 is then

$$\sum_{j=1}^{3} U_j \int_{-1}^{+1} \left(\frac{d\phi_j}{d\xi} \frac{d\xi}{dx} \right) \left(\frac{d\phi_2}{d\xi} \frac{d\xi}{dx} \right) (\det \mathbf{J}) \, d\xi = \int_{-1}^{+1} (-2)\phi_2 \, d\xi \tag{4.1.54}$$

Use of equations (4.1.49), (4.1.50), and (4.1.51) allows equation (4.1.54) to be solved for U_2. Figure 4.15 shows solutions $U(x)$ for different choices of X_2. As X_2 moves

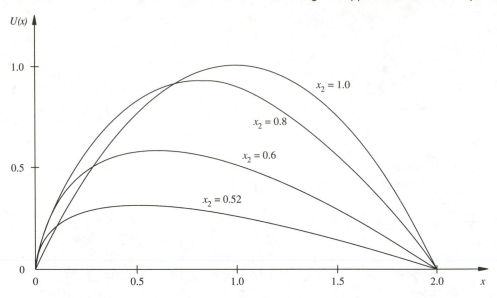

Figure 4.15 Finite element solutions to equation (4.1.53) using one quadratic
finite element, illustrated in Figure 4.14, with $x_1 = 0$, $x_3 = 2$, x_2 as indi-
cated above. (From M. A. Celia and W. G. Gray, "An Improved Isoparametric
Transformation for Finite Element Analysis," *Int. J. for Numerical Methods in
Engineering*, 20, 1443–1459, 1984. Reprinted by permission of John Wiley
& Sons, Ltd.)

away from the center of the element, the solution progressively deteriorates, while for
$X_2 = 1.0$ (element center), the finite element solution reproduces the exact solution.
The error in the finite element solutions is due entirely to the isoparametric coordinate
transformation.

Solution of the example problem directly in global space, without use of a coordinate map, reproduces the exact solution for all $X_1 < X_2 < X_3$. This demonstrates the
potential problems with the isoparametric coordinate transformation. It also points out
the following important rule: Unless there is a special reason for wanting distortion or
singular behavior in the numerical solution, or the one-dimensional domain is actually
a curved line, a nonlinear coordinate transformation should not be used when solving
one-dimensional problems.

The reason for the distortion problem in the quadratic example presented above is
the nonlinear nature of the isoparametric coordinate transformation. If a simple linear
(subparametric) mapping were to be used, with

$$x(\xi) = \frac{X_3 - X_1}{2}\xi + \frac{X_1 + X_3}{2} \tag{4.1.55}$$

all distortion problems would disappear. Alternatively, a modified quadratic transformation can also be defined to eliminate the distortion problem. The revised quadratic
map is based on modification of the prescribed nodal locations in the local space. The

new node locations are at $\xi_1 = -1$, $\xi_2 = \alpha$, and $\xi_3 = 1$, with α to be determined (see Figure 4.16). The basis functions in local space now have the following definitions:

$$\phi_1(\xi; \alpha) = \frac{(1 - \xi)(\alpha - \xi)}{2(1 + \alpha)} \tag{4.1.56a}$$

$$\phi_2(\xi; \alpha) = \frac{1 - \xi^2}{1 - \alpha^2} \tag{4.1.56b}$$

$$\phi_3(\xi; \alpha) = \frac{(1 + \xi)(\xi - \alpha)}{2(1 - \alpha)} \tag{4.1.56c}$$

where the notation implies that ϕ_j is a function of the independent variable ξ and the parameter α. The isoparametric coordinate transformation associated with these functions now takes the form

$$x(\xi) = \sum_{j=1}^{3} X_j \phi_j(\xi; \alpha) = \left[\frac{X_1}{2(1 + \alpha)} - \frac{X_2}{1 - \alpha^2} + \frac{X_3}{2(1 - \alpha)} \right] \xi^2 + \frac{X_3 - X_1}{2} \xi$$

$$+ \left[\frac{\alpha X_1}{2(1 + \alpha)} + \frac{X_2}{1 - \alpha^2} - \frac{\alpha X_3}{2(1 - \alpha)} \right] \tag{4.1.57}$$

This transformation can be made linear by setting the coefficient of ξ^2 to zero, resulting in the rule

$$\alpha \equiv \frac{\nabla X_2 - \Delta X_2}{\nabla X_2 + \Delta X_2} \tag{4.1.58}$$

where $\nabla X_2 \equiv X_2 - X_1$ and $\Delta X_2 \equiv X_3 - X_2$. This rule states that the nodes in global and local coordinates should be in the same relative positions, so that if X_2 is offset from the center of the global element, $\xi_2 = \alpha$ will be offset from its center in the same proportion. Use of rule (4.1.58) in equation (4.1.57) yields

$$x(\xi) = \frac{X_3 - X_1}{2} \xi + \frac{X_3 + X_1}{2} \tag{4.1.59}$$

This is the linear map of equation (4.1.55), which is known to completely eliminate the distortion problems and to produce exact results for all $X_1 < X_2 < X_3$.

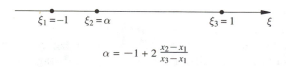

$$\alpha = -1 + 2\frac{x_2 - x_1}{x_3 - x_1}$$

Figure 4.16   Quadratic finite element with modified nodal location in local space.

The idea of unequally spaced nodes in the local space has been applied to two-dimensional quadratic elements, as discussed in Problem 4.18. The procedure applies to arbitrary quadratic elements with curved sides. Example calculations have shown that errors due to distortion are significantly reduced, and zero Jacobians that result from inappropriate node placement along element sides are effectively eliminated. An analogous development has also been presented for Lagrange cubic elements.

The important point in all of this analysis is that linear coordinate transformations should be used whenever possible. The only reason for using nonlinear coordinate transformations should be to map curved elements, unless the distortion or singular nature of higher-order maps is to be used to some special advantage. An example of such use is the deliberate generation of numerical singularities to model the physical singularity of, for example, a fracture in a continuous solid body.

Even when elements are chosen to have curved sides, the actual location of the curves in global space is not known a priori. A curved element side drawn onto a piece of paper (or a computer screen) during the grid design stage will almost never correspond to the actual location computed by the coordinate map, although it is usually close. This is because the coordinate map imparts a parametric representation of the curved sides which is not easily predicted. This problem is also avoided by use of elements with straight sides, since straight lines remain straight in both coordinate systems.

While high-order basis functions are easily accommodated in finite element methods, element geometries should be restricted to those with straight sides whenever possible. Linear coordinate transformations should then be used on the elements, unless solution distortion is desired. If nonlinear coordinate transformations are used, care must be taken to avoid singular maps and excessive distortion. This can be done by using the modified coordinate transformation presented above in which nodes in the local space are spaced unequally, in proportion to their associated global locations. This eliminates many of the zero Jacobian problems and greatly reduces distortion. If a standard isoparametric coordinate transformation is used, with equal spacing of nodes in the local space, then as a minimum the Jacobian should be evaluated at all corner nodes of an element and the values checked for a sign change. A change in sign indicates a zero Jacobian within the element, which means that the element must be redesigned.

4.2 TEMPORAL DISCRETIZATION

The time dimension is fundamentally different from the spatial dimensions in that the time domain is open ended and information can only propagate forward. Thus approximations to time derivatives must be inherently one-sided, always looking to the past for information to predict the future. Future information cannot propagate back in time to affect solutions at past times. Therefore, problems involving the time dimension are always initial value problems in time. Numerical algorithms that propagate information forward in time are called *time-marching* or *time-stepping algorithms*.

The analyses presented in Section 4.1.1 to derive simple guidelines for spatial grid design may be applied to time-marching algorithms as well. Thus Taylor series, coupled with some expectation of solution behavior, can provide insights into algorithm design and choice of time step size. Much of the underlying development and analysis of time-stepping methods has already been presented in Section 2.6. In that section, several general classes of time-marching algorithms were derived using combinations of Taylor series analysis and manipulation of the governing equation. The latter manipulation allowed truncation errors from different terms in the governing equation to be combined and canceled. Such procedures were also used in Section 4.1.1, for example in expressing derivatives of u as functions of the coefficient K and its derivatives [see equation (4.1.9)].

However, to consider only truncation error when designing time-marching algorithms is not sufficient. As illustrated in Sections 2.5 and 2.6, time-marching algorithms can also exhibit unstable behavior, characterized by unbounded growth of the finite difference solution as time increases. Consistent finite difference approximations, of any order, may be unstable. Therefore, when designing and analyzing time-marching algorithms, both consistency (order of accuracy) and stability must be considered. This section discusses both accuracy and stability, with emphasis on the latter. It concludes with presentation of the fundamental result that satisfaction of both consistency and stability leads to a convergent numerical approximation.

4.2.1 Choice of Time Step: Stability and Accuracy

Choice of time step size for a given time-stepping algorithm is dictated by accuracy considerations and stability constraints. Analysis of accuracy can be approached using Taylor series expansions in the ways presented in Sections 2.6 and 4.1. For example, it is known from the analytical solution of simple model problems that for first-order equations in time of the form

$$\frac{du}{dt} + Ku = 0 \tag{4.2.1a}$$

the solution is of the form $u \sim \exp(-Kt)$. Similar behavior is observed for systems of equations of the form of equation (4.2.1a), that is,

$$\frac{d\mathbf{u}}{dt} + \mathbf{A} \cdot \mathbf{u} = \mathbf{0} \tag{4.2.1b}$$

In the latter case, the solution is a linear combination of functions of the form $\exp(-\lambda_i t)$, where $\{\lambda_i\}$ are appropriate eigenvalues (see Appendix A, Section A.4). Whenever K in equation (4.2.1a), or the λ_i associated with equation (4.2.1b), are positive real numbers, the magnitude of the solution decreases with increasing time. This decay in the solution affects the truncation error terms, which are typically of the form

$$\frac{(\Delta t)^p}{(p+m)!} \left. \frac{d^{p+m}u}{dt^{p+m}} \right|_{t^n} \tag{4.2.2}$$

If $u \sim \exp(-Kt)$, then all derivatives of u also decrease exponentially in time. Thus the truncation error decreases as time increases, for a fixed time step Δt. This means that progressively larger time steps might be taken as time increases, because the derivatives in expression (4.2.2) are decreasing.

The strategy of using progressively larger time steps is often adopted for semidiscrete approximations to transient diffusion equations, in which the diffusive (second-order space derivative) process dominates any other lower-order spatial derivatives. For the pure diffusion case (no other spatial derivatives present in the governing equation), the eigenvalues associated with the semidiscrete approximation are usually real, and the above analysis applies. A typical algorithm is to increase Δt by a constant factor, so that $\Delta t^{n+1} = C \Delta t^n$. The multiplicative factor C is usually chosen to be between 1.0 and 1.2. Notice that this is analogous to the approach used for spatial discretization when the general solution behavior was known a priori, such as in the logarithm solution of Section 4.1.1.

The analysis presented above can be influenced by the nature of specified boundary conditions and the presence of right-side forcing functions. As Problem 4.19 points out, whenever boundary conditions or forcing functions are time variable, their specific forms need to be accounted for in the analysis. A more important consideration in problems such as equation (4.2.1b) is the case of complex eigenvalues. These generally lead to both dissipative and translational behavior in the solution. The dissipative nature results from the real component of λ_i and conforms to the analysis described above. The imaginary component of λ_i requires additional analysis. Such an analysis is presented in Section 4.2.3.

The important point to be made here in these introductory remarks is that the underlying idea of using information about the solution behavior to design grids applies to the temporal dimension as well as the spatial dimensions. However, because time and space are inherently different, other considerations arise in time-marching algorithms, in particular stability considerations. Thus additional tools and methods of analysis must be examined that allow understanding and prediction of stability behavior.

Stability can be formally defined by the constraint that the difference between the numerical and analytical solutions must remain bounded for all time. That is, for any finite time step size,

$$\|U^n - u^n\| < C$$

where U^n denoted the numerical approximation at time level n, u^n is the exact solution evaluated at $t = t^n$, and C is a finite-valued constant. For stable physical systems, u remains bounded. Therefore, the numerical stability constraint for stable physical systems may be restated as requiring the numerical solution U^n to remain bounded for arbitrarily large n. Because only stable physical systems are to be considered, the latter definition of stability will be used.

To demonstrate the analysis of stability, consider the simple linear initial value problem,

$$\frac{du}{dt} = -u, \qquad t > t^0 \qquad (4.2.3)$$

$$u(t^0) = U^0$$

In Section 2.6, general classes of approximations for initial value problems were presented. Any of these methods may be applied to equation (4.2.3). As a first example, consider the variably weighted, one-step Euler method, given by

$$\frac{U^{n+1} - U^n}{\Delta t} = -[\theta U^{n+1} + (1 - \theta)U^n]$$

This approximation is $\mathcal{O}((1 - 2\theta)\Delta t, (\Delta t)^2)$ (i.e., first order for all θ except $\theta = 0.5$, for which the approximation is second order). Example 2.9 of Section 2.5 presented solutions for the case of $\theta = 0$ (forward Euler) that demonstrated a stability bound of $0 \leq \Delta t \leq 2$. A similar analysis may be applied to the general weighted Euler approximation.

There are several ways to approach the question of stability. The first is to observe that for one-step approximations, U^{n+1} can be related to U^n by a multiplicative factor, call it λ. This factor depends on the time step size Δt and is constant for approximations to constant-coefficient linear equations that use constant time step size. In the case of the variably weighted Euler approximation,

$$U^{n+1} = \frac{1 - (1 - \theta)(\Delta t)}{1 + \theta(\Delta t)}U^n = \lambda U^n \tag{4.2.4}$$

Stability dictates that the approximate solution not grow without bound as time increases. By successive substitution for U^n in equation (4.2.4), U^{n+1} can be directly related to the initial condition by

$$U^{n+1} = (\lambda)^{n+1}U^0 \tag{4.2.5}$$

Examination of equation (4.2.5) indicates that λ serves to continually amplify the initial value if $|\lambda| > 1$, continually decrease the magnitude of the initial value if $|\lambda| < 1$, or maintain the magnitude of U^0 if $|\lambda| = 1$. The factor λ is therefore called the *amplification factor* associated with this numerical approximation. Because the solution grows without bound whenever the amplification factor is greater than 1, while it remains bounded when λ is less than or equal to 1, the condition for stability is

$$|\lambda| \leq 1 \quad \text{(stability)} \tag{4.2.6}$$

The case of $|\lambda| = 1$ is referred to as *neutral stability* because the magnitude of the solution neither grows nor decays. Notice that the magnitudes, and not the signs, of U^n and λ are the important factors. A numerical scheme can be stable with λ positive or negative as long as $|\lambda| \leq 1$. In addition, if λ is imaginary, it is the modulus (magnitude) of λ that dictates stability with $|\lambda| \leq 1$ again being the stability constraint.

Application of condition (4.2.6) to the variably weighted Euler approximation leads to

$$\left| \frac{1 - (1 - \theta)(\Delta t)}{1 + \theta(\Delta t)} \right| \leq 1 \tag{4.2.7a}$$

or,

$$-1 \leq \frac{1 - (1 - \theta)(\Delta t)}{1 + \theta(\Delta t)} \leq 1 \tag{4.2.7b}$$

If θ is restricted to $0 \leq \theta \leq 1$, then the positive bound in equation (4.2.7b) is always satisfied. The negative bound is respected whenever Δt satisfies the condition

$$(\Delta t)(1 - 2\theta) \leq 2 \tag{4.2.8}$$

Therefore, whenever $\theta \geq 0.5$, the variably weighted Euler approximation is stable for any value of Δt. When $0 \leq \theta < 0.5$, Δt is constrained by $\Delta t \leq 2/(1 - 2\theta)$. The $\theta = 0$ case corresponds to the forward Euler stability bound presented in Section 2.5.

When no stability constraint exists for a time-marching algorithm, the method is said to be *unconditionally stable*. When Δt is constrained to be less than a specified (positive) value for stability to be achieved, the approximation is called *conditionally stable*. If no stable solution exists for any positive value of Δt, the approximation is called *unconditionally unstable*. Thus the variably weighted Euler method is conditionally stable when $\theta < 0.5$, and is unconditionally stable when $\theta \geq 0.5$.

Any one-step method applied to a linear equation, using constant Δt, can be written in the form of equation (4.2.5). For these methods, $|\lambda| \leq 1$ is the stability constraint.

Next, consider a two-step approximation to equation (4.2.1), for example the two-step implicit Gear method presented in Section 2.6,

$$\frac{3U^{n+1} - 4U^n + U^{n-1}}{2(\Delta t)} = -U^{n+1} \tag{4.2.9}$$

As with all two-step methods, a start-up procedure is required for the first time level. Let the backward Euler method be applied for this start-up. Equation (4.2.9) is then applied for all $n \geq 1$, with $U^1 = U^0/(1 + \Delta t)$ and U^0 given.

In this case, a numerical amplification factor such that $U^{n+1} = \lambda U^n$ may again be sought. Assuming existence of such an amplification factor, $U^n = \lambda U^{n-1}$ and $U^{n+1} = \lambda U^n = \lambda^2 U^{n-1}$. Therefore, equation (4.2.9) may be rewritten in terms of λ as

$$[(3 + 2\Delta t)\lambda^2 - 4\lambda + 1]U^{n-1} = 0 \tag{4.2.10}$$

To avoid the trivial solution $U^{n-1} = 0$, the coefficient $(3 + 2\Delta t)\lambda^2 - 4\lambda + 1$ must be set to zero. This provides the equation for λ, namely

$$(3 + 2\Delta t)\lambda^2 - 4\lambda + 1 = 0 \tag{4.2.11}$$

This equation is of the general quadratic form

$$\alpha_2\lambda^2 + \alpha_1\lambda + \alpha_0 = 0 \tag{4.2.12}$$

which has two solutions (or roots), call them λ_1 and λ_2. Assume for now that these roots are distinct. Then these two solutions may be used to write the solution of the finite difference equations at any time level n in the following form,

$$U^n = C_1(\lambda_1)^n + C_2(\lambda_2)^n \tag{4.2.13}$$

where C_1 and C_2 are constants that are related to the two values provided, in this case U^0 (from the initial condition) and U^1 (from the start-up algorithm). Because each λ_i is raised to the power n, stability dictates that each λ_i must have magnitude no greater than 1. Notice that this procedure is analogous to the usual procedure for solving homogeneous, linear, constant-coefficient ordinary differential equations. In that procedure, the roots of the characteristic equation are determined, and the general solution is then formed as a linear combination of exponentials with the roots as exponents.

For the general quadratic equation (4.2.12), the stability constraints can be converted into relatively simple criteria based on the coefficients α_0, α_1, α_2 of equation (4.2.12). Solution of the quadratic equation for λ yields

$$\lambda = \frac{-\alpha_1}{2\alpha_2} \pm \left[\frac{(\alpha_1)^2}{4(\alpha_2)^2} - \frac{\alpha_0}{\alpha_2}\right]^{1/2} \tag{4.2.14}$$

Let $D \equiv (\alpha_1)^2/4(\alpha_2)^2 - \alpha_0/\alpha_2$. If $D < 0$, then two complex roots exist, as complex conjugates. Their magnitudes are equal and given by $|\lambda|^2 = (\alpha_0/\alpha_2)$. Thus the stability constraint is

$$\text{If } D < 0: \qquad \text{require:} \qquad \left|\frac{\alpha_0}{\alpha_2}\right| \leq 1 \tag{4.2.15a}$$

If $D > 0$, there are two distinct, real roots. Because $-\alpha_1/2\alpha_2$ has a positive number ($\sqrt{D}$) added to and subtracted from it, a minimum constraint is that $|\alpha_1/2\alpha_2| \leq 1$. When $\alpha_1/2\alpha_2 > 0$, then the most critical constraint is $-\alpha_1/2\alpha_2 - \sqrt{D} \geq -1$. This gives the stability criterion $-(\alpha_0/\alpha_2) \leq 1 - \alpha_1/\alpha_2$. Similarly, when $\alpha_1/2\alpha_2 < 0$, the constraint becomes $-(\alpha_0/\alpha_2) \leq 1 + \alpha_1/\alpha_2$. Thus the constraints for $D > 0$ are:

$$\text{If } D > 0: \qquad \text{require:} \qquad \left|\frac{\alpha_1}{2\alpha_2}\right| \leq 1 \tag{4.2.15b}$$

$$-\frac{\alpha_0}{\alpha_2} \leq 1 - \frac{\alpha_1}{\alpha_2} \qquad \left(\frac{\alpha_1}{2\alpha_2} > 0\right)$$

$$-\frac{\alpha_0}{\alpha_2} \leq 1 + \frac{\alpha_1}{\alpha_2} \qquad \left(\frac{\alpha_1}{2\alpha_2} < 0\right)$$

A final case is $D = 0$. When this occurs, $\lambda = -\alpha_1/2\alpha_2$ is a double root for the quadratic equation. Recall that when solving constant coefficient, second-order ordinary differential equations, a double root in the characteristic equation led to a solution of the form $C_1 e^{\lambda x} + C_2 x e^{\lambda x}$, with x the independent variable. Similarly, when solving the finite difference equation, the solution for the double root case is of the form

$$U^n = C_1 \lambda^n + C_2 n \lambda^n \tag{4.2.16}$$

For this case, $|U^n|$ does not grow without bound provided that $|\lambda|$ is strictly less than 1. The case of $|\lambda| = 1$ is no longer stable because of the multiplier n. When all roots are distinct, the criterion for stability allows $|\lambda| = 1$. This subtle distinction between strictly less than and less than or equal to is important because it is not uncommon to have characteristic values λ that are equal to one in magnitude.

The stability constraint when $D = 0$ is written as $|(\alpha_1/2\alpha_2)| < 1$. The constraints for the general quadratic equation $\alpha_2 \lambda^2 + \alpha_1 \lambda + \alpha_0 = 0$ can be summarized as follows, where $D \equiv (\alpha_1)^2/4(\alpha_2)^2 - \alpha_0/\alpha_2$:

$$\text{If } D < 0: \qquad \text{require:} \qquad \left|\frac{\alpha_0}{\alpha_2}\right| \leq 1 \tag{4.2.17}$$

$$\text{If } D \geq 0: \quad \text{require:} \quad \left| \frac{\alpha_1}{2\alpha_2} \right| \leq 1$$

$$-\frac{\alpha_0}{\alpha_2} \leq 1 - \left| \frac{\alpha_1}{\alpha_2} \right|$$

For the two-step Gear implicit approximation (4.2.9), $\alpha_2 = 3 + 2\Delta t$, $\alpha_1 = -4$, and $\alpha_0 = 1$. Because $|\alpha_0/\alpha_2| < 1$, $|\alpha_1/2\alpha_2| < 1$, and $-\alpha_0/\alpha_2 \leq 1 - |\alpha_1/\alpha_2|$, for all values of Δt, this approximation is unconditionally stable. Thus stability considerations do not influence the choice of time step size for this algorithm; time step size is dictated by accuracy considerations only.

The characteristic analysis described above can be applied to a wide variety of linear, constant-coefficient approximations. For a general p-step method, the characteristic equation is a pth-degree polynomial in λ. When the p roots of this equation are distinct, the finite difference solution is given by $U^n = \sum_{i=1}^{p} C_i (\lambda_i)^p$. If one of the roots has multiplicity m, then the solution becomes

$$U^n = \sum_{i=1}^{p-m} C_i (\lambda_i)^n + [C_{p-m+1} + nC_{p-m+2} + \cdots + n^{m-1} C_p](\lambda_{p-m+1})^n \quad (4.2.18)$$

Presence of multiplicity $m > 1$ requires strict inequality when bounding the characteristic value.

Application of this stability analysis is limited only by the ability to obtain roots of polynomials. Fortunately, a general class of rules for polynomials has been derived. These rules provide constraints under which all roots of a polynomial are guaranteed to be bounded by one in magnitude. They are usually referred to as Routh-Hurwitz criteria. For the one-step case,

$$\alpha_1 U^{n+1} + \alpha_0 U^n = 0 \quad (4.2.19)$$

define the quantities p_0 and p_1 as

$$p_0 \equiv \alpha_1 - \alpha_0 \quad (4.2.20a)$$

$$p_1 \equiv \alpha_1 + \alpha_0 \quad (4.2.20b)$$

Then the Routh-Hurwitz criterion, which is necessary and sufficient to guarantee $|\lambda| \leq 1$, is

$$p_i \geq 0, \quad i = 1, 2, \text{ with strict inequality for at least one } i \quad (4.2.20c)$$

This can be easily seen by the observation that $\lambda = \alpha_0/\alpha_1$ and the stability requirement of $|\lambda| \leq 1$.

The Routh-Hurwitz stability criteria for the quadratic case, $\alpha_2 \lambda^2 + \alpha_1 \lambda + \alpha_0 = 0$, are provided by the following. First define

$$p_0 = \alpha_2 - \alpha_1 + \alpha_0 \quad (4.2.21a)$$

$$p_1 = 2(\alpha_2 - \alpha_0) \quad (4.2.21b)$$

$$p_2 = \alpha_2 + \alpha_1 + \alpha_0 \quad (4.2.21c)$$

The Routh-Hurwitz conditions which guarantee that all nonmultiple roots will have magnitude less than or equal to 1, and all multiple roots strictly less than 1, are given by

$$p_i \geq 0, \qquad i = 0, 1, 2 \tag{4.2.21d}$$

with the condition that the following equalities *not* hold:

$$p_0 = p_1 = 0 \qquad \text{(simultaneously)} \tag{4.2.21e}$$

$$p_1 = p_2 = 0 \qquad \text{(simultaneously)} \tag{4.2.21f}$$

A complete list of criteria for first- through fourth-degree polynomials is given in Appendix B.

While the bounds of equations (4.2.17)–(4.2.21) assure a stable approximation, there is yet more information that can be extracted from this analysis. Consider again the first-order equation $du/dt = -u$. This equation has analytical solution

$$u(t) = C_1 e^{-t} \tag{4.2.22}$$

The change in u between times t and $t + \Delta t$ is equal to $C_1 e^{-\Delta t}$. Define this ratio as the analytical amplification factor, λ_A. This amplification factor can be expressed as an equivalent series as follows:

$$\lambda_A \equiv \frac{u(t + \Delta t)}{u(t)} = e^{-\Delta t} = 1 - \Delta t + \frac{(\Delta t)^2}{2!} - \frac{(\Delta t)^3}{3!} + \cdots \tag{4.2.23}$$

Next consider the one-step Euler approximation (4.2.4), which has amplification factor $\lambda = [1 - (1 - \theta)\Delta t]/[1 + \theta(\Delta t)]$, where λ is the ratio of numerical solutions at successive time steps, $\lambda = U^{n+1}/U^n$. This numerical amplification factor may also be expanded in a series as

$$\lambda = \frac{1 - (1 - \theta)\Delta t}{1 + \theta(\Delta t)} = 1 - \Delta t + \theta(\Delta t)^2 - \theta^2(\Delta t)^3 + \cdots \tag{4.2.24}$$

The numerical amplification factor can be seen to be an approximation to the analytical amplification factor. The approximation matches through $\mathcal{O}(\Delta t)$ when $\theta \neq 0.5$ and through $\mathcal{O}((\Delta t)^2)$ when $\theta = 0.5$. The numerical amplification therefore corresponds to the physical behavior of the system.

For the quadratic approximation, there are two values of λ. However, the physical system has only one. Examination of the expressions for λ_1 and λ_2 that result from the two-point Gear approximation shows that

$$\lambda_1 = \frac{4 + 2[1 - 2\Delta t]^{1/2}}{6 + 4(\Delta t)} = 1 - \Delta t + \frac{(\Delta t)^2}{2} - \frac{(\Delta t)^3}{2} + \cdots \tag{4.2.25a}$$

$$\lambda_2 = \frac{4 - 2[1 - 2\Delta t]^{1/2}}{6 + 4(\Delta t)} = \frac{1}{3} + \frac{\Delta t}{9} + \frac{5(\Delta t)^2}{54} + \cdots \tag{4.2.25b}$$

The first root is an approximation to the analytical (physical) amplification factor λ_A, while the second does not approximate the physical root. This second root is strictly an artifact of the numerical approximation. For the approximate solution to be close to the analytical solution, it should be dominated by the physical root λ_1 and should not be significantly influenced by the nonphysical root λ_2. Because the solution U^n is given by the linear combination $C_1(\lambda_1)^n + C_2(\lambda_2)^n$, the coefficients C_1 and C_2 are important in determining the relative influence of the two roots. The coefficients can be determined by noting that U^0 and U^1 are given from the initial condition and the start-up calculation, respectively. These known values can be used to determine C_1 and C_2 via evaluation of the general solution for $n = 0$ and $n = 1$, that is,

$$U^0 = C_1 + C_2 \qquad (4.2.26a)$$

$$U^1 = C_1\lambda_1 + C_2\lambda_2 \qquad (4.2.26b)$$

Solution of these equations for C_1 and C_2 yields

$$C_1 = \frac{U^1 - \lambda_2 U^0}{\lambda_1 - \lambda_2} \qquad (4.2.27a)$$

$$C_2 = \frac{U^1 - \lambda_1 U^0}{\lambda_2 - \lambda_1} \qquad (4.2.27b)$$

Recall that U^1 is calculated by a one-step start-up method. The start-up method has associated with it a numerical amplification factor, call it λ_S. Therefore, C_2 is equal to $(\lambda_S - \lambda_1)U^0/(\lambda_2 - \lambda_1)$. Because both λ_S and λ_1 approximate the physical root, they are approximately equal, and C_2 can be expected to be small compared to C_1. This relative difference in coefficients means that the physical root λ_1 will dominate the numerical solution. This result is general, because the expressions for C_1 and C_2 in equations (4.2.27) are not based on any specific two-step algorithm. Thus it is usually the case that the physical root dominates, given that stability limits are respected.

Because the governing equation has only one characteristic value λ_A, any approximation method that uses more than one step will generate spurious numerical characteristic values. Only one will correspond to the physical root. Fortunately, the physical root usually dominates the solution, as was shown above for the quadratic case. However, care must always be exercised to be sure that spurious roots are not adversely affecting the approximation.

Finally, by looking more closely at the characteristic values λ, estimates of accuracy may be obtained. This is done by comparing the numerical and analytical amplification factors. How well the numerical amplification factor matches the analytical factor is a measure of the accuracy of the approximation. For example, equation (4.2.24) indicates that the amplification factor for the variably weighted Euler method matches the analytical amplification factor through $\mathcal{O}(\Delta t)$ unless $\theta = 0.5$, in which case the $(\Delta t)^2$ term is matched as well. The method is $\mathcal{O}((1 - 2\theta)\Delta t, (\Delta t)^2)$. Similarly, the two-step Gear implicit method matches the amplification factor through $(\Delta t)^2$ and is a second-order approximation, $\mathcal{O}((\Delta t)^2)$. Stability analysis can therefore provide added insights into accuracy by comparison of numerical and analytical amplification factors.

Stability analysis is generally limited to linear approximating equations with constant coefficients. Some specific analyses may be applied to linear equations with nonconstant coefficients, although it is difficult to derive general stability constraints for such systems. For nonlinear problems, it is rare to be able to obtain an exact stability limit, although the stability limit given in Example 2.10 is one example. That example also demonstrates the specific nature of such bounds, in that it is influenced by the initial condition and it applies to the forward Euler method but cannot be readily extended to other approximations. In general, nonlinear equations are analyzed approximately by first linearizing the equations and then applying linear analysis. This linear analysis provides guidelines but must be used with some caution because the nonlinear solution may still be unstable even when the linearized equation is stable. If the linearized analysis predicts instability, application of the algorithm will almost certainly result in an unstable solution.

This stability analysis can be applied to any of the time-marching algorithms presented in Section 2.6. For example, one-step multistage methods, such as those in the Runge-Kutta family, are easily analyzed. The two-stage Runge-Kutta method of equation (2.6.7) has amplification factor $\lambda = 1 - \Delta t + \alpha_1 \alpha_3 (\Delta t)^2$ [demonstrating that the criterion for second order accuracy is $\alpha_1 \alpha_3 = 1/2$, as per equation (2.6.11b)], while the four-stage method of equation (2.6.12) has amplification factor $\lambda = 1 - \Delta t + (\Delta t)^2/2 - (\Delta t)^3/6 + (\Delta t)^4/24$. Analysis of other approximations from Section 2.6 are left as exercises at the end of this chapter.

4.2.2 Systems of Equations, Semidiscrete Approximations, and Fourier Analysis

The characteristic analysis of the preceding section carries directly to systems of linear equations. Consider the following set of coupled ordinary differential equations:

$$\frac{d\mathbf{u}}{dt} + \mathbf{B} \cdot \mathbf{u} = \mathbf{0} \tag{4.2.28}$$

$$\mathbf{u}(t^0) = \mathbf{U}^0$$

A variably weighted Euler approximation to this system can be written as

$$[\mathbf{I} + \theta\mathbf{B}] \cdot \mathbf{U}^{n+1} + [-\mathbf{I} + (1-\theta)\mathbf{B}] \cdot \mathbf{U}^n = \mathbf{0} \tag{4.2.29}$$

The amplification factor analysis now takes the form of searching for λ values such that $\mathbf{U}^{n+1} = \lambda\mathbf{U}^n$. Substitution of $\lambda\mathbf{U}^n$ for $\mathbf{U}^{n+1}$ in equation (4.2.29) results in the following equation:

$$\{\lambda(\mathbf{I} + \theta\mathbf{B}) + [-\mathbf{I} + (1-\theta)\mathbf{B}]\} \cdot \mathbf{U}^n = \mathbf{0} \tag{4.2.30}$$

To avoid the trivial solution $\mathbf{U}^n = \mathbf{0}$, the determinant of the coefficient matrix must be set to zero (see Theorem A.2.1). This provides the equation for λ:

$$\det\{\lambda(\mathbf{I} + \theta\mathbf{B}) + [-\mathbf{I} + (1-\theta)\mathbf{B}]\} = 0 \tag{4.2.31}$$

For a system of N unknowns, this equation is an Nth-degree polynomial in λ. Similarly, for any general two-step approximation of the form

$$\mathbf{A}_1 \cdot \mathbf{U}^{n+1} + \mathbf{A}_0 \cdot \mathbf{U}^n = \mathbf{0} \tag{4.2.32a}$$

the characteristic equation is

$$\det[\lambda \mathbf{A}_1 + \mathbf{A}_0] = |\lambda \mathbf{A}_1 + \mathbf{A}_0| = 0 \qquad (4.2.32b)$$

Note that this is equivalent to solving for the eigenvalues of the matrix $\mathbf{A}_1^{-1} \cdot \mathbf{A}_0$. For a system of N unknowns, there will be N values of λ.

For multistep methods, the approach is analogous to the single equation case. That is, seek values of λ such that $\mathbf{U}^{n+1} = \lambda \mathbf{U}^n = \lambda^2 \mathbf{U}^{n-1} = \cdots$. As an example, consider a general two-step algorithm of the form

$$\mathbf{A}_2 \cdot \mathbf{U}^{n+1} + \mathbf{A}_1 \cdot \mathbf{U}^n + \mathbf{A}_0 \cdot \mathbf{U}^{n-1} = \mathbf{0} \qquad (4.2.33a)$$

The characteristic equation associated with this approximation is

$$|\mathbf{A}_2 \lambda^2 + \mathbf{A}_1 \lambda + \mathbf{A}_0| = 0 \qquad (4.2.33b)$$

For a system of N unknowns, equation (4.2.33b) leads to $2N$ values of λ. In general, a p-step approximation applied to a system of N unknowns leads to pN characteristic values λ. Because the governing differential equations have N (analytical) characteristic values, p-step methods, with $p \geq 2$, lead to solutions with a set of physical roots and a set of spurious roots.

Solution of the determinant equation for the amplification factors λ_i is difficult, especially if analytical relationships between λ_i and Δt are desired (as opposed to inputting a specific number for Δt and calculating specific values for λ_i). While general relationships between matrix entries and the resulting characteristic values exist for very special cases, the general solution is usually extremely difficult, if not impossible.

There are other methods of testing for stability that apply specifically to systems of equations that arise from approximations of space-time partial differential equations. Recall that when a spatial approximation is applied to a space-time partial differential equation, the result is a set of coupled ordinary differential equations in time. The unknowns in these equations are the nodal values associated with the spatial discretization. Such systems are called *semidiscrete systems*, or *semidiscretizations*. Application of a time-marching algorithm to the resulting set of equations provides the final discrete (algebraic) system.

As an example, consider the model heat equation,

$$\frac{\partial u}{\partial t} - D \frac{\partial^2 u}{\partial x^2} = 0, \qquad 0 < x < \ell, \quad t > 0 \qquad (4.2.34)$$

$$u(x, 0) = G(x)$$

$$u(0, t) = g_0(t)$$

$$u(\ell, t) = g_\ell(t)$$

Application of the standard three-point finite difference approximation in space leads to the following semidiscretization:

$$\frac{dU_i}{dt} - D \frac{U_{i-1} - 2U_i + U_{i+1}}{(\Delta x)^2} = 0 \qquad (4.2.35)$$

where $U_i(t)$ are time-dependent values of the spatial finite difference approximation at node i. Next, let the time domain be approximated by the variably weighted Euler scheme, so that

$$\frac{U_i^{n+1} - U_i^n}{\Delta t} - D\left[\frac{\theta}{(\Delta x)^2}\delta_x^2 U_i^{n+1} + \frac{(1-\theta)}{(\Delta x)^2}\delta_x^2 U_i^n\right] = 0 \qquad (4.2.36)$$

where $\delta_x^2 U_i \equiv U_{i-1} - 2U_i + U_{i+1}$, with δ_x being the central difference operator defined with respect to the independent variable x (see Section 2.2). Equation (4.2.36) may be written in matrix form as

$$\mathbf{A}_1 \cdot \mathbf{U}^{n+1} + \mathbf{A}_0 \cdot \mathbf{U}^n = \mathbf{0} \qquad (4.2.37)$$

A typical row of matrix $\mathbf{A}_1$, say row i, has entries $(\alpha_1)_{i,i-1} = (\alpha_1)_{i,i+1} = -\rho\theta$, $(\alpha_1)_{i,i} = 1 + 2\rho\theta$, and $(\alpha_1)_{i,j} = 0$ for all other j, with $\rho \equiv D(\Delta t)/(\Delta x)^2$ being a dimensionless diffusion coefficient. Thus matrix $\mathbf{A}_1$ is tridiagonal. Similarly, $\mathbf{A}_0$ is tridiagonal with $(\alpha_0)_{i,i-1} = (\alpha_0)_{i,i+1} = -\rho(1-\theta)$, $(\alpha_0)_{i,i} = -1 + 2\rho(1-\theta)$, and all other $(\alpha_0)_{i,j} = 0$. The characteristic equation is

$$|\lambda\mathbf{A}_1 + \mathbf{A}_0| = 0 \qquad (4.2.38)$$

If first-type boundary conditions are specified at $x = x_1 = 0$ and at $x = x_N = \ell$, with N being the number of nodes in the spatial discretization, then the matrix problem reduces to $N - 2$ rows, with each row having identical entries (although rows 1 and N have only two entries due to the boundary effects). While in general the eigenvalues λ must be determined algebraically, there being no simple analytical formula for their evaluation, this case of identical entries in each row of the tridiagonal matrices allows an analytical expression to be written for λ based on the fact that the values of λ satisfying equation (4.2.38) are eigenvalues of the matrix $-\mathbf{A}_0 \cdot \mathbf{A}_1^{-1}$ (Ames, 1977, pp. 56–58). For matrices $\mathbf{A}_1$ and $\mathbf{A}_0$, with row entries $(-\rho\theta, 1 + 2\rho\theta, -\rho\theta)$ and $(-\rho(1-\theta), -1 + 2\rho(1-\theta), -\rho(1-\theta))$, respectively, the values of λ that satisfy equation (4.2.38) may be expressed as

$$\lambda_k = \frac{[-1 + 2\rho(1-\theta)] + 2[-\rho(1-\theta)]\cos[k\pi/(N-1)]}{1 + 2\rho\theta + 2(-\rho\theta)\cos[k\pi/(N-1)]}, \qquad k = 1, 2, \ldots, N-2$$

$$(4.2.39a)$$

Use of the formulas $(N-1) = \ell/\Delta x$; $k\pi/(N-1) = k\pi(\Delta x)/\ell \equiv \sigma_k(\Delta x)$ (where $\sigma_k \equiv k\pi/\ell$ is a *wave number*, which is a measure of spatial frequency, or period length); and $1 - \cos(\sigma_k \Delta x) = 2\sin^2(\sigma_k \Delta x/2)$, leads to the following expression for λ_k:

$$\lambda_k = \frac{-1 + 4\rho(1-\theta)\sin^2(\sigma_k\Delta x/2)}{1 + 4(\rho\theta)\sin^2(\sigma_k\Delta x/2)} \qquad (4.2.39b)$$

Stability considerations dictate that $|\lambda_k| \leq 1$ for all k. For equation (4.2.39b), the most restrictive case is when $\sin^2(\sigma_k\Delta x/2) = 1$. This leads to the stability constraint

$$\rho(1 - 2\theta) \leq 0.5 \qquad (4.2.40)$$

This constraint implies that the classic explicit approximation ($\theta = 0$) has a stability bound of $\rho \leq 0.5$, while approximations that use any value of $\theta \geq 0.5$ are unconditionally stable.

The matrix analysis presented above leads to general rules such as equation (4.2.40) only in special circumstances, in this case $\mathbf{A}_j$ being tridiagonal with identical entries in each row. In general, all stability analyses require that each equation have the same coefficients, because constant coefficients and constant grid spacing, which are general requirements for stability analysis, lead to approximating equations that have identical coefficients. The limitation of the matrix method is the requirement of explicit expressions for the eigenvalues. An alternative technique for stability analysis is based on Fourier series expansions, and goes by the name Fourier analysis (often referred to as *von Neumann analysis*, after the founder of the method, John von Neumann). This method is quite general in its application and will be the focus of the following discussion.

To explain the procedure, consider first analytical solution of equation (4.2.34). One way to solve this equation is to write the solution as a Fourier series in space. The theory of Fourier series guarantees that any continuous function $f(x) \in \mathbb{C}^0[0, \ell]$, defined over the interval $[0, \ell]$, can be written as a sum of trigonometric functions, that is,

$$f(x) = \frac{A_0}{2} + \sum_{k=1}^{\infty} A_k \cos \frac{k\pi x}{\ell} + B_k \sin \frac{k\pi x}{\ell} \qquad (4.2.41)$$

where A_k and B_k are Fourier coefficients, defined by

$$A_k = \frac{1}{\ell} \int_0^{\ell} f(x) \cos \frac{k\pi x}{\ell} \, dx \qquad (k = 1, 2, \ldots) \qquad (4.2.42a)$$

$$B_k = \frac{1}{\ell} \int_0^{\ell} f(x) \sin \frac{k\pi x}{\ell} \, dx \qquad (k = 1, 2, \ldots) \qquad (4.2.42b)$$

$$A_0 = \frac{1}{2\ell} \int_0^{\ell} f(x) \, dx \qquad (4.2.42c)$$

Notice that because any function $f(x) \in \mathbb{C}^0[0, \ell]$ can be written in the form of equation (4.2.41), the set $\{\cos(k\pi x/\ell), \sin(k\pi x/\ell)\}_{k=0}^{\infty}$ forms a basis for $\mathbb{C}^0[0, \ell]$. For references to discussions of other interesting properties of Fourier series, see Appendix C.

The Fourier series representation can be written equivalently using complex exponential notation. Recall the definition of a complex exponential given by the Euler relationship,

$$e^{\hat{i}\phi} \equiv \cos \phi + \hat{i} \sin \phi \qquad (4.2.43)$$

where $\hat{i} \equiv \sqrt{-1}$. Given this formula, $\cos \phi$ and $\sin \phi$ may be written in terms of complex exponentials as

$$\cos \phi = \frac{1}{2}(e^{\hat{i}\phi} + e^{-\hat{i}\phi}) \qquad (4.2.44a)$$

$$\sin \phi = \frac{-\hat{i}}{2}(e^{\hat{i}\phi} - e^{-\hat{i}\phi}) \tag{4.2.44b}$$

These relations can be substituted into equation (4.2.41) so that

$$f(x) = \sum_{k=0}^{\infty} A_k \left[\frac{1}{2}(e^{\hat{i}(k\pi x/\ell)} + e^{-\hat{i}(k\pi x/\ell)}) \right] + B_k \left[\frac{-\hat{i}}{2}(e^{\hat{i}(k\pi x/\ell)} - e^{-\hat{i}(k\pi x/\ell)}) \right]$$

$$= \sum_{k=-\infty}^{+\infty} C_k e^{\hat{i}\sigma_k x} \tag{4.2.45a}$$

where

$$\sigma_k \equiv \frac{k\pi}{\ell} \tag{4.2.45b}$$

$$C_0 = A_0 \tag{4.2.45c}$$

$$C_k = \frac{1}{2}(A_k - \hat{i}B_k), \qquad k > 0 \tag{4.2.45d}$$

$$C_k = \frac{1}{2}(A_{-k} + \hat{i}B_{-k}), \qquad k < 0 \tag{4.2.45e}$$

with σ_k referred to as the wave number. This is related to the wavelength of the Fourier component, L_k, by the relation $\sigma_k = k\pi/\ell = 2\pi/L_k$.

Consider expansion of the solution of equation (4.2.34), $u(x,t)$, in a Fourier series in space with time-dependent coefficients $\Lambda_k(t)$,

$$u(x,t) = \sum_{k=-\infty}^{+\infty} \Lambda_k(t) e^{\hat{i}\sigma_k x} \tag{4.2.46}$$

Substitution of this expansion into equation (4.2.34) yields

$$\sum_{k=-\infty}^{+\infty} \left[\frac{d\Lambda_k}{dt} + D(\sigma_k)^2 \Lambda_k \right] e^{\hat{i}\sigma_k x} = 0 \tag{4.2.47}$$

Because $\{e^{\hat{i}\sigma_k x}\}$ forms a basis for the solution space, it must be a linearly independent set. By definition of linear independence, the only way for equation (4.2.47) to be satisfied is for the coefficient of each $e^{\hat{i}\sigma_k x}$ to be zero (see Definition A.3.3). Thus the coefficients Λ_k must satisfy

$$\frac{d\Lambda_k}{dt} + D(\sigma_k)^2 \Lambda_k = 0 \tag{4.2.48a}$$

or

$$\Lambda_k(t) = C_k e^{-D\sigma_k^2 t} \tag{4.2.48b}$$

Then the general analytical solution to equation (4.2.34) is expressed as

$$u(x,t) = \sum_{k=-\infty}^{+\infty} C_k e^{i\sigma_k x} e^{-D\sigma_k^2 t} \tag{4.2.49}$$

The coefficients C_k are determined by Fourier series representation of the known initial condition $u(x,0)$. The important point here is that the solution is represented as a Fourier series, with the coefficient of each term (or component), $\Lambda_k(t)$, changing as a function of time, based on the governing equation.

This same idea can be used to describe mathematically the spatial structure of a numerical approximation. The coefficients of this numerical expansion, analogous to Λ_k, will change in time based on the discrete numerical approximation equations. Requirement that each of these coefficients remains bounded as time progresses will lead to stability constraints.

Consider expansion of the numerical solution in a Fourier series, such that

$$U(x,t) = \sum_{k=-(N-1)}^{N-1} \hat{\Lambda}_k(t) e^{i\sigma_k x} \tag{4.2.50}$$

where the numerical approximation has coefficients $\hat{\Lambda}_k(t)$, and the range of k is now limited to wavelengths greater than or equal to $2\Delta x$, because the numerical solution is incapable of resolving any wavelengths smaller than $2\Delta x$. The latter point is a consequence of the finite sampling theorem, as illustrated in Problem 4.21. Let the representation (4.2.50) be inserted into the finite difference approximation of equation (4.2.36). There results

$$\sum_{k=-(N-1)}^{N-1} \left\{ \hat{\Lambda}_k(t^{n+1})e^{i\sigma_k x_j} - \hat{\Lambda}_k(t^n)e^{i\sigma_k x_j} \right.$$

$$- \frac{D(\Delta t)}{(\Delta x)^2} \left[\theta\hat{\Lambda}_k(t^{n+1})(e^{i\sigma_k x_{j-1}} - 2e^{i\sigma_k x_j} + e^{i\sigma_k x_{j+1}}) \right.$$

$$\left. \left. + (1-\theta)\hat{\Lambda}_k(t^n)(e^{i\sigma_k x_{j-1}} - 2e^{i\sigma_k x_j} + e^{i\sigma_k x_{j+1}}) \right] \right\} = 0 \tag{4.2.51a}$$

or

$$\sum_{k=-(N-1)}^{N-1} e^{i\sigma_k x_j} \left\{ \hat{\Lambda}_k(t^{n+1}) \left[(-\rho\theta)e^{-i\sigma_k \Delta x} + (1 + 2\rho\theta) + (-\rho\theta)e^{i\sigma_k \Delta x} \right] \right.$$

$$\left. + \hat{\Lambda}_k(t^n) \left[[-\rho(1-\theta)]e^{i\sigma_k \Delta x} + [1 + 2\rho(1-\theta)] + [-\rho(1-\theta)]e^{i\sigma_k \Delta x} \right] \right\} = 0$$

$$\tag{4.2.51b}$$

Because of the linear independence of $\{e^{i\sigma_k x}\}$ and because equation (4.1.51) must hold for every node x_j, the coefficient of each term in the series must be equal to zero. Therefore,

$$\hat{\Lambda}_k(t^{n+1}) \left[(-\rho\theta)e^{-i\sigma_k \Delta x} + (1 + 2\rho\theta) + (-\rho\theta)e^{i\sigma_k \Delta x} \right]$$

$$+\hat{\Lambda}_k(t^n) \left[[-\rho(1-\theta)]e^{i\sigma_k \Delta x} + [-1 + 2\rho(1-\theta)] + [-\rho(1-\theta)]e^{i\sigma_k \Delta x} \right] = 0 \quad (4.2.52)$$

Next observe that the ratio $\Lambda_k(t^{n+1})/\Lambda_k(t^n)$ measures the analytical amplification of component number k over one time step, while the ratio $\hat{\Lambda}_k(t^{n+1})/\hat{\Lambda}_k(t^n)$ measures the numerical amplification. These ratios are referred to, respectively, as the *analytical amplification factor* λ_k^A and the *numerical amplification factor* λ_k^N. Because the solution is composed of a linear combination of Fourier components (wave numbers), a necessary condition for stability is that none of the components grows without bound. This must hold for both the analytical amplification factor $\lambda_k^A \equiv \Lambda_k(t^{n+1})/\Lambda_k(t^n)$ and the numerical amplification factor $\lambda_k^N \equiv \hat{\Lambda}_k(t^{n+1})/\hat{\Lambda}_k(t^n)$. It will be assumed that the physical systems to be examined are inherently stable, which means that $|\lambda_k^A| \leq 1$ for all k. The constraint on the numerical amplification factor, $|\lambda_k^N| \leq 1$, will provide stability bounds for numerical approximations.

As an example, consider the approximation (4.2.52). This equation may be rewritten as

$$\hat{\Lambda}_k(t^{n+1})[1 + 2\rho\theta - 2\rho\theta\cos(\sigma_k \Delta x)] = \hat{\Lambda}_k(t^n)[1 - 2\rho(1-\theta) + 2\rho(1-\theta)\cos(\sigma_k \Delta x)]$$

$$(4.2.53a)$$

Use of the trigonometric relation $1 - \cos(\sigma_k \Delta x) = 2\sin^2(\sigma_k \Delta x/2)$ leads to the following expression:

$$\hat{\Lambda}_k(t^{n+1}) \left(1 + 4\rho\theta\sin^2\frac{\sigma_k \Delta x}{2} \right) = \hat{\Lambda}_k(t^n) \left[1 - 4\rho(1-\theta)\sin^2\frac{\sigma_k \Delta x}{2} \right] \quad (4.2.53b)$$

or

$$\lambda_k^N = \frac{\hat{\Lambda}_k(t^{n+1})}{\hat{\Lambda}_k(t^n)} = \frac{1 - 4\rho(1-\theta)\sin^2(\sigma_k \Delta x/2)}{1 + 4\rho\theta\sin^2(\sigma_k \Delta x/2)} \quad (4.2.54)$$

Stability requires that $|\lambda_k^N| \leq 1$ for all k. This is satisfied whenever (see Problem 4.22)

$$\rho(1 - 2\theta) \leq 0.5 \quad (4.2.55)$$

This stability constraint indicates that the one-step forward (explicit) approximation is conditionally stable, with stability condition $\rho \equiv D(\Delta t)/(\Delta x)^2 \leq 0.5$, while the one-step backward Euler method is unconditionally stable. Equation (4.2.55) indicates that any one-step Euler method with $\theta \geq 0.5$ is unconditionally stable for the model equation (4.2.34). This result is identical to that which resulted from matrix analysis, as given by equations (4.2.39) and (4.2.40).

Because the one-dimensional heat equation is a standard model equation for diffusive processes, simple approximations to it have standard titles associated with them. The forward Euler approximation ($\theta = 0$) is usually referred to as the *classic explicit* approximation, while the backward Euler ($\theta = 1$) method is the *classic implicit* approximation. Both approximations are $\mathcal{O}(\Delta t, (\Delta x)^2)$, assuming constant node spacing Δx. In fact, all approximations of the form of equation (4.2.36) are $\mathcal{O}(\Delta t, (\Delta x)^2)$ except

$\theta = 0.5$, in which case the approximation is $\mathcal{O}((\Delta t)^2, (\Delta x)^2)$. This special case is usually referred to as a *Crank-Nicolson* approximation; it has the property of unconditional stability (albeit neutral stability for the $2\Delta x$ wavelength) and second-order accuracy in both space and time.

Fourier analysis has associated with it assumptions that must be met for it to be used. These include: linear governing equation with constant coefficients; constant node spacing (or a repeating pattern of nonconstant spacing) in both space and time; and effectively infinite spatial domain. In addition, the initial condition must be amenable to Fourier series representation, which means that some periodicity must be present in the initial condition. The assumption of infinite spatial domain means that the influence of boundary conditions is not captured in the analysis. This assumption is usually reasonable, although examples can be constructed wherein boundary conditions can influence the stability of a method. Inclusion of boundary effects in the matrix stability analysis is the only significant difference between stability results obtained using Fourier analysis and matrix analysis.

Notice that when analyzing for stability, all resolvable wavelengths must be checked, whether or not the Fourier representation of the initial condition includes all of the waves. This is because machine error and numerical round-off will, through introduction of random errors, generate waves of all resolvable lengths. Thus a wave, initially not present but introduced by the arithmetic, can destroy a computation if the numerical scheme being used is not stable for that wavelength. Thus, at times, a simulation may appear to give reasonable results for a computation of 5, 10, 100, or even 1000 time steps before an instability becomes apparent. This behavior can be avoided for linear equations by always defining the stability constraint with respect to the most limiting wavelength. In nonlinear equations for which an approximate linear stability analysis has been performed, the nonlinearity can sometimes drive this slow growth of an instability, typically corresponding to a short wave. Care should always be exercised when dealing with nonlinear equations.

A variety of numerical approximations can be written and analyzed for the model diffusion equation. For example, an $\mathcal{O}((\Delta t)^2, (\Delta x)^2)$ approximation for equation (4.2.34) can be written as

$$\frac{U_i^{n+1} - U_i^{n-1}}{2(\Delta t)} - \frac{D}{(\Delta x)^2} \delta_x^2 U_i^n = 0 \tag{4.2.56}$$

Notice that this is an explicit method in that only one unknown appears in each equation, U_i^{n+1}. Therefore, this $\mathcal{O}((\Delta t)^2, (\Delta x)^2)$ approximation appears to have very attractive computational properties. This is also a two-step method, involving three time levels $(n - 1, n, n + 1)$. As such, two families of amplification factors exist, $\{(\lambda_1)_k^N, (\lambda_2)_k^N\}$. Derivation of expressions for these amplification factors and subsequent analysis indicates that the approximation (4.2.56) is unconditionally unstable, because there is no positive time step for which all amplification factors can be guaranteed to be bounded by one in magnitude (see Problem 4.22). Therefore, an attractive algorithm is rendered useless because it is unstable. A two-step approximation that is unconditionally stable is the following scheme, based on a two-step Gear approximation for the time derivative:

$$\frac{3U_i^{n+1} - 4U_i^n + U_i^{n-1}}{2(\Delta t)} - \frac{D}{(\Delta x)^2}\delta_x^2 U_i^{n+1} = 0 \qquad (4.2.57)$$

Many other approximations may be proposed and analyzed.

Fourier analysis may also be used to analyze approximations for other types of equations. Problems 4.24 and 4.25 examine Fourier analysis applied to the first-order hyperbolic equation $\partial u/\partial t + V(\partial u/\partial x) = 0$ and the second-order hyperbolic equation $\partial^2 u/\partial t^2 - c^2(\partial^2 u/\partial x^2) = 0$. Because these equations satisfy the requirements necessary for Fourier analysis (linear, constant coefficient), discrete approximations that employ constant node spacing can be readily analyzed. For example, a standard finite difference approximation for the second-order hyperbolic (wave) equation is given by

$$\frac{U_i^{n+1} - 2U_i^n + U_i^{n-1}}{(\Delta t)^2} - c^2 \frac{U_{i+1}^n - 2U_i^n + U_{i-1}^n}{(\Delta x)^2} = 0 \qquad (4.2.58)$$

Fourier analysis (Problem 4.25) leads to the characteristic equation

$$\lambda^2 - \lambda \left(2 - 4\rho^2 \sin^2 \frac{\sigma_k \Delta x}{2}\right) + 1 = 0 \qquad (4.2.59)$$

Use of the general rules of equation (4.2.17) then leads to the stability constraint

$$\nu \equiv \frac{c(\Delta t)}{\Delta x} \leq 1 \qquad (4.2.60)$$

The dimensionless parameter ν is usually referred to as the *Courant number*. Notice that in this case, the characteristic equation is quadratic and thus each wavelength has associated with it two roots. While two roots implied existence of one physical root and one numerical artifact for first-order equations in time, the second-order-in-time wave equation has two physical roots associated with it (see the characteristic analysis of Chapter 1). Therefore, each numerical root corresponds to a physical root.

Fourier analysis can be used to extract much more information about an approximation than simply whether or not it is stable. The additional information provides valuable quantification and insight into accuracy of the numerical approximation and its behavior.

Recall the analysis of equations (4.2.23)–(4.2.25), in which the numerical amplification factor was compared to the analytical amplification factor for the simple case of an initial value, ordinary differential equation. This provided a measure of how well the numerical approximation was capturing the correct solution behavior. The same kind of analysis can be applied to the case of partial differential equations, in which spatial approximation leads to a semidiscrete system of coupled ordinary differential equations in time. As an example, consider the general parabolic equation with hyperbolic secondary characteristics (see Section 1.3 for a discussion of primary and secondary characteristics),

$$\frac{\partial u}{\partial t} + V \frac{\partial u}{\partial x} - D \frac{\partial^2 u}{\partial x^2} = 0 \qquad (4.2.61)$$

The general Fourier representation of the analytical solution $u(x, t)$ is

$$u(x, t) = \sum_k \Lambda_k(t) e^{\hat{i}\sigma_k x} = \sum_k C_k e^{(-\hat{i}V\sigma_k - D\sigma_k^2)t} e^{\hat{i}\sigma_k x} \tag{4.2.62}$$

The analytical amplification factor associated with wave number σ_k is defined by

$$\lambda_k^A \equiv \frac{\Lambda_k(t + \Delta t)}{\Lambda_k(t)} = e^{(-\hat{i}V\sigma_k - D\sigma_k^2)\Delta t} \tag{4.2.63}$$

The magnitude of each Fourier component k declines over one time step by the factor

$$|\lambda_k^A| = \left| e^{-\hat{i}\sigma_k V\Delta t} e^{-D\sigma_k^2 \Delta t} \right| = \left| e^{-\hat{i}\sigma_k V\Delta t} \right| \left| e^{-D\sigma_k^2 \Delta t} \right| = e^{-D\sigma_k^2 \Delta t} \tag{4.2.64}$$

This result is consistent with the physical behavior associated with equation (4.2.61): the advective (first-order hyperbolic) part of the equation is nondissipative and the diffusive (second-order parabolic) part of the equation is inherently dissipative. Equation (4.2.64) indicates that the diffusive part of the equation causes the amplitude of each wave to decay, while the advective part does not. Note in particular that the case of $D \to 0$ results in $|\lambda_k^A| = 1$ for all k, meaning that under pure advection no wave components are dissipated.

One measure of how well a numerical solution approximates the analytical solution is comparison of the magnitude of the numerical and analytical amplification factors. The ratio of these two factors, defined as the *amplitude ratio*, R_k, can be used to quantify this comparison, with

$$R_k \equiv \frac{|\lambda_k^N|}{|\lambda_k^A|} \tag{4.2.65}$$

When R_k is close to unity, the numerical representation of the amplitude of wave component k is close to the analytical behavior.

To illustrate the amplitude ratio, consider two approximations to equation (4.2.61) with $D = 0$:

Centered in time, centered in space (CTCS).

$$\frac{U_i^{n+1} - U_i^n}{\Delta t} + V\left[\left(\frac{1}{2}\right)\frac{U_{i+1}^{n+1} - U_{i-1}^{n+1}}{2(\Delta x)} + \left(\frac{1}{2}\right)\frac{U_{i+1}^n - U_{i-1}^n}{2(\Delta x)}\right] = 0 \tag{4.2.66a}$$

Forward in time, backward in space (FTBS).

$$\frac{U_i^{n+1} - U_i^n}{\Delta t} + V\frac{U_i^n - U_{i-1}^n}{\Delta x} = 0 \tag{4.2.66b}$$

If the dimensionless parameter $\nu \equiv V(\Delta t)/\Delta x$, which is the Courant number, is used, then Fourier analysis of equations (4.2.66a) and (4.2.66b) leads to

$$(\lambda_k^N)_C = \frac{1 - \hat{i}(\nu/2)\sin(\sigma_k \Delta x)}{1 + \hat{i}(\nu/2)\sin(\sigma_k \Delta x)} \tag{4.2.67a}$$

$$(\lambda_k^N)_F = [1 - \nu + \nu\cos(\sigma_k \Delta x)] - \hat{i}\sin(\sigma_k \Delta x) \tag{4.2.67b}$$

where subscripts C and F refer to approximations of equations (4.2.66a) and (4.2.66b), respectively. By definition, the amplitude ratio is $R_k \equiv |\lambda_k^N|/|\lambda_k^A|$. Because $|\lambda_k^A| = \left| e^{iV\sigma_k \Delta t} \right| = 1$, $R_k = |\lambda_k^N|$. The amplitude ratio may be expressed as a function of wave number σ_k, or as a function of wavelength L_k. These are related by the relationship

$$\sigma_k = \frac{2\pi}{L_k} \tag{4.2.68}$$

From equation (4.2.68), $\sigma_k \Delta x = 2\pi/(L_k/\Delta x)$, where $L_k/\Delta x$ is a dimensionless wavelength, normalized by the grid spacing Δx. Figure 4.17 is a plot of R_k as a function of $L_k/\Delta x$ for both finite difference approximations. The plots show results for all $L_k \geq 2\Delta x$, because a discrete grid cannot resolve wavelengths below $2\Delta x$. The figure shows that the CTCS approximation (4.2.66a) maintains the correct amplitude behavior for all wavelengths, independent of the choice of ν. The FTBS approximation (4.2.66b) has amplitude errors, especially at small wavelengths, for all values of ν except $\nu = 1$.

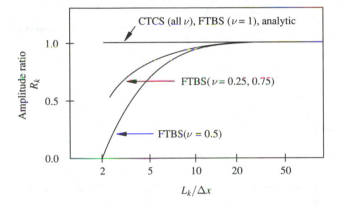

Figure 4.17 Amplitude ratio versus dimensionless wavelength for CTCS and FTBS approximations.

   In Figure 4.18 are shown numerical results using these two approximations. The boundary and initial conditions used are $u(0, t) = 1$, $u(x, 0) = 0$, and $u(\ell, t) = 0$.[1] Relevant parameters in these numerical simulations are $V = 1$, $\ell = 2$, $\Delta x = 0.02$, and $\Delta t = 0.01$ and 0.02 ($\nu = 0.5$ and 1.0). These numerical results indicate that while the CTCS approximations maintain perfect amplitude behavior, the actual numerical solutions exhibit significant oscillations. These oscillations are completely nonphysical, being artifacts of the numerical approximation. On the other hand, the FTBS method with $\nu = 1$, which also maintained perfect amplitude behavior, yields exact solutions. Thus the analysis of amplitude behavior is insufficient to characterize solution behavior adequately.

   When solving equations via Fourier decomposition, each Fourier component or wave can be modified by changes in both amplitude and phase. Dissipative processes

---

[1]Notice that this boundary condition is necessary when the CTCS approximation is used. This boundary condition overspecifies (mathematically) the partial differential equation whenever $D = 0$ (see Chapter 1); therefore, the CTCS scheme should be viewed with some skepticism.

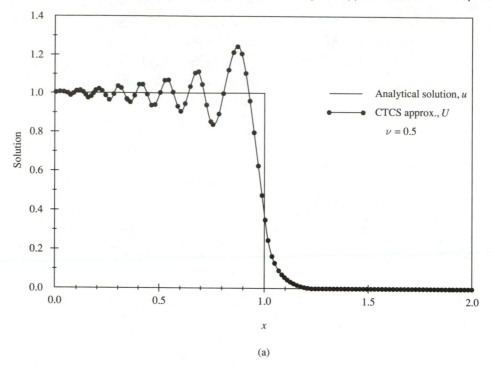

(a)

Figure 4.18   Numerical solutions using (a) CTCS, $\nu = 0.5$.

act to change (decrease) amplitude, while translational or advective processes act to translate, or change the phase of, the Fourier component. To this point, only amplitude changes have been considered. To complete the analysis, phase changes associated with the numerical and analytical solutions must be examined.

To analyze phase change, consider first the analytical phase behavior of equation (4.2.61). The amplification factor is given by equation (4.2.63) as

$$\lambda_k^A = e^{-i\sigma_k V \Delta t} e^{-D\sigma_k^2 \Delta t} \qquad (4.2.63)$$

Given this complex exponential representation, it is convenient to represent phase changes via phase plots, wherein the real and imaginary components of λ_k^A are plotted in the complex plane. As illustrated in Figure 4.19, the angle of phase change over one time step is measured by Φ_k^A, with

$$\tan \Phi_k^A = \frac{\text{Im}\lambda_k^A}{\text{Re}\lambda_k^A} = \frac{\sin(-V\sigma_k\Delta t)}{\cos(-V\sigma_k\Delta t)} = -\tan(V\sigma_k\Delta t)$$

$$= -\tan(\nu\sigma_k\Delta x) = -\tan\left(\nu\frac{2\pi}{L_k/\Delta x}\right) \qquad (4.2.69)$$

In equation (4.2.69), Im and Re refer to imaginary and real, respectively. From equation (4.2.69), Φ_k^A is defined by

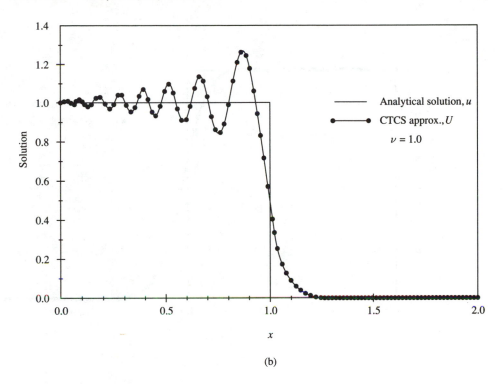

(b)

Figure 4.18 (cont'd.) Numerical solutions using (b) CTCS, $\nu = 1.0$.

$$\Phi_k^A = -\nu \frac{2\pi}{L_k/\Delta x} \tag{4.2.70}$$

Because the phase change per time step is defined by Φ_k^A, the number of time steps required to go through one entire phase cycle, equal to 2π radians, is $2\pi/\Phi_k^A$. This quantity is denoted by M_k^A,

$$M_k^A \equiv \frac{2\pi}{\Phi_k^A} \tag{4.2.71}$$

Comparison of numerical phase behavior to analytical behavior provides a measure of how well a numerical approximation propagates phase changes for each wave k. For example, the CTCS approximation has amplification factor

$$(\lambda_k^N)_C = \frac{1 - \hat{i}(\nu/2)\sin(\sigma_k \Delta x)}{1 + \hat{i}(\nu/2)\sin(\sigma_k \Delta x)} \tag{4.2.67a}$$

The ratio of imaginary to real parts of λ_k^N provides the measure of the numerical phase change per time step, Φ_k^N, via the relation

$$\tan \Phi_k^N = \frac{\mathrm{Im}\lambda_k^N}{\mathrm{Re}\lambda_k^N} = \frac{-\nu \sin(\sigma_k \Delta x)}{1 - (\nu^2/4)\sin^2(\sigma_k \Delta x)} = \frac{-\nu \sin[2\pi/(L_k/\Delta x)]}{1 - (\nu^2/4)\sin^2[2\pi/(L_k/\Delta x)]}$$

$$\tag{4.2.72}$$

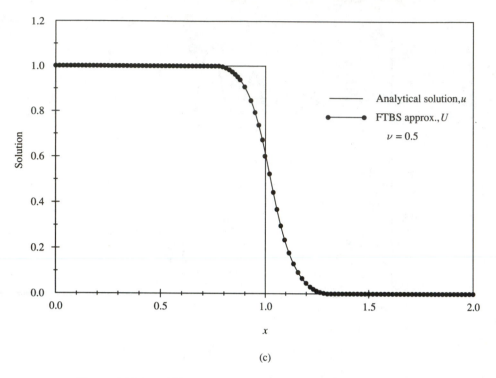

(c)

Figure 4.18 (cont'd.)   Numerical solutions using (c) FTBS, $\nu = 0.5$.

The difference between Φ_k^A and Φ_k^N can be measured as a simple ratio, called the *phase ratio*, as

$$\Gamma_k \equiv \frac{\Phi_k^N}{\Phi_k^A} \qquad (4.2.73)$$

Another measure commonly used is the difference between the numerical and analytical phase shifts after one complete (analytical) phase is completed. This is referred to as the *phase error* Γ_k' and defined by

$$\Gamma_k' \equiv M_k^A \Phi_k^N - M_k^A \Phi_k^A = M_k^A \Phi_k^N - 2\pi \qquad (4.2.74)$$

Figure 4.20a shows plots of Γ_k versus $L_k/\Delta x$ for the CTCS approximation, using $\nu = 0.5$ and $\nu = 1$. Other values of $\nu \le 1$ give very similar results. Notice that while the CTCS approximation showed exact amplitude behavior, the phase behavior is relatively poor, especially in the low L_k range. This means that upon reconstitution of the Fourier components at time $t + \Delta t$, the individual waves do not sum to produce a smooth solution, as indicated by the numerical solutions in Figure 4.18. The numerical solution exhibits nonphysical oscillations because of poor phase behavior.

Similar plots of Γ_k versus $L_k/\Delta x$ for the FTBS approximation are shown in Figure 4.20b. Here there are two values of ν that yield correct phase propagation: $\nu = 0.5$

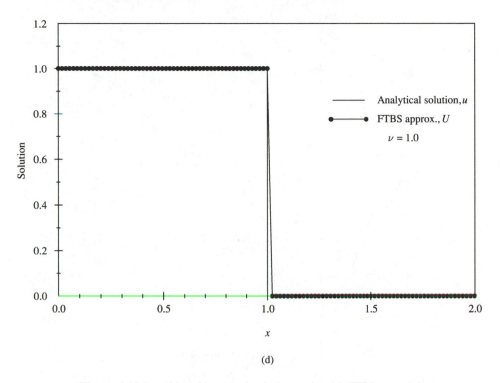

(d)

Figure 4.18 (cont'd.)   Numerical solutions using (d) FTBS, $\nu = 1.0$.

and $\nu = 1.0$. Other values of ν have associated with them phase propagation errors, some greater than 1 (Fourier waves propagate too rapidly) and others less than 1 (waves propagate too slowly). Notice that while the phase behavior for for $\nu = 0.5$ is exact, the actual solution using $\nu = 0.5$ (Figure 4.18) shows excessive smearing of the front. This is due to numerical damping, as shown by the Fourier amplitude plot in Figure 4.17. This dissipative behavior is often referred to as *artificial diffusion* or *numerical diffusion*. This phenomenon is examined in Problems 4.26 and 4.27. When phase errors are present (such as for $\nu = 0.25$ and $\nu = 0.75$), errors greater than 1 tend to induce oscillatory behavior ahead of a front, while errors less than 1 imply possible oscillations behind a front. Actual occurrence of oscillatory behavior depends on the damping characteristics of the governing equation as well as the damping characteristics (measured by the amplitude ratio) of the numerical approximation. Oscillatory behavior also depends on the functional form (shape) of the actual solution as discussed below. The term *numerical dispersion* has purposely been avoided because it is used in some disciplines, such as groundwater hydrology, to denote excessive damping (because *hydrodynamic dispersion* is a diffusive physical process), while in other fields, such as signal processing, it is used to denote phase errors.

Finally, consider the FTBS approximation with $\nu = 1$. For this case, the phase behavior is exact (Figure 4.20). Recall that the amplitude behavior is also exact for

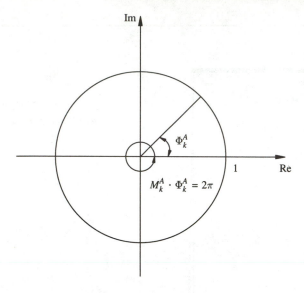

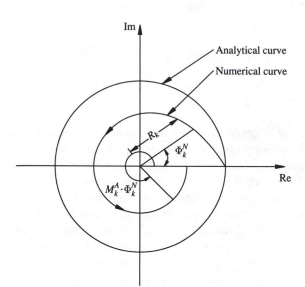

Figure 4.19 Propagation of Fourier components using the complex plane.

FTBS with $\nu = 1$. Because both amplitude and phase are correctly modeled, the resulting numerical solution produces exact nodal values (Figure 4.18). This can be verified by truncation error analysis (Problem 4.28) and by arguments based on the family of characteristic curves associated with the governing first-order hyperbolic partial differential equation (see Section 4.3).

These results indicate that Fourier analysis can be applied to obtain insight into numerical algorithms and to explain the behavior of the resulting numerical solutions.

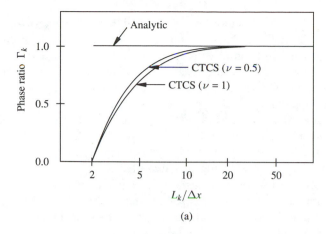

(a)

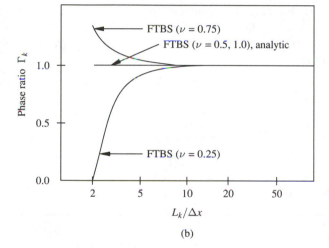

(b)

Figure 4.20 Phase error versus dimensionless wavelength for (a) CTCS and (b) FTBS approximations.

For example, examination of Figure 4.20 indicates that phase errors are most prominent in the short-wavelength (high-wave number) range, where "short" is defined with respect to the grid spacing Δx. (In general, short waves are considered to be wavelengths between $2\Delta x$ and approximately $20\Delta x$.) Short wavelengths are important in Fourier series representation of functions with steep gradients, while they are not very important for smooth, slowly varying functions (see Problem 4.29). These observations lead to the prediction that numerical solutions that use the CTCS approximation will exhibit oscillatory behavior when the true solution has steep gradients (relative to Δx), such as the extreme case of Figure 4.18. This fact may be demonstrated by application of the CTCS approximation to equation (4.2.61) with $D = 0$ and the following boundary and initial conditions: $u(0, t) = u(\ell, t) = 0$, $u(x, 0) = \exp[-(x - x_0)^2 / 2\sigma_0^2]$. The problem is set up so that the nonzero portion of the solution remains far from the boundaries (this is again because the boundary condition at $x = \ell$ is a numerical artifact). A domain of length 5 was used with the following parameters: $V = 1$, $\Delta x = 0.1$,

$\Delta t = 0.05 \, (\nu = 0.5)$, and $x_0 = 2$. Solutions were run to $t = 1$. Choice of $\sigma_0 = 0.1$ means that the initial exponential hill spans approximately $6\Delta x$. On a discrete grid, the *steepness* of a gradient is measured with respect to the discrete spacing Δx. This initial configuration is quite steep, as the resulting oscillations in the numerical solution of Figure 4.21 indicate. Conversely, if a standard deviation of $\sigma_0 = 0.4$ is used, the exponential spans approximately $20\Delta x$. The resulting numerical solution is essentially oscillation-free after time $t = 1$, as illustrated in Figure 4.22. Problems 4.30 and 4.31 explore these concepts further. In particular, those problems illustrate that the apparently smooth numerical solution of Figure 4.22 in fact develops oscillatory behavior as time becomes sufficiently large. This is representative of a phase error that is less severe (but nonetheless present) and therefore takes a longer time to affect the solution. Because the CTCS algorithm has no inherent dissipation (due to its unit amplitude of all wavelengths), phase errors will eventually produce oscillatory behavior no matter how fine the spatial discretization. However, for practical (finite time) simulations, discretizations can be defined that provide acceptable solutions. The only restriction might be one of computational resources, given the potentially large number of nodes that could be required. Alternatively, another approximation method might be chosen instead of the CTCS algorithm.

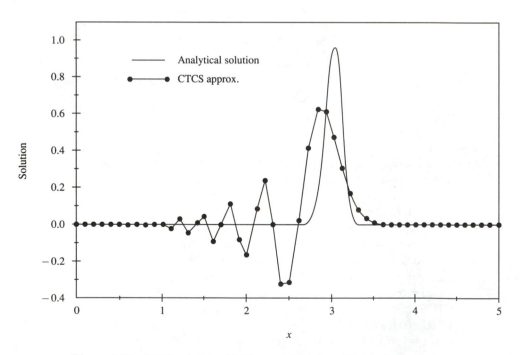

Figure 4.21 CTCS solution with Gaussian initial condition spanning approximately $6\Delta x$.

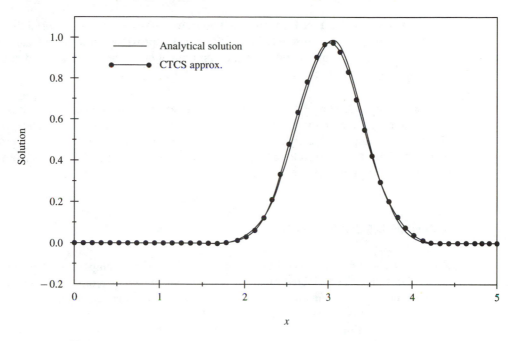

Figure 4.22   CTCS solution with Gaussian initial condition spanning approximately $20\Delta x$.

4.2.3 Convergence

A desirable property for any numerical approximate is that it should produce solutions that become arbitrarily close to the exact solution as the spatial and temporal steps are reduced toward zero. That is, the numerical modeler must have confidence that numerical errors can be controlled by sufficiently fine discretization. If this is not the case, then the numerical approximation is likely to be useless.

A numerical approximation to a differential equation that reproduces the exact solution upon continuous spatial and temporal grid refinement is said to be *convergent*. Mathematically, the criterion is stated as follows:

$$\lim_{\substack{\Delta \mathbf{x} \to 0 \\ \Delta t \to 0}} \|u(\mathbf{x}, t) - U(\mathbf{x}, t)\| = 0 \qquad \text{(convergence)} \qquad (4.2.75)$$

where $u(\mathbf{x}, t)$ denotes the exact solution and $U(\mathbf{x}, t)$ denotes the numerical approximation. Convergence is an important property for any numerical scheme.

While analytical tools exist to investigate properties of approximations such as consistency and stability, analogous tools to analyze for convergence are not readily available. Fortunately, there exists a very important theorem from which convergence may be implied by using consistency and stability analyses. In particular, the Lax equivalence theorem states that consistent and stable approximations are also convergent. Thus convergence may be shown by truncation error analysis (consistency) and by stability analysis. The formal statement of the theorem is as follows:

Theorem 4.2.1: Lax Equivalence Theorem.   Given a properly posed linear initial value problem and a discrete, linear numerical approximation to it that satisfies the consistency requirements, stability of the approximation is the necessary and sufficient condition for convergence.

References that present proof of this theorem are given in Appendix C. This theorem is very important because it allows the tools already developed in this and previous chapters to be applied directly to the question of convergence. Convergence is a property that should always be considered when choosing a numerical method. If an algorithm is not convergent, it should generally be avoided.

4.3 SPACE-TIME DISCRETIZATION

Sections 4.1 and 4.2 presented basic concepts for spatial and temporal grid design. Spatial grid design was considered for steady-state problems, while temporal design included some space-time problems but did not examine the spatial discretization beyond consideration of stability. The present section will look briefly at simultaneous analysis of both space and time discretizations. This is generally a complicated issue, but will be addressed briefly here using heuristic reasoning and simple truncation error analysis. Numerical treatment of grid design in the context of error analysis and error control is presented in the next chapter.

The presentation in this section will focus on two model problems, each of which corresponds to a transient extension of a problem for which optimal spatial approximations were derived in Section 4.1. These equations are

$$\frac{\partial u}{\partial t} - \frac{\partial}{\partial x}\left[(\alpha + \beta x)\frac{\partial u}{\partial x}\right] = 0 \tag{4.3.1}$$

$$\frac{\partial u}{\partial t} + V\frac{\partial u}{\partial x} - D\frac{\partial^2 u}{\partial x^2} = 0 \tag{4.3.2}$$

As in the previous sections, simple analytical results will be derived for these model equations. The resulting guidelines may provide insight into grid design for more complex equations that are similar in form to equations (4.3.1) and (4.3.2).

4.3.1 Static Grids

Consider first the transient diffusion equation (4.3.1). Absent the time derivative, truncation error analysis presented in Section 4.1 demonstrated that exact nodal solutions could be obtained using a three-point finite difference approximation if proper node placement is used. A similar truncation error analysis may be applied to finite difference approximations for equation (4.3.1). For example, consider the following one-step-in-time, three-points-in-space finite difference approximation,

$$\frac{U_i^{n+1} - U_i^n}{\Delta t^n} - \frac{K_{i+1/2}\dfrac{U_{i+1}^{n+\theta} - U_i^{n+\theta}}{\Delta x_i} - K_{i-1/2}\dfrac{U_i^{n+\theta} - U_{i-1}^{n+\theta}}{\nabla x_i}}{\delta x_i} = 0 \qquad (4.3.3)$$

where Δt^n denotes the nth time step, $K(x) \equiv \alpha + \beta x$, and equation (4.3.3) is derived by Taylor series expansions about the point $(x_i, t^{n+\theta})$. Taylor expansions and subsequent truncation error analysis show that the truncation error may be expressed as follows (Problem 4.32):

$$\text{T.E.} = \frac{1}{\delta x_i}\left[\frac{(\Delta x_i)^2}{24}\left(K\frac{\partial^3 u}{\partial x^3}\right)\Big|_{x_{i+1/2}}^{t^{n+\theta}} - \frac{(\nabla x_i)^2}{24}\left(K\frac{\partial^3 u}{\partial x^3}\right)\Big|_{x_{i-1/2}}^{t^{n+\theta}} + \cdots \right]$$

$$+ \left[\frac{1}{\delta x_i}\frac{(\Delta x_i)^2 - (\nabla x_i)^2}{8}\right]\frac{\partial^2 u}{\partial x\,\partial t}\Big|_{x_i}^{t^{n+\theta}}$$

$$+ \left[\frac{1}{\delta x_i}\frac{(\Delta x_i)^3 + (\nabla x_i)^3}{48}\right]\frac{\partial^3 u}{\partial x^2\,\partial t}\Big|_{x_i}^{t^{n+\theta}}$$

$$+ \left[\frac{1 - 2\theta}{2}(\Delta t)\right]\frac{\partial^2 u}{\partial t^2}\Big|_{x_i}^{t^{n+\theta}} + \mathcal{O}((\Delta t)^2, (\delta x)^3) \qquad (4.3.4)$$

From the governing equation,

$$K\frac{\partial u}{\partial x}(x, t) = q_0(t) + \int_0^x \frac{\partial u}{\partial t}dx, \quad \text{with } q_0 \equiv \left(K\frac{\partial u}{\partial x}\right)\Big|_{x=0}$$

Therefore,

$$K\frac{\partial^3 u}{\partial x^3} = \left[\frac{2}{K^2}\left(\frac{dK}{dx}\right)^2 - \frac{1}{K}\frac{d^2 K}{dx^2}\right]\left[q_0 + \int_0^x \frac{\partial u}{\partial t}dx\right] - \frac{2}{K}\frac{dK}{dx}\frac{\partial u}{\partial t} + \frac{\partial^2 u}{\partial x\,\partial t}$$

$$= \frac{\partial^2 u}{\partial x\,\partial t} - \frac{2}{K}\frac{dK}{dx}\frac{\partial u}{\partial t} + \kappa(x)\left[q_0 + \int_0^x \frac{\partial u}{\partial t}dx\right] \qquad (4.3.5)$$

Substitution of equation (4.3.5) into equation (4.3.4) and rearrangement leads to

$$\text{T.E.} = \frac{1}{\delta x_i}\left\{ \left[q_0^{n+\theta} + \int_0^{x_{i-1/2}}\frac{\partial u}{\partial t}dx\right]\left[\frac{\kappa_{i+1/2}(\Delta x_i)^2}{24} - \frac{\kappa_{i-1/2}(\nabla x_i)^2}{24}\right] \right\}$$

$$+ \frac{1}{\delta x_i}\left\{ \frac{(\Delta x_i)^2}{24}\left[\frac{\partial^2 u}{\partial x\,\partial t}\Big|_{x_{i+1/2}}^{t^{n+\theta}} - \left[\frac{2}{K}\left(\frac{dK}{dx}\right)\frac{\partial u}{\partial t}\right]\Big|_{x_{i+1/2}}^{t^{n+\theta}}\right] \right.$$

$$\left. - \frac{(\nabla x_i)^2}{24}\left[\frac{\partial^2 u}{\partial x\,\partial t}\Big|_{x_{i-1/2}}^{t^{n+\theta}} - \left[\frac{2}{K}\left(\frac{dK}{dx}\right)\frac{\partial u}{\partial t}\right]\Big|_{x_{i-1/2}}^{t^{n+\theta}}\right]\right.$$

$$
+ \kappa_{i+1/2} \frac{(\Delta x_i)^2}{24} \int_{x_{i-1/2}}^{x_{i+1/2}} \left. \frac{\partial u}{\partial t} \right|^{t^{n+\theta}} dx \bigg\}
$$

$$
+ \frac{1 - 2\theta}{2} (\Delta t) \left. \frac{\partial^2 u}{\partial t^2} \right|_{x_i}^{t^{n+\theta}} + \mathcal{O}((\Delta t)^2, (\delta x)^3) \tag{4.3.6}
$$

For arbitrary choices of node locations, the truncation error is $\mathcal{O}(\Delta t, \delta x)$. However, judicious choice of grid point locations may again be used to advantage. For example, choice of grid spacing ratio $\nabla x_i / \Delta x_i$ such that

$$
\frac{\nabla x_i}{\Delta x_i} = \sqrt{\frac{\kappa_{i+1/2}}{\kappa_{i-1/2}}} \tag{4.3.7}
$$

eliminates the first term in equation (4.3.6), while choice of $\theta = 0.5$ eliminates the $\partial^2 u / \partial t^2$ term. In addition, the other derivatives appearing in equation (4.3.6) may all be approximated using the six node points at x_{i-1}, x_i, x_{i+1} and t^n, t^{n+1}, which are the points that have been used in the original finite difference approximation. For example,

$$
\left. \frac{\partial^2 u}{\partial x \, \partial t} \right|_{x_{i+1/2}}^{t^{n+1/2}} = \frac{u_{i+1}^{n+1} - u_{i+1}^{n} - u_i^{n+1} + u_i^{n}}{(\Delta x_i)(\Delta t)} + \mathcal{O}((\Delta x)^2, (\Delta t)^2) \tag{4.3.8}
$$

Similar approximations may be written for the other terms, including the integral between $x_{i-1/2}$ and $x_{i+1/2}$ (Problem 4.33). Employment of these approximations leads to a spatial truncation error that is $\mathcal{O}((\delta x)^3)$ and temporal errors that are $\mathcal{O}((\Delta t)^2)$. Thus a high-order approximation may be derived using only two time levels and three spatial locations.

Notice that for this equation there is no way to eliminate additional higher-order terms in the truncation error without using more nodes in the finite difference approximation. In general, it is not possible to generate exact finite difference solutions for this equation. This is because the solution space for $u(x, t)$ is infinite dimensional, meaning that an infinite number of functions is required to represent the general solution u. Whenever this is the case, any numerical solution will be incapable of capturing the exact values. For the one-dimensional example [steady-state version of equation (4.3.1)], exact finite difference approximations are possible because the solution space is finite-dimensional (dimension 2, with two fundamental solutions $\{1, ln(\alpha + \beta x)\}$). While the analysis presented above results in improved approximations for the transient differential equation, the improvements are not significant (see Problem 4.34). The major influence is spatial node placement, and other (temporal) effects appear to be secondary.

As a second example of space-time analysis, consider the transient version of the advection-diffusion equation in one spatial dimension,

$$
\frac{\partial u}{\partial t} + V \frac{\partial u}{\partial x} - D \frac{\partial^2 u}{\partial x^2} = 0 \tag{4.3.9}
$$

The steady-state version of this equation was analyzed in Section 4.1. In that discussion, a finite difference approximation was offered that produces exact nodal values. This is possible because, for the steady-state equation in one dimension, the solution space is finite dimensional (dimension of 2). As stated above, this allows exact finite difference approximations to be derived. The transient partial differential equation has a solution space of infinite dimension, and therefore is not expected to admit finite difference approximations that yield exact solutions.

Consider application of the "optimal" rule derived in Section 4.1 to approximate the transient equation (4.3.9). This approximation may be written as a semidiscretization as

$$\frac{dU_i}{dt} + V\frac{U_{i+1} - U_i}{2(\Delta x)} - (D + D^*)\frac{U_{i+1} - 2U_i + U_{i-1}}{(\Delta x)^2} = 0 \qquad (4.3.10)$$

where $D^* \equiv \alpha_{opt}(V\Delta x/2)$, a constant space step, Δx, is assumed, and $\alpha_{opt} \equiv \coth(V\Delta x/2D) - (2D/V\Delta x)$ (see Section 4.1 and Problem 4.10). Because this choice of D^* yields a zero truncation error for the (combined) spatial derivatives, equation (4.3.10) has zero truncation error. However, the task of temporal discretization remains. It is here that nonzero truncation error is introduced.

Consider approximation of equation (4.3.10) by a one-step, variably weighted Euler method,

$$\frac{U_i^{n+1} - U_i^n}{\Delta t} + V\left[\theta\frac{U_{i+1}^{n+1} - U_{i-1}^{n+1}}{2(\Delta x)} + (1 - \theta)\frac{U_{i+1}^n - U_{i-1}^n}{2(\Delta x)}\right]$$

$$-(D + D^*)\left[\theta\frac{U_{i+1}^{n+1} - 2U_i^{n+1} + U_{i-1}^{n+1}}{(\Delta x)^2} + (1 - \theta)\frac{U_{i+1}^n - 2U_i^n + U_{i-1}^n}{(\Delta x)^2}\right] = 0 \qquad (4.3.11)$$

The truncation error associated with this approximation is $\mathcal{O}((1 - 2\theta)\Delta t, (\Delta t)^2)$, with the truncation error expression being

$$\text{T.E.} = \frac{1 - 2\theta}{2}(\Delta t)\left.\frac{\partial^2 u}{\partial t^2}\right|_{x_i}^{t^{n+\theta}} + \frac{1 - 3\theta(1 - \theta)}{3!}(\Delta t)^2\left.\frac{\partial^3 u}{\partial t^3}\right|_{x_i}^{t^{n+\theta}}$$

$$+ \frac{\theta(1 - \theta)}{2}(\Delta t)^2\frac{\partial^2}{\partial t^2}\left.\left(V\frac{\partial u}{\partial x} - D\frac{\partial^2 u}{\partial x^2}\right)\right|_{x_i}^{t^{n+\theta}} + \mathcal{O}\left((\Delta t)^3\right) \qquad (4.3.12)$$

While the steady-state solution led to exact nodal values, independent of the values of V, D, or Δx (i.e., independent of the grid Peclet number $\text{Pe}^G \equiv V\Delta x/D$), transient results based on equation (4.3.11) turn out to be quite sensitive to Pe^G. For example, Figure 4.23 shows results for the Gauss hill problem used at the end of Section 4.2, where approximation (4.3.11) is applied to equation (4.3.9) with boundary conditions $u(0, t) = u(\ell, t) = 0$ and initial condition $u(x, 0) = \exp[-(x - x_0)^2/(2\sigma_0^2)]$. The solution of Figure 4.23 can be seen to be excessively diffusive. The Fourier analysis plots for this approximation, shown in Figure 4.24, reveal the expected behavior, with the amplitude plots exhibiting excessive numerical damping and the phase plots illustrating phase shift error for the smaller wavelengths. Notice that the excessive damping (amplitude errors) of the short wavelengths serves to damp out the oscillatory behavior that might be

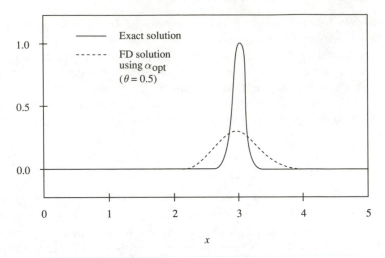

Figure 4.23 Transient finite difference solution based on optimal spatial approximation.

expected from the phase error analysis. This again demonstrates that amplitude and phase errors work in concert to define the final numerical solution. This example also demonstrates that for problems with relatively steep fronts, an optimal rule for the spatial part of the equation alone provides a relatively poor algorithm for the transient equation. Simple separation of space and time is not necessarily a good strategy for numerical approximations.

The root of the difficulty, when the Peclet number Pe^G is large and steep fronts are present, is the time truncation error. The optimal spatial discretization used above has as its foundation the idea of combining the advection, $V(\partial u/\partial x)$, and diffusion, $D(\partial^2 u/\partial x^2)$, approximations to cancel truncation errors, yielding no net truncation error. In transient problems involving large Peclet numbers, the solution at a fixed point in space may change quite rapidly. This means that derivatives with respect to time can be very large, and the time truncation error may therefore overwhelm the numerical solution.

To improve the approximation for the case of large Peclet numbers (which is the most severe case in terms of errors), consider adoption of a different strategy wherein both spatial and temporal truncation errors are allowed to be nonzero. However, let the strategy be adopted such that the leading components of the spatial error cancel with the leading terms in the temporal error. To demonstrate the idea, consider the limiting case of $D \to 0$ ($Pe^G \to \infty$). In this case, the governing equation (4.3.9) reverts to the pure advection case,

$$\frac{\partial u}{\partial t} + V\frac{\partial u}{\partial x} = 0 \tag{4.3.13}$$

Next consider a general three-point (in space), two-level (in time) approximation for the time and space derivatives, such that

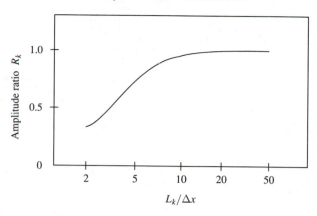

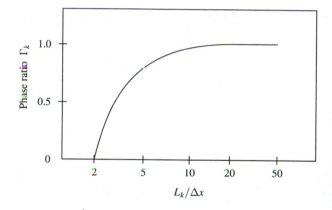

Figure 4.24 Amplitude and phase error plots for the solution shown in Figure 4.23.

$$\left.\frac{\partial u}{\partial t}\right|_{x_i}^{t^{n+\theta}} \simeq \gamma_{-1}\frac{U_{i-1}^{n+1}-U_{i-1}^{n}}{\Delta t} + (1-\gamma_{-1}-\gamma_1)\frac{U_i^{n+1}-U_i^{n}}{\Delta t} + \gamma_1\frac{U_{i+1}^{n+1}-U_{i+1}^{n}}{\Delta t} \quad (4.3.14a)$$

$$\left.\frac{\partial u}{\partial x}\right|_{x_i}^{t^{n+\theta}} \simeq \theta\left[\alpha\frac{U_i^{n+1}-U_{i-1}^{n+1}}{\Delta x} + (1-\alpha)\frac{U_{i+1}^{n+1}-U_{i-1}^{n+1}}{2\Delta x}\right]$$

$$+ (1-\theta)\left[\alpha\frac{U_i^{n}-U_{i-1}^{n}}{\Delta x} + (1-\alpha)\frac{U_{i+1}^{n}-U_{i-1}^{n}}{2\Delta x}\right] \quad (4.3.14b)$$

where the coefficients $(1-\gamma_{-1}-\gamma_1)$, $(1-\theta)$, and $(1-\alpha)$ are required for consistency (given γ_{-1}, γ_1, θ, and α). The truncation error associated with these approximations may be written as follows (see Problem 4.35):

$$\text{T.E.} = \left\{-V(\gamma_1-\gamma_{-1})(\Delta x) - V\frac{\alpha\Delta x}{2} + V^2\frac{1-2\theta}{2}(\Delta t)\right\}\left.\frac{\partial^2 u}{\partial x^2}\right|_{x_i}^{t^{n+\theta}}$$

$$+ \left\{V\frac{(\Delta x)^2}{6} - V(\gamma_1+\gamma_{-1})\frac{(\Delta x)^2}{2} + V^2(\gamma_1-\gamma_{-1})\frac{1-2\theta}{2}(\Delta x)(\Delta t)\right.$$

$$
+V^3 \frac{\theta(1-\theta)}{2}(\Delta t)^2 - V^3 \frac{1-3\theta(1-\theta)}{6}(\Delta t)^2 \bigg\} \frac{\partial^3 u}{\partial x^3}\bigg|^{t^{n+\theta}}_{x_i}
$$

$$
+ \bigg\{ -V\alpha\frac{(\Delta x)^3}{24} - V(\gamma_1 - \gamma_{-1})\frac{(\Delta x)^3}{6} + V^2(\gamma_1 - \gamma_{-1})\frac{1-2\theta}{2}(\Delta t)\frac{(\Delta x)^2}{2}
$$

$$
- V^3 \bigg[\alpha\frac{\theta(1-\theta)}{2} + (\gamma_1 - \gamma_{-1})\frac{1-3\theta(1-\theta)}{6}\bigg](\Delta x)(\Delta t)^2
$$

$$
+ V^4 \frac{(1-\theta)^4 - \theta^4}{24}(\Delta t)^3 \bigg\} \frac{\partial^4 u}{\partial x^4}\bigg|^{t^{n+\theta}}_{x_i} + \mathcal{O}((\Delta x)^p(\Delta t)^q)
$$

$$
(p + q = 4, \ p \geq 1, \ q \geq 1) \qquad (4.3.15)
$$

In deriving equation (4.3.15), use was made of the following equalities

$$
\frac{\partial u}{\partial t} = -V\frac{\partial u}{\partial x},
$$

$$
\frac{\partial^2 u}{\partial x\,\partial t} = -V\frac{\partial^2 u}{\partial x^2},
$$

$$
\frac{\partial^2 u}{\partial t^2} = V^2\frac{\partial^2 u}{\partial x^2}, \quad \text{etc.}
$$

The coefficients of the $\partial^2 u/\partial x^2$ and $\partial^4 u/\partial x^4$ terms in equation (4.3.15) may be forced to zero by specifying $\alpha = 0$, $\theta = 0.5$, and $\gamma_1 = \gamma_{-1} \equiv \Gamma$. A specific value of Γ may then be determined such that the coefficient of the $\partial^3 u/\partial x^3$ term is zero. The relevant equation is

$$
V\frac{(\Delta x)^2}{6} - V\Gamma(\Delta x)^2 + V^3\frac{(\Delta t)^2}{8} - V^3\frac{(\Delta t)^2}{24} = 0
$$

Division by $V(\Delta x)^2$ and use of the Courant number $\nu \equiv V(\Delta t)/\Delta x$ allows Γ to be determined as

$$
\Gamma = \frac{1}{6} + \frac{\nu^2}{12} \qquad (4.3.16)
$$

With these values for Γ, θ, and α, the resulting finite difference approximation is $\mathcal{O}((\Delta x)^4, (\Delta x)^2(\Delta t)^2, (\Delta t)^4)$ and takes the form

$$
\left(\frac{1}{6} + \frac{\nu^2}{12}\right)\frac{U_{i-1}^{n+1} - U_{i-1}^n}{\Delta t} + \left(\frac{2}{3} - \frac{\nu^2}{6}\right)\frac{U_i^{n+1} - U_i^n}{\Delta t} + \left(\frac{1}{6} + \frac{\nu^2}{12}\right)\frac{U_{i+1}^{n+1} - U_{i+1}^n}{\Delta t}
$$

$$
+ V\left[\left(\frac{1}{2}\right)\frac{U_{i+1}^{n+1} - U_{i-1}^{n+1}}{2(\Delta x)} + \left(\frac{1}{2}\right)\frac{U_{i+1}^n - U_{i-1}^n}{2(\Delta x)}\right] = 0 \qquad (4.3.17)
$$

Notice that this approximation can be viewed as a perturbed, or corrected, Galerkin approximation in that the Galerkin finite element method with piecewise linear basis functions produces a spatial weighting of the time derivative of (1/6, 2/3, 1/6), while the approximation for the advection term is identical to that in equation (4.3.17).

Based on this analysis, it should be expected that use of the weights $[(1/6 + \nu^2/12), (2/3 - \nu^2/6), (1/6 + \nu^2/12)]$ for the time derivative, with centered spatial approximations for the advection and diffusion terms, will produce improved solutions for the transient advection-diffusion equation in which advection dominates diffusion. Figure 4.25 presents a comparison of such a solution with a solution based on the optimal spatial approximation, equation (4.3.11). In the figure are shown example numerical solutions for the Gauss hill problem. Notice that the approximation based on equation (4.3.17) provides a significantly better approximation in terms of amplitude behavior, but it still suffers from oscillatory behavior. Fourier analysis can again provide the explanation of why this occurs.

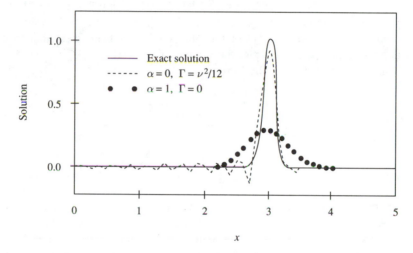

Figure 4.25   Solutions using equation (4.3.17), denoted by dashed line, and optimal spatial solution, denoted by •.

This last example problem demonstrates that application of optimal rules for steady-state problems to the related transient problem is often not a good strategy. It is important to have a sufficient understanding of the physical system so that the dominant terms in the equation can be identified. Then an algorithm should be devised that controls these errors, if possible. Error cancellation between terms must be understood, because this is a likely avenue for error control. For more complex problems, simple analytical control of errors may become impossible. In those cases, resort to numerical estimates of error is warranted; numerical error control is discussed in Chapter 5.

4.3.2 Dynamic Gridding

To this point, grid design has been restricted by the unstated assumption that spatial locations of node points are fixed for all time. Relaxation of this restriction can often yield approximations that more fully take advantage of the ideas of space-time error cancellation. Nonstationary grids may also provide significantly improved computational efficiencies by allocating the majority of nodes to regions of the domain where they are most needed, while using relatively few in regions where the solution is not changing much. Although these ideas seem both reasonable and very appealing, their practical implementation for general multidimensional problems remains an area of active research. This section will present a very brief introduction to this general topic, with the aim of providing an understanding of the basic ideas. Related topics are discussed in Sections 5.1.5 and 5.3.

As an introduction, reconsider the example of the transient transport equation presented in Section 4.3.1. In particular, for the relatively general approximation to the pure advection equation, given by equations (4.3.14), a choice was made for the parameters α, θ, γ_{-1}, and γ_1, such that a high-order approximation was achieved. The values of the parameters chosen were $\alpha = 0$, $\theta = 0.5$, $\gamma_{-1} = \gamma_1 = \nu^2/12$, where ν is the Courant number. However, this is not the only choice of parameters that gives a high-order approximation. For example, the choice of $\alpha = 1$, $\theta = 0$, $\gamma_{-1} = \gamma_1 = 0$ leads to a truncation error that has the form

$$
\text{T.E.} = \left\{ \frac{V(\Delta x)}{2}[\nu - 1] \right\} \frac{\partial^2 u}{\partial x^2}\bigg|_{x_i}^{t^n} - \left\{ \frac{V(\Delta x)^2}{6}[\nu^2 - 1] \right\} \frac{\partial^3 u}{\partial x^3}\bigg|_{x_i}^{t^n}
$$

$$
+ \left\{ \frac{V(\Delta x)^3}{24}[\nu^3 - 1] \right\} \frac{\partial^4 u}{\partial x^4}\bigg|_{x_i}^{t^n} + \cdots \qquad (4.3.18)
$$

Examination of equation (4.3.18) indicates that restriction of Δx and Δt such that $\nu \equiv V(\Delta t)/\Delta x = 1$ results in a truncation error of zero—that is, an exact solution. [Notice that this is the FTBS approximation of equation (4.2.67b) with $\nu = 1$, which was shown to be exact in Section 4.2.] The reason that this occurs is that the pure advection equation has a simple analytical solution: namely any function that has constant values along the space-time curves $x - Vt = $ constant. The curves $x - Vt = $ constant (i.e., $dx/dt = V$) define the characteristic curves of the first-order partial differential equation (see Chapter 1). When the numerical solution moves exactly along the analytical characteristics to define the numerical solution, exact values are obtained. This is easily seen to be the case in this example in that the finite difference approximation when $\nu = 1$ reduces to the simple expression $U_i^{n+1} = U_{i-1}^n$. Here $\Delta x/\Delta t = V$ is the numerical characteristic. Therefore, for pure advection, the optimal approximation is that which follows the characteristics of the governing equation.

This observation may be used to significant advantage when solving advection-dominated transport problems. In fact, this simple observation is the foundation of many numerical methods, including the so-called Eulerian-Lagrangian methods, method of characteristics, and particle tracking methods. Some representative references for these methods are provided in Appendix C. All of these are *characteristic methods* in that characteristic curves, defined by $dx/dt = V$, are tracked through space-time as part of the solution procedure. Detailed presentation of these methods is beyond the scope of this book. However, a simple example will be solved to demonstrate one possible use of characteristics in solving dynamic equations.

Consider solution of the advection-diffusion equation by a moving grid that incorporates the characteristic concept. Let the Gauss hill problem be solved, so that the governing equation is

$$\frac{\partial u}{\partial t} + V\frac{\partial u}{\partial x} - D\frac{\partial^2 u}{\partial x^2} = 0, \qquad 0 < x < \ell, \quad t > 0 \tag{4.3.19}$$

$$u(0, t) = 0$$

$$u(\ell, t) = 0$$

$$u(x, 0) = \exp\left[-\frac{(x - x_0)^2}{2\sigma_0^2}\right]$$

where $\ell = 10$ and the initial center of mass is $x_0 = 3.0$ with standard deviation $\sigma_0 = 0.3$. From previous arguments in this chapter, the important truncation errors are expected to occur in the vicinity of the hill; in regions where $u \simeq 0$, there is essentially no truncation error. Let the grid of Figure 4.26a be used as the initial grid. In this grid are 11 nodes, with spacing $\Delta x_1 = 2$, $\Delta x_k = 0.25\,(k = 2, 3, \ldots, 10)$, and $\Delta x_{10} = 6$. The cluster of nodes, numbered 2 through 10, are closely spaced to define the Gauss hill with relatively high resolution. This choice of initial grid points is purely heuristic. Let this cluster of nodes be moved to new locations at the next time level, t^1, so that $(x_k)^1 = (x_k)^0 + V(\Delta t)$, $k = 2, 3, \ldots, 10$. The resulting node locations at time $t^4 = 4\Delta t$ are shown in Figure 4.26b. Given this dynamic discretization, the appropriate finite difference approximation may be written as

$$\frac{U_i^{n+1} - U_i^n}{\Delta t} - D\frac{1}{\delta x_i^n}\left[\frac{1}{\nabla x_i^n}U_{i-1}^n - \left(\frac{1}{\nabla x_i^n} + \frac{1}{\Delta x_i^n}\right)U_i^n + \frac{1}{\Delta x_i^n}U_{i+1}^n = 0\right] \tag{4.3.20}$$

where a subscript i identifies a node number whose spatial location varies as a function of time. Spacing between nodes may also be time dependent, so that δx_i, ∇x_i, and Δx_i have a superscript n associated with them. In this equation, the first-order time and space derivatives are approximated using the characteristic concept while the diffusion term is evaluated explicitly at the old time level, t^n. The solution at the new time level is

$$U_i^{n+1} = U_i^n + \frac{D(\Delta t)}{\delta x_i^n}\left[\frac{1}{\nabla x_i^n}U_{i-1}^n - \left(\frac{1}{\nabla x_i^n} + \frac{1}{\Delta x_i^n}\right)U_i^n + \frac{1}{\Delta x_i^n}U_{i+1}^n\right] \tag{4.3.21}$$

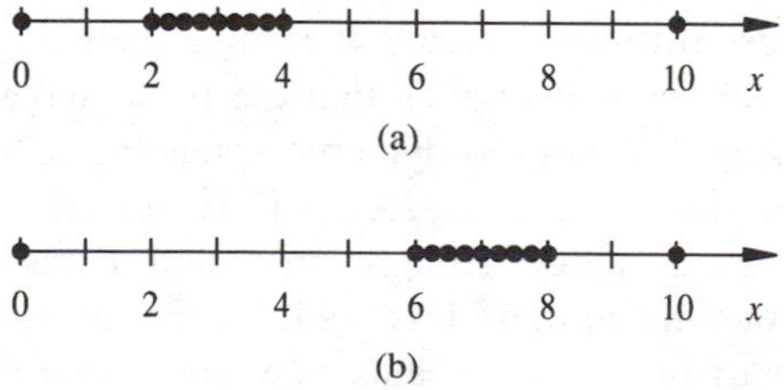

(a)

(b)

Figure 4.26 Dynamic grid, with (a) initial grid and (b) grid after $4\Delta t$.

Equation (4.3.21) demonstrates explicitly that the solution at time $n + 1$ is a result of pure translation (advection) as well as a diffusive component which tends to spread the solution profile spatially.

Figure 4.27 shows a profile calculated using this algorithm. It is compared to a solution that uses the same number of nodes but the nodes are static and equally spaced. The advantages of the proposed algorithm are obvious from the solutions shown in the figure.

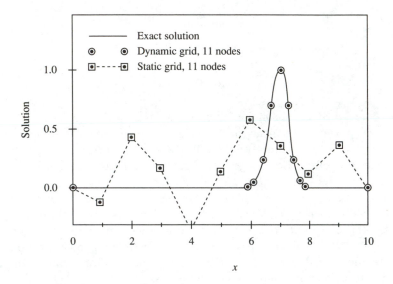

Figure 4.27 Dynamic grid solution versus static grid solution.

Notice that when $D \neq 0$, the governing partial differential equation is formally parabolic, with characteristic curves that are simply horizontal lines in space-time. What is actually being done numerically is to acknowledge the importance of the secondary characteristics (see Chapter 1), because for early times the solution is dominated by these secondary characteristics. Numerical methods that incorporate this behavior are able to produce good approximations, while methods that do not respect this behavior generally behave poorly.

While this method of tracking along secondary characteristics appears to be an efficient technique for obtaining very accurate solutions, it has several shortcomings. First, the spacing between the clustered nodes ideally should increase as time increases (assuming that $D \neq 0$) because diffusion spreads the pulse spatially as time increases. For this problem, the analytical solution implies that the pulse spreads as $\sim \sqrt{1/Dt}$. This knowledge might be used to design the dynamic spreading of the grid points. A more challenging problem occurs when the velocity V is not constant. In this case, the secondary characteristics are no longer straight lines, and numerical tracking along these characteristics may become much more involved. Furthermore, if care (sometimes extreme care) is not taken, variable-velocity fields may cause two nodes to cross one another, leading to a "tangled" grid, which causes the approximation to fail. This is especially problematic in complex multidimensional flow fields. This difficulty is one of the strongest motivations for incorporating characteristic-type approximations in the context of fixed spatial grids and for developing techniques for selective refinement on a fixed coarse grid. An example of a characteristic method on a fixed grid is discussed in Problem 4.36, while selective refinement on a fixed coarse grid is discussed in Sections 5.1.4 and 5.2.4.

As a final example, consider the transient equation

$$\frac{\partial u}{\partial t} - \frac{\partial}{\partial x}\left[(\alpha + \beta x)\frac{\partial u}{\partial x}\right] = 0, \qquad 0 < x < \ell, \quad t > 0 \qquad (4.3.22)$$

Static-grid rules for node placement were developed for this equation earlier in Section 4.3.1. However, this is another equation for which dynamic gridding might be employed to improve the numerical solution. For this problem, the concept of secondary characteristics does not apply. However, grid design rules based on the underlying physics of the problem may be attempted. For example, consider the case of the following boundary and initial conditions: $u(x,0) = C_0$, $u(\ell,t) = C_0$, and $u(0,t) = C_1$, with C_0 and C_1 constants. The solution is a disturbance that propagates into the domain from the left boundary, due to the imposed change $C_1 - C_0$. As time increases, this change propagates (diffuses) into the domain. While the characteristic analysis of Chapter 1 indicates that all points in the domain are influenced by the change at the boundary, for all $t > 0$, significant changes in u are initially restricted to areas local to $x = 0$. This is demonstrated qualitatively in Figure 4.28. If at a time t^*, the zone of disturbance [defined by, say, values of u greater than $C_0 + 0.01(C_1 - C_0)$] has moved to $x = \ell^* \le \ell$, then the grid generation algorithm of Section 4.1 might be applied using length ℓ^*. That is, if N^* nodes are to be used within this zone, they would be spaced geometrically according to equation (4.1.12a), with

$$\rho_i \equiv \frac{\nabla x_i}{\Delta x_i} = \left(1 - \frac{\beta\ell^*}{\alpha + \beta\ell^*}\right)^{1/(N^*-1)} \qquad (4.3.23)$$

Some practical implementation problems related to this algorithm are discussed in Problem 4.37.

As was stated at the beginning of this section, the presentation on dynamic gridding is meant to provide a simple introduction to the topic. This area of numerical methods is developing rapidly, and the interested reader is referred to the reading list of Appendix C for more detailed information. Dynamic local grid refinement on fixed coarse grids, as well as dynamic local time stepping, appear to hold significant promise for realizing the full potential of dynamic gridding while avoiding many of its inherent difficulties. In addition, variants of Eulerian-Lagrangian methods (Problem 4.36) which use the characteristic-tracking concept on fixed grids, also appear to hold significant promise.

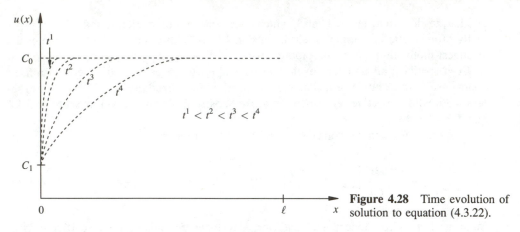

Figure 4.28 Time evolution of solution to equation (4.3.22).

4.4 ALTERNATIVE NUMERICAL PROCEDURES

To this point, finite difference theory has been the major focus for deriving simple rules for grid design and for high-order approximation development. More general systematic procedures exist for generating approximations with some "optimality" properties. This section briefly introduces several of these methods. All are presented in the context of the method of weighted residuals, and some will be shown to be slight generalization, or simply direct utilization, of the truncation error analysis presented above.

Petrov-Galerkin (P-G) methods are method of weighted residuals (MWR) techniques in which the test space (the space in which the weight, or test, functions reside) is different from the trial space. Under this definition, it can be seen that several Petrov-Galerkin methods have already been presented in Chapter 3, namely the subdomain method and the collocation method. The actual designation of a method as a Petrov-Galerkin method is usually reserved for formulations in which the test functions are constructed as the sum of the basis functions for the trial space and a perturbation term. In respect to this tradition, Section 4.4 is broken into three distinct subsections, even though all methods presented satisfy the general definition of a Petrov-Galerkin method. In Section 4.4.1, several P-G approximations developed for the transport equation will be presented. This is followed in Section 4.4.2 by presentation of a family of approximations designated as localized adjoint methods (LAMs), and then by presentation of the boundary element method in Section 4.4.3.

4.4.1 Petrov-Galerkin Methods

To present the initial Petrov-Galerkin approximations, consider the steady-state advection-diffusion equation in one dimension,

$$V\frac{du}{dx} - D\frac{d^2u}{dx^2} = 0 \qquad (4.4.1)$$

Many Petrov-Galerkin methods have this simple equation as their motivational foundation. As a first P-G formulation, consider approximation of this equation using a piecewise linear trial space with a piecewise quadratic test space. The piecewise quadratic test (weight) functions are defined as the original piecewise linear functions with a quadratic perturbation added to each nonzero piece in the following way:

$$
w_i(x) = \begin{cases}
\dfrac{x - x_{i-1}}{x_i - x_{i-1}} + 3\alpha\dfrac{(x - x_{i-1})(x_i - x)}{(x_i - x_{i-1})^2}, & x_{i-1} \le x \le x_i \\[3mm]
\dfrac{x_{i+1} - x}{x_{i+1} - x_i} - 3\alpha\dfrac{(x - x_i)(x_{i+1} - x)}{(x_{i+1} - x_i)^2}, & x_i \le x \le x_{i+1} \\[3mm]
0, & x \le x_{i-1}; \quad x \ge x_{i+1}
\end{cases}
\qquad (4.4.2)
$$

This test function is plotted in Figure 4.29. If this function is inserted into the MWR statement, using piecewise linear basis functions for the trial function U, the following expression results after performance of the integrations on a grid with constant node spacing:

$$
V\frac{U_{i+1} - U_{i-1}}{2(\Delta x)} - (D + D^*)\frac{U_{i+1} - 2U_i + U_{i-1}}{(\Delta x)^2} = 0 \qquad (i \text{ an interior node })\quad (4.4.3)
$$

where $D^* = V[\alpha(\Delta x)/2]$. Notice that this equation is exactly the form of the finite difference approximation (4.3.10). In Section 4.1 and Problem 4.10, it was shown that choice of $\alpha = \coth[V(\Delta x)/2D] + 2D/V(\Delta x)$ produces exact nodal values. Therefore, this choice of α in the definition of the test function $w_i(x)$ will produce a Petrov-Galerkin approximation that yields exact nodal values. Because this quadratic Petrov-Galerkin (QPG) approximation, with optimal choice of α, provides exact solutions, it can be seen as an optimal spatial method, just as the finite difference analog was in Section 4.3.

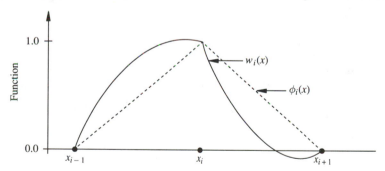

Figure 4.29   Quadratic test function $w_i(x)$ of equation (4.4.2).

If this algorithm is applied to the transient version of the transport equation, the following semidiscrete approximation results:

$$
\left(\frac{1}{6} + \frac{\alpha}{4}\right)\frac{dU_{i-1}}{dt} + \left(\frac{2}{3}\right)\frac{dU_i}{dt} + \left(\frac{1}{6} - \frac{\alpha}{4}\right)\frac{dU_{i+1}}{dt} + V\frac{U_{i+1} - U_{i-1}}{2(\Delta x)}
$$

$$
-(D + D^*)\frac{U_{i+1} - 2U_i + U_{i-1}}{(\Delta x)^2} = 0 \qquad (4.4.4)
$$

Examination of this equation indicates that the Petrov-Galerkin approximation distributes the time derivative in space, with weightings $[(1/6 + \alpha/4), (2/3), (1/6 - \alpha/4)]$. This compares to the standard finite difference method, which uses weightings $(0,1,0)$, and the standard Galerkin method, which has weightings $(1/6, 2/3, 1/6)$. Thus the asymmetry in the test function affects both the effective diffusion coefficient and the time weightings. Numerical solutions using this approximation (using optimal α) can show significant differences from those that do not use the modified time derivative term (see Figure 4.23 and Problem 4.38). Notice that the original Galerkin approximation is recovered when $\alpha = 0$.

The analysis of Section 4.3 demonstrated that use of an "optimal spatial approximation" is generally not the best strategy for transient problems. This must also be the case for the quadratic Petrov-Galerkin scheme. By equation (4.3.15), a high-order estimate requires that $\alpha = 0$ (unless a characteristic method is adopted, as discused in Section 4.3.2). The $\mathcal{O}((\Delta x)^4, (\Delta x)^2(\Delta t)^2, (\Delta t)^4)$ approximation of equation (4.3.17) requires a symmetric spatial distribution of the time derivative, with no artificial diffusion added. To achieve this in the context of a Petrov-Galerkin method, a piecewise linear trial space may be coupled with a piecewise cubic test space with test functions defined by

$$
w_i(x) = \begin{cases}
\dfrac{x - x_{i-1}}{x_i - x_{i-1}} - 5\Gamma\dfrac{(x - x_{i-1})(x_i - x)(x_i + x_{i-1} - 2x)}{2(x_i - x_{i-1})^3}, & x_{i-1} \leq x \leq x_i \\[3mm]
\dfrac{x_{i+1} - x}{x_{i+1} - x_i} + 5\Gamma\dfrac{(x - x_i)(x_{i+1} - x)(x_i + x_{i+1} - 2x)}{2(x_{i+1} - x_i)^3}, & x_i \leq x \leq x_{i+1} \\[3mm]
0, & x \leq x_{i-1}, \ x \geq x_{i+1}
\end{cases}
$$

$$(4.4.5)$$

This test function is plotted in Figure 4.30. Examination of equation (4.4.5) indicates that the test function is a cubic perturbation of the piecewise linear functions. Upon evaluation of the MWR integrals, the following semidiscrete approximation results:

$$
\left(\frac{1}{6} + \Gamma\right)\frac{dU_{i-1}}{dt} + \left(\frac{2}{3} - 2\Gamma\right)\frac{dU_i}{dt} + \left(\frac{1}{6} + \Gamma\right)\frac{dU_{i+1}}{dt}
$$

$$
+ V\frac{U_{i+1} - U_{i-1}}{2(\Delta x)} - D\frac{U_{i+1} - 2U_i + U_{i-1}}{(\Delta x)^2} = 0 \qquad (4.4.6)
$$

By the analysis of Section 4.3.1, the parameter Γ should be chosen as $\Gamma = \nu^2/12$, where ν is the Courant number, $\nu \equiv V(\Delta t)/\Delta x$. This approximation, and related extensions in multiple spatial dimensions, is currently in use for a variety of applications, as indicated by the reference list in Appendix C.

A variety of other Petrov-Galerkin methods also exist for solution of the advection-diffusion equation, some of which are referenced in Appendix C. It is interesting to note that the quadratic and cubic P-G methods presented above, which are quite popular among finite element modelers, may be derived from relatively simple truncation error analysis. This again reinforces the point that ability to understand and effectively

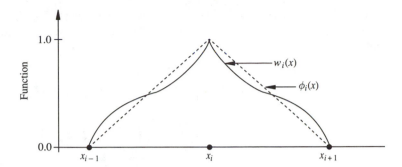

Figure 4.30   Cubic test function $w_i(x)$ of equation (4.4.5).

manipulate truncation error terms is very important to development of good numerical approximations.

4.4.2 Localized Adjoint Methods

Localized adjoint methods (LAMs) are Petrov-Galerkin approximations in which the specific form of the test functions is determined as part of the solution procedure. The general idea is to choose test functions that are specific to the governing equation. This is accomplished by judicious use of the adjoint operator associated with the governing differential operator (see Appendix A for a definition of adjoint operators).

To demonstrate the general idea of the method, consider the steady state, one-dimensional advection-diffusion equation,

$$\mathcal{L}u \equiv V\frac{du}{dx} - D\frac{d^2u}{dx^2} = 0, \qquad 0 < x < \ell \tag{4.4.7}$$

A general Petrov-Galerkin (method of weighted residuals) approximation can be written as

$$\int_\Omega \mathcal{L}(u)w(x)\,dx = 0 \tag{4.4.8}$$

Let the domain $\Omega = [0, \ell]$ be discretized using N nodes, $\{x_1, x_2, \ldots, x_N\}$, with $E = N - 1$ elements defined by $\Omega_e = [x_e, x_{e+1}]$. Under the smoothness assumptions $u(x) \in \mathbb{C}^1[\Omega]$, $w(x) \in \mathbb{C}^{-1}[\Omega]$, the domain integral of equation (4.4.8) may be replaced by a simple sum of element integrals, that is,

$$\int_\Omega \mathcal{L}(u)w\,dx = \sum_{e=1}^E \int_{\Omega_e} \mathcal{L}(u)w\,dx = \sum_{e=1}^E \int_{x_e}^{x_{e+1}} \mathcal{L}(u)w\,dx = 0 \tag{4.4.9}$$

Notice that the continuity restriction is very important in writing equation (4.4.9). This equation does not hold when u is less smooth (e.g., $u(x) \in \mathbb{C}^0[\Omega]$). Problem 4.39 examines this issue in some detail.

Given equation (4.4.9), the first key to localized adjoint methods is repeated application of integration by parts to each of the elemental integrals until all derivatives are applied to the test function w and not the unknown function u. This leads directly to the adjoint operator. In this case, integration by parts applied twice leads to the following equation:

$$\int_{x_e}^{x_{e+1}} \mathcal{L}(u)w\,dx = \int_{x_e}^{x_{e+1}} \left(V\frac{du}{dx} - D\frac{d^2u}{dx^2}\right)w\,dx$$

$$= -\int_{x_e}^{x_{e+1}} u\left(V\frac{dw}{dx} + D\frac{d^2w}{dx^2}\right)dx$$

$$+ \left[\left(Vu - D\frac{du}{dx}\right)w + Du\frac{dw}{dx}\right]\Bigg|_{x_e}^{x_{e+1}} \tag{4.4.10}$$

The resulting integral on the right side of equation (4.4.10) has as an integrand the product of u and the formal adjoint operator $\mathcal{L}^*$ acting on w. That is, given the operator $\mathcal{L}$ of equation (4.4.7), its formal adjoint is given by

$$\mathcal{L}^* \equiv -\left(V\frac{d}{dx} + D\frac{d^2}{dx^2}\right) \tag{4.4.11}$$

In addition, when the remaining boundary terms are summed [see equation (4.4.9)], they may be written as

$$\sum_{e=1}^{E}\left[\left(Vu - D\frac{du}{dx}\right)w + Du\frac{dw}{dx}\right]\Bigg|_{x_e}^{x_{e+1}} = \left[\left(Vu - D\frac{du}{dx}\right)w + Du\frac{dw}{dx}\right]\Bigg|_{0}^{\ell}$$

$$- \sum_{j=2}^{N-1}\left\{\left(V[\![w]\!]_j + D\left[\!\!\left[\frac{dw}{dx}\right]\!\!\right]_j\right)u_j - D[\![w]\!]_j\frac{du_j}{dx}\right\} \tag{4.4.12}$$

where the double bracket denotes a jump operator, $[\![w]\!]_j \equiv \lim_{\epsilon\to 0}[w(x_j + \epsilon) - w(x_j - \epsilon)]$, and u_j and du_j/dx denote nodal evaluations of the unknown function u and its derivative.

The second key to localized adjoint methods is the choice of test functions. Examination of equation (4.4.10) indicates that if $w(x)$ were specified such that $\mathcal{L}^*w = 0$ within each element, then all integrals appearing in the equation would be zero. The only remaining terms are nodal evaluations, and the summations in equation (4.4.9) or equation (4.4.12) lead directly to linear algebraic equations for the nodal unknowns. Choice of test functions from the solution space of local (elemental), homogeneous adjoint equations leads to LAM. The name corresponds to this fact.

For the equation at hand, $\mathcal{L}^*w = 0$ has two independent solutions, $w = 1$ and $w = \exp[-(Vx/D)]$. A variety of possibilities exist for combination of these two functions into a set of test functions. One such choice is shown in Figure 4.31. This function has the definition

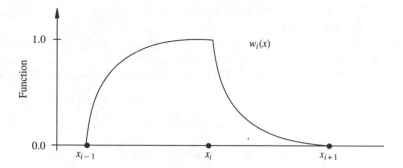

Figure 4.31   Exponential test function $w_i(x)$ of equation (4.4.13).

$$
w_i(x) =
\begin{cases}
\dfrac{1 - \exp\left[-(V/D)(x - x_{i-1})\right]}{1 - \exp\left[-(V/D)(x_i - x_{i-1})\right]}, & x_{i-1} \leq x \leq x_i \\[2em]
\dfrac{-\exp\left[-(V/D)(x_{i+1} - x_i)\right] + \exp\left[-(V/D)(x - x_i)\right]}{1 - \exp\left[-(V/D)(x_{i+1} - x_i)\right]}, & x_i \leq x \leq x_{i+1} \\[2em]
0, & x \leq x_{i-1} \quad \text{or} \\[1em]
 & x \geq x_{i+1}
\end{cases}
$$

$$(4.4.13)$$

As the figure indicates, this function is $C^0[\Omega]$, and closely resembles an upstream-biased, quadratic Petrov-Galerkin function. Application of this set of exponential test functions leads to exact nodal values in the resulting solution. This method for generating exact nodal values is somewhat more general than those presented previously because it applies to a more general class of equations. For example, application of the LAM procedure to the nonhomogeneous equation

$$
V \frac{du}{dx} - D \frac{d^2 u}{dx^2} = f(x) \tag{4.4.14}
$$

leads directly to exact nodal values. This is in contrast to derivation of exact nodal solutions by use of Taylor series expansions in the context of finite difference theory, which for this equation constitutes a very complicated task. While the LAM approach leads to exact solutions for a somewhat broader class of equations, it is still generally restricted by the condition that exact numerical solutions may only be obtained for equations for which exact analytical solutions may be written. For LAM, this is clear from the observation that solutions must be determined for the adjoint operator. When exact solutions cannot be found for the adjoint operator, or when the solutions used as test functions do not span the entire solution space (this is generally the case for partial differential equations), exact nodal values will not result. However, simplified model equations may again be used to guide the development of approximations for more complex equations.

The LAM approach will be discussed only briefly in the context of partial differential equations. A much more complete presentation can be found in some of the references listed in Appendix C. As an example, consider the transient version of equation (4.4.7), namely

$$\mathcal{L}u \equiv \frac{\partial u}{\partial t} + V\frac{\partial u}{\partial x} - D\frac{\partial^2 u}{\partial x^2} = 0 \tag{4.4.15}$$

In this case, the adjoint operator is also a partial differential operator, given by

$$\mathcal{L}^*w = -\frac{\partial w}{\partial t} - V\frac{\partial w}{\partial x} - D\frac{\partial^2 w}{\partial x^2} \tag{4.4.16}$$

The solution space for this operator is infinite-dimensional (for $D \neq 0$), so that an infinite number of solutions exist for the homogeneous adjoint equation $\mathcal{L}^*w = 0$. Use of different subsets of solutions for test functions leads to different families of approximations. One such solution, which is developed in Problem 4.40, leads to a general semidiscrete approximation, with the exponential functions of equation (4.4.13) applied in the spatial dimension. This therefore becomes another example of an optimal spatial approximation applied to a transient version of the governing equation. As was the case previously with the Allen-Southwell finite difference scheme, or the quadratic Petrov-Galerkin method, this semidiscrete LAM approximation does not perform very well for the transient case. Recent developments in LAM techniques have led to a fully space-time approximation that embeds the idea of secondary characteristic tracking in a very systemmatic way. The interested reader is referred to the reference list in Appendix C.

4.4.3 Boundary Element Methods

The boundary element method (BEM) is related to the LAM technique in that the adjoint operator is again a central consideration. However, boundary elements seek global (domain-wide) solutions to the adjoint equation instead of localized solutions over only one element. The overall objective is reduction of the dimension of the problem by one, so that a three-dimensional problem is solved by a numerical approximation defined in only two dimensions, a two-dimensional problem is solved in only one dimension, and so on. This section provides a brief overview of the BEM concept.

To explain the idea of boundary elements, consider solution of the steady-state diffusion equation in a homogeneous but geometrically irregular two-dimensional region, subject to a nonzero source or sink term,

$$\mathcal{L}u \equiv \nabla^2 u = f(x, y), \qquad \mathbf{x} \in \Omega \tag{4.4.17}$$

$$u(\mathbf{x}) = u_B(\mathbf{x}), \qquad \mathbf{x} \in \partial\Omega_1$$

$$\frac{\partial u}{\partial n}(\mathbf{x}) = q_B(\mathbf{x}), \qquad \mathbf{x} \in \partial\Omega_2$$

where the boundary of Ω, denoted by $\partial\Omega$, is composed of the two segments: $\partial\Omega_1$, along which first-type boundary conditions are specified, and $\partial\Omega_2$, along which second-type boundary conditions are specified. The BEM approach begins with a weighted residual statement,

$$\int_\Omega \mathcal{L}(u)w(\mathbf{x})\,d\mathbf{x} = \int_\Omega \nabla^2 u\, w\, d\mathbf{x} = \int_\Omega f(\mathbf{x})w(\mathbf{x})\,d\mathbf{x} \qquad (4.4.18)$$

Recall that the LAM approach broke the domain into elements and applied the integration over each element. The BEM does not break the domain into any subregions, but rather applies integration by parts (Green's theorem) over the entire domain to arrive at an equivalent equation in terms of the adjoint operator,

$$\int_\Omega \nabla^2 u\, w\, d\mathbf{x} = \int_{\partial\Omega}\left(\frac{\partial u}{\partial n}w - u\frac{\partial w}{\partial n}\right)ds + \int_\Omega u\,\nabla^2 w\, d\mathbf{x}$$

$$= \int_{\partial\Omega}\left(\frac{\partial u}{\partial n}w - u\frac{\partial w}{\partial n}\right)ds + \int_\Omega u\mathcal{L}^* w\, d\mathbf{x} \qquad (4.4.19)$$

Instead of next searching for test functions that satisfy the homogeneous adjoint equation at all points, the BEM is based on test functions that satisfy the following singular equation (whose solution is the so-called Green's function of the operator),

$$\mathcal{L}^* w = \delta(\mathbf{x} - \mathbf{x}^*)$$

or

$$\nabla^2 w = \delta(\mathbf{x} - \mathbf{x}^*) \qquad (4.4.20)$$

where $\delta(\mathbf{x} - \mathbf{x}^*)$ is the multidimensional version of the Dirac delta function. The general solution to equation (4.4.20) in two-dimensional space is

$$w(\mathbf{x}) = \ell n(|\mathbf{x} - \mathbf{x}^*|) \qquad (4.4.21)$$

If a set of points $\{\mathbf{x}_i^*\}_{i=1}^N$ is defined, then an associated set of test functions may be defined by $w_i(\mathbf{x}) \equiv \ell n(|\mathbf{x} - \mathbf{x}_i^*|)$. Location of these points is the key to the BEM algorithm.

Examination of equation (4.4.19) reveals the important idea of BEM. Choice of $w_i(\mathbf{x})$ as defined above implies that the interior integral in the equation may be replaced, by definition of the Dirac delta function, by

$$\int_\Omega u\,\mathcal{L}^* w_i\, d\mathbf{x} = u(\mathbf{x}_i^*) \qquad (4.4.22)$$

Therefore equation (4.4.19) can be written equivalently as

$$\int_{\partial\Omega}\left(\frac{\partial u}{\partial n}w_i - u\frac{\partial w_i}{\partial n}\right)ds = -u(\mathbf{x}_i^*) \qquad (4.4.23)$$

This equation now involves only a boundary integral (which is a one-dimensional line integral) and a point evaluation. If the boundary values of u and $\partial u/\partial n$ were known, then equation (4.4.23) could be used to solve for the unknown u at any point $\mathbf{x}_i^*$ interior to Ω. Conversely, equation (4.4.23) may also be used to solve for (approximate) values of u and $\partial u/\partial n$ along the boundary of Ω. This approximate solution constitutes the boundary element method, and is accomplished as follows.

Consider placement of N nodes along the boundary of Ω, as illustrated in Figure 4.32. Associated with each node are approximate values of the function u and of the normal derivative $\partial u/\partial n$, denoted respectively by U_j and $\partial U_j/\partial n$. At each node, either u or $\partial u/\partial n$ will be known from boundary conditions. Therefore, N unknowns remain to be determined. The BEM produces a set of N algebraic equations, written in terms of these nodal values, by writing equation (4.4.23) for $\{\mathbf{x}_i^*\}$ corresponding to the set of N boundary nodes. Given the definition of $w_i(\mathbf{x})$, the resulting system takes the form

$$\sum_{j=1}^{N}\left\{(\gamma_{i1})_j U_j + (\gamma_{i2})_j \frac{\partial U_j}{\partial n}\right\} = f_i \tag{4.4.24}$$

Determination of the coefficients γ_{i1} and γ_{i2} requires careful treatment of the geometry of the problem (see Problem 4.41), but in general involves straightforward function evaluations. Therefore, the BEM algorithm provides a solution for the unknown at any interior point [via equation (4.4.22)] while requiring numerical solution of an effectively one-dimensional problem.

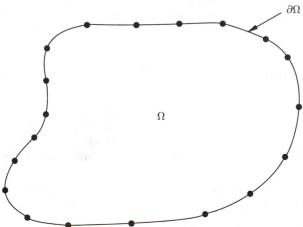

$\partial\Omega$

Ω

Figure 4.32 Nodal placement for boundary element method.

While this method appears to be very attractive, there are a variety of limitations. The most severe is the existence of a solution for the singular equation (4.4.20). This usually requires that the equation have constant coefficients (i.e., homogeneous material properties). In addition, while there are only N unknowns, the matrix that needs to be solved to determine these unknowns is full. This is in contrast to other (interior) methods which have more unknowns but whose matrices are usually sparse and banded. The BEM remains difficult to apply to transient problems, although recent advances have been made on this front. More details may be found in the references and in the problems at the end of this chapter. Overall, the BEM is an attractive option for a restricted class of problems. It also serves as another excellent example of an alternative numerical procedure based on the fundamental ideas of MWR.

4.5 CONCLUSION

This chapter has presented a variety of analytical techniques for improving numerical approximations. The topics covered included geometric considerations as well as truncation error analysis. Geometric considerations included use of irregular grids, leading to the general ideas of coordinate maps and finite element formulations. Potential problems in unrestricted irregular finite elements were pointed out, and improved coordinate transformations were presented.

An important concept stressed in the chapter is that application of relatively simple analysis can lead to important general rules for discretization strategies and choice of numerical approximation. The simple analysis that is the basis for both grid design and definition of approximation is truncation analysis. When applicable, this is a very powerful tool. It also provides qualitative guidelines for approximations to more complex problems.

An additional important concept that was introduced and explained in this chapter is stability. Analysis of stability, including Fourier analysis, is important for all time-marching algorithms. Fourier analysis also provides important insights into the behavior of numerical approximations by examining both amplitude and phase errors. With this information, quantitative evaluation of numerical approximations is greatly enhanced. Finally, truncation error (consistency) and stability combine to give convergence. For any numerical approximation, convergence is a necessary attribute.

When the basic concepts of finite difference approximations, the method of weighted residuals, and the analysis techniques presented in this chapter are thoroughly understood, a variety of specialized techniques may be derived. Examples presented in this chapter include Petrov-Galerkin methods, localized adjoint methods, and boundary element methods.

Although only relatively simple model problems, amenable to analytical manipulations, were treated in this chapter, the material presented applies to a wide variety of problems. However, when the problems become sufficiently complex such that analytical manipulations may not be sufficient, analysis tools based on numerical computations need to be developed. That is the topic of Chapter 5.

PROBLEMS

4.1. Show that the finite element method applied to the equation

$$\frac{d}{dx}\left[K(x)\frac{du}{dx}\right] = 0 \tag{4.6.1}$$

yields equation (4.1.3b), that is,

$$\frac{\left[\dfrac{1}{\Delta x_i}\displaystyle\int_{x_i}^{x_{i+1}} K(x)dx\right]\dfrac{U_{i+1} - U_i}{\Delta x_i} - \left[\dfrac{1}{\nabla x_i}\displaystyle\int_{x_{i-1}}^{x_i} K(x)dx\right]\dfrac{U_i - U_{i-1}}{\nabla x_i}}{\delta x_i} = 0 \qquad (4.6.2)$$

4.2. (a) Using Taylor series analysis, derive the truncation error expression for the approximation to

$$\frac{d}{dx}\left[K(x)\frac{du}{dx}\right] = 0$$

given by equation (4.1.3a), that is,

$$\frac{K_{i+1/2}\dfrac{U_{i+1} - U_i}{\Delta x_i} - K_{i-1/2}\dfrac{U_i - U_{i-1}}{\nabla x_i})}{\delta x_i} = 0 \qquad (4.6.3)$$

(b) Show that this is the approximation that results from the finite element approximation when a one-point integration rule is used to evaluate the integrals of conductivity $K(x)$. Perform a truncation error analysis for the approximation that results if the integrals of conductivity are evaluated using a trapezoidal rule, such that

$$\int_{x_i}^{x_{i+1}} K(x)\,dx \simeq \frac{1}{2}(K_i + K_{i+1})$$

4.3. Write a computer code to solve the finite difference approximation given by equation (4.5.3). Demonstrate that the code is working properly by solving the simple example of $K(x) = 1$, using both constant and nonconstant node spacing (the finite difference solution should produce exact nodal values for this test case).

4.4. Using the computer code of Problem 4.3, perform a convergence test by measuring rate of error decrease as a function of Δx. Plot log(error) versus log(Δx) and use the slope of the resulting line as an estimate of the order of the approximation. Be sure that the measure of error uses an appropriate norm. Use $K(x) = 1 + x$.

4.5. Show that the optimal gridding rule

$$\rho_i = \frac{\nabla x_i}{\Delta x_i} = \left(\frac{\kappa_{i+1/2}}{\kappa_{i-1/2}}\right)^{1/2} \qquad (4.6.4)$$

where

$$\kappa(x) \equiv K(x)\frac{d^3u}{dx^3} = \frac{2}{K^2}\left(\frac{dK}{dx}\right)^2 - \frac{1}{K}\frac{d^2K}{dx^2}$$

is independent of i when $K(x)$ is a linear function, $K(x) = \alpha + \beta x$. That is, $\cdots = \rho_{i-1} = \rho_i = \rho_{i+1} = \cdots$.

4.6. Using the truncation error result of Problem 4.2, show that all terms in the truncation error expression vanish whenever the optimal rule of Problem 4.5 is applied.

4.7. Given that there exists an optimal value of $\rho_i \equiv \nabla x_i/\Delta x_i$, call it ρ_{opt}, for the case of $K(x) = \alpha + \beta x$, show that for a grid that uses N nodes over $[0, \ell]$, the appropriate geometric formulas are those of equations (4.1.12),

$$\rho_{\text{opt}} = \left(1 - \frac{\beta\ell}{\alpha + \beta\ell}\right)^{1/(N-1)} \qquad (4.6.5a)$$

$$\nabla x_N = \frac{1}{\beta}(\alpha + \beta\ell)(1 - \rho_{\text{opt}}) \qquad (4.6.5b)$$

[*Hint:* Begin with ∇x_N, then $\nabla x_{N-1} = \rho\nabla x_N$, $\nabla x_{N-2} = \rho^2\nabla x_N$, ..., $\nabla x_2 = \rho^{N-2}\nabla x_N$. Use the relations $\sum_{i=2}^{N}\nabla x_i = \ell$ and $(1 + \rho + \rho^2 + \cdots + \rho^{N-2}) = (1 - \rho^{N-1})/(1 - \rho)$.] Attempt to develop similar criteria when $K(x)$ is not linear in x.

4.8. For the equation

$$\frac{d^2u}{dx^2} = f(x) = \delta(x - 0.5)$$

with $\delta(x - 0.5)$ being the Dirac delta function, write the approximating equations on a uniform discretization using (a) finite elements with piecewise linear basis functions, and (b) finite differences with the standard approximation for the second derivative. Use a general discretization with spacing Δx such that $x = 0.5$ is always a node location. When fnite elements are used, the numerical solution at $x = 0.5$ is -0.25, independent of Δx. If the finite difference approximation is used with the right side of the difference equation at $x = 0.5$ set equal to 1, the resulting numerical solution at $x = 0.5$ is equal to $-(\Delta x)/4$. The correct solution is $u(0.5) = -0.25$. Explain these results and propose a proper finite difference approximation for this equation.

4.9. Consider extension of the truncation error analysis of the homogeneous equation

$$\frac{d}{dx}\left[K(x)\frac{du}{dx}\right] = 0$$

to the nonhomogeneous equation

$$\frac{d}{dx}\left[K(x)\frac{du}{dx}\right] = f(x)$$

Let the finite difference approximation to $f(x)$ be given by

$$f|_{x_i} \simeq \gamma_1 f_{i-1} + (1 - \gamma_1 - \gamma_2)f_i + \gamma_2 f_{i+1} \qquad (4.6.6)$$

with γ_1 and γ_2 being arbitrary parameters. Using truncation error analysis, show that one of the leading error terms is

$$\frac{(\Delta x_i)^2}{24}\left[\kappa_{i+1/2}\left(q_0 + \int_0^{x_{i+1/2}} f(x)\,dx\right)\right] - \frac{(\nabla x_i)^2}{24}\left[\kappa_{i-1/2}\left(q_0 + \int_0^{x_{i-1/2}} f(x)\,dx\right)\right]$$

$$= \left(q_0 + \int_0^{x_{i-1/2}} f(x)\,dx\right)\left[\frac{(\Delta x_i)^2}{24}\kappa_{i+1/2} - \frac{(\nabla x_i)^2}{24}\kappa_{i-1/2}\right]$$

$$+ \frac{(\Delta x_i)^2}{24}\kappa_{i+1/2}\int_{x_{i-1/2}}^{x_{i+1/2}} f(x)\,dx \qquad (4.6.7)$$

where

$$q_0 \equiv \left(K\frac{du}{dx}\right)\Big|_{x_0}$$

Choice of $\nabla x_i / \Delta x_i = (\kappa_{i+1/2}/\kappa_{i-1/2})^{1/2}$ is still viable for this problem. If this rule is chosen, propose other rules, including but not limited to choice of γ_1 and γ_2, to eliminate other truncation error terms.

4.10. For the one-dimensional steady state advection-diffusion equation,

$$V\frac{du}{dx} - D\frac{d^2u}{dx^2} = 0 \qquad (4.6.8)$$

show that when constant node spacing is used in the finite difference approximation (4.1.20), the resulting equation may be written as

$$V\frac{U_{i+1} - U_{i-1}}{2(\Delta x)} - \left(D + \alpha\frac{V\Delta x}{2}\right)\frac{U_{i+1} - 2U_i + U_{i-1}}{(\Delta x)^2} = 0 \qquad (4.6.9)$$

where the parameter β in equation (4.1.20) is related to the parameter α in equation (4.6.9) by $\alpha = 1 - 2\beta$. Thus the approximation (4.1.20) is equivalent to adding an *artificial diffusion* D^* equal to $\alpha(V\Delta x/2)$ to the physical diffusion coefficient D. Prove that the criterion first proposed by Allen and Southwell (1955), $\alpha = \coth(V\Delta x/2D) - (2D/V\Delta x)$, does in fact yield exact nodal values.

4.11. Derive a more general family of exact approximations for equation (4.6.8) by allowing both ρ and β to vary in equation (4.1.20).

4.12. Consider an irregular domain Ω, within which the Poisson equation governs a physical process of interest. A portion of the boundary of Ω, $\partial\Omega$, is shown below. Along this portion of $\partial\Omega$, a flux boundary condition is specified such that $\partial u/\partial n = q_n(x, y)$. Using the stepped discretization shown, write the appropriate approximating equations at nodes 1, 2, 3, and 4.

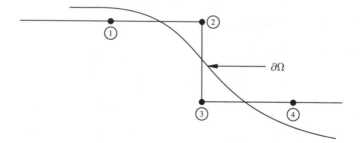

4.13. Show that the finite difference approximation of equation (4.1.24) is strictly consistent while the approximation (4.1.25) is only conditionally consistent. Determine the consistency category of the final approximation to the Laplace equation given by equation (4.1.26).

4.14. Write a computer code to evaluate the integral

$$\int_{\hat{\Omega}_e} \nabla\phi_j \cdot \nabla\phi_i \, dx \, dy \qquad (4.1.10)$$

for an arbitrary quadrilateral (four-node) element. Use as input the four-node coordinates $(X_k, Y_k), k = 1, 2, 3, 4$. The integration should accommodate 1×1, 2×2, 3×3, and 4×4 Gaussian quadrature. Using this code, with the combinations $j = 1, i = 1; j = 2, i = 4$; and $j = 3, i = 4$, evaluate the integral for the element shown in the accompanying figure. Observe the number of integration points required to obtain an accurate solution.

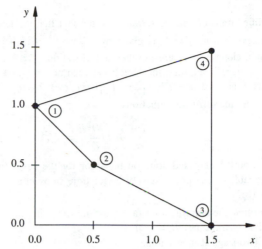

4.15. Modify the computer code of Problem 4.14 to calculate values of the Jacobian (det **J**) at each of the four nodes. Calculate nodal values of the Jacobian for the element of Problem 4.14.

4.16. Consider the element shown in the figure, where node 3 has variable coordinates. Calculate the Jacobian at all four nodes using (a) $X_3 = Y_3 = 1.0$; (b) $X_3 = Y_3 = 1.5$; (c) $X_3 = Y_3 = 0.5$; (d) $X_3 = Y_3 = 0.4$. Observe and comment on the behavior of the integral for these four cases.

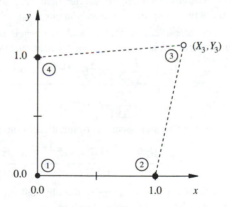

4.17. Propose a functional form for an isoparametric coordinate transformation using Hermite cubic polynomials in two dimensions. Because Hermite polynomials interpolate nodal values of both function and derivatives, it should be expected that terms such as $\partial X_j / \partial \xi$ will arise. Discuss options for estimating these geometric derivatives. [The references Frind and Pinder (1979) and Celia and Pinder (1990), given in Appendix C discuss this topic in detail.]

4.18. Consider the general curved quadratic element of Figure 4.12c. For this element, write the standard isoparametric coordinate transformation equations. Next consider application of the modified coordinate map related to equations (4.1.56) and (4.1.57). Propose a formulation that applies this rule along each of the curved sides. Given this formulation, define a set of modified two-dimensional basis functions, in the local space (ξ, η), that must be used in the modified transformation. (*Hint:* Use the fact that the length of a curved side, say the side corresponding to $\eta = 1$, is given by $\ell_{13} = \int_{-1}^{1}[(\partial x/\partial \xi)^2 + (\partial y/\partial \xi)^2]^{1/2}d\xi$. If the nodes located along $\eta = 1$ are numbered 1 (location $\xi = -1$, $\eta = 1$), 2 ($\xi = \alpha$, $\eta = 1$) and 3 ($\xi = 1$, $\eta = 1$), then the length between nodes 1 and 3 is given above while the length between nodes 1 and 2 is $\ell_{12} = \int_{-1}^{\alpha}[(\partial x/\partial \xi)^2 + (\partial y/\partial \xi)^2]^{1/2}d\xi$.)

4.19. Consider the diffusion equation

$$\frac{\partial u}{\partial t} - D\frac{\partial^2 u}{\partial x^2} = C(1 - \sin t)$$

Describe the expected solution behavior for the cases (a) $C = 0$ and (b) $C = 10$. Is it reasonable to use progressively larger time steps in a numerical solution for case (a)? for case (b)?

4.20. Determine the amplification factor for the following time-stepping algorithms applied to the model equation $du/dt = -u$.
   (a) Two-stage Runge-Kutta.
   (b) Four-stage Runge-Kutta.
   (c) Two-step Adams-Moulton.
   (d) Two-value, Adams-Moulton multivalue method.

4.21. Show diagramatically that a discrete system of nodes with spacing Δx cannot resolve wavelengths shorter than $2(\Delta x)$. For a grid $x_1 = 0$, $x_2 = \Delta x$, ..., what wavelength is implied by sampling only at nodes for the wave $\sin(50\pi x/\Delta x)$ (wavelength $= \Delta x/25$)? for the wave $\sin(10\pi x/\Delta x)$? for the wave $\sin(2\pi x/\Delta x)$? for the wave $\sin(\pi x/2\Delta x)$? The process whereby wavelengths shorter than $2\Delta x$ appear as wavelengths greater than $2\Delta x$ due to discrete sampling is called *aliasing*.

4.22. Derive the amplification factors and associated stability bounds for the following finite difference approximations to the model heat equation:
   (a) $\dfrac{U_i^{n+1} - U_i^n}{\Delta t} - \dfrac{D}{(\Delta x)^2}\left[\theta\delta_x^2 U_i^{n+1} + (1 - \theta)\delta_x^2 U_i^n\right] = 0$
   (b) $\dfrac{U_i^{n+1} - U_i^{n-1}}{2(\Delta t)} - \dfrac{D}{(\Delta x)^2}\delta_x^2 U_i^n = 0$

4.23. Show that the two-step Gear approximation to the model heat equation,

$$\frac{3U_i^{n+1} - 4U_i^n + U_i^{n-1}}{2(\Delta t)} - \frac{D}{(\Delta x)^2}\delta_x^2 U_i^{n+1} = 0$$

is unconditionally stable. Identify the physical root and the spurious (numerical) root, and determine which of the two is dominant.

4.24. Consider the variably weighted approximation to the advection equation

$$\frac{\partial u}{\partial t} + V\frac{\partial u}{\partial x} = 0$$

given by

$$\frac{U_i^{n+1} - U_i^n}{\Delta t} + V\left[\theta\frac{U_{i+1}^{n+1} - U_{i-1}^{n+1}}{2(\Delta x)} + (1 - \theta)\frac{U_{i+1}^n - U_{i-1}^n}{2(\Delta x)}\right] = 0$$

Determine the stability limits for this approximation, written in terms of the Courant number $\nu \equiv V(\Delta t)/\Delta x$, as a function of θ.

4.25. Determine stability constraints for the following finite difference approximation to the second-order wave equation,

$$\frac{\partial^2 u}{\partial t^2} - c^2 \frac{\partial^2 u}{\partial x^2} = 0$$

given by

$$\frac{U_i^{n+1} - 2U_i^n + U_i^{n-1}}{(\Delta t)^2} - c^2 \frac{U_{i+1}^n - 2U_i^n + U_{i-1}^n}{(\Delta x)^2} = 0$$

Compare the two numerical roots to the two analytical (physical) characteristics associated with the governing partial differential equation.

4.26. Perform a truncation error analysis for the FTBS approximation to the advection equation, given by

$$\frac{U_i^{n+1} - U_i^n}{\Delta t} + V \frac{U_i^n - U_{i-1}^n}{\Delta x} = 0$$

Show that the finite difference approximation is consistent, to $\mathcal{O}((\Delta x)^2)$, with the modified partial differential equation

$$\frac{\partial u}{\partial t} + V \frac{\partial u}{\partial x} - D^* \frac{\partial^2 u}{\partial x^2} = 0$$

where

$$D^* \equiv \frac{V(\Delta x)}{2} - \frac{V^2(\Delta t)}{2} = \frac{V(\Delta x)}{2} \left(1 - \frac{V(\Delta t)}{\Delta x} \right) = \frac{V(\Delta x)}{2}(1 - \nu)$$

The coefficient D^* is usually referred to as a *numerical diffusion* or *artificial diffusion*. How does the expression for D^* change when a backward Euler time-stepping scheme is used?

4.27. Repeat Problem 4.26 for the CTCS approximation

$$\frac{U_i^{n+1} - U_i^n}{\Delta t} + V \left[\left(\frac{1}{2} \right) \frac{U_{i+1}^{n+1} - U_{i-1}^{n+1}}{2(\Delta x)} + \left(\frac{1}{2} \right) \frac{U_{i+1}^n - U_{i-1}^n}{2(\Delta x)} \right] = 0$$

4.28. Using the truncation error result of Problem 4.26, show that the choice $\nu = 1$ yields exact results for the model advection equation.

4.29. Consider the *Gauss hill function* $f(x) = \exp[-(x - x_0)^2 / 2\sigma_0^2]$. For $x_0 = 0$ and $\sigma_0 = 1$, expand $f(x)$ in a Fourier series over the interval $[-100, 100]$. Observe the Fourier series representation for partial sums of 5 terms, 10 terms, and 50 terms. Repeat the same exercise for the interval $[-5, 5]$. Comment on the difference between the number of terms needed to obtain a reasonable representation of $f(x)$ and how this relates to a numerical approximation over each domain that is constrained to use a fixed number of nodes N.

4.30. Write a computer code to solve the equation

$$\frac{\partial u}{\partial t} + V \frac{\partial u}{\partial x} - D \frac{\partial^2 u}{\partial x^2} = 0, \qquad 0 < x < \ell, \quad t > 0$$

$$u(x, 0) = u_{\text{init}}(x)$$

$$u(0, t) = C_1$$

$$u(\ell, t) = C_2$$

Allow u_{init} to be a Gaussian distribution, $u_{\text{init}} = \exp[-(x - x_0)^2/2\sigma_0^2]$. Write the code to allow for variable upstream weighting and variable time weighting, so that the finite difference approximation is

$$\frac{U_i^{n+1} - U_i^n}{\Delta t} + \theta \left\{ V \left[\alpha \frac{\nabla U_i^{n+1}}{\Delta x} + (1 - \alpha) \frac{\delta \mu U_i^{n+1}}{2\Delta x} \right] - D \frac{\delta_x^2 U_i^{n+1}}{(\Delta x)^2} \right\}$$

$$+ (1 - \theta) \left\{ \left[\alpha \frac{\nabla U_i^n}{\Delta x} + (1 - \alpha) \frac{\delta \mu U_i^n}{2\Delta x} \right] - D \frac{\delta_x^2 U_i^n}{(\Delta x)^2} \right\} = 0$$

4.31. Solve the equation of Problem 4.30 using $\ell = 10$, $V = 1$, $D = 0$, $\Delta x = 0.1$, $\Delta t = 0.05$, $x_0 = 2$, $\sigma_0 = 0.1$, $\alpha = 0$, and $\theta = 0.5$. Observe the solution at times $t = 1, 2$, and 5. Comment on the presence of oscillations in the solution. How does the solution behavior change when σ_0 increases? when σ_0 decreases? when D increases? when α increases? when θ increases? Explain your observations based on truncation error analysis and Fourier analysis.

4.32. Show that the truncation error analysis of the transient heat equation with $K(x) = \alpha + \beta x$ leads to the expression given in equation (4.3.4).

4.33. Write all derivatives of u appearing in the truncation error expression (4.3.6) as discrete approximations, using only the six nodal values U_{i-1}^n, U_i^n, U_{i+1}^n, U_{i-1}^{n+1}, U_i^{n+1}, U_{i+1}^{n+1}. For the integral term, use a finite difference approximation for the time derivative and either a one-point (at x_i) or a trapezoidal estimate for the integral. Show that the resulting equation is an $\mathcal{O}((\Delta t)^2, (\delta x)^3)$ approximation.

4.34. Given the expression derived in Problem 4.33, write a computer code to solve for an approximate solution. Devise a test problem to test the improvements (if they exist) in the new approximation.

4.35. Derive the truncation expression given in equation (4.3.15).

4.36. Consider a static grid in space-time, that is, all nodes remain stationary as time increases. Consider a change of variable defined by $\tau = x - Vt$, so that

$$\frac{\partial u}{\partial t} + V \frac{\partial u}{\partial x} = \frac{\partial u}{\partial \tau}$$

Then the governing equation may be written as

$$\frac{\partial u}{\partial \tau} - D \frac{\partial^2 u}{\partial x^2} = 0$$

Propose a numerical approximation algorithm based on this modified equation, involving three discrete points in space at time t^{n+1} (say, nodes x_{i-1}, x_i, x_{i+1}). Explain what values are required at time level t^n, and propose an algorithm to calculate these values. How must the approximation be modified to accommodate boundary conditions? Discuss the advantages and disadvantages of this type of algorithm. This procedure is an example of an *Eulerian-Lagrangian method* (ELM), in that the advective term is treated in a Lagrangian framework (via the change of variable, τ) while the diffusive term is in an Eulerian frame. See Appendix C for references that present and discuss ELMs.

4.37. Consider a transport equation in which the coefficients are not constant, for example $V = V(x, t)$. For this case, write the expression for the secondary characteristics. Use this expression to define nodal velocities for a dynamic grid, such that each node is moved from position $(x_j(t^n), t^n)$ to position $(x_j(t^{n+1}), t^{n+1})$ via $x_j(t^{n+1}) = x_j(t^n) + V(x_j(t^n), t^n) \cdot$

(Δt). Demonstrate the potential problem of "tangled grids" by choosing an appropriate velocity field and applying the grid motion equation. Can a bound on Δt be derived to avoid this problem?

4.38. Write a computer code to solve equation (4.4.4). Compare solutions using this equation to the analogous solutions in Figure 4.23, which were calculated by a modified version of equation (4.4.4) in that the $\alpha/4$ factor in the time derivative terms was not present. Perform a Fourier analysis for both approximations to explain the differences between the two numerical solutions.

4.39. Consider the integral of equation (4.4.8) for the case of $u \in \mathbb{C}^0[0, \ell]$, $w \in \mathbb{C}^0[0, \ell]$. Use the concept of Dirac delta functions (Section 3.1) to express the integral as a sum of nodal quantities and element integrals involving the adjoint operator acting on w. Prove that equation (4.4.12) results. Show how the development changes when $w \in \mathbb{C}^{-1}[0, \ell]$.

4.40. Consider application of LAM to equation (4.4.15) using rectangular space-time elements. Let $w_i(x, t)$ be chosen such that it is equal to $w_i(x)$ defined by equation (4.4.13) whenever $t^n < t < t^{n+1}$. When $t > t^{n+1}$ or $t < t^n$, $w_i(x, t) = 0$. Apply the LAM concept in space-time to arrive at an expression for the unknowns evaluated along the (space-time) element boundaries. Perform a further discretization to arrive at a discrete system of equations involving only nodal values of the unknowns.

4.41. For the boundary element method approximation to the Laplace equation on a semicircular domain, derive expressions for the coefficients γ_{i1} and γ_{i2} in equation (4.4.24).

Chapter 5 _____

Accuracy
and Error
Reduction

5.0 INTRODUCTION

Differential equations with known analytical solutions are often solved numerically as a means of investigating the behavior of a numerical procedure or to verify that an algorithm has been correctly coded. These types of tests can provide insight to numerical methods which may be effective for simulating a particular physical process. One way that a numerical model of a complex system is commonly developed is by successively adding aspects of the problem into the differential equation. For example, a nonlinear, multidimensional equation describing flow in an irregularly shaped region could first be simplified to a related linear form and solved in one dimension. Then features such as nonlinearity, multiple dimensions, and complex geometry could be added and verified sequentially. By proceeding in this manner, the author of a model simultaneously gains new insights into numerics, physics, and their interaction.

Despite this idealized scenario for growth of knowledge and understanding, the ultimate goal of a serious modeler is to simulate a problem for which the analytical solution to the governing differential equation in a certain domain with appropriate boundary conditions is not known. The computer can generate as many numbers as desired and transform these numbers into impressive multicolor graphical output. At times the output can be so attractive that one loses sight of an important question: How closely does the numerical simulation mirror the physical system?

In order to affirm that the computer has provided a reasonable simulation, a number of aspects of the problem need to be properly posed. The differential equation must describe the process; the parameters used in the model must be correct; the boundary conditions must be known and sufficient for providing a unique solution; round-off errors by the computer must be unimportant; the truncation errors of the difference approximations must be negligible; and the intended use of the simulation results must be consistent with the degree of refinement of the model. This is a large problem, one beyond the scope of a single book. Nevertheless, it may be stated that desired increased precision of a simulation requires increasing complexity of the governing differential equations and increased creativity in developing numerical procedures capable of effectively solving these equations.

The portion of the simulation problem that will be discussed here is the control of numerical truncation error based solely on the numerical solution, without recourse to analytical solution. The presentation follows naturally from simplified analytical derivations presented in Chapter 4. Quantitative techniques will be developed that enable the modeler to demand accurate solution of a differential equation within a certain tolerance. The presentation again deals with fundamental principles and basic techniques as applied to simplified systems. However, an understanding of these methods will provide an entrance into the more complex and specialized literature dealing with general error control and multidimensional, adaptive grid, mesh refinement schemes. Two principal techniques are emphasized: (1) refinement of the mesh without altering the order of accuracy of the discrete approximation to the differential equation, and (2) the use of higher-order approximations on a fixed grid. The method of choice for error control and reduction depends on the problem being solved, the variability in problem parameters, and the behavior of the solution. Flexibility requires that a modeler have facility with both methods. In the subsequent sections, mesh refinement and higher-order approaches will be explained and then illustrated through simple examples. The formalisms and procedures of these methods, fully developed, are highly specialized and beyond the present scope.

This chapter builds on the concepts presented in Chapter 4. However, one important distinction must be kept in mind. Chapter 4 derived analytical results as aids in obtaining optimal grids and generating good numerical results. The material in that chapter demonstrates the importance of tailoring an approximation and its related discretization to a problem. The current chapter examines the same issues from a completely numerical perspective, without recourse to analytical solutions. Although the examples to be worked here may have analytical solutions, these will be used only in hindsight, not as aids in generating the solutions or assessing the error.

The goal of this chapter, then, is to present strategies which, when used in concert with the previously presented numerical methods and algorithms, control the magnitude of the truncation error. Furthermore, some estimate of the magnitude of this error must be obtained without recourse to a known analytical solution.

5.1 IMPROVED ACCURACY THROUGH MESH REFINEMENT

Perhaps the simplest method, conceptually, for investigating convergence of a numerical solution is the method of mesh refinement. In its simplest form, implementation of the method involves first solving the differential equation using one step size, changing the step size, resolving the problem, and then comparing the solutions. For the procedure to be effective in yielding information about the quality of the solution, it must be applied carefully and systematically. For example, solving a problem on a grid of N evenly distributed nodes and then resolving the problem on a grid of $N + n$ evenly distributed nodes where $N >> n$ is not likely to yield significantly different results. However, drawing the conclusion that the grid has been refined to the point where the solution is insensitive to grid size would be unjustified. Uniform refinement in a dimension requires roughly doubling the number of nodes in that dimension for a comparison of the solution to yield significant information concerning the error. Selective refinement of a nonuniform grid requires rationale for choice of the zone of refinement and careful interpretation of the significance of results obtained.

Mesh refinements made in the time domain are intrinsically different from those made in the spatial domain. Time is open-ended and the future does not affect the present. Thus as time marching proceeds, depending on the behavior of the solution, the time step may be modified without making requirements on any values of Δt used earlier in the simulation or to be used in the future. In particular, one-step methods such as Runge-Kutta and Euler, as well as one-step multivalue methods, require information only at one time location. Therefore, calculation to a new time location is independent of previous time steps used. Multistep methods may also employ variable time stepping, although this presents complexities in comparison to the constant time step case.

Mesh refinement in the spatial domain is affected by the fact that for parabolic and elliptic problems, information from the boundaries is transmitted instantaneously throughout the domain (as discussed in Chapter 1). Thus refinement in one part of space affects the solution throughout the space. The spatial domain should therefore be considered as an entity in locating nodes.

The interaction between space and time discretization is also very important. The condition on stability of a time integration procedure is dependent on the relative sizes of Δt and $\Delta \mathbf{x}$ as well as problem parameters. Thus very fine spatial discretization in part of the region can dictate a maximum time step well below that necessary for stability in most of the domain and well below that needed for accuracy based on truncation error considerations. Either a spatially constant very small time step must be applied over the entire grid, or an algorithm should be implemented that allows for different values of Δt in different regions of space.

Some problems require that more than one dependent variable be solved for in space. For example, simulation of a groundwater contamination event may require that fluid pressure, fluid velocities, and concentrations of multiple chemical species be considered. In this case, a spatial grid that is suitable for velocity simulation may not be suitable for simulating the movement of chemical species. If some of the species react or adsorb, these processes may require consideration and provide conflicting demands of the grid. In addition, processes such as change in fluid pressure and chemical spreading may have different time scales. For example, the flow field may only change significantly on a monthly basis, while the contamination changes much faster. Thus different time-stepping algorithms might be needed to simulate these processes.

The preceding narrative is intended to indicate that the discretization and solution of important problems by numerical procedures is difficult, although certainly not hopeless. Furthermore, if one has insight and physical understanding of the dynamics of the problem under consideration, this can be of assistance in developing an accurate model. Also if one has insight and understanding of the numerical procedures being applied to a problem, this can be of great value in better understanding the dynamics of the problem.

5.1.1 Interval Halving in Time

Consider the ordinary differential equation

$$\frac{du}{dt} = f(u, t)$$
$$u(t^0) = u^0 \tag{5.1.1}$$

which is to be solved numerically. The analyses of Chapter 2 have provided a number of sets of solution procedures that give approximate solutions to u^n (indicated as U^n). For a single step, these approximations are related to the true solution by

$$U^1 = u^1 + C_p \left. \frac{d^{p+1}u}{dt^{p+1}} \right|_{t^{*1}} (\Delta t^0)^{p+1} \tag{5.1.2}$$

where $\Delta t^0 \equiv t^1 - t^0$, $t^0 \leq t^{*1} \leq t^1$, C_p is a constant that depends upon the method being implemented, and p is the integer order of accuracy of the approximation. The parameters p and C_p can be determined analytically from a Taylor series expansion for a particular method. Alternatively, because some methods are tedious to evaluate analytically, the error expression can be approximated by a numerical procedure as described subsequently.

In the procedure to be used, a differential equation with a known analytical solution is employed to determine p and C_p. The results obtained may be generalized to the case where the analytical solution is not known. An algorithm to be examined is used to solve equation (5.1.1) using a constant time step with $f(u, t)$ sequentially taking on the specific forms

$$f(u, t) = (k + 1)(t)^k, \qquad k = 0, 1, ..., p \tag{5.1.3a}$$

such that

$$u = u^0 + (t)^{k+1} - (t^0)^{k+1}, \qquad k = 0, 1, ..., p \tag{5.1.3b}$$

where p is the unknown order of accuracy of the numerical procedure as given in equation (5.1.2). The functional form of $f(u, t)$ selected in equation (5.1.3a) is convenient because for $k < p$, the error term in equation (5.1.2) will be zero. In solving the differential equation, a consistent numerical solution will equal the exact solution with $k = 0$.

Therefore, by sequentially increasing k, the order of the error term, p, can be determined as equal to the lowest value of k that produces a nonzero error in the solution. When $k = p$, the $k+1$ derivative of u is constant and equal to $(p+1)!$ such that equation (5.1.2) becomes

$$U^1 - u^1 = C_p(p + 1)!\,(\Delta t)^{p+1} \tag{5.1.4a}$$

Repeated application of this equation for n steps, assuming constant Δt, leads to

$$U^n - u^n = nC_p(p + 1)!\,(\Delta t)^{p+1} \tag{5.1.4b}$$

To be precise, a single algorithm such as equation (5.1.4a) can be used for all n steps to obtain equation (5.1.4b) only for a one-step, single-value method. For multistep methods, which require information at earlier times than t^i to compute a solution at t^{i+1}, a start-up algorithm must be used on early time steps so that values of U are generated at the needed positions in t to enable full implementation of the computational method. For multivalue methods, the compensating errors in computed derivatives that contribute to the accuracy of the method are absent in the first steps. Thus for these approximations, equations (5.1.4) may not be exact. However, these complications arise only in the early steps of computation and can be negated by considering the change in error between steps after the total start-up error has been introduced.

To evaluate C_p, solutions obtained on two consecutive steps will be analyzed. Subtraction of the error in equation (5.1.4b) on two consecutive steps yields

$$(U^{n+1} - u^{n+1}) - (U^n - u^n) = C_p(p + 1)!(\Delta t)^{p+1} \tag{5.1.5}$$

such that C_p may be calculated from

$$C_p = \frac{(U^{n+1} - u^{n+1}) - (U^n - u^n)}{(p + 1)!(\Delta t)^{p+1}} \tag{5.1.6}$$

This procedure is illustrated in the following example.

Example 5.1

Problem   Determine the leading truncation error term for the three-value Adams-Moulton multivalue method.

Solution   The coefficients for the three-value Adams-Moulton method were derived in Example 2.13 and are also given in Table B.6. The coefficients are $\{\alpha_{1,0}, \alpha_{1,1}, \alpha_{1,2}\} = \{5/12, 1, 1/2\}$. Solution of the differential equation

$$\frac{du}{dt} = (k + 1)(t)^k$$
$$u(0) = 0 \tag{5.1.7}$$

using the three-value Adams-Moulton method is exact with $k = 0$ and 1. For $k = 2$ and $k = 3$, the solutions are as in the following table, where a step size of $\Delta t = 1$ has been employed:

t^n	n	$k = 2$		$k = 3$	
		u^n	U^n	u^n	U^n
0.0	0	0.	0.	0.	0.
1.0	1	1.	1.25	1.	1.6666667
2.0	2	8.	8.25	16.	17.666667
3.0	3	27.	27.25	81.	83.666667
4.0	4	64.	64.25	256.	259.66667
5.0	5	125.	125.25	625.	629.66667

With $k = 2$, an error of 0.25 can be seen to be introduced on the first step. (Experience indicates that in an m-value Adams-Moulton method, the first $m - 2$ steps are susceptible to this anomalous start-up error.) However, $U^n - u^n$ for $n \geq 1$ is constant when $k = 2$ and equation (5.1.6) provides $C_2 = 0$. For the next solution, $k = 3$ and with $n = 2$, equation (5.1.6) becomes

$$C_3 = \frac{(83\frac{2}{3} - 81) - (17\frac{2}{3} - 16)}{4!(1)^4} = \frac{1}{4!} \tag{5.1.8}$$

Equation (5.1.2) for the truncation error per time step now takes the form

$$U^1 = u^1 + \frac{1}{4!} \left. \frac{d^4 u}{dt^4} \right|_{t^{*1}} (\Delta t)^4 \tag{5.1.9}$$

indicating that the three-value Adams-Moulton method is third-order accurate.

Equation (5.1.2) is an expression of the error for one step. If U^n is computed numerically from an initial condition at t^0 to time t^n using a step size Δt, then this error will apply at each step and may be summed over n steps to give the error in U^n, or

$$U^n - u^n = \sum_{i=1}^{n} C_p \left. \frac{d^{p+1} u}{dt^{p+1}} \right|_{t^{*i}} (\Delta t)^{p+1} \tag{5.1.10}$$

where t^{*i} is the time of evaluation of the derivative for step i. Example 5.1 used a constructed solution such that $d^{p+1}u/dt^{p+1}$ was constant; therefore, the location t^{*i} was not important. However, in this general case, t^{*i} must be considered.

With C_p and Δt as constants, the sum of the derivatives can be rewritten

$$n \left. \frac{d^{p+1} u}{dt^{p+1}} \right|_{t_{\Delta t}^{*n}} = \sum_{i=1}^{n} \left. \frac{d^{p+1} u}{dt^{p+1}} \right|_{t^{*i}} \tag{5.1.11}$$

where $t^0 < t_{\Delta t}^{*n} < t^n$ and $t_{\Delta t}^{*n}$ is the time of evaluation of the derivative, which ensures that the equality holds when the time step is Δt. Therefore, the error expression for n time steps is obtained by substitution of equation (5.1.11) into equation (5.1.10) as

$$U^n - u^n = C_p n(\Delta t) \left. \frac{d^{p+1} u}{dt^{p+1}} \right|_{t_{\Delta t}^{*n}} (\Delta t)^p \tag{5.1.12}$$

where $n(\Delta t) = t^n - t^0$. At any value of $t = i\,\Delta t$ where $0 < i \le n$, the error can be written as

$$U^i - u^i = C_p i(\Delta t)\left.\frac{d^{p+1}u}{dt^{p+1}}\right|_{t^{*i}_{\Delta t}} (\Delta t)^p, \qquad i = 1, 2, ..., n \qquad (5.1.13)$$

For the simple equation considered in Example 5.1, where the analytical solution is known, the error could be evaluated exactly. Equation (5.1.13) provides an expression that theoretically gives the error in a numerical solution to a differential equation for any smooth function at each step. In that equation, the step size, Δt, and the numerically computed value U^i will be known; the parameters p and C_p can be obtained for a numerical procedure. However, this leaves two unknowns, u^i and $d^{p+1}u/dt^{p+1}|_{t^{*i}_{\Delta t}}$, which must be dealt with to obtain the error in the solution at step i. These are generally unknown at any step. Additionally, $t^{*i}_{\Delta t}$, the points of evaluation of the derivative, generally depend on Δt. Thus the value of the derivative that enters the equation depends on both t^i and the magnitude of the time step. Explicit evaluation of the error term is seen to be quite complex.

Despite these difficulties, a measure of the error may be obtained using the method of interval halving. This analysis of the error makes use of the L_2 discrete norm, defined in Appendix A as

$$\|A^i\|_{(i,n)} = \left[\sum_{i=1}^{n} w_i(A^i)^2\right]^{1/2} \qquad (5.1.14)$$

Some understanding of this norm is required before proceeding with the current formalism. Define $U(t^i; \Delta t)$ as the approximation to $u(i\,\Delta t + t^0)$ obtained using a step size Δt. Thus equation (5.1.13) may be used to approximate $u(i\,\Delta t + t^0)$ obtained using time steps of Δt and $\Delta t/2$, respectively, as

$$U(t^i; \Delta t) = u(i\,\Delta t + t^0) + C_p i(\Delta t)\left.\frac{d^{p+1}u}{dt^{p+1}}\right|_{t^{*i}_{\Delta t}} (\Delta t)^p \qquad (5.1.15a)$$

and

$$U(t^{2i}; \Delta t/2) = u(i\,\Delta t + t^0) + C_p i(\Delta t)\left.\frac{d^{p+1}u}{dt^{p+1}}\right|_{t^{*2i}_{\Delta t/2}} \left(\frac{\Delta t}{2}\right)^p \qquad (5.1.15b)$$

Equation (5.1.15b) is written to account for the fact that using a step size of $\Delta t/2$, twice as many steps must be taken to approximate $u(i\,\Delta t + t^0)$ as with a step size Δt. Now subtraction of these two equations to eliminate $u(i\,\Delta t + t^0)$ yields

$$U(t^i; \Delta t) - U(t^{2i}; \Delta t/2) = C_p i(\Delta t)\left[\left.\frac{d^{p+1}u}{dt^{p+1}}\right|_{t^{*i}_{\Delta t}} - \left(\frac{1}{2}\right)^p \left.\frac{d^{p+1}u}{dt^{p+1}}\right|_{t^{*2i}_{\Delta t/2}}\right] (\Delta t)^p$$

$$(5.1.16)$$

If the assumption is made that the value of the quantity in brackets on the right side of equation (5.1.16) is relatively insensitive to differences in value between the two derivatives, then let

$$\left.\frac{d^{p+1}u}{dt^{p+1}}\right|_{t^{*1}_{\Delta t}} \simeq \left.\frac{d^{p+1}u}{dt^{p+1}}\right|_{t^{*2i}_{\Delta t/2}} \equiv \left.\frac{d^{p+1}u}{dt^{p+1}}\right|_{(i^*\Delta t)} \tag{5.1.17a}$$

where $(i^*\Delta t)$ is such that $t^0 \leq (i^*\Delta t) \leq (i\,\Delta t) + t^0$. This assumption may be better understood, perhaps, by noting that the purpose of its introduction is to change the point of evaluation of the derivatives on the right side of equation (5.1.16) to a common point. Thus, as an alternative to equation (5.1.17a), one could define this point to be $(i^*\Delta t)$ such that

$$\left.\frac{d^{p+1}u}{dt^{p+1}}\right|_{(i^*\Delta t)} = \frac{\left.\dfrac{d^{p+1}u}{dt^{p+1}}\right|_{t^{*i}_{\Delta t}} - \left(\dfrac{1}{2}\right)^p \left.\dfrac{d^{p+1}u}{dt^{p+1}}\right|_{t^{*2i}_{\Delta t/2}}}{1 - \left(\dfrac{1}{2}\right)^p} \tag{5.1.17b}$$

where the denominator on the right side of this equation is a normalizing factor chosen to ensure that the equality holds when $d^{p+1}u/dt^{p+1}$ is a constant. With either equation (5.1.17a) or (5.1.17b) invoked, equation (5.1.16) simplifies to

$$U(t^i; \Delta t) - U(t^{2i}; \Delta t/2) = C_p i(\Delta t) \left[\left.\frac{d^{p+1}u}{dt^{p+1}}\right|_{(i^*\Delta t)}\right] \left[1 - \left(\frac{1}{2}\right)^p\right] (\Delta t)^p \tag{5.1.18}$$

The discrete L_2 norm for equation (5.1.18) is

$$\|U(t^i; \Delta t) - U(t^{2i}; \Delta t/2)\|_{(i,n)} = \left\|C_p i(\Delta t)\frac{d^{p+1}u}{dt^{p+1}}\right|_{(i^*\Delta t)}\Bigg\|_{(i,n)} \left[1 - \left(\frac{1}{2}\right)^p\right](\Delta t)^p \tag{5.1.19}$$

A discrete error norm can also be derived from equation (5.1.15b) as

$$\|U(t^{2i}; \Delta t/2) - u(i\,\Delta t + t^0)\|_{(i,n)} = \left\|C_p i(\Delta t)\frac{d^{p+1}u}{dt^{p+1}}\right|_{(i^*\Delta t)}\Bigg\|_{(i,n)} \left(\frac{\Delta t}{2}\right)^p \tag{5.1.20}$$

The norms on the right side of equations (5.1.19) and (5.1.20) are equal and may be eliminated between the equations to obtain

$$\|U(t^{2i}; \Delta t/2) - u(i\,\Delta t + t^0)\|_{(i,n)} = \frac{1}{[(2)^p - 1]}\|U(t^i; \Delta t) - U(t^{2i}; \Delta t/2)\|_{(i,n)} \tag{5.1.21}$$

This equation provides a reliable error norm provided that the restriction imposed in the form of either equation (5.1.17a) or (5.1.17b) is satisfied. In the limit as Δt becomes small, the equality stipulated in equation (5.1.17) is more closely realized. If Δt is sequentially halved to $\Delta t/2, \Delta t/4, \Delta t/8, ...$, equations corresponding to equation (5.1.19) can be obtained as

$$\|U(t^{mi}; \Delta t/m) - U(t^{2mi}; \Delta t/2m)\|_{(i,n)}$$

$$= \left\| C_p i(\Delta t) \frac{d^{p+1}u}{dt^{p+1}} \Big|_{(i*\Delta t)} \right\|_{(i,n)} \left[1 - \left(\frac{1}{2} \right)^p \right] \left(\frac{\Delta t}{m} \right)^p, \qquad m = 1, 2, 4, 8, ... \quad (5.1.22)$$

The ratio between norms on the left of equation (5.1.22) obtained using consecutive values of m is

$$\frac{\|U(t^{mi}; \Delta t/m) - U(t^{2mi}; \Delta t/2m)\|_{(i,n)}}{\|U(t^{2mi}; \Delta t/2m) - U(t^{4mi}; \Delta t/4m)\|_{(i,n)}} = (2)^p \qquad m = 1, 2, 4, 8, ... \quad (5.1.23)$$

Therefore, when assumption (5.1.17) is valid, the ratio defined above will be a constant. This will be the case when m is large enough ($\Delta t/m$ small enough). When this condition is reached, no further decrease of the step size is necessary to obtain the error norm. The most accurate solution will be that obtained with the largest value of p, and its error norm follows directly from equation (5.1.21) as

$$\|U(t^{2mi}; \Delta t/2m) - u(i\,\Delta t + t^0)\|_{(i,n)}$$

$$= \frac{1}{[(2)^p - 1]} \|U(t^{mi}; \Delta t/m) - U(t^{2mi}; \Delta t/2m)\|_{(i,n)} \qquad m = 1, 2, 4, ... \quad (5.1.24)$$

This equation provides a direct measure of the accuracy of the numerical solution to an equation. The root-mean-square error may be obtained by dividing the norm by $(\sum_{i=1}^{n} w_i)^{1/2}$, where the w_i are those used in equation (5.1.14) in evaluating the norm.

Note that equation (5.1.23) also serves as a check of a derivation of order of accuracy or of the correctness of a programmed algorithm. For example, if a fourth-order method ($p = 4$) is being used and the ratio in (5.1.23) approaches a value of 2 when m increases, the possibility that the numerical procedure has been incorrectly implemented or that the equation being solved has a nonsmooth solution should be investigated.

Example 5.2

   Problem   Determine the solution to the differential equation

$$\frac{du}{dt} = -u^2, \qquad 1 < t \le 11$$

$$u(1) = 1 \qquad \qquad (5.1.25)$$

with an average error (in the root-mean-square sense) of less than 1.0×10^{-5}. Use the three-value Adams Moulton method. (This method was derived in Example 2.13; coefficients needed also appear in Table B.6.)

Solution   The error criterion can be satisfied by doing a succession of simulations and sequentially halving the time step. If the initial time step chosen in the sequence is Δt, then those criteria for accuracy stated above can be written in terms of the norms in equation (5.1.24). For each of the sequence of simulations, the time step is constant and thus a constant value of $w_i = \Delta t$ is chosen in evaluating the norms (see Problems 5.2 and 5.3 for insights on selection of w_i). The root-mean-square error is obtained by dividing equation (5.1.14) by

$$\left(\sum_{i=1}^{n} w_i \right)^{1/2} = \sqrt{n(\Delta t)}$$

The required average error is

$$1.0 \times 10^{-5} \geq \frac{1}{\sqrt{n(\Delta t)}} \|U(t^{2mi}; \Delta t/2m) - u(i\,\Delta t + t^0)\|_{(i,n)} \qquad (5.1.26a)$$

or, based on the norm in terms of calculated solutions,

$$1.0 \times 10^{-5} \geq \frac{1}{\sqrt{n(\Delta t)}} \frac{1}{[(2)^p - 1]} \|U(t^{mi}; \Delta t/m) - U(t^{2mi}; \Delta t/2m)\|_{(i,n)} \qquad (5.1.26b)$$

As a first guess, Δt was set equal to 2.0 and the approximate solution to $u(t)$ was obtained at the five discrete locations $t = 3.0, 5.0, 7.0, 9.0,$ and 11.0. Thus $n = 5$ and solutions obtained only at these five locations in time are utilized in the calculation of norms such that n and Δt are constants in equation (5.1.26b) while m varies. Calculated results at these locations are compiled in the following table using a step size $\Delta t/m$ with $\Delta t = 2$ and $m = 1, 2, 4, 8, 16,$ and 32. It should be noted that, for example, with a step size of $\Delta t/32 = 1/16$, solutions must be obtained at 160 time steps, although only the values computed at the five points in time are presented here.

	$m = 1$	$m = 2$	$m = 4$
$U(3; \Delta t/m)$	0.379795897	0.358151121	0.336011939
$U(5; \Delta t/m)$	0.285981489	0.209518290	0.201194612
$U(7; \Delta t/m)$	0.175351606	0.147961492	0.143495669
$U(9; \Delta t/m)$	0.133199776	0.114247676	0.111504139
$U(11; \Delta t/m)$	0.105409016	0.093021098	0.091174376

	$m = 8$	$m = 16$	$m = 32$
$U(3; \Delta t/m)$	0.333671738	0.333375635	0.333338616
$U(5; \Delta t/m)$	0.200147097	0.200018188	0.200002260
$U(7; \Delta t/m)$	0.142935572	0.142866829	0.142858346
$U(9; \Delta t/m)$	0.111159377	0.111117071	0.111111851
$U(11; \Delta t/m)$	0.090941675	0.090913114	0.090909590

From these solutions, five norms can be calculated with $\Delta t = 2$ and $n = 5$ as

m	$\|U(t^{mi}; \Delta t/m) - U(t^{2mi}; \Delta t/2m)\|_{(i,5)}$
1	1.2311×10^{-1}
2	3.4360×10^{-2}
4	3.7578×10^{-3}
8	4.7249×10^{-4}
16	5.8919×10^{-5}

The ratio of consecutive entries in the preceding table is used to evaluate 2^P in equation (5.1.23). The following table of values is obtained.

m	2^P
1	3.5829
2	9.1437
4	7.9531
8	8.0194

Because the numerical procedure being used is third order, 2^P should approximately equal 8 if equation (5.1.17) is a reasonable approximation. This is the case for m of 4 and 8. Hence the norms calculated with $m = 4, 8$, and 16 are accurate norms. Now with $2^P = 8$ and $n = 5$, equation (5.1.26b) becomes

$$1 \times 10^{-5} \geq \frac{1}{\sqrt{10}} \frac{1}{7} \|U(t^{mi}; \Delta t/m) - U(t^{2mi}; \Delta t/2m)\|_{(i,n)} \quad (5.1.27a)$$

or

$$2.21 \times 10^{-4} \geq \|U(t^{mi}; \Delta t/m) - U(t^{2mi}; \Delta t/2m)\|_{(i,n)} \quad (5.1.27b)$$

This constraint is satisfied by the norm in the table with $m = 16$. Thus, from equation (5.1.26a), a solution of the required accuracy will be obtained with a step size as large as $\Delta t/32 = 1/16$. If none of the solutions tabulated here had satisfied the constraint condition, then additional interval halving would have been necessary in search of the needed Δt. Note that if the base Δt for these calculations were chosen to be 1 rather than 2, the calculations of the norm could involve up to 10 values from each grid.

Typically, in solving a problem of interest, the analysis would end here. The evaluation of discrete error norms has provided a criterion for accurate solution of a differential equation without recourse to the analytical solution. In the current case, because the analytical solution is known, the curious or skeptical reader may compare the predicted mean-square error with that actually obtained.

The norms developed above can be applied to an entire region or to only a portion of a domain. For example, if a function u is expected to have a large value of du/dt in some region of time, the method of interval halving can be applied just to that region to obtain an estimate of step size that provides the accuracy required. Thus different step sizes could be used in different regions of time. This concept can be implemented efficiently, as discussed in the next subsection.

5.1.2 Time Step Control in Predictor-Corrector Methods

In contrast to the method of interval halving that requires successive solutions of the problem in order to obtain a satisfactory step size, predictor-corrector methods allow the time step to be adjusted as the calculations proceed. A satisfactory time step for obtaining the solution to the differential equation at $t^{i-1} + \nabla t^i$ is obtained based on the differences between the predicted and corrected solution at t^i. Application of the method requires that the predictor step and the corrector step be of the same order of accuracy. In the following, an expression for the error norm is first derived. Then the procedure for controlling the step size is explained.

For solution of a differential equation, $du/dt = f(u, t)$, a pth-order explicit or predictor method is applied such that for one step, a solution $\hat{U}^1$ is predicted with

$$\hat{U}^1 = u^1 + \hat{C}_p \frac{d^{p+1}u}{dt^{p+1}}\bigg|_{\hat{t}^{*1}} (\nabla t^1)^{p+1} \tag{5.1.28}$$

where the time step, $\nabla t^i = t^i - t^{i-1}$, may vary for subsequent steps, the carat indicates that the method is a predictor, and $\hat{C}_p$ is the coefficient of the truncation error term. Let a pth-order corrector be such that for one step the numerical and analytical solutions are related by

$$U^1 = u^1 + C_p \frac{d^{p+1}u}{dt^{p+1}}\bigg|_{t^{*1}} (\nabla t^1)^{p+1} \tag{5.1.29}$$

Assume, similarly to equation (5.1.17), that the differences between the derivatives in these last two expressions are negligible for the step considered. Subtraction of these last two equations to eliminate u^1 then yields

$$U^1 - \hat{U}^1 = (C_p - \hat{C}_p) \frac{d^{p+1}u}{dt^{p+1}}\bigg|_{t^{*1}} (\nabla t^1)^{p+1} \tag{5.1.30}$$

Additionally, the time derivative may be removed using the last two equations when $C_p \neq \hat{C}_p$ to provide an expression for the error of a time step as

$$U^1 - u^1 = \frac{C_p}{C_p - \hat{C}_p}(U^1 - \hat{U}^1) \tag{5.1.31}$$

If calculations proceed for i steps, the error between U^i and u^i is obtained by summing over the error of each step as

$$U^i - u^i = \frac{C_p}{C_p - \hat{C}_p} \sum_{j=1}^{i} (U^j - \hat{U}^j) \tag{5.1.32}$$

The discrete L_2 norm of the error follows directly as

$$\|U^i - u^i\|_{(i,n)} = \left| \frac{C_p}{C_p - \hat{C}_p} \right| \left\| \sum_{j=1}^{i} (U^j - \hat{U}^j) \right\|_{(i,n)} \tag{5.1.33}$$

This expression provides a useful measure of the error of a solution when n time steps have been completed. The time step size is not restricted to being constant but is included as the weighting function in computation of the norm with $w_j = \nabla t^j$. For this case the root-mean-square error is calculated as the right side of equation (5.1.33) divided by $\sqrt{t^n - t^0}$. Although the last equation is useful in assessing the errors after the fact, it does not assist in a priori selection of the time step that will satisfy an error criterion.

To predict a reasonable time step, first note that the expression containing the derivative on the right side of equation (5.1.29) is the additional error added to the solution in advancing one time step. This term, for step j rather than step 1, is a measure of

$$|U^j - u^j| - |U^{j-1} - u^{j-1}| = \nabla |U^j - u^j| = \left| C_p \frac{d^{p+1} u}{dt^{p+1}} \right|_{t^{*j}} (\nabla t^j)^{p+1} \tag{5.1.34}$$

If the assumption is made that the time derivative in equation (5.1.34) is approximately constant in computing the error committed in steps j and $j-1$ (which is true when ∇t^j is small), then division of $\nabla |U^j - u^j|$ by $\nabla |U^{j-1} - u^{j-1}|$ yields

$$\nabla |U^j - u^j| = \nabla |U^{j-1} - u^{j-1}| \left(\frac{\nabla t^j}{\nabla t^{j-1}} \right)^{p+1} \tag{5.1.35}$$

Note that the quantity $\nabla |U^{j-1} - u^{j-1}|$ is the additional error made during step $j-1$ and is not the total difference at time t^{j-1} between the numerical and analytical solutions. The error made during a single time step can be obtained as an analog to equation (5.1.31) and substituted into this last equation, leaving

$$\nabla |U^j - u^j| = \left| \frac{C_p}{C_p - \hat{C}_p} (U^{j-1} - \hat{U}^{j-1}) \right| \left(\frac{\nabla t^j}{\nabla t^{j-1}} \right)^{p+1} \tag{5.1.36}$$

The next step is to specify some condition on the size of this error. A first possibility is to require that $\nabla |U^j - u^j|$, the error introduced in the time step, be less than some constant. Although this constraint is easy to apply, it does not restrict the total error present in a solution at some fixed time. Perhaps a more realistic condition is to require that

$$\epsilon \geq \frac{\nabla |U^j - u^j|}{\nabla t^j} \tag{5.1.37}$$

where ϵ is a constant. This condition, restricting the rate of error introduction into the solution, allows a simulation to be carried out with a specified maximum error at any point in time. Substitution of equation (5.1.36) into equation (5.1.37) yields

$$\epsilon \geq \left| \frac{C_p(U^{j-1} - \hat{U}^{j-1})}{(C_p - \hat{C}_p)(\nabla t^{j-1})} \right| \left(\frac{\nabla t^j}{\nabla t^{j-1}} \right)^p \qquad (5.1.38)$$

or

$$\nabla t^j \leq \left| \frac{\epsilon(\nabla t^{j-1})(C_p - \hat{C}_p)}{C_p(U^{j-1} - \hat{U}^{j-1})} \right|^{1/p} (\nabla t^{j-1}) \qquad (5.1.39)$$

Based on the predicted and corrected solution for step $j-1$, this equation allows selection of time step ∇t^j such that the error will be controlled. This is a very useful relationship, although it must be used with some care and only when $C_p \neq \hat{C}_p$.

The condition (5.1.39) is based only on accuracy considerations and does not account for the possibility of a method becoming unstable when the time step becomes large. Unlimited growth of the time step should be avoided. Also note that this condition on step size is only approximate in that it assumes constancy of the $p + 1$ derivative of u over consecutive time steps. Additionally, when this derivative is of a different sign in different regions of the solution domain, this condition fails to account for positive errors made in one region canceling negative errors made in another region. Thus the step size condition may be overly conservative and restrict the error more than necessary. Furthermore, even though multivalue methods facilitate adjustment of the time step, the accuracy of these methods is best when some cancellation of errors occurs between the derivatives. This cancellation seems to take $k - 2$ steps to become fully operative in Adams-Moulton k-value methods and is only approached in the limit of a large number of steps for Gear's multivalue methods. Therefore, the step size should not be changed at every step. The predicted step size is an extrapolation; and, because extrapolations tend to be very sensitive to minor variations within the solution, the step size changes recommended should be considered as possibly excessive. For instance, the step size ratio between consecutive time steps might be wisely constrained to be no more than two even if a larger ratio is predicted to be acceptable.

One remaining problem in determining a solution with a specified accuracy is to decide on an initial time step. If too large a value is selected, the constraints on rate of change of time step might preclude obtaining a solution with the needed accuracy. If too small a step is selected, excessive computations may be necessary. One way of obtaining an estimate of the needed initial time step is to use the method of interval halving on an initial subregion of the grid of length Δt. If ϵ is the average rate of error introduction into the solution, then the error introduced over grid length Δt starting from the specified initial condition must be constrained such that

$$\epsilon \Delta t > \frac{1}{\sqrt{\Delta t}} \| U(t^{2mi}; \Delta t/2m) - u(\Delta t + t^0) \|_{(i,1)}, \qquad m = 1, 2, 4, 8, \ldots \qquad (5.1.40)$$

But equation (5.1.24) provides an expression for this norm based on the numerical solution of order p, such that

$$\epsilon \Delta t > \frac{1}{2^p - 1} \|U(t^{mi}; \Delta t/m) - U(t^{2mi}; \Delta t/2m)\|_{(i,1)}, \qquad m = 1, 2, 4, 8, \ldots$$

$$(5.1.41)$$

The largest value of $\Delta t/2m$ which satisfies this constraint would seem to be an appropriate step size for beginning computations although a more conservative choice of $\Delta t/4m$ might also be considered.

Finally, the actual error obtained in the full solution may be obtained using the L_2 discrete norm of equation (5.1.33). This norm is a useful tool in verifying that the time step solution algorithm has achieved its purpose.

Example 5.3

Problem   Solve the differential equation

$$\frac{du}{dt} = -u^2, \qquad 1 < t \leq 11$$

$$u(1) = 1$$

$$(5.1.25)$$

using both the two-value and three-value Adams-Moulton methods with an average rate of error introduction, ϵ, less than 1×10^{-6}.

Solution   The predictor form of these methods is given by equation (2.6.51) and the corrector form is equation (2.6.49). The needed coefficients $\alpha_{1,k}$ were derived in Example 2.13 and are also provided in Appendix B. The coefficients $\hat{C}_p$ and C_p may be derived following the procedure of Section 5.1 (see Problem 5.6) and appear, as well, in Table B.6. For the two value Adams-Moulton method, $p = 2$, $\hat{C}_2 = -5/12$, and $C_2 = 1/12$. For the three-value Adams method, $p = 3$, $\hat{C}_3 = -9/24$, and $C_3 = 1/24$. For this study, the initial time step to be used is obtained from an interval halving computation over the range $1 < t < 1.1$ with an initial time step of $\Delta t = 0.1$. Thus the error introduced should be such that $\epsilon \Delta t \leq 1.0 \times 10^{-7}$. The set of norms presented in the following table were computed for the two methods.

$$\frac{1}{\sqrt{\Delta t}} \|U(t^{mi}; \Delta t/m) - U(t^{2mi}; \Delta t/2m)\|_{(i,1)}$$

m	Norm for Ad-2	Norm for Ad-3
1	2.8469×10^{-4}	1.6007×10^{-4}
2	7.0618×10^{-5}	1.6940×10^{-5}
4	1.7620×10^{-5}	1.9781×10^{-6}
8	4.4029×10^{-6}	$\rightarrow 2.3880 \times 10^{-7}$
16	1.1006×10^{-6}	2.9330×10^{-8}
32	$\rightarrow 2.7514 \times 10^{-7}$	3.6341×10^{-9}
64	6.8785×10^{-8}	4.5226×10^{-10}
128	1.7196×10^{-8}	5.6407×10^{-11}
256	4.2991×10^{-9}	7.0434×10^{-12}
512	1.0748×10^{-9}	8.7885×10^{-13}

The estimated appropriate starting time step is the lowest value of $\Delta t/2m$ for which

$$\frac{1}{\sqrt{\Delta t}}\|U(t^{mi};\Delta t/m) - U(t^{2mi};\Delta t/2m)\|_{(i,1)} < (2^p - 1) \cdot 1 \times 10^{-7} \qquad (5.1.42)$$

For the Adams-2 case, $(2^p - 1) \cdot \epsilon \Delta t = 3 \times 10^{-7}$, and this criterion is closely satisfied with $m = 32$, indicating that an initial step size of $\Delta t/2m = 0.1/64$ is satisfactory. For the Adams-3 case, $(2^p - 1) \cdot \epsilon \Delta t = 7 \times 10^{-7}$ and condition (5.1.26) is comfortably satisfied with $m = 8$ and an initial step size of $\Delta t/2m = 0.1/16$.

For these p-value methods, the step size was tested for potential alteration only every p steps. As a conservative application of equation (5.1.39) for step size adjustment, a coefficient of 0.8 was used such that

$$\nabla t^j = 0.8 \left| \frac{\epsilon(\nabla t^{j-1})(C_p - \hat{C}_p)}{C_p(U^{j-1} - \hat{U}^{j-1})} \right|^{1/p} (\nabla t^{j-1}) \qquad (5.1.43)$$

The change in time step was also restricted to not increase or decrease on one adjustment by more than a factor of 2. Also, if the predicted allowable or necessary change in time step was less than 20%, the adjustment was not made. These restrictions were aimed at preventing the time step from changing at every opportunity, thereby preventing the multivalue methods from suffering excessive error introduction at time step change points.

The solution to equation (5.1.25) obtained using the second order Adams-Moulton formula appears in the following table. The values of i, ∇t^i, and U^i included are those that were obtained immediately after any time step change occurred (as well as the values for the final step).

Step # i	∇t^i	t^i	$U(t^i)$
3	1.1349×10^{-3}	1.0043	0.995758160
87	1.3623×10^{-3}	1.0998	0.909240206
165	1.6383×10^{-3}	1.2064	0.828943519
237	1.9744×10^{-3}	1.3246	0.754917546
303	2.3820×10^{-3}	1.4554	0.687112648
363	2.8729×10^{-3}	1.5988	0.625478006
417	3.4576×10^{-3}	1.7545	0.569963443
467	4.1727×10^{-3}	1.9281	0.518647490
513	5.0450×10^{-3}	2.1209	0.471496287
555	6.1037×10^{-3}	2.3339	0.428475190
593	7.3774×10^{-3}	2.5671	0.389548942
627	8.8898×10^{-3}	2.8194	0.354683287
659	1.0775×10^{-2}	3.1058	0.321980553
687	1.2970×10^{-2}	3.4097	0.293282768
713	1.5664×10^{-2}	3.7496	0.266694652
737	1.8964×10^{-2}	4.1288	0.242198084
759	2.2993×10^{-2}	4.5501	0.219775372

Step # i	∇t^i	t^i	$U(t^i)$
779	2.7877×10^{-2}	5.0148	0.199408028
797	3.3738×10^{-2}	5.5225	0.181077370
813	4.0657×10^{-2}	6.0692	0.164765490
829	4.9856×10^{-2}	6.7289	0.148611342
843	6.0737×10^{-2}	7.4378	0.134447650
855	7.3223×10^{-2}	8.1791	0.122261401
867	8.9837×10^{-2}	9.0744	0.110198716
877	1.0849×10^{-1}	9.9914	0.100084174
887	1.3340×10^{-1}	11.1013	0.090077945
888	1.3340×10^{-1}	11.2347	0.089008284

Note that for this solution, the code reduced the time step from 1.5625×10^{-3} to 1.1349×10^{-3} at the first opportunity. The time step was not increased to more than its initial value until 165 steps into the simulation. This indicates that the first time step was too large and raises the possibility that the error introduced in the first two steps may be excessive for the error criterion. Perhaps this behavior could have been anticipated because equation (5.1.42) was only closely satisfied. A more judicious choice for the first step might have been $\Delta t = 0.1/128$. Note that time step changes occurred more frequently at large time. This is not surprising, as when du/dt becomes small, as it does in this problem with increasing time, the solution becomes more constant and is more easily simulated. Overall, the simulation ran for 888 steps and terminated with $t^{888} = 11.234$. The norm, weighted with the time step and computed by equation (5.1.33), is

$$\|U^i - u^i\|_{(i,888)} = 8.8614 \times 10^{-6} \tag{5.1.44}$$

The solutions obtained using the three-value Adams-Moulton formula are presented in the following table.

Step # i	∇t^i	t^i	$U(t^i)$
4	8.0657×10^{-3}	1.0268	0.973884509
19	9.7726×10^{-3}	1.1495	0.869937073
34	1.1940×10^{-2}	1.2983	0.770258472
49	1.4817×10^{-2}	1.4802	0.675563376
61	1.7893×10^{-2}	1.6611	0.602001226
73	2.1923×10^{-2}	1.8799	0.531950639
85	2.7288×10^{-2}	2.1483	0.465481679
97	3.4592×10^{-2}	2.4831	0.402727765
106	4.2079×10^{-2}	2.8019	0.356902840
115	5.2019×10^{-2}	3.1905	0.313427512

Step # i	∇t^i	t^i	$U(t^i)$
124	6.5412×10^{-2}	3.6721	0.272324474
133	8.3903×10^{-2}	4.2793	0.233683826
139	1.0075×10^{-2}	4.7996	0.208352887
145	1.2290×10^{-2}	5.4262	0.184291464
151	1.5214×10^{-2}	6.1928	0.161477778
157	1.9158×10^{-1}	7.1450	0.139956911
163	2.4606×10^{-1}	8.3490	0.119775023
169	3.2347×10^{-1}	9.9028	0.100982040
174	3.2347×10^{-1}	11.5201	0.086805145

Again, the values that appear are those obtained on the first step after a time step change (as well as the solution and parameter values obtained on the last time step computed). Here, the time step was increased by the code at the first opportunity by about 30% and then remained constant for the next 15 steps. This indicates that the initial selection of time step was a very reasonable selection. Similarly to the second-order method, the step size changes became more frequent at larger times due to the smoothness of the solution there and the slower rate of error generation. Note that with the higher-order method, the solution was obtained in only 174 steps, as opposed to 888 steps for the second-order procedure. For this higher-order method, the time step weighted norm computed using equation (5.1.33) is

$$\|U^i - u^i\|_{(i,174)} = 6.7669 \times 10^{-6} \tag{5.1.45}$$

As a measure of the success of both of these methods in producing solutions with the desired accuracy, assume that some method with constant time step Δt could be devised that produces precisely an error of $\epsilon \Delta t$ at each step. Then at some time $i\,\Delta t$,

$$U(t^i; \Delta t) - u(i\,\Delta t) = \epsilon i\,\Delta t \tag{5.1.46}$$

The norm of this expression is

$$\|U(t^i; \Delta t) - u(i\,\Delta t)\|_{(i,n)} = \epsilon\,\Delta t\|i\|_{(i,n)} \tag{5.1.47}$$

When Δt is used as a weight function, this norm can be evaluated as

$$\|U(t^i; \Delta t) - u(i\,\Delta t)\|_{(i,n)} = \epsilon \left[\frac{(n\Delta t)[2(n\Delta t) + \Delta t][(n\Delta t) + \Delta t]}{6} \right]^{1/2} \tag{5.1.48}$$

But $n\,\Delta t$ is the interval of simulation, denoted here as T, so that

$$\|U(t^i; \Delta t) - u(i\,\Delta t)\|_{(i,n)} = \epsilon \left[\frac{T(2T + \Delta t)(T + \Delta t)}{6} \right]^{1/2} \tag{5.1.49}$$

When Δt in this expression approaches zero, n approaches infinity and the norm is a continuous L_2 norm with

$$\|U(t^i; \Delta t) - u(i\,\Delta t)\|_{(i,\infty)} = \epsilon \left[\frac{T^3}{3} \right]^{1/2} \tag{5.1.50}$$

On the other hand, when $\Delta t = T$, the approximation is that for a one-term discretization and

$$\|U(t^i; \Delta t) - u(i \, \Delta t)\|_{(i,1)} = \epsilon T^{3/2} \tag{5.1.51}$$

Therefore, for a simulation to be carried out with an error entry rate less than ϵ but greater than 0.1ϵ, a reasonable condition to expect might be

$$0.1\epsilon \left[\frac{T^3}{3} \right]^{1/2} < \|U^i - u^i\|_{(i,n)} < \epsilon T^{3/2} \tag{5.1.52}$$

For the Adams-2 case with actual $T = 11.23 - 1.00 = 10.23$ and $\epsilon = 1.0 \times 10^{-6}$, this condition becomes

$$1.889 \times 10^{-6} < \|U^i - u^i\|_{(i,888)} < 3.272 \times 10^{-5} \tag{5.1.53}$$

The actual norm computed of 8.861×10^{-6} falls within this range. For the Adams-3 case with an actual $T = 11.52 - 1.00 = 10.52$ and $\epsilon = 1.0 \times 10^{-6}$,

$$1.970 \times 10^{-6} < \|U^i - u^i\|_{(i,174)} < 3.412 \times 10^{-5} \tag{5.1.54}$$

Here also, the actual norm of 6.767×10^{-6} falls nicely within this range.

This example must be viewed as a simple illustration. The fact that u and its derivatives all decrease monotonically in magnitude makes the simulation relatively straightforward. In more complex problems, the actual step size used might decrease as well as increase. Also, oscillatory behavior can cause some cancellation of error. Nevertheless, the tools for analysis presented here demonstrate the effectiveness of time step control in predictor-corrector methods.

In the last two sections, methods have been presented for assessing and controlling the error in a solution in time-stepping problems. Both the method of interval halving and the use of predictor-corrector methods rely on obtaining different solutions at points in time with the same order of accuracy. Because the error terms are of the same order, they may be evaluated between pairs of solutions to gain an estimate of the error norm. The same approach may also be applied in the spatial domain, as will be illustrated in the next subsection.

5.1.3 Interval Halving for Spatial Problems

In theory, the use of interval halving in the spatial domain to assess the accuracy of a solution is the same as in the time domain. However, in application there are some important differences. First, the spatial domain is a closed domain for elliptic, parabolic, and many hyperbolic partial differential equations. Boundary conditions are applied along the entire boundary of the region and influence the interior solution at all points within the domain. For these cases, the solution at a node in space generally depends on the solution at neighboring nodes in all spatial directions. This is in contrast to the time domain, which is open-ended such that the numerical procedure constantly must project forward with no influence from a specified solution at a future time. Second, the approximations at different nodes may be of different orders of accuracy, depending on the numerical analogs applied and the regularity of spacing between nodes. An analysis for the form and coefficients of the truncation error in the approximation at every node on an irregular grid is an impractically large task. Finally, in multiple dimensions truncation error terms are sums of spatial derivatives.

The need exists to determine which directions are introducing the most error and if interval halving is necessary in all or only some of the directions. When the order of accuracy of an approximation to a differential equation on a regular grid is different in one coordinate direction from another, the effectiveness of interval halving (i.e., the number of halvings that must be applied to achieve satisfactory convergence) will be different in each direction.

In refining a grid to examine accuracy, the concepts of convergence and conditional consistency must be kept in mind. In Chapter 2 it was shown that on a multidimensional grid, mesh refinement in only one coordinate direction may lead to divergence of the numerical approximation from the actual differential equation (see strict versus weak consistency in Section 2.7). Therefore, when applying interval halving, one may have to refine the mesh in all directions simultaneously or at a different rate in different directions. On the other hand, applications of interval halving to each grid direction independently may provide insight into the consistency of the numerical approximation utilized.

Development of the error norms in space results in equations similar to (5.1.23) and (5.1.24). However, because the order of accuracy of an approximation used may be dependent on the direction or on the location on the grid, the interpretation of the norm and the results requires some caution. To illustrate this fact, consider the numerical solution of a differential equation where x and y, denoted as $\mathbf{x}$, are the independent variables. If an arbitrary grid is used in the domain of the solution, then at point i the numerical solution will be related to the exact solution by

$$U(\mathbf{x}_i; \Delta\mathbf{x}) = u(\mathbf{x}_i) + A\frac{\partial^m u}{\partial x^m}\bigg|_{\mathbf{x}_x^*} (\Delta x)^m + B\frac{\partial^k u}{\partial y^k}\bigg|_{\mathbf{x}_y^*} (\Delta y)^k + C\frac{\partial^{r+s} u}{\partial x^r \partial y^s}\bigg|_{\mathbf{x}_{xy}^*} (\Delta x)^r (\Delta y)^s$$

$$(5.1.55)$$

where $U(\mathbf{x}_i; \Delta\mathbf{x})$ is used to indicate the numerical solution at $\mathbf{x}_i$ with a grid characterized by a set of values of Δx and Δy throughout the region; A, B, and C are constants; the last three terms on the right side of the equation are taken to represent typical leading or lowest-order error terms; $\mathbf{x}_x^*$, $\mathbf{x}_y^*$, and $\mathbf{x}_{xy}^*$ are the locations where the lowest-order error terms are evaluated; and Δx and Δy in these terms are indicative of the grid size. The description of terms in equation (5.1.55) is somewhat vague, as necessitated when an irregular grid is used in multiple dimensions. If the grid is now refined by halving all the intervals, the numerical solution at $\mathbf{x}_i$ can be represented as

$$U(\mathbf{x}_i; \Delta\mathbf{x}/2) = u(\mathbf{x}_i) + \left(\frac{1}{2}\right)^m A\frac{\partial^m u}{\partial x^m}\bigg|_{\mathbf{x}_x^*} (\Delta x)^m + \left(\frac{1}{2}\right)^k B\frac{\partial^k u}{\partial y^k}\bigg|_{\mathbf{x}^* y} (\Delta y)^k$$

$$+ \left(\frac{1}{2}\right)^{r+s} C\frac{\partial^{r+s}}{\partial x^r \partial y^s}\bigg|_{\mathbf{x}_{xy}^*} (\Delta x)^r (\Delta y)^s \qquad (5.1.56)$$

where $\mathbf{x}_x^*$, $\mathbf{x}_y^*$, and $\mathbf{x}_{xy}^*$ are assumed to be approximately the same points, respectively, in both solutions. Note that if m, k, and/or $r + s$ have different values, equations (5.1.55) and (5.1.56) cannot be combined to eliminate error terms. As the grid is refined, the dominant error term will become the one with the smallest positive value of m, k, or $r + s$. However, this term may not be dominant in the first refinements. Furthermore, as the interval size on an irregular grid is successively halved, the order of approximation at an increasing number of nodes becomes that of a regular approximation. Thus if error norms over the full spatial domain are used as a measure of convergence, the order of acuracy of an irregular grid will approach that of the regular grid. Thus the very predictable behavior of the error norm, demonstrated in Sections 5.1.1 and 5.1.2 for time stepping, is more difficult to achieve in multidimensions. For a regular grid with all terms in a governing differential equation approximated to the same order of accuracy, the behavior of the norms with interval halving will be similar to that demonstrated in the time domain in Section 5.1.1. In any event, the norm of equation (5.1.24) (with time replaced by space) and root-mean-square error norms are valuable tools in assessing the accuracy of a numerical solution.

Example 5.4

Problem   Solve the differential equation

$$\frac{d}{dx}\left(K\frac{du}{dx}\right) = a(u)^r, \qquad 0 < x < 4 \tag{5.1.57a}$$

$$u(0) = 0.0 \tag{5.1.57b}$$

$$u(4) = 4.0 \tag{5.1.57c}$$

when $K = 0.1x + 5.0$, $a = 0.1$, and $r = 0.3$.

Solution   This equation will be solved using linear finite elements, and the method of interval halving will be used to assess the accuracy of the calculations. Because equation (5.1.57a) is nonlinear, the numerical solution must be obtained for a particular grid by iteration. The iteration scheme requires that an initial estimate of the solution be made and then checked to determine if it satisfies the discrete equation. Depending on how well the solution satisfies the difference equation, a new solution may have to be estimated and then checked. The method of obtaining a new estimate of the solution should be systematic such that convergence is obtained. The problem considered in this example is relatively simple, but the methods for solution described subsequently have proven useful in many nonlinear problems.

First expand u and $(u)^r$ in terms of piecewise linear basis functions $\phi_j(x)$ for the case when the domain is discretized using N nodes:

$$u \simeq U = \sum_{j=1}^{N} U_j \phi_j(x) \tag{5.1.58a}$$

$$(u)^r \simeq \sum_{j=1}^{N} (U_j)^r \phi_j(x) \tag{5.1.58b}$$

Note that an expression for $(u)^r$ can alternatively be written by raising equation (5.1.58a) to the rth power. However, the increased complexity of this type of expression usually does not result in an improved solution and creates convergence difficulties in many cases. Thus equation (5.1.58b) is chosen. Substitution of these last expressions into (5.1.57a) and application of the Galerkin finite element method yields

$$\sum_{j=1}^{N} \int_0^4 \frac{d}{dx}\left(KU_j \frac{d\phi_j}{dx}\right)\phi_i dx - \sum_{j=1}^{N} \int_0^4 a(U_j)^r \phi_j \phi_i dx = 0,$$

$$i = 1, 2, ..., N \qquad (5.1.59a)$$

or, after application of integration by parts to the first integral,

$$\sum_{j=1}^{N} \int_0^4 KU_j \frac{d\phi_j}{dx}\frac{d\phi_i}{dx}\,dx + \sum_{j=1}^{N} \int_0^4 a(U_j)^r \phi_j \phi_i\,dx + \hat{q}\phi_i \Big|_{x=0}^{x=4} = 0,$$

$$i = 1, 2, ..., N \qquad (5.1.59b)$$

where $\hat{q} \simeq -K(du/dx)$ denotes the boundary flux. Equation (5.1.59b) is nonlinear in U_j when r is not equal to 0 or 1 and cannot be solved directly. An iterative scheme can be derived by setting U_j equal to an estimate, $\hat{U}_j$, plus an error, e_j, or

$$U_j = \hat{U}_j + e_j \qquad (5.1.60a)$$

and

$$(U_j)^r = (\hat{U}_j + e_j)^r \qquad (5.1.60b)$$

Binomial expansion of $(U_j)^r$ yields

$$(U_j)^r = (\hat{U}_j)^r + re_j(\hat{U}_j)^{r-1} + \frac{1}{2}r(r-1)(e_j)^2(\hat{U}_j)^{r-2} + \cdots \qquad (5.1.61)$$

The iterative scheme to be implemented is intended to converge $\hat{U}_j$ to U_j such that e_j goes to zero. Thus only the first two terms on the right side of equation (5.1.61) will be retained with terms in e_j^2, e_j^3, and so on, being very small when e_j is small. Substitution of approximation (5.1.60a) back into (5.1.59b) then gives

$$\sum_{j=1}^{N} \int_0^4 Ke_j \frac{d\phi_j}{dx}\frac{d\phi_i}{dx}\,dx + \sum_{j=1}^{N} \int_0^4 are_j(\hat{U}_j)^{r-1}\phi_j \phi_i\,dx + \hat{q}\phi_i \Big|_{x=0}^{x=4}$$

$$= -\sum_{j=1}^{N} \int_0^4 K\hat{U}_j \frac{d\phi_j}{dx}\frac{d\phi_i}{dx}\,dx - \sum_{j=1}^{N} \int_0^4 a(\hat{U}_j)^r \phi_j \phi_i\,dx, \quad i = 1, 2, ..., N \quad (5.1.62)$$

With $\hat{U}_j$ estimated, the terms on the right side of this equation are known. The left side is linear in e_j and thus the equation may be solved directly. Because u is specified at $x = 0$ and $x = 4$, only $N - 2$ values of U_j are unknown and the weighting with respect to ϕ_1 and ϕ_N is not done. Therefore, $\hat{q}$ will not enter into the solution for U_j. After obtaining U_j, equation (5.1.62) or equation (5.1.59b) may be used with $i = 1$ and N to determine $\hat{q}|_{x=0}$ and $\hat{q}|_{x=4}$, respectively. Computation proceeds by specifying $\hat{U}_j$, solving equation set (5.1.62) for e_j, and then obtaining a new estimate for $\hat{U}_j$ as $\hat{U}_j + e_j$. For a convergent computation, successive solutions for e_j will approach zero and thus $\hat{U}_j$ will approach U_j. Note that e_j is not a measure of error between the exact solution u and the numerical solution for a particular grid. It is an approximation of the error between estimated and converged numerical solutions. In general, when evaluating the integrals in equation (5.1.62), either the known functional form for K or an approximation to K in terms of basis functions may be used. For the current problem, where K has been specified as a linear function of x, K is exactly represented in terms of the linear basis functions as

$$K = \sum_{j=1}^{N} K_j \phi_j(x) \tag{5.1.63}$$

The problem was solved using an initial step size of $\Delta x = 2$ (i.e., 3 nodes) and then by successive interval halving. The solutions obtained at $x = 2$, the middle point of the grid, are tabulated below.

m	$\Delta x/m$	$U(2; \Delta x/m)$
1	2	2.9668
2	1	3.1345
4	1/2	3.2545
8	1/4	3.3359
16	1/8	3.3879
32	1/16	3.4177
64	1/32	3.4318
128	1/64	3.4371
256	1/128	3.4387
512	1/256	3.4392
1024	1/512	3.4393

These solutions were obtained using the iteration scheme described previously with iteration terminating when

$$\|e_j\|_{(j, 2m+1)} < 1.0 \times 10^{-8} \|U(x_j; \Delta x/m)\|_{(j, 2m+1)} \tag{5.1.64}$$

where $2m + 1$ is the number of nodes in the grid. This convergence criterion inspects all nodes, not just nodes of the original coarse grid, and requires the root-mean-square average correction to be less than 1×10^{-8} of the root-mean-square solution. This may also be seen as equivalent to requiring the solution to converge with more than seven places of accuracy. Note that this is convergence to the numerical solution, U, of the nonlinear equation (5.1.59) and provides no indication of the quality of agreement between U and u. For each grid only two or three iterations were required to achieve convergence with an initial estimate of the solution as a linear function of x.

Equations (5.1.23) and (5.1.24) provide estimates of the norm using time marching. These expressions exploit the fact that at the initial point, the numerical solution is equal to the applied initial condition. For boundary value problems in space, if a second- or third-type boundary condition is applied, the solution for the dependent variable at the boundary may only approximate the analytical solution. Therefore, in writing spatial domain analogs to equations (5.1.23) and (5.1.24), the boundary nodes must be included. For the current one-dimensional problem (even though the grid spacing is equal and Dirichlet conditions are applied at the boundary nodes), the analogs to equations (5.1.23) and (5.1.24) that account for the boundary nodes are, respectively,

$$\frac{\|U(x_i; \delta x_i/m) - U(x_i; \delta x_i/2m)\|_{(i,N)}}{\|U(x_i; \delta x_i/2m) - U(x_i; \delta x_i/4m)\|_{(i,N)}} = (2)^p, \qquad m = 1, 2, 4, 8, \ldots \qquad (5.1.65)$$

and

$$\|U(x_i; \delta x_i/2m) - u(x_i)\|_{(i,N)} = \frac{1}{(2)^p - 1} \|U(x_i; \delta x_i/m) - U(x_i; \delta x_i/2m)\|_{(i,N)},$$

$$m = 1, 2, 4, 8, \ldots \qquad (5.1.66)$$

In these expressions, N is the number of nodes on the coarsest grid, regardless of the value of p. Correspondingly, the subscripts i also are used to indicate locations on the coarse grid, regardless of renumbering of nodes that may occur when the intervals are halved.

If the weighting factor for computing the norm is δx_i for interior nodes and $\delta x_i/2$ for the two boundary nodes, then the root-mean-square error is obtained by dividing the error norm on the left side of equation (5.1.66) by $\sqrt{x_N - x_1}$.

The following quantities may be obtained from equations (5.1.65) and (5.1.66) based on solutions to equation (5.1.57) where $\delta x_i = 2.0$.

m	$\|U(x_1; \delta x_i/m) - U(x_i; \delta x_i/2m)\|_{(i,3)}$	$(2)^p$	p
1	2.3722×10^{-1}	1.3988	0.4842
2	1.6959×10^{-1}	1.4731	0.5589
4	1.1512×10^{-1}	1.5631	0.6444
8	7.3650×10^{-2}	1.7507	0.8079
16	4.2069×10^{-2}	2.1078	1.0757
32	1.9959×10^{-2}	2.6571	1.4099
64	7.5114×10^{-3}	3.2709	1.7097
128	2.2964×10^{-3}	3.7126	1.8924
256	6.1855×10^{-4}	3.9124	1.9681
512	1.5810×10^{-4}	—	—

The term 2^p appears to approach 4 as the mesh is refined, indicating that p approaches 2 and the solution is second-order accurate. The root-mean-square error, computed from the error norm in equation (5.1.56) for the case of $m = 128$ is 3.8273×10^{-4}. This indicates that with $m = 256$, the numerical solution is, on the average, accurate to three decimal places, in comparison to the actual solution to the differential equation.

Example 5.5

Problem   Solve the two-dimensional heat conduction equation

$$\nabla^2 u = 0, \qquad 0 < x < 2, \quad 0 < y < 2 \tag{5.1.67a}$$

with

$$u(0, y) = 2y - y^2 \tag{5.1.67b}$$

$$u(x, 2) = 0 \tag{5.1.67c}$$

$$u(2, y) = (2 - y)^2 \tag{5.1.67d}$$

$$u(x, 0) = x^2 \tag{5.1.67e}$$

Solution   This rather simple equation will be solved using linear triangular finite elements. Two different 3×3 grids will be used as starting points and the method of interval halving will be employed to demonstrate the convergence of the solution. One grid will start with equispaced nodes and similar triangular elements, while the other will use triangles that are not of equal size.

Expansion of u in terms of basis functions yields

$$u \simeq U = \sum_{j=1}^{N} U_j \phi_j(x, y) \tag{5.1.68}$$

Substitution of this expression into equation (5.1.67a), followed by application of the Galerkin finite element method and of Green's theorem, provides

$$\sum_{j=1}^{N} \int_{\Omega} U_j \nabla \phi_j \cdot \nabla \phi_i d\Omega - \int_{\Gamma} \nabla U \cdot \mathbf{n} \phi_i d\Gamma = 0, \qquad i = 1, 2, ..., N \tag{5.1.69}$$

Because the problem posed is a Dirichlet problem with values of u specified along the entire boundary of the domain, Γ, equation (5.1.69) will not be applied when node i is on the boundary. Use of equation (5.1.69) at all interior nodes plus application of equations (5.1.67b) through (5.1.67e) to the boundary nodes completely determines the solution.

The mesh to be used in solving this problem is depicted in Figure 5.1a. An equispaced grid is obtained by setting $\gamma = 1$. For comparison, a second set of solutions will be generated using $\gamma = 0.75$. The discrete approximations that arise in this instance are the same as one would obtain using three-point finite difference approximations to $\partial^2 u / \partial x^2 |_{x_i}$ and $\partial^2 u / \partial y^2 |_{x_i}$. Note that in interval halving with a triangular grid, many options exist for connecting nodes to form elements. Two possibilities for the current problem are shown in Figure 5.1b and c. For the solutions here, in all halvings, the diagonals were added such that all extend from lower left to upper right (i.e., as in Figure 5.1b).

The solutions obtained at the point $(\gamma, \gamma) = (1, 1)$ and $(\gamma, \gamma) = (0.75, 0.75)$ for the two original grids, respectively, and for these points when the intervals are halved in both the x and y directions are tabulated below.

m	Number of nodes	$U(1,1;\delta x_i/m,\delta y_i/m)$	$U(0.75,0.75;\delta x_i/m,\delta y_i/m)$
1	9	0.60000	0.61709
2	25	0.60212	0.63060
4	81	0.60271	0.63636
8	289	0.60287	0.63806
16	1089	0.60291	0.63851
32	4225	0.60292	0.63862

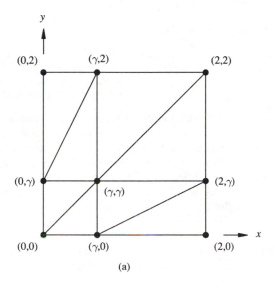

(a)

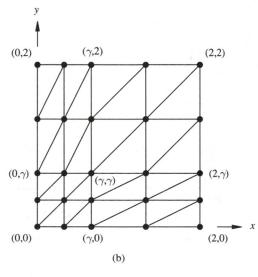

(b)

Figure 5.1 Interval halving of a two-dimensional finite element grid. (a) Nine-node triangular finite element grid. (b) Option for interval halving of original grid (used in computations of Example 5.5).

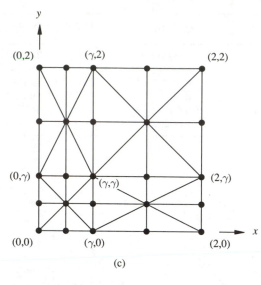

Figure 5.1 (cont'd.) Interval halving of a two-dimensional finite element grid. (c) Alternative halving of intervals of original grid.

As would be expected, the solutions in the two columns converge to different values because they correspond to different locations in space. Interval halving in two dimensions quickly gives rise to a grid with a very large number of nodes. (This situation would be even worse if a three-dimensional spatial problem were being considered.) For the grid with nonconstant spacing, $\delta x_i/m$ and $\delta y_i/m$ will be different at different nodal locations. Computationally, this is not a problem; but conveying the grid discretization for which a solution is generated at $\mathbf{x}_i$ in concise notation is difficult because the solution at node i depends on the various values of δx_j and δy_j at all nodes in the mesh.

The norms in equations (5.1.65) and (5.1.66) can be changed notationally to forms appropriate for multidimensions by replacing x_i and δx_i with $\mathbf{x}_i$ and $\delta \mathbf{x}_i$, respectively. For these equations, the following quantities are obtained:

UNIFORM GRID WITH $(\gamma, \gamma) = (1.0, 1.0)$

m	$\|U(\mathbf{x}_i; \delta\mathbf{x}_i/m) - U(\mathbf{x}_i; \delta\mathbf{x}_i/2m)\|_{(i,9)}$	2^p	p
1	2.11911×10^{-3}	3.56805	1.8351
2	5.93912×10^{-4}	3.85188	1.9456
4	1.54187×10^{-4}	3.95894	1.9851
8	3.89466×10^{-5}	3.98944	1.9962
16	9.76243×10^{-6}	—	—

NONUNIFORM GRID WITH $(\gamma, \gamma) = (0.75, 0.75)$

m	$\|U(\mathbf{x}_i; \delta\mathbf{x}_i/m) - U(\mathbf{x}_i; \delta\mathbf{x}_i/2m)\|_{(i,9)}$	2^p	p
1	1.35112×10^{-2}	2.34652	1.2305
2	5.75799×10^{-3}	3.37296	1.7540
4	1.70710×10^{-3}	3.82317	1.9348
8	4.46515×10^{-4}	3.95467	1.9836
16	1.12908×10^{-4}	—	—

Note that for both grids, convergence is approaching second order. For the uniform grid, this behavior is seen at an earlier stage of refinement because for the nonuniform grid, the approximations near the node at (0.75,0.75) are first order. When the mesh becomes highly refined, the region of the lower-order approximation is small and the near second-order convergence for the solution is obtained. Additionally, for corresponding levels of refinement, the error norm is roughly one order of magnitude smaller for the uniform grid. Because the weighting function $w_i = \delta x_i \, \delta y_i$ was used in computing the error norm, the root-mean-square error is obtained from equation (5.1.66) by dividing by the square root of the area of the domain. With $m = 8$, the root-mean-square errors are 6.49×10^{-6} and 7.44×10^{-5} for the uniform and nonuniform grids, respectively. This means that the $m = 16$ solution provides, on average, five decimal places of accuracy for the uniform grid and four places of accuracy for the nonuniform grid.

This last example, though simple, illustrates a few points that are important for simulation of real systems. Sequential interval halving of a multidimensional discretization quickly leads to a grid with a very large number of nodes, which greatly increases the computational work and storage. For the linear problem here where no iteration was necessary, the execution time of the code increased by a factor of about 16 in going from the $m = 16$ to the $m = 32$ case using a banded matrix solver. Since simulation of real systems may involve use of tens or even hundreds of thousands of nodes, interval halving is impractical. Additionally, the computation illustrates that although the rate of convergence is the same for both grids, the error in the solution is less for a uniform grid. Thus a uniform distribution of nodes is desirable.

Note that the preceding observations are somewhat at odds with each other. The way to keep a uniform grid uniform is by interval halving. However, this approach is too expensive, suggesting that selective refinement may be a better option. On the other hand, selective refinement produces a nonuniform grid and a lower rate of convergence. This paradox is illustrative of a very important principle in numerical simulation: Trade-offs among various optimal computational strategies are necessary in order to achieve a simulation that provides adequate accuracy at a reasonable cost. Interval halving is one strategy for providing error estimates and is useful for small problems. However, for large problems, a procedure for nonuniform introduction of nodes in regions of the grid where the solution is poor is valuable.

5.1.4 Nonuniform Introduction of Nodes in Space: Mesh Enrichment

The preceding subsection refined meshes in space by halving the grid size and examining the change in the solution. This procedure provides excellent guidance on the accuracy of a solution and the rate of convergence to an analytical solution. Unfortunately, the method of interval halving, when applied a few times, increases the number of nodes substantially such that speed of computation of a solution becomes slow and the computer storage requirements become excessive. The drawbacks become especially important in multidimensional problems. For example, if an $N \times N \times N$ three-dimensional grid is subjected to interval halving, the number of nodes increases by a factor of 8. A second refinement, as would be needed to apply equation (5.1.65), would increase the number of nodes to approximately $64N^3$. Further refinement adds additional computational burden.

The potential for uncontrolled growth of the work of simulation due to interval reduction can be diminished if, rather than indiscriminately halving the grid size, the mesh is enriched with nodes only at locations where the error is greatest. The problem with this approach is that the estimate of the error in a solution developed previously requires comparison of successive solutions obtained from interval halving. Of course, if the exact solution to a problem were known, the location of the greatest error would be easily identified; but there would be no need for a numerical solution in that case.

Effective methods for determination of the portions of a discretized region most in need of refinement is an active area of research. This is a complex problem whose full treatment is well beyond the scope of the fundamental material presented here. Nevertheless, examples will be presented that convey some underlying concepts. For steady-state cases, as considered in this section, the most difficult part of the problem is the determination of the portion of the mesh to be refined. For some linear equations, nonuniform mesh refinement is rather straightforward. For nonlinear equations and for simulation of singularities, the mesh refinement strategy may be very complex. Here, simple examples will hint at some of the power of nonuniform refinement.

Although mesh enrichment can be performed in the context of both finite difference and finite element formulations, it is more readily performed with the latter. Selective addition of nodes produces nonuniform meshes which are, in general, more conveniently handled with finite elements.

The first difficulty with a mesh enrichment strategy is deciding which elements to enrich. The method of interval halving for spatial problems allows a hindcast of error to be made based on a comparison of two approximate solutions to a problem. For effective mesh enrichment, an indicator of those elements in the grid most in need of refinement is needed based on a single solution. A number of criteria for mesh refinement have been developed for specific problems based on norms, particularly the energy norm for Poisson equations. Besides enriching an element with nodes based on error considerations, other somewhat arbitrary conditions may be applied based on experience. For example, a smooth transition of element size from small to large is typically deemed preferable to an abrupt transition. Therefore, if one region of space is heavily enriched with nodes because of error considerations, neighboring regions may also be enriched simply to force a gradual transition of element sizes. Procedures that take into account singularities in the solution domain have also been developed. Indeed, the development of optimal mesh refinement strategies is a highly specialized and complex field.

For exposition here, a relatively simple but nonetheless powerful method for identifying regions of a grid that need refinement is presented. The method will be developed in the context of $\mathbb{C}^0$ basis functions, although variants for basis function with higher degrees of continuity can also be formed. Consider a second-order differential equation of the form

$$\nabla \cdot (\mathbf{K} \cdot \nabla u) - f(\mathbf{x}, u, \nabla u) = 0 \qquad (5.1.70)$$

where the tensor $\mathbf{K}$ may be a function of space as well as of u and its first derivatives. This may be a one-, two-, or three-dimensional problem. Equations of this form have application in a wide variety of engineering and scientific applications. Solution of this equation, with appropriate boundary conditions, is carried out over a region Ω that is discretized using finite elements. The function u is expanded in terms of the $\mathbb{C}^0$ basis functions ϕ_j:

$$u \simeq \sum_{j=1}^{N} U_j \phi_j(\mathbf{x}) \tag{5.1.71}$$

where N is the number of nodes and N_e will indicate the number of elements. After solution for the coefficients U_j, an estimate of error is obtained by considering differences between fluxes calculated from equation (5.1.71) using two different methods.

The dissipative flux of u is defined as

$$\mathbf{q} = -\mathbf{K} \cdot \nabla u \tag{5.1.72}$$

From the approximation of (5.1.71), an approximation, $\mathbf{Q}$, to $\mathbf{q}$ can be calculated as

$$\mathbf{Q} = -\mathbf{K} \cdot \sum_{j=1}^{N} U_j \nabla \phi_j \tag{5.1.73}$$

Because ϕ_j is $\mathbb{C}^0$ continuous, $\mathbf{Q}$ will generally be discontinuous at element boundaries. An alternative estimate of $\mathbf{q}$ that is continuous across element boundaries may be obtained from equation (5.1.72) using the weighted residual equation

$$\int_{\Omega} (\mathbf{q} + \mathbf{K} \cdot \nabla u) \phi_i d\Omega = 0, \qquad i = 1, 2, \dots, N \tag{5.1.74}$$

Expansion of $\mathbf{q}$ in terms of the basis functions yields

$$\mathbf{q} \simeq \hat{\mathbf{Q}} = \sum_{j=1}^{N} \hat{\mathbf{Q}}_j \phi_j \tag{5.1.75}$$

so that (5.1.74) becomes

$$\sum_{j=1}^{N} \int_{\Omega} (\hat{\mathbf{Q}}_j \phi_j + \mathbf{K} \cdot U_j \nabla \phi_j) \phi_i \, d\Omega = 0, \qquad i = 1, 2, \dots, N \tag{5.1.76}$$

With U_j known, this equation may be solved for the coefficients $\hat{\mathbf{Q}}_j$ to provide an estimate for $\mathbf{q}$. Note that $\hat{\mathbf{Q}}$ and $\mathbf{Q}$ are different approximations of the same quantity. Therefore, the difference between these functions may be used as a measure of error in the solution for u. Specifically, a root-mean-square error for each element k with element region Ω_k may be computed from

$$e_k^{\text{rms}} = \left(\frac{1}{\Omega_k} \int_{\Omega_k} (\hat{\mathbf{Q}} - \mathbf{Q}) \cdot (\hat{\mathbf{Q}} - \mathbf{Q}) d\Omega \right)^{1/2} = \frac{1}{\Omega_k^{1/2}} \|\hat{\mathbf{Q}} - \mathbf{Q}\|_{\Omega_k}, \qquad k = 1, 2, \dots, N_e$$

$$\tag{5.1.77}$$

Elements in which e_k^{rms} is largest are also presumed to have the greatest error in u and can be refined by adding nodes. Calculations may then be performed on the refined grid followed by new estimates of e_k^{rms} for each element and further mesh enrichment. In this manner, a discretization of a region can be achieved in which the root-mean-square error is approximately constant over the solution domain.

Once a portion of a grid has been identified as a candidate for mesh enrichment, various methods may be adopted to implement the new grid. In this section, only procedures that do not involve changing to a higher-order approximation are considered. Essentially, the technique of interval halving is applied, but is restricted to only some of the elements. Such methods which reduce error by decreasing the element sizes are referred to as *h-convergence techniques*, because for a numerical method with order of accuracy indicated by $\mathcal{O}((h)^p)$, where h is a measure of grid size (i.e., h corresponds to a characteristic value of δx_i), convergence to the true solution is achieved by decreasing h. Alternatively, and as will be presented in Section 5.2, p-convergence can be achieved by enriching the mesh such that the order of accuracy of an approximation, p, is increased while h remains constant.

In applying h-convergence techniques, the most obvious approach is to subdivide a grid and completely re-solve the problem. For a one-dimensional grid, this is not a particularly difficult task, as indicated with reference to Figure 5.2. Here linear basis functions are being used on an N-node grid, and element i in Figure 5.2a is to be enriched. This is done by adding node $N + 1$ midway between nodes i and $i + 1$ as shown in Figure 5.2b, thereby breaking element i into two elements, labeled as elements i and N. Basis functions can now be written for the new grid and the calculation performed. However, if the nodes are numbered as in Figure 5.2b, the matrix that arises will not have the tridiagonal structure that is convenient for efficient solution. Therefore, either the matrix solution algorithm must make use of reordering of rows and columns to maximize efficiency or the nodes should be renumbered as indicated in Figure 5.2c. (The elements are also renumbered for convenience.)

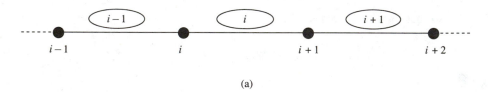

(a)

Figure 5.2 Enrichment of a one-dimensional finite element grid. (a) One-dimensional finite element grid with N nodes.

Typically, mesh refinement is not restricted to one element at a time. After elements are evaluated for a root-mean-square error estimate such as that of equation (5.1.77), any number of them may be refined. Furthermore, if an element appears to yield a particularly poor solution, it may be subdivided into more than two elements. As a practical consideration, adjacent elements sometimes behave poorly if the ratio of their lengths becomes large. Therefore, an enrichment strategy might include a criterion that

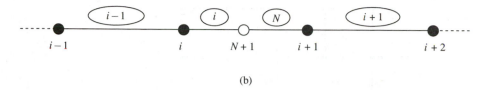

(b)

Figure 5.2 (cont'd.)   Enrichment of a one-dimensional finite element grid. (b) Enrichment by adding node $N + 1$ to element i.

forces this ratio to remain less than a certain value by refining elements neighboring a region of interest as needed.

When refining a mesh in multiple dimensions, the need for node renumbering/matrix reordering remains and is essential for efficient solution. In the subsequent discussion, recognition of this fact will be implicit, while other facets of multidimensional enrichment will be presented. The issues that arise in two-dimensional enrichment are the same as those in the three-dimensional case. Thus, for simplicity, these issues will be presented only in the two-dimensional context.

Consider the portion of a bilinear rectangular finite element mesh as in Figure 5.3a, where the shaded element has been identified as a candidate for enrichment. A proposed subdivision of the element into four smaller elements is indicated in Figure 5.3b, where the new nodes added are indicated as open circles. This mesh, however, is not acceptable because the nodes A, B, C, and D are corner nodes in some elements but lie at the midsides of other elements. For example, the element containing node A on its right boundary should exhibit linear variation along this boundary. However, the two other elements containing node A would allow the variation to be composed of two piecewise linear segments. This inconsistency is not acceptable because it may lead to $\mathbb{C}^{-1}$ continuity in the trial function, thereby causing the finite element integral to be undefined.

One way to overcome this problem is to further refine the mesh of Figure 5.3b, as indicated in Figure 5.3c. These two grids contain the same number and locations of nodes, but four of the rectangular elements have each been subdivided into three linear triangular elements. This formulation of a mesh containing a mix of triangular and quadrilateral elements preserves $\mathbb{C}^0$ continuity across element boundaries and is acceptable. However, if additional refinement is to be performed, such as in one of the rectangular elements diagonal to the principal refined region, the strategy for subdivision into legal elements that are not excessively deformed is not obvious.

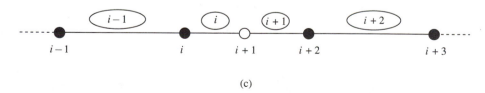

(c)

Figure 5.2 (cont'd.)   Enrichment of a one-dimensional finite element grid. (c) Renumbered nodes and elements following enrichment.

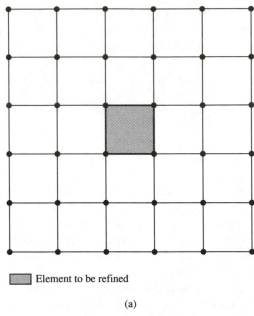

▨ Element to be refined

(a)

Figure 5.3 Enrichment of a bilinear rectangular grid. (a) Portion of a bilinear grid with shaded element to be enriched.

Figure 5.3d depicts a second option for completing the mesh refinement begun in Figure 5.3b. Here four additional nodes, indicated as open squares, have been added and element subdivisions are also indicated. The new open square nodes are called *slave nodes*. They are restricted such that the continuity of a function in the direction tangent

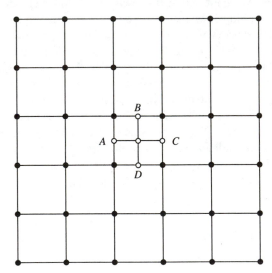

○ Nodes added to refine the grid of part (a), producing an unacceptable grid.

(b)

Figure 5.3 (cont'd.) Enrichment of a bilinear rectangular grid. (b) Incomplete refinement of original mesh.

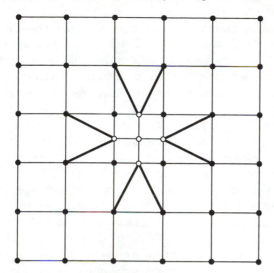

— Element boundaries added to the grid of part
(b) which make it acceptable.

(c)

Figure 5.3 (cont'd.)   Enrichment
of a bilinear rectangular grid.
(c) Modification to grid of (b) resulting
in acceptable elements.

to the element side containing the slave node is unaltered in the refinement process. For
example, at the leftmost slave node,

$$U_S = \frac{U_M + U_P}{2} \tag{5.1.78}$$

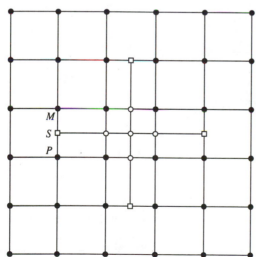

□ Slave nodes used in completing refinement of
the grid of part (b), resulting in an acceptable
finite element mesh.

(d)

Figure 5.3 (cont'd.)   Enrichment of a
bilinear rectangular grid. (d) Grid with
slave nodes resulting in acceptable
elements.

With this constraint, the approximation to u is linear along side $M - P$ and the presence of a node that is a corner node for two elements and a midside position for another element does not violate $\mathbb{C}^0$ continuity constraints. Constraint (5.1.78) is imposed in the coefficient matrix of the finite element problem as a replacement for the equation that would be generated by applying the finite element procedure using ϕ_s, the basis function for node s, as the weighting function.

The use of the slave node concept is very effective in allowing for additional mesh refinement based on an identical refinement algorithm. The mesh in Figure 5.4 is obtained by refining the shaded region from its configuration in Figure 5.3d. Note that to make this refinement, the rightmost slave node in Figure 5.3d was converted to a regular enrichment node. For the grid in Figure 5.4, approximation equations for the dependent variables are generated by the finite element method using basis functions associated with the original and enriching nodes. Additional conditions are provided by slave node conditions that preserve linear variation along the sides. If the grid considered had been composed of general quadrilaterals rather than rectangles, the mesh refinement scheme would be unaltered. Problem 5.16 presents some of the issues of importance in refinement of a mesh composed of quadratic elements on quadrilaterals.

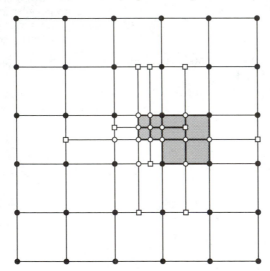

● Original nodes (grid of Figure 5.3a)
○ Enrichment nodes
□ Slave nodes used in enrichment   **Figure 5.4**   Additional enrichment of
▨ Region of grid of Figure 5.3d enriched here   the grid of Figure 5.3(d).

Now consider strategies for mesh enrichment on a triangular grid. Suppose that the shaded linear triangular element in the grid of Figure 5.5a is to be refined. One strategy would be to add a single node at the centroid of this element and then form new elements by connecting this node with the vertices of the original element as in Figure 5.5b. This procedure does not create a need for slave nodes as $\mathbb{C}^0$ continuity across element boundaries is assured. However, a significant drawback to the procedure

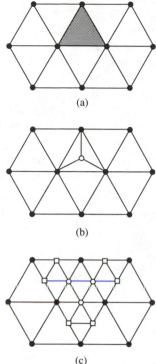

(a)

(b)

(c)

Figure 5.5 Enrichment of a linear triangular mesh. (a) Shaded region to be refined. (b) One option for enrichment by addition of one node. (c) Alternative enrichment strategy using three nodes plus six slave nodes.

- ● Nodes for original grid
- ○ Enrichment nodes
- □ Slave nodes

is the shape of the new elements. Triangular grids are most accurate when the angles at the vertices are all 60° such that the triangle is equilateral. If the region that is enriched were an equilateral triangle, the new elements would be isoceles triangles with angles of 30°, 30°, and 120°. Additional refinement would cause further deviations from the ideal triangular element shape. To avoid this problem, the shaded region can be discretized by adding nodes at the midpoints of the sides of the element to be refined. Then subdivision of the region as in Figure 5.5c by connecting these new nodes subdivides the original element into four elements that are similar to the original element. This procedure has the drawback that a need for slave nodes is created to preserve necessary continuity restrictions at element boundaries. However, these drawbacks are less severe than the element distortion which results from the previous method, and the effectiveness of the enrichment is greater. Problems 5.17 and 5.18 involve enrichment with higher-order triangles and on a grid that is a mix of triangles and quadrilaterals.

Once a decision has been made to enrich a mesh and the revised mesh has been determined, the next step is to reconvert the solution of the differential equation to the solution of a matrix problem, typically by the finite element method. The more apparent way to do this is to treat each added node as a location where an approximation to the dependent variable will be obtained directly. This approach makes no use of the solution obtained on the unenriched mesh to solve the problem. Furthermore, this approach requires either node renumbering or matrix reordering to assure that the matrix problem is solved efficiently (as discussed previously in the context of a one-dimensional mesh). Another way to obtain a solution on the enriched mesh is to seek that solution as a modification of the original solution. This approach has advantages in that the matrix problem for the coarse mesh is retained as a subset of the new problem. Additionally, consideration of the new solution as a perturbation on the previous one directly suggests an iterative matrix solution.

To illustrate the underlying idea behind the solution for deviations, consider interpolation in $\xi - \eta$ space over the element I in Figure 5.6a. For this element

$$u \simeq \sum_{j=1}^{4} U_j \phi_j(\xi, \eta), \qquad \begin{array}{l} -1 \leq \xi \leq 1 \\ -1 \leq \eta \leq 1 \end{array} \qquad (5.1.79)$$

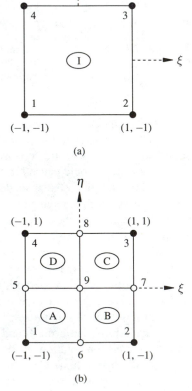

(a)

(b)

Figure 5.6 Mesh enrichment using deviation functions. (a) Bilinear element I. (b) Division of element I into four bilinear elements.

where $\phi_j = \frac{1}{4}(1+\xi\xi_j)(1+\eta\eta_j)$. Now if the element is enriched as depicted in Figure 5.6b, the appropriate representation would be

$$u \simeq \sum_{j=1}^{9} U_j \omega_j(\xi, \eta), \qquad \begin{array}{l} -1 \le \xi \le 1 \\ -1 \le \eta \le 1 \end{array} \qquad (5.1.80)$$

Note that in this expression, the basis function ω_j is different from that in equation (5.1.79). Each basis function ω_j is defined to equal 1 at node j and 0 at all other nodes. Thus, for example,

$$\phi_1 = \frac{1}{4}(1 - \xi)(1 - \eta), \qquad \begin{array}{l} -1 \le \xi \le 1 \\ -1 \le \eta \le 1 \end{array} \qquad (5.1.81)$$

whereas

$$\omega_1 = \xi\eta, \qquad \begin{array}{l} -1 \le \xi \le 0 \\ -1 \le \eta \le 0 \end{array} \qquad (5.1.82a)$$

and

$$\omega_1 = 0, \qquad\qquad\qquad \xi, \eta \text{ in elements } B, C, \text{ or } D \qquad (5.1.82b)$$

The coefficients U_j in equations (5.1.79) and (5.1.80) all correspond to the approximation to u at node j. For the grid of Figure 5.6a, u is approximated as varying linearly along each of the element sides. The introduction of nodes 5 through 8 in the refined grid breaks the variation into two linear pieces on each side. Thus the nodes allow the original linear interpolation to "kink" or deviate from the linearity. Therefore, one could write the interpolation in terms of the approximation to u at nodes 1 through 4 and the magnitude of the deviation as

$$u \simeq \sum_{j=1}^{4} U_j \phi_j(\xi, \eta) + \sum_{j=5}^{9} V_j \omega_j(\xi, \eta) \qquad (5.1.83)$$

where ϕ_j are the basis functions as defined for the grid in Figure 5.6a used in equation (5.1.79) and ω_j are the linear basis functions defined for the grid in Figure 5.6b and used in equation (5.1.80). The basis functions ϕ_j are thus nonzero over the entire region in Figure 5.6b and are nonzero at some nodes besides node j. Although the U_j's are approximations to u at node j, the V_j's are only measures of deviation from the bilinear approximation. For example, at node 5, where $(\xi, \eta) = (-1, 0)$, approximation (5.1.83) yields

$$u(-1, 0) \simeq \frac{1}{2}(U_1 + U_4) + V_5 \qquad (5.1.84)$$

When $V_5 = 0$, the variation of U along side 1-5-4 is linear.

Suppose that a problem of interest is defined by the differential equation

$$\mathcal{L}u - f = 0 \qquad (5.1.85)$$

where $\mathcal{L}$ is the differential operator. If the domain of the solution is discretized by finite elements using N nodes, then

$$u \simeq U = \sum_{j=1}^{N} U_j \phi_j \tag{5.1.86a}$$

and the Galerkin finite element approximation will be

$$\langle \mathcal{L}U - f, \phi_i \rangle = 0, \quad i = 1, 2, \ldots, N \tag{5.1.86b}$$

Evaluation of the integrals in this expression leads to the $N \times N$ matrix problem

$$\mathbf{A} \cdot \mathbf{U} = \mathbf{R}_1 \tag{5.1.86c}$$

where boundary conditions are assumed accounted for by modifying $\mathbf{A}$ without condensing out any known values of U_j, and the unknowns $\mathbf{U}$ are estimates of u at the N nodes. If the mesh is refined and the basis functions are reformulated for the new grid by adding M nodes, then a formulation following equation (5.1.80) would give

$$u \simeq U^* = \sum_{j=1}^{N+M} U_j \omega_j \tag{5.1.87a}$$

with Galerkin finite element approximation

$$\langle \mathcal{L}U^* - f, \omega_i \rangle = 0, \quad i = 1, , 2, \ldots, N + M \tag{5.1.87b}$$

leading to the $(N + M) \times (N + M)$ matrix problem

$$\mathbf{B} \cdot \mathbf{U}^* = \mathbf{R}_2 \tag{5.1.87c}$$

The unknown, $\mathbf{U}^*$, corresponds to estimates of u at the $N + M$ nodes. In regions of the mesh where no refinement is made, rows in matrix equation (5.1.87c) correspond to rows in equation (5.1.86c). However, no use of the estimate obtained on the coarse grid is utilized by the refined grid.

Instead of using expansion (5.1.87a), the approximate solution for the refined grid can be expressed using the idea of corrections to a solution as

$$u \simeq U^{**} = \sum_{j=1}^{N} U_j \phi_j + \sum_{k=N+1}^{M} V_k \omega_k \tag{5.1.88a}$$

The basis functions ϕ_j and ω_j are those that appear in equations (5.1.86a) and (5.1.87a). Although the unknown coefficient, U_j, corresponds to an estimate of u at node j, the coefficient V_k is a measure of the correction to the estimate of u at the location of node k interpolated using only the first summation in equation (5.1.88a). The Galerkin finite element approximation obtained using the expansion (5.1.88a) is

$$\langle \mathcal{L}U^{**} - f, \phi_i \rangle = 0, \quad i = 1, 2, \ldots, N \tag{5.1.88b}$$

and

$$\langle \mathcal{L}U^{**} - f, \omega_i \rangle = 0, \quad i = N + 1, \ldots, M \tag{5.1.88c}$$

The resultant matrix problem can be written as

$$\begin{bmatrix} \mathbf{A} & \mathbf{C} \\ \mathbf{D} & \mathbf{G} \end{bmatrix} \begin{bmatrix} \mathbf{U} \\ \mathbf{V} \end{bmatrix} = \begin{bmatrix} \mathbf{R}_1^* \\ \mathbf{R}_3 \end{bmatrix} \tag{5.1.88d}$$

Here **A** is the same $N \times N$ matrix obtained on the unrefined grid, **C** is an $N \times M$ matrix, **D** is an $M \times N$ matrix, and **G** is an $M \times M$ matrix. The vector $\mathbf{R}_1^*$ is $N \times 1$ and $\mathbf{R}_3$ is $M \times 1$. Note that $\mathbf{R}_1^*$ may be slightly different from $\mathbf{R}_1$, depending on the procedure used for integration of f over the refined grid. Equation (5.1.88d) may be solved directly or by an iterative scheme that makes use of the original solution for U_j. The U_j's calculated from equation (5.1.88d) will be different from those in equation (5.1.86c) because of the effects of V_k.

Let the solution to the problem $\mathbf{A} \cdot \mathbf{U} = \mathbf{R}_1$ which is available from the original mesh solution be designated $\mathbf{U}^{(0)}$. Then from equation (5.1.88d), with **U** estimated as $\mathbf{U}^{(0)}$,

$$\mathbf{G} \cdot \mathbf{V}^{(0)} = \mathbf{R}_3 - \mathbf{D} \cdot \mathbf{U}^{(0)} \tag{5.1.89}$$

Solution of this equation for $\mathbf{V}^{(0)}$ allows the next iteration to be performed as

$$\mathbf{A} \cdot \mathbf{U}^{(1)} = \mathbf{R}_1^* - \mathbf{C} \cdot \mathbf{V}^{(0)} \tag{5.1.90}$$

The revised solution, $\mathbf{U}^{(1)}$, is then used to obtain a revised solution for **V**. The iteration procedure may be written, in general, as

$$\mathbf{G} \cdot \mathbf{V}^{(n)} = \mathbf{R}_3 - \mathbf{D} \cdot \mathbf{U}^{(n)} \tag{5.1.91a}$$

$$\mathbf{A} \cdot \mathbf{U}^{(n+1)} = \mathbf{R}_1^* - \mathbf{C} \cdot \mathbf{V}^{(n)} \tag{5.1.91b}$$

The iteration proceeds until consecutive solution for **U** and **V** differ by less than some preselected tolerance.

The principal advantages of the iterative scheme over the direct solution of equation (5.1.87d) is that the matrix problems which must be solved are smaller and thus can be solved faster using less computer storage. The trade-off is that a smaller problem must be solved a number of times to obtain the same result as one solution of a large problem. If the iteration is slow to converge, the direct solution may be preferable.

The structure proposed as equation (5.1.88a) is very attractive. Further refinements of the mesh are obtained by adding one row (and column) to equation (5.1.88d) for each deviation variable V_k included. The initial unrefined mesh can be considered as providing a solution in which all deviation variables for any enriched mesh are held at zero. Then, if the deviation variables are uncoupled from each other and treated as if only one is added with all the others held at zero, they may be estimated from $\mathbf{U}^{(0)}$ and equation (5.1.91a) as

$$g_{N+i,N+i} V_i^{\text{est}} = r_{3_{N+i}} - \sum_{j=1}^{N} d_{N+i,j} U_j^{(0)} \tag{5.1.92}$$

Locations where V_i^{est} is largest are those where the mesh is most in need of refinement. Equation (5.1.92) suggests the idea that rather than the algorithm of (5.1.91) being the only iterative scheme, a variety of approaches are possible which allow for concurrent mesh refinement and matrix iterative schemes. Development of optimal procedures is an evolving and challenging area of investigation.

Example 5.6

Problem   Solve the differential equation of Example 5.4:

$$\frac{d}{dx}\left(K\frac{du}{dx}\right) = a(u)^r, \qquad 0 < x < 4 \tag{5.1.57a}$$

$$u(0) = 0.0 \tag{5.1.57b}$$

$$u(4) = 4.0 \tag{5.1.57c}$$

when $K = 0.1x+5.0$, $a = 0.1$, and $r = 0.3$. Use the concepts of selective mesh enrichment to refine the mesh and estimate the error in the solution.

Solution   The problem will be solved using linear finite elements. When enriching a mesh, the strategy may involve simultaneous refinement in many elements, many refinements in one element, or some combination of the two strategies. Here, for illustration purposes, only one element will be refined after obtaining a converged solution; and this will be achieved by adding just one independent variable to the element. After obtaining the next solution on the refined grid, the same procedure will be applied again. This strategy is adopted solely because it provides a convenient format for presentation of the results.

The initial grid used is composed of three equispaced nodes, as depicted in Figure 5.7a. The expansion for u follows equation (5.1.88a) as

$$u \simeq U(x) = \sum_{j=1}^{3} U_j\phi_j(x) + \sum_{k=4}^{M} V_k\omega_k(x) \tag{5.1.93}$$

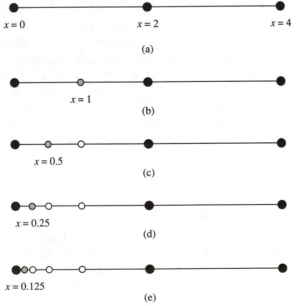

Figure 5.7   Meshes for Example 5.6. (a) Initial mesh. (b) First refinement. (c) Second refinement. (d) Third refinement. (e) Fourth refinement.

Note that for the initial grid composed of three nodes, all V_k will be set to zero. Introduction of nodes where deviation can be computed is equivalent to allowing the V_k's to be computed. As with Example 5.4, equation (5.1.58b), an expansion is also made in terms of $(U)^r$ as

$$(u)^r \simeq \hat{U}^r(x) = \sum_{j=1}^{3}(U_j)^r \phi_j(x) + \sum_{k=4}^{M} W_k \omega_k(x) \qquad (5.1.94)$$

Note that W_k is the deviation in $(U_j)^r$ at a location so that at position x_k, it is not simply equal to the deviation in U_j raised to the rth power [i.e., $(V_k)^r$]. In fact, the relation between V_k and W_k is an approximation that can be obtained by defining constraints requiring some correspondence between $\hat{U}^r$ and $(U)^r$. Here, for example, if x_ℓ is the point such that $\omega_\ell(x_\ell) = 1$, then V_ℓ may be related to W_ℓ by requiring that

$$[U(x_\ell)]^r - [\hat{U}^r(x_\ell)] = 0, \qquad \ell = 4, 5, \ldots, M \qquad (5.1.95)$$

This expression and some alternative constraints are explored in more detail in Problems 5.19 and 5.20.

The Galerkin finite element approximations are obtained using equations (5.1.88b) and (5.1.88c), respectively. Green's theorem is also applied as in Example 5.4, equation (5.1.59b), to obtain

$$\sum_{j=1}^{3}\int_0^4 KU_j \frac{d\phi_j}{dx}\frac{d\phi_i}{dx}\,dx + \sum_{k=4}^{M}\int_0^4 KV_k \frac{d\omega_k}{dx}\frac{d\phi_i}{dx}\,dx + \sum_{j=1}^{3}\int_0^4 a(U_j)^r \phi_j \phi_i\,dx$$

$$+ \sum_{k=4}^{M}\int_0^4 aW_k \omega_k \phi_i\,dx + \hat{q}\phi_i\Big|_{x=0}^{x=4} = 0, \qquad i = 1, 2, 3 \qquad (5.1.96a)$$

and

$$\sum_{j=1}^{3}\int_0^4 KU_j \frac{d\phi_j}{dx}\frac{d\omega_i}{dx}\,dx + \sum_{k=4}^{M}\int_0^4 KV_k \frac{d\omega_k}{dx}\frac{d\omega_i}{dx}\,dx + \sum_{j=1}^{3}\int_0^4 a(U_j)^r \phi_j \omega_i\,dx$$

$$+ \sum_{k=4}^{M}\int_0^4 aW_k \omega_k \omega_i\,dx = 0, \qquad i = 4, \ldots, M \qquad (5.1.96b)$$

The term involving the flux at the boundary, $\hat{q} \simeq -K(du/dx)$, is not present in the second expression because all ω_i are zero at the boundary.

The first solution to this problem was obtained by setting all V_k and W_k to zero. This solution is that for linear finite elements on a three-node grid. The same iterative scheme as described in Example 5.4 was employed. The flux, $\hat{Q}_j$, at each node was obtained from equation (5.1.59b) for the end nodes and equation (5.1.76) for the interior nodes with all U_j's known. After obtaining this solution, the root-mean-square error for the flux was obtained for each element using equation (5.1.77). Next an estimate was made for the size of V_k in each element, holding U_j at the value obtained. This corresponds to applying equation (5.1.92) to equation (5.1.96b) or, for element e,

$$
V^{\text{est}} \int_{\Omega_e} K \frac{d\omega_k}{dx} \frac{d\omega_k}{dx} \, dx + W_k^{\text{est}} \int_{\Omega_e} a\omega_k \omega_k \, dx
$$

$$
= -\sum_{j=1}^{3} \int_{\Omega_e} K U_j \frac{d\phi_j}{dx} \frac{d\omega_k}{dx} \, dx - \sum_{j=1}^{3} \int_{\Omega_e} a(U_j)^r \phi_j \omega_k \, dx, \qquad k = 4, 5 \qquad (5.1.97)
$$

Here k indexes the deviation variable, V or W, and basis function ω associated with element e. The superscript designation "est" appears in this equation to emphasize that V_k is being estimated based on the solution obtained previously for the coefficients U_j. Additionally, equation (5.1.95) is applied to relate W_k to V_k. Thus for each element, a pair of equations is solved to obtain an estimate of the deviation size for the element.

For this first grid, the solution obtained is

x_j	U_j	Q_j
0.0	0.0	−7.5192
2.0	2.9668	−8.4887
4.0	4.0	−7.9479

and the error measures are

Element	Element location	e_k^{rms}	V_k^{est}
1	$0 \leq x \leq 2$	4.0263	7.19×10^{-1}
2	$2 \leq x \leq 4$	1.6995	8.07×10^{-2}

By both error measures, the error in the element $0 \leq x \leq 2$ is greater than in the element $2 \leq x \leq 4$. Thus the mesh is enriched by adding a node at $x = 1$ as depicted in Figure 5.7b. The basis function ω_4 is defined for this position and deviation variables V_4 and W_4 are allowed to be nonzero at this location. Revised solutions for U_1, U_2, and U_3 are obtained in conjunction with V_4. After these variables are determined, the solution at $x = 1.0$ is

$$
U(1.0) = \frac{U_1 + U_2}{2} + V_4 \qquad (5.1.98)
$$

The flux-based root-mean-square error may also be computed, and projected values of deviation variables for each of the three elements may be obtained holding U_1, U_2, U_3, and V_4 constant from

$$V_k^{est} \int_{\Omega_e} K \frac{d\omega_k}{dx} \frac{d\omega_k}{dx} dx + W_k^{est} \int_{\Omega_e} a\omega_k \omega_k \, dx \simeq -\sum_{j=1}^{3} \int_{\Omega_e} KU_j \frac{d\phi_j}{dx} \frac{d\omega_k}{dx} dx$$

$$- \int_{\Omega_e} KV_4 \frac{d\omega_4}{dx} \frac{d\omega_k}{dx} dx - \sum_{j=1}^{3} \int_{\Omega_e} a(U_j)^r \phi_j \omega_k \, dx$$

$$- \int_{\Omega_e} aW_4\omega_4\omega_k \, dx, \qquad k = 5,6,7 \qquad (5.1.99)$$

where the terms on the right side of this equation are all known.
For this second grid, the solution is

x_j	U_j	Q_j
0.0	0.0	-6.0571
1.0	2.3379	-6.7682
2.0	3.1521	-6.0854
4.0	4.0	-6.5494

and the error measures are

Element	Element location	e_k^{rms}	V_k^{est}
1	$0 \le x \le 1$	3.1868	5.58×10^{-1}
2	$1 \le x \le 2$	1.3930	6.47×10^{-2}
3	$2 \le x \le 4$	1.0931	6.53×10^{-3}

It is interesting to note that based on the original three-node solution, $U(1.0)$ would be the average of U_1 and U_2 or 1.4834. The projected correction based on this solution was 7.19×10^{-1}, such that, from equation (5.1.98), $U(1.0)$ would equal 2.202. When the value of U_2 is updated, taking into account the "kink" in the solution at $x = 1.0$, the actual value of $U(1.0)$ obtained is 2.338. Thus the V_k^{est} coefficients are seen to indeed provide an estimate of the solution change which can be expected by enriching the mesh. Note also that the root-mean-square error, as well as the size of the estimated correction, decreases from the first to the second solution.

For the five subsequent solutions obtained by enriching the mesh in the element where e_k^{rms} and V_k^{est} were largest, the element that was enriched was the one which had one node at $x = 0$ (i.e., refinement always occurred in the element at the $x = 0$ boundary).

The seventh solution obtained is

SOLUTION 7

x_j	U_j	Q_j
0.0	0.0	−3.8240
1/32	0.6710	−3.9562
1/16	1.0286	−3.6955
1/8	1.4497	−3.6985
1/4	1.9126	−3.7143
1/2	2.4019	−3.7513
1.0	2.9102	−3.8309
2.0	3.4389	−3.9988
4.0	4.0	−4.3857

with error measures (presented in order based on magnitude of e_k^{rms})

Element	Location	e_k^{rms}	V_k^{est}
1	$0 \leq x \leq 1/32$	0.9326	7.35×10^{-2}
7	$1 \leq x \leq 2$	0.7221	4.11×10^{-2}
6	$1/2 \leq x \leq 1$	0.7213	4.02×10^{-2}
5	$1/4 \leq x \leq 1/2$	0.7080	3.82×10^{-2}
8	$2 \leq x \leq 4$	0.6996	4.15×10^{-2}
4	$1/8 \leq x \leq 1/4$	0.6774	3.46×10^{-2}
3	$1/16 \leq x \leq 1/8$	0.6216	2.88×10^{-2}
2	$1/32 \leq x \leq 1/16$	0.5915	2.09×10^{-2}

Here, still, the largest error is apparently occurring in element 1, even though it is the smallest element. Note that the relative size of the error is not always the same using the two measures listed. For example, e_k^{rms} projects a larger error in element 6 than in element 8, while V_k^{est} predicts the reverse. This should not be surprising as projections are often imprecise. Both measures predict relatively uniform errors in elements 2 through 8 with element 1 clearly having the largest error. The computation of e_k^{rms} requires solution of a matrix problem while projections of V_k^{est} for each element are decoupled. Thus the price for more accuracy in obtaining the root-mean-square error measure is more work. However, since the use of these error measures is merely as a guide in mesh discretization, the extra work producing a more precise measure may not be worthwhile.

Based on the seventh solution, the first element was enriched and the solutions obtained for U_j and Q_j are

SOLUTION 8

x_j	U_j	Q_j
0.0	0.0	−3.7905
1/64	0.4259	−3.8550
1/32	0.6987	−3.6719
1/16	1.0533	−3.6636
1/8	1.4707	−3.6667
1/4	1.9296	−3.6826
1/2	2.4147	−3.7197
1.0	2.9188	−3.7994
2.0	3.4432	−3.9673
4.0	4.0	−4.3531

with error measures, again presented in order based on the magnitude of e_k^{rms},

Element	Location	e_k^{rms}	V_k^{est}
8	$1 \leq x \leq 2$	0.7157	4.08×10^{-2}
7	$1/2 \leq x \leq 1$	0.7150	3.98×10^{-2}
6	$1/4 \leq x \leq 1/2$	0.7018	3.79×10^{-2}
9	$2 \leq x \leq 4$	0.6937	4.12×10^{-2}
5	$1/8 \leq x \leq 1/4$	0.6715	3.43×10^{-2}
4	$1/16 \leq x \leq 1/8$	0.6163	2.86×10^{-2}
1	$0 \leq x \leq 1/64$	0.5970	2.99×10^{-2}
3	$1/32 \leq x \leq 1/16$	0.5294	2.07×10^{-2}
2	$1/64 \leq x \leq 1/32$	0.4475	1.23×10^{-2}

This solution, using three primary nodes and six enrichment nodes, is the first that does not recommend element 1 as the best candidate for enrichment. In going from solution 7 to solution 8, the maximum value of e_k^{rms} decreased from 0.9326 to 0.7157, a decrease of over 23%. Based on the results of solution 8, element 8 was enriched. For the solution then obtained, the largest root-mean-square error was 0.7125. Thus refining element 8 to obtain solution 9 decreased the maximum root-mean-square error by only 0.4%. This seems to be a point of diminishing returns for selective refinement. Therefore, rather than applying selective refinement to solution 8, the method of interval halving will be used twice, creating grids of 19 and 37 nodes, respectively, so that error norms may be calculated using equations (5.1.65) and (5.1.66) for direct comparison with the solution to Example 5.4.

If the norms are calculated, as with Example 5.4, using only the solution at $x = \{0, 2, 4\}$, then with the initial grid from solution 8:

m	$\|U(x_i; \delta x_i/m) - U(x_i; \delta x_i/2m)\|_{(i,3)}$	$(2)^p$	p
1	3.8915×10^{-3}	3.2907	1.7184
2	1.1826×10^{-3}	—	—

Here 2^p is approaching 4 but additional halvings are needed to show second-order convergence. With the irregular grid in which all approximations are first order, it is reasonable to anticipate that more than two halving operations would need to be performed to enable second-order accurate approximation to dominate. What is striking is that the error norm above with $m = 1$ made use of grids containing 10 and 19 nodes, while in Example 5.4, a comparable norm required grids of 257 and 513 nodes ($m = 128$). Thus by making use of selective enrichment, significant improvements in accuracy are obtained with much less computational work.

As an interesting side note, the convergence in the flux error norm can be examined. Note that for the computation of the error norm in U, successive solutions are required, making use of solutions on two grids. However, a flux norm for the entire region may be computed for a single grid making use of the two different elementwise estimates, Q and $\hat{Q}$, on the same grid.

m	$\|Q_i - \hat{Q}_i\|_\Omega$	$(2)^p$	p
1	1.396740	1.9850	0.9891
2	0.703664	1.9703	0.9784
4	0.357129	—	—

Here $(2)^p$ is the ratio of consecutive norms, as with computation for U. Because p approaches 1, the convergence of Q is first order. This result demonstrates that the order of convergence of a derivative of a function approximated using discrete values of the function is one order less than the order of convergence of the function.

This example concludes the discussion here of selective mesh refinement without altering the order of approximation of the test function. Although the example presented is for a small one-dimensional problem, it serves to introduce the underlying concepts and method of implementation of the refinement strategy. Two criteria for enrichment, one based on two estimates of flux or first derivative of the solution function and the other based on a projected correction to the solution within a refined element, have provided useful guidance for enrichment.

The methods of this subsection have dealt exclusively with h-refinement of a fixed, coarse, base grid. An interesting topic deserving of some mention is the selection of nodal locations for the base grid itself. This is the topic of the next subsection.

5.1.5 Optimal Node Placement for Base Grids

The preceding two subsections indicate that accuracy of a numerical solution to a differential equation can be improved by refining a mesh either globally using interval halving or locally by reducing the interval in only a portion of the domain. By increasing the number of nodes, both of these techniques increase the number of nodal coefficients that must be solved for. As an alternative to these strategies, one might attempt to obtain the best possible solution using a fixed number of degrees of freedom (i.e., nodes) by a judicious selection of node locations. This topic was examined to some extent in Chapter 4, where simple analytical rules for grid design were derived. While these rules are very useful for certain types of problems, more complex systems require more general numerical procedures for designing optimal grids. If an initial estimate can be made for a grid design, subsequent mesh enrichment strategies may be used to refine this base optimal grid, if desired. The main topic to be discussed in this subsection is general numerical procedures for making a "judicious" choice of base node locations.

For some problems, the proper discretization of the domain is strongly dependent on the parameters of the system being simulated. For example, to develop a physically reasonable model of flow in a large body of water, the geometry of the bottom of the water body must be represented accurately. Therefore, in regions where the gradients in bathymetry are large (where bathymetry is the distance from the bottom of the water body to a reference datum), nodes must be placed closer together than in regions where the bathymetry is smooth. Caution must be exercised, however, as other phenomena, such as a sharp saltwater front, may require a highly resolved grid in regions where the bathymetry is smooth. Nevertheless, by considering a system under study and estimating where large gradients in system properties or the dependent variable are likely to occur, one may be able to make a reasonable guess at portions of the system where a relatively fine mesh might be needed. These concepts were discussed in Chapter 4.

The concept of trying to obtain a preliminary physical understanding of a problem being studied prior to simulation is an excellent one. However, it is certainly not a fail-safe way of designing an optimal mesh. The most obvious drawback is that some important phenomena may be overlooked. Furthermore, knowing that some portion of the system should be modeled using a grid that is "relatively fine" compared to another portion does not pin down the actual discretization needed in either region.

Sometimes numerical simulations are performed to simultaneously determine interacting dependent variables. For example, in environmental problems one often wishes to determine the flow field as well as concentrations of various chemicals and pollutants. In some cases these must be calculated simultaneously because the flow field greatly affects chemical movement; and the chemicals, if present in high enough concentrations, affect the flow field by altering the fluid density and viscosity. The flow field computation may require a fine mesh in some part of the domain of interest, while the contaminant distribution might require a fine mesh in a different part. Additionally, if a number of pollutants are present and interacting with the system in different ways, they may each dictate different mesh discretization strategies. Further confounding the mesh selection process is the fact that for transient problems, the optimal discretization of a domain may be a function of time. The determination of an optimal grid is thus seen to be one that cannot typically be readily solved by mere inspection.

In general, the optimal grid problem is a very difficult one that requires significant computer power and clever programming to be solved effectively. In some cases, for instance when factors compete such that a single optimal grid does not exist, the best way to address the problem is to lay out a rather uniform base grid. Then selective enrichment (and deenrichment) of different portions of the grid, in time and space, for different variables using the techniques of Section 5.1.4 may be the best way to proceed. In this manner, all variables would be solved for on the same base grid, with various enrichments of the grid being tailored as appropriate for each variable. In this book, however, discussion is limited to an examination of basic aspects of derivation of an optimal grid for a problem with a single dependent variable. Furthermore, the complications of a time-dependent optimal grid in space are not treated in detail. In addition, it is worthwhile to emphasize that optimal node placement is a useful, though not universally applicable, technique. Whether or not an optimal grid can be found, the methods of mesh enrichment and interval halving remain powerful tools for assurance of the accuracy of any solution obtained.

In some cases, a discretization is to be determined for a region of interest prior to and independent of the differential equation to be solved. To accomplish this, mesh generation algorithms have been developed that try to optimize the grid based on three desirable attributes: smoothness such that distances between nodes do not vary abruptly, minimal deformation such that quadrilaterals are nearly square and triangles are equilateral, and strategic node concentration such that node density is greatest where system properties are rapidly varying. These criteria compete with each other; and typically, the mesh designer must use judgment to modify coefficients in an optimization algorithm until the mesh obtained appears to be satisfactory. Mesh generation programs are attractive interactive procedures for developing a mesh in an irregularly shaped region, certainly a necessary and vital advancement over manual discretization and compilation of data indicating node locations and how these nodes are connected to form elements. However, the mesh generation procedure is most effective when understanding of the system can be incorporated into the final acceptance of a grid generated.

One way to ensure that the system under study has a sufficient impact on the grid generation process is to simultaneously solve the differential equation system and generate the mesh. Formulation of this problem generally leads to coupled nonlinear equations that must be solved for both nodal positions and the unknowns of interest at the nodes. Because the problem is nonlinear, it must be solved iteratively. During the iteration step, the possibility of nodes moving such that they cross each other, hopelessly deforming the mesh, must be avoided. For multidimensional problems and for transient problems where, perhaps, a new mesh is generated each time step, the design and implementation of efficient and effective algorithms constitute a highly specialized field of study.

One point that is very important to keep in mind is that a solution for nodal locations need not be achieved with the same high precision as that for dependent variables. A differential equation can be solved on a suboptimal as well as an optimal grid. Therefore, an iterative solution for nodal locations need not be continued to the same accuracy as the solution for the nodal variables on the grid obtained.

The discussion that follows is a limited introduction to optimal mesh generation. Techniques are presented that have applicability to multiple dimensions, but the worked examples are restricted to one-dimensional steady-state problems. Although unacceptable nodal movement that causes nodes to cross must be avoided, the even more difficult problem of excessive deformation of elements in multiple dimensions does not arise. Additionally, the complexity of the task of generating an algorithm that efficiently converges to the best grid for the problem under study is much reduced. Nevertheless, the material presented does demonstrate the great computational advantage that can be obtained by designing a grid for a specific problem.

At the heart of any method for grid adaptation is the specification of some criteria for node placement. A very reasonable criterion is to require that some measure of error be equal for each element such that the error is distributed evenly over the entire domain of interest. A number of error measures are possible, but here the two used in Section 5.1.4 for mesh enrichment will be employed.

The discussion in this paragraph is based on equations (5.1.70) through (5.1.77). Suppose that the equation to be solved is

$$\nabla \cdot (\mathbf{K} \cdot \nabla u) - f(\mathbf{x}, u, \nabla u) = 0, \qquad \mathbf{x} \in \Omega \tag{5.1.70}$$

and that the solution is to be obtained using the finite element method as

$$u \simeq U = \sum_{j=1}^{N} U_j \phi_j(\mathbf{x}) \tag{5.1.71}$$

where U_j are nodal coefficients, $\phi_j(\mathbf{x})$ are the basis functions, and N is the number of nodes. Now the flux may be approximated two alternative ways as

$$\mathbf{Q} = -\mathbf{K} \cdot \nabla U = -\mathbf{K} \cdot \sum_{j=1}^{N} U_j \nabla \phi_j \tag{5.173}$$

and

$$\hat{\mathbf{Q}} = \sum_{j=1}^{N} \hat{\mathbf{Q}}_j \phi_j \tag{5.1.75}$$

with the values of $\hat{\mathbf{Q}}_j$ obtained in terms of U_j by solving the following equation:

$$\sum_{j=1}^{N} \int_{\Omega} (\hat{\mathbf{Q}}_j \phi_j + \mathbf{K} \cdot U_j \nabla \phi_j) \phi_i \, d\Omega = 0, \qquad i = 1, 2, \ldots, N \tag{5.1.76}$$

A measure of the error in element Ω_k, denoted $\|e\|_{\Omega_k}$, may be obtained in terms of the difference between $\hat{\mathbf{Q}}$ and $\mathbf{Q}$ as

$$\|e\|_{\Omega_k} = \|\hat{\mathbf{Q}} - \mathbf{Q}\|_{\Omega_k}, \qquad k = 1, \ldots, N_e \tag{5.1.100}$$

where N_e is the number of elements. A reasonable error criterion would be to require that this norm be equal in all elements, or

$$\|e\|_{\Omega_k} = \|e\|_{\Omega_{k+1}}, \qquad k = 1, \ldots, N_e - 1 \tag{5.1.101}$$

Unfortunately, a means for directly enforcing this equation to fix the grid is not obvious. A grid with N nodes will have N x-coordinates and N y-coordinates to be determined, but equation (5.1.101) provides $N_e - 1$ constraints. Therefore, the number of constraints provided above will not necessarily be adequate for determining the node locations. To work around this problem, a procedure commonly called *elliptic mesh generation* has been developed over the last few years. An introduction to this method follows which is presented in the context of a two-dimensional situation.

Consider the bilinear grid of Figure 5.8a, for which nodes are to be moved such that the error of solution of a differential equation is evenly distributed over the grid. The node positions in **x**-space are mapped into the grid on Figure 5.8b in **X**-space. In **X**-space, all the elements are taken to be squares. A correspondence between nodes in the two spaces can be written in terms of basis function in **X**-space as

$$x = \sum_{j=1}^{N} x_j \phi_j(X, Y) \tag{5.1.102a}$$

and

$$y = \sum_{j=1}^{N} y_j \phi_j(X, Y) \tag{5.1.102b}$$

where $\phi_j(X, Y)$ are bilinear basis functions and (x_j, y_j) are node locations in **x**-space.

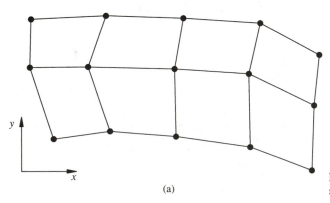

(a)

Figure 5.8 (a) Bilinear grid in **x** space.

At this point, differential equations will be postulated that are to be solved for node locations in **x**-space as functions of **X**. The equations that will be presented are not the only ones that could be selected but are chosen because of knowledge of the behavior of elliptic equations. Let the **x**-coordinates be related to **X**-coordinates by

$$\frac{\partial}{\partial X}\left(w_1 \frac{\partial x}{\partial X}\right) + \frac{\partial}{\partial Y}\left(w_1 \frac{\partial x}{\partial Y}\right) = 0 \tag{5.1.103a}$$

and

$$\frac{\partial}{\partial X}\left(w_2 \frac{\partial y}{\partial X}\right) + \frac{\partial}{\partial Y}\left(w_2 \frac{\partial y}{\partial Y}\right) = 0 \tag{5.1.103b}$$

where $w_1(\mathbf{X})$ and $w_2(\mathbf{X})$ are weighting functions to be selected which are everywhere positive. Note that each of these equations may be thought of as a steady-state diffusion or heat conduction equation with $w_\ell(\mathbf{X})$ coresponding to the diffusivity or thermal conductivity. With reference to equation (5.1.103a), the domain of solution for "temperature," x, is the grid in **X**-space of Figure 5.8b. Where the "conductivity," w_1, is large, the gradient of "temperature" will be small. Thus the change in x is small across regions of large $w_1(\mathbf{X})$. In terms of the grid in Figure 5.8a, when the change in x is small, the nodes are close together. These observations, and similar ones for equation (5.1.103b), suggest that for solution of equation (5.1.70), $w_1(\mathbf{X})$ and $w_2(\mathbf{X})$ should be selected to be large in regions of the solution domain where the gradient in u is large (thereby moving nodes close together) and small where the gradient of u is small.

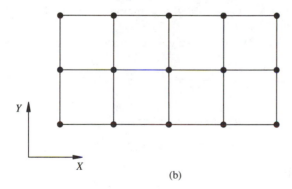

Y

X

(b)

Figure 5.8 (cont'd.)   (b) Bilinear grid mapped into **X** space.

Solution for u on a grid with optimal node positions requires simultaneous solution of the governing system equations along with the node position equations. If equation (5.1.70) is to be solved in two dimensions, over domain Ω with boundary Γ, then the resulting set of equations, after application of the Galerkin finite element method and integration by parts, is

$$\sum_{j=1}^{N} \int_{\Omega} \nabla \phi_i \cdot \mathbf{K} U_j \cdot \nabla \phi_j \, d\Omega - \int_{\Omega} f \phi_i \, d\Omega - \int_{\Gamma} \mathbf{q} \cdot \mathbf{n} \phi_i \, d\Gamma = 0,$$

$$i = 1, 2, \ldots, N \tag{5.1.104a}$$

$$-\sum_{j=1}^{N}\int_{\hat{\Omega}} w_1 x_j (\hat{\boldsymbol{\nabla}}\phi_j \cdot \hat{\boldsymbol{\nabla}}\phi_i)\, d\hat{\Omega} + \int_{\hat{\Gamma}} w_1 \hat{\mathbf{N}} \cdot \hat{\boldsymbol{\nabla}} x\phi_i \, d\hat{\Gamma} = 0,$$

$$i = 1, 2, \ldots, N \qquad (5.1.104\text{b})$$

$$-\sum_{j=1}^{N}\int_{\hat{\Omega}} w_2 y_j (\hat{\boldsymbol{\nabla}}\phi_j \cdot \hat{\boldsymbol{\nabla}}\phi_i)\, d\hat{\Omega} + \int_{\hat{\Gamma}} w_2 \hat{\mathbf{N}} \cdot \hat{\boldsymbol{\nabla}} y\phi_i \, d\hat{\Gamma} = 0,$$

$$i = 1, 2, \ldots, N \qquad (5.1.104\text{c})$$

where $\hat{\Omega}$ and $\hat{\Gamma}$ are the domain and boundary in the **X**-coordinate system, $\hat{\boldsymbol{\nabla}}$ is the gradient operator in the **X**-coordinate system, $\mathbf{n}$ is the unit normal to boundary Γ, and $\hat{\mathbf{N}}$ is the unit normal to boundary $\hat{\Gamma}$. Equations (5.1.104) are coupled equations for N values of U_j, x_j, and y_j. Depending on the functions selected for w_1 and w_2, the last two equations may be highly nonlinear. At least one boundary nodal location (x_j, y_j) must be specified; and depending on the region under study, the position of some other boundary nodes may be specified. The boundary conditions for equations (5.1.104b) and (5.1.104c) are examined further in Problem 5.24.

The equations (5.1.104b) and (5.1.104c) for nodal positioning should be viewed as guides for nodal positions and not equations that must be solved exactly. For example, these equations may produce a highly irregular grid which is not satisfactory. The equations can thus be further constrained by conditions limiting deformation in an element. Remember, these equations were postulated as providing guidelines to grid development; they are not essential equations to the solution of equation (5.1.104a) but are subject to further arbitrary modification as desired.

Still in need of specification are the weighting functions w_1 and w_2. Here, four possibilities will be examined:

1. For the entire domain:

$$w_1 = \text{nonzero constant} \qquad (5.1.105\text{a})$$

$$w_2 = \text{nonzero constant} \qquad (5.1.105\text{b})$$

2. Within each element:

$$w_1(\mathbf{X}) = w_2(\mathbf{X}) = (\hat{\mathbf{Q}} - \mathbf{Q}) \cdot (\hat{\mathbf{Q}} - \mathbf{Q}) \qquad (5.1.106)$$

3. Within each element:

$$w_1(\mathbf{X}) = [(\hat{\mathbf{Q}} - \mathbf{Q}) \cdot \mathbf{e}_x]^2 \qquad (5.1.107\text{a})$$

$$w_2(\mathbf{X}) = [(\hat{\mathbf{Q}} - \mathbf{Q}) \cdot \mathbf{e}_y]^2 \qquad (5.1.107\text{b})$$

4. Within each element k:

$$w_1(\mathbf{X}) = w_2(\mathbf{X}) = \frac{1}{\Omega_k}(U^{\text{est}} - U)^2 \qquad (5.1.108)$$

The notation will be explained in the subsequent paragraphs, which describe the impact of each of these options.

The first case, where w_1 and w_2 are constant, does not weight one portion of the solution domain more than another. This method favors grids where element sizes are approximately equal and nodal spacing is uniform. The judicious placement of nodes on the boundary is important when a uniform grid is desired. With this weighting scheme, the node locations are not dependent on the approximate solution for U and equations (5.1.104) are linear.

The second case, equation (5.1.106), produces elements for which the error norm given by equation (5.1.100) is equal. This is achieved, using an initial grid, by reducing element sizes where the norm is large and increasing the size of elements where the norm is small.

The third case, equation (5.1.107), is similar to the second. However, this procedure accounts for directional dependence of the error. The quantities $\mathbf{e}_x$ and $\mathbf{e}_y$ are unit normal vectors in the x and y directions, respectively. For example, if w_1 is constant, the node distribution in the x-direction will be uniform, while if w_2 is variable, the nodes will distribute such that they are closer together in y where w_2 is large.

In the fourth set of weighting schemes proposed here, Ω_k is the area of element k and U^{est} is an estimate of an improved solution for U if mesh enrichment were used. The estimated solution could be one obtained by enriching all the elements for a particular grid configuration. However, because grid configurations are obtained iteratively and the entire process is somewhat arbitrary, it is probably not worthwhile to expend a lot of computational effort to get a precise solution for U^{est}. In fact, the algorithm of equation (5.1.92), where the kink sizes, V_i^{est}, are decoupled from each other and projected based on the solution, U, is probably an excellent way to obtain an estimated improved solution with minimum work.

A large number of additional weighting schemes could be selected. Neither the node position equations (5.1.104) nor weighting schemes (5.1.105) through (5.1.108) are unique or necessarily truly optimal. The actual weighting scheme used could be some combination of the four schemes presented here. Furthermore, nothing has been incorporated here to assure that element distortion is not unacceptably severe. In fact, if w_1 or w_2 is zero over an element, the nodal location problem becomes indeterminate. Thus, as insurance against this, a small positive constant might be added to w_1 and w_2 in equations (5.1.106) through (5.1.108) to guarantee a solution. The size of this constant must be small enough so that it does not overwhelm the spatially varying parts of w_1 and w_2 and thereby reduce the weighting scheme to that of equation (5.1.105).

Example 5.7

> **Problem** In Example 5.6, starting with three equispaced nodes, mesh enrichment was applied to obtain a grid of 10 nodes. Now compute the optimal 10 node grids for the same problem using the methods of this section. Use linear finite elements.
>
> **Solution** The problem to be solved is
>
> $$\frac{d}{dx}\left(K\frac{du}{dx}\right) = a(u)^r, \qquad 0 < x < 4 \qquad\qquad (5.1.57a)$$

$$u(0) = 0.0 \qquad\qquad (5.1.57\text{b})$$

$$u(4) = 4.0 \qquad\qquad (5.1.57\text{c})$$

when $K = 0.1x + 5.0$, $a = 0.1$, and $r = 0.3$. Because this is a one-dimensional problem, only x node locations need to be calculated.

The solution is generated first on a uniform grid of 10 nodes with $\Delta x = 4/9$. The solution algorithm is exactly that described in Example 5.4 using equations (5.1.58) through (5.1.63). Next, with node 1 fixed at $x = 0.0$ and node 10 fixed at $x = 4$, equation (5.1.104b) must be applied at each interior node. The X domain is selected to extend from $X = 1$ to $X = 10$ with $\Delta X = 1.0$. Therefore, equation (5.1.104b) becomes

$$-\sum_{j=1}^{N} \int_{1}^{10} w_1 x_j \frac{d\phi_j}{dX}\frac{d\phi_i}{dX}\, dX = 0, \qquad i = 2, 3, \ldots, 9 \qquad (5.1.109)$$

The derivatives of the linear basis functions are constants within each element so that integration of equation (5.1.109) yields

$$-(x_i - x_{i-1}) \int_{i-1}^{i} w_1\, dX + (x_{i+1} - x_i) \int_{i}^{i+1} w_1\, dX = 0, \qquad i = 2, 3, \ldots, 9 \quad (5.1.110)$$

For the case $w_1 = constant$, this equation becomes

$$x_{i+1} - 2x_i + x_{i-1} = \delta^2 x_i = 0, \qquad i = 2, 3, \ldots, 9 \qquad (5.1.111)$$

With $x_1 = 0.0$ and $x_{10} = 4.0$ the solution to this equation is an evenly spaced grid with

$$x_i = \frac{4(i-1)}{9}, \qquad i = 1, 2, \ldots, 10 \qquad (5.1.112)$$

Because the solution for U was obtained on this equispaced grid, the grid and the solution for U are consistent and no further iteration is required. The solution of the governing equation (5.1.57a) on a regular grid was already treated in some detail in Example 5.4 and therefore will not be pursued further here.

The second case, with w_1 given by equation (5.1.106), is equivalent to using w_1 of equation (5.1.107) since the problem (5.1.57) is one-dimensional. Substitution of expression (5.1.106) into equation (5.1.110) yields

$$-(x_i - x_{i-1}) \int_{i-1}^{i} (\hat{Q} - Q)^2\, dX + (x_{i+1} - x_i) \int_{i}^{i+1} (\hat{Q} - Q)^2\, dX = 0, \qquad i = 2, 3, \ldots, 9$$

$$(5.1.113)$$

or

$$\|\hat{Q} - Q\|_{\Omega_{i-1}} = \|\hat{Q} - Q\|_{\Omega_i}, \qquad i = 2, 3, \ldots, 9 \qquad (5.1.114)$$

Therefore, this case requires the norm of the difference between flux estimates [calculated using equations (5.1.71) through (5.1.77)] to be equal for every element. This is the same condition as hypothesized in equation (5.1.101). Because $\hat{Q}$ and Q depend on x, equation (5.1.113) is nonlinear. As a convenient, though not necessarily most efficient, method of computing new node locations, equation set (5.1.113) is solved for new values of x_i with $(\hat{Q} - Q)^2$ obtained from U and the original grid. Thus the matrix problem involves the tridiagonal matrix **A** with

$$\mathbf{A} \cdot \mathbf{x} = \mathbf{f} \qquad\qquad (5.1.115\text{a})$$

where $\mathbf{A}$ is a 10×10 matrix and $\mathbf{f}$ is a 10×1 vector where

$$a_{1,1} = 1 \quad \text{and} \quad f_1 = x_1 = 0.0 \tag{5.1.115b}$$

and the nonzero entries of $\mathbf{A}$ and $\mathbf{f}$ are

$$a_{i,i-1} = \int_{i-1}^{i} (\hat{Q} - Q)^2 \, dX, \qquad i = 2, 3, \ldots, 9 \tag{5.1.115c}$$

$$a_{i,i} = -\int_{i-1}^{i+1} (\hat{Q} - Q)^2 \, dX, \qquad i = 2, 3, \ldots, 9 \tag{5.1.115d}$$

$$a_{i,i+1} = \int_{i}^{i+1} (\hat{Q} - Q)^2 \, dX, \qquad i = 2, 3, \ldots, 9 \tag{5.1.115e}$$

$$a_{10,10} = 1.0 \quad \text{and} \quad f_{10} = x_{10} = 4.0 \tag{5.1.115f}$$

After the new estimates of x are obtained, they are checked to ensure that no node is predicted to move so far that it crosses a neighbor. In fact, in the computer code the nodes are constrained such that if a node is predicted to move more than a fraction (e.g., 0.5) of the distance separating it from its neighbor, it is taken to move only the fractional distance. This constraint is applied sequentially to the nodes, such that no nodes end up crossing. The grid thus obtained is used to generate a new solution for U. Iteration proceeds in this manner until the flux difference norm is equal over each element to three places of accuracy. For this problem the solution obtained is

i	x_i	U_i
1	0.0	0.0000
2	5.55×10^{-2}	9.0383×10^{-1}
3	1.68×10^{-1}	1.5687
4	3.53×10^{-1}	2.0846
5	6.28×10^{-1}	2.5102
6	1.01	2.8746
7	1.52	3.1957
8	2.18	3.4852
9	3.00	3.7515
10	4.00	4.0000

and the error norm for each element is

$$\|\hat{Q} - Q\|_{\Omega_e} = 3.16 \times 10^{-1}, \qquad e = 1, 2, \ldots, 9$$

The nodes are seen to concentrate toward $x = 0.0$, as might be expected in light of Example 5.6.

The third weighting function selected is given in equation (5.1.108). Substitution of the expression for w_1 into equation (5.1.110) gives

$$-\int_{i-1}^{i} (U^{\text{est}} - U)^2 \, dX + \int_{i}^{i+1} (U^{\text{est}} - U)^2 \, dX = 0, \qquad i = 2, 3, \ldots, 9 \quad (5.1.116)$$

If U^{est} is taken to be the original U with the addition of a variable per element, V_e^{est}, which allows the linear U profile over an element to kink, then, from equation (5.1.88),

$$U^{\text{est}} = \sum_{j=1}^{10} U_j \phi_j + \sum_{e=1}^{9} V_e^{\text{est}} \omega_e \qquad (5.1.117)$$

Substitution of this expression back into equation (5.1.116) yields

$$-\int_{i-1}^{i} \left(\sum_{e=1}^{9} V_e^{\text{est}} \omega_e \right)^2 dX + \int_{i}^{i+1} \left(\sum_{e=1}^{9} V_e^{\text{est}} \omega_e \right)^2 dX = 0, \qquad i = 2, 3, \ldots, 9$$

$$(5.1.118)$$

Because ω_e is nonzero only over element e, this expression reduces to

$$-\left(V_{i-1}^{\text{est}} \right)^2 \int_{i-1}^{i} \omega_{i-1}^2 \, dX + \left(V_i^{\text{est}} \right)^2 \int_{i}^{i+1} \omega_i^2 \, dX = 0, \qquad i = 2, 3, \ldots, 9 \quad (5.1.119)$$

The integrals in this expression are equal so that equation (5.1.119) becomes

$$-\left(V_{i-1}^{\text{est}} \right)^2 + \left(V_i^{\text{est}} \right)^2 = 0, \qquad i = 2, 3, \ldots, 9 \qquad (5.1.120)$$

This criterion for nodal positioning thus requires that the predicted magnitude of the correction due to enriching an element be the same in each element. The base node positioning required to satisfy this condition may be obtained by solving for V_i^{est} as a function of U_i, U_{i+1}, x_i, and x_{i+1} using equation (5.1.92). Then equation (5.1.110) may be applied to obtain a matrix problem in x. This is illustrated by the method of Problem 5.25. Iteration between the predicted x and U values ultimately provides the solution as follows:

i	x_i	U_i
1	0.0	0.0000
2	1.60×10^{-2}	4.3265×10^{-1}
3	4.49×10^{-2}	8.6558×10^{-1}
4	9.69×10^{-2}	1.2990
5	1.91×10^{-1}	1.7334
6	3.59×10^{-1}	2.1697
7	6.64×10^{-1}	2.6097
8	1.21	3.0564
9	2.21	3.5161
10	4.00	4.0000

and the magnitude of V_e^{est} for each element is

$$\left| V_e^{\text{est}} \right| = 3.092 \times 10^{-2}, \qquad e = 1, 2, \ldots, 9$$

Note that in comparison to the flux weighting function, this method skews the nodal distribution even further toward $x = 0$.

As a final step in this example, the method of interval halving was applied twice to each of three 10-node grids: one with equispaced nodes and the other two obtained using the flux difference and constant $\left|V_k^{est}\right|$ criteria, respectively. The norms computed and values of $(2)^p$ are as follows:

EQUISPACED NODES ON BASE GRID

m	$\|U(x_i; \delta x_i/m) - U(x_i; \delta x_i/2m)\|_{(i,10)}$	$(2)^p$	p
1	2.1271×10^{-1}	1.5354	0.6186
2	1.3854×10^{-1}	—	—

EQUALITY OF $\|\hat{Q} - Q\|_{\Omega_e}$ FOR BASE GRID

m	$\|U(x_i; \delta x_i/m) - U(x_i; \delta x_i/2m)\|_{(i,10)}$	$(2)^p$	p
1	5.0393×10^{-2}	2.7688	1.4693
2	1.8200×10^{-2}	—	—

EQUALITY OF $|V_e^{est}|$ FOR BASE GRID

m	$\|U(x_i; \delta x_i/m) - U(x_i; \delta x_i/2m)\|_{(i,10)}$	$(2)^p$	p
1	1.6435×10^{-4}	3.2569	1.7035
2	5.0462×10^{-5}	—	—

Based on an examination of the error norm, the criterion of equal $\left|V_e^{est}\right|$ is seen to have produced the grid for which the most accurate solution is obtained. The fact that this criterion is superior for this problem does not necessarily mean that it will be superior for all problems. The example here is relatively simple, involving a one-dimensional problem with a smooth, monotonic solution. Nevertheless, the example does demonstrate some of the aspects of generation of an optimal base grid. Note that here the solutions for U_j and x_j were obtained by iterating back and forth between governing differential equations. An alternative iteration scheme could also be developed that updates U_j and x_j simultaneously. Such a scheme would involve larger matrices than considered here but might provide an enhanced rate of convergence to the final grid, especially for multidimensional problems.

The grid refinement techniques presented thus far—interval halving, mesh enrichment, and base grid generation—have been developed here only for ordinary differential equations and for partial differential equations in space. In Section 5.3, some remarks will be made concerning grid refinement of space-time (i.e., parabolic and hyperbolic) problems.

5.2 IMPROVED ACCURACY THROUGH HIGHER-ORDER APPROXIMATION

In the preceding section, accuracy estimates and improvements in solutions were obtained by refining the mesh, adding nodes, but leaving the order of accuracy of the approximations unchanged. Because the error in an approximate solution is proportional to the discretization step size raised to a positive exponent, p, the error decreases as step size decreases. The method of interval halving, of reducing all the step sizes by one-half, was shown to lead to an error norm and information concerning the order of accuracy of a solution.

An alternative approach to interval halving (or mesh enrichment) for improving the accuracy of a numerical solution to a differential equation is to increase the order of accuracy of the approximation. This method can be applied universally to the entire solution domain or selectively in portions of the grid where the accuracy is poorest.

One way to implement this method is to leave node positions unchanged on a grid but change the approximation equation used. In the context of finite differences, this is equivalent to incorporating more locations at which a function is evaluated into the Taylor series approximations using the methods of Chapter 2. In the finite element context, this is accomplished by changing the element connectivity such that more nodes are included within or on the sides of an element. Higher-order basis functions are then employed for interpolation, as presented in Chapter 3. Using finite elements, one could instead keep a grid intact but improve the order of accuracy by increasing the degree of continuity of the basis functions.

Another way to improve the accuracy of a solution is to enrich a mesh selectively using higher-order approximations to deviations or "kinks" in the computed solution. Higher-order selective enrichment is commonly called p-convergence because the error term of order $(h)^p$ (where h is the grid step size) is decreased by increasing the value of p.

The analysis of error in Section 5.1 was facilitated by the fact that as the step size decreased, the form and order of the error term were unchanged. Thus two approximate solutions to a differential equation on grids employing interval halving could be combined to provide equations, such as equation (5.1.21), where the unknown parts of the error term have been canceled; and an error norm is obtained for the solution on the refined grid. In this section, where use is made of approximations of successively higher order, the form of the error term changes with each approximation. Thus manipulation to cancel portions of the error term is not possible. Error norms based on two solutions obtained on the same grid using approximations of different order cannot, in general, be obtained. Error norms will be obtained by the method of interval halving using a specific approximation to demonstrate the improvement in accuracy obtained by using higher-order methods.

5.2.1 Inclusion of More Nodes in a Finite Difference Approximation

Generalized formulations of finite difference approximations have been presented in Sections 2.4 and 2.7 for one- and two-dimensional problems, respectively. Use of those formulations demonstrated that the inclusion of additional nodes in an approximation to a differential operator at a point may increase the order of the truncation error of the approximation. For problems with smooth solutions, higher-order approximations are typically more accurate. Thus the alteration of difference formulas on a particular grid to include more nodes in the approximation may improve accuracy. This technique will be demonstrated in the following example.

Example 5.8

Problem   Solve the two-dimensional heat conduction problem previously posed as Example 5.5.

$$\nabla^2 u = 0, \qquad 0 < x < 2, \quad 0 < y < 2 \tag{5.1.67a}$$

with

$$u(0, y) = 2y - y^2 \tag{5.1.67b}$$

$$u(x, 2) = 0 \tag{5.1.67c}$$

$$u(2, y) = (2 - y)^2 \tag{5.1.67d}$$

$$u(x, 0) = x^2 \tag{5.1.67e}$$

Use the method of finite differences to demonstrate the effect of using higher-order differences on a fixed grid.

Solution   The grid to be employed is depicted in Figure 5.9a and consists of a 5×5 uniform distribution of nodes. Because the solution for u has been specified on the boundary, approximate solutions must be generated at each of the nine nodes on the interior of the mesh. To generate difference approximations for this grid, the methods of Chapter 2 will be employed, particularly equations (2.7.10) through (2.7.12).

To develop finite difference approximations to equation (5.1.67a), a set of 13 nodes located as indicated in Figure 5.9b was selected. The approximation will be developed for node 7. For Γ_i being the coefficient of U_i in the discretization of the heat conduction equation, the constraint equations based on equations (2.7.12) and (2.7.13), which must be satisfied for a consistent approximation, are based on the expression

$$B_{r,s} = \sum_{i=1}^{13} \frac{1}{r!\,s!}(x_i - x_7)^r (y_i - y_7)^s \Gamma_i, \qquad r = 0, 1, \ldots \tag{5.2.1a}$$

$$s = 0, 1, \ldots$$

and take the forms

$$B_{0,0} = B_{1,0} = B_{0,1} = B_{1,1} = 0 \tag{5.2.1b}$$

and

$$B_{2,0} = B_{0,2} = 1 \tag{5.2.1c}$$

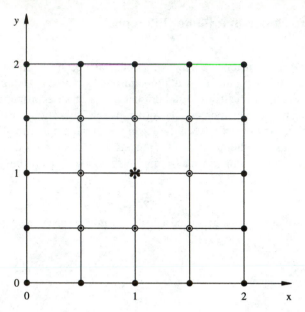

✳ Center node

◉ Node adjacent to the boundary where case III
  approximation cannot be applied

● Boundary node with solution specified

(a)

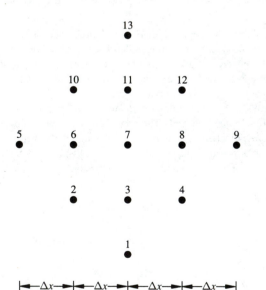

(b)

Figure 5.9 (a) Finite difference grid
for Example 5.8. (b) Nodes used in
developing approximations to the
two-dimensional Laplacian operator.

Higher-order approximations to the heat equation are obtained by constraining $B_{r,s}$ to be zero for $r + s > 2$ as possible. Equations (5.2.1b) and (5.2.1c) impose six constraints on the 13 independent values of Γ_i. Therefore, seven more conditions may be applied to obtain consistent approximations. Here, three different possibilities will be examined.

Case I.   For case I, the four nodes farthest from the position of interest, node 7, are not included in the approximation. Therefore, the coefficients Γ_1, Γ_5, Γ_9, and Γ_{13} are required to be zero. With these conditions, $B_{3,0}$ and $B_{0,3}$ are zero. Then after selecting the constraints $B_{1,2} = B_{2,1} = 0$ in order to eliminate first-order truncation error terms, equation (5.2.1a) for $r + s < 5$ provides the following:

$$\Gamma_2 = \Gamma_4 = \Gamma_{10} = \Gamma_{12} \tag{5.2.2a}$$

$$\Gamma_3 = \Gamma_{11} \tag{5.2.2b}$$

$$\Gamma_6 = \Gamma_8 \tag{5.2.2c}$$

$$4\Gamma_2 + 2\Gamma_3 + 2\Gamma_6 + \Gamma_7 = 0 \tag{5.2.2d}$$

$$(\Delta y)^2 (2\Gamma_2 + \Gamma_3) = 1 \tag{5.2.2e}$$

$$(\Delta x)^2 (2\Gamma_2 + \Gamma_3) = 1 \tag{5.2.2f}$$

$$B_{4,0} = \frac{(\Delta x)^2}{12} \tag{5.2.2g}$$

$$B_{2,2} = (\Delta x)^2 (\Delta y)^2 \Gamma_2 \tag{5.2.2h}$$

$$B_{0,4} = \frac{(\Delta y)^2}{12} \tag{5.2.2i}$$

$$B_{r,s} = 0, \qquad r + s = 5 \tag{5.2.2j}$$

One parameter remains to be selected. The obvious choice is to eliminate the error term $\mathcal{O}((\Delta x)(\Delta y))$ by selecting $\Gamma_2 = 0$. This results in

$$\Gamma_{11} = \Gamma_3 = \frac{1}{(\Delta y)^2} \tag{5.2.3a}$$

$$\Gamma_8 = \Gamma_6 = \frac{1}{(\Delta x)^2} \tag{5.2.3b}$$

$$\Gamma_7 = -\left[\frac{2}{(\Delta x)^2} + \frac{2}{(\Delta y)^2} \right] \tag{5.2.3c}$$

with the other Γ_i being zero. The difference approximation is thus

$$\frac{U_5 - 2U_7 + U_9}{(\Delta x)^2} + \frac{U_{11} - 2U_7 + U_3}{(\Delta y)^2} = 0 \tag{5.2.4a}$$

Because $\Delta x = \Delta y$ in the current problem, this expression may also be written as

$$U_3 + U_5 + U_9 + U_{11} - 4U_7 = 0 \tag{5.2.4b}$$

Equation (5.2.4a) is the same approximation obtained previously in Example 2.21 by considering each of the derivatives in equation (5.1.67a) separately. The truncation error term is second order and takes the form

$$\text{T.E.} = -B_{4,0} \frac{\partial^4 u}{\partial x^4}\bigg|_{\mathbf{x}_x^*} - B_{0,4} \frac{\partial^4 u}{\partial y^4}\bigg|_{\mathbf{x}_y^*} = -\frac{(\Delta x)^2}{12} \frac{\partial^4 u}{\partial x^4}\bigg|_{\mathbf{x}_x^*} - \frac{(\Delta y)^2}{12} \frac{\partial^4 u}{\partial y^4}\bigg|_{\mathbf{x}_y^*} \tag{5.2.5}$$

Case II.   This case builds upon case I and demonstrates the advantage that may be gained in some cases by considering all terms in an equation simultaneously rather than individually. Note that based on equations (5.2.2), the lowest-order truncation error term for the nine-node finite difference approximation to the heat equation is

$$\text{T.E.} = \frac{(\Delta x)^2}{12} \frac{\partial^4 u}{\partial x^4}\bigg|_{\mathbf{x}_x^*} + (\Delta x)^2 (\Delta y)^2 \Gamma_2 \frac{\partial^4 u}{\partial x^2 \partial y^2}\bigg|_{\mathbf{x}_{xy}^*} + \frac{(\Delta y)^2}{12} \frac{\partial^4 u}{\partial y^4}\bigg|_{\mathbf{x}_y^*} \tag{5.2.6}$$

where Γ_2 has not yet been selected. The Laplacian of heat equation (5.1.67a) may be taken to obtain

$$\nabla^2(\nabla^2 u) = 0 = \frac{\partial^4 u}{\partial x^4} + 2\frac{\partial^4 u}{\partial x^2 \partial y^2} + \frac{\partial^4 u}{\partial y^4} \tag{5.2.7}$$

This equation must be exactly satisfied by the solution u. It may be rearranged to

$$\frac{\partial^4 u}{\partial x^2 \partial y^2} = -\frac{1}{2}\left(\frac{\partial^4 u}{\partial x^4} + \frac{\partial^4 u}{\partial y^4}\right) \tag{5.2.8}$$

Substitution of this expression into equation (5.2.6) with the assumption that the differences among $\mathbf{x}_x^*$, $\mathbf{x}_y^*$, and $\mathbf{x}_{xy}^*$ are negligible or will be accounted for in higher-order terms results in

$$\begin{aligned}
\text{T.E.} = &-\frac{(\Delta x)^2(\Delta y)^2}{2}\left[\frac{1}{6(\Delta y)^2} - \Gamma_2\right]\frac{\partial^4 u}{\partial x^4}\bigg|_{\mathbf{x}_x^*} \\
&-\frac{(\Delta x)^2(\Delta y)^2}{2}\left[\frac{1}{6(\Delta x)^2} - \Gamma_2\right]\frac{\partial^4 u}{\partial y^4}\bigg|_{\mathbf{x}_y^*}
\end{aligned} \tag{5.2.9}$$

In general, selection of Γ_2 as inversely proportional to the grid spacing squared results in a finite difference approximation with error $\mathcal{O}[(\Delta x)^2] + \mathcal{O}[(\Delta y)^2]$. However, for this particular problem, where $h = \Delta x = \Delta y$, selection of $\Gamma_2 = 1/6h^2$ causes the second-order error terms in equation (5.2.9) to drop out. Because $B_{r,s} = 0$ for $r + s = 5$, no third-order truncation error terms appear either and the error is fourth order. The values of Γ_i are thus

$$\Gamma_1 = \Gamma_5 = \Gamma_9 = \Gamma_{13} = 0 \tag{5.2.10a}$$

$$\Gamma_2 = \Gamma_4 = \Gamma_{10} = \Gamma_{12} = \frac{1}{6h^2} \tag{5.2.10b}$$

$$\Gamma_3 = \Gamma_6 = \Gamma_8 = \Gamma_{11} = \frac{2}{3h^2} \tag{5.2.10c}$$

$$\Gamma_7 = \frac{-10}{3h^2} \tag{5.2.10d}$$

The difference approximation is

$$U_2 + U_4 + U_{10} + U_{12} + 4(U_3 + U_6 + U_8 + U_{11}) - 20U_7 = 0 \tag{5.2.11}$$

and the truncation error of the approximation to the equation is (see problem 5.26).

$$\text{T.E.} = \frac{-h^4}{360}\left[\frac{\partial^6 u}{\partial x^6} + 5\left(\frac{\partial^6 u}{\partial x^4 \partial y^2} + \frac{\partial^6 u}{\partial x^2 \partial y^4}\right) + \frac{\partial^6 u}{\partial y^6}\right]\Bigg|_{\mathbf{x}^*} \qquad (5.2.12)$$

where the subscript on $\mathbf{x}^*$ has been dropped for convenience. Thus case II provides a fourth-order accurate approximation.

Case III.   For this case, the four nodes diagonally adjacent to center node 7 are excluded from the approximation by setting $\Gamma_2 = \Gamma_4 = \Gamma_{10} = \Gamma_{12} = 0$. The remaining nine nodes are included. This stipulation causes $B_{r,s}$ to be zero if neither r nor s is zero. If $B_{3,0}$ and $B_{0,3}$ are set to zero to force the approximation to be at least second-order accurate, the conditions provided by equation (5.2.1) are

$$\Gamma_1 = \Gamma_{13} = \frac{12B_{0,4} - (\Delta y)^2}{12(\Delta y)^4} \qquad (5.2.13a)$$

$$\Gamma_5 = \Gamma_9 = \frac{12B_{4,0} - (\Delta x)^2}{12(\Delta x)^4} \qquad (5.2.13b)$$

$$\Gamma_3 = \Gamma_{11} = \frac{4(\Delta y)^2 - 12B_{0,4}}{3(\Delta y)^4} \qquad (5.2.13c)$$

$$\Gamma_6 = \Gamma_8 = \frac{4(\Delta x)^2 - 12B_{4,0}}{3(\Delta x)^4} \qquad (5.2.13d)$$

$$\Gamma_7 = \frac{12B_{4,0} - 5(\Delta x)^2}{2(\Delta x)^4} + \frac{12B_{0,4} - 5(\Delta y)^2}{2(\Delta y)^4} \qquad (5.2.13e)$$

If $B_{4,0}$ and $B_{0,4}$ are chosen to be zero, the approximation is fourth-order accurate and takes the form

$$\frac{-U_5 + 16U_6 - 30U_7 + 16U_8 - U_9}{(\Delta x)^2} + \frac{-U_1 + 16U_2 - 30U_7 + 16U_{11} - U_{13}}{(\Delta y)^2} = 0 \quad (5.2.14)$$

or, for the current case where $\Delta x = \Delta y$,

$$-(U_1 + U_5 + U_9 + U_{13}) + 16(U_2 + U_6 + U_8 + U_{11}) - 60U_7 = 0 \qquad (5.2.15)$$

The truncation error of approximation (5.2.14) is obtained by calculating $B_{6,0}$ and $B_{0,6}$ (since all $B_{r,s}$ are zero with $r + s = 5$) and is given by

$$\text{T.E.} = \frac{1}{90}\left[(\Delta x)^4 \frac{\partial^6 u}{\partial x^6} + (\Delta y)^4 \frac{\partial^6 u}{\partial y^6}\right]\Bigg|_{\mathbf{x}^*} \qquad (5.2.16)$$

The approximations developed for these three cases are to be applied to the interior nodes of the grid of Figure 5.9a and grids obtained from interval halving. Each of the three approximations can be applied directly at the center node. The case I and case II approximations can also be applied at the nodes adjacent to the boundary. However, the case III formula cannot be applied directly at nodes adjacent to the boundary because this will result in some of the calculation points falling outside the solution domain. One attractive way to remedy this situation would be to derive alternative fourth-order approximations at nodes adjacent to the boundary. For the current discretization where $\Delta x = \Delta y$, the case II approximation is a viable candidate for implementation at these nodes. However, for a rectangular grid where $\Delta x \neq \Delta y$, this approximation would not be fourth order and additional nodes inside the domain would have to be drawn into the difference approximation. These specialized approximations can destroy the regular structure of the coefficient matrix that must be solved and cause a considerable increase in the amount of computational work that must be done.

A different approach is to use a simpler approximation at nodes adjacent to the boundary, such as case I equation (5.2.4a). With this approximation the matrix structure is unaltered but the approximation near the boundary is only second-order accurate. When employing case III, equation (5.2.15) is used at nodes at least two increments from the boundary, three-point centered approximations to second derivatives with respect to x are used at nodes adjacent to the x-boundaries, and three-point centered approximations to the second derivatives with respect to y are used at nodes adjacent to the y-boundaries (see Problem 5.27). This implementation will provide some insight into the effects of low-order approximations on convergence rates when a higher-order approximation is implemented at most locations.

The heat conduction equation (5.1.67) was solved on the regular 5×5 grid of Figure 5.9a with $\Delta x = \Delta y = 0.5$ using the approximations of case I, case II, and case III. The method of interval halving was applied three times so that the problem was also solved on a 9×9, 17×17, and 33×33 grid. The norm of the difference between consecutive solutions, $\|U(\mathbf{x}_i; \delta\mathbf{x}/m) - U(\mathbf{x}_i; \delta\mathbf{x}/2m)\|_{(i,25)}$, was calculated for each of the cases and the results are plotted in Figure 5.10. The fourth-order case II solution is seen to have the smallest difference norm and is thus the most accurate. The slope of the log-log plot for fourth-order cases II and III are similar. On the original 5×5 grid, the case III approximation of equation (5.2.14) could be applied at only the center node. At all other interior nodes, the second-order case I approximation was used. Thus for $m = 1$ it is not surprising that the norms for cases I and III are almost equal. As the intervals are halved, however, the fourth-order character of case III predominates; and the difference norm for case III decreases faster than for case I and at a rate similar to case II. From equation (5.1.65) with $m = 1$ and $m = 2$, p is calculated for each of the three cases. This is equivalent to calculating the negative of the slopes in Figure 5.10, and the results are tabulated below.

m	p(case I)	p(case II)	p(case III)
1	1.87	4.07	3.25
2	1.96	4.05	3.63

Thus the orders of accuracy of cases I and II are near their theoretical values of 2 and 4, respectively, while case III also is approaching fourth-order accuracy as anticipated.

For the example presented here, the higher-order approximations provide better accuracy using the same discretization of the region as well as faster convergence to the true solution as the mesh increment is decreased. This result indicates the advantage that may be obtained by using difference approximations that make use of more than the minimum number of nodes at the expense of generating a matrix to be solved with a higher density of nonzero entries (see Problem 5.28). For problems where the solution or

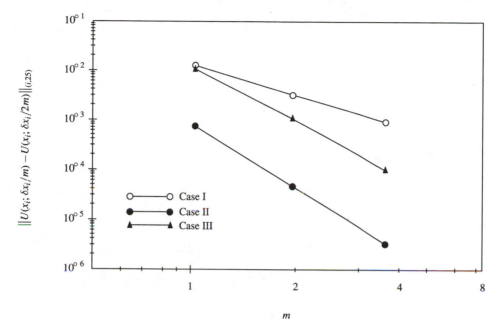

Figure 5.10   Error norms for three cases considered in Example 5.8.

parameters contain discontinuities or sharp fronts, the gains in accuracy from high-order approximations may not be as dramatic as found here. The computational advantage of using a higher-order approximation must be carefully weighed against the increased work required. In some situations, a solution on one mesh using second-order approximations can be obtained for the same cost and with comparable accuracy to a solution on a coarser mesh using higher-order approximations. Also, efficiency may dictate that high-order approximations should be applied in some portion of the grid, while lower-order approximations are suitable in other portions. Development of criteria for switching from one difference formula to another is an interesting topic for further study in modeling of physical problems.

5.2.2 Higher-Order Basis Functions in a Finite Element Approximation

For a particular distribution of nodes in a region to be modeled using the finite element method, the order of accuracy of an approximation can be altered by changing the basis functions. In this section this concept is discussed for the case where the total number of unknowns that must be solved for is kept constant. The process of enriching a mesh by adding unknowns using higher-order basis functions is postponed to Section 5.2.3.

Consider, for example, the meshes in Figure 5.11, which depict identical distributions of nodes. In Figure 5.11a, the nodes are connected such that they lie only at the corners of elements. For this grid, bilinear basis functions that are C^0 continuous

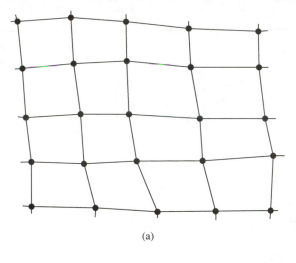

(a)

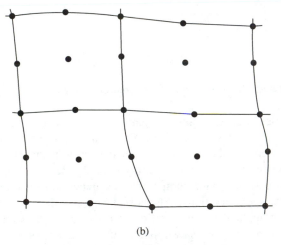

(b)

Figure 5.11   Alternative grids
using identical node distributions.
(a) Bilinear grid. (b) Biquadratic grid.

could be employed. However, with the nodes connected as in Figure 5.11b, biquadratic
interpolation would be appropriate. In general, grids may be constructed to contain a mix
of basis function types, but here the purpose of the discussion is to explore the merits of
one basis function type versus another.

The grids in Figure 5.11 raise several interesting points. In Figure 5.11a, the nodes
are connected by straight lines. However, in Figure 5.11b, the nodes must be connected by smooth curves along the element sides. For the quadrilateral grids, coordinate
transformations are used to facilitate computations as discussed in Section 4.1.3. These
transformations determine the actual shape of the curve connecting corner nodes and can
influence the overall order of accuracy of an approximation.

Also of note are the types of discrete approximations that arise using the two grids.
In Figure 5.11a, each node lies in four elements. When the Galerkin finite element method

is applied to approximate a derivative by weighting with respect to basis function ϕ_i, the discrete representation generally involves values of the dependent variable at all nodes in elements that contain node i. For the grid of Figure 5.11a, nine nodes would be involved in each representation. However, with reference to Figure 5.11b, when i is a corner node of an element, the approximation uses information at 25 nodes; when i is an element side node, 15 nodes are involved in the approximation; and when i is in the interior of an element, only 9 nodes are involved. Therefore, in contrast to higher-order finite difference approximations that may be applied at each node, higher-order finite element approximations are different at different nodes in the grid.

A comprehensive and satisfying discussion of the relative merits of higher-order to lower-order finite element approximation is difficult to formulate. The variety of element shapes, geometric transformations, basis functions, weighting functions, and integration formulas available make the subject a very broad one. Here the one-dimensional model problem first considered in Example 5.4 will be utilized to provide a sample of improved accuracy using higher-order finite elements.

Example 5.9

Problem   Solve the differential equation

$$\frac{d}{dx}\left[K\frac{du}{dx}\right] = a(u)^r, \qquad 0 < x < 4 \tag{5.1.57a}$$

$$u(0) = 0.0 \tag{5.1.57b}$$

$$u(4) = 4.0 \tag{5.1.57c}$$

when $K = 0.1x + 5.0$, $a = 0.1$, and $r = 0.3$, using linear, quadratic, and cubic basis functions on a regular grid. Examine the accuracy and error of the solution by the method of interval halving.

Solution   The initial grid used to solve this problem consisted of seven equispaced nodes with $\delta x = 2/3$. This nodal layout provides six linear, three quadratic, or two cubic finite elements. Interval halving was applied eight times so that the finest grid examined contained 1537 nodes. The norm of the difference between consecutive solutions, $\|U(x_i; \delta x/m) - U(x_i; \delta x/2m)\|_{(i,3)}$ was calculated using the computed results for each of the finite element approximations; these norms are plotted in Figure 5.12. For any value of m, the norm is smallest for the cubic basis functions and largest for the linear basis function. The shape of the curve should approach an asymptotic value of 2^p as $\delta x/m$ becomes small. However, even with the finest discretization of $\delta x/m = 1/1536$, only the curve obtained for linear basis functions seems to be approaching a constant slope. In fact, the cubic approximation provides seven places of accuracy, yet still does not give an indication that it is approaching an asymptotic slope. Furthermore, calculation of a solution with seven places of accuracy apparently is nearing the accuracy of the computational algorithms due to machine round-off. The norm with $m = 128$ for the cubic case was calculated to be 1.7275×10^{-7} but does not appear on the plot.

The ratio of consecutive norms as given by equation (5.1.65) was obtained in order to plot 2^p versus m in Figure 5.13. The curve obtained for linear elements appears to be approaching $2^p = 4$ (for $m = 64$, $2^p = 3.853$), while for the quadratic and cubic cases, the asymptotic values of 2^p cannot be discerned readily.

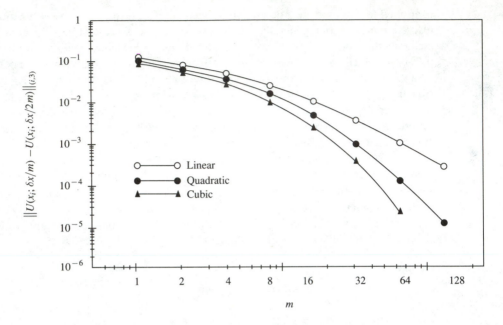

Figure 5.12 Error norms for calculations of Example 5.9.

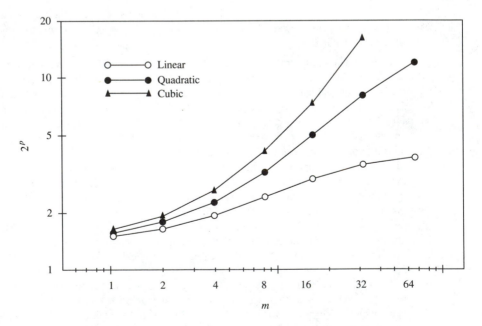

Figure 5.13 Ratio of consecutive error norms for calculations of Example 5.9.

The results of Example 5.9 are somewhat unsatisfactory in that the solution on a highly resolved grid does not provide definitive information on the behavior of the high-order approximations. This is in contrast to calculations performed in Example 5.8, which showed very satisfying agreement between theory and implementation in the context of higher-order finite difference approximations. Based on these two experiments, one should not draw the conclusion that higher-order approximations are better using finite differences than finite elements. The reason for the disparity in results is the near-logarithmic behavior of the solution to the one-dimensional problem, which gives high gradients near $x = 0$. This type of functional shape is very difficult to model using polynomial interpolations. Therefore, both finite difference and finite element methods approach their theoretical asymptotic behavior very slowly for this problem. Prediction of whether the accuracy of a numerical solution to a complex problem can best be improved by increasing the order of accuracy of an approximation or by retaining a low-order approximation but refining the mesh is not easy. Because of some advantages from the point of view of computer algorithm design and error assessment, the latter approach is more commonly employed.

To obtain additional empirical information concerning the asymptotic order of accuracy of the finite element approximations, equation (5.1.57a) was solved with $K = 1$, $a = 1$, and $r = 1$. Here as the mesh was refined, p asymptotically approached values of 2, 4, and 6 for the linear, quadratic, and cubic cases, respectively (see Problem 5.29). This result, however, may be utilized only with caution. First, although theoretical convergence rates can often be derived, they may not be achieved in practice, depending on the behavior of the solution. This is particularly true when large gradients, discontinuities, or shock fronts are part of the phenomena under study. Second, and perhaps even more important, the convergence rates computed here are misleading. The norm used in computing the error estimates was $\|U(x_i; \delta x/m) - U(x_i; \delta x/2m)\|_{(i,3)}$. This is a very simple norm to compute in that the values of U employed are exact at the two end positions, and thus the only computed solutions contributing to the magnitude of this norm are those at the center node, $U(2.0; \delta x/m)$. This node is an interelement node, a node whose basis function spans two elements. On the other hand, the basis functions for the interior nodes of the quadratic and cubic elements span only one element. Based on this empirical observation, one might expect the solutions at corner nodes to be better than those at interior nodes and perhaps better than at any other locations in the grid. A large amount of theoretical work has gone into proving that with the finite element method where the approximations used are not the same at all locations, the rate of convergence indeed is different at different locations. These proofs are complex and are specific to particular types of differential equations. Indeed, for the differential equation given by equation (5.1.57) under the special conditions that K and a are constant and $r = 1$, use of a $\mathbb{C}^0$ basis function of degree $p - 1$ results in convergence rates nominally of order p but of order $2p - 2$ at the interelement nodes. Thus, for complex problems being solved on irregular grids, determination of the rate of convergence of solution at various locations in the region of interest or overall are commonly obtained empirically rather than based on a full theoretical analysis.

5.2.3 Nonuniform Addition of Variables: p-Convergence

Section 5.1.4 considered mesh enrichment as it is implemented by refining a mesh without changing the order of the basis functions used. Here a slightly different approach will be introduced wherein an element is enriched by adding higher-order basis functions and variables to elements where mesh refinement is desired. For example, if a one-dimensional element with linear basis functions is to be refined, the refinement can be accomplished by adding a node in the center of the element and using quadratic basis functions, as developed in Chapter 3. Alternatively, and preferably, the refinement may be achieved by retaining the linear basis functions but adding a quadratic interpolating function that acts as a perturbation term and accounts for deviation from linear behavior in the element. To obtain additional refinement, higher-degree perturbation functions (i.e., cubics, quartics, quintics, etc.) can also be added in an element. This approach raises the order of the truncation error in the element and hence is referred to as *p-convergence* where the error is of order $\mathcal{O}((h)^p)$ and h is the grid spacing. Recall that the method of Section 5.1, for which the node spacing is reduced while p is held constant, is called *h-convergence*. The approach of using higher-degree basis functions defined by higher-degree perturbation terms combined with the original lower-order basis functions is called a *hierarchic formulation*. It is somewhat analogous to the refinement strategy developed in Section 5.1.4, where refinement variables provided a measure of "kinking" or deviation from linear variation. Here the kinking is rather a measure of deviation from linear behavior which takes the form of a smooth curve.

When using the approach of Section 5.1.4, addition of more interpolation functions to accomplish a mesh refinement is equivalent to subdividing an element into more elements. This can be done as many times as desired. For instance, in Example 5.6, the mesh initially consisted of two elements. Seven subdivisions of one element were performed while the other element was not refined at all. In the current subsection, where each refinement corresponds to an increase in the degree of interpolation in an element, seven refinements of a single linear element would result in eighth-degree interpolation over the element. Typically, interpolation of this degree is not used because it can allow a solution to oscillate excessively in an element. Furthermore, a loss of precision in computer arithmetic performed with high-order basis functions occurs. Although the discussion here does not restrict the order of the basis function added, the example problem worked is limited to third-order interpolation. If p-refinement of this degree is insufficient to obtain a solution with the desired accuracy, either a new base grid should be considered or the concepts of p-convergence could be combined with h-convergence strategy.

The development of higher-order enrichment that follows is structured to facilitate a comparison with enrichment using basis functions of the same order as described in Section 5.1.4. Again, for simplicity, two-dimensional elements will be considered. The addition of higher-order functions in a hierarchical manner, however, is conceptually easier, as the kinks do not lead to discontinuities at element boundaries and preserve the smooth interpolation within an element. No new corner nodes are introduced, and interelement continuity is preserved without resorting to slave nodes. Thus the need to consider the propagation of enrichment effects, as done in Figures 5.3 and 5.4 and the accompanying discussion, is much reduced. The presentation here begins with a single element that has been transformed into $\xi - \eta$ space as depicted in Figure 5.14a. For simplicity, the element in **x** space is considered to have straight sides.

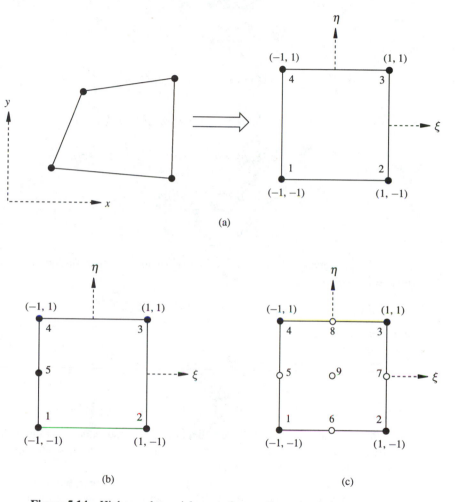

Figure 5.14   Higher-order enrichment of a two-dimensional element. (a) Transformation of a bilinear element in x-y space to a square in ξ-η space. (b) Addition of node 5 to the original grid. (c) Positions associated with deviation functions.

The bilinear interpolation of a function u over this element is

$$u \simeq U = \sum_{j=1}^{4} U_j \phi_j(\xi, \eta), \qquad \begin{array}{l} -1 \leq \xi \leq 1 \\ -1 \leq \eta \leq 1 \end{array} \qquad (5.1.79)$$

where $\phi_j = (1/4)(1 + \xi\xi_j)(1 + \eta\eta_j)$. If it were desired to enrich the element such that quadratic variation in U is allowed along the side connecting nodes 1 and 4, this could be done by adding node 5 as depicted in Figure 5.14b and letting

$$u \simeq U = \sum_{j=1}^{5} U_j \omega_j(\xi, \eta) \tag{5.2.17}$$

where

$$\omega_1(\xi, \eta) = -\frac{1}{4}(1 - \xi)\eta(1 - \eta) \tag{5.2.18a}$$

$$\omega_2(\xi, \eta) = \phi_2(\xi, \eta) = \frac{1}{4}(1 + \xi)(1 - \eta) \tag{5.2.18b}$$

$$\omega_3(\xi, \eta) = \phi_3(\xi, \eta) = \frac{1}{4}(1 + \xi)(1 + \eta) \tag{5.2.18c}$$

$$\omega_4(\xi, \eta) = \frac{1}{4}(1 - \xi)\eta(1 + \eta) \tag{5.2.18d}$$

$$\omega_5(\xi, \eta) = \frac{1}{2}(1 - \eta)(1 + \eta)(1 - \xi) \tag{5.2.18e}$$

These expressions are obtained by allowing linear variation in ξ and quadratic variation in η such that

$$\omega_j(\xi, \eta) = \alpha_{0j} + \alpha_{1j}\xi + \alpha_{2j}\eta + \alpha_{3j}\xi\eta + \alpha_{4j}\xi\eta^2, \qquad j = 1, 2, \ldots, 5 \tag{5.2.19a}$$

and then requiring that

$$\omega_j(\xi_j, \eta_j) = 1, \qquad j = 1, 2, \ldots, 5 \tag{5.2.19b}$$

with

$$\omega_j(\xi_k, \eta_k) = 0, \qquad k = 1, 2, \ldots, 5 \quad \text{but } k \neq j \tag{5.2.19c}$$

Note that the forms of ω_j will vary depending on the nodes in Figure 5.14c that are included in an approximation. Thus the procedure is very clumsy and would result in an inefficient mesh-enrichment computer algorithm.

This situation can be improved by retaining the original basis functions, ϕ_j, at the four corner nodes and letting the variables computed along the midside and interior of the element correspond to deviations from the bilinear approximations. The perturbation functions for these additional variables should be equal to zero at the corner nodes and exhibit higher-degree variation in the direction tangent to the side for side variables and in both directions for variables on the interior. Thus, with reference to the element in figure 5.14c, the approximation for u is

$$u \simeq U = \sum_{j=1}^{4} U_j \phi_j(\xi, \eta) + \sum_{j=5}^{8} \sum_{k=2}^{S_j} V_{j,k} \omega_{j,k}(\xi, \eta) + \sum_{k=2}^{S_9} \sum_{\ell=2}^{R_9} V_{9,k,\ell} \omega_{9,k,\ell}(\xi, \eta) \tag{5.2.20}$$

where, for $j = 5, \ldots, 8$, S_j is the highest-degree perturbation polynomial along the element side containing point j; and S_9 and R_9 are the highest degrees of the perturbation polynomials associated with point 9 in ξ and η, respectively. Note that if S_j or R_9 is less than 2, the summation is neglected (i.e., no perturbation variable is considered). In equation (5.2.20), the perturbation functions are

$$\omega_{5,k} = \frac{1}{2}(1 - \xi)f_k(\eta) \tag{5.2.21a}$$

$$\omega_{6,k} = \frac{1}{2}(1 + \eta)f_k(\xi) \tag{5.2.21b}$$

$$\omega_{7,k} = \frac{1}{2}(1 + \xi)f_k(\eta) \tag{5.2.21c}$$

$$\omega_{8,k} = \frac{1}{2}(1 - \eta)f_k(\xi) \tag{5.2.21d}$$

$$\omega_{9,k,\ell} = f_k(\xi)f_\ell(\eta) \tag{5.2.21e}$$

where

$$f_k(z) = \begin{cases} \dfrac{1}{k!}(z^k - 1) & \text{for } k \text{ even} \\[2ex] \dfrac{1}{k!}(z^k - z) & \text{for } k \text{ odd} \end{cases} \tag{5.2.21f}$$

These basis functions have been developed sequentially such that inclusion of a function in equation (5.2.20) does not alter the interpretation of any lower-order functions that have previously been included. The coefficients of these basis functions in equation (5.2.20) are thus approximations to derivatives of u such that

$$\left. \frac{\partial^k U}{\partial \eta^k} \right|_{(-1,0)} = V_{5,k} \tag{5.2.22a}$$

$$\left. \frac{\partial^k U}{\partial \xi^k} \right|_{(0,-1)} = V_{6,k} \tag{5.2.22b}$$

$$\left. \frac{\partial^k U}{\partial \eta^k} \right|_{(1,0)} = V_{7,k} \tag{5.2.22c}$$

$$\left. \frac{\partial^k U}{\partial \xi^k} \right|_{(0,1)} = V_{8,k} \tag{5.2.22d}$$

$$\frac{\partial^{k+\ell} U}{\partial \xi^k \, \partial \eta^\ell} = V_{9,k,\ell} \tag{5.2.22e}$$

Note that the open circles in Figure 5.14c are positions in the element rather than true nodes. They are convenient locations for use in interpreting the meaning of the deviation coefficients but are not nodes in the usual sense as employed with basis function families in Chapter 3. The general form of (5.2.20) has the following hierarchical analogs to commonly used basis function families:

$$S_5 = S_6 = S_7 = S_8 = S_9 = R_9 = 1 \qquad \text{bilinear}$$
$$S_5 = S_6 = S_7 = S_8 = 2; S_9 = R_9 = 1 \qquad \text{serendipity quadratics}$$
$$S_5 = S_6 = S_7 = S_8 = S_9 = R_9 = 2 \qquad \text{Lagrangian quadratics}$$
$$S_5 = S_6 = S_7 = S_8 = 3; S_9 = R_9 = 1 \qquad \text{serendipity cubics}$$
$$S_5 = S_6 = S_7 = S_8 = S_9 = R_9 = 3 \qquad \text{Lagrangian cubics}$$

When a side position variable is added to an element, it must also be added in the adjacent element which shares that side to preserve the continuity of U across the element boundary. Interior variables, $V_{9,k,\ell}$, have no effect on the interpolation required in adjacent elements.

Each of the deviation coefficients in equation (5.2.20) may also be thought of as a measure of the deviation of the solution using interpolation of degree k from the solution calculated using interpolation of degree $k - 1$ at a particular point. For example, examination of equation (5.2.21a) leads to the conclusion that its maxima occur at $(\xi, \eta) = (-1, 0)$ when k is even and at $(\xi, \eta) = (-1, \pm(k)^{[1/(1-k)]})$ when k is odd. Thus the maximum deviation due to perturbations with k even will be

$$\left| V_{5,k} \omega_{5,k}(-1, 0) \right| = \left| \frac{V_{5,k}}{k!} \right| \tag{5.2.23a}$$

and when k is odd the maximum deviation terms will be

$$\left| V_{5,k} \omega_{5,k}(-1, \pm(k)^{[1/(1-k)]}) \right| = \left| \frac{V_{5,k}(1 - k)(k)^{[k/(1-k)]}}{k!} \right| \tag{5.2.23b}$$

Similar relations can be obtained for the other deviation variables (see Problem 5.30). The use of the deviation functions in a computation will be demonstrated subsequently in Example 5.10. However, prior to that example, some remarks comparing h- and p-refinement are in order.

Implementation of algorithms that selectively add deviation variables in elements is analogous to that presented in Section 5.1.4 for mesh enrichment. Selection of the elements most in need of improved approximations may be based on an error norm for each element, such as in equation (5.1.77). Alternatively, candidate elements for improved approximations may be identified from estimates of the coefficients $V_{j,k}$ and $V_{9,k,\ell}$. These coefficients are related to maximum deviations as indicated in equation (5.2.23). Thus projected estimates of the lowest-order deviation variables may be used to select regions to enrich with higher-order approximations. The discussion from equations (5.1.79) through (5.1.93) is applicable if this strategy is to be employed.

Recall that h-refinement strategies are roughly equivalent to selective halving of element increment lengths. Application of this procedure is usually accomplished while requiring that length ratios of adjacent elements do not exceed a factor of about 2 or 3. On the other hand, application of p-refinement is typically accomplished by restricting the degree of the higher-order interpolation polynomial. Thus h-refinement of a particular region can be virtually unlimited, provided that geometric constraints are observed by also enriching neighboring regions, while p-refinement of a region is limited by the allowed degree of the deviation polynomial. If, as is typical, deviation functions are restricted to cubics or quadratics, then p-convergence alone is incapable of producing a highly refined approximation but must be used in concert with another technique, such as h-convergence. These concepts are illustrated in the following one-dimensional example.

Example 5.10

Problem   Once again, solve the differential equation

$$\frac{d}{dx}\left[K\frac{du}{dx}\right] = a(u)^r, \qquad 0 < x < 4 \tag{5.1.57a}$$

$$u(0) = 0.0 \tag{5.1.57b}$$

$$u(4) = 4.0 \tag{5.1.57c}$$

when $K = 0.1x + 5.0$, $a = 0.1$, and $r = 0.3$. Use the concepts of nonuniform addition of variables in conjunction with mesh enrichment strategies to improve the accuracy of the solution.

Solution   The initial grid to be employed will use linear finite elements throughout and allow the option of including higher-order deviation variables. In general, more than one deviation variable may be added to an element and to many elements on successive calculations. However, here the attempts to improve accuracy will be very limited in scope from one calculation to the next in order to illustrate the effects of various strategies. Furthermore, deviation functions of only second, third, and fourth degree will be considered with actual p-refinement limited to third-degree interpolation.

The initial grid to be employed is composed of three equispaced nodes located at $x = \{0, 2, 4\}$ and two elements. The basis functions and deviation functions will be written in the global coordinate system for convenience.

The approximation for u that follows from equation (5.2.20) is

$$u \simeq U(x) = \sum_{j=1}^{3} U_j \phi_j(x) + \sum_{e=1}^{2}\sum_{k=2}^{4} V_{e,k}\omega_{e,k}(x) \tag{5.2.24}$$

where j refers to the node number, e is the element number, and k is the degree of the deviation function. For example, in element 1 ($0 \le x \le 2$), the functions have the forms

$$\phi_1 = \frac{x_2 - x}{\Delta x_1}, \qquad\qquad\qquad x_1 \le x \le x_2 \quad \text{(5.2.25a)}$$

$$\phi_2 = \frac{x - x_1}{\Delta x_1}, \qquad\qquad\qquad x_1 \le x \le x_2 \quad \text{(5.2.25b)}$$

$$\phi_3 = 0, \qquad\qquad\qquad\qquad x_1 \le x \le x_2 \quad \text{(5.2.25c)}$$

$$\omega_{1,2} = \frac{1}{2}(x - x_1)(x - x_2) \qquad\qquad x_1 \le x \le x_2 \quad \text{(5.2.25d)}$$

$$\omega_{1,3} = \frac{1}{6}(x - x_1)(x - x_2)\left[x - \left(\frac{x_1 + x_2}{2}\right)\right], \qquad x_1 \le x \le x_2 \quad \text{(5.2.25e)}$$

$$\omega_{1,4} = \frac{1}{24}(x - x_1)(x - x_2)\left[x^2 - (x_1 + x_2)x + \frac{1}{2}(x_2^2 + x_1^2)\right], \quad x_1 \le x \le x_2 \quad \text{(5.2.25f)}$$

$$\omega_{2,k} = 0, \qquad k = 2, 3, 4 \qquad\qquad x_1 \le x \le x_2 \quad \text{(5.2.25g)}$$

Note that $\omega_{1,k}$ is zero at the ends of element 1 and that its first through $(k-1)$st derivatives are zero at the midpoint of element 1 for all k. These properties assure that each higher-order basis function included in the approximation contributes only a deviation to the lower-order approximation. The coefficients U_j are estimates of u at node j and $V_{e,k}$ are the deviation variables. If $V_{e,2}$, $V_{e,3}$, and $V_{e,4}$ are all set to zero in element e, U is a linear function of x in that element. If $V_{e,3}$ and $V_{e,4}$ are set to zero, but $V_{e,2}$ is allowed to take on nonzero values, U is quadratic in element e; and if both $V_{e,2}$ and $V_{e,3}$ are allowed to be nonzero while $V_{e,4}$ is zero, U is cubic in element e. In the current example, $V_{e,4}$ will not be incorporated into any approximations to u. However, $V_{e,4}$ will be used as an estimate of error in an element using a cubic approximation. An expansion for $(u)^r$ is made with

$$(u)^r \simeq \hat{U}^r(x) = \sum_{j=1}^{3}(U_j)^r \phi_j(x) + \sum_{e=1}^{2}\sum_{k=2}^{4} W_{e,k}\omega_{e,k}(x) \qquad \text{(5.2.26)}$$

Expansions (5.2.26) and (5.2.24) do not provide equality of $\hat{U}^r$ and $(U)^r$ for all values of x. However, as in the discussion leading to (5.1.95), constraints may be imposed that allow approximate equality. Relations must also be developed between $W_{e,k}$ and $V_{e,k}$. This process is somewhat arbitrary and the conditions to be imposed here are only one possible set. Require that at the center of element e, $\hat{U}^r = AU$, where A is a function of proportionality that depends on U_e and U_{e+1}. This stipulation, though not necessarily optimum, does possess the property that the relationship between $W_{e,2}$ and $V_{e,2}$ will be linear. Thus with equation (5.2.24) proportional to (5.2.26) at the center of element e,

$$\frac{1}{2}\left[(U_e)^r + (U_{e+1})^r\right] + W_{e,2}\frac{(\Delta x_e)^2}{8} = A\left[\frac{1}{2}(U_e + U_{e+1}) + V_{e,2}\frac{(\Delta x_e)^2}{8}\right] \qquad \text{(5.2.27)}$$

Stipulate further that when $V_{e,2} = 0$, $W_{e,2}$ must also equal zero. Therefore,

$$A = \frac{(U_e)^r + (U_{e+1})^r}{U_e + U_{e+1}} \qquad \text{(5.2.28)}$$

and substitution back into equation (5.2.27) yields

$$W_{e,2} = V_{e,2} \frac{(U_e)^r + (U_{e+1})^r}{U_e + U_{e+1}} \qquad (5.2.29a)$$

Equation (5.2.29a) provides the relation between $W_{e,2}$ and $V_{e,2}$ so that if U_e, U_{e+1}, and $V_{e,2}$ are known, $(U_e)^r$, $(U_{e+1})^r$, and $W_{e,2}$ may be obtained directly. Similar manipulations, as encouraged in Problems 5.31 and 5.32, lead to the relations

$$W_{e,3} = V_{e,3} \frac{(U_e)^r - (U_{e+1})^r}{U_e - U_{e+1}} \qquad (5.2.29b)$$

and

$$W_{e,4} = \frac{4[(U_e)^r + (U_{e+1})^r] - W_{e,2}(\Delta x_e)^2}{4(U_e + U_{e+1}) - V_{e,2}(\Delta x_e)^2} V_{e,4} \qquad (5.2.29c)$$

Galerkin finite element approximations are obtained by substitution of equations (5.2.24) and (5.2.26) into equation (5.1.57a) and weighting with respect to ϕ_j and $\omega_{j,k}$. Green's theorem is applied to the equations so that the forms obtained are similar to equation (5.1.97) (although the deviation coefficients and functions have different interpretations):

$$\sum_{j=1}^{3} \int_0^4 KU_j \frac{d\phi_j}{dx} \frac{d\phi_i}{dx}\, dx + \sum_{e=1}^{2}\sum_{k=2}^{4} \int_0^4 KV_{e,k} \frac{d\omega_{e,k}}{dx} \frac{d\phi_i}{dx}\, dx + \sum_{j=1}^{3} \int_0^4 a(U_j)^r \phi_j \phi_i\, dx$$

$$+ \sum_{e=1}^{2}\sum_{k=2}^{4} \int_0^4 aW_{e,k}\omega_{e,k}\phi_i\, dx + \hat{q}\phi_i \Big|_{x=0}^{x=4} = 0, \qquad i = 1,2,3 \qquad (5.2.30a)$$

and

$$\sum_{j=1}^{3} \int_0^4 KU_j \frac{d\phi_j}{dx} \frac{d\omega_{\ell,i}}{dx}\, dx + \sum_{e=1}^{2}\sum_{k=2}^{4} \int_0^4 KV_{e,k} \frac{d\omega_{e,k}}{dx} \frac{d\omega_{\ell,i}}{dx}\, dx$$

$$+ \sum_{j=1}^{3} \int_0^4 a(U_j)^r \phi_j \omega_{\ell,i}\, dx + \sum_{e=1}^{2}\sum_{k=2}^{4} \int_0^4 aW_{e,k}\omega_{e,k}\omega_{\ell,i}\, dx = 0, \qquad \begin{aligned}\ell &= 1,2 \\ i &= 2,3,4\end{aligned}$$

$$(5.2.30b)$$

These equations are solved first with all the $V_{e,k}$ and $W_{e,k}$ coefficients set to zero. This solution will be identical to that obtained in Example 5.6 for the three-node linear grid. Since the interpolation is linear, an estimate of the coefficient $V_{e,2}$ multiplied by the maximum value of $\omega_{e,2}$ will provide an approximation to the change in solution by including a quadratic term. The estimate may be obtained from equation (5.2.30b) with $V_{e,3}$, $W_{e,3}$, $V_{e,4}$, and $W_{e,4}$ zero such that

$$V_{e,2}^{\text{est}} \int_{x_e}^{x_{e+1}} K \frac{d\omega_{e,2}}{dx} \frac{d\omega_{e,2}}{dx}\, dx + W_{e,2}^{\text{est}} \int_{x_e}^{x_{e+1}} a\omega_{e,2}\omega_{e,2}\, dx$$

$$= -\sum_{j=1}^{3} \int_{x_e}^{x_{e+1}} KU_j \frac{d\phi_j}{dx} \frac{d\omega_{e,2}}{dx}\, dx - \sum_{j=1}^{3} \int_{x_e}^{x_{e+1}} a(U_j)^r \phi_j \omega_{e,2}\, dx \qquad (5.2.31)$$

where the limits of integration apply because $\omega_{e,2}$ and $d\omega_{e,2}/dx$ are zero outside this range, and $V_{e,2}^{\text{est}}$ and $W_{e,2}^{\text{est}}$ are related by equation (5.2.29a). This expression is only approximate because the values of U_j used are obtained from equation (5.2.30a) with $V_{e,2}$ and $W_{e,2}$ assumed to be zero. However, these estimates do provide insight into the improvement in solution that can be expected if the higher-order enrichment is utilized. When a decision is made to incorporate a deviation function into an element, the solution for the coefficients U_j must be updated. The matrix procedure for accomplishing this is the same as used for h-enrichment and described following equation (5.1.88). Sequential updates of the estimates of error may also be obtained from equation (5.2.30b) for cubic and quartic coefficients. The form employed to obtain estimates is

$$
V_{e,k}^{\text{est}} \int_{x_e}^{x_{e+1}} K \frac{d\omega_{e,k}}{dx} \frac{d\omega_{e,k}}{dx} \, dx + W_{e,k}^{\text{est}} \int_{x_e}^{x_{e+1}} a\omega_{e,k}\omega_{e,k} \, dx
$$

$$
= -\sum_{j=1}^{3} \int_{x_e}^{x_{e+1}} KU_j \frac{d\phi_j}{dx} \frac{d\omega_{e,k}}{dx} \, dx - \sum_{j=1}^{3} \int_{x_e}^{x_{e+1}} a(U_j)^r \phi_j \omega_{e,k} \, dx
$$

$$
- \sum_{\ell=2}^{k-1} \int_{x_e}^{x_{e+1}} KV_{e,\ell} \frac{d\omega_{e,\ell}}{dx} \frac{d\omega_{e,k}}{dx} \, dx - \sum_{\ell=2}^{k-1} \int_{x_e}^{x_{e+1}} aW_{e,\ell}\omega_{e,\ell}\omega_{e,k} \, dx \qquad (5.2.32)
$$

When $k = 2$, the last two summations are each defined to be zero and this equation is identical to equation (5.2.31). All terms listed on the right side of the equation are known before the estimates of the impact of further refinement are made.

The presentation of results that follows is comprised of a set of solutions that are sequentially refined. For illustrative purposes, only one modification is done between solutions. That modification is either higher-order enrichment of an element, splitting of an element (h-enrichment), or redistribution of the deviation functions between elements. As applied here, the first two options increase the number of dependent variables by one, while the second option keeps the number of variables fixed. The use of h-enrichment in conjunction with p-enrichment is done to allow sufficient refinement of the mesh without using interpolation functions higher than third order. All decisions to refine the mesh are based on examination of the estimated maximum improvement to a solution within an element as predicted by $V_{e,k}^{\text{est}}$, where e is the element number and k is the order of interpolation currently applied in an element plus 1.

For the initial three-node grid with linear interpolation, the solution obtained is

j	x_j	U_j
1	0.0	0.0
2	2.0	2.9668
3	4.0	4.0

Based on equation (5.2.31) [or equation (5.2.32) with $k = 2$], the following estimates of higher-order correction are obtained:

Element	Element location	Interpolation	k	$\left\vert V_{e,k}^{\text{est}}\omega_{e,k}\right\vert_{\max}$
1	$0 \leq x \leq 2.0$	Linear	2	7.18×10^{-1}
2	$2.0 \leq x \leq 4.0$	Linear	2	8.06×10^{-2}

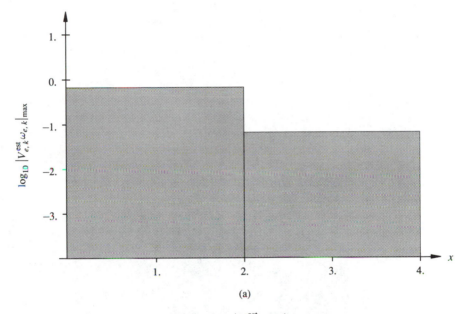

(a)

Figure 5.15   Semilog plots of $\left\vert V_{e,k}^{\text{est}}\omega_{e,k}\right\vert_{\max}$ versus element for successive h- and p- refinements of the initial three-node linear grid of Example 5.10. Light gray indicates a linear element; medium gray indicates a quadratic approximation; and dark gray indicates a region of cubic approximation.

The data in this last list are used to generate Figure 5.15a. This semilog bar graph depicts the value of the maximum deviation for each element. The light gray shading indicates that the elements are using linear interpolation such that $k = 2$ in the estimates of correction. The figure predicts that the improvement to the solution will be greatest if element 1 is enriched. Therefore, the second solution generated employs p-enrichment such that element 1 is quadratic and the solution obtained is as follows:

j	x_j	U_j
1	0.0	0.0
2	2.0	3.2215
3	4.0	4.0

with

Element	Element location	Interpolation	k	$\left\vert V_{e,k}^{\text{est}}\omega_{e,k}\right\vert_{\max}$
1	$0 \le x \le 2.0$	Quadratic	3	1.94×10^{-1}
2	$2.0 \le x \le 4.0$	Linear	2	5.95×10^{-2}

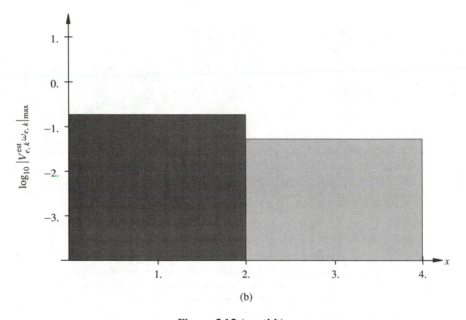

(b)

Figure 5.15 (cont'd.)

Note that incorporation of the parameter $V_{1,2}$ into the solution improves the accuracy as indicated by the magnitude of the estimate of the impact of further higher-order refinement. The data in the preceding table are plotted in Figure 5.15b. The darker gray shading for element 1 is used to indicate that quadratic interpolation is used in that element so that the predicted correction is based on cubic p-refinement. The data suggest that even though elements 1 and 2 are of the same size and element 1 has been refined to quadratic, further refinement of element 1 will most improve the solution. Use of cubic interpolation in element 1 and linear interpolation in element 2 provides the information used to construct Figure 5.15c. The plot suggests use of a fourth-order deviation function in element 1 is an appropriate refinement. However, the restriction arbitrarily imposed that interpolation will not be higher order than cubic precludes this approach. Alternatively, element 1 may be refined using h-convergence techniques such that a kink is allowed at $x = 1$, while p-convergence is applied such that interpolation is quadratic in both halves of the $0 \le$

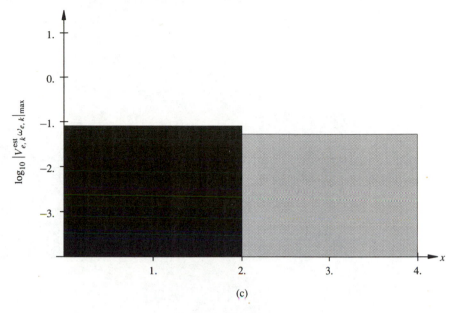

(c)

Figure 5.15 (cont'd.)

$x \leq 2$ domain. Interpolation is kept linear in the region $2 \leq x \leq 4$, and the solution is calculated as

j	x_j	U_j
1	0.0	0.0
2	1.0	2.6519
3	2.0	3.3210
4	4.0	4.0

with information concerning corrections as

Element	Element location	Interpolation	k	$\left|V_{e,k}^{\text{est}}\omega_{e,k}\right|_{\max}$
1	$0 \leq x \leq 1.0$	Quadratic	3	1.55×10^{-1}
2	$1.0 \leq x \leq 2.0$	Quadratic	3	4.46×10^{-3}
3	$2.0 \leq x \leq 4.0$	Linear	2	5.13×10^{-2}

This last set of correction data is also plotted in Figure 5.15d and suggests that the use of quadratic interpolation in element 2 is excessive. As an alternative, which uses no

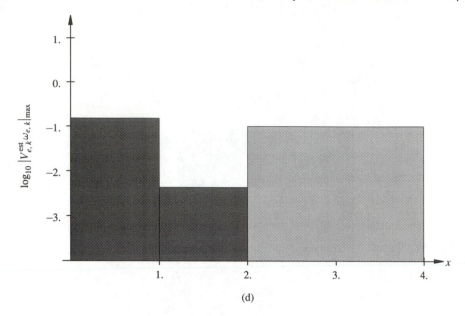

(d)

Figure 5.15 (cont'd.)

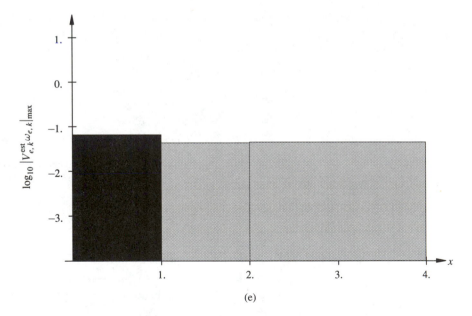

(e)

Figure 5.15 (cont'd.)

additional independent variables, cubic interpolation might be used in element 1 with linear interpolation in element 2. Application of this strategy provides the plot of Figure 5.15e which, indeed, indicates a more uniform distribution of estimated error than Figure 5.15d.

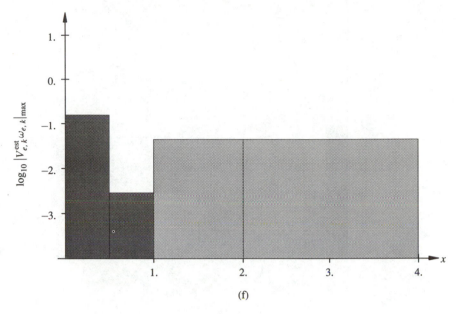

(f)

Figure 5.15 (cont'd.)

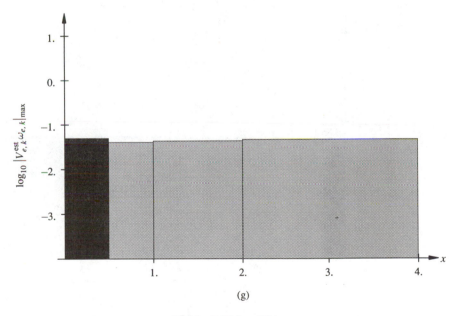

(g)

Figure 5.15 (cont'd.)

The plots in Figure 5.15f through i provide profiles of estimated error by two subsequent splittings of element 1 into two quadratic elements and the redistribution of interpolation to being cubic in the first element and linear in the second. The solution that led to the

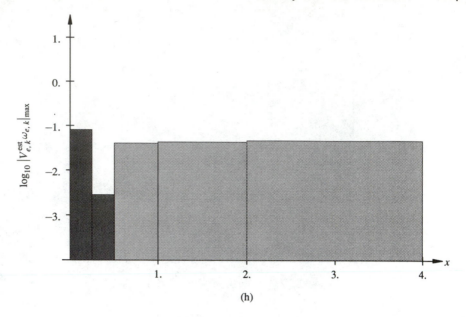

(h)

Figure 5.15 (cont'd.)

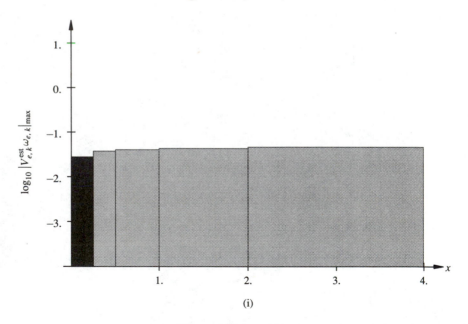

(i)

Figure 5.15 (cont'd.)

correction profile of Figure 5.15i is the first to suggest that an optimal refinement strategy might involve an element other than that closest to $x = 0$. (Note that this suggestion arose using the current combined p- and h-refinement strategy with eight dependent variables,

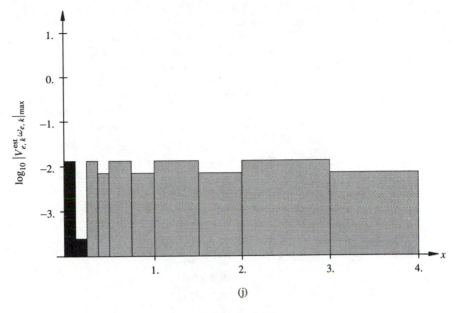

(j)

Figure 5.15 (cont'd.)

while in Example 5.6, using only h-convergence, the suggestion did not arise until ten dependent variables were in use.) The solution is

j	x_j	U_j
1	0.0	0.0
2	0.25	1.9124
3	0.50	2.4017
4	1.0	2.9101
5	2.0	3.4388
6	4.0	4.0

while the information plotted in Figure 5.15i is

Element	Element location	Interpolation	k	$\left\| V^{est}_{e,k} \omega_{e,k} \right\|_{max}$
1	$0 \leq x \leq 0.25$	Cubic	4	3.04×10^{-2}
2	$0.25 \leq x \leq 0.50$	Linear	2	3.82×10^{-2}
3	$0.50 \leq x \leq 1.0$	Linear	2	4.02×10^{-2}
4	$1.0 \leq x \leq 2.0$	Linear	2	4.11×10^{-2}
5	$2.0 \leq x \leq 4.0$	Linear	2	4.15×10^{-2}

At this point, rather than proceed with selective refinement, all five elements were divided in half using h-refinement. This refinement was performed without altering the order of interpolation over the various regions of the grid. The plot of the error estimates appears as Figure 5.15j. This plot is interesting in that it suggests that the halving of each element resulted in pairs of elements for which the part closer to $x = 0$ is in greater need of refinement. This kind of behavior is indicative of the fact that the largest gradients in the solution are at smaller x values. The interval halving was applied to the five-element grid six times and norms calculated as in equations (5.1.65) and (5.1.66) based on information at the six nodes $x_i = \{0, 1/4, 1/2, 1, 2, 4\}$.

m	$\|U(x_i; \delta x_i/m) - U(x_i; \delta x_i/2m)\|_{(i,6)}$	$(2)^p$	p
1	4.3115×10^{-3}	21.895	4.45
2	1.9692×10^{-4}	0.2300	-2.12
3	8.5601×10^{-4}	2.2235	1.15
4	3.8497×10^{-4}	3.4933	1.80
5	1.1020×10^{-4}	3.9304	1.97
6	2.8039×10^{-5}	—	—

(*Note*: In Example 5.6, the norm computed starting from the 10-node grid was calculated using only three nodal points, $x_i = \{0, 2, 4\}$. An alternative calculation of that norm using all the node points gives a value of 8.92×10^{-3}. This point is raised to facilitate additional comparison between Example 5.6 and the current example.)

The fact that the norm does not converge to zero monotonically is an effect of the use of different degree interpolation functions in different portions of the grid. As mesh refinement proceeds, the convergence rate is that of the linear basis functions. The reason for the peculiar behavior of the apparent value of p might be thought to be related to the nonlinearity of the problem and the poor quality of the approximate representation of $W_{e,k}$ in terms of $V_{e,k}$ provided by equation (5.2.29). However, the linear problem related to equation (5.1.57a) which arises when $r = 1$ rather than 0.3 produces virtually the same behavior. The reason for the apparently anomalous result is the varying degrees of interpolation used in the grid. The derivation of the norm in Section 5.1.1 was based on the assumption that p is the same for all approximations used. When, for example, cubics are used in one portion of the domain and linear interpolation is applied in another portion, this assumption is violated. Both the nonlinear ($r = 0.3$) and linear ($r = 1.0$) problems were solved starting with the six-node grid using quadratic interpolation for all elements and using cubic interpolation for all elements. For these cases, the convergence of p towards its expected value occurred with mesh refinement.

The preceding example illustrates that p-refinement, refinement using higher-order approximations, may be implemented on selected finite elements that are least accurate in approximating a solution. The estimated value of $V_{e,k}$ is useful in determining candidate elements for refinement. Alternatively, one could use estimates of root-mean-square error as was done in Example 5.6 to determine which regions should be refined. Although p-refinement is a very powerful tool and increases the rate of convergence as compared to h-refinement, calculation of the error norm between successive solutions is not, in general, possible. This difficulty points out the value of studying simple problems for which analytical solutions are known in order to gain insight into a numerical procedure (as in Chapter 4). If convergence is studied using a differential equation along with its known analytical solution, error norms may be calculated directly and the power of the procedure under study can be ascertained. Those methods that work well on simple problems are good candidates for implementation with complex problems. On the other hand, if a method performs poorly for a case where the solution is known, its extension to complex problems where the accuracy of a solution must be ascertained using comparison of successive solutions is, at best, very risky. The higher-order convergence of p-refinement interpolation functions makes these functions valuable tools in assuring an accurate solution. The projected correction that will be obtained by adding a higher-order correction function serves as a useful practical guide to the value of refinement in a particular region of the mesh.

5.3 CONSIDERATIONS FOR SPACE-TIME PROBLEMS: DYNAMIC GRIDDING

The preceding two sections have considered the issues of h-refinement, optimal mesh layout and p-refinement. The discussion considered the treatment of open-ended domains, such as time, separately from the treatment of closed domains, such as space. The general concepts described can be combined directly in space-time problems, but the implementation may lead to relatively complex and specialized algorithms. As a solution to a problem of interest develops as a function of time, the spatial gradients of the dependent variable may be largest in different parts of the grid. Thus the need arises to allow the grid, the deviation variables, and even the computational algorithm to evolve with the solution. Some fundamental considerations will be provided here, with details of specific applications left to the more specialized literature. Two general approaches may be applied: movement of the nodes as a function of time and p- or h-enrichment of a base grid. These approaches may, of course, be used in concert, but they will be discussed separately here.

5.3.1 Node Movement for a Time-Dependent Optimal Grid

The idea of moving nodes around so that the density of nodes in a portion of the grid is highest where needed at any particular time has appeal because of its elegance. However, in practice, this procedure is very complex and relies on imposition of some external criteria for proper implementation. This procedure is usually used to move nodes around in space as a function of time while the time step is uniform through space. Although the concept may be extended to finite difference methods, the fact that the grid becomes irregular makes the method particularly suited to the finite element framework. Nevertheless, drawbacks to efficient implementation of the method are numerous.

When the locations of the nodes are to be obtained as a function of time, the overhead cost of the computations becomes high. The interdependence of nodal position and solution variable results in a highly nonlinear problem that requires significant iteration for solution at each time step. The idea of moving nodes with the advective velocity (i.e., the characteristic of a hyperbolic equation or the secondary characteristics of a parabolic problem) might seem to suggest a straightforward algorithm for nodal movement; but such a plan can lead to severe grid distortion such that computation becomes impossible. For example, even in a computation where the primary advective velocity is in one direction, if the boundary of the region being simulated is fixed, the nodes will bunch up on one edge of the domain. In general, the distribution of the velocity throughout the domain commonly leads to severe element distortion and nodes crossing element boundaries such that the grid becomes unusable. This tendency can be countered by placing a value on grids that are regular and have uniformly shaped elements, but incorporation of this value into a moving-grid framework is somewhat arbitrary.

Perhaps the greatest drawback to moving grids is the fact that the criteria for optimal nodal placement depend on only one dependent variable. For example, consider the case where a few contaminants are being transported in an estuary that has a complex bottom geometry. The grid for solution of this problem could be selected as a stationary one that captures the most important features of the geometry. Alternatively, the time-varying flow field might be used to determine a deforming mesh that best captures the features of the flow. Finally, the need to model the movement of one of the chemical constituents very accurately might be the major concern so that the mesh should have the highest concentration of nodes in regions where the concentration gradient of this species is largest. The difficulty with using any one of these criteria for nodal placement is that it may preclude obtaining a good solution for another variable. Thus in solving multivariable problems, the best strategy seems to be to work with a convenient base grid that is not especially biased in favor of one variable and then use mesh refinement, as needed for each variable. This approach will be the focus of Section 5.3.2.

If a situation exists where only one variable is of interest and a dynamic grid is to be used, the movement of the nodes must be accounted for in the finite element approximation. Consider a basis function ϕ_i associated with a node in an element that is expressed as the function $\phi_i(\boldsymbol{\xi})$ in local space using an isoparametric transformation. This function may also be written as $\phi_i(\mathbf{x}; \mathbf{x}_j)$ where $\mathbf{x}_j$ are the nodal locations of the element and may depend on time. If the element has N_e nodes, then the isoparametric transformation may be expressed as

$$\mathbf{x} = \sum_{j=1}^{N_e} \mathbf{x}_j(t)\phi_j(\boldsymbol{\xi}) \tag{5.3.1}$$

Because $\mathbf{x}$ is a function of the nodal positions $\mathbf{x}_j$ and $\boldsymbol{\xi}$, both arguments of the basis function $\phi_i(\mathbf{x}; \mathbf{x}_j)$ depend on the nodal positions. Therefore, differentiation of ϕ_i with respect to $\mathbf{x}_k$ while holding $\boldsymbol{\xi}$ constant requires that the chain rule be used to obtain

$$\frac{\partial \phi_i}{\partial \mathbf{x}_k}\bigg|_\xi = \nabla \phi_i \cdot \frac{\partial \mathbf{x}}{\partial \mathbf{x}_k}\bigg|_\xi + \sum_{j=1}^{N_e} \frac{\partial \phi_i}{\partial \mathbf{x}_j} \frac{\partial \mathbf{x}_j}{\partial \mathbf{x}_k}\bigg|_\xi \tag{5.3.2}$$

where $\nabla \phi_i = \partial \phi_i / \partial \mathbf{x}$. The value of ϕ_i at a point in ξ-space is independent of the global location of the nodes, so the left side of this equation is zero. Also, from equation (5.3.1),

$$\frac{\partial \mathbf{x}}{\partial \mathbf{x}_k}\bigg|_\xi = \sum_{j=1}^{N_e} \frac{\partial \mathbf{x}_j}{\partial \mathbf{x}_k} \phi_j \tag{5.3.3}$$

Substitution of this expression into equation (5.3.2) yields

$$0 = \sum_{j=1}^{N_e} \left[\phi_j \nabla \phi_i + \frac{\partial \phi_i}{\partial \mathbf{x}_j} \right] \cdot \frac{\partial \mathbf{x}_j}{\partial \mathbf{x}_k}\bigg|_\xi \tag{5.3.4}$$

The last factor in this expression is a Kronecker delta equal to 1 when $j = k$ and 0 otherwise; therefore, equation (5.3.4) becomes

$$\frac{\partial \phi_i}{\partial \mathbf{x}_k} = -\phi_k \nabla \phi_i \tag{5.3.5}$$

This expression is very important for proper representation of time derivatives in a finite element formulation with moving nodes.

Consider a function $u(\mathbf{x}, t)$ that is to be approximated using finite element basis functions as

$$u \simeq U = \sum_{j=1}^{N} U_j(t) \phi_j(\mathbf{x}; \mathbf{x}_k) \tag{5.3.6}$$

where the N nodal positions $\mathbf{x}_k$ are functions of time. The partial derivative of U with respect to time at a fixed point in space is therefore

$$\frac{\partial U}{\partial t} = \sum_{j=1}^{N} \frac{dU_j}{dt} \phi_j + \sum_{j=1}^{N} U_j \left(\sum_{k=1}^{N} \frac{\partial \phi_j}{\partial \mathbf{x}_k} \cdot \frac{d\mathbf{x}_k}{dt} \right) \tag{5.3.7}$$

Substitution of equation (5.3.5) into this relation yields

$$\frac{\partial U}{\partial t} = \sum_{j=1}^{N} \frac{dU_j}{dt} \phi_j - \left(\sum_{j=1}^{N} U_j \nabla \phi_j \right) \cdot \left(\sum_{k=1}^{N} \frac{d\mathbf{x}_k}{dt} \phi_k \right) \tag{5.3.8}$$

The last term in parentheses involves the movement of nodes and can be identified as the nodal velocity. The next-to-last term in parentheses is the gradient of U such that equation (5.3.8) becomes

$$\frac{\partial U}{\partial t} = \sum_{j=1}^{N} \frac{dU_j}{dt} \phi_j - \mathbf{V}^{\text{nodes}} \cdot \boldsymbol{\nabla} U \qquad (5.3.9)$$

In this expression, remember that U_j is the approximation of U at node j regardless of the actual position of node j. For the case of a fixed grid, the last term in equation (5.3.9) will be zero and the usual expression for $\partial U / \partial t$ results.

If the velocities of all nodes can be specified independently of a solution for U, equation (5.3.9) may be used directly in the finite element formulation of U. However, if $\mathbf{V}^{\text{nodes}}$ is to be calculated such that some error norm on U is minimized, the interdependence of U and $\mathbf{V}^{\text{nodes}}$ will complicate the problem. This concept is explored further in Problem 5.39.

When the node positioning is to be obtained as a function of time based on some error criterion, equations such as (5.1.103) will have to be solved at each time step using specified values of w_1 and w_2 such as those in equations (5.1.105) through (5.1.108). Typically, the equations for nodal positions are formulated through arbitrary modification of w_1 and w_2 or by adding additional terms to equation (5.1.103), so that severe grid distortion is avoided. Remember that a precise solution for nodal positions is not essential as a differential equation for a problem of interest may be solved for any reasonable nodal movement. The objective of moving the nodes is to provide an optimal grid for solution. However, if a near optimal grid can be obtained more conveniently, it may be the grid of choice.

The velocity of a node over a time step may be specified aribtrarily to be a constant such that for node $\mathbf{x}_j$,

$$\frac{d\mathbf{x}_j}{dt} = \frac{\mathbf{x}_j(t + \Delta t) - \mathbf{x}_j(t)}{\Delta t} \qquad (5.3.10)$$

If desired, an alternative higher-order specification of nodal velocity may be imposed. A relatively simple moving-node example appears as Problem 5.41.

One of the difficult aspects of solving moving-grid problems is the specification of an initial grid. For example, if the initial distribution of the dependent variable within the domain is uniform, one might expect to begin computation with a uniform mesh. However, in fact, if the dependent variable is uniform, it may be represented just as well on a nonuniform grid as on a uniform grid. The initial placement of nodes must be determined to allow for the propagation of the disturbances from the boundary. For a hyperbolic problem where pulses are sent into the system from the boundary at some random frequency, the need exists for nodes to be near the boundary to follow the pulse as it enters the system. Quanititative determination of an adequate number of nodes to apply near the boundary or of their actual initial distribution is a difficult problem. The behavior of problems with a strong hyperbolic character (i.e., hyperbolic problems or parabolic problem with an important secondary characteristic) can be captured well within the domain using moving nodes, but propagation of information from the boundaries creates a need to be able to introduce nodes at the boundary or adapt the grid to account for these effects while retaining good performance in the interior of the domain. For parabolic problems with a small or no advective component (e.g., the transient heat conduction equation), the node movement is easier to specify. However, the arbitrariness in specifying the initial grid configuration remains (see Problem 5.41).

The discussion in this section has concentrated on movement or redistribution of nodes in the spatial domain. In the open-ended time domain, nodal movement is not performed. Rather, time steps are simply increased or decreased as computations proceed in order to obtain an accurate solution. As discussed in Section 5.1.2, the change in the time step affects only future computations and not previous calculations. Further discussion of dynamic time step size determination belongs more properly in the next subsection, which deals with dynamic p- and h-refinement.

5.3.2 Time-Dependent Implementation of h- and p-Refinement

As an alternative to moving nodes in order to refine a computational mesh, selective use of p- and h-refinement of a fixed base grid has significant appeal. By this method, refinement of a particular region can be obtained by solving for deviation variables, denoted here as $V_{e,k}$, in element e. Furthermore, if the refinement becomes unnecessary, it may be eliminated by requiring $V_{e,k}$ to be zero. Another extremely attractive feature of applying this method is the ability to use a single base grid for all dependent variables (such as velocity, chemical concentration, and temperature in modeling a large water body) while implementing refinement for each variable only as needed. Criteria for h- or p-refinement may be developed for each variable based on an error norm or an estimate of $V_{e,k}$.

In contrast to the moving-node formulation, where the basis functions are dependent on time, all basis functions and deviation functions are time independent for the current approach. The solution procedure differs from the steady-state problems discussed in Sections 5.1 and 5.2 in that a determination must be made at each time step as to whether or not a particular refinement variable will be used. Issues related to nodal crossing or element distortion do not arise, although extreme cases of the juxtaposition of a highly refined element with one that is unrefined may cause round-off errors. This problem may be avoided by placing constraints on the difference in refinement between neighboring elements.

The basic idea behind time-dependent h- and p-convergence is virtually the same as for steady problems. On implementation, some caution must be exercised. The algorithm used should not add and subtract variables in large numbers at each time step. This is akin to the conservative refinement criterion developed in Example 5.3, which requires some persistence of a call for refinement and that the effect of refinement will not be trivial. Second, refinement in space may lead to instabilities if the time step is not reduced. As discussed in Section 4.2, some computational approaches require that a ratio of the time step to the spatial step size raised to a power, $\Delta t/(h)^m$, be smaller than a critical value in order to retain stability. The methods of h- and p-refinement reduce the effective grid size and thus can strain a stability constraint. Therefore, the time step may need to be adjusted in concert with the spatial step size for reasons of stability as well as accuracy. This adjustment will be most effective computationally if the time step can vary over the spatial domain.

The efficient employment of dynamic p- and h-convergence is conceptually simple but requires efficient and creative programming for actual implementation. This is particularly true when complex, coupled, nonlinear equations, difficult to solve in their own right, are being solved on a dynamic grid. Ironically, these are just the kinds of problems whose solution accuracy stands to be most improved when time-dependent p- and h-refinement is successfully implemented.

5.4 CONCLUSION

This chapter has presented some basic techniques for assessing and improving the accuracy of a numerical solution to a differential equation. Of underlying importance in the discussion is the need to be able to determine that the numbers and graphs generated during numerical simulation do, in fact, provide a solution to the problem of interest with enough precision to be useful. Methods for improving the accuracy of a solution include implementation of higher-order approximations, uniform mesh refinement through interval halving, optimal mesh generation, and selective mesh enrichment. The material in the current chapter addresses only relatively simple problems as a mechanism for exposing fundamental principles and techniques for error reduction.

This chapter shows that one does not need to know the analytical solution to a problem in order to assess the accuracy of a numerical solution. Nevertheless, three important points must be kept in mind when performing the simulation of a field problem. First, the equations that are used to describe the problem must capture and account for the important operative physical processes. Second, the parameters, or at least the range of parameters, in the equation must be known; and solutions covering a realistic range of these parameters need to be investigated. Third, any numerical solution technique employed should be stable, consistent, and convergent and should minimize the introduction of spurious phenomena attributable to the form of numerical approximation used. If any one of these three features is absent, a modeling exercise will be, at best, misleading.

PROBLEMS

5.1. Determine the leading error term for
    (a) The four-value implicit Adams-Moulton multivalue method
    (b) The three-value implicit Gears multivalue method
    (c) The five-value implicit Adams-Moulton multivalue method
    (d) The four-value explicit Gears multivalue method
    (e) The four-value explicit Adams-Bashforth multivalue method

5.2. The L_2 discrete norm is defined in Appendix A and by equation (5.1.14) as

$$\|A^i\|_{(i,n)} = \left[\sum_{i=1}^{n} w_i (A^i)^2\right]^{1/2} \qquad (5.5.1)$$

This norm is the discrete analog to the L_2 norm

$$\|A\|_\Omega = \left[\int_\Omega A^2 d\Omega \right]^{1/2} \tag{5.5.2}$$

where Ω is the domain of A.

(a) If Ω is a one-dimensional domain $0 \le x \le 1$ and A^i is evaluated at n data points where $x_i = (i-1)\Delta x$ and $\Delta x = 1/(n-1)$, what values of the w_i's will make equation (5.5.1) a trapezoidal rule approximation to the integral in equation (5.5.2)?

(b) For the condition of part (a), what values of the coefficients w_i and n will make equation (5.5.1) a Simpson's rule approximation to equation (5.5.2)?

(c) If Ω is a two-dimensional domain $0 \le x \le a$ and $0 \le y \le b$ with Δx and Δy as constants, what values of w_i in equation (5.5.1) allow equation (5.5.2) to be approximated by a trapezoidal rule?

(d) Should one select w_i to provide a very high order approximation of equation (5.5.1) to (5.5.2)? Give your answer in the context of evaluating an error norm such as that on the right side of equation (5.1.24).

5.3. If values of A^i are available on an irregular grid, provide a set of reasonable values of the coefficients w_i for use in equation (5.5.1). (*Note*: This problem does not necessarily have a unique answer.)

5.4. Program Example 5.2 using Gear's three-value multivalue method. How does the required step size compare with that of the method used in Example 5.2?

5.5. Program Example 5.2 using the explicit Adams-Bashforth three-value method starting with $\Delta t = 2$. Compare the accuracy and rate of convergence with that found in the example. Explain differences.

5.6. The error term coefficients $\hat{C}_p$ and C_p (as provided in Appendix B) for the Adams-Moulton multivalue method are the same as for the Adams-Bashforth and Adams-Moulton multistep predictor-corrector methods. Demonstrate this for the $p = 3$ methods.

5.7. For Gear's method with $p = 2$, demonstrate that $\hat{C}_p$ and C_p, the error term coefficients, are the same for multistep and multivalue methods.

5.8. Instead of interval halving, it is proposed to refine a mesh by splitting the intervals into thirds.

(a) How will this strategy cause equations (5.1.22) through (5.1.24) to be altered? Derive the appropriate forms.

(b) The standard procedure of dividing an interval in 2 to examine convergence is arbitrary. Discuss possible advantages and disadvantages of selecting an alternative factor for subdividing a mesh.

5.9. Program a solution to the problem described in Example 5.3. Use the Adams-Moulton four-value method. Compare your results with those of Example 5.3.

5.10. Predictor and corrector forms of multivalue methods are given by equations (2.6.51) and (2.6.49), respectively (with some specific forms tabulated in Appendix B). Efficient implementation requires only knowledge of $\alpha_{1,k}$, C_p, and $\hat{C}_p$ for the method of interest.

(a) Program a general multivalue solution algorithm for equation (5.1.25) that allows the coefficients above to be specified as input.

(b) Demonstrate your model by solving the differential equation of Example 5.3 using Gear's three- and five-value methods. Compare your results with those of Example 5.3.

5.11. The shooting method is sometimes used to solve a boundary value problem using an algorithm that is actually appropriate for initial value problems. Consider the simple boundary value problem of Example 5.4:

$$\frac{d}{dx}\left(K\frac{du}{dx}\right) = 0.1(u)^{0.3}, \qquad 0 < x < 4 \tag{5.5.3a}$$

where

$$K = 0.1x + 5.0 \tag{5.5.3b}$$

with

$$u(0) = 0.0 \tag{5.5.3c}$$

and

$$u(4) = 4.0 \tag{5.5.4}$$

Instead of solving this problem directly, as in Example 5.4, the shooting method replaces condition (5.5.4) with an additional initial condition of the form

$$\left.\frac{du}{dx}\right|_{x=0} = a \tag{5.5.5}$$

where a is some assumed constant. Thus with $u(0)$ and $du/dx|_{x=0}$ specified, equation (5.5.3a) may be solved using a multivalue or multistep method over the region $0 < x < 4$. The solution calculated at $x = 4$ is compared with condition (5.5.4) to determine if the solution to the initial value problem is also the solution to the original boundary value problem. If $U(4)$ is not a satisfactory approximation of $u(4)$, a new value of a is selected and the problem is solved again. The second-order equation (5.5.3a) subject to conditions (5.5.3c) and (5.5.5) may be rewritten as two first-order equations:

$$\frac{du}{dx} = \frac{w}{K} \qquad \text{with} \quad u(0) = 0 \tag{5.5.6a}$$

$$\frac{dw}{dx} = 0.1(u)^{0.3} \qquad \text{with} \quad w(0) = K\left.\frac{du}{dx}\right|_{x=0} = Ka \tag{5.5.6b}$$

This system of equations may be solved as described in Section 2.6.5. Solve the problem described as equations (5.5.3) and (5.5.4) by the shooting method and obtain the root mean square error of your solution. Your solution technique should be

(a) Runge-Kutta fourth order

(b) Adams-Moulton four-step method

(c) Gear's four-value method

(d) Adams-Moulton three-value method with predictor-corrector error control

5.12. For the data presented in Example 5.4, make a log-log plot of $\|U(x_i; \delta x_i/m) - U(x_i; \delta x_i/2m)\|_{(i,3)}$ versus $\delta x_i/m$ and determine the value of p from this plot in the limit as $\delta x_i/m$ becomes small. Relate this method of evaluating p to the use of equation (5.1.65) in determining p.

5.13. Program a solution to the problem described in Example 5.4. Produce all the information provided there when quadratic $\mathbb{C}^0$ finite elements are used (rather than the linear ones employed in the example).

5.14. Program a solution to the problem described in Example 5.4, producing similar information, when Hermitian cubic $\mathbb{C}^1$ finite elements are used.

5.15. Program a solution to the problem described in Example 5.5 on a regular grid, producing similar information, using $\mathbb{C}^1$ Hermitian cubic basis functions.

5.16. Consider the following serendipity quadratic quadrilateral grid. The shaded region is to be refined into four quadratic quadrilaterals. This refinement, an h-refinement, requires that neighboring elements also be refined. If all regions are to retain serendipity quadratic interpolation, the enrichment will require addition of quadratic basis functions associated with the open circle positions and with the slave nodes indicated as squares. Note that in contrast to refinement on bilinear elements, as discussed in Section 5.1.4 in conjunction with Figure 5.3, new basis functions added to the grid produce quadratic kinking along the sides of the original elements of the grid.

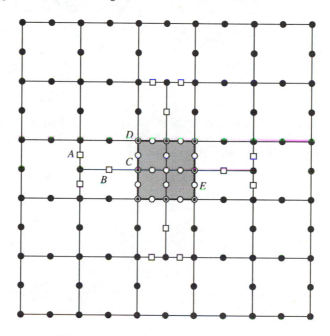

●   Original node

○   Location of h-refinement node

◉   Location of original node most affected by h-refinement

□   Slave node

▨   Element to be refined

Let the interpolation for a function u be approximated using a form

$$u \simeq U = \sum_{j=1}^{N} U_j \phi_j + \sum_{k=N+1}^{M} V_k \omega_k$$

where ϕ_j are the basis functions associated with the original grid, U_j is the approximation to u at node j, ω_k is a refinement basis function, and V_k is a deviation variable. Determine ω_k for nodes A, B, C, D, and E.

5.17. Enrich the following quadratic triangle grid by subdividing the shaded region into four quadratic triangles. Indicate enrichment nodes and slave nodes in adjacent elements such that $\mathbb{C}^0$ continuity is preserved at element boundaries. Provide expressions for typical deviation functions ω_j.

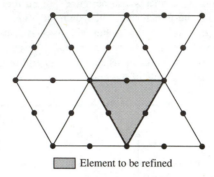

Element to be refined

5.18. Enrich the shaded region in the following grid by subdividing into four linear quadrilaterals. Indicate enrichment nodes and slave nodes that will be needed such that the refinement will be effective and $\mathbb{C}^0$ continuity preserved. Provide expressions for typical deviation functions.

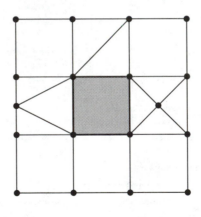

Element to be refined

5.19. In Example 5.6, equations (5.1.94) and (5.1.95) provided approximations to u and $(u)^r$, respectively. Discussion following equation (5.1.75) indicated the need to relate the deviation variables in these two expressions. Consider a single element that extends from x_1 to x_2 such that

$$u \simeq U = U_1 \frac{x_2 - x}{x_2 - x_1} + U_2 \frac{x - x_1}{x_2 - x_1} + \sum_{k=3}^{M} V_k \omega_k(x) \qquad (5.5.7)$$

and

$$(u)^r \simeq \hat{U}^r = (U_1)^r \frac{x_2 - x}{x_2 - x_1} + (U_2)^r \frac{x - x_1}{x_2 - x_1} + \sum_{k=3}^{M} W_k \omega_k(x) \qquad (5.5.8)$$

Examine some constraints that relate W_3 to V_3 when W_k and V_k are zero for $k = 4, \ldots, M$. Note that ω_3 is given by

$$\omega_3 = \frac{x - x_1}{x^* - x_1}, \qquad x_1 \le x \le x^* \qquad (5.5.9a)$$

$$\omega_3 = \frac{x_2 - x}{x_2 - x^*}, \qquad x^* \le x \le x_2 \qquad (5.5.9b)$$

where $x^* = (x_1 + x_2)/2$. Relate W_3 to V_3 as a function of U_1 and U_2 for the following cases and discuss the relative merits of each in light of appropriateness and ease with which it may be applied computationally.

(a) $[U(x^*)]^r = \hat{U}^r(x^*)$

(b) $\int_{x_1}^{x_2} [U]^r \, dx = \int_{x_1}^{x_2} \hat{U}^r \, dx$

(c) $\int_{x_1}^{x_2} U \, dx = \int_{x_1}^{x_2} [\hat{U}^r]^{1/r} \, dx$

(d) $\int_{x_1}^{x_2} U \, \omega_3 \, dx = \int_{x_1}^{x_2} [\hat{U}^r]^{1/r} \omega_3 \, dx$

(e) Postulate a reasonable constraint of your own.

5.20. State conditions under which pairs of constraints given in Problem 5.19 will be identical. (For example, when $r = 1$, all constraints give the same relation between W_3 and V_3.)

5.21. As refinement of the grid proceeds in Problem 5.19, V_4 and W_4 will come into play. Determine appropriate relations between these variables and argue for a computationally convenient form of the approximation.

5.22. Consider a solution to Example 5.6 making use of quadratic basis functions. The implementation of h-refinement thus involves division of a quadratic element into two quadratic elements.

(a) Provide reasonable relationships between V_k and W_k for the first enrichment of an element.

(b) Program a solution which parallels that given in the example.

5.23. The solution presented in Example 5.6 suggests an alternative to equation (5.1.77) may be useful for obtaining a root-mean-square error estimate. In any element i, V_k^{est} for that element is an error estimate of the solution variable. Thus one might propose

$$e_i^{\text{rms}} = \frac{1}{\Omega_i^{1/2}} \| V_k^{\text{est}} \omega_k \|_{\Omega_i}, \qquad i = 1, 2, \ldots, N_e \qquad (5.5.10)$$

(a) What is the detailed expression for

$$e^{\text{rms}} = \frac{1}{\Omega^{1/2}} \| V_k^{\text{est}} \omega_k \|_{\Omega}$$

(the root-mean-square error for the entire domain) in terms of e_i^{rms}?

(b) The problem posed as Example 5.6 was solved using interval halving. Starting with the two-element grid, the values of V_k^{est} obtained are as indicated.

SOLUTION 1

Element location	V_k^{est}
$0 \le x \le 2$	7.1944×10^{-1}
$2 \le x \le 4$	8.0704×10^{-2}

SOLUTION 2

Element location	V_k^{est}
$0 \le x \le 1$	5.5534×10^{-1}
$1 \le x \le 2$	6.4361×10^{-2}
$2 \le x \le 3$	2.3346×10^{-2}
$3 \le x \le 4$	1.1934×10^{-2}

Based on these data, compute an estimate of

$$\|U(x^{mi}; \Delta x/m) - U(x^{2mi}; \Delta x/2m)\|, \qquad m = 1, 2 \tag{5.5.11}$$

(c) If the ratio of the two norms calculated in part (b) is called R, the rate of convergence of this norm is $p = \log_2 R$. Explain the value of p obtained.

(d) Does the proposed norm provide information on the rate of convergence of the solution?

5.24. Solution of equations (5.1.103) for nodal locations requires specification of boundary conditions. Comment on the following statements and provide mathematical justification as needed or appropriate.

(a) Specification of all boundary node locations is necessary.

(b) The conditions on a portion of the boundary

$$\hat{\mathbf{N}} \cdot \hat{\boldsymbol{\nabla}} \mathbf{r} \cdot \hat{\boldsymbol{\Lambda}} = 0 \tag{5.5.12a}$$

and

$$\hat{\boldsymbol{\Lambda}} \cdot \hat{\boldsymbol{\nabla}} \mathbf{r} \cdot \hat{\mathbf{N}} = 0 \tag{5.5.12b}$$

(where $\mathbf{r}$ is the position vector of the boundary of Ω, $\hat{\mathbf{N}}$ is the unit normal to the boudary of $\hat{\Omega}$, and $\hat{\boldsymbol{\Lambda}}$ is the unit tangent to the boundary of $\hat{\Omega}$) assure that the nodes are equispaced on the boundary and that the element sides intersecting the boundary are orthogonal to the boundary.

(c) The solution of the 2N equations (5.1.104b) and (5.1.104c) may be approximated by making the following specifications.

(i) When node i is on the interior of the region, the boundary integral drops out.

(ii) For a smooth segment of the boundary, fix the position of nodes at the end of the segment and prescribe the number of nodes that will lie on the boundary. Use the equation of the boundary to relate y_i to x_i. Another equation for each boundary node along the segment is obtained by multiplying equation (5.1.104b) by α_i and equation (5.1.104c) by β_i and adding the two equations to obtain

$$\sum_{j=1}^{N} \int_{\hat{\Omega}} (w_1 \alpha_i x_j + w_2 \beta_i y_i)(\hat{\boldsymbol{\nabla}} \phi_j \cdot \hat{\boldsymbol{\nabla}} \phi_i)\, d\hat{\Omega}$$

$$+ \int_{\hat{\Gamma}} (w_1 \alpha_i \hat{\mathbf{N}} \cdot \hat{\boldsymbol{\nabla}} x + w_2 \beta_i \hat{\mathbf{N}} \cdot \hat{\boldsymbol{\nabla}} y)\phi_i\, d\hat{\Gamma} = 0 \qquad (5.5.13)$$

Then if α_i and β_i are chosen for each node i so that $w_1 \alpha_i \hat{\mathbf{i}} + w_2 \beta_i \hat{\mathbf{j}} \simeq \hat{\boldsymbol{\Lambda}}_i$, where $\hat{\mathbf{i}}$ and $\hat{\mathbf{j}}$ are unit vectors in $\mathbf{X}$, the integral over $\hat{\Gamma}$ may be neglected since the portion of the integrand in parentheses is an approximation to $\hat{\mathbf{N}} \cdot \hat{\boldsymbol{\nabla}} \mathbf{r} \cdot \hat{\boldsymbol{\Lambda}}$ which is zero along the boundary.

Equation (5.5.13) for node i on the boundary (with the integral over $\hat{\Gamma}$ neglected) in conjunction with the equation for the boundary curve and equations (5.1.104b) and (5.1.104c) for node i on the interior may now be solved to obtain an optimal grid.

5.25. In order to understand the manipulations involved in Example 5.7, determine an optimal three-node grid for the problem studied there.

    (a) Let the initial grid have nodes at $x = \{0, 2, 4\}$ such that the end nodes are fixed but the interior node will be allowed to move.

    (b) The discussion of solution of this problem for a fixed grid in Example 5.4 will provide guidance for obtaining the solution $U(2) = 2.9668$.

    (c) Next calculate V_1^{est} from equation (5.1.92) when V_2^{est} is required to be zero and then calculate V_2^{est} from the same equation when V_1^{est} is set to zero.

    (d) Let the weighting function for nodal movement be given by equation (5.1.108) such that for each element, e,

$$w_1\big|_e = \frac{1}{L_e} \left[V_e^{\text{est}} \omega_e(x) \right]^2 \qquad (5.5.14)$$

    where L_e is the length of the element and ω_e is the deviation function associated with V_e^{est}.

    (e) Use the one-dimensional analog to equation (5.1.104b) to obtain

$$\sum_{j=1}^{3} \int_0^4 w_1 x_j \frac{d\phi_j}{dX} \frac{d\phi_2}{dX}\, dX = 0 \qquad (5.5.15)$$

    and solve this equation for x_2.

    (f) Use the new value of x_2 and return to part (b) to solve the differential equation for $U(x_2)$ and proceed through step (f) until the value of x_2 used in (b) is approximately the same as that calculated in part (e).

    (g) Note that when the x value converges, V_i^{est} will be the same for both elements. Also note that the solution obtained in part (b) is the solution for the nodal configuration used. Further calculations try to obtain a better solution by using a different x_2 location. Thus use of a suboptimal node position may still provide reasonable results.

5.26. For a regular grid with $\Delta x = \Delta y = h$, show that the approximation to $\nabla^2 u = 0$, where ∇^2 is the two-dimensional Laplacian operator, given by equation (5.2.11) has a fourth-order truncation error as given by equation (5.2.12).

5.27. For the grid of Figure 5.9a, derive finite difference approximations to the two-dimensional equation $\nabla^2 u = 0$ using the techniques described in Section 2.7.

    (a) For the node at $(1, 0.5)$ derive a centered approximation that is $\mathcal{O}[(\Delta x)^4 + (\Delta y)^2]$.

(b) For the node at $(0.5, 1)$ derive a centered approximation that is $\mathcal{O}[(\Delta x)^2 + (\Delta y)^4]$.

5.28. With respect to Example 5.7, determine the number of nonzero entries in the coefficient matrix formed to solve the problem by case I, case II, and case III, respectively.

5.29. The discussion following Example 5.9 alluded to the solution to the following equation.

$$\frac{d^2 u}{dx^2} = u, \qquad 0 < x < 4 \tag{5.5.16a}$$

$$u(0) = 0 \tag{5.5.16b}$$

$$u(4) = 4 \tag{5.5.16c}$$

The statement is made that as the mesh was refined using interval halving, the order of convergence was 2, 4, or 6, depending on whether linear, quadratic, or cubic basis functions, respectively, were used. This result was obtained by considering a discrete L_2 norm that used only the solution at the nodes.

(a) Formulate a quadratic finite element solution to equation (5.5.16) and use the method of interval halving to examine the rate of convergence of the solution at an arbitrary point in the domain.

(b) Repeat part (a) using cubic elements.

The higher rate of convergence obtained at the nodes on interelement boundaries is called *superconvergence*.

5.30. Find the maximum of the basis functions defined in equations (5.2.21). Show that in the limit of large k, the maximum value of $\omega_{5,k}(\xi, \eta)$ is $1/k!$ for both even and odd k.

5.31. Obtain equation (5.2.29b) by requiring $W_{e,3} = 0$ when $V_{e,3} = 0$ and $d\hat{U}^r/dx$ to be proportional to dU/dx at the center of an element.

5.32. Obtain equation (5.2.29c) by requiring $W_{e,4} = 0$ when $V_{e,4} = 0$ and also requiring $\hat{U}^r$ to be proportional to U at the center of the element.

5.33. Propose alternative (and hopefully more accurate) approximations to relations (5.2.29). Also develop criteria for conditions where (5.2.29) are reasonable approximations.

5.34. Consider a linear one-dimensional finite element with nodes at x_1 and x_2. This element is to be refined using a mix of p-convergence and h-convergence techniques. It is desirable to include mesh refinement in a hierarchicial fashion such that each interpolation function added accounts for a correction to the previous system. Let the approximation over the element of a function u be

$$u \simeq U = \sum_{j=1}^{2} U_j \phi_j + \sum_{k=3}^{M} V_k \omega_k \tag{5.5.17}$$

where ϕ_j's are the linear basis functions, U_j is the values of U at node j, ω_k is a deviation function, and V_k is a deviation coefficient. Determine ω_k and provide an interpretation of V_k for each of the following refinement strategies.

(a) Start with the linear interpolation. The first refinement (for ω_3) is of the h-type, which keeps interpolation over the element piecewise linear but allows a kink at $(x_1 + x_2)/2$. The next refinement (for ω_4) introduces quadratic interpolation over the range $x_1 \leq x \leq (x_1 + x_2)/2$. The final refinement (using ω_5) introduces quadratic interpolation over the range $(x_1 + x_2)/2 \leq x \leq x_2$.

(b) Start with linear interpolation. The first refinement (using w_3) is of p-type and provides quadratic interpolation over the range $x_1 \leq x \leq x_2$. The second refinement introduces an h-type piecewise linear kink at $(x_1 + x_2)/2$. The final refinement (using w_5) allows the interpolation to contain an h-type quadratic kink at $x = (x_1 + x_2)/2$.

(c) Are the interpolations in parts (a) and (b) different?

5.35. Piecewise linear interpolation is being used on a one-dimensional grid. A p-refinement of the mesh is proposed by which one cubic deviation function is added to each element. Determine the form of a typical deviation function. May the quadratic refinement be bypassed?

5.36. A one-dimensional element makes use of three quadratic basis functions. Is it possible to add a deviation function or functions to this element so that the net interpolation order is reduced to linear? If so, find the appropriate deviation function(s)? Is there a way to achieve this result without adding a deviation function?

5.37. It is desired to use h-refinement with Hermitian cubics such that the $\mathbb{C}^1$ continuity of the basis functions is preserved. Determine the deviation functions for a one-dimensional element.

5.38. It is desired to use p-refinement with Hermitian cubics such that the $\mathbb{C}^1$ continuity of the basis functions is preserved. Determine the deviation functions for a one-dimensional element.

5.39. It is desired to model the concentration profile of a contaminant in a fluid flowing in a converging pipe with cross-sectional area $A(x)$, where x is the position along the axis of the tube. The fluid is incompressible so that wA is independent of x (but not necessarily time), where w is the average axial velocity of the fluid. The equation that governs the contaminant motion is

$$\frac{\partial cA}{\partial t} + \frac{\partial wAc}{\partial x} = \frac{\partial}{\partial x}\left(\mathcal{D}A\frac{\partial c}{\partial x}\right) \tag{5.5.18a}$$

where $\mathcal{D}$ is the dispersion coefficient and $c(x, t)$ is the concentration of contaminant. The boundary and initial conditions imposed on this problem are

$$c(0, t) = f(t) \tag{5.5.18b}$$

$$\frac{\partial c(L, t)}{\partial x} = 0.0 \tag{5.5.18c}$$

$$c(x, 0) = 0.0 \tag{5.5.18d}$$

(a) Assume that an algorithm can be developed which allows nodes to enter and leave the system. Determine a form for $\mathbf{V}^{\text{nodes}}$ in equation (5.3.9) that is convenient for a moving-grid solution.

(b) In this case, will the nodes ever cross?

(c) If the computer algorithm developed does not allow nodes to enter or leave the system, suggest criteria for obtaining a time-dependent optimal grid and comment on any complications that these criteria present which were not present in your answer to part (a).

5.40. Determine a form analogous to equation (5.3.9) for $\partial^2 U/\partial t^2$.

5.41. Formulate a solution to the following diffusion problem making use of moving-node concepts:

$$\frac{\partial u}{\partial t} = \frac{\partial}{\partial x}\left(K\frac{\partial u}{\partial x}\right), \qquad \begin{matrix} t > 0 \\ 0 < x < 4 \end{matrix} \tag{5.5.19}$$

where $K = 0.1 + 5x$. Use a three-node grid (i.e., two finite elements) and linear basis functions. Let the initial and boundary conditions for the problem be

$$u(0, t) = 0.0 \tag{5.5.20a}$$

$$u(4, t) = 4.0 \tag{5.5.20b}$$

$$u(x, 0) = 0.0 \tag{5.5.20c}$$

Let the equation for nodal positions be the one-dimensional form of equation (5.1.103a):

$$\frac{\partial}{\partial X}\left(w_1 \frac{\partial x}{\partial X}\right) = 0 \tag{5.5.21}$$

where w_1 is given by equation (5.1.109):

$$w_1 = \frac{1}{\Omega_e}(U^{\text{est}} - U)^2 \tag{5.5.22}$$

and the two end nodes are first at $x = 0$ and $x = 4$. Let U^{est} be calculated using the concepts of h- or p-convergence (i.e., projected if the element is allowed to kink or is enriched with a quadratic interpolant).

(a) Determine a reasonable initial time step size.
(b) Calculate the solution (i.e., location of the internal node and estimate of u at that node) for five time steps.
(c) Provide arguments that justify your selection of an initial grid configuration.

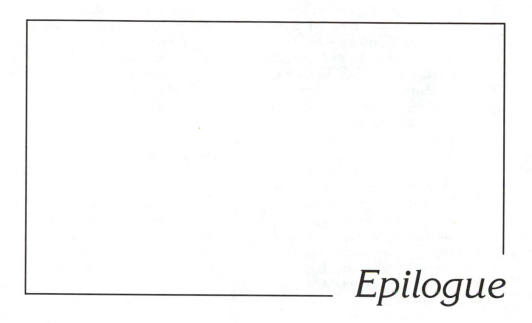

Epilogue

One usually reaches the end of a text with a sense of relief and of accomplishment. The authors of this text hope that such a sense is gained by the reader of the current book who has studied the material and worked through the problems. However, we also hope that the reader will have a sense of having only been introduced to the topics treated in the various chapters. The field of numerical methods and numerical simulation is vast, and the serious student should appreciate that expanse.

In hindsight, the book may be seen to treat three different topics: characteristics and boundary conditions in Chapter 1, approximation procedures in Chapters 2 and 3, and analysis of solutions obtained in Chapters 4 and 5. In Chapter 1, characteristics and their utility in determining boundary conditions were introduced. The concept of secondary characteristics was also presented to help explain that classification of a partial differential equation does not necessarily provide sufficient information to decide on an appropriate solution algorithm, nor is classification sufficient to completely understand the behavior of the physical processes described by the equation. The material presented was limited to relatively simple cases designed to provide both understanding and the ability to delve further into more complex topics such as nonlinear waves and shock fronts.

Chapter 2 presented finite difference formulas as sets of approximations that are systematically derived from Taylor series expansions. Emphasis was on the common origin of such formulas rather than the particular advantages of certain specific difference representations. Chapter 3 considered the finite element method in a weighted residuals context, within which approximations were derived from polynomial interpolations. By comparing and contrasting the features of finite difference and finite element formulas of Chapters 2 and 3, the reader may come to an understanding that these are not two totally different methods but rather are approximation approaches that share many common features. An appreciation of this commonality is very helpful in placing specific numerical approximations into the broader context of general numerical methods.

Chapter 4 demonstrated the value of applying analytical methods in the context of relatively simple problems in order to gain quantitative insight into the behavior of numerical schemes. Examples were presented to illustrate potential shortcomings of various numerical approximations, even when applied to simple problems, and to motivate the concept of designing a grid and an approximation to suit the particular problem under study. Analytical techniques, specifically truncation error analysis and Fourier analysis, were also used to explain much of the numerical difficulties encountered. Chapter 5 addressed the ultimate question raised in numerical computation: How good is the approximate solution? The material in this chapter provides some of the ways of obtaining improved solutions and estimating the order of accuracy of the approximate solution when the actual solution is unknown.

After reading these five chapters, and especially working the problems at the ends of the chapters, the reader will have gained an understanding of some of the fundamental principles which must be kept in mind when performing a simulation of an actual system of interest. However, this book alone is not sufficient to allow a reader to become an expert at actually developing such simulations. Specialized work in modeling requires an understanding of the physical system under study, knowledge of the relevant literature in that particular area so that previously developed numerical techniques may be identified, and understanding and exploitation of the capabilities of the specific computer to be used in the simulation. In all three of these areas, advances occur very rapidly. The material presented in this book is not intended to keep pace or even be concerned with these advances. Rather the material provides fundamental techniques and information that are necessary in any simulation effort and are applicable regardless of the technological advances that occur.

This Epilogue, then, might be more appropriately titled Interlude. It is a cautionary statement warning the reader not to overestimate the knowledge gained from this book. It is also a launching statement encouraging the reader into the references and journals listed in Appendix C to obtain information developed for specific problem types. It is hoped that the material in this book will provide the foundation upon which the reader may develop an interest in and understanding of numerical models, which are increasingly important tools for technological advancement.

Appendix A

Fundamental Concepts of Linear Algebra

A.0 INTRODUCTION

Linear algebra is fundamental to the study of numerical methods and is used throughout this textbook. The field of linear algebra covers a spectrum of topics, ranging from standard matrix equations and Euclidean spaces to more abstract function spaces and application to differential equations. This appendix presents fundamental concepts that underlie the subject of linear algebra.

The presentation begins by reviewing the basic concepts related to solution of systems of linear algebraic equations. Vectors, matrices, matrix algebra, determinants, and existence and uniqueness of solutions to systems of linear algebraic equations are discussed. Next, the definition of linear algebra is expanded, beginning with the formal definition of a linear vector space. The fundamentally important concepts of linear independence, generating sets, and basis vectors are discussed. Examples are provided that include the cases of standard finite-dimensional Euclidean spaces as well as more general function spaces. Finally, the notion of linear operators and general mappings is presented. Examples range from simple matrix equations to partial differential equations. The appendix closes with a discussion of eigenvalues and eigenvectors in the context of both algebraic and differential equations.

A.1 SYSTEMS OF LINEAR EQUATIONS

A system of linear equations consists of a number of equations (say, m equations) that are written in terms of a set of unknowns (say, n unknowns). All unknowns appearing in the equations are raised to the first power only. The determination of the n unknowns is usually the desired goal.

A generic set of linear algebraic equations may be written as

$$
\begin{aligned}
\alpha_{11}U_1 + \alpha_{12}U_2 + \cdots + \alpha_{1n}U_n &= \beta_1 \\
\alpha_{21}U_1 + \alpha_{22}U_2 + \cdots + \alpha_{2n}U_n &= \beta_2 \\
\vdots \qquad \vdots \qquad\qquad \vdots \qquad\ \ \vdots& \\
\alpha_{m1}U_1 + \alpha_{m2}U_2 + \cdots + \alpha_{mn}U_n &= \beta_m
\end{aligned}
\tag{A.1.1}
$$

where α_{ij} and $\beta_i (i = 1, 2, \ldots, m; \ j = 1, 2, \ldots, n)$ are known real numbers, and $U_j (j = 1, 2, \ldots, n)$ are the unknowns that are to be determined. A standard shorthand representation of equation (A.1.1) is

$$
\mathbf{A} \cdot \mathbf{u} = \mathbf{b} \tag{A.1.2}
$$

where $\mathbf{A}$ represents an $m \times n$ array of real numbers and is called a *matrix*. The array representation is

$$
\mathbf{A} =
\begin{bmatrix}
\alpha_{11} & \alpha_{12} & \cdots & \alpha_{1n} \\
\alpha_{21} & \alpha_{22} & \cdots & \alpha_{2n} \\
\vdots & \vdots & & \vdots \\
\alpha_{m1} & \alpha_{m2} & \cdots & \alpha_{mn}
\end{bmatrix}
= [\alpha_{ij}]
\tag{A.1.3}
$$

Similarly, $\mathbf{u}$ is an $n \times 1$ matrix and $\mathbf{b}$ an $m \times 1$ matrix,

$$
\mathbf{u} =
\begin{bmatrix}
U_1 \\
U_2 \\
\vdots \\
U_n
\end{bmatrix},
\qquad
\mathbf{b} =
\begin{bmatrix}
\beta_1 \\
\beta_2 \\
\vdots \\
\beta_m
\end{bmatrix}
\tag{A.1.4}
$$

The bold upper case notation indicates a matrix, while a bold lower case character refers to the special matrix that has only one column, that being referred to as a *vector*. Thus $\mathbf{u}$ and $\mathbf{b}$ are vectors. Equation (A.1.2) is the standard matrix equation that represents general systems of linear algebraic equations.

A.1.1 Matrices

An $m \times n$ matrix is defined as an ordered array of real numbers having m rows and n columns. Examples are given by equations (A.1.3) and (A.1.4). Certain matrices possess special properties and are thereby called by special names. For example, equations (A.1.4) contain special matrices that have only one column. These matrices are called vectors (or *column vectors*). Similarly, matrices with only one row are called *row vectors*. There follows a list of other special matrices, defined in terms of the general matrix $\mathbf{A}(m \times n)$.

Square matrix	$m = n$
Identity matrix ($\mathbf{I}$)	$\alpha_{ii} = 1, \quad \alpha_{ij} = 0 \,(i \neq j), \quad m = n$
Zero or null matrix ($\mathbf{0}$)	$\alpha_{ij} = 0, \quad i = 1, 2, \ldots, m; \quad j = 1, 2, \ldots, n$
Symmetric matrix	$\alpha_{ij} = \alpha_{ji}, \quad m = n$
Skew-symmetric matrix	$\alpha_{ij} = -\alpha_{ji}, \quad m = n$
Upper triangular matrix	$\alpha_{ij} = 0, \quad i > j$
Lower triangular matrix	$\alpha_{ij} = 0, \quad j > i$

The symbol α_{ij} represents the entry in the ith row and jth column of the matrix $\mathbf{A}$.

Arithmetic operations can be defined for matrices, just as they are for real numbers. To define these operations, consider the two matrices $\mathbf{A}(m \times n)$ and $\mathbf{M}(p \times q)$, with $\mathbf{A} = [\alpha_{ij}]$, $\mathbf{M} = [\mu_{ij}]$. Matrix addition is defined by

$$\mathbf{H} = [\eta_{ij}] = \mathbf{A} + \mathbf{M} \tag{A.1.5a}$$

$$\eta_{ij} = \alpha_{ij} + \mu_{ij} \tag{A.1.5b}$$

where η_{ij} and μ_{ij} are the entries in row i and column j of the matrices $\mathbf{H}$ and $\mathbf{M}$, respectively. For matrix addition to be a meaningful operation, the matrices $\mathbf{A}$ and $\mathbf{M}$ must be the same size ($m = p$ and $n = q$). The resulting matrix $\mathbf{H}$ is also of size $m \times n$. Scalar multiplication of a matrix results when each entry is multiplied by a given scalar. Symbolically, this is represented by

$$\mathbf{M} = \theta \mathbf{A} \tag{A.1.6a}$$

$$\mu_{ij} = \theta \alpha_{ij}, \qquad \theta \text{ scalar} \tag{A.1.6b}$$

In addition to scalar multiplication, matrices can sometimes multiply one another. Matrix multiplication of two matrices $\mathbf{A}(m \times n)$ and $\mathbf{M}(p \times q)$ is defined by

$$\mathbf{H} = \mathbf{A} \cdot \mathbf{M} \tag{A.1.7a}$$

$$\eta_{ij} = \sum_{k=1}^{n} \alpha_{ik} \mu_{kj} \tag{A.1.7b}$$

For matrix multiplication to be meaningful, it is required that $n = p$. That is, the number of columns in $\mathbf{A}$ must be the same as the number of rows in $\mathbf{M}$. The resulting matrix $\mathbf{H}$ is $(m \times p)$. Notice that equation (A.1.2) contains a very common example of matrix multiplication, with $\mathbf{A}$ being $(m \times n)$, $\mathbf{u}(n \times 1)$, and $\mathbf{b}(m \times 1)$. Using the definition of equations (A.1.7), it can be shown that matrix multiplication is both associative and distributive, but it is *not* commutative. For $\mathbf{A}$, $\mathbf{M}$, and $\mathbf{H}$, each $(n \times n)$,

$$\mathbf{A} \cdot (\mathbf{H} \cdot \mathbf{M}) = (\mathbf{A} \cdot \mathbf{H}) \cdot \mathbf{M}$$

$$\mathbf{A} \cdot (\mathbf{H} + \mathbf{M}) = \mathbf{A} \cdot \mathbf{H} + \mathbf{A} \cdot \mathbf{M} \tag{A.1.8}$$

$$\mathbf{A} \cdot \mathbf{M} \neq \mathbf{M} \cdot \mathbf{A}$$

Finally, the following matrices, derived from the general square matrix $\mathbf{A}(n \times n)$, are defined.

1. Transpose of $\mathbf{A} \equiv \mathbf{A}^T$:

$$\alpha_{ij}^T = \alpha_{ji} \tag{A.1.9a}$$

2. Inverse of $\mathbf{A} \equiv \mathbf{A}^{-1}$:

$$\mathbf{A} \cdot \mathbf{A}^{-1} = \mathbf{A}^{-1} \cdot \mathbf{A} = \mathbf{I} \tag{A.1.9b}$$

where $\mathbf{I}$ is the identity matrix.

With these definitions, a number of fundamental properties can be proven. For example:

1. $(\mathbf{A}^T)^T = \mathbf{A}$
2. $\mathbf{A} \cdot \mathbf{I} = \mathbf{I} \cdot \mathbf{A} = \mathbf{A}$
3. $(\mathbf{A} \cdot \mathbf{M})^T = \mathbf{M}^T \cdot \mathbf{A}^T$
4. $(\mathbf{A} \cdot \mathbf{M})^{-1} = \mathbf{M}^{-1} \cdot \mathbf{A}^{-1}$
5. $(\mathbf{A} \cdot \mathbf{A}^T)^T = \mathbf{A} \cdot \mathbf{A}^T$ (the matrix $\mathbf{A} \cdot \mathbf{A}^T$ is symmetric)
6. $(\mathbf{A} \pm \mathbf{A}^T)^T = \pm(\mathbf{A} \pm \mathbf{A}^T)$ [the matrix $(\mathbf{A} + \mathbf{A}^T)$ is symmetric; the matrix $(\mathbf{A} - \mathbf{A}^T)$ is skew-symmetric]
7. $(\mathbf{A} \pm \mathbf{M})^T = \mathbf{A}^T \pm \mathbf{M}^T$

Example A.1

     Problem   Prove that $(\mathbf{A} \cdot \mathbf{M})^T = \mathbf{M}^T \cdot \mathbf{A}^T$.

     Solution   Let $\mathbf{H} \equiv \mathbf{A} \cdot \mathbf{M}$. Then $\eta_{ij} = \sum_{k=1}^{n} \alpha_{ik}\mu_{kj}$. Let $\mathbf{H}^T = (\mathbf{A} \cdot \mathbf{M})^T \equiv \mathbf{L} = [\lambda_{ij}]$. Then $\lambda_{ij} = \eta_{ji}^T = \sum_{k=1}^{n} \alpha_{jk}\mu_{ki}$. Finally, let $\mathbf{G} \equiv \mathbf{M}^T \cdot \mathbf{A}^T$. Then

$$\gamma_{ij} = \sum_{k=1}^{n} \mu_{ik}^T \alpha_{kj}^T = \sum_{k=1}^{n} \mu_{ki} a_{jk} = \sum_{k=1}^{n} a_{jk}\mu_{ki} = \lambda_{ij}$$

Thus $\gamma_{ij} = \lambda_{ij}$, so that $(\mathbf{A} \cdot \mathbf{M})^T = \mathbf{M}^T \cdot \mathbf{A}^T$.

A.1.2 Determinants

The determinant of a square matrix $\mathbf{A}(n \times n)$ is a scalar that is defined in terms of the entries of the matrix. This scalar value characterizes a matrix and plays an important role in the analysis of linear systems. Determinants appear throughout this appendix and in many parts of the main text.

     Before defining the determinant, two preliminary definitions are needed. Consider the square matrix $\mathbf{A}(n \times n)$. The minor matrix $\mathbf{M}_{ij}$, associated with the element α_{ij} of matrix **A**, is the $(n-1) \times (n-1)$ matrix that results from deletion of row i and column j from the original matrix **A**. The associated cofactor matrix is defined by the following scalar multiplication:

$$\mathbf{C}_{ij} \equiv (-1)^{i+j} \mathbf{M}_{ij} \qquad (A.1.10)$$

Given these definitions, the determinant of $\mathbf{A}(n \times n)$ is defined as follows:

> **Definition A.1.1: Determinant.**   The *determinant* of **A**, denoted by det **A** or $|\mathbf{A}|$, is a scalar that is equal to the sum of the products of each element in any row (or column) and the determinant of that element's cofactor matrix. The determinant of a 1×1 matrix is defined as the element of the matrix.

Computationally, the determinant is derived by successively reducing the size of the submatrices involved in the cofactors until a 1×1 matrix is reached. Since the determinant of a 1×1 matrix is just equal to the entry of that matrix, at this point the actual value of the determinant of the original matrix can be computed algebraically. The procedure is illustrated in the following examples.

Example A.2

   Problem   Derive the algebraic formula for the determinant of a 2×2 matrix.

   Solution   The determinant of the general 2×2 matrix **A** is denoted by

$$\det \mathbf{A} = |\mathbf{A}| = \begin{vmatrix} \alpha_{11} & \alpha_{12} \\ \alpha_{21} & \alpha_{22} \end{vmatrix}$$

Formation of the cofactor matrices as per the definition of the determinant, and subsequent addition of the products of $|\mathbf{C}_{ij}|$ and matrix entry α_{ij}, along one row or column (the choice is arbitrary; in what follows, the first column is chosen), produces

$$|\mathbf{A}| = \alpha_{11}(-1)^2 \det [\alpha_{22}] + \alpha_{21}(-1)^3 \det [\alpha_{12}]$$

$$= \alpha_{11}\alpha_{22} - \alpha_{12}\alpha_{21}$$

Since all determinants in this equation involve only 1×1 matrices, which are simply equal to the matrix entry, $|\mathbf{A}|$ can be written algebraically as shown. Notice that choice of any other row or column along which to perform the expansion produces the same result, as can be verified by simple calculation.

Example A.3

   Problem   Derive the algebraic formula for the determinant of a 3×3 matrix.

   Solution   For $\mathbf{A}(3 \times 3)$, the relevant formula is obtained as follows, using expansion about the first row.

$$\det \mathbf{A} = \begin{vmatrix} \alpha_{11} & \alpha_{12} & \alpha_{13} \\ \alpha_{21} & \alpha_{22} & \alpha_{23} \\ \alpha_{31} & \alpha_{32} & \alpha_{33} \end{vmatrix} = \alpha_{11}(-1)^2 \begin{vmatrix} \alpha_{22} & \alpha_{23} \\ \alpha_{32} & \alpha_{33} \end{vmatrix}$$

$$+ \alpha_{12}(-1)^3 \begin{vmatrix} \alpha_{21} & \alpha_{23} \\ \alpha_{31} & \alpha_{33} \end{vmatrix} + \alpha_{13}(-1)^4 \begin{vmatrix} \alpha_{21} & \alpha_{22} \\ \alpha_{31} & \alpha_{32} \end{vmatrix}$$

$$= \alpha_{11}(\alpha_{22}\alpha_{33} - \alpha_{23}\alpha_{32}) - \alpha_{12}(\alpha_{21}\alpha_{33} - \alpha_{31}\alpha_{23})$$

$$+ \alpha_{13}(\alpha_{21}\alpha_{32} - \alpha_{22}\alpha_{31})$$

Example A.4

Problem   Find the determinant of the following matrix:

$$\mathbf{A} = \begin{bmatrix} 5 & 3 & 9 & 7 \\ 0 & 1 & 10 & 2 \\ 0 & 0 & 2 & 0 \\ 0 & 0 & 0 & 2 \end{bmatrix}$$

Solution   The definition of the determinant allows for choice of any row or column for the expansion in minors. It is usually convenient to choose the row or column that has the most zero entries, since this minimizes computation. Therefore, the first column of **A** is chosen for the expansion. This choice leads directly to the result,

$$|\mathbf{A}| = 5 \cdot 1 \cdot 2 \cdot 2 = 20$$

This example illustrates the fact that the determinant of triangular matrices (upper or lower) is simply the product of the entries along the main diagonal.

Determinants, like matrices, conform to a variety of rules. Several of the more important ones are listed below, for the determinant of the general matrix $\mathbf{A}(n \times n)$.

1. If all elements of any row or column of **A** are zero, then the determinant of **A** is zero, $\det \mathbf{A} = 0$.
2. The determinant of the transpose of **A** is equal to the determinant of **A**, $\det(\mathbf{A}^T) = \det(\mathbf{A})$.
3. If two rows (or two columns) of **A** are interchanged, then the sign of $\det \mathbf{A}$ is changed, although the magnitude is unaffected.
4. If all elements of one row (or one column) are multiplied by a constant k, the determinant is multiplied by the same factor k.
5. If corresponding elements of two rows (or two columns) are equal or in a constant ratio, then $\det \mathbf{A} = 0$.
6. If k times the elements of one row (column) are added to the corresponding elements of any other row (column), the determinant is unchanged.

One of the major roles that determinants play is determination of whether or not a general set of linear algebraic equations, such as equation (A.1.2), possesses a solution. Existence and uniqueness of solutions are the next topics.

A.1.3 Solution of Linear Algebraic Equations

A large number of techniques exist for the solution of the system of linear algebraic equations

$$\mathbf{A} \cdot \mathbf{u} = \mathbf{b} \tag{A.1.11}$$

Some of these techniques are reviewed in the references listed in Appendix C. The present discussion addresses the question of whether a solution to equation (A.1.11) exists and, if so, whether the solution is unique.

Existence and uniqueness of a solution for $\mathbf{u}$ in equation (A.1.11) can be determined by using a property known as the rank of a matrix.

> **Definition A.1.2: Rank.**   The *rank* of an $(m \times n)$ matrix $\mathbf{A}$, denoted by Rank($\mathbf{A}$), is the number of rows or columns (r) in the largest square submatrix $\mathbf{A}'(r \times r)$, formed from the original matrix $\mathbf{A}$ by deleting rows and/or columns, that possesses a nonzero determinant.

An immediate consequence of this definition is that the rank of a nonsquare matrix $\mathbf{A}(m \times n)$ is, at most, the smaller of the number of rows (m) and the number of columns (n). Furthermore, the rank of a square matrix $\mathbf{A}(n \times n)$ is always less than or equal to n.

Example A.5

   Problem   Determine the rank of the following matrix:

$$\mathbf{A} = \begin{bmatrix} 1 & 2 & 3 \\ 2 & 4 & 6 \\ 1 & 0 & 0 \end{bmatrix}$$

   Solution   Since det $\mathbf{A} = 0$, Rank($\mathbf{A}$) cannot equal 3. If a 2×2 submatrix can be found such that its determinant is nonzero, then Rank($\mathbf{A}$) = 2. This is easily constructed as the lower left 2×2 submatrix (delete the first row and third column of $\mathbf{A}$); that is, $\mathbf{A}' = \begin{bmatrix} 2 & 4 \\ 1 & 0 \end{bmatrix}$, so that det($\mathbf{A}'$) = $-4 \neq 0$. Thus Rank($\mathbf{A}$) = 2. Notice that not every 2×2 submatrix of $\mathbf{A}$ possesses a nonzero determinant. For example, the upper right submatrix, $\begin{bmatrix} 2 & 3 \\ 4 & 6 \end{bmatrix}$, has a zero determinant, as does the lower right submatrix $\begin{bmatrix} 4 & 6 \\ 0 & 0 \end{bmatrix}$. The definition of rank does not require every $(r \times r)$ submatrix to have a nonzero determinant; only one such submatrix must possess a nonvanishing determinant.

Existence of a solution to equation (A.1.11) depends on the rank of $\mathbf{A}$ and also on the rank of the associated augmented matrix, which is defined as follows.

> **Definition A.1.3: Augmented Matrix.**   The *augmented matrix* associated with the matrix equation $\mathbf{A} \cdot \mathbf{u} = \mathbf{b}$, denoted by $\mathbf{A;b}$, is the $(m \times (n+1))$ matrix formed by adding an additional column to the matrix $\mathbf{A}$, that column being the right-side vector $\mathbf{b}$. The vector $\mathbf{b}$ is placed in the $(n+1)$st column.

With this definition in hand, the following fundamental theorem can be stated for general linear algebraic systems.

> **Theorem A.1.1.** For the system of linear algebraic equations $\mathbf{A} \cdot \mathbf{u} = \mathbf{b}$, with $\mathbf{A}(m \times n)$, $\mathbf{u}(n \times 1)$, and $\mathbf{b}(m \times 1)$, a solution for $\mathbf{u}$ exists if and only if the rank of the coefficient matrix $\mathbf{A}$ is equal to the rank of the augmented matrix $\mathbf{A};\mathbf{b}$. One and only one solution exists—that is, the solution is unique—if and only if the rank of both the coefficient matrix $\mathbf{A}$ and the augmented matrix $\mathbf{A};\mathbf{b}$ are equal to n, the number of entries in the unknown vector. Thus:
>
> Existence of a solution: $\text{Rank}(\mathbf{A}) = \text{Rank}(\mathbf{A};\mathbf{b})$
> Uniqueness of the solution: $\text{Rank}(\mathbf{A}) = \text{Rank}(\mathbf{A};\mathbf{b}) = n$

A large number of conclusions follow directly from this very important theorem. Four of the more important ones are stated as corollaries.

> **Corollary A.1.1.1.** For the square matrix $\mathbf{A}(n \times n)$, a unique solution to the system $\mathbf{A} \cdot \mathbf{u} = \mathbf{b}$ exists if and only if $\det \mathbf{A} \neq 0$.

This corollary follows from the definition of rank and is a fundamentally important result in the solution of linear algebraic systems.

> **Corollary A.1.1.2.** For the homogeneous equation $\mathbf{A} \cdot \mathbf{u} = \mathbf{0}$, existence of a unique solution implies that $\mathbf{u}$ must equal the zero, or null, vector.

> **Corollary A.1.1.3.** For the system of equations $\mathbf{A} \cdot \mathbf{u} = \mathbf{b}$, $\mathbf{A}(m \times n)$, $\mathbf{u}(n \times 1)$, $\mathbf{b}(m \times 1)$, if $\text{Rank}(\mathbf{A}) = \text{Rank}(\mathbf{A};\mathbf{b}) = r$, and if r is less than n, then an infinite number of solutions exist for the unknown $\mathbf{u}$. These solutions can be represented by an $(n - r)$-parameter family of vectors.

> **Corollary A.1.1.4.** If the number of unknowns, n, is larger than the number of equations, m, a unique solution for $\mathbf{u}$ cannot exist.

Some of these principles are illustrated in the following examples.

Example A.6

   Problem   Determine existence and uniqueness of solution for the following system:

$$\begin{bmatrix} 1 & 2 \\ 2 & 4 \\ 1 & 3 \end{bmatrix} \begin{bmatrix} U_1 \\ U_2 \end{bmatrix} = \begin{bmatrix} 3 \\ 6 \\ 4 \end{bmatrix}$$

   Solution $\mathbf{A}$ is (3×2), so that $m = 3$ and $n = 2$. $\text{Rank}(\mathbf{A}) = 2$. $\text{Rank}(\mathbf{A};\mathbf{b}) = 2$. Since $\text{Rank}(\mathbf{A}) = \text{Rank}(\mathbf{A};\mathbf{b})$, a solution must exist. Since these ranks are the same as n, a unique solution must exist. In fact, the (unique) solution is given by $U_1 = 1$, $U_2 = 1$.

Example A.7

Problem   Determine the existence and uniqueness of the solution for

$$\begin{bmatrix} 1 & 2 \\ 2 & 4 \end{bmatrix} \begin{bmatrix} U_1 \\ U_2 \end{bmatrix} = \begin{bmatrix} 3 \\ 6 \end{bmatrix}$$

Solution   Definition of **A**, **u**, and **b** as the coefficient matrix, the unknown vector, and the right-side vector, respectively, leads to the following equations: $n = 2$, det $\mathbf{A} = 0$, Rank($\mathbf{A}$) = 1, Rank($\mathbf{A;b}$) = 1. Thus Rank($\mathbf{A}$) = Rank($\mathbf{A;b}$) = 1 = $r < n = 2$. Since $r < n$, a multiplicity of solutions exists, which can be written as an $(n - r) = 1$ parameter family. These solutions are given

$$U_1 = \kappa$$

$$U_2 = \frac{1}{2}(3 - \kappa)$$

Any set (U_1, U_2) that satisfies these equations (where the value of κ is arbitrary) also satisfies the original matrix equation.

When formulating algebraic approximations to differential equations, it is generally required that at the very least, the algebraic solution be unique. Theorem A.1.1, and its associated corollaries, provide criteria by which algebraic systems can be tested. The most frequently used result is Corollary A.1.1.1, which deals specifically with square matrices.

While the presentation to this point has focused on linear algebraic systems, it is very useful to expand the concept of linear algebra to a more general setting. Definition and analysis of generalized linear vector spaces allows for a more unified approach in the development of approximation methods for differential equations. These generalized concepts encompass function spaces as well as the standard finite-dimensional Euclidean vector spaces that have been discussed to this point.

A.2 LINEAR VECTOR SPACES

In mathematics, a linear vector space has a very precise meaning. It is a collection, or set, of mathematical elements that always conform to given rules for both addition and scalar multiplication. The definition of the operations of addition (denoted by the standard symbol "+") and of scalar multiplication (i.e., a real number multiplying an element of the set) form part of the definition of a vector space. The axioms that every linear vector space satisfies are listed in the following definition.

Definition A.2.1: Linear Vector Space.   Let S denote a set of mathematical elements, with u, v, and w being elements of S. Further, assume that both addition and scalar multiplication are defined on S. Then S is a *linear vector space*, with each element of S being a (generalized) vector, if the following axioms are satisfied,

1. $u + v = v + u$ $\qquad\qquad\qquad \forall u, v \in S$
2. $(u + v) + w = u + (v + w)$ $\qquad \forall u, v, w \in S$

3. There exists a zero vector, denoted by 0, such that
$$0 + v = v \qquad\qquad \forall v \in S$$

4. For each $v \in S$, there exists a vector $-v$ such that
$$v + (-v) = 0 \qquad\qquad \forall v \in S$$

5. $\alpha(u + v) = \alpha u + \alpha v \qquad\qquad \forall u, v \in S,\ \alpha$ scalar

6. $(\alpha + \beta)v = \alpha v + \beta v \qquad\qquad \forall v \in S,\ \alpha, \beta$ scalar

7. $\alpha(\beta v) = (\alpha\beta)v \qquad\qquad\qquad \forall v \in S,\ \alpha, \beta$ scalars

8. $(1)v = v \qquad\qquad\qquad\qquad \forall v \in S$

In the definition, standard mathematical notation is used, so that the symbol $\forall$ means "for every," and $\in$ means "belongs to" or "is an element of." The operations of addition and scalar multiplication must satisfy the conditions that the sum of two vectors in S yields a vector that is also in S, and the product of a real number with a vector in S produces a vector that is in S. These conditions can be used to define precisely the operations of addition and scalar multiplication, although the formality is not undertaken here. For practical purposes, the operations of addition and scalar multiplication are taken as the obvious ones. Examples of linear vector spaces include the following.

1. The n-dimensional Euclidean space, denoted by $\mathbb{R}^n$, wherein a vector **a** is defined by the n-tuple $(\alpha_1, \alpha_2, \ldots, \alpha_n)$. Addition and scalar multiplication are defined in the usual way for Euclidean vectors [see equations (A.1.5) and (A.1.6)]. Notice that only for finite-dimensional Euclidean spaces is the bold face notation applied to denote a vector.

2. The set $M_{m \times n}$ of all $m \times n$ matrices, where addition and scalar multiplication are again taken in standard ways [equations (A.1.5) and (A.1.6)].

3. The space $\mathbb{C}^n[\omega_1, \omega_2]$, which is the set of all functions of x whose first n derivatives are continuous on the interval $\omega_1 \leq x \leq \omega_2$. Addition and scalar multiplication of functions are taken in the usual way. Let the functions $g_1 \equiv u + v$, and $g_2 \equiv \alpha u$, with $u, v \in S$, and α scalar. Then

$$g_1(x) = u(x) + v(x) \qquad \forall u(x), v(x) \in S \qquad\qquad \text{(A.2.1a)}$$

$$g_2(x) = \alpha[u(x)] \qquad \forall u(x) \in S, \quad \alpha \text{ scalar} \qquad\qquad \text{(A.2.1b)}$$

For a multidimensional region $\Omega \in \mathbb{R}^N$, $\mathbb{C}^n[\Omega]$ denotes functions whose mixed derivatives through order n are continuous within Ω; that is, if $u(x, y) \in \mathbb{C}^n[\Omega]$, then $\partial^k u / \partial x^m \partial y^{k-m}$ is continuous for all $k = 0, 1, 2, \ldots, n$ and $m = 0, 1, 2, \ldots, k$.

4. The space $P_n[\omega_1, \omega_2]$ of polynomials of degree less than or equal to n that are defined over the interval $\omega_1 \leq x \leq \omega_2$.

Example A.8

Problem   Prove that $\mathbb{C}^0[\omega_1, \omega_2]$, the set of continuous functions defined on $\omega_1 \leq x \leq \omega_2$, forms a linear vector space.

Solution   Satisfaction of the eight axioms given in Definition A.2.1 is necessary and sufficient for the proof. That each is satisfied is easily shown as follows. Let $f(x)$, $g(x)$, and $h(x)$ be continuous functions on $\omega_1 \leq x \leq \omega_2$. Axioms 1 and 2 are satisfied by the commutative and associative properties of addition of real numbers. The zero vector is simply $z(x) = 0$. The negative vector is $F(x) = -f(x)$. Finally, axioms 5 through 8 are satisfied by the definition of scalar multiplication of functions [equation (A.2.1b)]. Thus the function space $\mathbb{C}^0[\omega_1, \omega_2]$ constitutes a linear vector space.

It is reasonable at this point to drop the explicit reference to the actual definitions of the addition and the scalar multiplication operations when referring to particular linear vector spaces. In virtually all cases, the operations are self-evident and are taken in standard ways. Only when the definition of these operations is unclear will explicit recognition be given to their definition.

For any linear vector space, there are several important properties that particular sets of vectors possess. These properties underlie the foundation of linear algebra and linear analysis. Included are the concepts of linear combinations, linear independence, generating sets, basis vectors, and the dimension of a linear vector space. Each of these important concepts is now defined and demonstrated via examples.

Definition A.2.2: Linear Combination.   Let $u_1, u_2, \ldots, u_n$ be n elements of a linear vector space S. A vector of the form $\gamma_1 u_1 + \gamma_2 u_2 + \cdots + \gamma_n u_n$, where the γ_i are scalars, is a *linear combination* of the vectors $u_1, u_2, \ldots, u_n$ in S, with coefficients $\gamma_1, \gamma_2, \ldots, \gamma_n$.

It follows from the fundamental properties of addition and scalar multiplication that a linear combination of vectors in S is itself a vector in S. This is due to the facts that each $\gamma_i u_i$ is in S, by the definition of scalar multiplication, and that the sum of any pair of vectors in S is again in S. Successive application of these facts leads to the desired result, which is restated as a theorem.

Theorem A.2.1.   A linear combination of vectors contained in S is itself contained in S.

Definition A.2.3: Linear Independence.   The vectors $u_1, u_2, \ldots, u_n$, with each $u_i \in S$, are *linearly independent* if and only if the only values of scalars γ_i for which

$$\gamma_1 u_1 + \gamma_2 u_2 + \cdots + \gamma_n u_n = 0 \qquad (A.2.2)$$

are $\gamma_1 = \gamma_2 = \cdots = \gamma_n = 0$. If one or more γ_i can be nonzero and equation (A.2.2) still holds, then the vectors $u_1, u_2, \ldots, u_n$ are *linearly dependent*.

From this definition, two important results follow directly. These are stated as theorems.

Theorem A.2.2.   A set of linearly independent vectors cannot include the zero vector.

Theorem A.2.3.   If a set of vectors is linearly dependent, then at least one of the vectors can be expressed as a linear combination of the others.

Theorem A.2.2 follows from the fact that any scalar γ multiplied by the zero vector always produces the zero vector. Thus, if $u_i = 0$, multiplication by any $\gamma_i \neq 0$ still yields the zero vector. Thus linear independence can never be achieved. Theorem A.2.3 is easily shown as follows. Assume $\gamma_k (1 \leq k \leq n)$ to be nonzero in the linear combination (A.2.2). Then

$$u_k = \frac{-1}{\gamma_k} \sum_{\substack{i=1 \\ i \neq k}}^{n} \gamma_i u_i \tag{A.2.3}$$

which expresses the vector u_k as a linear combination of the other $n - 1$ vectors.

Example A.9

Problem   Consider the Euclidean space $\mathbb{R}^2$. Determine whether or not the following sets of vectors are linearly independent.

> 1. $\mathbf{u}_1 = (1, 0)$, $\mathbf{u}_2 = (0, 1)$
> 2. $\mathbf{u}_1 = (\alpha_1, \beta_1)$, $\mathbf{u}_2 = (\alpha_2, \beta_2)$

Solution   The procedure is to form a linear combination of the vectors and to test for the possibility of nonzero scalar coefficients that satisfy equation (A.2.2). This is accomplished as follows.

> 1. $\gamma_1 \mathbf{u}_1 + \gamma_2 \mathbf{u}_2 = (\gamma_1, \gamma_2) = \mathbf{0} = (0, 0)$. This can only be true if $\gamma_1 = \gamma_2 = 0$. Therefore, the vectors are linearly independent.
> 2. $\gamma_1 \mathbf{u}_1 + \gamma_2 \mathbf{u}_2 = (\gamma_1 \alpha_1 + \gamma_2 \alpha_2, \gamma_1 \beta_1 + \gamma_2 \beta_2) = \mathbf{0} = (0, 0)$. The question is whether or not γ_1 and γ_2 must equal zero for the equation to hold. The relevant equations are

$$\gamma_1 \alpha_1 + \gamma_2 \alpha_2 = 0$$

$$\gamma_1 \beta_1 + \gamma_2 \beta_2 = 0$$

or

$$\begin{bmatrix} \alpha_1 & \alpha_2 \\ \beta_1 & \beta_2 \end{bmatrix} \begin{bmatrix} \gamma_1 \\ \gamma_2 \end{bmatrix} = \begin{bmatrix} 0 \\ 0 \end{bmatrix}$$

By Corollary A.1.1.3, $\gamma_1 = \gamma_2 = 0$ if and only if the determinant of the coefficient matrix is nonzero. Thus u_1 and u_2 are linearly independent whenever $\alpha_1 \beta_2 \neq \alpha_2 \beta_1$.

An idea that complements linear independence is that of a generating set. The following definition pertains.

Definition A.2.4: Generating Set.   The set of vectors $\{u_1, u_2, \ldots, u_n\}$, with $u_i \in S$, is said to *span* the space S if all elements of S can be expressed as linear combinations of $u_1, u_2, \ldots, u_n$. In this case, $\{u_1, u_2, \ldots, u_n\}$ is called a *generating set* for the linear vector space S.

Example A.10

Problem   Consider the vectors $\mathbf{u}_1 = (1, 0)$, $\mathbf{u}_2 = (0, 1)$, $\mathbf{u}_3 = (\alpha, \beta)$. Does this set constitute a generating set for $\mathbb{R}^2$? Is the set $\mathbf{u}_1 = (1, 1)$, $\mathbf{u}_2 = (2, 2)$, $\mathbf{u}_3 = (3, 3)$ a generating set?

Solution   Any vector (ρ_1, ρ_2) in $\mathbb{R}^2$ can be expressed as a linear combination of the first set, $(\rho_1, \rho_2) = (\gamma_1 + \alpha\gamma_3, \gamma_2 + \beta\gamma_3)$, since there exist constants γ_1, γ_2, and γ_3 such that $\gamma_1 + \alpha\gamma_3 = \rho_1$ and $\gamma_2 + \beta\gamma_3 = \rho_2$, for any given values of α, β, ρ_1, and ρ_2. This follows from the fact that the system

$$\begin{bmatrix} 1 & 0 & \alpha \\ 0 & 1 & \beta \end{bmatrix} \begin{bmatrix} \gamma_1 \\ \gamma_2 \\ \gamma_3 \end{bmatrix} = \begin{bmatrix} \rho_1 \\ \rho_2 \end{bmatrix}$$

possesses an infinite number of solutions by Theorem A.1.1 and its related corollaries. The second set of vectors fails to be a generating set because a solution for the relevant system of equations,

$$\begin{bmatrix} 1 & 2 & 3 \\ 1 & 2 & 3 \end{bmatrix} \begin{bmatrix} \gamma_1 \\ \gamma_2 \\ \gamma_3 \end{bmatrix} = \begin{bmatrix} \rho_1 \\ \rho_2 \end{bmatrix}$$

fails to exist except for the special case of $\rho_1 = \rho_2$. This result is again a direct consequence of the fundamental Theorem A.1.1.

A set of vectors that is both a generating set and linearly independent is called by a special name, as the following definition indicates.

Definition A.2.5: Basis.   A set of vectors $\{u_1, u_2, \ldots, u_n\}$, with each $u_i \in S$, is a *basis* for S if the following two conditions are met:

1. The vectors $u_1, u_2, \ldots, u_n$ are linearly independent.
2. The vectors $u_1, u_2, \ldots, u_n$ form a generating set for the space S.

A set of basis vectors can be viewed as the fundamental building block for the given linear vector space. Since it is a generating set, all vectors in the space can be expressed as linear combinations of the basis (or base) vectors. Furthermore, since the basis vectors are linearly independent, none of them can be expressed as a linear combination of the others. This means that removal of one vector from the set leaves a set that, while linearly independent, is no longer a generating set, and therefore no longer a basis. The next theorem therefore follows.

Theorem A.2.4.   The number of vectors in a basis is the smallest number that can form a generating set for the space.

The choice of a basis for any given linear vector space is not unique. In fact, there is generally an infinite number of choices, each of which satisfies Definition A.2.5. However, each basis set must have the same number of basis vectors. This common number, which is the smallest number of vectors required to form a generating set, defines the dimension of the space.

> **Definition A.2.6: Dimension.** The *dimension* of the linear vector space S, denoted by dim S, is the number of elements in any basis of S.

Dimensions of common linear vector spaces are listed below.

1. $\dim \mathbb{R}^n = n$
2. $\dim P_n(x) = n + 1$
3. $\dim \mathbb{C}^0[\omega_1, \omega_2]$ is infinite

Example A.11

Problem   Show that the dimension of $P_n(x)$ is $n + 1$.

Solution   A basis for $P_n(x)$ is the set $\{1, x, x^2, x^3, \ldots, x^n\}$. A linear combination of these vectors (functions) can produce any nth-degree polynomial; therefore, the set is a generating set. Furthermore, the functions are linearly independent, since all coefficients of a polynomial must be zero if the polynomial is equal to zero for all values of x. Since the set is a basis, and there are $n + 1$ elements in the set, the dimension of the linear vector space $P_n(x)$ must be $n + 1$.

A.2.1 Inner Product Spaces

Most linear vector spaces that are of practical interest have associated with them a particular operation called an *inner product*. Such spaces are referred to as *inner product spaces*. The following definition pertains.

> **Definition A.2.7: Inner Product.**   For a given linear vector space S, with elements u, v, an *inner product* is a scalar-valued function, denoted symbolically by $\langle u, v \rangle$, that satisfies the following conditions,
>
> 1. $\langle u, v \rangle = \langle v, u \rangle \qquad \forall u, v \in S$
> 2. $\langle \alpha u + \beta v, w \rangle = \alpha \langle u, w \rangle + \beta \langle v, w \rangle \qquad \forall u, v, w \in S, \quad \alpha, \beta \text{ scalar}$
> 3. $\langle u, u \rangle > 0 \qquad \forall u \neq 0$
> $\langle 0, 0 \rangle = 0$

Any relationship that satisfies these three criteria is, by definition, an inner product on the space S. Common examples are as follows.

1. For the space $\mathbb{R}^2$, let $\mathbf{a} = (\alpha_1, \alpha_2)$ and $\mathbf{b} = (\beta_1, \beta_2)$. The most common inner product is the standard dot product of the two vectors, given by

$$\langle \mathbf{a}, \mathbf{b} \rangle = \mathbf{a} \cdot \mathbf{b} = \alpha_1 \beta_1 + \alpha_2 \beta_2$$

2. For the space $\mathbb{C}^0[\omega_1, \omega_2]$, let $f(x), g(x) \in \mathbb{C}^0[\omega_1, \omega_2]$. The standard inner product is defined by the following integral

$$\langle f(x), g(x) \rangle = \int_a^b f(x) g(x) \, dx$$

These two are by far the most commonly used inner products, the first for finite-dimensional Euclidean spaces, and the second for function spaces. A final definition related to inner products involves the case when two vectors have an inner product equal to zero. Such vectors are said to be orthogonal.

> **Definition A.2.8: Orthogonality.**   Two vectors are *orthogonal* if their inner product is zero.

In n-dimensional Euclidean space, $\mathbb{R}^n$, orthogonal vectors are those that are perpendicular to each other.

Inner product spaces play a very important role in numerical analysis. For example, the formulation of classical finite element methods is based on the concept of inner product spaces. Another important consideration in numerical approximation theory is a measure of distance between two vectors. An example of this is the distance between an approximate solution to a differential equation and the corresponding exact solution. A tool that provides for a systematic definition of length in a vector space is a norm. The following definition pertains.

> **Definition A.2.9: Norm.**   A *norm* of a vector $u \in S$ is a scalar-valued function, denoted by $\|u\|$, that satisfies the following conditions.
>
> 1. $\|\alpha u\| = |\alpha| \, \|u\|$ $\forall u \in S, \quad \alpha$ scalar
> 2. $\|u\| > 0$ $\forall u \neq 0$
> $\|0\| = 0$
> 3. $\|u + v\| \leq \|u\| + \|v\|$ $\forall u, v \in S$

It is easy to show that a norm which is always valid is defined by

$$\|u\| = \sqrt{\langle u, u \rangle} \tag{A.2.4}$$

Therefore, every inner product space is also a normed space. Standard examples of norms are listed below.

1. Euclidean norm (also called discrete L_2 norm)
   Let $S = \mathbb{R}^n$, and let $\mathbf{a} = (\alpha_1, \alpha_2, \dots, \alpha_n)$. Then

$$\|\mathbf{a}\| = \left[w_1 \alpha_1^2 + w_2 \alpha_2^2 + \cdots + w_n \alpha_n^2 \right]^{1/2} \tag{A.2.5a}$$

with $\{w_i\}$ being a set of arbitrary positive weights. These are sometimes normalized such that $\sum_{i=1}^{n} w_i = 1$, or if this norm is used as an approximation to a continuous L_2 norm [equation (A.2.5b)], a normalization such that $\sum_{i=1}^{n} w_i = b - a$ is appropriate, where $b - a$ is the length of the integration interval. When computing the length of a vector in Euclidean space, each w_i is set equal to 1. The specific notation $\|a_i\|_{(i,n)}$ is used in Chapters 4 and 5 and means summation over index i, from $i = 1$ to $i = n$,

$$\|a_i\|_{(i,n)} = \sum_{i=1}^{n} [w_i (a_i)^2]^{1/2}$$

2. L_2 Norm
Let $S = \mathbb{C}^0[a, b]$, and $f(x) \in S$. Then the L_2 norm is defined as

$$\|f(x)\|_2 = \left[\int_a^b w(x) [f(x)]^2 \, dx \right]^{1/2} \qquad \text{(A.2.5b)}$$

where $w(x)$ is now an arbitrary weight function such that $w(x) > 0$ for all $x \in [a, b]$. The weight $w(x)$ is often set to unity, $w(x) = 1$, or is chosen as a normalized weight such that

$$\int_a^b w(x) \, dx = \left(\frac{1}{b - a} \right)^2$$

3. L_∞ Norm (also called Chebyshev norm and maximum norm)
Let $S = \mathbb{C}^n[a, b]$, with $g(x) \in S$. Then the L_∞ norm is defined as

$$\|g(x)\|_\infty = \max_{a \leq x \leq b} |g(x)| \qquad \text{(A.2.5c)}$$

Throughout this book, normed inner product spaces are used to formulate and solve numerical approximations to differential equations of science and engineering.

A.2.2 Linear Operators

An operator is a mathematical device that transforms, or maps, vectors in one space to vectors in another space. More precisely,

Definition A.2.10: Operator. An *operator* (or *transformation*), denoted symbolically by $\mathcal{L}: \mathcal{D} \rightarrow \mathcal{R}$, where $\mathcal{L}$ is the operator, is a mapping from a vector space $\mathcal{D}$, called the domain, to another vector space $\mathcal{R}$, called the range. This is often written as

$$\mathcal{L}u = f, \qquad u \in \mathcal{D}, \quad f \in \mathcal{R}$$

The vector f is referred to as the image of u under the operator $\mathcal{L}$.

The concept of linearity is crucial to many mathematical developments. This is especially true of operators. A linear operator has the following definition.

Definition A.2.11: Linearity.   An operator $\mathcal{L}: \mathcal{D} \to \mathcal{R}$ is *linear* if the following two conditions hold.

  1. $\mathcal{L}(u + v) = \mathcal{L}u + \mathcal{L}v \qquad \forall u, v \in \mathcal{D}$
  2. $\mathcal{L}(\alpha u) = \alpha \mathcal{L}u \qquad \forall u \in \mathcal{D}, \quad \alpha$ scalar

This is sometimes written in one combined condition as follows:

$$\mathcal{L}(\alpha u + \beta v) = \alpha \mathcal{L}u + \beta \mathcal{L}v \qquad \forall u, v \in \mathcal{D}, \quad \alpha, \beta \text{ scalar} \qquad (A.2.6)$$

Examples of linear operators abound; the following are provided.

  1. The $m \times n$ matrix $\mathbf{A}(m \times n)$ maps a vector in $\mathbb{R}^n$ to a vector in $\mathbb{R}^m$. The operator equation is written as $\mathbf{A} \cdot \mathbf{u} = \mathbf{f}$, with $\mathbf{u} \in \mathbb{R}^n$ and $\mathbf{f} \in \mathbb{R}^m$, and the mapping is denoted symbolically by $\mathcal{L}: \mathbb{R}^n \to \mathbb{R}^m$.
  2. The differential operator equation

$$\mathcal{L}u(x) = \frac{d^2u}{dx^2} + \alpha(x)\frac{du}{dx} + \beta(x)u = f(x), \qquad x \in [\omega_1, \omega_2]$$

with, for example, $u(x) \in \mathbb{C}^2[\omega_1, \omega_2]$, $f(x) \in \mathbb{C}^0[\omega_1, \omega_2]$, maps twice-differentiable functions $u(x)$ to continuous functions $f(x)$. The linear mapping is denoted by $\mathcal{L}: \mathbb{C}^2[\omega_1, \omega_2] \to \mathbb{C}^0[\omega_1, \omega_2]$.
  3. The Laplacian operator,

$$\mathcal{L}u \equiv \nabla^2 u = \frac{\partial^2 u}{\partial x^2} + \frac{\partial^2 u}{\partial y^2}, \qquad (x, y) \in \Omega$$

where Ω denotes some closed, two-dimensional region, is linear. One possible choice of domain and range is the following: $\mathcal{L} : \mathbb{C}^2[\Omega] \to \mathbb{C}^0[\Omega]$.
  4. The identity operator, denoted by I, not only maps vectors from a given vector space to vectors in that same space, but the mapped vector remains unchanged. Thus $Iu = u$. This definition of the identity operator holds for any linear vector space.

Any other transformations that satisfy the criteria of Definition A.2.11 qualify as linear operators.

There are two important definitions that are related to linear operators defined on inner product spaces. The first is a property of the operator itself, while the second is a definition of an associated operator that derives from the original linear operator.

Definition A.2.12: Positive Definite.   A linear operator $\mathcal{L}$, defined with respect to two inner product spaces $\mathcal{D}$ and $\mathcal{R}$, is *positive definite* if and only if $\langle \mathcal{L}u, u \rangle > 0$ for all $u \in \mathcal{D}$ and $u \neq 0$.

Proof that an operator is positive definite is sometimes a difficult proposition. Criteria exist for the case of $\mathcal{L}$ being a real, symmetric matrix (see Jennings, 1977, pp. 32–34). The following example demonstrates a standard procedure used for the case of differential operators.

Example A.12

Problem   Determine whether or not the operator $\mathcal{L} = -\nabla^2$, defined on the two-dimensional space of infinitely differentiable functions over a finite region of $\mathbb{R}^2$, denoted by Ω, and that satisfy homogeneous boundary conditions on $\partial\Omega$ (the boundary of the domain Ω), is positive definite. Assume the standard inner product.

Solution   The standard definition of inner product on function spaces is $\langle f, g \rangle = \int_\Omega f(x, y)g(x, y)\,dx\,dy$. Thus it is required to prove that $\int_\Omega (\mathcal{L}u)u\,dx\,dy$ is always positive whenever $u \neq 0$. By Green's theorem (multidimensional integration by parts), the integral is expressed as follows:

$$\int_\Omega (-\nabla^2 u)u\,dx\,dy = -\int_{\partial\Omega} u\frac{\partial u}{\partial n}\,ds + \int_\Omega \boldsymbol{\nabla} u \cdot \boldsymbol{\nabla} u\,dx\,dy$$

$$= \int_\Omega \left[\left(\frac{\partial u}{\partial x}\right)^2 + \left(\frac{\partial u}{\partial y}\right)^2\right]dx\,dy$$

where the boundary integral vanishes due to the homogeneous Dirichlet boundary condition. The integrand is clearly nonnegative, so that the integral is also nonnegative. Furthermore, the integral is zero for any constant value of u. However, the only constant that satisfies the boundary conditions is $u = 0$. Thus the only value of $u(x, y)$ for which the inner product is zero is $u = 0$, so that the operator is positive definite. If other values of u had produced zero inner products, the less restrictive property $\langle \mathcal{L}u, u \rangle \geq 0$ would apply. In such a case, the operator is called *positive semidefinite*.

Definition A.2.13: Adjoint Operator.   The *adjoint operator* $\mathcal{L}^*$, associated with the linear operator $\mathcal{L}$ and the inner product $\langle \cdot, \cdot \rangle$, is defined as the operator that satisfies the following equality:

$$\langle \mathcal{L}u, v \rangle = \langle u, \mathcal{L}^* v \rangle$$

If $\mathcal{L}^* = \mathcal{L}$, then the operator is called *self-adjoint*.

Example A.13

Problem   Show that for the case of matrix operators, with $\mathcal{L}: \mathbb{R}^n \to \mathbb{R}^n$, the adjoint operator is simply the transpose of the matrix operator.

Solution   Consider the standard inner product on $\mathbb{R}^n$, defined by $\langle \mathbf{a}, \mathbf{b} \rangle \equiv \mathbf{b}^T \cdot \mathbf{a}$. Then $\langle \mathbf{A} \cdot \mathbf{u}, \mathbf{v} \rangle = \mathbf{v}^T \cdot \mathbf{A} \cdot \mathbf{u} = (\mathbf{A}^T \cdot \mathbf{v})^T \cdot \mathbf{u} = \langle \mathbf{u}, \mathbf{A}^T \cdot \mathbf{v} \rangle$. Thus it must be that $\mathbf{A}^* = \mathbf{A}^T$. Notice that real, symmetric matrices are self-adjoint.

Example A.14

Problem   Find the adjoint operator associated with the differential operator d^2/dx^2, defined on the space of $\mathbb{C}^2$-continuous functions over $\omega_1 \leq x \leq \omega_2$ that satisfy the boundary conditions

$$u(\omega_1) = \frac{du}{dx}(\omega_2) = 0$$

Solution   Let $u(x) \in \mathbb{C}^2[a, b]$ with

$$u(\omega_1) = \frac{du}{dx}(\omega_2) = 0$$

and assume the standard inner product. The adjoint operator is formed by (repeatedly) invoking integration by parts. Thus

$$\langle \mathcal{L}u, v \rangle = \int_{\omega_1}^{\omega_2} (\mathcal{L}u)v \, dx = \int_{\omega_1}^{\omega_2} \frac{d^2u}{dx^2} v \, dx$$

$$= \left[v \frac{du}{dx} \right]_{\omega_1}^{\omega_2} - \int_{\omega_1}^{\omega_2} \frac{du}{dx} \frac{dv}{dx} dx$$

$$= \left[v \frac{du}{dx} - u \frac{dv}{dx} \right]_{\omega_1}^{\omega_2} + \int_{\omega_1}^{\omega_2} u \frac{d^2v}{dx^2} dx$$

$$= \left[v \frac{du}{dx} - u \frac{dv}{dx} \right]_{\omega_1}^{\omega_2} + \int_{\omega_1}^{\omega_2} u(\mathcal{L}^* v) \, dx$$

For this last expression to equal the inner product $\langle u, \mathcal{L}^* v \rangle$, the boundary terms must vanish. Since $u(\omega_1) = du(\omega_2)/dx = 0$, the conditions on v must be that $v(\omega_1) = dv(\omega_2)/dx = 0$. For two operators to be equivalent, they must have the same (differential) form and must also have the same domain. In this case $\mathcal{L}^*$ has the same form as $\mathcal{L}$ and their domains are the same. Thus the operator $\mathcal{L}: \mathcal{D} \to \mathcal{R}$ is self-adjoint. When the form, or "action," of the adjoint operator is the same as that of the original operator but the associated boundary terms differ, the operator is called *formally self-adjoint*. This is often a more important consideration than the fully self-adjoint condition.

A.3 EIGENVALUES AND EIGENVECTORS

Eigenvalues and eigenvectors are special scalars and vectors, respectively, that are associated with a given linear operator. Specifically, for an operator $\mathcal{L}: \mathcal{D} \to \mathcal{D}$, an eigenvector is a vector $v \in \mathcal{D}$ whose image under $\mathcal{L}$ is a scalar multiple of itself. The scalar multiple is called the *eigenvalue*. This concept is formalized in the following definition.

Definition A.3.1: Eigenvalue Problem.   For the linear operator $\mathcal{L}: \mathcal{D} \to \mathcal{D}$, the general *eigenvalue problem* consists of finding all nontrivial (nonzero) values of the pair (λ, v), with $v \in \mathcal{D}$ and λ scalar, such that

$$\mathcal{L}v = \lambda v \tag{A.3.1}$$

Vectors v that satisfy equation (A.3.1) are called *eigenvectors*, with the companion scalars λ being called *eigenvalues*.

Eigenvalue problems are very important in many physical and mathematical applications. For example, determination of buckling loads, or of principal stresses, involves solution of an eigenvalue problem. Analysis of stability and convergence for numerical approximations also relies on eigenvalue properties.

When $\mathcal{L}$ is a matrix operator, $\mathcal{L}: \mathbb{R}^n \to \mathbb{R}^n$, the eigenvalues and associated eigenvectors are determined algebraically. Specifically, consider the matrix $\mathbf{A}(n \times n)$. Then, equation (A.3.1) is written as

$$\mathbf{A} \cdot \mathbf{v} = \lambda \mathbf{v}$$

or, equivalently,

$$(\mathbf{A} - \lambda \mathbf{I}) \cdot \mathbf{v} = \mathbf{0} \tag{A.3.2}$$

By Theorem A.1.1 and Corollary A.1.1.2, nontrivial solutions of equation (A.3.2) exist only if the determinant of the coefficient matrix, $\mathbf{A} - \lambda \mathbf{I}$, is equal to zero. The requirement that eigenvectors be nontrivial leads to the algebraic expression that is called the *characteristic equation*,

$$|\mathbf{A} - \lambda \mathbf{I}| = 0 \tag{A.3.3}$$

This equation is an nth-degree polynomial in λ, the roots of which are the eigenvalues of $\mathbf{A}$.

Example A.15

Problem   Find the eigenvalues of the 3×3 matrix

$$\mathbf{A} = \begin{bmatrix} 3 & 2 & 0 \\ 2 & 0 & 0 \\ 1 & 0 & 2 \end{bmatrix}$$

Solution   The characteristic equation for this matrix is

$$|\mathbf{A} - \lambda \mathbf{I}| = \det \begin{bmatrix} 3 - \lambda & 2 & 0 \\ 2 & -\lambda & 0 \\ 1 & 0 & 2 - \lambda \end{bmatrix} = -\lambda^3 + 5\lambda^2 - 2\lambda - 8 = 0$$

Solution of the characteristic equation for λ is $\lambda = 2, 4, -1$. Thus there are three real, distinct eigenvalues,

$$\lambda_1 = 2, \qquad \lambda_2 = 4, \qquad \lambda_3 = -1$$

The eigenvectors associated with each eigenvalue are computed by solving equation (A.3.2) for $\mathbf{v}$. For $\lambda_1 = 2$ the appropriate equation for $\mathbf{v}_1$ is

$$\begin{bmatrix} 3 - 2 & 2 & 0 \\ 2 & -2 & 0 \\ 1 & 0 & 2 - 2 \end{bmatrix} \begin{bmatrix} v_{1,1} \\ v_{1,2} \\ v_{1,3} \end{bmatrix} = \begin{bmatrix} 0 \\ 0 \\ 0 \end{bmatrix}$$

The number of unknowns is 3, the rank of the 3×3 matrix is two; therefore, a one-parameter family of solutions exists. These solutions are expressed by $\mathbf{v}_1 = [0, 0, \alpha]^T$, with α an arbitrary scalar. Similarly, solution of the system (A.3.2) leads to the other two eigenvectors,

$$\lambda_2 = 4, \qquad \mathbf{v}_2 = [2\beta, \beta, \beta]^T$$

$$\lambda_3 = -1, \qquad \mathbf{v}_3 = [-3\gamma, 6\gamma, \gamma]^T$$

When $\mathcal{L}: \mathcal{D} \to \mathcal{D}$ is a differential operator and $\mathcal{D}$ is a function space, the eigenvalue problem involves solution of a differential equation.

Example A.16

Problem   Find the eigenvalues and associated eigenvectors for the differential operator $\mathcal{L} = -d^2/dx^2$, with associated boundary conditions $u(0) = u(\ell) = 0$, for $u \in \mathbb{C}^2[0, \ell]$.

Solution   The eigenvalue problem is expressed as $\mathcal{L}u = \lambda u$, or

$$\frac{d^2 u}{dx^2} + \lambda u = 0$$

The general solution to this equation is given by

$$u(x) = C_1 \cos(\sqrt{\lambda}x) + C_2 \sin(\sqrt{\lambda}x)$$

The boundary condition $u(0) = 0$ implies that $C_1 = 0$. The condition $u(\ell) = 0$ implies that either $C_2 = 0$ (which leads to the trivial solution and thus not to the eigens) or that $\sin(\sqrt{\lambda}\ell) = 0$. Choice of the latter constraint implies that $(\sqrt{\lambda}\ell) = n\pi$, or $\lambda_n = n^2\pi^2/\ell^2$, where n is an integer. The eigenvalues are given by the (infinite) set $\left\{ n^2\pi^2/\ell^2 \right\}_{n=1}^{\infty}$, with associated eigenvectors (eigenfunctions) $\{\sin(n\pi x/\ell)\}$.

Series expansion of functions in terms of eigenfunctions is the foundation of Fourier series. Eigenvalue solutions also form the basis of Sturm-Liouville theory for ordinary differential equations.

The following theorems are stated, without proof, to indicate some of the more important properties of eigenvalues. The first two pertain to general linear operators, while the next two deal specifically with the matrix operator case.

Theorem A.3.1.   For any self-adjoint operator $\mathcal{L}$, defined on a finite-dimensional linear vector space $\mathcal{D}$, the associated eigenvalues constitute a basis for $\mathcal{D}$.

Theorem A.3.2.   For any self-adjoint operator $\mathcal{L}$, defined on a finite-dimensional domain $\mathcal{D}$, there exist m mutually orthogonal eigenvectors for each eigenvalue of multiplicity m.

Theorem A.3.3.   If the eigenvalues of a matrix are distinct, then the associated eigenvectors are linearly independent.

Theorem A.3.4.   If the matrix $\mathbf{A}(n \times n)$ is real and symmetric, then:

1. The eigenvalues of $\mathbf{A}$ are real,
2. The eigenvectors associated with distinct eigenvalues are mutually orthogonal,

3. An eigenvalue of multiplicity m has associated with it m linearly independent eigenvectors,

4. The matrix is positive definite if each eigenvalue is positive, $\lambda_i > 0$, and positive semidefinite if each $\lambda_i \geq 0$.

PROBLEMS

A.1. Prove that $(\mathbf{AB})^{-1} = \mathbf{B}^{-1}\mathbf{A}^{-1}$.

A.2. An *elementary row (or column) operation* is the process of replacing each element of a row (column) by the sum of that element and k times the corresponding element of another row (column). This is precisely the procedure that is used in standard matrix solution procedures such as Gauss elimination. Prove that the application of elementary row or column operations does not change the determinant of the matrix. (*Hint:* Begin with the 2×2 case and work up to the $n \times n$ case by induction.)

A.3. Determine the existence and uniqueness of the solution(s) to the following systems of linear algebraic equations:

(a) $\begin{bmatrix} 1 & 2 & 0 \\ 3 & 1 & 4 \\ 0 & 5 & -4 \end{bmatrix} \begin{bmatrix} u_1 \\ u_2 \\ u_3 \end{bmatrix} = \begin{bmatrix} 3 \\ 8 \\ -1 \end{bmatrix}$

(b) $\begin{bmatrix} 1 & 2 & 0 \\ 3 & 1 & 4 \\ 0 & 5 & -4 \end{bmatrix} \begin{bmatrix} u_1 \\ u_2 \\ u_3 \end{bmatrix} = \begin{bmatrix} 3 \\ 8 \\ 1 \end{bmatrix}$

A.4. For the linear vector space $\mathbb{R}^n$, derive a criterion by which the vectors $\mathbf{u}_1, \mathbf{u}_2, \ldots, \mathbf{u}_n$, with $\mathbf{u}_i = (\alpha_{i1}, \alpha_{i2}, \ldots, \alpha_{in})$, can be tested for linear independence.

A.5. For the linear vector space $P_n[\alpha, \beta]$, derive a criterion by which the set of vectors $\{p_i(x)\}_{i=1}^{n+1}$, with $p_i(x) = \alpha_{i0} + \alpha_{i1}x + \alpha_{i2}x^2 + \cdots + \alpha_{in}x^n$, can be tested for linear independence.

A.6. An nth-degree Lagrange polynomial is a polynomial whose coefficients are chosen so that the polynomial passes through a specified function value at each of $n + 1$ locations $x_1, x_2, \ldots, x_{n+1}$. A different Lagrange polynomial is defined for each "node" x_i; the polynomial associated with node k is denoted by $\ell_{nk}(x)$ and is required to take on the value of 1 at $x = x_k$ and zero at each of the other node points $x_i (i \neq k)$. The functional form is thus

$$\ell_{nk}(x) = \frac{(x - x_1)(x - x_2) \cdots (x - x_{k-1})(x - x_{k+1}) \cdots (x - x_{n+1})}{(x_k - x_1)(x_k - x_2) \cdots (x_k - x_{k-1})(x_k - x_{k+1}) \cdots (x_k - x_{n+1})}$$

$$= \prod_{\substack{i=1 \\ i \neq k}}^{n+1} \frac{x - x_i}{x_k - x_i}$$

Develop an argument to demonstrate that $\{\ell_{nk}(x)\}_{i=1}^{n+1}$ forms a basis for $P_n[\alpha, \beta]$. Is it required that each $x_i \in [\alpha, \beta]$?

A.7. Lagrange polynomials are often used to interpolate data. Consider $n+1$ data points $\{U_i\}_{i=1}^{n+1}$, measured at discrete locations $\{x_i\}_{i=1}^{n+1}$. An nth-degree interpolation polynomial can then be defined by

$$U(x) = \sum_{i=1}^{n+1} U_i \ell_{ni}(x)$$

Show that $U(x)$ exactly matches the measurements at each node point. An alternative interpolation procedure is to use piecewise Lagrange polynomials. These are standard Lagrange polynomials that are of degree less than n and are defined over only "pieces" of the domain. For example, to "connect the data points by straight lines," piecewise linear Lagrange polynomials are used as follows:

$$U(x) = \sum_{i=1}^{n+1} U_i \phi_i(x)$$

where $\phi_i(x)$ is a piecewise linear Lagrange polynomial defined as

$$\phi_i(x) = \begin{cases} \dfrac{x - x_{i-1}}{x_i - x_{i-1}}, & x_{i-1} \le x \le x_i \\[2mm] \dfrac{x_{i+1} - x}{x_{i+1} - x_i}, & x_i \le x \le x_{i+1} \\[2mm] 0, & \text{all other } x \end{cases}$$

This interpolation retains the property that $U(x_k) = U_k$ but differs from the previous one in that $U(x)$ is only $\mathbb{C}^0[x_1, x_{n+1}]$ rather than $\mathbb{C}^\infty[x_1, x_{n+1}]$. Furthermore, the value of $U(x)$ at any $x_i \le x \le x_{i+1}$ is dependent only on the values U_i and U_{i+1} in the piecewise case, while in the previous case the dependence is on all of the U_j, $j = 1, 2, \ldots, n+1$. For the data points below, compute $U(x)$ using both of the interpolation methods above, and sketch the results.

i	x_i	U_i
1	0	1
2	2	1
3	3	2
4	4	0

A.8. Given a linear vector space S, a subspace of S, call it S', is defined as a subset of the elements of S which itself forms a linear vector space. Show that the set of piecewise linear Lagrange polynomials forms a subspace of $\mathbb{C}^0[x_1, x_{n+1}]$.

A.9. Prove that the solution of an $n \times n$ matrix equation is unique if and only if the set of vectors in $\mathbb{R}^n$ formed by each row, as well as the set formed by each column, are linearly independent.

A.10. Prove that the expression

$$\langle f(x), g(x) \rangle = \int_\alpha^\beta w(x) f(x) g(x)\, dx, \qquad w(x) > 0$$

where $w(x), f(x), g(x) \in \mathbb{C}^0[\alpha, \beta]$ is a valid inner product for the space $\mathbb{C}^0[\alpha, \beta]$.

A.11. Determine whether or not the differential operator

$$\mathcal{L} \equiv \frac{d^2}{dx^2} + (x^2)\frac{d}{dx}$$

is linear. State an appropriate domain and range for this operator.

A.12. Show that the expression

$$\|u(x)\| = \int_\alpha^\beta \left\{ [u(x)]^2 + \left[\frac{du}{dx}\right]^2 \right\}^{1/2} dx$$

is a valid norm for $u(x) \in \mathbb{C}^1[\alpha, \beta]$. Is this a valid norm for $u(x) \in \mathbb{C}^0[\alpha, \beta]$?

Appendix B

Tables of Formulas and Coefficients

TABLE B.1   STANDARD DIFFERENCE FORMULAS

Nonconstant Spacing	Constant Spacing	Order
	Approximations for $du/dx\vert_{x_i}$	

$$\frac{u_{i+1} - u_i}{x_{i+1} - x_i} = \frac{\Delta u_i}{\Delta x_i}$$ (same) $\mathcal{O}(\Delta x)$

$$\frac{u_i - u_{i-1}}{x_i - x_{i-1}} = \frac{\nabla u_i}{\nabla x_i}$$ (same) $\mathcal{O}(\Delta x)$

$$\alpha_{-1} u_{i-1} + \alpha_0 u_i + \alpha_1 u_{i+1}$$

$$\frac{u_{i+1} - u_{i-1}}{x_{i+1} - x_{i-1}} = \frac{\mu\, \delta u_i}{\mu\, \delta x_i} \qquad \mathcal{O}((\Delta x)^2)$$

$$\alpha_{-1} = \frac{-1}{\nabla x_i (\nabla x_i / \Delta x_i + 1)}$$

$$\alpha_1 = \frac{1}{\Delta x_i (\Delta x_i / \nabla x_i + 1)}$$

$$\alpha_0 = -\alpha_{-1} - \alpha_1$$

$$\beta_{-2} u_{i-2} + \beta_{-1} u_{i-1} + \beta_0 u_i$$

$$\frac{u_{i-2} - 4u_{i-1} + 3u_i}{2(\Delta x)} = \frac{\nabla u_i + \nabla^2 u_i / 2\Delta x}{2\Delta x} \qquad \mathcal{O}((\Delta x)^2)$$

$$\beta_{-2} = \frac{1}{4\delta x_{i-1}(\delta x_{i-1} / \nabla x_i - 1/2)}$$

$$\beta_{-1} = \frac{-1}{\nabla x_i (1 - \nabla x_i / 2\delta x_{i-1})}$$

$$\beta_0 = -\beta_{-2} - \beta_{-1}$$

| | Approximations for $d^2 u/dx^2\vert_{x_i}$ | |

$$\frac{u_{i-1}}{\nabla x_i\, \delta x_i} - \frac{2u_i}{\Delta x_i\, \nabla x_i} - \frac{u_{i+1}}{\Delta x_i\, \delta x_i}$$

$$\frac{u_{i-1} - 2u_i + u_{i+1}}{(\Delta x)^2} = \frac{\delta^2 u_i}{(\Delta x)^2}$$

$\mathcal{O}(\Delta x)$ for nonconstant spacing $\mathcal{O}((\Delta x)^2)$ for constant spacing

$$\frac{u_{i-2}}{\nabla x_{i-1}\, \delta x_{i-1}} - \frac{2u_{i-1}}{\nabla x_i\, \nabla x_{i-1}} + \frac{u_i}{\nabla x_i\, \delta x_{i-1}}$$

$$\frac{u_{i-2} - 2u_{i-1} + u_i}{(\Delta x)^2} = \frac{\delta^2 u_{i-1}}{(\Delta x)^2}$$

$\mathcal{O}(\Delta x)$

TABLE B.2 pth-ORDER ADAMS-BASHFORTH (OPEN) MULTISTEP FORMULAS

Differential Equation.

$$\frac{du}{dt} = f(u, t)$$

Adams-Bashforth Formula.

$$U^{n+1} = U^n + \frac{\Delta t}{A_p} \sum_{k=0}^{p-1} \alpha_{n-k} F^{n-k}$$

Leading Error Term.

$$U^{n+1} = u^{n+1} + (n+1)\Delta t \, \hat{C}_p \left. \frac{d^{p+1} u}{dt^{p+1}} \right|_{t^{*n+1}_{\Delta t}} (\Delta t)^p$$

p	A_p	α_n	α_{n-1}	α_{n-2}	α_{n-3}	α_{n-4}	α_{n-5}	$\hat{C}_p$
1	1	1						$-1/2$
2	2	3	-1					$-5/12$
3	12	23	-16	5				$-9/24$
4	24	55	-59	37	-9			$-251/720$
5	720	1901	-2744	2616	-1274	251		$-475/1440$
6	1440	4277	-7923	9982	-7298	2877	-475	$-19{,}087/60{,}480$

TABLE B.3 pth-ORDER ADAMS-MOULTON (CLOSED) MULTISTEP FORMULAS

Differential Equation.

$$\frac{du}{dt} = f(u, t)$$

Adams-Moulton Formula.

$$U^{n+1} = U^n + \frac{\Delta t}{A_p} \sum_{k=0}^{p-1} \alpha_{n+1-k} F^{n+1-k}$$

Leading Error Term.

$$U^{n+1} = u^{n+1} + (n+1)\Delta t\, C_p \left.\frac{d^{p+1}u}{dt^{p+1}}\right|_{t^{*n+1}_{\Delta t}} (\Delta t)^p$$

p	A_p	α_{n+1}	α_n	α_{n-1}	α_{n-2}	α_{n-3}	α_{n-4}	C_p
1	1	1						1/2
2	2	1	1					1/12
3	12	5	8	−1				1/24
4	24	9	19	−5	1			19/720
5	720	251	646	−264	106	−19		27/1440
6	1440	475	1427	−798	482	−173	27	863/60,480

TABLE B.4 pth-ORDER GEAR OPEN MULTISTEP FORMULAS

Differential Equation.

$$\frac{du}{dt} = f(u, t)$$

Gear Open Formula.

$$U^{n+1} = \frac{1}{A_p} \sum_{k=0}^{p-1} \beta_{n-k} U^{n-k} + \frac{\Delta t}{A_p} \alpha_n F^n$$

Leading Error Term.

$$U^{n+1} = u^{n+1} + (n+1)\Delta t\, \hat{C}_p \left. \frac{d^{p+1}u}{dt^{p+1}} \right|_{t^{*n+1}_{\Delta t}} (\Delta t)^p$$

p	A_p	α_n	β_n	β_{n-1}	β_{n-2}	β_{n-3}	β_{n-4}	β_{n-5}	$\hat{C}_p$
1	1	1	1						$-1/2$
2	1	2	0	1					$-1/3$
3	2	6	-3	6	-1				—
4	3	12	-10	18	-6	1			—
5	12	60	-65	120	-60	20	-3		—
6	10	60	-77	150	-100	50	-15	2	—

TABLE B.5 pth-ORDER GEAR CLOSED MULTISTEP FORMULAS

Differential Equation.

$$\frac{du}{dt} = f(u, t)$$

Gear Closed Formula.

$$U^{n+1} = \frac{1}{A_p} \sum_{k=0}^{p-1} \beta_{n-k} U^{n-k} + \frac{\Delta t}{A_p} \alpha_{n+1} F^{n+1}$$

Leading Error Term.

$$U^{n+1} = u^{n+1} + (n+1)\Delta t\, C_p \left. \frac{d^{p+1} u}{dt^{p+1}} \right|_{t^{*n+1}_{\Delta t}} (\Delta t)^p$$

p	A_p	α_{n+1}	β_n	β_{n-1}	β_{n-2}	β_{n-3}	β_{n-4}	β_{n-5}	C_p
1	1	1	1						1/2
2	3	2	4	−1					1/3
3	11	6	18	−9	2				1/4
4	25	12	48	−36	16	−3			1/5
5	137	60	300	−300	200	−75	12		1/6
6	147	60	360	−450	400	−225	72	−10	1/7

TABLE B.6 pth-ORDER ADAMS MULTIVALUE FORMULAS

Differential Equation.

$$\frac{du}{dt} = f(u, t)$$

Taylor Series Constraint.

$$\frac{d^k \tilde{U}^m}{dt^k} = \sum_{l=k}^{p-1} \frac{(\Delta t)^{l-k}}{(l-k)!} \frac{d^l U^{m-1}}{dt^l} \tag{2.6.48}$$

$$\text{where } m = n \text{ or } n+1; \ k = 0, 1, \ldots, p-1$$

Predictor Formula.

$$\frac{(\Delta t)^k}{k!} \frac{d^k \hat{U}^{n+1}}{dt^k} = \frac{(\Delta t)^k}{k!} \frac{d^k \tilde{U}^{n+1}}{dt^k} + \alpha_{1,k}(\Delta t) \left[F^n - \frac{d\tilde{U}^n}{dt} \right] \tag{2.6.50}$$

$$\text{where } k = 0, 1, \ldots, p-1$$

Leading Error Term, Predictor.

$$U^{n+1} = u^{n+1} + (n+1)\Delta t \, \hat{C}_p \left. \frac{d^{p+1} u}{dt^{p+1}} \right|_{t^{*n+1}_{\Delta t}} (\Delta t)^p$$

Corrector Formula.

$$\frac{(\Delta t)^k}{k!} \frac{d^k U^{n+1}}{dt^k} = \frac{(\Delta t)^k}{k!} \frac{d^k \tilde{U}^{n+1}}{dt^k} + \alpha_{1,k}(\Delta t) \left[F^{n+1} - \frac{d\tilde{U}^{n+1}}{dt} \right] \tag{2.6.49}$$

$$\text{where } k = 0, 1, \ldots, p-1$$

Leading Error Term, Corrector.

$$U^{n+1} = u^{n+1} + (n+1)\Delta t \, C_p \left. \frac{d^{p+1} u}{dt^{p+1}} \right|_{t^{*n+1}_{\Delta t}} (\Delta t)^p$$

p	$\alpha_{1,0}$	$\alpha_{1,1}$	$\alpha_{1,2}$	$\alpha_{1,3}$	$\alpha_{1,4}$	$\alpha_{1,5}$	$\hat{C}_p$	C_p
1	1						$-1/2$	$1/2$
2	1/2	1					$-5/12$	$1/12$
3	5/12	1	1/2				$-9/24$	$1/24$
4	3/8	1	3/4	1/6			$-251/720$	$19/720$
5	251/720	1	11/12	1/3	1/24		$-475/1440$	$27/1440$
6	95/288	1	25/24	35/72	5/48	1/120	$-19,087/60,480$	$863/60,480$

TABLE B.7 pth-ORDER GEAR MULTIVALUE FORMULAS

Differential Equation.

$$\frac{du}{dt} = f(u, t)$$

Taylor Series Constraint.

$$\frac{d^k \tilde{U}^m}{dt^k} = \sum_{l=k}^{p} \frac{(\Delta t)^{l-k}}{(l-k)!} \frac{d^l U^{m-1}}{dt^l} \qquad (2.6.48)$$

$$\text{where } m = n \text{ or } n+1; \; k = 0, 1, \ldots, p$$

Predictor Formula.

$$\frac{(\Delta t)^k}{k!} \frac{d^k \hat{U}^{n+1}}{dt^k} = \frac{(\Delta t)^k}{k!} \frac{d^k \tilde{U}^{n+1}}{dt^k} + \alpha_{1,k}(\Delta t) \left[F^n - \frac{d\tilde{U}^n}{dt} \right] \qquad (2.6.50)$$

$$\text{where } k = 0, 1, \ldots, p$$

Leading Error Term, Predictor.

$$U^{n+1} = u^{n+1} + (n+1)\Delta t \, \hat{C}_p \left. \frac{d^{p+1} u}{dt^{p+1}} \right|_{t^{*n+1}_{\Delta t}} (\Delta t)^p$$

Corrector Formula.

$$\frac{(\Delta t)^k}{k!} \frac{d^k U^{n+1}}{dt^k} = \frac{(\Delta t)^k}{k!} \frac{d^k \tilde{U}^{n+1}}{dt^k} + \alpha_{1,k}(\Delta t) \left[F^{n+1} - \frac{d\tilde{U}^{n+1}}{dt} \right] \qquad (2.6.49)$$

$$\text{where } k = 0, 1, \ldots, p$$

Leading Error Term, Corrector.

$$U^{n+1} = u^{n+1} + (n+1)\Delta t \, C_p \left. \frac{d^{p+1} u}{dt^{p+1}} \right|_{t^{*n+1}_{\Delta t}} (\Delta t)^p$$

p	$\alpha_{1,0}$	$\alpha_{1,1}$	$\alpha_{1,2}$	$\alpha_{1,3}$	$\alpha_{1,4}$	$\alpha_{1,5}$	$\alpha_{1,6}$	$\hat{C}_p$	C_p
1	1	1						1/2	1/2
2	2/3	1	1/3					1/3	1/3
3	6/11	1	6/11	1/11				1/4	1/4
4	12/25	1	7/10	1/5	1/50			1/5	1/5
5	60/137	1	225/274	85/274	15/274	1/274		1/6	1/6
6	20/49	1	58/63	5/12	25/252	1/84	1/1764	1/7	1/7

TABLE B.8   ELEMENTWISE BASIS FUNCTIONS: ONE DIMENSION

Piecewise Linear Lagrange.

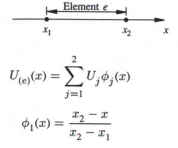

$$U_{(e)}(x) = \sum_{j=1}^{2} U_j \phi_j(x)$$

$$\phi_1(x) = \frac{x_2 - x}{x_2 - x_1}$$

$$\phi_2(x) = \frac{x - x_1}{x_2 - x_1}$$

$$U_{(e)}(\xi) = \sum_{j=1}^{2} U_j \phi_j(\xi)$$

$$\phi_1(\xi) = \frac{1 - \xi}{2}$$

$$\phi_2(\xi) = \frac{1 + \xi}{2}$$

Piecewise Quadratic Lagrange.

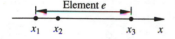

$$\left[\alpha = -1 + 2 \left(\frac{x_2 - x_1}{x_3 - x_1} \right) \right]$$

$$U_{(e)}(x) = \sum_{j=1}^{3} U_j \phi_j(x)$$

$$\phi_1(x) = \frac{(x - x_2)(x - x_3)}{(x_1 - x_2)(x_1 - x_3)}$$

$$\phi_2(x) = \frac{(x - x_1)(x - x_3)}{(x_2 - x_1)(x_2 - x_3)}$$

$$\phi_3(x) = \frac{(x - x_1)(x - x_2)}{(x_3 - x_1)(x_3 - x_2)}$$

$$\left[\phi_j(x) = \prod_{\substack{i=1 \\ i \neq j}}^{3} \frac{x - x_j}{x_i - x_j} \right]$$

$$U_{(e)}(\xi) = \sum_{j=1}^{3} U_j \phi_j(\xi; \alpha)$$

$$\phi_1(\xi; \alpha) = \frac{(\xi - \alpha)(1 - \xi)}{2(1 + \alpha)}$$

$$\phi_2(\xi; \alpha) = \frac{1 - \xi^2}{1 - \alpha^2}$$

$$\phi_3(\xi; \alpha) = \frac{(\xi - \alpha)(1 + \xi)}{2(1 - \alpha)}$$

Note: α is often chosen as $\alpha = 0$, independent of x_1, x_2, and x_3. See pages 210–214.

TABLE B.8 (continued)   ELEMENTWISE BASIS FUNCTIONS: ONE DIMENSION

Piecewise Cubic Lagrange.

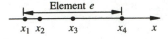

$$\left[\alpha = -1 + 2\left(\frac{x_2 - x_1}{x_4 - x_1}\right)\right]$$

$$\left[\beta = -1 + 2\left(\frac{x_3 - x_1}{x_4 - x_1}\right)\right]$$

$$U_{(e)}(x) = \sum_{j=1}^{4} U_j \phi_j(x)$$

$$U_{(e)}(\xi) = \sum_{j=1}^{4} U_j \phi_j(\xi)$$

$$\phi_1(\xi; \alpha, \beta) = \frac{(\xi - \alpha)(\xi - \beta)(1 - \xi)}{2(1 + \alpha)(1 + \beta)}$$

$$\phi_j(x) = \prod_{\substack{i=1 \\ i \neq j}}^{4} \frac{x - x_j}{x_i - x_j}$$

$$\phi_2(\xi; \alpha, \beta) = \frac{(1 - \xi^2)(\xi - \beta)}{(1 - \alpha^2)(\alpha - \beta)}$$

$$(j = 1, 2, 3, 4)$$

$$\phi_3(\xi; \alpha, \beta) = \frac{(1 - \xi^2)(\xi - \alpha)}{(1 - \beta^2)(\beta - \alpha)}$$

$$\phi_4(\xi; \alpha, \beta) = \frac{(\xi - \alpha)(\xi - \beta)(1 + \xi)}{2(1 - \alpha)(1 - \beta)}$$

Note: (α, β) often chosen as $\alpha = -1/3$, $\beta = 1/3$ independent of x_1, x_2, x_3, x_4.

TABLE B.8 (continued)   ELEMENTWISE BASIS FUNCTIONS: ONE DIMENSION

Piecewise Cubic Hermite.

$$U_{(e)}(x) = \sum_{j=1}^{2} U_j \phi_{0j}(x) + \frac{dU_j}{dx} \phi_{1j}(x)$$

$$U_{(e)}(\xi) = \sum_{j=1}^{2} U_j \phi_{0j}(\xi) + \frac{dU_j}{d\xi} \phi_{1j}(\xi)$$

$$= \sum_{j=1}^{2} U_j \phi_{0j}(\xi) + \frac{dU_j}{dx} \left(\frac{x_2 - x_1}{2} \right) \phi_{1j}(\xi)$$

$$\phi_{01}(x) = \frac{(x_2 - x)^2}{(x_2 - x_1)^3} [3(x_2 - x_1) - 2(x_2 - x)]$$

$$\phi_{01}(\xi) = \frac{1}{4}(1 - \xi)^2(2 + \xi)$$

$$\phi_{02}(x) = \frac{(x - x_1)^2}{(x_2 - x_1)^3} [2(x_2 - x) + (x_2 - x_1)]$$

$$\phi_{02}(\xi) = \frac{1}{4}(1 + \xi)^2(2 - \xi)$$

$$\phi_{11}(x) = \frac{(x_2 - x)^2(x - x_1)}{(x_2 - x_1)^2}$$

$$\phi_{11}(\xi) = \frac{1}{4}(1 - \xi)^2(1 + \xi)$$

$$\phi_{12}(x) = \frac{(x - x_1)^2(x_2 - x)}{(x_2 - x_1)^2}$$

$$\phi_{12}(\xi) = -\frac{1}{4}(1 + \xi)^2(1 - \xi)$$

$$\left[\begin{array}{l} \phi_{0j}(\xi) = \frac{1}{4}(1 + \xi\xi_j)^2(2 - \xi\xi_j) \\ \phi_{1j}(\xi) = -\frac{1}{4}(\xi_j)(1 + \xi\xi_j)^2(1 - \xi\xi_j) \end{array} \right]$$

TABLE B.9   ELEMENTWISE (MASTER) BASIS FUNCTIONS: TWO DIMENSIONS

Piecewise Bilinear.

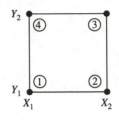

$$U_{(e)}(x, y) = \sum_{j=1}^{4} U_j \phi_j(x, y)$$

$$U_{(e)}(\xi, \eta) = \sum_{j=1}^{2} U_j \phi_j(\xi, \eta)$$

$$\phi_1(x, y) = \left(\frac{X_2 - x}{X_2 - X_1} \right) \left(\frac{Y_2 - y}{Y_2 - Y_1} \right)$$

$$\phi_1(\xi, \eta) = \frac{1}{4}(1 - \xi)(1 - \eta)$$

$$\phi_2(x, y) = \left(\frac{x - X_1}{X_2 - X_1} \right) \left(\frac{Y_2 - y}{Y_2 - Y_1} \right)$$

$$\phi_2(\xi, \eta) = \frac{1}{4}(1 + \xi)(1 - \eta)$$

$$\phi_3(x, y) = \left(\frac{x - X_1}{X_2 - X_1} \right) \left(\frac{y - Y_1}{Y_2 - Y_1} \right)$$

$$\phi_3(\xi, \eta) = \frac{1}{4}(1 + \xi)(1 + \eta)$$

$$\phi_4(x, y) = \left(\frac{X_2 - x}{X_2 - X_1} \right) \left(\frac{y - Y_1}{Y_2 - Y_1} \right)$$

$$\phi_4(\xi, \eta) = \frac{1}{4}(1 - \xi)(1 + \eta)$$

$$\left[\phi_j(\xi, \eta) = \frac{1}{4}(1 + \xi\xi_j)(1 + \eta\eta_j) \right]$$

TABLE B.9 (continued)   ELEMENTWISE (MASTER) BASIS FUNCTIONS: TWO DIMENSIONS

Eight-Node Quadratic Element.

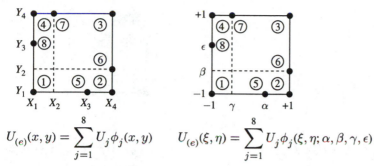

$$U_{(e)}(x, y) = \sum_{j=1}^{8} U_j \phi_j(x, y) \qquad U_{(e)}(\xi, \eta) = \sum_{j=1}^{8} U_j \phi_j(\xi, \eta; \alpha, \beta, \gamma, \epsilon)$$

Obtain $\phi_j(x, y)$ from
$\phi_j(\xi, \eta; \alpha, \beta, \gamma, \epsilon)$ by
substitution of the
following:

$$\xi = \frac{2x - (X_4 + X_1)}{X_4 - X_1}$$

$$\phi_1 = \frac{1}{4}(1 - \xi)(1 - \eta)\frac{(1 + \alpha)(1 + \epsilon) - (1 + \alpha)(1 + \eta) - (1 + \epsilon)(1 + \xi)}{(1 + \alpha)(1 + \epsilon)}$$

$$\eta = \frac{2y - (Y_4 + Y_1)}{Y_4 - Y_1}$$

$$\phi_2 = \frac{1}{4}(1 + \xi)(1 - \eta)\frac{(1 - \alpha)(1 + \beta) - (1 - \alpha)(1 + \eta) - (1 + \beta)(1 - \xi)}{(1 - \alpha)(1 + \beta)}$$

$$\alpha = -1 + 2\left(\frac{X_2 - X_1}{X_4 - X_1}\right)$$

$$\phi_3 = \frac{1}{4}(1 + \xi)(1 + \eta)\frac{(1 - \gamma)(1 - \beta) - (1 - \gamma)(1 - \eta) - (1 - \beta)(1 - \xi)}{(1 - \gamma)(1 - \beta)}$$

$$\beta = -1 + 2\left(\frac{Y_2 - Y_1}{Y_4 - Y_3}\right)$$

$$\phi_4 = \frac{1}{4}(1 - \xi)(1 + \eta)\frac{(1 + \gamma)(1 - \epsilon) - (1 + \gamma)(1 - \eta) - (1 - \epsilon)(1 + \xi)}{(1 + \gamma)(1 - \epsilon)}$$

$$\gamma = -1 + 2\left(\frac{X_3 - X_1}{X_4 - X_1}\right)$$

$$\phi_5 = \frac{1}{2}(1 - \eta)\frac{1 - \xi^2}{1 - \alpha^2}$$

$$\epsilon = -1 + 2\left(\frac{Y_3 - Y_1}{Y_4 - Y_1}\right)$$

$$\phi_6 = \frac{1}{2}(1 + \xi)\frac{1 - \eta^2}{1 - \beta^2}$$

$$\phi_7 = \frac{1}{2}(1 + \eta)\frac{1 - \xi^2}{1 - \gamma^2}$$

$$\phi_8 = \frac{1}{2}(1 - \xi)\frac{1 - \eta^2}{1 - \epsilon^2}$$

TABLE B.9 (continued)   ELEMENTWISE (MASTER) BASIS FUNCTIONS: TWO DIMENSIONS

Nine-Node Quadratic Element.

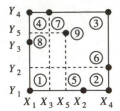

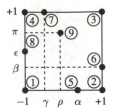

$$U_{(e)}(x, y) = \sum_{j=1}^{8} U_j \phi_j(x, y) + U_9^* \phi_9(x, y)$$

$$U_{(e)}(\xi, \eta) = \sum_{j=1}^{8} U_j \phi_j(\xi, \eta; \alpha, \beta, \gamma, \epsilon)$$

$$+ U_9^* \phi_9(\xi, \eta; \alpha, \beta, \gamma, \epsilon, \rho, \pi)$$

Obtain $\phi_j(x, y)$, $j = 1, 2, \ldots, 8$, from $\phi_j(\xi, \eta; \alpha, \beta, \gamma, \epsilon)$ given above for an eight-node element.

$\phi_j(\xi, \eta; \alpha, \beta, \gamma, \epsilon)$, $j = 1, 2, \ldots, 8$, same as those above for an eight-node element.

For ϕ_9, use the following substitutions:

$$\phi_9(\xi, \eta; \alpha, \beta, \gamma, \epsilon, \rho, \pi) = \frac{(1 - \xi^2)(1 - \eta^2)}{(1 - \rho^2)(1 - \pi^2)}$$

$$\rho = -1 + 2 \left(\frac{X_5 - X_1}{X_4 - X_1} \right)$$

$$U_9^* = U_9 - \sum_{j=1}^{8} U_j \phi_j \Bigg|_{(\rho, \pi)}$$

$$\pi = -1 + 2 \left(\frac{Y_5 - Y_1}{Y_4 - Y_1} \right)$$

$$= U_9 - \sum_{j=1}^{8} U_j \phi_j(\rho, \pi; \alpha, \beta, \gamma, \epsilon)$$

$$U_9^* = U_9 - \sum_{j=1}^{8} U_j \phi_j(X_5, Y_5)$$

Note: These functions reduce to standard biquadratic polynomials when $X_2 = X_3 = X_5$ and $Y_2 = Y_3 = Y_5$. In this case, $\alpha = \gamma = \rho$ and $\beta = \epsilon = \pi$.

TABLE B.9 (continued)   ELEMENTWISE (MASTER) BASIS FUNCTIONS: TWO DIMENSIONS

Linear Triangular Element.

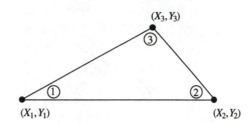

$$U_{(e)}(x, y) = \sum_{j=1}^{3} U_j \phi_j(x, y)$$

$$\phi_1(x, y) = \frac{1}{2A}[(X_2 Y_3 - X_3 Y_2) + (Y_2 - Y_3)x + (X_3 - X_2)y]$$

$$\phi_2(x, y) = \frac{1}{2A}[(X_3 Y_1 - X_1 Y_3) + (Y_3 - Y_1)x + (X_1 - X_3)y]$$

$$\phi_3(x, y) = \frac{1}{2A}[(X_1 Y_2 - X_2 Y_1) + (Y_1 - Y_2)x + (X_2 - X_1)y]$$

$$A = \frac{1}{2}[(X_2 Y_3 - X_3 Y_2) - (X_1 Y_3 - X_3 Y_1) + (X_1 Y_2 - X_2 Y_1)]$$

TABLE B.9 (continued)   ELEMENTWISE (MASTER) BASIS FUNCTIONS: TWO DIMENSIONS

Quadratic Triangular Element.

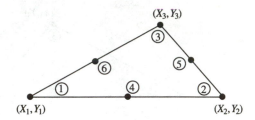

$$U_{(e)}(x, y) = \sum_{j=1}^{6} U_j \phi_j(x, y)$$

Let the three basis functions associated with a linear triangular element be denoted by $\Psi_1(x, y)$, $\Psi_2(x, y)$, and $\Psi_3(x, y)$. Then the quadratic basis functions are defined by the following:

$$\phi_1(x, y) = \Psi_1(2\Psi_1 - 1)$$

$$\phi_2(x, y) = \Psi_2(2\Psi_2 - 1)$$

$$\phi_3(x, y) = \Psi_3(2\Psi_3 - 1)$$

$$\phi_4(x, y) = 4\Psi_1\Psi_2$$

$$\phi_5(x, y) = 4\Psi_2\Psi_3$$

$$\phi_6(x, y) = 4\Psi_3\Psi_1$$

Note: Node 4 is assumed to be midway between nodes 1 and 2. Nodes 5 and 6 must also be at the midpoint of their respective sides.

TABLE B.10   NUMERICAL INTEGRATION FORMULAS

1. Gaussian Quadrature in One Dimension.

$$\int_{-1}^{+1} f(\xi)\, d\xi \simeq \sum_{i=1}^{N} W_i\, f(\xi_i)$$

$$\int_{x_1}^{x_2} F(x)\, dx = \int_{-1}^{+1} F(x(\xi)) \frac{dx}{d\xi}\, d\xi = \frac{x_2 - x_1}{2} \int_{-1}^{+1} F(x(\xi))\, d\xi$$

$$\simeq \frac{x_2 - x_1}{2} \sum_{i=1}^{N} W_i\, F(x(\xi_i))$$

$\{\xi_i\}_{i=1}^{N}$ = integration points, which are the N roots of the Nth-degree Legendre polynomial defined over $[-1, 1]$. These points are often referred to as *Gauss points*.

$\{W_i\}_{i=1}^{N}$ = weightings associated with the N integration points, defined as the values of the integrals over $[-1, 1]$ of the N Lagrange polynomials associated with the N interpolation points $\{\xi_i\}_{i=1}^{N}$.

Piecewise Gaussian Integration

$$\int_{a}^{b} F(x)\, dx = \sum_{e=1}^{E} \int_{x_e}^{x_{e+1}} F(x)\, dx \simeq \sum_{e=1}^{E} \frac{x_{e+1} - x_e}{2} \sum_{i_e=1}^{N_e} W_{i_e}\, F(x_{(e)}(\xi_{i_e}))$$

where $x_1 = a$, $x_{E+1} = b$, $x_e \in [a, b]$ and $x_{e+1} > x_e$ for $e = 2, 3, \ldots, E$, and

$$x_{(e)}(\xi) \equiv \frac{x_e + x_{e+1}}{2} + \frac{x_{e+1} - x_e}{2} \xi$$

TABLE B.10 (continued) NUMERICAL INTEGRATION FORMULAS

LIST OF GAUSS POINTS AND WEIGHTS

N	$\{\xi_i\}_{i=1}^{N}$	$\{W_i\}_{i=1}^{N}$
1	0.	2.
2	$\pm(1/\sqrt{3})$	1.
	$= \pm 0.57735027$	
3	$0., \pm\sqrt{(3/5)}$	$\dfrac{8}{9}, \dfrac{5}{9}$
	$= 0., \pm 0.77459667$	
4	$\pm\sqrt{\dfrac{30 - \sqrt{480}}{70}}, \pm\sqrt{\dfrac{30 + \sqrt{480}}{70}}$	$\left[\dfrac{\xi_2^2 - \frac{1}{3}}{\xi_2^2 - \xi_1^2}\right], \left[\dfrac{\frac{1}{3} - \xi_1^2}{\xi_2^2 - \xi_1^2}\right]$
	$= \pm 0.3399810, \pm 0.86113631$	$= 0.65214515, 0.3478485$
5	$0., \pm\sqrt{\dfrac{70 - \sqrt{1120}}{126}}, \pm\sqrt{\dfrac{70 + \sqrt{1120}}{126}}$	$\dfrac{6 - 5(\xi_2^2 + \xi_3^2) + 15\xi_2^2\xi_3^2}{15\xi_2^2\xi_3^2},$
		$\left[\dfrac{6 - 10\xi_3^2}{30\xi_2^2(\xi_2^2 - \xi_3^2)}\right], \left[\dfrac{6 - 10\xi_2^2}{30\xi_3^2(\xi_3^2 - \xi_2^2)}\right]$
	$= 0., \pm 0.5384693, \pm 0.9061798$	$= 0.568889, 0.47862867, 0.2369269$

2. Integration Based on Linear Interpolation in One Dimension.

$$\int_{x_1}^{x_2} F(x)\, dx \simeq \frac{F(x_1) + F(x_2)}{2}(x_2 - x_1)$$

Piecewise Linear Integration

$$\int_a^b F(x)\, dx = \sum_{e=1}^{E} \int_{x_e}^{x_{e+1}} F(x)\, dx \simeq \sum_{e=1}^{E} \frac{F(x_e) + F(x_{e+1})}{2}(x_{e+1} - x_e)$$

$$= \frac{x_2 - x_1}{2} F(x_1) + \frac{x_3 - x_1}{2} F(x_2) + \cdots + \frac{x_{E+1} - x_{E-1}}{2} F(x_E) + \frac{x_{E+1} - x_E}{2} F(x_{E+1})$$

For constant spacing, such that $x_{e+1} - x_e = h$, this is the *trapezoidal rule:*

$$\int_a^b F(x)\, dx \simeq \left(\frac{h}{2}\right) [F(a) + 2F(x_2) + 2F(x_3) + \cdots + 2F(x_E) + F(b)]$$

TABLE B.10 (continued)   NUMERICAL INTEGRATION FORMULAS

3. Integration Based on Quadratic Interpolation in One Dimension.

$$\int_{x_1}^{x_2} F(x)\, dx \simeq \alpha_1 F(x_1) + \alpha_1^* F(x_1^*) + \alpha_2 F(x_2)$$

where: $\alpha_1 = \dfrac{x_2 - x_1}{x_1^* - x_1} \left(\dfrac{x_1^* - x_1}{2} - \dfrac{x_2 - x_1}{6} \right)$

$$\alpha_1^* = \dfrac{(x_2 - x_1)^3}{6(x_2 - x_1^*)(x_1^* - x_1)}$$

$$\alpha_2 = \dfrac{x_2 - x_1}{x_1^* - x_1} \left(\dfrac{x_2 - x_1}{3} - \dfrac{x_1^* - x_1}{2} \right)$$

and x_1^* is restricted only by $x_1 < x_1^* < x_2$.

Piecewise Quadratic Integration

$$\int_a^b F(x)\, dx = \sum_{e=1}^{E} \int_{x_e}^{x_{e+1}} F(x)\, dx \simeq \sum_{e=1}^{E} [\alpha_{e,1} F(x_e) + \alpha_{e,1}^* F(x_e^*) + \alpha_{e,2} F(x_{e+1})]$$

$$= \alpha_{1,1} F(x_1) + \alpha_{1,1}^* F(x_1^*) + (\alpha_{1,2} + \alpha_{2,1}) F(x_2) + \alpha_{2,1}^* F(x_2^*) + \cdots$$

For constant spacing, such that $x_{e+1} - x_e = h$, this is *Simpson's rule:*

$$\int_a^b F(x)\, dx \simeq \dfrac{h}{6} \left[F(a) + 4F\left(x_1 + \dfrac{h}{2}\right) + 2F(x_2) + 4F\left(x_2 + \dfrac{h}{2}\right) + 2F(x_3) + \ldots + 4F\left(x_E + \dfrac{h}{2}\right) + F(b) \right]$$

4. Gaussian Quadrature in Two Dimensions: Rectangles.

$$\int_{-1}^{+1} \int_{-1}^{+1} f(\xi, \eta)\, d\xi\, d\eta \simeq \sum_{i=1}^{N_\xi} \sum_{j=1}^{N_\eta} W_i W_j f(\xi_i, \eta_j)$$

$$\int_{x_1}^{x_2} \int_{y_1}^{y_2} F(x, y)\, dx\, dy \simeq \left(\dfrac{x_2 - x_1}{2} \right) \left(\dfrac{y_2 - y_1}{2} \right) \sum_{i=1}^{N_x} \sum_{j=1}^{N_y} W_i W_j F(x(\xi_i), y(\eta_j))$$

where: $x(\xi) = \dfrac{x_1 + x_2}{2} + \dfrac{x_2 - x_1}{2} \xi$

$$y(\eta) = \dfrac{y_1 + y_2}{2} + \dfrac{y_2 - y_1}{2} \eta$$

(Piecewise Gaussian as well as bilinear and biquadratic integration rules follow in an analogous way.)

TABLE B.10 (continued)   NUMERICAL INTEGRATION FORMULAS

5. *Numerical Integration on Triangles.*

$$\int_{\Delta} F(x, y)\, dx\, dy \simeq A_{\Delta} \sum_{i=1}^{N} W_i F(x_i, y_i)$$

where Δ denotes an arbitrary triangle with area A_{Δ}. Let the standard planar basis functions be denoted by $\{\Psi_1, \Psi_2, \Psi_3\}$. The locations $\{(x_i, y_i)\}_{i=1}^{N}$ and associated weights $\{W_i\}$ are given by the following table:

TABLE OF INTEGRATION POINTS AND WEIGHTS FOR TRIANGLES

N	$\{(x_i, y_i)\}_{i=1}^{N}$	$\{W_i\}_{i=1}^{N}$
1	Location where $\Psi_1 = \Psi_2 = \Psi_3 = \dfrac{1}{3}$ (center of triangle; see figure)	1.

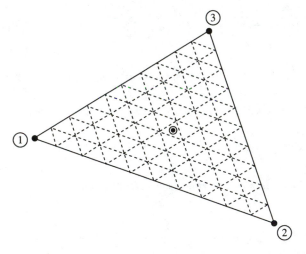

3	Locations where $\Psi_1 = \dfrac{2}{3}, \quad \Psi_2 = \Psi_3 = \dfrac{1}{6}$ $\Psi_2 = \dfrac{2}{3}, \quad \Psi_1 = \Psi_3 = \dfrac{1}{6}$ $\Psi_3 = \dfrac{2}{3}, \quad \Psi_1 = \Psi_2 = \dfrac{1}{6}$ (see figure)	$\dfrac{1}{3}$ $\dfrac{1}{3}$ $\dfrac{1}{3}$

TABLE B.10 (continued)   NUMERICAL INTEGRATION FORMULAS

N	$\{(x_i, y_i)\}_{i=1}^{N}$	$\{W_i\}_{i=1}^{N}$

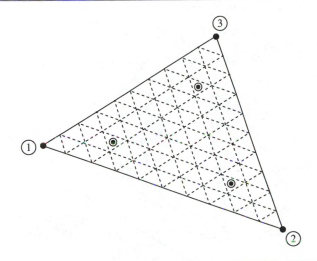

3	Locations where	
	$$\Psi_1 = \Psi_2 = \frac{1}{2}, \quad \Psi_3 = 0$$	$\dfrac{1}{3}$
	$$\Psi_1 = \Psi_3 = \frac{1}{2}, \quad \Psi_2 = 0$$	$\dfrac{1}{3}$
	$$\Psi_2 = \Psi_3 = \frac{1}{2}, \quad \Psi_1 = 0$$	$\dfrac{1}{3}$
	(see figure)	

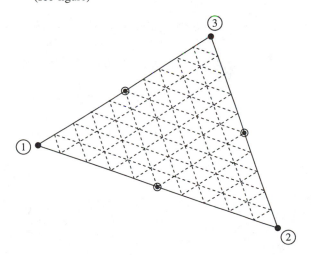

TABLE B.10 (continued) NUMERICAL INTEGRATION FORMULAS

N	$\{(x_i, y_i)\}_{i=1}^N$	$\{W_i\}_{i=1}^N$
4	Locations where	
	$\Psi_1 = \Psi_2 = \Psi_3 = \dfrac{1}{3}$	-0.5625
	$\Psi_1 = 0.6, \ \Psi_2 = \Psi_3 = 0.2$	0.5208333
	$\Psi_2 = 0.6, \ \Psi_1 = \Psi_3 = 0.2$	0.5208333
	$\Psi_3 = 0.6, \ \Psi_1 = \Psi_2 = 0.2$	0.5208333
	(see figure)	

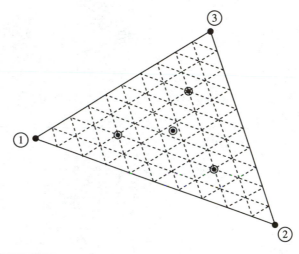

6	Locations where	
	$\Psi_1 = 0.659028, \quad \Psi_2 = 0.231934, \quad \Psi_3 = 0.109039$	$\dfrac{1}{6}$
	$\Psi_1 = 0.659028, \quad \Psi_2 = 0.109039, \quad \Psi_3 = 0.231934$	$\dfrac{1}{6}$
	$\Psi_1 = 0.231934, \quad \Psi_2 = 0.659028, \quad \Psi_3 = 0.109039$	$\dfrac{1}{6}$
	$\Psi_1 = 0.231934, \quad \Psi_2 = 0.109039, \quad \Psi_3 = 0.659028$	$\dfrac{1}{6}$
	$\Psi_1 = 0.109039, \quad \Psi_2 = 0.231934, \quad \Psi_3 = 0.659028$	$\dfrac{1}{6}$
	$\Psi_1 = 0.109039, \quad \Psi_2 = 0.659028, \quad \Psi_3 = 0.231934$	$\dfrac{1}{6}$
	(see figure)	

TABLE B.10 (continued)   NUMERICAL INTEGRATION FORMULAS

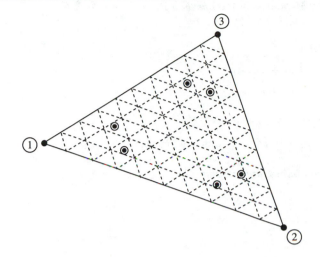

TABLE B.11   ROUTH-HURWITZ STABILITY CRITERIA

1. One-Step Method with Amplification Factor Given by:

$$\alpha_1 \lambda + \alpha_0 = 0$$

Define

$$p_0 \equiv \alpha_1 - \alpha_0$$
$$p_1 \equiv \alpha_1 + \alpha_0$$

Stability Requirements

$p_i \geq 0$, $i = 0, 1$, with strict inequality for at least one i.

2. Two-Step Method with Amplification Factor Given by:

$$\alpha_2 \lambda^2 + \alpha_1 \lambda + \alpha_0 = 0$$

Define

$$p_0 \equiv \alpha_2 - \alpha_1 + \alpha_0$$
$$p_1 \equiv 2(\alpha_2 - \alpha_0)$$
$$p_2 \equiv \alpha_2 + \alpha_1 + \alpha_0$$

Stability Requirements

$p_i \geq 0$, $i = 0, 1, 2$, with the condition that the following equations *not* hold:

$$p_0 = p_1 = 0 \quad \text{(simultaneously)}$$
$$p_1 = p_2 = 0 \quad \text{(simultaneously)}$$

3. Three-Step Method with Amplification Factor Given by:

$$\alpha_3 \lambda^3 + \alpha_2 \lambda^2 + \alpha_1 \lambda + \alpha_0 = 0$$

Define

$$p_0 \equiv \alpha_3 - \alpha_2 + \alpha_1 - \alpha_0$$
$$p_1 \equiv 3\alpha_3 - \alpha_2 - \alpha_1 + 3\alpha_0$$
$$p_2 \equiv 3\alpha_3 + \alpha_2 - \alpha_1 - 3\alpha_0$$
$$p_3 \equiv \alpha_3 + \alpha_2 + \alpha_1 + \alpha_0$$
$$\Delta_3 \equiv p_1 p_2 - p_0 p_3$$

Stability Requirements

$p_i \geq 0$, $i = 0, 1, 2, 3$ and $\Delta_3 \geq 0$ with the condition that the following equalities *not* hold:

$$p_0 = p_1 = 0 \quad \text{(simultaneously)}$$
$$p_2 = p_3 = 0 \quad \text{(simultaneously)}$$

TABLE B.11 (continued)   ROUTH–HURWITZ STABILITY CRITERIA

4. Four-Step Method with Amplification Factor Given by:

$$\alpha_4 \lambda^4 + \alpha_3 \lambda^3 + \alpha_2 \lambda^2 + \alpha_1 \lambda + \alpha_0 = 0$$

Define

$$p_0 \equiv \alpha_4 - \alpha_3 + \alpha_2 - \alpha_1 + \alpha_0$$

$$p_1 \equiv 2(2\alpha_4 - \alpha_3 + \alpha_1 - 2\alpha_0)$$

$$p_2 \equiv 2(3\alpha_4 - \alpha_2 + 3\alpha_0)$$

$$p_3 \equiv 2(2\alpha_4 + \alpha_3 - \alpha_1 - 2\alpha_0)$$

$$p_4 \equiv \alpha_4 + \alpha_3 + \alpha_2 + \alpha_1 + \alpha_0$$

$$\Delta_4 \equiv p_1 p_2 p_3 - p_1^2 p_4 - p_2^2 p_0$$

Stability Requirements

$p_i \geq 0$, $i = 0, 1, 2, 3, 4$, and $\Delta_4 \geq 0$ with the condition that the following equalities *not* hold:

$$p_1 = p_3 = 0 \text{ and } p_2^2 < 4p_0 p_4 \qquad \text{(simultaneously)}$$

$$p_0 = p_1 = 0 \qquad \text{(simultaneously)}$$

$$p_3 = p_4 = 0 \qquad \text{(simultaneously)}$$

$$p_3 = p_1 = p_2^2 - 4p_0 p_4 \qquad \text{(simultaneously)}$$

Note: See Chapter 4 of Kinnmark (1986) for more details.

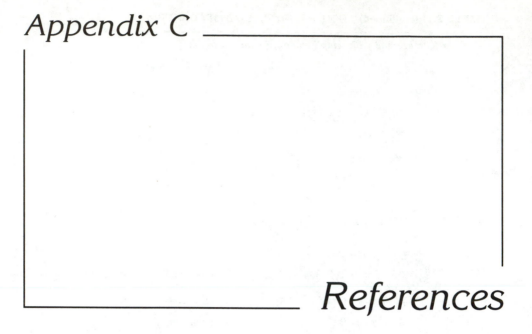

Appendix C

References

CHAPTER 1

ABBOTT, M. B., *Computational Hydraulics*, Pitman, London, 1979.

COURANT, R., and D. HILBERT, *Methods of Mathematical Physics*, Vols. I and II, Wiley Classics Edition, Wiley, New York, 1989.

DAVIS, J. L., *Finite Difference Methods in Dynamics of Continuous Media*, Macmillan, New York, 1986.

HILDEBRAND, F. B., *Advanced Calculus for Applications*, Prentice-Hall, Englewood Cliffs, N.J., 1976.

MORSE, P. M., and H. FESHBACH, *Methods of Theoretical Physics*, Vols. I and II, McGraw-Hill, New York, 1953.

SMITH, G. D., *Numerical Solution of Partial Differential Equations*: *Finite Difference Methods*, Oxford University Press, New York, 1985.

CHAPTER 2

AMES, W. F., *Numerical Methods for Partial Differential Equations*, 2nd Edition, Academic Press, New York, 1977.

426

DAHLQUIST, G., A. BJORCK, and N. ANDERSON, *Numerical Methods*, Prentice-Hall, Englewood Cliffs, N.J., 1974.

DAVIS, P. J., *Interpolation and Approximation*, Dover, New York, 1975.

FERZIGER, J. H., *Numerical Methods for Engineering Application*, Wiley, New York, 1981.

GEAR, C. W., *Numerical Initial Value Problems in Ordinary Differential Equations*, Prentice-Hall, Englewood Cliffs, N.J., 1971.

KAHANER, D., C. MOLER, and S. NASH, *Numerical Methods and Software*, Prentice-Hall, Englewood Cliffs, N.J., 1989.

LEITHOLD, L., *The Calculus with Analytical Geometry*, Harper & Row, New York, 1972.

MICKENS, R. E., *Difference Equations*, Van Nostrand Reinhold, New York, 1987.

NAKAMURA, S., *Applied Numerical Methods with Software*, Prentice-Hall, Englewood Cliffs, N.J., 1991.

ROACHE, P. J., *Computational Fluid Dynamics*, Hermosa, Albuquerque, N.Mex., 1982.

SKEEL, R. D., "Equivalent forms of multistep methods," *Mathematics of Computation*, 33(148), 1129–1250, 1979.

SMITH, G. D., *Numerical Solution of Partial Differential Equations: Finite Difference Methods*, Oxford University Press, New York, 1985.

CHAPTER 3

AHLIN, A. C., "A bivariate generalization of Hermite's interpolation formula," *Mathematics of Computation*, 18, 264–273, 1964.

BAKER, A. J., and D. W. PEPPER, *Finite Elements 1-2-3*, McGraw-Hill, New York, 1991.

BECKER, E. B., G. F. CAREY, and J. T. ODEN, *Finite Elements: An Introduction*, Vol. 1 of the Texas Finite Element Series, Prentice-Hall, Englewood Cliffs, N.J., 1981.

BICKFORD, W. B., *A First Course in the Finite Element Method*, Richard D. Irwin, Homewood, Ill., 1990.

BURNETT, D. S., *Finite Element Analysis*, Addison-Wesley, Reading, Mass., 1987.

CAREY, G. F., and J. T. ODEN, *Finite Elements: A Second Course*, Vol. 2 of the Texas Finite Element Series, Prentice-Hall, Englewood Cliffs, N.J., 1983.

CAREY, G. F., and J. T. ODEN, *Finite Elements: Computational Aspects*, Vol. 3 of the Texas Finite Element Series, Prentice-Hall, Englewood Cliffs, N.J., 1984.

GRAY, W. G., and M. A. CELIA, "On the use of generalized functions in engineering analysis," *International Journal of Applied Engineering Education*, 6(1), 89–96, 1990.

HUGHES, T. J. R., *The Finite Element Method*, Prentice-Hall, Englewood Cliffs, N.J., 1987.

LAPIDUS, L., and G. F. PINDER, *Numerical Solution of Partial Differential Equations in Science and Engineering*, Wiley, New York, 1982.

MIKHLIN, S. G., *Variational Methods in Mathematical Physics*, Pergamon Press, Elmsford, N.Y., 1964.

PRENTER, P. M., *Splines and Variational Methods*, Wiley, New York, 1975.

STRANG, G., and G. J. FIX, *An Analysis of the Finite Element Method*, Prentice-Hall, Englewood Cliffs, N.J., 1973.

ZIENKIEWICZ, O. C., and R. L. TAYLOR, *The Finite Element Method*, 4th Edition, McGraw-Hill, London, 1989.

CHAPTER 4

ALLEN, D., and R. SOUTHWELL, "Relaxation methods applied to determining the motion in two dimensions of a fluid past a fixed cylinder," *Quarterly Journal of Mechanics and Applied Mathematics*, 8, 129–145, 1955.

AMES, W. F., *Numerical Methods for Partial Differential Equations*, 2nd Edition, Academic Press, New York, 1977.

ATLURI, S. N., "Higher order, special and singular finite elements," in N. K. Noor and W. Pilkey (eds.), *State-of-the-Art Surveys on Finite Element Technology*, American Society of Mechanical Engineers, New York, 87–126, 1983.

BREBBIA, C. A., and J. DOMINGUEZ, *Boundary Elements: An Introductory Course*, Computational Mechanics Publications, Southampton, Hampshire, England, 1989.

BROOKS, A. N., and T. J. R., HUGHES, "Streamline upwind/Petrov-Galerkin formulation for convection dominated flows with particular emphasis on the incompressible Navier-Stokes equations," *Computer Methods in Applied Mechanics and Engineering*, 32, 199–259, 1982.

CELIA, M. A., and W. G. GRAY, "An improved isoparametric transformation for finite element analysis," *International Journal for Numerical Methods in Engineering*, 20, 1443–1459, 1984.

CELIA, M. A., and W. G. GRAY, "Improved co-ordinate transformations for finite elements: the Lagrange cubic case," *International Journal for Numerical Methods in Engineering*, 23, 1529–1545, 1986.

CELIA, M. A., T. F. RUSSELL, I. HERRERA, and R. E. EWING, "An Eulerian-Lagrangian localized adjoint method for the advection-diffusion equation," *Advances in Water Resources*, 13(4), 187–206, 1990.

CELIA, M. A., and G. F. PINDER, "Generalized alternating-direction collocation methods for parabolic equations. III. Nonrectangular domains," *Numerical Methods for Partial Differential Equations*, 6, 231–243, 1990.

CHRISTIE, I., D. F. GRIFFITHS, A. R. MITCHELL, and O. C. ZIENKIEWICZ, "Finite element methods for second order differential equations with significant first derivatives," *International Journal for Numerical Methods of Engineering*, 10, 1389–1396, 1976.

DICK, E., "Accurate Petrov-Galerkin methods for transient convective diffusion problems," *International Journal for Numerical Methods in Engineering*, 19, 1425–1433, 1983.

FLETCHER, C. A. J., *Computational Galerkin Methods*, Springer-Verlag, New York, 1984.

FRIND, E. O., and G. F. PINDER, "A collocation finite element method for potential problems in irregular domains," *International Journal for Numerical Methods in Engineering*, 14, 681–701, 1979.

GRESHO, P. M., and R. L. LEE, "Don't suppress the wiggles—they are telling you something," *Computers and Fluids*, 9, 213–253, 1981.

HEMKER, P. W., "A numerical study of stiff two point boundary value problems," Ph.D. thesis, Mathematisch Centrum, Amsterdam, 1977.

KINNMARK, I., *The Shallow Water Wave Equations: Formulation, Analysis and Application*, Lecture Notes in Engineering Series, C. A. Brebbia and S. A. Orszag, eds., Springer-Verlag, Berlin, 1986.

LIGGETT J. A., and P. L. F. LIU, *The Boundary Integral Equation Method for Porous Media Flow*, Allen & Unwin, London, 1983.

PEYRET, R., and T. D. Taylor, *Computational Methods for Fluid Flow*, Springer-Verlag, New York, 1983.

TOLSTOV, G. P., *Fourier Series*, translated from Russian by R. A. Silverman, Dover, New York, 1962.

VICHNEVETSKY, R., and J. B. BOWLES, *Fourier Analysis of Numerical Approximations of Hyperbolic Equations*, Society for Industrial and Applied Mathematics, Philadelphia, 1982.

WESTERINK, J. J., and D. SHEA, "Consistent higher degree Petrov-Galerkin methods for the solution of the transient convection-diffusion equation," *International Journal for Numerical Methods in Engineering*, 28(5), 1077–1101, 1989.

CHAPTER 5

BURNETT, D. S., *Finite Element Analysis*, Addison-Wesley, Reading, Mass., 1987.

GELINAS, R. J., S. K. DOSS, and K. MILLER, "The moving finite element method: applications to general partial differential equations with multiple large gradients," *Journal of Computational Physics*, 40(1), 202–249, 1981.

HIRSCH, C., *Numerical Computation of Internal and External Flows*, Vol. I: *Fundamentals of Numerical Discretization*, Wiley, Chichester, West Sussex, England, 1988.

HUGHES, T. J. R., *The Finite Element Method*, Prentice-Hall, Englewood Cliffs, N.J., 1987.

JALURIA, Y., and K. E. TORRANCE, *Computational Heat Transfer*, Hemisphere, Washington, D.C., 1986.

PRESS, W. H., B. P. FLANNERY, S. A. TEUKOLSKY, and W. T. VETTERLING, *Numerical Recipes*, Cambridge University Press, Cambridge, 1986.

THOMPSON, J. F., "A survey of dynamically-adaptive grids in the numerical solution of partial differential equations," *Applied Numerical Mathematics*, 1, 3–27, 1985.

THOMPSON, J. F., Z. U. A. WARSI, and C. W. MASTIN, *Numerical Grid Generation: Foundations and Applications*, Elsevier, New York, 1985.

ZIENKIEWICZ, O. C., and A. CRAIG, "Adaptive refinement, error estimates, multigrid solution, and hierarchic finite element method concepts," Chapter 2 in *Accuracy Estimates and Adaptive Refinements in Finite Element Computations*, I. Babuska, O. C. Zienkiewicz, J. Gago, and E. R. de A. Oliveira, eds., Wiley, Chichester, West Sussex, England, 1986.

ZIENKIEWICZ, O. C., and R. L. TAYLOR, *The Finite Element Method*, 4th Edition, McGraw-Hill, London, 1989.

APPENDIX A

GREENBERG, M. D., *Foundations of Applied Mathematics*, Prentice-Hall, Englewood Cliffs, N.J., 1978.

HILDEBRAND, F. B., *Methods of Applied Mathematics*, 2nd Edition, Prentice-Hall, Englewood Cliffs, N.J., 1965.

JENNINGS, A., *Matrix Computation for Engineers and Scientists*, Wiley, New York, 1977.

PETTOFREZZO, A. J., *Matrices and Transformations*, Dover, New York, 1966.

STRANG, G., *Introduction to Applied Mathematics*, Wellesley-Cambridge Press, Wellesley, Mass., 1986.

WESTLAKE, J. R., *A Handbook of Numerical Matrix Inversion and Solution of Linear Equations*, R. E. Krieger, Melbourne, Fla., 1975.

APPENDIX B

ABRAMOWITZ, M., and I. A. STEGUN, *Handbook of Mathematical Functions*, National Bureau of Standards Applied Mathematics Series, NBS, Washington, D.C., 1964.

GRADSHTEYN, I. S., and I. M. RYZHIK, *Table of Integrals, Series, and Products*, Academic Press, New York, 1980.

KINNMARK, I., *The Shallow Water Wave Equations: Formulation, Analysis and Application*, Lecture Notes in Engineering Series, C. A. Brebbia and S. A. Orszag, eds., Springer-Verlag, Berlin, 1986.

PRESS, W. H., B. P. FLANNERY, S. A. TEUKOLSKY, and W. T. VETTERLING, *Numerical Recipes*, Cambridge University Press, Cambridge, 1986.

PARTIAL LISTING OF RELATED JOURNALS

Applied Mathematical Modeling, Butterworth-Heinemann, 80 Montvale Avenue, Stoneham, MA 02180 USA.

Applied Numerical Mathematics, Elsevier Sciences Publishers, B.V., P.O. Box 211, 1000 AE Amsterdam, The Netherlands.

BIT, Computer Science and Numerical Mathematics, Postbox 113, DK-1004 Copenhagen K, Denmark.

Communications in Applied Numerical Methods, John Wiley & Sons, Ltd., Baffins Lane, Chichester, Sussex PO19 1UD, England.

Computer Methods in Applied Mechanics and Engineering, Elsevier Science Publishers, B.V., P.O. Box 1991, 1000 BZ Amsterdam, The Netherlands.

Engineering Analysis with Boundary Elements, Computational Mechanics Publications, Ashurst Lodge, Ashurst, Southampton SO4 2AA, England.

Engineering Computations, Pineridge Press, Ltd., 54 Newton Rd., Mumbles, Swansea, SA3 4BQ, Wales.

IMA Journal of Numerical Analysis, Institute of Mathematics and Its Applications, 16 Newton Street, Southend-on-Sea, Essex SS1 1EF, England.

International Journal for Numerical Methods in Engineering, John Wiley & Sons, Ltd., Baffins Lane, Chichester, Sussex PO19 1UD, England.

International Journal of Computer Mathematics, Gordon & Breach Science Publishers Inc., c/o STBD Ltd., 1 Bedford Street, London, WC2E 9PP, England.

Journal of Computational Physics, Academic Press, Inc., 1 East First Street, Duluth, MN 55802 USA.

Journal of Scientific Computing, Plenum Publishing Corp., 233 Spring Street, New York, NY 10033, USA.

Numerical Methods for Partial Differential Equations, John Wiley & Sons, Inc., 605 Third Avenue, New York, NY 10158 USA.

Numerische Mathematik, Springer-Verlag KG, Heidelberger Platz 3, 1000 Berlin 33 Germany.

SIAM Journal on Numerical Analysis, Society for Industrial and Applied Mathematics, 3600 University City Science Center, Philadelphia, PA 19104-2688 USA.

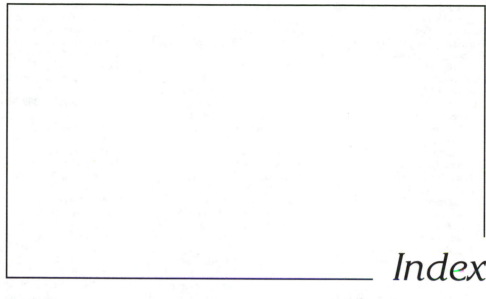

Index